THIS REGISTRATION CODE GIVES YOU ACCESS TO

 book | InQuizitive

For *Essentials of Cultural Anthropology*, Second Edition

ACTIVATE YOUR REGISTRATION CODE!

1) Scratch the foil to view your code.

2) Go to http://digital.wwnorton.com/essculturalanthro2.
3) Follow the instructions to register your code.

A code can be registered to only one user.
Used codes are nontransferable and nonrefundable.

For more help, see the back of this card.

What if my code is scratched off?

You can purchase access at
http://digital.wwnorton.com/essculturalanthro2.

What if I need more help?

For additional support, visit **support.wwnorton.com.**

ISBN 978-0-393-63125-8

9 780393 631258

90000

THE HOBO-DYER MAP

Can a map challenge your assumptions about the world?
The Hobo–Dyer map reorients the world, placing south at the
top and, like the Peters map that follows, uses an equal-area
presentation, presenting accurate proportions of countries,
continents, and oceans in relation to one another, rather than
emphasizing shape or compass bearings. What do you see
differently from this new perspective?

Falkland
Islands (U.K.)

New
Zealand

Argentina

Chile

Uruguay

SOUTH
PACIFIC
OCEAN

New
Caledonia
(Fr.)

Paraguay

Bolivia

Peru

Fiji

Vanuatu

Samoa

S

B r a z i l

E ─ W

Solomon
Islands

N

Ecuador

Equator

Kiribati

French Guiana
Suriname

Guyana

Colombia

Trinidad and Tobago
Grenada
St. Vincent and
the Grenadines
Barbados
St. Lucia
(Fr.) Martinique
Dominica
(Fr.) Guadeloupe
Antigua and Barbuda
St. Kitts & Nevis
(U.S.) Puerto Rico

Venezuela

Panama

Costa Rica
Nicaragua
El Salvador
Honduras
Guatemala

Caribbean
Sea

Jamaica

Belize

Dom.
Rep.

Haiti

Cuba

Bahamas

Hawaii
(U.S.)

Mexico

Gulf of
Mexico

NORTH
ATLANTIC
OCEAN

NORTH
PACIFIC
OCEAN

United States

Canada

Bering
Sea

Labrador
Sea

Hudson
Bay

Alaska (U.S.)

Greenland

Beaufort Sea

ARCTIC OCEAN

THE PETERS WORLD MAP

How do maps shape the way you think about the world and its people? The Earth is round. So every flat, rectangular map involves distortions. But which distortions? The Peters world map is an equal-area map, showing countries and continents in accurate proportion with one another and reducing the visual dominance of the Northern Hemisphere by shifting the equator to the middle of the map, both in sharp contrast to the more familiar Mercator projection.

WORLD · POLITICAL

NATIONAL BOUNDARIES

While humanity's impact is quite evident, and even striking, on many remotely sensed scenes, sometimes, as in the case with most political boundaries, it is invisible. State, provincial, and national boundaries can follow natural features, such as mountain ridges, rivers, or coastlines. Artificial constructs that possess no physical reality—for example, lines of latitude and longitude—can also determine political borders. This world political map represents the results of humanity's efforts to slice and divide Earth into discrete spheres of influence.

The National Geographic Society recognizes 192 independent states in the world as represented here. Of those nations, 185 are members of the United Nations.

Winkel Tripel Projection

Longitude West of Greenwich

Essentials of Cultural Anthropology

Second Edition

Essentials of Cultural Anthropology

A Toolkit for a Global Age

Second Edition

Kenneth J. Guest

Baruch College
The City University of New York

W. W. Norton & Company
New York ▪ London

W. W. Norton & Company has been independent since its founding in 1923, when William Warder Norton and Mary D. Herter Norton first published lectures delivered at the People's Institute, the adult education division of New York City's Cooper Union. The firm soon expanded its program beyond the Institute, publishing books by celebrated academics from America and abroad. By midcentury, the two major pillars of Norton's publishing program—trade books and college texts—were firmly established. In the 1950s, the Norton family transferred control of the company to its employees, and today—with a staff of four hundred and a comparable number of trade, college, and professional titles published each year—W. W. Norton & Company stands as the largest and oldest publishing house owned wholly by its employees.

Editor: Peter Lesser

Project Editor: Caitlin Moran

Associate Editor: Samantha Held

Managing Editor, College: Marian Johnson

Managing Editor, College Digital Media: Kim Yi

Production Manager: Ashley Horna

Media Editor: Eileen Connell

Media Associate Editor: Mary Williams

Media Assistant Editor: Grace Tuttle

Marketing Managers: Julia Hall and Erin Brown

Design Director: Hope Miller Goodell

Book Design: Kiss Me I'm Polish LLC

Photo Editor: Aga Millhouse

Permissions Manager: Megan Schindel

Permissions Associate: Elizabeth Trammell

Composition: Jouve

Manufacturing: LSC Crawfordsville

Permission to use copyrighted material is included on p A:23.

Library of Congress Cataloging-in-Publication Data

Names: Guest, Kenneth J., author.

Title: Essentials of cultural anthropology : a toolkit for a global age / Kenneth J. Guest, Baruch College, The City University of New York.

Description: Second Edition. | New York : W.W. Norton & Company, [2018] | Includes bibliographical references and index.

Identifiers: LCCN 2017038033 | **ISBN 9780393624618 (paperback)**

Subjects: LCSH: Ethnology. | Applied anthropology. | Globalization.

Classification: LCC GN316 .G845 2018 | DDC 301—dc23 LC record available at https://lccn.loc.gov/2017038033

W. W. Norton & Company, Inc., 500 Fifth Avenue, New York, NY 10010-0017

wwnorton.com

W. W. Norton & Company Ltd., Castle House, 75/76 Wells Street, London W1T 3QT

2 3 4 5 6 7 8 9 0

About the Author

Kenneth J. Guest is Professor of Anthropology at Baruch College, CUNY, and author of *God in Chinatown: Religion and Survival in New York's Evolving Immigrant Community* (2003). His research focuses on immigration, religion, globalization, ethnicity, and entrepreneurialism.

Professor Guest's ethnographic research in China and the United States traces the immigration journey of recent Chinese immigrants from Fuzhou, southeast China, who, drawn by restaurant, garment shop, and construction jobs and facilitated by a vast human smuggling network, have revitalized New York's Chinatown. His writing explores the role of Fuzhounese religious communities in China and the United States; the religious revival sweeping coastal China; the Fuzhounese role in the rapidly expanding U.S. network of all-you-can-eat buffets and take-out restaurants; the higher education experiences of the Fuzhounese second generation; and the contestation over Chinatown's future in the face of Manhattan's rapid gentrification.

A native of Florida, Professor Guest studied Chinese at Beijing University and Middlebury College. He received his B.A. from Columbia University (East Asian Languages and Cultures), an M.A. from Union Theological Seminary (Religious Studies), and the M.A., M.Phil., and Ph.D. from The City University of New York Graduate Center (Anthropology).

Brief Contents

Contents

Chapter 3: Fieldwork and Ethnography 60

Chapter 4: Language   90

Part 2: Unmasking the Structures of Power

Chapter 5: Race and Racism   118

Chapter 7: Gender — 176

Chapter 8: Sexuality — 204

Chapter 14: Health, Illness, and the Body — 394

Preface

Anthropology may be the most important course you take in college. That may seem like a bold statement. But here's what I mean.

CULTURAL ANTHROPOLOGY: A TOOLKIT

The world in the twenty-first century is changing at a remarkable pace. We are experiencing an interaction with people, ideas, and systems that is intensifying at breathtaking speed. Communication technologies link people instantaneously across the globe. Economic activities challenge national boundaries. People are on the move within countries and between them. As a result, today we increasingly encounter the diversity of humanity, not on the other side of the world but in our schools, workplaces, neighborhoods, religious communities, and families. How will we develop the skills and strategies for engaging and navigating the complex, multicultural, global, and rapidly changing reality of the world around us?

Anthropology is the toolkit you are looking for. Cultural anthropology is the study of humans, particularly the many ways people around the world today and throughout human history have organized themselves to live together: to get along, to survive, to thrive, and to have meaningful lives. This second edition of *Essentials of Cultural Anthropology: A Toolkit for a Global Age* will introduce you to the fascinating work of anthropologists and the research strategies and analytical perspectives that anthropologists have developed—our tools of the trade—that can help you better understand and engage today's world as you move through it.

I teach Introduction to Cultural Anthropology to hundreds of students every year at Baruch College, a senior college of The City University of New York. Baruch has an incredibly diverse student body, with immigrants from more than a hundred countries, speaking dozens of languages and thinking about culture, race, gender, and family in as many different ways. Some of my students will become anthropology majors. More will become anthropology minors. But at Baruch, in fact, most students will become business majors.

This book emerges from my efforts to make anthropology relevant to all of my students as they navigate their everyday lives, think about the world as it is and as it is becoming, and consider tackling the crucial issues of our times. On a practical level, we all employ the skills of anthropology on a daily basis. Every time you walk into a room and try to figure out how to fit into a new group of people—in your classroom, in a student club, at the office, at a party, in your religious community, when your new love interest takes you home to meet the family—how in the world do you deduce what the rules are? Where you fit in? What you're supposed to do? What the power dynamics are? What you can contribute to the group? *Essentials of Cultural Anthropology: A Toolkit for a Global Age, Second Edition* is designed to help you develop those skills—to think more deeply and analyze more carefully—and to prepare you to use them in a diversity of settings at home or around the world.

WHY A NEW TEXTBOOK?

The world has changed dramatically in the past forty years and so has the field of anthropology. *Essentials of Cultural Anthropology: A Toolkit for a Global Age, Second Edition*—like the parent version, *Cultural Anthropology*—presents the theoretical, methodological, and pedagogical innovations that are transforming anthropology and highlights both historical and contemporary research that can provide students with insight into the ways in which anthropologists approach the crucial challenges and questions of our times. *Essentials* contains 15 concise chapters that I hope will easily fit into most courses—either as a stand-alone text or paired with additional primary readings and assignments. My goal with *Essentials* is to place at students' fingertips a lively, compelling presentation of the key concepts and debates at the heart of anthropology today in a shorter text—written without boxes and special features—that allows faculty increased flexibility in course development and design.

Globalization. As the world is changing, so too are the people anthropologists study. Even the way anthropologists conduct research is changing. In the contemporary period of rapid globalization, the movement, connection, and interrelatedness that have always been a part of human reality have intensified and become more explicit, reminding us that our actions have consequences for the whole world, not just for our own lives and those of our families and friends. This book integrates globalization into every chapter, analyzing its effects throughout the text rather than in a series of boxes, icons, or the occasional extra chapter so commonly seen in contemporary textbooks. The introductory chapter, "Anthropology in a Global Age," establishes an analytical framework of globalization that is developed in every succeeding chapter—whether the topic is fieldwork, language, ethnicity, economics, or kinship—and gives students the tools to understand its impact on people's lives as they encounter them in ethnographic examples throughout the book.

Reframing the Culture Concept. The concept of culture has been central to anthropological analysis since the beginning of our field. But anthropologists have significantly reframed our thinking about culture over the past forty years. In the 1960s, Clifford Geertz synthesized anthropological thinking about culture as a system of meaning—shared norms, values, symbols, and categories. In the ensuing years, anthropologists have paid increasing attention to the relationship of power to culture, building on the work of Antonio Gramsci, Michel Foucault, and Eric Wolf to examine the ways cultural meanings are created, learned, taught, enforced, negotiated, and contested. *Essentials of Cultural Anthropology: A Toolkit for a Global Age, Second Edition* integrates this holistic and complex concept of culture into every chapter, exploring both meaning and power in human culture. Chapter 5, for example, is titled "Race and Racism," acknowledging that not only is race a social construction of ideas but also that ideas of race can be expressed and made real through cultural processes, institutions, and systems of power—racism—in ways that create patterns of stratification and inequality in U.S. culture and in cultures around the world.

Anthropology for the Twenty-First Century. *Essentials of Cultural Anthropology: A Toolkit for a Global Age, Second Edition* reflects the field of anthropology as it is developing in the twenty-first century. While carefully covering the foundational work of early anthropologists, every chapter has been designed to introduce the cutting-edge research and theory that make anthropology relevant to today's world. Chapters on classic anthropological topics such as language, religion, and kinship incorporate contemporary research and help students understand why anthropological thinking matters in day-to-day life. Chapters on sexuality, the global economy, class and inequality, and health, illness, and the body give students a sense of historical and contemporary research in the field and bring the presentation of anthropology fully into the twenty-first century.

Ethnography. Anthropologists conduct fascinating research about the lives of people all over the world. In many ways ethnography is at the heart of anthropology, reflecting our unique research strategies, our analytical methodologies, and our deep commitment to the project of cross-cultural understanding and engagement in our attempts to make the world a better place. But ethnographies often get lost in introductory textbooks. *Essentials of Cultural Anthropology: A Toolkit for a Global Age, Second Edition* introduces scores of ethnographic studies set in dozens of different countries, presenting both new research and classic studies in ways that are accessible to undergraduates so that the rich work of anthropologists comes alive over the course of the semester.

Relevance. *Essentials of Cultural Anthropology, Second Edition* responds to my students' request for relevance in a textbook. Each chapter opens with a recent event that raises central questions about the workings of human culture. Key questions throughout the chapter guide students through an introduction to the anthropological strategies and analytical frameworks that can enable them to think more deeply about the chapter-opening event and the underlying issues they may confront in their own lives. "Thinking Like an Anthropologist" sections wrap up each chapter and challenge students to apply what they have learned.

What's New in the Second Edition

Reflecting the dynamic nature of cultural anthropology, this new, second edition of *Essentials of Cultural Anthropology: A Toolkit for a Global Age* includes revisions and updates to every chapter that introduce cutting edge developments in the discipline, new theoretical frameworks, and new ethnographies. New chapter openers and examples continue the book's pedagogical approach to engage students in thinking like an anthropologist and provide them with an anthropological toolkit for analyzing and engaging the world around them.

NEW CHAPTER ON ART AND MEDIA

A new chapter on art and media explores the unique approach anthropologists take to the study of art, the many ways in which art reflects and transforms culture, and the ways in which globalization and new forms of media are transforming art and its dissemination. Through ethnographies of Brazil, west Africa, the Middle East, and the United States, the chapter explores how art is embedded in communities, how it connects to social norms and values, as well as economic and political systems and events.

NEW CHAPTER OPENING STORIES ON FAMILIAR TOPICS AND CURRENT EVENTS

Ferguson, the Flint water crisis, a Happy Meal, Bangladesh's Sundarban tidal forest, women Army Rangers, protesting sexual violence on campus, football concussions, Pope Francis and the television show *Transparent*: Nine new chapter openers challenge students to ask big questions and apply their anthropological toolkit to the real world challenges of today.

NEW ETHNOGRAPHIES ADDED THROUGHOUT THE TEXT

Ethnographies are at the heart of anthropological inquiry. This edition introduces new ethnographies set in places including: Bolivia, Brazil, Denmark and Sweden, Egypt, Eritrea, India, Japan, Taiwan, the United States, and Tanzania.

NEW COVERAGE OF ENGAGING, CUTTING-EDGE TOPICS

- **The environment and climate change.** Humans are reshaping the natural environment, leading scholars to rename the current geological period the Anthropocene. The book's focus on the environment begins in chapter one with a new section on the Anthropocene, and ethnographies and explorations of current issues and events throughout the book, including: A Coca-Cola bottling factory in India; water crises in Flint, Michigan and Mumbai, India; environment and health disparities in Harlem; and climate activists in Bangladesh, Paris, and U.S. college campuses.

- **The anthropology of the body.** Cross-cultural anthropological studies have challenged the notion of the body as isolated, natural, and universal and revealed a more complex picture of human bodies as products of specific environments, cultural experiences, and historical contexts. In addition to discussion of health and illness, the second edition adds new material on sickness.

- **Disabilities.** Anthropology's increasing attention to the body has been accompanied by a recent expansion of work on issues of disability. Anthropologists have begun to bring their distinctive ethnographic methods to the task of understanding the embodied experiences of people with impairments and analyzing those experiences within broader forms of social inequality. New content has been added in chapters on Health, Illness, and the Body and Sexuality.

- **The anthropology of food.** Always central to anthropological studies, food has received increased attention in recent years. The anthropology of food is explored throughout the book, including food production; food and colonialism; religious symbolism of food; water and inequality in Flint, Michigan and Mumbai, India; soda bottling; the social life of a chocolate bar; the global trade in tuna; food and ethnic identity; migration of Chinese restaurant workers; and a new chapter opener on the Happy Meal.

- **Anthropology's biocultural perspective.** *Essentials of Cultural Anthropology* presents the latest thinking on human evolution, development, and adaptation as an ongoing biocultural process in which biology, culture, and the environment are deeply intertwined in an ongoing interplay and interaction through which humans are continually evolving and changing, both on a species level and in our individual lifespans.

- **The anthropology of global financial markets.** The 2008 fiscal crisis revealed how global financial markets, firms, and financial instruments like derivatives are reshaping the global economy. New content provides insight into the value that anthropological perspectives bring to analyzing these changes.

Additional Resources

Learn more at *wwnorton.com/instructors* and *digital.wwnorton.com/essculturalanthro2*

CULTURAL ANTHROPOLOGY: A READER FOR A GLOBAL AGE

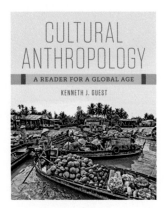

In *Cultural Anthropology: A Reader for a Global* Age, Ken Guest presents the essential readings and diverse voices that will help students understand and engage their rapidly globalizing world. This concise, affordable reader is designed to complement any introductory syllabus and is the perfect companion for *Essentials of Cultural Anthropology: A Toolkit for a Global Age, Second Edition*. Each chapter in the *Reader* includes two or three readings that correspond directly to the chapters in *Essentials*. Selections focus on cutting edge topics that students care about, like the environment, the body, income inequality, sexuality, race and racism, migration, and more. In addition, Guest's rich headnotes and smart discussion questions help students understand important contexts and apply what they learn in the readings to the world around them.

(NEW) INQUIZITIVE
Available at *digital.wwnorton.com/essculturalanthro2*

Norton's award-winning, easy-to-use adaptive learning tool personalizes the learning experience for students and helps them master—and retain—the learning goals outlined in each chapter of *Essentials of Cultural Anthropology*. Used as a prelecture tool, InQuizitive helps students improve their reading comprehension and critical thinking skills so that they come to class better prepared to think like anthropologists. InQuizitive can also improve students' test grades when assigned consistently for points, as a part of the overall course grade. The convenience of LMS integration saves you time by allowing InQuizitive scores to report right to your LMS gradebook.

CULTURAL ANTHROPOLOGY FIELDWORK JOURNAL

Ethnographic fieldwork is one of the most fundamental (and for students sometimes daunting) tools for anthropological study. Ken Guest's *Cultural Anthropology Fieldwork Journal*, Second Edition, provides 17 step-by-step exercises to help students apply the concepts they are learning in class while out in the real world. Designed to complement *Essentials of Cultural Anthropology: A Toolkit for a Global Age, Second Edition*, every activity in the *Fieldwork Journal* enhances students' understanding of the concepts covered in the parent textbook. Compact and easy to use, the *Fieldwork Journal* includes space to write notes and record data. The *Fieldwork Journal* can be packaged for free with *Essentials of Cultural Anthropology*, Second Edition.

The media package for *Essentials of Cultural Anthropology: A Toolkit for a Global Age, Second Edition* provides additional pedagogical tools that inspire students to *do* anthropology and apply it to their own lives. Instructors have everything they need to make traditional and online classes easier to manage: documentary film clips that will enliven lectures and spark discussion; illustrated PowerPoints that include instructor-view lecture notes; and a fully customizable coursepack for Blackboard and other course-management systems. The coursepack includes optional access to InQuizitive, our new adaptive learning system.

EBOOK

Available at *digital.wwnorton.com/esssculturalanthro2*

Essentials of Cultural Anthropology is also available as an ebook. An affordable and convenient alternative, the ebook retains the content of the print book and allows students to highlight and take notes with ease.

POWERPOINTS

David Anderson, Radford University/Roanoke College

Downloadable from wwnorton.com/instructors and perfect for classroom presentation, these resources include:

- **Lecture PowerPoints:** Illustrated with images from the text, these lecture PowerPoint slides feature a suggested classroom lecture outline in the notes field that will be particularly helpful to first-time teachers.

- **Art PowerPoints and JPEGs:** All of the art from the book and from the coursepack is sized for classroom display.

DOCUMENTARTY VIDEO CLIPS

Russell Sharman

These documentary and ethnographic film clips are ideal for initiating classroom discussion and showing students how anthropology is relevant to their lives. Filmmaker and anthropologist Russell Sharman has selected clips that are both engaging and pedagogically useful. Each clip is available in the coursepack and is accompanied by an exercise.

COURSEPACK

David Anderson, Radford University/Roanoke College; Chad T. Morris, Roanoke College; and Maisa C. Taha, Montclair State University

Essentials of Cultural Anthropology's coursepack offers assessment and review materials for instructors who use Blackboard, Moodle, Canvas, and other learning-management systems. In addition to chapter-based assignments, test banks and quizzes, and an optional ebook, the coursepack includes interactive learning tools that will enliven hybrid, online, or traditional classrooms. Features include:

- A pre-test for each chapter
- Review and key term quizzes for each chapter
- "Thinking like an Anthropologist" and "Your Turn: Fieldwork" exercises and activities
- Streaming film clips from the Instructor DVD, each supported by a quiz or exercise
- InQuizitive (Optional)

TEST BANK

Alexandra Lancey, University of South Florida; Pilar Rau, Rutgers University

The test bank for *Essentials of Cultural Anthropology* is designed to help instructors prepare exams. Devised according to Bloom's taxonomy, the test bank includes 50–60 multiple-choice questions per chapter. In addition to Bloom's, each question is tagged with metadata that place it in the context of the chapter, as well as difficulty level, making it easy to construct tests that are meaningful and diagnostic.

INTERACTIVE INSTRUCTOR'S GUIDE

Now in a newly redesigned and easier-to-navigate platform, the Interactive Instructor's Guide makes lecture development easy with an array of teaching resources that can be searched and browsed according to a number of criteria. Resources include chapter outlines and summaries; lecture ideas; discussion questions, recommended readings, author videos, and websites; video exercises with streaming video; and activities with downloadable handouts. Instructors can subscribe to a mailing list to be notified of periodic updates and new content.

Acknowledgments

Writing a book of this scope is a humbling experience. I have been awed by the remarkable work of the anthropologists I have encountered, whether through written texts, films, or one-on-one conversations. And I have been inspired by the commitment of my fellow anthropologists to deep understanding of people and cultures, to the search for insights into how the world really works, and to engagement with the world and its people in ways that may help make the world a better place. I have learned a great deal, personally and professionally, on this journey. Along the way it has been my privilege to have the support and encouragement of a remarkable array of people.

First, I would like to thank those colleagues whose invaluable feedback at many stages of the revision process led to the creation of this book. I have adopted many of the recommendations that they made.

Kathleen Adams, Loyola University Chicago

Sabrina Adleman, Lansing Community College

Augustine Agwuele, Texas State University

Hayder Al-Mohammad, University of Wisconsin, Madison

Mark Allen, California State Polytechnic University, Pomona

Peter Allen, Rhode Island College

Deborah Altamirano, State University of New York, Plattsburgh

Myrdene Anderson, Purdue University

Tracy J. Andrews, Central Washington University

Iván Arenas, University of Illinois at Chicago

Kristi Arford, Northern Essex Community College

James D. Armstrong, State University of New York, Plattsburgh

Elizabeth Arnold, Grand Valley State University

Christine B. Avenarius, East Carolina University

Bridget Balint, Indiana University

Data Barata, California State University, Sacramento

Diane Baxter, University of Oregon

AnnMarie Beasley, Cosumnes River College

Sara Becker, York College of Pennsylvania

Monica Bellas, Cerritos College

O. Hugo Benavides, Fordham University

David Beriss, University of New Orleans

Ethan Bertrando, Cuesta College

Catherine Besteman, Colby College

Brad Biglow, Florida State College at Jacksonville

Krista Billingsley, University of Tennessee

Maggie Bodemer, California Polytechnic State University

Deborah A. Boehm, University of Nevada, Reno

Laurian Bowles, Davidson College

Angela Bratton, Georgia Regents University

Elise Brenner, Bridgewater State University

Caroline B. Brettell, Southern Methodist University

Mary Jill Brody, Louisiana State University

Keri Brondo, University of Memphis

Boyd Brown III, Nichols College

Susan Brownell, University of Missouri, St. Louis

Ronda Brulotte, University of New Mexico

Jan Brunson, University of Hawai'i at Manoa

Kathleen Bubinas, University of Wisconsin – Waukesha

Pem Davidson Buck, Elizabethtown Community and Technical College

Liam Buckley, James Madison University

Andrew Buckser, State University of New York, Plattsburgh

Anne Buddenhagen, John Jay College of Criminal Justice

Jennie Burnet, University of Louisville

Noah Butler, Loyola University Chicago

Maria Leonor Cadena, Fullerton College

Walter Calgaro, Prairie State College

Jerome Camal, University of Wisconsin, Madison

Jennifer Chase, University of North Texas

Leo Chavez, University of California, Irvine

Kristen Check, University of South Carolina

Kun Chen, California State Polytechnic University, Pomona

Aldo Civico, Rutgers University

Paula Clarke, Columbia College

Kimberley Coles, University of Redlands

Elizabeth E. Cooper, University of Alabama

Susan Bibler Coutin, University of California, Irvine

Mark Cozin, Raritan Valley Community College

Mary Lou Curran, Mount Wachusett Community College

Joanna Davidson, Boston University

Sasha David, Los Angeles Harbor College

Christina Davis, Western Illinois University

Dona Davis, University of South Dakota

Allan Dawson, Drew University

Jeanne de Grasse, Butler Community College

Jeffrey Debies-Carl, University of New Haven

Teresa Delfin, Whittier College

Rene M. Descartes, State University of New York at Cobleskill

Rosemary Diaz, Southern Connecticut State University

William Doonan, Sacramento City College

Haley Duschinski, Ohio University

Paulla Ebron, Stanford University

Terilee Edwards-Hewitt, Montgomery College

Kenneth Ehrensal, Kutztown University

Tracy Evans, Fullerton College

Susan Falls, Savannah College of Art and Design

Tessa Farmer, Whittier College

Jason Fancher, Mt. Hood Community College

Derick Fay, University of California, Riverside

Rick Feinberg, Kent State University

Doug Feldman, The College at Brockport, State University of New York

Elena Filios, Charter Oak State College

Mike Folan, New Hampshire Technical Institute

Allison Foley, Indiana University, South Bend

Ben Ford, Indiana University of Pennsylvania

Carla Freeman, Emory University

Todd French, Depauw University

Jonathan Friedman, University of California, San Diego

John Fritz, Salt Lake Community College

Cynthia Gabriel, Eastern Michigan University

Sue-Je Gage, Ithaca College

Ismael García Colón, College of Staten Island

Carlos Garcia-Quijano, University of Rhode Island

Peter M. Gardner, University of Missouri

Laura Gonzalez, San Diego Miramar College

Daniel Goldstein, Rutgers University

Julie Goodman, California Baptist University

Henri Gooren, Oakland University

Mark Gordon, Pasadena City College

Thomas Gordon, Monroe College

Alexis Gray, Norco College

Peter B. Gray, University of Nevada, Las Vegas

Thomas Gregor, Vanderbilt University

Hugh Gusterson, George Washington University

Joyce D. Hammond, Western Washington University

Melissa D. Hargrove, University of North Florida

Amy Harper, Central Oregon Community College

Adam Harr, St. Lawrence University

Tina Harris, University of Amsterdam

K. David Harrison, Swarthmore College

Kimberly Hart, Buffalo State, State University of New York

Angelique Haugerud, Rutgers University

Bridget Hayden, University of Southern Mississippi, Hattiesburg

Gary Heidinger, Roane State Community College

Deanna Heikkinen, Los Angeles Valley College

Gilbert Herdt, San Francisco State University

Nicole Hess, Washington State University, Vancouver

Josiah Heyman, University of Texas at El Paso

Jude Higgins, Salt Lake Community College

Servando Z. Hinojosa, University of Texas – Pan American

Dorothy L. Hodgson, Rutgers University

David Hoffman, Mississippi State University

Derek Honeyman, University of Arizona

Sherman Horn, Tulane University

Kendall House, Boise State University

Brian Howell, Wheaton College

Jayne Howell, California State University, Long Beach

Douglas William Hume, Northern Kentucky University

Arianne Ishaya, De Anza College

Alice James, Shippensburg University

Paul James, Western Washington University

Alana Jolley, Saddleback College

Patricia Jolly, University of Northern Colorado

Carla Jones, University of Colorado

Barbara Jones, Brookdale Community College

Jessica Jones-Coggins, Madison Area Technical College

Hannah Jopling, Fordham University

Ingrid Jordt, University of Wisconsin – Milwaukee

Karen Kapusta-Pofahl, Washburn University

Peta Katz, University of North Carolina at Charlotte

Neal B. Keating, College at Brockport, State University of New York

Grace Keyes, St. Mary's University

Diane E. King, University of Kentucky

Melissa King, San Bernardino Valley College

Alice Kingsnorth, American River College

Ashley Kistler, Rollins College

Christine Kitchin, Ocean County College

Chhaya Kolavalli, University of Kentucky

Kathryn Kozaitis, Georgia State University

Kathy Koziol, University of Arkansas

Don Kulick, Uppsala University

Ruth Laird, Mission College

Clark Larsen, Ohio State University

Gabriel Lataianu, Bergen Community College

Ida Leggett, Middle Tennessee State University

Elinor Levy, Raritan Valley Commmunity College

Pierre Liénard, University of Nevada, Las Vegas

Linda Light, California State University, Long Beach

Pamela Lindell, Sacramento City College

David M. Lipset, University of Minnesota

Chris Loeffler, Irvine Valley College

Aurolyn Luykx, University of Texas at El Paso

Pamela Maack, San Jacinto College

Yvette Madison, Pennsylvania Highlands Community College

Kathe Managan, Louisiana State University

Valentina Martinez, Florida Atlantic University

Scott Matter, University of Vermont

Michael Mauer, College of the Canyons

Kathryn Maurer, Foothill College

Siobhan McCollum, Buffalo State, State University of New York

Jack McCoy, Monmouth University

Reece McGee, Texas State University

Bettie Kay McGowan, Eastern Michigan University

Melanie Medeiros, State University of New York at Geneseo

Karletty Medina, Northern Essex Community College

Arion Melidonis, Oxnard College

Seth Messinger, University of Maryland, Baltimore County

Jim Mielke, University of Kansas

Ryan Moore, Florida Atlantic University

Scotty Moore, Houston Community College

Juliet Morrow, Arkansas State University

Amy Mountcastle, State University of New York, Plattsburgh

Martin Muller, University of New Mexico

Joylin Namie, Utah Valley University

Chris Nelson, University of North Carolina at Chapel Hill

Neil Nevins, New Hampshire Technical Institute

Rachel Newcomb, Rollins College

Evelyn Newman Phillips, Central Connecticut State University

Carol Nickolai, Community College of Philadelphia

Jeremy Nienow, Inver Hills Community College

Jennifer Oksenhorn, Suffolk County Community College

Michael O'Neal, St. Louis Community College

Erik Ozolins, Mount San Jacinto College

Liana Padilla-Wilson, Los Medanos College

Eric Paison, Golden West College

Craig Palmer, University of Missouri

Anastasia Panagakos, Cosumnes River College

Amanda Paskey, Cosumnes River College

Phyllis Passariello, Centre College

Crystal Patil, University of Illinois at Chicago

Mike Pavlik, Joliet Junior College

Linda Pelon, McLennan Community College

Ramona Pérez, San Diego State University

Dana Pertermann, Blinn College

Holly Peters-Golden, University of Michigan

Mieka Brand Polanco, James Madison University

Wayne Politsch, Lewis and Clark Community College

Lin Poyer, University of Wyoming

Marla Prochnow, College of the Sequoias

Erica Prussing, University of Iowa

James Quesada, San Francisco State University

Sharon Rachele, California State Polytechnic University, Pomona

Michelle Raisor, Blinn College

Amanda Reinke, University of Tennessee, Knoxville

Michael Robertson, Los Angeles Harbor College

Daniel Robinson, University of Florida

Monica Rothschild-Boros, Orange Coast College

Frances Rothstein, Montclair State University

Stephanie Sadre-Orafai, University of Cincinnati

Kristin Safi, Washington State University

Rita Sakitt, Suffolk County Community College

Maureen Salsitz, Cypress College

Bruce Sanchez, Lane Community College

Keri Sansevere, Monmouth University

Antonia Santangelo, York College, City University of New York

Richard Sattler, University of Montana

Naomi Schiller, Brooklyn College

Jennifer Schlegel, Kutztown University

Scott Schnell, University of Iowa

Kathy Seibold, The College of Idaho

Frank Shih, Suffolk County Community College

Gregory Simon, Pierce College

Suzanne Simon, University of North Florida

Michael Simonton, University of Cincinnati

Nancy Smith, South Plains College

Sarah Smith, Delta College

Brian Spooner, University of Pennsylvania

Chelsea Starr, University of Phoenix

Erin E. Stiles, University of Nevada, Reno

Karen Stocker, California State University, Fullerton

Michelle Stokely, Indiana University Northwest

Richard Stuart, University of North Carolina at Greensboro

Circe Sturm, University of Texas at Austin

Noelle Sullivan, Northwestern University

Rania Sweis, University of Richmond

Patricia Taber, Ventura College

Orit Tamir, New Mexico Highlands University

Arthur Tolley, Indiana University East

Patricia Tovar, John Jay College of Criminal Justice

Mark Tracy, Minneapolis Community and Technical College

Susan Trencher, George Mason University

Monica Udvardy, University of Kentucky

Lisa Valkenier, Merritt College

Jay VanderVeen, Indiana University South Bend

Katherine Wahlberg, Florida Gulf Coast University

Salena Wakim, Mount San Jacinto College

Renee Walker, State University of New York at Oneonta

Deana Weibel, Grand Valley State University

Nicole Weigel, State University of New York College at Oneonta

Margaret Weinberger, Bowling Green State University

Jill Wenrick, California State Polytechnic University, Pomona

Chelsi West, University of Texas at Austin

Max White, Piedmont College

Cassandra White, Georgia State University

Jennifer Wies, Eastern Kentucky University

Rebecca Wiewel, University of Arkansas, Fort Smith

Laura Wilhelm, University of Nevada, Reno

Benjamin Wilreker, College of Southern Nevada

Scott Wilson, California State University, Long Beach

Jessica Winegar, Northwestern University

Paul C. Winther, Eastern Kentucky University

Katrina Worley, American River College

Aníbal Yáñez-Chávez, California State University, San Marcos

Laura Zeeman, Red Rocks Community College

I would also like to thank the editors and staff at W. W. Norton who took a chance on this project to rethink the way anthropology is learned and taught. Julia Reidhead years ago encouraged me to keep my lecture notes in case I might write a textbook someday. Peter Lesser, my first editor, embraced the vision of the original book, signed me, brought me into the Norton fold and, with associate editor Samantha Held, has guided the creation of *Essentials*. Karl Bakeman advised me throughout the writing and production of the Full book, and has been integral to its continued success among my colleagues and students. Jackie Estrada has been an excellent copyeditor. Ted Szczepanski, Trish Marx, Aga Millhouse, and the Norton photo research department have worked hard to find engaging and beautiful illustrations. Caitlin Moran and Ashley Horna handled every part of the manuscript and managed to keep the many pieces of the book moving through production. Norton's cultural anthropology marketing and sales team, Julia Hall, Erin Brown, Natasha Zabohonski, Julie Sindel, Jonathan Mason, and Roy McClymont have advocated for the book with enthusiasm and boundless energy. Eileen Connell, Mary Williams, Grace Tuttle, and Alice Garrard put together all of the media resources that accompany the textbook. When it comes to creating new digital resources to help anthropologists teach in the classroom or teach online, I couldn't ask for a better team of people. Thanks to you all.

Heartfelt thanks to my many colleagues who have helped me think more deeply about anthropology, including members of the Sociology and Anthropology Department at Baruch College, especially Glenn Petersen, Robin Root, Carla Bellamy, Barbara Katz-Rothman, Angie Beeman, Myrna Chase, Nancy Aries, Greg Snyder and Shelley Watson, as well as Jane Schneider, Louise Lennihan, Ida Susser, Peter Kwong, Angelique Haugerud, Hugh Gusterson, Carol Greenhouse, Sydel Silverman, Michael Blim, Jonathan Shannon, Christa Salamandra, Russell Sharman, Dana Davis, Jeff Maskovsky, Rudi Gaudio, Charlene Floyd, and Zoë Sheehan Saldana. Members of the New York Academy of Sciences Anthropology Section helped me think more deeply about the relationship of culture and power. Leslie Aiello and the staff of the Wenner-Gren Foundation provided a vibrant venue to engage the cutting edges of anthropological research. The board of the American Ethnological Society allowed me to explore the theme of anthropologists engaging the world through their spring 2012 conference. My research assistants Alessandro Angelini, Andrew Hernann, Chris Grove, Suzanna Goldblatt, Lynn Horridge, and Chris Baum continually introduced me to the richness of contemporary scholarship and creative strategies for teaching and learning. Thanks also to a wonderful group of friends and family who have supported and encouraged me during this fascinating and challenging journey: K and Charlene, Douglas, Marybeth, Julia, Asher, Dayna, Zoë, Sally and Steve, Marty and Linda, the guys at the Metro Diner—Nick, Marco, and Antonio—the SPSA community, the Ajax soccer family, Shari, Vicki, Frances Helen, and Thomas Luke.

Finally, I would like to thank my students at Baruch College who every class ask to be introduced to an anthropology that is relevant to their daily lives, that tackles significant contemporary issues, and that provides them the tools of analysis and empowerment to live awake, conscious, and engaged. This book is dedicated to you and your potential to make the world a better place.

Perhaps the quintessential human task is to pass to the next generation the accumulated insights, understandings, and knowledge that will empower them to live life fully and meaningfully and to meet the challenges confronting humanity and the planet. I hope this book might contribute to that existential endeavor.

Essentials of Cultural Anthropology

Second Edition

Part 1

Anthropologists in the twenty-first century engage a world that is experiencing an unprecedented interaction of people, ideas, images, and things that continues to intensify. Communication technologies link people instantaneously across the globe. Economic activities challenge national boundaries. People are on the move between countries and within them. How can you use the tools of anthropology to engage this world on the move?

Anthropology for the 21st Century

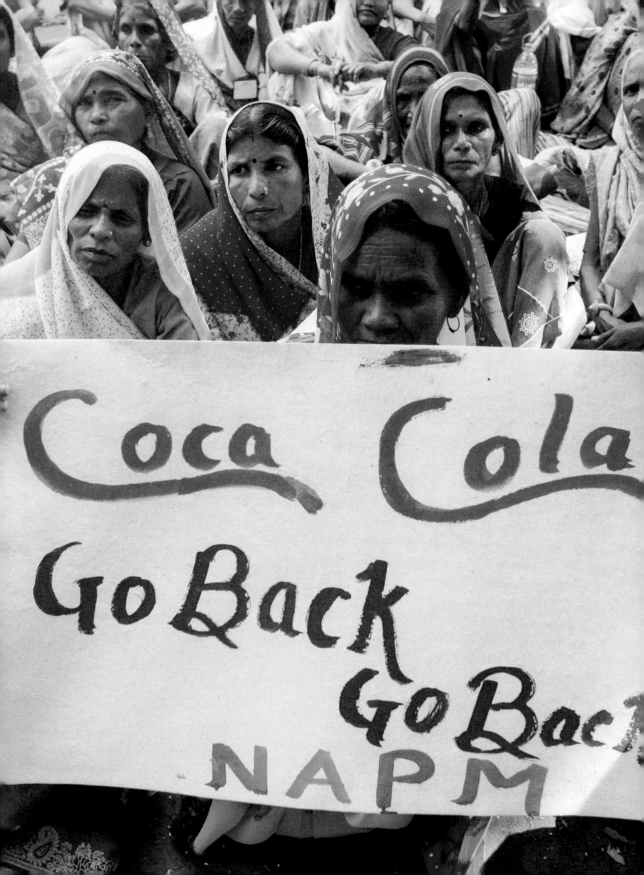

Chapter 1
Anthropology in a Global Age

Every morning the women of Plachimada, a rural area in southern India, begin a 5-kilometer (3-mile) trek in search of fresh water. The morning journey for water is a common task for many women across the world, for one-third of the planet's population live with water scarcity. But such scarcity is new for the people of Plachimada, an area of typically rich agricultural harvests.

Local residents trace the changes to March 2000, when the Coca-Cola Company opened a bottling plant in the village. The plant is capable of producing 1.2 million bottles of Coke, Sprite, and Fanta every day. Nine liters of fresh water are needed to make one liter of Coke, so Plachimada's large underground aquifer was an attractive resource for the company. But according to local officials, when the company began to drill more wells and install high-powered pumps to extract groundwater for the factory, the local water table fell dramatically—from

Indian village women protest the Coca-Cola company's exploitation of underground water supplies.

45 meters (147.5 feet) below the surface to 150 meters (492 feet), far more than could be explained by periods of limited rainfall. Hundreds of local non–Coca-Cola wells ran dry, and harvests became much less productive. Local residents also claimed that Coca-Cola workers were dumping chemical wastes on land near the factory and that the runoff was polluting the groundwater. Local women organized protests and a sit-in at the factory gates.

With the assistance of local media and international human rights networks, the protestors' activism drew national and international attention. It even spurred solidarity actions, including support from university students in the United States, Canada, the United Kingdom, and Norway. As a result, the local village council withdrew the Coca-Cola factory's license. But the state government maintained its support. The case finally reached the highest state court, which ruled that Coca-Cola must cease illegal extraction of groundwater in Plachimada. Coca-Cola closed the bottling plant in 2005. But similar battles over water use and pollution have erupted across India in the years since (Aiyer 2007; India Resource Center 2015; Shiva 2006).

MAP 1.1
Plachimada

For those of us who often enjoy a Coke with lunch or dinner—or breakfast—the story of the women of Plachimada offers a challenge to consider how our lives connect to theirs. It is a challenge to explore how a simple soft drink, made by a U.S. corporation with global operations, may link people halfway around the world in ways both simple and profound. This is also the challenge of anthropology today: to understand the rich diversity of human life and to see how our particular life experiences connect to those of others. By bringing these perspectives together, we can grasp more fully the totality and potential of human life.

At the same time, the world is changing before our eyes. Whether we call it a global village or a world without borders, we in the twenty-first century are experiencing a level of interaction among people, ideas, and systems that is intensifying at a breathtaking pace. Communication technologies link people instantaneously across the globe. Economic activities challenge national boundaries. People are on the move within countries and among them. Violence and terrorism disrupt lives. Humans have had remarkable success at feeding a growing world population, yet income inequality continues to increase—among nations and also within them. And increasing human diversity on our doorstep opens possibilities for both deeper understanding and greater misunderstanding. Clearly, the human community in the twenty-first century is being drawn further into a global web of interaction.

For today's college student, every day can be a cross-cultural experience. This may manifest itself in the most familiar places: the news you see on television, the music you listen to, the foods and beverages you consume, the women or men you date, the classmates you study with, the religious communities you attend. Today you can realistically imagine contacting any of our 7.2 billion co-inhabitants on the planet. You can read their posts on Facebook and watch their videos on YouTube. You can visit them. You wear clothes that they make. You make movies that they view. You can learn from them. You can affect their lives. How do you meet this challenge of deepening interaction and interdependence?

Anthropology provides a unique set of tools, including strategies and perspectives, for understanding our rapidly changing, globalizing world. Most of you are already budding cultural anthropologists without realizing it. Wherever you may live or go to school, you are probably experiencing a deepening encounter with the world's diversity. This phenomenon leads to broad questions such as: How do we approach human diversity in our universities, businesses, families, and religious communities? How do we understand the impact of global transformations on our lives?

Whether our field is business or education, medicine or politics, we all need a skill set for analyzing and engaging a multicultural and increasingly interconnected world and workplace. *Essentials of Cultural Anthropology: A Toolkit for a Global Age* introduces the anthropologist's tools of the trade to help you to better understand and engage the world as you move through it and, if you so choose, to apply those strategies to the challenges confronting us and our neighbors around the world. To begin our exploration of anthropology, we'll consider four key questions:

- **What is anthropology?**
- **Through what lenses do anthropologists gain a comprehensive view of human cultures?**

What Is Anthropology?

anthropology

The study of the full scope of human diversity, past and present, and the application of that knowledge to help people of different backgrounds better understand one another.

Anthropology is the study of the full scope of human diversity, past and present, and the application of that knowledge to help people of different backgrounds better understand one another. The word *anthropology* derives from the Greek words *anthropos* ("human") and *logos* ("thought," "reason," or "study"). The roots of anthropology lie in the eighteenth and nineteenth centuries, as Europeans' economic and colonial expansion increased that continent's contact with people worldwide.

BRIEF BACKGROUND

Technological breakthroughs in transportation and communication during the eighteenth and nineteenth centuries—shipbuilding, the steam engine, railroads, the telegraph—rapidly transformed the long-distance movement of people, goods, and information, in terms of both speed and quantity. As colonization, communication, trade, and travel expanded, groups of merchants, missionaries, and government officials traveled the world and returned to Europe with reports and artifacts of what seemed to them to be "exotic" people and practices. More than ever before, Europeans encountered the incredible diversity of human cultures and appearances. *Who are these people?* they asked themselves. *Where did they come from? Why do they appear so different from us?*

From the field's inception in the mid-1800s, anthropologists have conducted research to answer specific questions confronting humanity. And they have applied their knowledge and insights to practical problems facing the world.

Franz Boas (1858–1942), one of the founders of American anthropology, became deeply involved in early-twentieth-century debates on immigration, serving for a term on a presidential commission examining U.S. immigration policies. In an era when many scholars and government officials considered the different people of Europe to be of distinct biological races, U.S. immigration policies privileged immigrants from northern and western Europe over those from southern and eastern Europe. Boas worked to undermine these racialized views of immigrants. He conducted studies that showed the wide variation of physical forms within groups of the same national origin, as well as the marked physical changes in the children and grandchildren of immigrants as they adapted to the environmental conditions in their new country (Baker 2004; Boas 1912).

Audrey Richards (1899–1984), studying the Bemba people in the 1930s in what is now Zambia, focused on issues of health and nutrition among women and children, bringing concerns for nutrition to the forefront of anthropology. Her ethnography, *Chisungu* (1956), featured a rigorous and detailed study of the coming-of-age rituals of young Bemba women and established new standards for the conduct of anthropological research. Richards's research is often credited with opening a pathway for the study of nutritional issues and women's and children's health in anthropology.

Today anthropologists apply their knowledge and research strategies to a wide range of social issues. For example, they study HIV/AIDS in Africa, immigrant farmworkers in the United States, ethnic conflict in the Dominican Republic, financial firms on Wall Street, street children in Brazil, and Muslim judicial courts in Egypt. Anthropologists trace the spread of disease, promote economic development in underdeveloped countries, conduct market research, and lead diversity-training programs in schools, corporations, and community organizations. Anthropologists also study our human origins, excavating and analyzing the bones, artifacts, and DNA of our ancestors from millions of years ago to gain an understanding of who we are and where we've come from.

More than half of anthropologists today work in *applied anthropology*—that is, they work outside of academic settings to apply the strategies and insights of anthropology directly to current world problems (American Anthropological Association 2015). Even many of us who work full time in a college or university are deeply involved in public applied anthropology.

ANTHROPOLOGY'S UNIQUE APPROACH

Anthropology today retains its core commitment to understanding the richness of human diversity. Specifically, anthropology challenges us to move beyond **ethnocentrism**—the strong human tendency to believe that one's own culture or way of life is normal, natural, and superior to the beliefs and practices of others. Instead, as we will explore throughout this book, the anthropologist's toolkit of research strategies and analytical concepts enables us to appreciate, understand, and engage the diversity of human cultures in an increasingly global age. To that end, anthropology has built upon the key concerns of early generations to develop a set of characteristics unique among the social sciences.

ethnocentrism

The belief that one's own culture or way of life is normal and natural; using one's own culture to evaluate and judge the practices and ideals of others.

Anthropology Is Global in Scope. Our work covers the whole world and is not constrained by geographic boundaries. Anthropology was once noted for the study of faraway, seemingly exotic villages in developing countries. But from the beginning, anthropologists have been studying not only in the islands of the South Pacific, in the rural villages of Africa, and among indigenous peoples in Australia and North America, but also among factory workers in Britain and France, among immigrants in New York, and in other communities in the industrializing world. Over the last thirty years, anthropology has turned significant attention to urban communities in industrialized nations. With the increase of studies in North America and Europe, it is fair to say that anthropologists now embrace the full scope of humanity—across geography and through time.

Anthropologists Start with People and Their Local Communities. Although the whole world is our field, anthropologists are committed to understanding the local, everyday lives of the people we study. Our unique perspective focuses on the details and patterns of human life in the local community and then examines how particular cultures connect with the rest of humanity. Sociologists, economists, and political scientists primarily analyze broad trends, official organizations, and national policies, but anthropologists— particularly cultural anthropologists—adopt **ethnographic fieldwork** as their primary research strategy (see Chapter 3). They live with a community of people over an extended period to better understand their lives by "walking in their shoes."

Anthropologists have constantly worked to bring often-ignored voices into the global conversation. As a result, the field has a history of focusing on the cultures and struggles of non-Western and nonelite people. In recent years, some

ethnographic fieldwork

A primary research strategy in cultural anthropology typically involving living and interacting with a community of people over an extended period to better understand their lives.

Once noted for the study of seemingly far-away and "exotic" people and places, anthropologists today increasingly study the complex interaction of diverse communities in global cities like New York.

anthropologists have conducted research on elites—"studying up," as some have called it—by examining financial institutions, aid and development agencies, medical laboratories, and doctors (Gusterson 1997; Ho 2009; Nader 1972; Tett 2010). But the vast majority of our work has addressed the marginalized segments of society.

Anthropologists Study People and the Structures of Power.

Human communities are full of people, the institutions they have created for managing life in organized groups, and the systems of meaning they have built to make sense of it all. Anthropology maintains a commitment to studying both the people and the larger structures of power around them. These include families, governments, economic systems, educational institutions, militaries, the media, and religions, as well as ideas of race, ethnicity, gender, class, and sexuality.

To comprehensively examine people's lives, anthropologists consider the structures that empower and constrain those people, both locally and globally. At the same time, anthropologists seek to understand the "agency" of local people—in other words, the central role of individuals and groups in determining their own lives, even in the face of overwhelming structures of power.

Anthropologists Believe That All Humans Are Connected.

Anthropologists believe that all humans share connections that are biological, cultural, economic, and ecological. Despite fanciful stories about the "discovery" of isolated, seemingly lost tribes of "stone age" people, anthropologists suggest

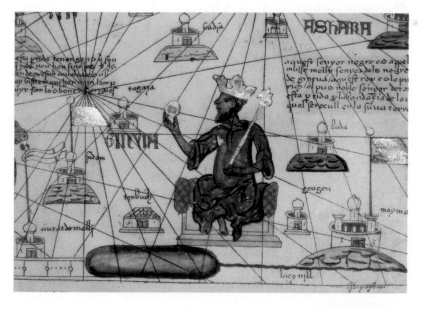

The King of Mali, West Africa, in 1375, is shown seated at the center of his vast kingdom—a key point along trade routes stretching across Africa and into the Middle East and beyond.

that there are no truly isolated people in the world today and that there rarely, if ever, were any in the past. Clearly, some groups of people are less integrated than others into the global system under construction today. But none are completely isolated. And for some, their seeming isolation may be of recent historical origins. In fact, when we look more closely at the history of so-called primitive tribes in Africa and the Americas we find that many were complex state societies before colonialism and the slave trade led to their collapse.

Human history is the story of movement and interaction, not of isolation and disconnection. Although some anthropology textbooks show "tribal"-looking people in brightly colored, seemingly exotic clothing holding cell phones, which suggests the recent and rapid integration of isolated people into a high-tech, global world, anthropological research indicates that this imagined isolation never really existed. Yes, today's period of rapid globalization is intensifying the interactions among people and the flow of goods, technology, money, and ideas within and across national boundaries, but interaction and connection are not new phenomena. They have been central to human history. Our increasing connection today reminds us that our actions have consequences for the whole world, not just for our own lives and those of our families and friends.

Through What Lenses Do Anthropologists Gain a Comprehensive View of Human Cultures?

One of the unique characteristics of anthropology in the United States is that it has developed four "lenses" for examining humanity. Constituting the **four-field approach**, these interrelated fields are physical anthropology, archaeology, linguistic anthropology, and cultural anthropology. In Europe, the four fields are quite separate, but the history of anthropology in the United States (see Chapter 3) has fostered a holistic approach for examining the complexity of human origins and human culture, past and present.

Holism refers to anthropology's commitment to look at the whole picture of human life—culture, biology, history, and language—across space and time. The field's cross-cultural and comparative approach considers the life experiences of people in every part of the world, comparing and contrasting cultural beliefs and practices to understand human similarities and differences on a global scale. Anthropologists conduct research on the contemporary world and also look deep into human history.

four-field approach
The use of four interrelated disciplines to study humanity: physical anthropology, archaeology, linguistic anthropology, and cultural anthropology.

holism
The anthropological commitment to look at the whole picture of human life—culture, biology, history, and language—across space and time.

Because we analyze both human culture and biology, anthropologists are in a unique position to offer insights into debates about the roles of "nature" and "nurture." How do biology, culture, and the environment interact to shape who we are as humans, individually and as groups? The four-field approach is key to implementing this holistic perspective within anthropology.

PHYSICAL ANTHROPOLOGY

Physical anthropology, sometimes called *biological anthropology*, is the study of humans from a biological perspective—in particular, how they have evolved over time and have adapted to their environments. Both the fossil record and genetic evidence suggest that the evolutionary line leading to modern humans split, between five and six million years ago, from the one leading to modern African apes. Modern humans thus share a common ancestor with other primates such as chimpanzees, apes, and monkeys. In fact, genetic studies reveal that humans share 97.7 percent of DNA with gorillas and 98.7 percent with chimpanzees. Through a complex evolutionary process that we are learning more about every day, *Homo sapiens* (the group of modern humans to which you and I belong) evolved in Africa fairly recently in the grand scheme of things—probably less than 200,000 years ago—and gradually spread across the planet (Larsen 2014).

Physical anthropology has several areas of specialization. **Paleoanthropology** traces the history of human evolution by reconstructing the human fossil record. Thus, paleoanthropologists excavate the teeth, skulls, and other bones of our human ancestors and analyze them to track changes in human physical form over time. From these fossils they map changes in key categories such as overall body size, cranial capacity, hand structure, head shape, and pelvic position.

physical anthropology
The study of humans from a biological perspective, particularly how they have evolved over time and adapted to their environments.

paleoanthropology
The study of the history of human evolution through the fossil record.

Paleoanthropologists trace the history of human evolution by reconstructing the human fossil record. Here, Ketut Wiradyana unearths a fossilized human skeleton buried in a cave in Indonesia's Aceh province.

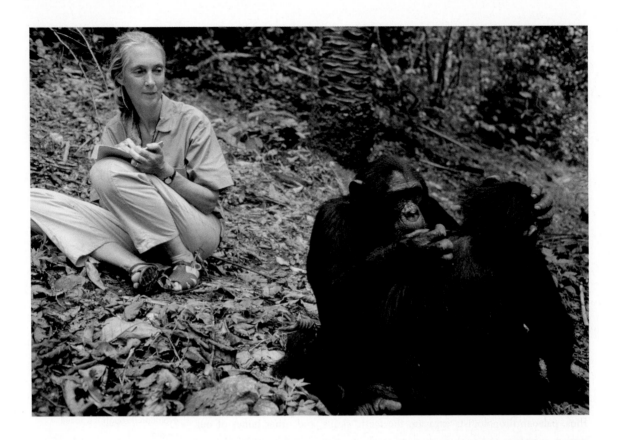

primatology

The study of living nonhuman
primates as well as primate
fossils to better understand
human evolution and early human
behavior.

Such changes reveal developments in walking, diet, intelligence, and capacity for cultural adaptation. Since the late 1970s, paleoanthropologists have also used molecular genetics to trace changes in human ancestors over time. The sequencing of DNA allows us to measure how closely humans are related to other primates and even to follow the movement of groups of people through the flow of genes. For instance, mitochondrial DNA (passed on from mother to daughter) indicates that modern *Homo sapiens* first appeared in Africa around 150,000 years ago and migrated out of Africa 100,000 years ago. This DNA evidence generally matches the findings of the archaeological record.

Primatology is another specialization within physical anthropology. Primatologists study living, nonhuman primates and primate fossils—including monkeys, apes, chimpanzees, and gorillas—to see what clues their biology, evolution, behavior, and social life might provide about our own, particularly our early human behavior. Careful observation of primates in their natural habitats and in captivity has offered significant insights into sexuality, parenting, male/female differences, cooperation, intergroup conflict, aggression, and problem solving.

Physical anthropologists also study the diversity of human physical forms that have evolved over time. Humans come in all shapes and sizes. Our differences range from body size and facial shape to skin color, height, blood chemistry, and susceptibility to certain diseases. Physical anthropologists attribute general patterns of human physical variation to adaptation to different physical environments as humans spread from Africa across the other continents. Variations in skin color, for instance, can be traced to the need to adapt to different levels of ultraviolet light as humans migrated away from the equator (see Chapter 5).

However, studies of human biology show that the physical similarities among the world's people far outweigh the differences. In fact, there is more variation *within* what are assumed to be "groups" than *between* groups. This is clearly evident in terms of the thorny concept of race (see Chapter 5). A biologically distinct race would include people in a group who share a greater statistical frequency of genes and physical traits than people outside the group. Physical anthropologists find no evidence of distinct, fixed, biological races. Rather, there is only one human race. Attempts to identify distinct biological races are flawed and arbitrary, as no clear biological lines exist to define different races. Racial categories, which vary significantly from culture to culture, are loosely based on a few visible physical characteristics such as skin color, but they have no firm basis in genetics (Larsen 2014; Mukhopadhyay, Henze, and Moses 2007). We will return to this discussion of the biological and social dimensions of race in Chapter 5.

ARCHAEOLOGY

Archaeology involves the investigation of the human past by means of excavating and analyzing material remains (artifacts). The goal is not to recover buried treasure, but to understand past human life. Some archaeologists study the emergence of early states in places such as Egypt, India, China, and Mexico. They have unearthed grand sites such as the pyramids of Egypt and Mexico and the terra-cotta warriors guarding the tomb of China's Qin Dynasty emperor. Others focus on the histories of less spectacular sites that shed light on the everyday lives of people in local villages and households.

Archaeology is our only source of information about human societies before writing began (around 5,500 years ago). Because we are unable to travel back through time to observe human behavior, **prehistoric archaeology** seeks to reconstruct human behavior in the distant past (before written records) from artifacts that give significant clues about our ancestors' lives. Campsites, hunting grounds, buildings, burials, and especially garbage dumps are rich sources of material. There, archaeologists find tools, weapons, pottery, human and animal bones, jewelry, seeds, charcoal, ritual items, building foundations, and even coprolites (fossilized fecal matter). Through excavation and analysis of these material remains, archaeologists reconstruct family and work life. What animals did the people eat? What seeds did they plant? What tools and crafts did they make? Coprolites reveal a great deal about the local diet. Burial sites provide significant

archaeology
The investigation of the human past by means of excavating and analyzing artifacts.

prehistoric archaeology
The reconstruction of human behavior in the distant past (before written records) through the examination of artifacts.

Prehistoric garbage dumps provide rich sources of material for understanding the cultural practices of human ancestors. Today, "garbologists" also learn about contemporary culture by examining what people throw away, including in large trash landfills like the one pictured here. What might an anthropologist 200 years from now learn about your community by studying its garbage?

data about how people treated their elders and their dead, what rituals they may have practiced, and their ideas about the afterlife. Archaeological evidence can suggest trade patterns, consumption habits, gender roles, and power stratification.

Unlike prehistoric archaeology, which looks at the time before writing, **historic archaeology** explores the more recent past and often combines the examination of physical remains and artifacts with that of written or oral records. Historic archaeologists excavate houses, stores, factories, sunken slave ships, and even polar ice caps to better understand recent human history and the impact of humans on the environment. For example, recent excavations of former slave plantations in the southern United States, combined with historical records such as deeds, census forms, personal letters, and diaries, have provided rich insight into the lives of African slaves in the seventeenth and eighteenth centuries. Students in the North Atlantic Biocultural Organisation's international field school conduct excavations in Iceland that reveal not only historical information about the settling of the North Atlantic but also data on major changes in the contemporary global climate. Core samples from borings drilled through the glaciers reveal sediments deposited from the air over thousands of years as the glaciers formed; such samples allow archaeologists to track global warming and the impact of greenhouse gases on climate change.

historic archaeology

The exploration of the more recent past through an examination of physical remains and artifacts as well as written or oral records.

LINGUISTIC ANTHROPOLOGY

linguistic anthropology

The study of human language in the past and the present.

Linguistic anthropology involves the study of human language in the past and the present. Languages are complex, vibrant, and constantly changing systems of symbols through which people communicate with one another. (Think about how hard it is to get your ideas across in your college papers, in text messages, or even in conversation with your parents.) Languages are very flexible and inventive. (Consider how English has adapted to the rise of the Internet to include such new words and concepts as *spam, instant messages, texting, Googling, Skyping, snapchat,* and *facetime.*) A language clearly reflects a people's ideas of and experiences with the world. But linguistic anthropologists suggest that language may also limit and constrain a people's views of the world. In other words, can we think clearly about something if we don't have an adequately sophisticated language?

Language is perhaps the most distinctive feature of being human. It is the key to our ability to learn and share culture from generation to generation, to cooperate in groups, and to adapt to our environment. While some animals—including dolphins and whales, bees, and ravens—have a limited range of communication, human language is more complex, creative, and extensively used.

Linguistic anthropology includes three main areas of specialization. **Descriptive linguists** work to carefully describe spoken languages and preserve them as written languages. For example, some descriptive linguists spend years in rural areas helping local people construct a written language from their spoken language. **Historic linguists** study how language changes over time within a culture and as it moves across cultures. **Sociolinguists** study language in its social and cultural contexts. They examine how different speakers use language in different situations or with different people. They explore how language is affected by factors such as race, gender, age, class, or other relationships of power. Consider the so-called "N-word"—a very controversial word in the United States today. Sociolinguists would explore the word's usage in American English: Where did it come from? Who uses it, and in what situations? How does its meaning change according to the speaker and the context? When is it a term of racial hatred? When is it a term of camaraderie? We will explore these issues further in Chapter 4.

CULTURAL ANTHROPOLOGY

Cultural anthropology is the study of people's everyday lives and their communities—their behaviors, beliefs, and institutions. Cultural anthropologists explore all aspects of human culture, such as war and violence, love and sexuality, child rearing and death. They examine what people do and how they live, work, and play together. But they also search for patterns of meaning embedded within each culture, and they develop theories about how cultures work. Cultural anthropologists examine the ways in which local communities interact with global forces.

Ethnographic fieldwork is at the heart of cultural anthropology. Through **participant observation**—living and working with people on a daily basis, often

descriptive linguists
Those who analyze languages and their component parts.

historic linguists
Those who study how language changes over time within a culture and how languages travel across cultures.

sociolinguists
Those who study language in its social and cultural contexts.

cultural anthropology
The study of people's communities, behaviors, beliefs, and institutions, including how people make meaning as they live, work, and play together.

participant observation
A key anthropological research strategy involving both participation in and observation of the daily life of the people being studied.

for a year or more—the cultural anthropologist strives to see the world through the eyes of others. Intensive fieldwork has the power to educate the anthropologist by (1) making what may at first seem very unfamiliar into something that ultimately seems quite familiar, and (2) taking what has seemed very familiar and making it seem very strange. Through fieldwork, anthropologists look beyond the taken-for-granted, everyday experience of life to discover the complex systems of power and meaning that all people construct. These include the many systems we will cover throughout this book: gender, sexuality, race, ethnicity, religion, kinship, class, and economic and political systems.

Cultural anthropologists analyze and compare ethnographic data across cultures in a process called **ethnology**. This process looks beyond specific local realities to see more general patterns of human behavior and to explore how local experiences intersect with global dynamics. Ultimately, through intensive ethnographic fieldwork and cross-cultural comparison, cultural anthropologists seek to help people better understand one another and the way the world works.

ethnology

The analysis and comparison of ethnographic data across cultures.

What Is Globalization, and Why Is It Important for Anthropology?

The term **globalization** refers to the worldwide intensification of interactions and increased movement of money, people, goods, and ideas within and across national borders. Growing integration of the global economy has driven the

globalization

The worldwide intensification of interactions and increased movement of money, people, goods, and ideas within and across national borders.

Syrian refugees land on the coast of Greece in 2015.

intense globalization of the past forty years. Corporations are relocating factories halfway around the world. People are crossing borders legally and illegally in search of work. Goods, services, and ideas are flowing along high-speed transportation and communication networks. People, organizations, and nations are being drawn into closer connection.

Globalization is not an entirely new phenomenon. Intensification of global interaction occurred in earlier eras as breakthroughs in communication and transportation brought the world's people into closer contact. The present period of globalization, however, has reached a level of intensity previously unknown.

Although globalization is often portrayed in a positive light in the media and popular discourse, the realities are much more complicated. The new technologies associated with globalization may indeed allow more and more people to interact and communicate, but billions of other people are being left out of these advances. Moreover, along with the economic expansion and growth associated with globalization, there are equally significant global economic inequalities.

GLOBALIZATION AND ANTHROPOLOGY

Globalization and anthropology are intricately intertwined, both in history and in the contemporary world. As we have noted, the field of anthropology emerged in the mid-nineteenth century during a time of intense globalization. At that time, technological inventions in transportation and communication were consolidating a period of colonial encounter, the slave trade, and the emerging capitalist economic system and were enabling deeper interactions of people across cultures. Early anthropologists sought to organize the vast quantity of information being accumulated about people across the globe, though, unlike most contemporary anthropologists, who conduct research in the field, they did so primarily from the comfort of their own homes and meeting halls.

Today another era of even more intense globalization is transforming the lives of the people whom anthropologists study in every part of the world. And, as we will see throughout this book, it is also transforming the ways anthropologists conduct research and communicate their findings. To understand these sweeping changes, we must understand the key dynamics of globalization at play in the world today (Inda and Rosaldo 2002; Kearney 1995; Lewellen 2002; Trouillot 2003).

GLOBALIZATION: KEY DYNAMICS

Globalization today is characterized by several key dynamics: time-space compression, flexible accumulation, increasing migration, and uneven development, all of which are happening at in increasingly rapid pace. These dynamics are reshaping the ways humans adapt to the natural world, and the ways the natural world is adapting to us.

Time-Space Compression. According to the theory of **time-space compression**, the rapid innovation of communication and transportation technologies has transformed the way we think about space (distances) and time. Jet travel, supertankers, superhighways, high-speed railways, telephones, computers, the Internet, digital cameras, and cell phones have condensed time and space, changing our sense of how long it takes to do something and how far away someplace or someone is. The world is no longer as big as it used to be.

Consider these examples of a changing sense of time. Today we can fly from New York to Paris in eight hours or from Los Angeles to Hong Kong in twelve. A letter that once took ten days to send from Texas to Kenya can now be attached as a PDF and emailed with a few clicks of a mouse. We instant message, text message, Skype, videoconference, and FaceTime. These kinds of changes have transformed not only how long it takes us to do something, but also how quickly we expect other people to do things. For example, how much time do you have to respond to an email or a text message before someone thinks you are rude or irresponsible?

Flexible Accumulation. A second characteristic of today's globalization, **flexible accumulation**, reflects the fact that advances in transportation and communication have enabled companies to move their production facilities and activities around the world in search of cheaper labor, lower taxes, and fewer environmental regulations—in other words, to be increasingly flexible about the way they accumulate profits (see Chapter 11). Companies in developed countries move their factories to export-processing zones in the developing world, a process called *offshoring*. Other corporations shift part of their work to employees in other parts of the world, a process called *outsourcing*. For example, General Motors used to make all of its automobiles in Flint, Michigan, but now the company has factories in Mexico, Brazil, China, and Thailand. Walmart, once known for its advertising campaign "Made in America," now has 7,000 factories in China.

Other examples span the globe as well: Phone and computer companies hire English-speaking operators and technicians in Bangalore, India, to answer customers' questions called in on 800 numbers. A company based in Sierre Leone, West Africa, processes traffic tickets issued in New York City. X-rays, CT scans, and MRIs taken in Colorado may be read and interpreted by doctors in Manila, the Philippines. Clearly, flexible accumulation allows corporations to maximize profits, while time-space compression enables the efficient management of global networks and distribution systems (Harvey 1990).

Increasing Migration. A third characteristic of globalization is **increasing migration**, the accelerated movement of people both within countries and between countries. In fact, recent globalization has spurred the international migration of more than 232 million people, 46 million of them to the United States alone (see Chapter 11) (United Nations Department of Economic and Social Affairs, Population Division 2013). An estimated 700 million more are internal migrants within their own countries, usually moving from rural to urban areas in search of work. The Chinese government counts nearly 250 million internal migrants floating in China's cities, drawn by construction projects, service jobs, and export-oriented factories (Armstrong 2013; Liang, Li, and Ma 2014).

In countries from Pakistan to Kenya to Peru, rural workers migrate to urban areas seeking to improve their lives and the lives of their families back home. This movement of people within and across national borders is stretching out human relationships and interactions across space and time. Immigrants send money home, call and email friends and family, and sometimes even travel back and forth. Migration is building connections between distant parts of the world, replacing face-to-face interactions with more remote encounters and potentially reducing the hold of the local environment over people's lives and imaginations.

Uneven Development. Globalization is also characterized by **uneven development**. Although many people associate globalization with rapid economic development and progress, globalization has not brought equal benefits to the world's people. Some travel the globe for business or pleasure; others are limited to more local forms of transportation. Although 3.2 billion people now have Internet access, the distribution is uneven. 4 billion people in developing countries remain offline, representing two-thirds of their population. And only 9.5 percent of the 940 million people living in the least-developed countries have Internet access. Europe, North America, and Asia account for the vast majority of high-tech consumption, while areas of Africa are marginalized and excluded from the globalization process (International Telecommunication Union 2015). Such uneven development and uneven access to the benefits of globalization reflect the negative side of changes in the world today.

Although the global economy is creating extreme wealth, it is also creating extreme poverty. Excluding China (which has experienced rapid economic growth), global poverty has increased over the past twenty years. Fully 40 percent of the world's population live in poverty, defined as income of less than $2.00 per day. And nearly 1 billion people live in extreme poverty, surviving on less than $1.25 each day (United Nations 2015). Even in the United States, the wealthiest country in the world, some full-time workers who earn the minimum wage make so little money that they must rely on state welfare programs for food stamps and medical care for themselves and their children. In Chapter 11, we will explore the possibility that the rapid growth seen in globalization actually *depends on* uneven development—extracting the resources of some to fuel the success of others.

uneven development
The unequal distribution of the benefits of globalization.

GLOBALIZATION AND THE ENVIRONMENT

Of course, modern humans and our ancestors have been adapting to changes in the environment for millions of years. In fact, perhaps our most distinctive characteristic is our ability to adapt—to figure out how to survive and thrive in a world that is rapidly changing. Although change has been a constant, so has human adaptation, both biological and cultural.

Our species has successfully adapted genetically to changes in the natural environment over millions of years. We walk upright on two legs. We have binocular vision and see in color. We have opposable thumbs for grasping. Our bodies also adapt temporarily to changes in the environment on a daily basis. We sweat to keep cool in the heat, tan to block out the sun's ultraviolet rays, shiver to generate warmth in the cold, and breathe rapidly to take in more oxygen at high altitudes.

As our ancestors evolved and developed greater brain capacity, they invented cultural adaptations—tools, the controlled use of fire, and weapons—to navigate the natural environment. Today our use of culture to adapt to the world around us is incredibly sophisticated. In the United States, we like our air conditioners on a hot July afternoon and our radiators in the winter. Oxygen masks deploy for us in sky-high airplanes, and sunscreen protects us against sunburn and skin cancer. These are just a few familiar examples of adaptations our culture has made. Looking more broadly, the worldwide diversity of human culture itself is a testimony to human flexibility and adaptability to particular environments.

Shaping the Natural World. To say that humans adapt to the natural world is only part of the story, for humans actively shape the natural world as well. Humans have planted, grazed, paved, excavated, and built on at least 40 percent of Earth's surface. Our activities have caused profound changes in the atmosphere, soil, and oceans. Human impact on the planet is so extensive that scholars in many disciplines have come to refer to the current historical period as the **Anthropocene**—a distinct era in which human activity is reshaping the planet in permanent ways. Whereas our ancestors struggled to adapt to the uncertainties of heat, cold, solar radiation, disease, natural disasters, famines, and droughts, today we confront changes and social forces that we ourselves have set in motion. These changes include climate change, water scarcity, overpopulation, extreme poverty, biological weapons, and nuclear missiles. These pose the greatest risks to human survival. As globalization intensifies, it escalates the human impact on the planet and on other humans, further accelerating the pace of change.

Human activity already threatens the world's ecological balance. We do not need to wait to see the effects. For instance, population growth and consumption

Anthropocene

The current historical era in which human activity is reshaping the planet in permanent ways.

patterns have placed incredible stress on Earth's water resources, both fresh water and saltwater. As the opening story of Plachimada, India, reveals, the struggle to gain access to the fresh water in lakes, rivers, and aquifers can be a source of conflict. Private companies are buying up rights to water in many countries, and bottled water sales have grown to a $50 billion global business. The seemingly vast oceans are also experiencing significant distress. The oil spill created by the British Petroleum Deepwater Horizon disaster in 2010 poured 210 million gallons of crude oil into the Gulf of Mexico over the course of two months. In the middle of the Pacific Ocean sits a floating island of plastic the size of Texas, caught in an intersection of ocean currents. The plastic originates mainly from consumers in Asia and North America. Pollution from garbage, sewage, and agricultural fertilizer runoff, combined with overfishing and spills from offshore oil drilling, may kill off edible sea life completely by 2048 (Worm et al. 2006). These sobering realities are characteristic of today's global age and the impacts of increasing globalization.

Actual stomach contents of a baby albatross on the remote north Pacific Midway Atoll, 2,000 miles from the nearest continent. Thousands die as their parents feed them lethal quantities of floating plastic trash that they mistake for food as they forage over the polluted Pacific Ocean. © Chris Jordan, courtesy of Kopeikin Gallery, Los Angeles.

Humans and Climate Change. Human activity is also producing rapid **climate change**. Driven by the increase of greenhouse gases in the atmosphere, largely from the burning of fossil fuels, global warming is already reshaping the physical world and threatening to radically change much of modern human civilization. Scientists predict a rise in average global temperatures of between 2.5 and 10 degrees Fahrenheit by 2100 (National Aeronautics and Space Administration 2015). Changing weather patterns have already begun to alter agricultural patterns and crop yields. Global warming has spurred rapid melting of polar ice and glaciers, well before most scientists had predicted, and the pace is increasing.

Melting glaciers mean rising sea levels. Given the current speed of melting, a one- to four-foot sea-level rise by 2100 is entirely possible (National Aeronautics and Space Administration 2015). Half of the world's population lives within fifty miles of the coast, so the implications are enormous—especially in low-lying delta regions. Bangladesh, home to more than 150 million people, will be largely underwater. Miami—parts of which already flood during heavy rain storms—will have an ocean on both sides. Should all the glacier ice on Greenland melt, sea levels would rise an estimated twenty-three feet.

How will the planet cope with the growth of the human population from 7.2 billion in 2015 to more than 9 billion in 2050? Our ancestors have successfully adapted to the natural world around us for millions of years, but human activity and technological innovation now threaten to overwhelm the natural world beyond its ability to adapt to us.

How Is Globalization Transforming Anthropology?

The field of anthropology has changed significantly in the past thirty years as the world has been transformed by globalization. Just as the local cultures and communities we study are changing in response to these forces, our focus and strategies must also change.

CHANGING COMMUNITIES

Globalization is changing the communities we study. Today vulnerable people and cultures are encountering powerful economic forces that are reshaping family, gender roles, ethnicity, sexuality, love, and work patterns. Debates over the effects of globalization on local cultures and communities are intense. Critics of globalization warn of the dangers of homogenization and the loss of traditional local cultures as products marketed by global companies flood into local communities.

(Many of these brands originate in Western countries, including Coca-Cola, Microsoft, McDonald's, Levi's, Disney, Walmart, CNN, and Hollywood.) Yet globalization's proponents note the new exposure to diversity that is now available to people worldwide, opening possibilities for personal choice that were previously unimaginable. As with the case of Plachimada, India—and as we will see throughout this book—although global forces are increasingly affecting local communities, local communities are also actively working to reshape encounters with globalization to their own benefit: fighting detrimental changes, negotiating better terms of engagement, and embracing new opportunities.

CHANGING RESEARCH STRATEGIES

Anthropologists are also changing research strategies to reflect the transformations affecting the communities we study (see Chapter 3). Today it is impossible to study a local community without considering the global forces that affect it. Thus, anthropologists are engaging in more multi-sited ethnographies, comparing communities linked, for instance, by migration, production, or communication. My own research is a case in point.

Rural Fuzhou villagers worship at a Chinese temple constructed with funds sent home by community members working in the United States.

MAP 1.2
Fuzhou/New York

Multi-sited Ethnography: China and New York. When I began my fieldwork in New York City's Chinatown in 1997, I anticipated conducting a year-long study of Chinese immigrant religious communities—Christian, Buddhist, and Daoist—and their role in the lives of new immigrants. I soon realized, however, that I did not understand why tens of thousands of immigrants from Fuzhou, China, were taking such great risks—some hiring human smugglers at enormous cost—to come and work in low-paying jobs in restaurants, garment shops, construction trades, and nail salons. To figure out why so many were leaving China, one summer I followed their immigrant journey back home.

I boarded a plane from New York to Hong Kong and on to Fuzhou, the capital of Fujian Province on China's southeast coast. From Fuzhou, I took a local bus to a small town at the end of the line. A ferry carried me across a river to a three-wheeled motor taxi that transported me across dirt roads to the main square of a rural fishing village at the foot of a small mountain. I began to hike up the slope and finally caught a ride on a motorcycle to my destination.

Back in New York, I had met the master of a temple, an immigrant from Fuzhou who was raising money from other immigrant workers to rebuild their temple in China. He had invited me to visit their hometown and participate in a temple festival. Now, finally arriving at the temple after a transcontinental journey, I was greeted by hundreds of pilgrims from neighboring towns and villages. "What are you doing here?" one asked. When I told them that I was an anthropologist from the United States, that I had met some of their fellow villagers in New York, and that I had come to learn about their village, they began to laugh. "Go back to New York!" they said. "Most of our village is there already, not here in this little place." Then we all laughed together, acknowledging the irony of my traveling to China when they wanted to go to New York—but also marveling at the remarkable connection built across the 10,000 miles between this little village and one of the most urban metropolises in the world.

Over the years I have made many trips back to the villages around Fuzhou. My research experiences have brought alive the ways in which globalization is transforming the world and the practice of anthropology. Today 70 percent of the village population resides in the United States, but the villagers live out time-space compression as they continue to build strong ties between New York and China. They travel back and forth. They build temples, roads, and schools back home. They transfer money by wire. They call, text, Skype, and post videos online. They send children back to China to be raised by grandparents in the village. Parents in New York watch their children play in the village using webcams and the Internet.

Back home, local factories built by global corporations produce toys for Disney and McDonald's and Mardi Gras beads for the city of New Orleans. The local jobs provide employment alternatives, but they have not replaced migration out of China as the best option for improving local lives.

These changes are happening incredibly rapidly, transforming people's lives and communities on opposite sides of the world. But globalization brings uneven benefits that break down along lines of ethnicity, gender, age, language, legal status, kinship, and class. These disparities give rise to issues that we will address in depth throughout this book. Such changes mean that I as an anthropologist have to adjust my own fieldwork to span my subjects' entire reality, a reality that now encompasses a village in China, the metropolis of New York City, and many people and places in between (Guest 2003, 2011). And as you will discover throughout this book, other anthropologists are likewise adapting their strategies to meet the challenges of globalization. Learning to think like an anthropologist will enable you to better navigate our increasingly interconnected world.

Toolkit

Thinking Like an Anthropologist:
Living in a Global Age

As you begin your exploration of anthropology, the women of Plachimada discussed in the chapter opening may provide you with a powerful image to keep in mind and challenge you to think more anthropologically about the world and its people. *Essentials of Cultural Anthropology: A Toolkit for a Global Age* is designed to help you explore the richness of human diversity, uncover your conscious and subconscious ideas of how the world works (or should work), and develop some strategies for living, working, and learning in an environment where diversity is a part of daily life.

Solving the challenges that face the human race in your lifetime will require greater engagement, interaction, and cooperation—not more isolation and ignorance. The future of the planet requires everyone to develop the skills of an anthropologist if our species is to thrive and, perhaps, even to survive. These skills include cross-cultural knowledge and sensitivity; perceptiveness of other people; understanding of systems of meaning and systems of power; and consciousness of one's own culture, assumptions, beliefs, and power. By the end of this book, you will have many of the skills needed to think carefully about these questions:

- **What is anthropology?**
- **Through what lenses do anthropologists gain a comprehensive view of human cultures?**
- **What is globalization, and why is it important for anthropology?**
- **How is globalization transforming anthropology?**

You also will discover that the study of anthropology helps you rethink many of your assumptions about the world and how it works. For the magic of anthropology lies in unmasking the underlying structures of life, in spurring the analytical imagination, and in providing the skills to be alert, aware, sensitive, and successful in a rapidly changing—and often confusing—multicultural and global world.

Key Terms

Chapter 2
Culture

What can you learn about culture—particularly American culture—from a McDonald's Happy Meal? The Happy Meal is perhaps the most iconic menu item for the world's largest chain of hamburger fast-food restaurants, serving 68 million customers in 119 countries. What can we learn by looking a little more carefully?

Opening up the bright red box with the broad yellow smile, you find a paper-wrapped hamburger and a miniature side of French Fries. A choice of yogurt or apple slices, juice or soda, and a toy for a boy or a girl complete the menu. The packaging is covered with games and advertisements. All this for just over $3.00. Clearly, many people like their food fast, cheap, processed, predictable, and entertaining—high in saturated fat, sugar, and salt followed by a chaser of sugary, carbonated, and caffeinated soda.

Each element of the Happy Meal has its own elaborate journey. Imagine its point of origin, the hands it has passed through, the aspects of economic and political

What can you learn about culture from a McDonald's Happy Meal?

systems it intersects, its place on the table and in our mouths, and its steps to a final resting spot. By the time it reaches our table the Happy Meal has been shaped by ideas of the American diet, government regulation, industrial agricultural production, the environment, social movements, health concerns, labor practices, gender norms, and connections to workers and consumers across the globe.

For instance, the U.S. Department of Agriculture regulates what can go into a hamburger. The tiny box of fries and apple slices are a response to consumer pressure for healthier food. The amount of water required to produce 10 pounds of beef is equivalent to that used by the average American family in a year. Expanding cattle ranching destroys climate-cooling rainforests in Central and South America. Young women in Chinese sweatshop factories make the toys. The costs of producing a Happy Meal far exceed its sale price. And McDonald's' gender assumptions determine which toy your child receives.

Turning an anthropological eye to food opens a window on the complex thing we call culture: the intricate patterns of ideas and behaviors humans create to live together in groups. Although we may consider eating as "doing what comes naturally," as an instinctive impulse, eating varies widely across cultures. What you eat, how you eat, and even who you eat with are shaped by culture, including ideas about religion, gender, race, ethnic identity, immigration, class, and age.

Eating is an intensely intimate cultural practice with complicated social meanings. Consider the role of food in your own family gatherings, romantic encounters, celebratory events, and religious rituals—the elaborate rules and deep significances.

Food is also closely linked to power. Who eats and who doesn't? In a time of unprecedented abundance, still 11 percent of the population do not have enough to eat on any given day, 663 million people lack access to safe drinking water, and 30 percent of the world's children are undernourished (World Health Organization 2015a). The study of food can illuminate the deep fault lines and often entrenched patterns of stratification and inequality within and between cultures.

As anthropologists, we can begin to see that a Happy Meal is not simply a happy meal. It is deeply embedded in processes central to American cultural life, and in this increasingly globalized world, to processes that affect every person on our planet (Anderson 2005; Counihan and Van Esterik, 2013; Robbins 2013; Watson and Caldwell, 2004).

In this chapter, we will apply an anthropologist's viewpoint to culture and consider its crucial role in shaping how we behave and what we think. In particular, we will consider:

- **What is culture?**
- **How has the culture concept developed in anthropology?**
- **How are culture and power related?**

- **How much of who you are is shaped by biology, and how much by culture?**

- **How is culture created?**

- **How is globalization transforming culture?**

By the end of the chapter you should have a clear sense of how anthropologists think about culture and use culture to analyze human life. By exploring this seemingly familiar concept, you can become conscious of the many unconscious patterns of belief and action that you accept as normal and natural. You can also begin to see how such patterns shape your everyday choices and even your basic conceptions of what is real and what isn't. By examining the rich diversity and complexity of human cultural expressions, you may also begin to grasp more fully the potential and possibilities for your own life.

All humans must eat. But what we eat, how we eat, and who we eat with are shaped by local cultures. (*Top left*) a street market in Bangkok; Thailand; (*right*) an interfaith Passover Seder with Muslims and Jews in Guba, Azerbaijan; (*bottom left*) planning a business startup in London.

What Is Culture?

When people hear the word *culture*, they often think about the material goods or artistic forms produced by distinct groups of people—Chinese food, Middle Eastern music, Indian clothing, Greek architecture, African dances. Sometimes people assume that culture means elite art forms such as those displayed in museums, operas, or ballets. But for anthropologists, culture is much more: It encompasses people's entire way of life.

Culture is a system of knowledge, beliefs, patterns of behavior, artifacts, and institutions that are created, learned, shared, and contested by a group of people. Culture is our manual for understanding and interacting with the people and the world around us. It includes shared norms, values, symbols, mental maps of reality, and material objects as well as structures of power—including the media, education, religion, and politics—in which our understanding of the world is shaped, reinforced, and negotiated. A cultural group may be large or small, and it may have within it significant diversity of region, religion, race, gender, sexuality, class, generation, and ethnic identity. It may not be accepted by everyone, even those living in a particular place or time. But ultimately, the culture that we learn has the potential to shape our ideas of what is normal and natural, what we can say and do, and even what we can think.

culture

A system of knowledge, beliefs, patterns of behavior, artifacts, and institutions that are created, learned, shared, and contested by a group of people.

CULTURE IS LEARNED AND TAUGHT

Humans do not genetically inherit culture. We learn culture throughout our lives from the people and cultural institutions that surround us. Anthropologists call the process of learning culture **enculturation**. Some aspects of culture we learn through formal instruction: English classes in school, religious instruction, visits to the doctor, history lessons, dance classes. Other processes of enculturation are informal and even unconscious as we absorb culture from family, friends, and the media. All humans are equally capable of learning culture and of learning any culture they are exposed to.

enculturation

The process of learning culture.

The process of social learning, passing cultural information within populations and across generations, is not unique to humans. Many animals learn social behavior from their immediate group: Wolves learn hunting strategies from the wolf pack. Whales learn to produce and distinguish the unique calls of their pod. Among monkeys and apes, our closest biological relatives, learned behaviors are even more common. Chimpanzees have been observed teaching their young to create rudimentary tools, stripping bark from a twig that they then insert into an anthill to extract a tasty and nutritious treat. But the human capacity to learn culture is unparalleled.

Culture is taught as well as learned. Humans establish cultural institutions as mechanisms for enculturating their members. Schools, medical and legal systems, media, and religious institutions promote the ideas and concepts that are considered central to the culture. Rules, regulations, laws, teachers, doctors, religious leaders, police officers, and sometimes militaries promote and enforce what is considered appropriate behavior and thinking.

How is culture learned and taught? Here, kindergartners learn Mandarin Chinese at the New York Chinese School.

CULTURE IS SHARED YET CONTESTED

No individual has his or her own culture. Culture is a shared experience developed as a result of living as a member of a group. Through enculturation, humans learn how to communicate and establish patterns of behavior that allow life in community, often in close proximity and sometimes with limited resources. Cultures may be shared by groups, large and small. For example, anthropologists may speak of Indian culture (1 billion people), of U.S. culture (300 million people) or of the culture of the Yanomami tribe (several thousand people) living in the Amazonian rainforest. There may be smaller cultures within larger cultures. For instance, your college classroom has a culture, one that you must learn in order to succeed academically. A classroom culture includes shared understandings of what to wear, how to sit, when to arrive or leave, how to communicate with classmates and the instructor, and how to challenge authority, as well as formal and informal processes of enculturation.

Although culture is shared by members of groups, it is also constantly contested, negotiated, and changing. Culture is never static. Just as cultural institutions serve as structures for promoting enculturation, they also serve as arenas for challenging, debating, and changing core cultural beliefs and behaviors. Intense debates erupt over school curriculums, medical practices, media content, religious practices, and government policies as members of a culture engage in sometimes dramatic confrontations about their collective purpose and direction.

CULTURE IS SYMBOLIC AND MATERIAL

Through enculturation, over time the members of a culture develop a shared body of cultural knowledge and patterns of behavior. Though anthropologists no longer think of culture as a completely separate, unique possession of a specific group of people, most argue that a common cultural core exists, at least among the dominant segments of the culture. Norms, values, symbols, and mental maps of reality are four elements that an anthropologist may consider in attempting to understand the complex workings of a culture. These are not universal; they vary from culture to culture. Even within a culture not everyone shares equally in that cultural knowledge, nor does everyone agree completely on it. But the elements of a culture powerfully frame what its participants can say, what they can do, and even what they think is possible and impossible, real or unreal.

Norms. **Norms** are ideas or rules about how people should behave in particular situations or toward certain other people—what is considered "normal" and appropriate behavior. Norms may include what to wear on certain occasions such as weddings, funerals, work, and school; what you can say in polite company; how younger people should treat older people; and who you can date or, as the opening anecdote demonstrated, what you can eat when. Many norms are assumed, not written down. We learn them over time—consciously and unconsciously— and incorporate them into our patterns of daily living. Other norms are formalized in writing and made publicly available, such as a country's laws, a system of medical or business ethics, or the code of academic integrity in your college or university. Norms may vary for segments of the population, imposing different expectations on men and women, for instance, or children and adults. Cultural norms may be widely accepted, but they may also be debated, challenged, and changed, particularly when norms enforced by a dominant group disadvantage or oppress a minority within the population.

Consider the question of whom you can marry. You may consider the decision to be a matter of personal choice, but in many cultures the decision is not left to the whims of young people. The results are too important. Often it is two families who arrange the marriage, not two individuals, although these patterns are under pressure from the globalization of Western cultural practices.

Cultures have clear norms, based on ideas of age, kinship, sexuality, race, religion, class, and legal status, that specify what is normal and what is not. Let's consider some extreme cases. In Nazi Germany, the Nuremburg Laws passed in 1935 banned marriage or sexual relations between German Jews and persons with German or related blood. From 1949 to 1985, South Africa's apartheid government, dominated by white lawmakers, declared marriage and sex between whites and "coloreds" (people of mixed race), Asians, and blacks to be a crime under the Prohibition of Mixed Marriages Act and the Immorality Act. In the history of the United States, as many as forty states passed anti-miscegenation laws—that is, laws barring interracial marriage and sex. Such laws targeted marriages between whites and nonwhites—primarily blacks, but also Asians and Native Americans. Only in 1967 did the U.S. Supreme Court unanimously rule (in *Loving v. Virginia*)

norms

Ideas or rules about how people should behave in particular situations or toward certain other people.

that these laws were unconstitutional, thereby striking down statutes still on the books in sixteen states (all the former slave states plus Oklahoma).

Cultural norms may discourage *exogamy* (marriage outside one's "group") and encourage *endogamy* (marriage within one's "group"). Think about your own family. Who could you bring home to your parents? Could you cross boundaries of race, ethnicity, nationality, religion, class, or gender? Although U.S. culture has very few formal rules about whom one can marry—with some exclusions around age, sexuality, and certain kinship relations—cultural norms still powerfully inform and enforce our behavior.

Most people, though not all, accept and follow a culture's norms. If they choose to challenge the norms, other members of the culture have means for enforcing its standards, whether through shunning, institutionalized punishment such as fines or imprisonment, or, in more extreme cases, violence and threats of violence.

Values.
Cultures promote and cultivate a core set of **values**—fundamental beliefs about what is important, what makes a good life, and what is true, right, and beautiful. Values reflect shared ultimate standards that should guide people's behavior, as well as goals that people feel are important for themselves, their families, and their community. What would you identify as the core values of U.S. culture? Individualism? Independence? Care for the most vulnerable? Freedom of speech, press, and religion? Equal access to social mobility?

As with all elements of culture, cultural values are not fixed. They can be debated and contested. And they may have varying degrees of influence. For example, if you pick up a newspaper in any country you will find a deep debate about cultural values. Perhaps the debate focuses on modesty versus public displays of affection in India, economic growth versus environmental pollution in China, or land settlement versus peace in the Middle East. In the United States, while the value of privacy is held dear, so is the value of security. The proper balance of the two is constantly being contested and debated. Under what conditions should the U.S. government be able to breach your privacy by eavesdropping on telephone calls and emails, or unlocking your iPhone, in order to ensure your safety?

Ultimately, values are not simply platitudes about people's ideals about the good life. Values are powerful cultural tools for clarifying cultural goals and motivating people to action. When enshrined in law, values can become powerful political and economic tools. Values can be so potent that some people are willing to kill or die for them.

Symbols.
Cultures include complex systems of symbols and symbolic actions—in realms such as language, art, religion, politics, and economics—that convey meaning to other participants. In essence, a **symbol** is something that stands for something else. For example, language enables humans to communicate abstract ideas through

values
Fundamental beliefs about what is important, what makes a good life, and what is true, right, and beautiful.

symbol
Anything that represents something else.

Money is symbolic, and only 10 percent of the world's money exists in tangible form. Here traders move money electronically at Euronext stock exchange in Amsterdam, the Netherlands.

the symbols of written and spoken words, as well as unspoken sounds and gestures (see Chapter 4). People shake hands, wave, whistle, nod, smile, give two thumbs up, give thumbs down, give someone the middle finger. These symbols are not universal, but within their particular cultural context they convey certain meanings.

Much symbolic communication is nonverbal, action-based, and unconscious. Religions include powerful systems of symbols that represent deeper meanings to their adherents. Consider mandalas, the Koran, the Torah, the Christian cross, holy water, statues of the Buddha—all carry greater meanings and value than the physical material they are constructed of. National flags, which are mere pieces of colored cloth, are symbols that stir deep political emotions. Even money is simply a symbolic representation of value guaranteed by the sponsoring government. It has no value, except in its symbolism. Estimates suggest that only about 10 percent of money today exists in physical form. The rest moves electronically through banks, stock markets, and credit accounts (Graeber 2011). Symbols change in meaning over time and from culture to culture. Not understanding another culture's collective understandings—sets of symbolic actions—can lead to embarrassing misunderstandings and cross-cultural miscues.

Mental Maps of Reality. Along with norms, values, and symbols, another key component of culture is **mental maps of reality**. These are "maps" that humans construct of what kinds of people and what kinds of things exist. Because the world presents overwhelming quantities of data to our senses, our brains create shortcuts—maps—to navigate our experience and organize all the data that come our way. A roadmap condenses a large world into a manageable format (one that you can hold in your hands or view on your portable GPS system) and helps us navigate the territory. Likewise, our mental maps organize the world into categories that help us sort out our experiences and what they mean. We do not want all the details all the time. We could not handle them anyway. From our general mental maps we can then dig deeper as required.

mental maps of reality

Cultural classifications of what kinds of people and things exist, and the assignment of meaning to those classifications.

Our mental maps are shaped through enculturation, but they are not fixed. Like other elements of culture, they can be challenged and redrawn. Today, globalization continues to put pressure on mental maps of reality as people on the planet are drawn into closer contact with the world's diversity. We will examine these transformations throughout this book, especially in chapters on language, race, ethnicity, gender, sexuality, and kinship.

Mental maps have two important functions. *First, mental maps classify reality.* Starting in the eighteenth century, European naturalists such as Carolus Linnaeus (1707–1778) began creating systems of classification for the natural world. These systems included five kingdoms subdivided into phylum, class, order, family, genus, and species. Through observation (this was before genetics), these naturalists sought to organize a logical framework to divide the world into kinds of things and kinds of people. In a similar way, our cultures' mental maps seek to classify reality—though often a culture's mental maps are drawn from the distinct vantage point of those in power.

A culture creates a concept such as time. Then we arbitrarily divide it into millennia, centuries, decades, years, seasons, months, weeks, hours, morning, afternoon, evening, minutes, seconds. Categories of time are assumed to be scientific, universal, and "natural." But mostly they are cultural constructs. The current Gregorian calendar, which is used in much of the world, was introduced in 1582 by the Catholic Church, but its adoption occurred gradually; it was accepted in the United States in 1756, replacing the earlier Julian calendar, and in China in 1949. Until 1949 and still today, much of China relies on a lunar calendar in which months and days align with the waxing and waning of the moon. New Year's Day shifts each year. So do Chinese holidays and festivals. Even in the Gregorian calendar, the length of the year is modified to fit into a neat mental map of reality. A year (how long it takes Earth to orbit the sun) is approximately 365.2425 days long, so every four years the Gregorian calendar must add a day, creating a leap year of 366 days rather than 365.

Now check your watch. Even the question of what time it is depends on accepting a global system of time zones centered at the Greenwich meridian in England. But countries regularly modify the system according to their needs. The mainland United States has four time zones. China, approximately the same physical size, uses only one time zone. Russia has eleven. There is a time change of three and a half hours when you cross the border between China and Afghanistan. As these examples demonstrate, categories that seem completely fixed and "natural" are in reality flexible and variable, showing the potential role of culture in defining our fundamental notions of reality.

Mental maps of reality become problematic when people treat cultural notions of difference as being scientifically or biologically "natural." Race is a key example. As we will see in Chapter 5, the notion of race is assumed in popular culture and conversation to have a biological basis. There is, however, no scientific

What does it mean to be a child laborer in your culture? (*left*) a boy in Dhaka, Bangladesh, makes balloons for export; (*right*) a girl in Nangarhar province, Afghanistan, works at a brick-making factory.

basis for this assumption. The particular racial categories in any given culture do not correlate directly to any biological differences. Although most people in the United States would name whites, blacks, Hispanics, Asians, and perhaps Native Americans as distinct races, no genetic line marks clear differences among these categories. The classifications are created by our culture and are specific to our culture. Other cultures draw different mental maps of the reality of human physical variation. The Japanese use different racial categories than the United States. Brazilians have more than 500 racial classifications.

Second, mental maps assign meaning to what has been classified. Not only do people in a culture develop mental maps of things and people, they also place values and meanings on those maps. For example, we divide the life span into categories—infants, children, adolescents, teenagers, young adults, adults, and seniors, for example—but then we give different values to different ages. Some carry more respect, more protection, and more rights, privileges, and responsibilities. In the United States, these categories determine at what age you can marry, have sex, drink alcohol, drive, vote, go to war, stand trial, retire, or collect Social Security and Medicare benefits.

In considering the earlier discussion of time, we can see how these classifications gain value and meaning. U.S. culture puts a premium on time, discourages idle leisure, and encourages people to work hard and stay busy. "Time is money!" we often hear, and so it should not be wasted. Assuming that our mental maps of reality are natural can cause us to disregard the cultural values of others. For instance, we may see as lazy those whose cultures value a midday nap. This effect of our mental maps is important for anthropologists to understand (Wolf-Meyer 2012).

To fully grasp the anthropological understanding of culture, we will examine the historical development of the culture concept before turning our attention to more recent notions of culture as a system of meaning and as a system of power.

How Has the Culture Concept Developed in Anthropology?

The concept of culture has been central to anthropology ever since the English anthropologist Edward Burnett Tylor (1832–1917) crafted his definition in the opening paragraph of his book *Primitive Culture* in 1871: "Culture or Civilization, taken in its wide ethnographic sense, is that complex whole which includes knowledge, belief, art, morals, law, custom and any other capabilities and habits acquired by man as a member of society."

Tylor understood culture to be a unified and complex system of ideas and behavior learned over time, passed down from generation to generation, and shared by members of a particular group. Over the past century and a half, culture has become more than a definition; it is now a key theoretical framework for anthropologists attempting to understand humans and their interactions.

EARLY EVOLUTIONARY FRAMEWORKS

Edward Burnett Tylor and James Frazer (1854–1941) of England and Lewis Henry Morgan (1818–1881) of the United States were among the leading early anthropologists who sought to professionalize a field long dominated by wealthy collectors of artifacts. They sought to organize the vast quantities of data about the diversity of cultures worldwide that were being accumulated through colonial and missionary enterprises during the nineteenth century. These anthropologists were influenced by Charles Darwin's theory of biological evolution, which maintains that the diversity of biological species resulted from gradual change over time in response to environmental pressures. Thus, they suggested that the vast diversity of cultures represented different stages in the evolution of human culture.

Early anthropologists suggested that all cultures would naturally evolve through the same sequence of stages, a concept known as **unilineal cultural evolution**. They set about plotting the world's cultures along a continuum from most simple to most complex, using the terms *savage*, *barbarian*, and *civilized*. Western cultures were, perhaps too predictably, considered the most evolved or civilized. By arranging all of the world cultures along this continuum, the early anthropologists believed that they could trace the path of human cultural evolution, understand where some cultures had come from, and predict where other cultures were headed.

While Tylor and others developed the theory of unilineal cultural evolution at least in part to combat the prevalent racist belief that many non-Europeans were of a different species, the theory has itself been criticized as racist for ranking different cultural expressions in a hierarchy with European culture, considered the ideal, at the apex (Stocking 1968). Franz Boas, the founder of American anthropology, and Bronislaw Malinowski, a Polish anthropologist who spent

British anthropologist Edward Burnett Tylor.

unilineal cultural evolution

The theory proposed by nineteenth-century anthropologists that all cultures naturally evolve through the same sequence of stages from simple to complex.

most of his life teaching in England, represent two main schools of anthropology that moved beyond the evolutionary framework for viewing cultural differences.

AMERICAN HISTORICAL PARTICULARISM

Franz Boas (1858–1942) conducted fieldwork among the Kwakiutl indigenous people of the Pacific Northwest of the United States and Canada before becoming a professor of anthropology at Columbia University in New York and a curator of the American Museum of Natural History. Boas rejected unilineal cultural evolution, its generalizations, and its comparative method. Instead he advocated for an approach called **historical particularism**. He claimed that cultures arise from different causes, not uniform processes. According to Boas, anthropologists could not rely on an evolutionary formula to explain differences among cultures but must study the particular history of each culture to see how it developed. Evolutionists such as Tylor, Frazer, and Morgan argued that similarities among cultures emerged through independent invention as different cultures independently arrived at similar solutions to similar problems. Boas, in contrast, while not ruling out some independent invention, turned to the idea of *diffusion*—the borrowing of cultural traits and patterns from other cultures—to explain apparent similarities.

historical particularism
The idea, attributed to Franz Boas, that cultures develop in specific ways because of their unique histories.

Boas's belief in the powerful role of culture in shaping human life exhibited itself in his early-twentieth-century studies of immigrants. His research with the children of immigrants from Europe revealed the remarkable effects of culture and environment on their physical forms, challenging the role of biology as a tool for discrimination. As a Jewish immigrant himself, Boas was particularly sensitive to the dangers of racial stereotyping, and his work throughout his career served to challenge white supremacy, the inferior ranking of non-European people, and other expressions of racism.

Boas's students Ruth Benedict (1887–1948) and Margaret Mead (1901–1979) continued his emphasis on the powerful role of culture in shaping human life and the need to explore the unique development of each culture. Benedict's popular studies, *Patterns of Culture* (1934) and *The Chrysanthemum and the Sword* (1946), explored the ways in which cultural traits and entire cultures are uniquely patterned and integrated. Mead conducted research in Samoa, Bali, and Papua New Guinea and became perhaps the most famous anthropologist of the twentieth century, promoting her findings and the unique tools of anthropology to the general American public.

American anthropologist Ruth Benedict.

Mead turned her attention particularly to enculturation and its powerful effects on cultural patterns and personality types. In her book *Coming of Age in Samoa* (1928), she explored the seeming sexual freedom and experimentation of Samoan young people and compared it with the repressed sexuality of young people in the United States, suggesting the important role of enculturation in shaping behavior—even behavior that is imagined to have powerful biological origins. Mead's controversial research and findings over her career challenged biological assumptions about gender, demonstrating cross-cultural variations in expressions of what it meant to be male or female, and contributing to heated debates about the roles of women and men in U.S. culture in the twentieth century.

BRITISH STRUCTURAL FUNCTIONALISM

Between the 1920s and 1960s, in a rejection of unilineal cultural evolution, many British social anthropologists viewed anthropology more as a science and field-work more as a science experiment that could focus on the specific details of a local **society**. These anthropologists viewed human societies as living organisms, and through fieldwork they sought to analyze each part of the "body." Each part of society—including the kinship, religious, political, and economic structures—fit together and had its unique function within the larger structure. Like a living organism, a society worked to maintain an internal balance, or equilibrium, that kept the system working. Under this conceptual framework, called **structural functionalism**, British social anthropologists employed a synchronic approach to control their science experiments—analyzing contemporary societies at a fixed point in time without regard to historical context. By isolating as many variables as possible, especially by excluding history and outside influences such as neighboring groups or larger national or global dynamics, these anthropologists sought to focus narrowly on the culture at hand.

Early practitioners of this approach included Bronislaw Malinowski (1884–1942), who used an early form of functionalism in his ethnography of the Trobriand Islands, *Argonauts of the Western Pacific* (1922), discussed in more detail in Chapter 3; and E. E. Evans-Pritchard (1902–1973) in his classic ethnography of the Sudan, *The Nuer* (1940), which we will consider further in Chapters 3 and 9. Later, British anthropologists, including Max Gluckman (1911–1975) in his work on rituals of rebellion, and Victor Turner (1920–1983) in his work on religious symbols and rituals, critiqued earlier structural functionalists for ignoring the dynamics of conflict, tension, and change within the societies they studied. Their intervention marked a significant turn in the study of society and culture by British anthropologists.

CULTURE AND MEANING

One predominant view within anthropology in recent decades sees culture primarily as a set of ideas or knowledge shared by a group of people that provides a common body of information about how to behave, why to behave that way, and what that behavior means. The anthropologist Clifford Geertz (1926–2006), a key figure in this **interpretivist approach**, urged anthropologists to explore culture primarily as a symbolic system in which even simple, seemingly straight-forward actions can convey deep meanings.

In a classic example, Geertz (1973c) examines the difference between a wink and a twitch of the eye. Both involve the same movement of the eye muscles, but the wink

society

The focus of early British anthropological research whose structure and function could be isolated and studied scientifically.

structural functionalism

A conceptual framework positing that each element of society serves a particular function to keep the entire system in equilibrium.

MAP 2.1
Trobriand Islands

interpretivist approach

A conceptual framework that sees culture primarily as a symbolic system of deep meaning.

carries a meaning, which can change depending on the context in which it occurs. A wink can imply flirting, including a friend in a secret, or slyly signaling agreement. Deciphering the meaning requires a complex, collective (shared) understanding of unspoken communication in a specific cultural context. Collective understandings of symbols and symbolic actions enable people to interact with one another in subtle yet complex ways without constantly stopping to explain themselves.

Geertz's essay "Deep Play: Notes on the Balinese Cockfight" (1973a) describes in intricate detail a cockfight—a common activity even today in local communities across Bali, a small island in the South Pacific. Geertz describes the elaborate breeding, raising, and training of the roosters; the scene of bedlam at the fight; the careful selection of the birds; the rituals of the knife man, who provides the razors for the birds' feet; the fight itself; the raucous betting before and during the fight; and the aftermath, with the cutting up of the losing cock and the dividing of its parts among participants in the fight.

Geertz argues that such careful description of cultural activity is an essential part of understanding Balinese culture. But it is not enough. He claims that we must engage in **thick description**, looking beneath the surface activities to see the layers of deep cultural meaning in which those activities are embedded. The cockfight is not simply a cockfight. It also represents generations of competition among the village families for prestige, power, and resources within the community. It symbolizes the negotiation of those families' prestige status and standing within the larger groups. For Geertz, all activities of the cockfight reflect these deeper webs of meaning, and their analysis requires extensive description that uncovers those deeper meanings. Indeed, according to Geertz, every cultural action is more than

MAP 2.2
Bali

thick description

A research strategy that combines detailed description of cultural activity with an analysis of the layers of deep cultural meaning in which those activities are embedded.

Preparations for a cockfight outside a Hindu temple in Bali. How do you analyze the deep webs of meaning at play in any cultural event?

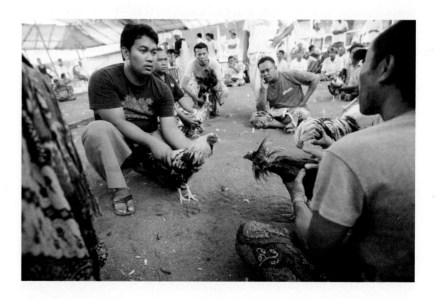

the action itself; it is also a symbol of deeper meaning. (Even the seemingly simple act of eating, as described in the chapter opener, carries a deeper cultural meaning.)

Geertz's culture concept has provided a key theoretical framework for much of the anthropological research in subsequent decades. But, as we will see in the following section, it has also been criticized for not adequately considering the relations of power within a culture and the contested processes by which cultural meanings—norms, values, symbols, mental maps of reality—are established.

How Are Culture and Power Related?

For many years, anthropologists focused primarily on culture as a system of ideas, as represented in the section you have just read. But more recent scholarship has pushed anthropology to consider the deep interconnections between culture and power in more sophisticated ways (Foucault 1977; Gramsci 1971; Wolf 1982), and the chapters of this book take this challenge seriously.

Power is often described as the ability or potential to bring about change through action or influence, either one's own or that of a group or institution. This may include the ability to influence through force or the threat of force. Power is embedded in many kinds of social relations, from interpersonal relations, to institutions, to structural frameworks of whole societies. In effect, power is everywhere and individuals participate in systems of power in complex ways. Throughout this book we will work to unmask the dynamics of power embedded in culture, including systems of power such as race and racism, ethnicity and nationalism, gender, human sexuality, economics, and family.

power

The ability or potential to bring about change through action or influence.

The anthropologist Eric Wolf (1923–1999) urged anthropologists to see power as an aspect of all human relationships. Consider the relationships in your own life: teacher/student, parent/child, employer/employee, landlord/tenant, lender/borrower, boyfriend/girlfriend. Wolf (1990, 1999) argued that all such human relationships have a power dynamic. Though cultures are often assumed to be composed of groups of similar people who uniformly share norms and values, in reality people in a given culture are usually diverse and their relationships are complicated.

Power in a culture reflects **stratification**—uneven distribution of resources and privileges—among participants that often persists over generations. Some people are drawn into the center of the culture. Others are ignored, marginalized, or even annihilated. Power may be stratified along lines of gender, racial or ethnic group, class, age, family, religion, sexuality, or legal status. These structures of power organize relationships among people and create a framework through which access to cultural resources is distributed. As a result, some people are able

stratification

The uneven distribution of resources and privileges among participants in a group or culture.

A young Muslim woman with two French flags pulled over her head covering marches in Paris against a French ban on religious symbols, including head coverings, in public schools.

to participate more fully in the culture than others. This balance of power is not fixed; it fluctuates over time. By examining the way access to the resources, privileges, and opportunities of a culture are shared unevenly and unequally, we can begin to use culture as a conceptual guide to power and its workings.

POWER AND CULTURAL INSTITUTIONS

One key to understanding the relationship between culture and power is to recognize that a culture is more than a set of ideas or patterns of behavior shared among a collection of individuals. A culture also includes the powerful institutions that these people create to promote and maintain their core values. Ethnographic research must consider a wide range of institutions that play central roles in the enculturation process. For example, schools teach a shared history, language, patterns of social interaction, notions of health, and scientific ideas of what exists in the world and how the world works. Religious institutions promote moral and ethical codes of behavior. The various media convey images of what is considered normal, natural, and valued. Other prominent cultural institutions that reflect and shape core norms and values include the family, medicine, government, courts, police, and the military.

These cultural institutions are also locations where people can debate and contest cultural norms and values. In 2003, an intense debate erupted in France about Muslim girls wearing headscarves to public schools. Although few girls actually wore headscarves, the controversy took on particular intensity in the aftermath of the events of September 11, 2001, the invasions of Afghanistan and Iraq, and terrorist incidents in Europe. For many non-Muslim people in France, the wearing of head coverings represented a grave danger to French society, particularly its commitment to equality for women, its history of ethnic assimilation, and its tradition of the separation of church and state. Passage of a law banning the headscarf from public schools was intended as a signal (to people both inside and outside France) of the country's commitment to these principles. But many Muslim girls believed that wearing the headscarf also expressed a commitment to French values—the country's commitment to religious freedom and liberty.

Despite legal challenges, strikes by students, and street demonstrations in opposition to the law, in 2004 the French government banned any clothing in public schools that indicates particular religious beliefs. Although the language of the law was broadly stated to include all religions, everyone understood that the headscarves of Muslim girls were the target. France's public schools had become the venue for debating, contesting, and enforcing key French cultural norms and values (Bowen 2006). As we will see, cultural institutions such as schools are not only places where norms are enforced, but also places where powerful ideas of what is normal and natural are shaped.

HEGEMONY

The Italian political philosopher Antonio Gramsci (1891–1937) described two aspects of power. *Material power,* the first component, includes political, economic, or military power. It exerts itself through coercion or brute force. The second aspect of power involves the ability to create consent and agreement within a population, a condition that Gramsci (1971) called **hegemony**.

Gramsci recognized the tremendous power of culture—particularly the cultural institutions of media, schools, and religion—to shape, often unconsciously, what people think is normal, natural, and possible, and thereby directly influence the scope of human action and interaction. Cultures, which develop slowly over time, include a shared belief system of what is right and what is wrong, and what is normal and appropriate. In this hegemony of ideas, some thoughts and actions become unthinkable, and group members develop a set of "beliefs" about what is normal and appropriate that come to be seen as natural "truths." The French sociologist Michel Foucault (1926–1984), in *Discipline and Punish* (1977), described this hegemonic aspect of power as the ability to make people discipline their own behavior so that they believe and act in certain "normal" ways—often against their own interests, even without a tangible threat of punishment for misbehavior.

Earlier in this chapter we discussed anti-miscegenation laws in the history of the United States. These laws drew upon cultural beliefs in "natural" biological differences among races and the seemingly unnatural, deviant practice of intermarriage. Despite the elimination of these formal laws, a certain hegemony of thought remains: Many in U.S. culture still see interracial marriage as unthinkable and undoable. As evidence, consider current intermarriage rates in

hegemony
The ability of a dominant group to create consent and agreement within a population without the use or threat of force.

FIGURE 2.1
U.S. Interracial Marriage Patterns, 2010

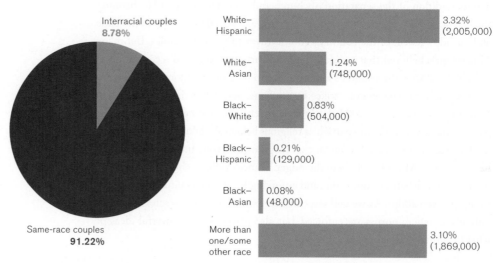

INTERRACIAL MARRIAGES

Interracial couples
8.78%

Same-race couples
91.22%

White–Hispanic	3.32% (2,005,000)
White–Asian	1.24% (748,000)
Black–White	0.83% (504,000)
Black–Hispanic	0.21% (129,000)
Black–Asian	0.08% (48,000)
More than one/some other race	3.10% (1,869,000)

Source: U.S. Census Bureau. 2010. "America's Families and Living Arrangements: 2010," Table FG3. www.census.gov/hhes /families/files/cps2010/tabFG4-all.xls.

the United States (Figure 2.1). According to the U.S. Census Bureau (2010), there were 5,303,000 interracial married couples in 2010, only 8.78 percent of all marriages in the U.S.

Clearly, although U.S. culture has very few formal rules about whom one can marry, cultural norms combined with long-term geographic and institutional patterns of segregation still powerfully inform and enforce our behavior. As this example shows, views against interracial marriage do not require legal sanction to remain dominant, hegemonic norms.

HUMAN AGENCY

Although hegemony can be very powerful, it does not completely dominate people's thinking. Individuals and groups have the power to contest cultural norms, values, mental maps of reality, symbols, institutions, and structures of power—a potential known as **agency**. Cultural beliefs and practices are not timeless; they change and can be changed. Cultures are not biologically determined; they are created over time by particular groups of people. By examining human agency, we see how culture serves as a realm in which battles over power take place—where people debate, negotiate, contest, and enforce what is considered normal, what people can say, do, and even think.

Although a dominant group may have greater access to power, resources, rights, or privileges, the systems of power they create are never absolute, and their

agency

The potential power of individuals and groups to contest cultural norms, values, mental maps of reality, symbols, institutions, and structures of power.

dominance is never complete. Individuals and groups with less power or no power may contest the dominant power relationships and structures, whether through political, economic, religious, or military means. At times these forms of resistance are visible, public, and well organized, including negotiations, protests, strikes, or rebellions. At other times the resistance may be more subtle, discreet, and diffuse. For example, James Scott's book *Weapons of the Weak: Everyday Forms of Peasant Resistance* (1985) identifies strategies—such as foot dragging, slowdowns, theft, sabotage, trickery, arson, and false compliance with regulations—that people in very weak positions use to express their agency and to resist the dominant group.

Resistance to unfair conditions takes many forms. (*left*) Egyptian protestors in Tahrir Square, Cairo, demonstrate against their government. (*right*) Malaysian farmers conduct a slowdown to protest working conditions.

How Much of Who You Are Is Shaped by Biology, and How Much by Culture?

Biology is important. We live in our bodies, after all. We feel, smell, taste, hear, and see the world around us through our bodies. We communicate with and through our bodies. And, yes, we have certain biological drives that are essential for survival. All humans must eat, drink, and sleep. But no matter how strong our biological needs or our hormones, odors, and appetites might be, culture and the environment in which we live also exert powerful influences on what we think, on how we behave, and even on the shape and functions of our bodies.

NATURE AND NURTURE

Popular American discourse often assigns biology—and usually genes—the primary role in determining who we are. Anthropological research, however, consistently reveals the powerful role culture and environment also play in shaping our lives and bodies. Human genetic codes are 99.9 percent identical, so if behavior were entirely driven by our genes, we should expect to find very similar—even universal—behavioral responses to biological influences. Instead we find remarkable physical and behavioral variety across cultures. Even the most basic human activities, such as eating, drinking, and sleeping, are carried out in remarkably distinct ways. All humans must do these things. But shared biological needs do not ensure shared cultural patterns.

Of course, food and liquid enter the body through the mouth and get digested in the stomach and intestines. But what goes in and how it goes in are other stories. Perhaps you find dog or snake or pony to be inedible, although these are delicacies in other cultures. Many Chinese dislike cheese, a staple of North American and European diets. Even how and where you eat and drink, or how many times a day, varies from culture to culture. You may use forks, knives, spoons, chopsticks, or hands. You may eat once a day, three times a day, or—like many Americans—six times a day (breakfast, "coffee break," lunch, afternoon snack, dinner, midnight snack). You may prefer caviar or a Happy Meal.

Everyone sleeps each day, but some people sleep six hours a night, others eight. Americans nap, Argentinians take a siesta, and Chinese *xiu-xi*. Many college students average six hours of sleep a night during the week and ten on the weekend. Whom you sleep with also varies by culture, with variations including husbands and wives, parents and children, siblings, mothers and children, grandparents and grandchildren. All these patterns vary by culture, and even within a culture they may vary by age, gender, and class. Despite the cross-cultural evidence of human behavioral variation, many popular debates continue to claim that basic patterns of human behavior, intellectual capacity, and psychological tendencies are determined by biology, from warfare and sexuality to the shortage of women in math and science careers.

Most anthropologists have been highly critical of approaches that significantly overstate the importance of a genetic inheritance fixed in deep evolutionary time and that underestimate the role of culture and the environment in shaping human physical and behavioral diversity (McKinnon and Silverman 2005). Although contemporary genetic discoveries are opening new realms of understanding about human biology, we are not close to linking certain genes or groups of genes with particular behaviors or characteristics. At best, we can imagine these connections based on contemporary patterns of behavior. But it often appears just as likely that contemporary notions of human nature are being projected back onto a version of human prehistory that never existed. We do have, however, much clearer indications of the ways cultural patterns and beliefs shape human behavior. In the debate over the origins of gender inequality in the upper echelons of math and science careers, we might look instead to gender stereotyping in the classroom, enculturation of girls, and conscious and unconscious gender bias in hiring and promotion practices. It may feel more comfortable to trace inequality to innate biological differences; a link might enable us to dismiss or excuse the inequality as "natural." But there is no biological evidence of this link. The current evidence is that these patterns of inequality and stratification are culturally constructed and completely changeable (Hopkins 1999; Pollitt 2005).

FROM HUMAN BEINGS TO HUMAN BECOMINGS: A BIOCULTURAL PROCESS

Contemporary anthropological research calls for a much more complex view of human evolution and individual development over a lifetime that incorporates multiple architects of the human physical form and behavior. An emerging synthesis looks at genes as part of a developmental history in which biology and culture are deeply intertwined and entangled in a dynamic and ongoing biocultural process of change (Fuentes 2013). For instance, the emerging field of **epigenetics** explores ways in which the environment into which one is born can directly affect the expression of genes during one's lifetime. In particular, epigenetics examines variations caused not by changes in the actual DNA sequence but by environmental factors that switch genes on and off and affect how cells read genes. These epigenetic marks may change in response to many of the processes anthropologists frequently study—nutrition, stress, disease, social inequality, and migration (Fuentes 2013; Thayer and Non 2015; Wade and Ferree 2015). Additionally, research shows that our bodies do not function in isolation as discrete biological units, despite what our popular culture narratives would lead us to believe. The human body contains approximately 100 trillion cells. About 90 percent are independent microorganisms that live within our bodies and form what has come to be known as the **human microbiome**. This microbiome plays a key role in many bodily functions, including human digestion, vitamin production, drug metabolism, and immunity (Palsson 2013; Warinner and Lewis 2015). Some scholars (see Ingold and Palsson 2013) suggest that these new formulations should lead us to think of ourselves not as human beings—shaped long ago by a completed evolutionary process—but as human *becomings* who are continually evolving and adapting, both on the species level and within the individual lifespan (Ingold and Palsson 2013).

epigenetics
An area of study in the field of genetics exploring how environmental factors directly affect the expression of genes in ways that may be inherited between generations.

human microbiome
The complete collection of microorganisms in the human body's ecosystem.

CONNECTING CULTURE AND BEHAVIOR

While direct links between specific genes and behavior have proven difficult to identify, we have much clearer indications of the ways cultural patterns and beliefs shape human behavior. Culture is learned from the people around us. It is not written into our DNA. Instead we are born with the ability to learn any culture that we might be born into or move into. We have the ability to learn any language and master any set of beliefs, practices, norms, or values. This may seem obvious, but it is a crucial principle to understand as we examine the many cultural patterns in our own experience that we regard as normal, even natural. Such cultural practices are not universal to all humans. Rather, they are uniquely created in each culture. Recognition of this fact allows us to question the biological basis for most if not all of human behavior and to consider how learned patterns of belief and practice have been created and how they might be changed. Later in this book, in the chapters on race, ethnicity, gender, family, and human sexuality, we will explore the intersections of biology and culture in further detail.

As popular as it may be to think that nature has driven our development as humans, even our long evolutionary process has been deeply influenced by culture. Ultimately, it is culture that has made us human, enabling us to evolve physically and in our patterns of relationship with others. For example, with the development of simple stone tools as early as 2.5 million years ago, culture allowed our ancestors to adapt to the world around them. Stone tools (in particular, hand axes and choppers) enabled our ancestors to butcher meat more quickly and efficiently, thereby providing higher quantities of protein for the developing brain and influencing the direction of our physical adaptation. In cases such as these, the power of culture to direct and modify biological instincts is indisputable. Over time, cultural adaptations—from the control of fire, to the development of language, to the invention of condoms and birth control pills—have replaced genetic adaptations as the primary way humans adapt to and manipulate their physical and social environments.

How Is Culture Created?

Culture does not emerge out of the blue. It is created over time, shaped by people and the institutions they establish in relationship to the environment around them. Culture is not fixed. It is invented, changed, contested, and negotiated. Nor is it bounded. It moves and flows across regions and between people. Just as we have examined the relationship between culture and power, we can analyze the processes through which culture is created by considering the origins of a consumer culture as part of twentieth-century capitalism.

MANUFACTURING THE DESIRE TO CONSUME

As capitalism has grown and shifted over the centuries into its present global form, so has the culture that supports and shapes it. Twentieth-century and early twenty-first-century global capitalism is deeply tied to a culture of consumerism that has emerged with the support and promotion of corporations, governments, and financial institutions. The culture of consumerism includes norms, values, beliefs, practices, and institutions that have become commonplace and accepted as normal and that cultivate the desire to acquire consumer goods to enhance one's lifestyle (McCracken 1991, 2005).

Advertising, marketing, and financial services industries work to transform the cultural values of frugality, modesty, and self-denial of the old Protestant ethic into patterns of spending and consumption associated with acquiring the material goods of a middle-class lifestyle. The culture of consumerism promotes spending and consumption even when people don't have money. Today, through global marketing and media advertising campaigns, increased trade, and rising migration, the desire for this lifestyle is being promoted around the world. Over the last few decades, following economic and political reforms in India, China, Russia, and the Middle East, hundreds of millions more people are now seeking that middle-class lifestyle seen on television and advertised on the Internet. This trend is placing incredible stress on the planet's natural resources and environment.

In many parts of the world, consumerism has become more than an economic activity. It is a way of life, a way of looking at the world—a culture. In fact, many key cultural rituals now focus on consumption. In the United States, holidays such as Christmas, Valentine's Day, Mother's Day, and Father's Day all promote the purchase of gifts, as do birthdays, weddings, and anniversaries.

Advertising. The advertising industry is key in arousing our desires for goods and services. Consider that children in the United States watch up to 40,000 television commercials a year (Vitelli 2013). In addition, they are bombarded with advertising on the Internet, cell phones, mp3 players, video games, and YouTube videos. Many children's television programs are themselves thinly disguised advertisements for products featuring their characters, from lunch boxes to clothing to action figures. Advertising appears before and during movies in the theater, at sporting events, in department stores and shopping malls, on billboards, and in store windows. Your favorite websites and social media are covered with advertisements. So are your clothes. Even your classroom is full of advertisements that you most likely do not notice: all the labels and tags on computers, pens, notebooks, backpacks, food packaging, and soda cans.

Advertising is a powerful tool of enculturation, teaching us how to be "successful" in consumer culture, how to be cool and normal. If only we could dress like the people in the adverstisement and imitate their lifestyles, then we would be more desirable. The culture of consumerism tells us that having these things will bring us better friends, better sex, stronger families, higher-paying jobs, fancier houses, faster cars, sharper picture definition, and truer sound quality. Do you find yourself believing this is true?

Financial Services and Credit Cards. The financial services industry makes sure that once our desires are aroused, we have access to money to make our dreams a reality—at a small price. In 2015, the average American carried 2.24 credit cards, and U.S. credit card debt was $712 billion, an average of $15,355 per household (DiGangi 2016; El Issa 2015).

College students are a key target of the credit industry, which promotes credit cards on campus and through the mail regardless of students' ability to repay. Credit cards grease the wheels of consumer culture. And so contemporary capitalism invests heavily to arouse our desire and promote the expansion of the culture of consumerism.

How Is Globalization Transforming Culture?

Cultures have never been made up of completely isolated or bounded groups of people located in a particular place. As we discussed in Chapter 1, anthropologists resist the myths of isolated and "primitive" groups who have lived on their own without contact. Encounter, interaction, movement, and exchange have been much more fundamental aspects of humanity. Cultures have always been influenced by the flow of people, ideas, and goods, whether through migration, trade, or invasion. Today's flows of globalization are intensifying the exchange and diffusion of people, ideas, and goods, creating more interaction and engagement among cultures. Let's consider three key interrelated effects of globalization on local cultures: homogenization, the global flows of culture through migration, and increased cosmopolitanism.

A McDonald's restaurant in downtown Manila, capital of the Philippines, advertises the McDo Rice Burger, a local product added to McDonald's standard global menu.

THE GLOBAL AND LOCAL IN TENSION: HOMOGENIZING OR DIVERSIFYING

The development of global corporations, products, and markets has led some anthropologists and cultural activists to warn of a homogenized, global culture dominated by McDonald's, Levi's, Coca-Cola, CNN, Hollywood, and U.S. cultural values. Will the spread of this culture—fueled by goods, images, and ideas from Western cultures—create a homogenizing process that will diminish the diversity of the world's cultures as foreign influences inundate local practices, products, and ways of thinking?

Let's consider McDonald's. Launched in the 1940s in San Bernardino, California, today McDonald's operates in 119 countries. As the company has expanded globally, it has adapted its menu in response to local tastes and culinary traditions, local laws, and religious beliefs. In Egypt the menu includes McFalafel Sandwiches. In Morocco the McArabia, a grilled chicken sandwich, is served on flatbread. McDonald's serves a teriyaki McBurger in Japan, McSpaghetti in the Philippines, and certified halal food in Malaysia. It has kosher stores in Israel, McCurrywurst hot sausages in Germany, and the McBurrito in Mexico. Clearly local cultures need not be homogenized by global encounters but may instead transform global practices and commodities to reflect their local character.

To many people in developing countries, the elements of global culture symbolically represent the opportunity for economic advancement and participation in the idealized middle-class lifestyle of consumption associated with these consumer products. In *Golden Arches East: McDonald's in East Asia* (1998), James Watson suggests that East Asians in Tokyo, Japan; Seoul, Korea; Hong Kong; Beijing, China; and Taipei, Taiwan, go to McDonald's not so much for the food but to participate in what they view as a middle-class activity. By eating out and eating Western fast food, they hope to align themselves with the Western middle-class norms and values to which they aspire (Yan 2004).

MIGRATION AND THE GLOBAL FLOWS OF CULTURE

The movement of people in large numbers within and across national boundaries associated with contemporary globalization reveals that cultures are not necessarily bound to a particular geographic location. People migrate with their cultural beliefs and practices. They incorporate the cultural practices of their homelands into their new communities. They build links to their homelands through which culture continues to be exchanged.

Robert Smith's book *Mexican New York* (2006) reveals one example of the deep transnational connections—links across national borders—that have become increasingly common in today's globalizing world. Direct flights physically link immigrants living in the suburbs of New York City to their hometowns in Mexico in five hours. Telephone calls, emails, and videoconferences connect families and communities. The Mexican town of Tihuateca relies heavily on money sent back from villagers in New York City to build roads, water systems, and schools. Community leaders travel between countries to strengthen relationships, promote projects, and raise funds. This story and many others reveal how global flows of people are transforming local cultures in both the sending and the receiving countries (see also Chapter 11).

INCREASING COSMOPOLITANISM

A third significant effect of globalization on culture is that the increasing flow of people, ideas, and products has allowed worldwide access to cultural patterns that are new, innovative, and stimulating. Local cultures are exposed to a greater range of cultural ideas and products—such as agricultural strategies and medicines, to name just two. Globalization means that communities in the most remote parts of the world increasingly participate in experiences that bridge and link cultural practices, norms, and values across great distances, leading to what some scholars have called a new cosmopolitanism.

Cosmopolitanism is a very broad, sometimes global, outlook, rather than a limited, local one—an outlook that combines both universality and difference (Appiah 2006). The term is usually used to describe sophisticated urban professionals who travel and feel at home in different parts of the world. But anthropologist Lila Abu-Lughod's study *Dramas of Nationhood: The Politics of Television in Egypt* (2005) explores the emergence of cosmopolitanism even among Egypt's rural poor. Her book explores the role of television dramas—much like American soap operas, but more in tune with political and social issues—in creating ideas

In a globalizing age, local cultures are increasingly exposed to a vast array of people, ideas, and products. Here, a montage of images from a day on Egyptian television, with channels from Egypt and across the Middle East, includes comedy and music from Lebanon, old Egyptian films, American entertainment, and news and religious discussion programs.

of a national culture, even among rural Egyptians, and crafting the identity of the new Egyptian citizen.

Abu-Lughod's ethnography of television pushes us to move beyond notions of single cultures sharing a set of ideas and meanings distinct from other cultures in an era of mass media, migration, and globalization. Television, she argues, "is an extraordinary technology for breaking the boundaries and intensifying and multiplying encounters among life-worlds, sensibilities and ideas" (2005, 45). By the 1990s, there were 6 million television sets in Egypt, and more than 90 percent of the population had access. In this reality, television provides material—produced somewhere else—that is consumed locally; it is inserted into, mixed up with, and interpreted by local knowledge and systems of meaning.

Even though poverty prevents the people in Abu-Lughod's study from fully participating in the consumer culture of commodities promoted by television programming and commercials, they are not untouched by these features of cosmopolitanism.

The influences of globalization ensure that even in rural Egyptian peasant culture, the knowledge of other worlds comes not only from television but also from foreign friends, tourists, visiting scholars/anthropologists, relatives migrating to find work in cities, imported movies and electronics, and even teachers trained by the Egyptian state and their approved textbooks. This is just one example of the powerful effects of the intersection of culture and globalization. No matter where you look in the twenty-first century, you are sure to find some elements of this intersection.

MAP 2.3
Egypt

Toolkit

Thinking Like an Anthropologist:
Unpacking a Happy Meal

Every day, culture is all around us. It informs our thoughts and actions; guides us through complex interactions in our families, schools, jobs, and other personal relationships; and even shapes the way we perceive reality. Thinking like an anthropologist can help you to better understand yourself and those around you, and to analyze your own culture and other cultures you encounter in this globalizing world.

In thinking about the Happy Meal and the anthropology of food discussed in the chapter opener, consider the questions we have raised about culture:

- **What is culture?**

- **How has the culture concept developed in anthropology?**

- **How are culture and power related?**

- **How much of who you are is shaped by biology, and how much by culture?**

- **How is culture created?**

- **How is globalization transforming culture?**

Perhaps you have worked in a food-related industry at some point in your life—as a waiter, cook, cleaner, cashier, or delivery person. Drawing on your own experience, how can the key questions of this chapter help you think more deeply about the journey of a Happy Meal from production through distribution, consumption, and disposal? You have participated in cultural food practices at home: shopping, preparing, eating, discussing, disposing of, and perhaps even growing your food. When you think carefully about the experience, how would you begin to explain the complex interactions that go into your food and the cultural practices surrounding it? How is food tied into your culture? How are food and power related? How are biology and culture both shaping your experience with food? How was your food culture created? And how is your experience with food being transformed by globalization?

After putting these questions into anthropological perspective, take a moment to think again about the Happy Meal. Perhaps the last time you ate at McDonald's you did not think particularly deeply about the complex social life of the food that you were eating. But now that you are thinking like an anthropologist, you can.

Key Terms

culture (p. 34)

enculturation (p. 34)

norms (p. 36)

values (p. 37)

symbol (p. 37)

mental maps of reality (p. 38)

unilineal cultural evolution (p. 41)

historical particularism (p. 42)

society (p. 43)

structural functionalism (p. 43)

interpretivist approach (p. 43)

thick description (p. 44)

power (p. 45)

stratification (p. 45)

hegemony (p. 47)

agency (p. 48)

epigenetics (p. 51)

human microbiome (p. 51)

Chapter 3
Fieldwork and Ethnography

Over many years, Nancy Scheper-Hughes, now a professor of cultural anthropology at the University of California, Berkeley, invested herself in trying to understand the lives of the women and children of one particular shantytown in Brazil. Her research resulted in numerous articles and an award-winning ethnography, *Death without Weeping: The Violence of Everyday Life in Brazil* (1992). Scheper-Hughes's efforts reflect the deep commitment of anthropologists to ethnographic fieldwork—a research strategy for understanding the world through intense interaction with a local community of people over an extended period.

Scheper-Hughes first arrived in Brazil's Alto do Cruzeiro (Crucifix Hill) in 1965 as a Peace Corps volunteer to assist in community development and health promotion. That year, a severe drought had created food and water shortages and a military coup had spread political and economic chaos throughout the country. In the Alto, more

Mother and child in a Rio de Janeiro favela, Brazil.

than 350 babies died in 1965, out of a total population of a little more than 5,000. Scheper-Hughes later wrote, "There were reasons enough for the deaths in the miserable conditions of shanty-town life. What puzzled me was the seeming indifference of Alto women to the death of their infants and their willingness to attribute to their own tiny offspring an aversion to life that made their deaths seem wholly natural, indeed all but anticipated" (1989, 10).

This puzzle crystallized her research agenda as she returned to the Alto many times over the ensuing years to conduct ethnographic fieldwork. Scheper-Hughes found it was possible to reduce diarrhea and dehydration-induced death among infants and toddlers in the shantytown with a simple solution of sugar, salt, and water. But it was more difficult to convince a mother to rescue a child she perceived as likely to die, a baby she already thought of as "an angel rather than a son or daughter." The high expectancy of death led mothers to differentiate between infants whom they saw as "thrivers and survivors" and those seen as born already "wanting to die." Scheper-Hughes found that in this environment, part of learning to be a mother was learning which babies to let go of and which ones it was safe to love.

Scheper-Hughes's experience in the Alto led her to a rethinking of "mother love." What does the idea of mother love mean in the impoverished context of Alto do Cruzeiro?

Scheper-Hughes suggests that Alto women were doing what must be done, given their context where the real dangers were "poverty, deprivation, sexism, chronic hunger, and economic exploitation." Reflecting on this high-risk environment, she asks, "If mother love is, as many psychologists and some feminists believe, a seemingly natural and universal maternal script, what does it mean to women for whom scarcity, loss, sickness, and deprivation have made that love frantic and robbed them of their grief, seeming to turn hearts to stone?" (1989, 14).

Their experience, suggests Scheper-Hughes, compares more aptly to a battlefield or an overcrowded emergency room where actions are guided by the practice of triage—prioritizing the treatment of those who can be saved. "In their slowness to anthropomorphize and personalize their infants, everything is mobilized so as to prevent maternal overattachment and, therefore, grief at death. The bereaved mother is told not to cry, that her tears will dampen the wings of her little angel so that she cannot fly up to her heavenly home" (16). Scheper-Hughes suggests that in these difficult conditions, Alto women are left with no choice but to find the best way to carry on with their lives and nurture those children who have the best chance of survival.

What can you learn about fieldwork by reading about Nancy Scheper-Hughes's research? A middle-class woman from the United States, she traveled to one of the poorest places in the world, learned the language, lived in the community, built relationships of trust, accompanied local people through the births

MAP 3.1
Brazil

Burial of an infant in the Alto do Cruzeiro favela in northeast Brazil. How did anthropologist Nancy Scheper-Hughes make sense of the "death without weeping" that she found in this poor community?

and deaths of their children, and searched for meaning in the midst of the pain. As you might imagine, the fieldwork experience can become more than a strategy for understanding human culture. Fieldwork has the potential to radically transform the anthropologist. Can you imagine making the same commitment Scheper-Hughes did?

The term *fieldwork* implies going out to "the field" to do extensive research. Although in the history of anthropology this may have meant going a long way from home, as Scheper-Hughes did, contemporary anthropologists also study human culture and activities in their own countries and local contexts. By exploring the practice of fieldwork, you will gain a deeper understanding of how anthropologists go about their work. In particular, in this chapter we will consider:

- **What is unique about ethnographic fieldwork, and why do anthropologists conduct this kind of research?**
- **How did the idea of fieldwork develop?**
- **How do anthropologists get started conducting fieldwork?**
- **How do anthropologists write ethnography?**
- **What moral and ethical concerns guide anthropologists in their research and writing?**
- **How are fieldwork strategies changing in response to globalization?**

By the end of the chapter you will see both how professional anthropologists employ fieldwork strategies and how fieldwork can provide a valuable toolkit for gathering information to make decisions in your own life. Fieldwork skills and strategies can help you navigate the many unfamiliar or cross-cultural experiences you will encounter at work or school, in your neighborhood, or in your family. And hopefully you will see how key fieldwork strategies can help you become a more engaged and responsible citizen of the world.

What Is Unique about Ethnographic Fieldwork, and Why Do Anthropologists Conduct This Kind of Research?

ethnographic fieldwork
A primary research strategy in cultural anthropology typically involving living and interacting with a community of people over an extended period to better understand their lives.

Ethnographic fieldwork is the unique set of practices that anthropologists—particularly cultural anthropologists—have developed to put people first as we analyze how human societies work. Chemists conduct experiments in laboratories. Economists analyze financial trends. Demographers crunch census data. Historians pore over records and library archives. Sociologists, economists, and political scientists analyze trends, quantifiable data, official organizations, and national policies. But anthropologists start with people and their local communities. Even though the whole world is our field, our unique perspective first focuses on the details and patterns of human life in the local setting.

FIELDWORK BEGINS WITH PEOPLE

Through fieldwork, we try to understand people's everyday lives, to see what they do and to understand why. By living with others over an extended period, we seek to understand their experience through their eyes. We participate in their activities, take careful notes, conduct interviews, take photographs, and record music. We make maps of communities, both of the physical environment and of family and social relationships. Although careful observation of the details of daily life is the first step, through intensive fieldwork anthropologists look beyond the taken-for-granted, everyday experience of life to discover the complex systems of power and meaning that people construct to shape their existence. These include the many systems discussed throughout this book: gender, sexuality, race, ethnicity, religion, kinship, and economic and political systems. As we extend our analysis as anthropologists, we try to see how local lives compare to others and fit into larger human patterns and global contexts.

FIELDWORK SHAPES THE ANTHROPOLOGIST

Fieldwork experience is considered an essential part of an anthropologist's training. It is the activity through which we learn the basic tools of our trade, earn credibility as effective observers of culture, and establish our reputation as full members of the discipline. Through the process, we learn the basic research strategies of our discipline and hone those skills: careful listening and observation, engagement with strangers, cross-cultural interaction, and deep analysis of human interactions and systems of power and inequality. Through fieldwork we learn empathy for those around us, develop a more global consciousness, and uncover our own ethnocentrism. Indeed, fieldwork is a rite of passage, an initiation into our discipline, and a common bond among anthropologists who have been through the experience.

Fieldwork transforms us. In fact, it is quite common for anthropologists entering the field to experience culture shock—a sense of disorientation caused by the overwhelmingly new and unfamiliar people and experiences encountered every day. Over time, the disorientation may fade as the unfamiliar becomes familiar. But then, many anthropologists feel culture shock again when returning home, where their new perspective causes previously familiar people and customs to seem very strange.

The Nacirema. In a now-famous article, "Body Ritual among the Nacirema" (1956), anthropologist Horace Miner helps readers understand the dichotomy between familiar and strange that anthropologists face when studying other cultures. Miner's article examines the cultural beliefs and practices of a group in North America that has developed elaborate and unique practices focusing on care of the human body. He labels this group the "Nacirema."

Miner hypothesizes that underlying the extensive rituals he has documented lies a belief that the human body is essentially ugly, is constantly endangered by forces of disease and decay, and must be treated with great care. Thus, the Nacirema have established extensive daily rituals and ceremonies, rigorously taught to their children, to avoid these dangers. For example, Miner describes the typical household shrine—the primary venue for Nacirema body rituals:

> While each family has at least one shrine, the rituals associated with it are not family ceremonies but are private and secret. . . . The focal point of the shrine is a box or chest which is built into the wall. In this chest are kept the many charms and magical potions without which no native believes he could live. . . . Beneath the charm-box is a small font. Each day every member of the family, in succession, enters the shrine room, bows his head before the charm-box, mingles different sorts of holy water in the font, and proceeds with a brief rite of ablution. (Miner 1956, 503–4)

In addition, the Nacirema regularly visit medicine men and "holy-mouth men." These individuals are specialists who provide ritual advice and magical potions.

> The Nacirema have an almost pathological horror of and fascination with the mouth, the condition of which is believed to have a supernatural influence on all social relationships. Were it not for the rituals of the mouth, they believe that their teeth would fall out, their gums bleed, their jaws shrink, their friends desert them and their lovers reject them. The daily body ritual performed by everyone includes a mouth-rite. It was reported to me that the ritual consists of inserting a small bundle of hog hairs into the mouth, along with certain magical powders, and then moving the bundle in a highly formalized series of gestures. (504)

Do these exotic rituals of a seemingly distant tribe sound completely strange to you, or are they vaguely familiar? Miner's descriptions of the Nacirema are intended to make the strange seem familiar and the familiar strange. "Nacirema" is actually "American" spelled backward. Miner's passages describe the typical American bathroom and personal hygiene habits: "Holy water" pours into the sink. The "charm-box" is a medicine cabinet. The Nacirema medicine men are doctors, and the "holy-mouth men" are dentists. The "mouth-rite" is toothbrushing.

Development of the anthropological perspective through fieldwork, in which we investigate the beliefs and practices of other cultures, enables us to perceive our own cultural activities in a new light. Even the most familiar aspects of our lives may then appear exotic, bizarre, or strange when viewed through the lens of anthropology. Through this cross-cultural training, anthropology offers the opportunity to unlock our ability to imagine, see, and analyze the incredible diversity of human cultures. It also enables us to avoid the tendencies of ethnocentrism, in which we often view our own cultural practices as "normal" and against which we are inclined to judge the cultural beliefs and practices of others.

FIELDWORK AS SOCIAL SCIENCE AND AS ART

A healing specialist conducts an elaborate ceremony, the facial treatment, a key body ritual among the Nacirema.

Fieldwork is simultaneously a social scientific method and an art form. It is a strategy for gathering data about the human condition, particularly through the life experiences of local people in local situations. Fieldwork is an experiment for testing hypotheses and building theories about the diversity of human behavior and the interaction of people with systems of power—a scientific method for examining how the social world really works. As such, anthropologists have developed techniques such as participant observation, field notes, interviews, kinship and social network analysis, life histories, and mapping—all of which we will discuss in this chapter.

But fieldwork is also an art. Its success depends on the anthropologist's more intuitive ability to negotiate complex interactions, usually in an unfamiliar cultural environment, to build relationships of trust, to make sense of patterns of behavior, to be conscious of one's own biases and particular vantage point. Ethnographic fieldwork depends on the ability of an outsider—the anthropologist—to develop close personal relationships over time in a local community and to understand the everyday experiences of often-unfamiliar people. It requires the anthropologist to risk being changed in the process—the risk of mutual transformation. Successful ethnographic fieldwork also depends on the anthropologist's ability to tell the subjects' stories to an audience that has no knowledge of them and in ways that accurately reflect the subjects' lives and shed light on the general human condition. This is also an art.

FIELDWORK INFORMS DAILY LIFE

Anthropologist Brackette Williams suggests that fieldwork can even be a kind of "homework"—a strategy for gathering information that will help the anthropologist make informed decisions in order to act morally and to weigh in advance the likely consequences of her or his actions. Williams studied homelessness and begging in New York City and Tucson, Arizona, over a period of several years. She began with some very practical questions about whether to give money to homeless people begging on the subway she took to work in New York City every day.

Her research started with careful observation of all the people involved, including homeless individuals and all the others on the subway. She continued with informal and formal interviews, careful note taking, and background reading. In the process she began to identify a clear set of stories and begging styles and to examine the complicated set of responses made by people on the subway who were being asked for money.

Williams suggests that this approach to her daily dilemma was not only an interesting use of her ethnographic fieldwork skills and training but also "socially required homework" for anyone who confronts complex problems in daily life, whether with family, friends, school, work, or politics (Williams 1995, 25). Can you imagine using this strategy to explore a problem, puzzle, or question in your life?

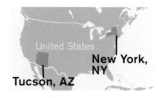

MAP 3.2
Tucson/New York

Early anthropologists encountered a world of people already in motion. The 1375 Catalan Atlas shows the world as it was then known. It depicts the location of continents and islands as well as information on ancient and medieval tales, regional politics, astronomy, and astrology.

How Did the Idea of Fieldwork Develop?

EARLY ACCOUNTS OF ENCOUNTERS WITH OTHERS

Descriptive accounts of other cultures existed long before anthropologists came on the scene. For centuries, explorers, missionaries, traders, government bureaucrats, and travelers recorded descriptions of the people they encountered. For example, nearly 2,500 years ago, the Greek historian Herodotus wrote about his travels in Egypt, Persia, and the area now known as Ukraine. In the thirteenth century, the Venetian explorer Marco Polo chronicled his travels from Italy across the silk route to China. And the Chinese admiral Zheng He reported on his extended voyages to India, the Middle East, and East Africa in the fifteenth century, seventy years before Columbus arrived in the Americas. These are just a few of the many early accounts of encounters with other peoples across the globe.

NINETEENTH-CENTURY ANTHROPOLOGY AND THE COLONIAL ENCOUNTER

The roots of anthropology and of fieldwork lie in the intense globalization of the late nineteenth century. At that time, the increased international movement of Europeans—particularly merchants, colonial administrators, and missionaries—generated a broad array of data that stimulated scientists and philosophers of the day to make sense of the emerging picture of humanity's incredible diversity (Stocking 1983). They asked questions like these: Who are these other people? Why are their foods, clothing, architecture, rituals, family structures, and political and economic systems so different from ours and from one another's? Are they related to us biologically? If so, how?

Fieldwork was not a common practice at the beginning of our discipline. In fact, many early anthropologists, such as Edward Burnett Tylor (1832–1917), are now considered "armchair anthropologists" because they did not conduct their own research; instead they worked at home in their armchairs analyzing the reports of others. One early exception was Louis Henry Morgan (1818–1881), who conducted fieldwork among Native Americans in the United States. As we discussed in Chapter 2, Tylor and Morgan were leading figures in attempts to organize the data that was accumulating, to catalogue human diversity, and to make sense of the many questions it stimulated. These men applied the theory of unilineal cultural evolution—the idea that all cultures would naturally evolve through the same sequence of stages from simple to complex and that the diversity of human cultural expressions represented different stages in the evolution of human culture, which could be classified in comparison to one another.

THE PROFESSIONALIZATION OF SOCIAL SCIENTIFIC DATA GATHERING AND ANALYSIS

Succeeding generations of anthropologists in Europe and North America rejected unilineal cultural evolution as being too Eurocentric, too ethnocentric, too hierarchical, and lacking adequate data to support its grand claims. Anthropologists in the early twentieth century developed more sophisticated research methods—particularly ethnographic fieldwork—to professionalize social scientific data gathering.

Franz Boas: Fieldwork and the Four-Field Approach. In the United States, Franz Boas (1858–1942) and his students focused on developing a four-field approach to anthropological research, which included gathering cultural, linguistic, archaeological, and biological data. Boas's early work among the indigenous Kwakiutl people of the Pacific Northwest of the United States and Canada firmly grounded him in the fieldwork process, as he learned about others' culture through extensive participation in their daily lives, religious rituals, and economic activities. After settling in New York City in the early twentieth century as a professor of anthropology at Columbia University and curator of the American Museum of Natural History, Boas (and his students) embarked on a massive project to document Native American cultures being devastated by the westward expansion of European settlers across the continent.

Often called **salvage ethnography**, Boas's approach involved the rapid gathering of all available material, including historical artifacts, photographs, recordings of spoken languages, songs, and detailed information about cultural beliefs and practices—from religious rituals to family patterns, from gender roles to political structures. With limited time and financial resources, these ethnographers often met with a small number of elderly informants and focused on conducting oral interviews rather than observing actual behavior. Despite the limitations of this emerging fieldwork, these early projects built upon Boas's commitment to historical particularism when investigating local cultures (see Chapter 2) and defined a continuing characteristic of American anthropology: a combined focus on culture, biology, artifacts, and language that today we call the four-field approach (see Chapter 1).

Another key contribution of Boas and his students was a commitment to the development of **cultural relativism** as a basic fieldwork perspective: to see each culture on its own merits; to understand it first from the inside, according to its own logic and structure. This rejection of ethnocentrism became a cornerstone of anthropology for generations to come (Stocking 1989).

Bronislaw Malinowski: The Father of Fieldwork.

Across the Pacific Ocean, Bronislaw Malinowski (1884–1942), considered by many to be the "father of fieldwork," went even further than Boas in developing cultural anthropology's research methods. Malinowski, a Polish citizen who later became a leading figure in British anthropology, found himself stuck for a year on the Trobriand Islands as a result of World War I. His classic ethnography, *Argonauts of the Western Pacific* (1922), has become most famous for its examination of the Kula ring, an elaborate system of exchange. The ring involved thousands of individuals across many islands, some of whom traveled hundreds of miles by canoe to exchange Kula valuables (in particular, shell necklaces and armbands).

Argonauts also set new standards for fieldwork. In the opening chapter, Malinowski proposes a set of guidelines for conducting fieldwork based on his own experience. He urges fellow anthropologists to stay for a long period in their field sites, learn the local language, get off the veranda (that is, leave the

American anthropologist Franz Boas in Inuit clothing during fieldwork in the Pacific Northwest of North America, 1883.

salvage ethnography

Fieldwork strategy developed by Franz Boas to collect cultural, material, linguistic, and biological information about Native American populations being devastated by the westward expansion of European settlers.

cultural relativism

Understanding a group's beliefs and practices within their own cultural context, without making judgments.

British anthropologist Bronislaw Malinowski at a bachelor's house in Kasanai, Trobriand Islands, ca. 1915–18.

safety of their front porch to mingle with the local people), engage in participant observation, and explore the "mundane imponderabilia"—the seemingly commonplace, everyday items and activities of local life. Using these strategies enabled Malinowski to analyze the complex dynamics of the Kula ring, both its system of economic exchange and its social networking.

Although some of these suggestions may seem obvious to us nearly a century later, Malinowski's formulation of a comprehensive strategy for understanding local culture was groundbreaking and has withstood the test of time. Of particular importance has been his conceptualization of **participant observation** as the cornerstone of fieldwork. For anthropologists, it is not enough to observe from a distance. We must learn about people by participating in their daily activities, walking in their shoes, seeing through their eyes. Participant observation gives depth to our observations and helps guard against mistaken assumptions based on observation from a distance (Kuper 1983).

participant observation

A key anthropological research strategy involving both participation in and observation of the daily life of the people being studied.

E. E. Evans-Pritchard and British Social Anthropology. Between

the 1920s and 1960s, many British social anthropologists viewed anthropology more as a science designed to discover the component elements and patterns of society (see Chapter 2). Fieldwork was their key methodology for conducting their scientific experiments. Adopting a *synchronic approach*, they sought to control their experiments by limiting consideration of the larger historical and social context in order to isolate as many variables as possible.

E. E. Evans-Pritchard (1902–1973), one of the leading figures during this period, wrote a classic ethnography in this style. In *The Nuer* (1940), based on his research with a Sudanese "tribe" over eleven months between 1930 and 1936, Evans-Pritchard systematically documents the group's social structure—political, economic, and kinship—capturing the intricate details of community life. But later

MAP 3.3
The Nuer Region of East Africa

British anthropologist E. E. Evans-Pritchard seated among Nuer men and boys in southern Sudan, ca. 1930.

anthropologists have criticized his failure to consider the historical context and larger social world. Indeed, the Nuer in Evans-Pritchard's study lived under British occupation in the Sudan, and many Nuer participated in resistance to British occupation despite an intensive British pacification campaign against the Sudanese during the time of Evans-Pritchard's research. Later anthropologists have questioned how he could have omitted such important details and ignored his status as a British subject when it had such potential for undermining his research success.

Margaret Mead: Fieldwork and Public Anthropology. Margaret Mead conducted pioneering fieldwork in the 1920s, famously examining teen sexuality in *Coming of Age in Samoa* (1928) and, later, the wide diversity of gender roles in three separate groups in Papua New Guinea (1935). Perhaps most significant, however, Mead mobilized her fieldwork findings to engage in crucial scholarly and public debates at home in the United States. At a time when

MAP 3.4
Samoa

American anthropologist Margaret Mead with a mother and child in the Admiralty Islands, South Pacific, 1953.

many in the United States argued that gender roles were biologically determined, Mead's fieldwork testified to the fact that U.S. cultural norms were not found cross-culturally but were culturally specific. Mead's unique blending of fieldwork and dynamic writing provided her with the authority and opportunity to engage a broad public audience and made her a powerful figure in the roiling cultural debates of her generation.

The People of Puerto Rico: A Turn to the Global. During the 1950s a team of anthropologists headed by Julian Steward, and including Sydney Mintz and Eric Wolf, engaged in a collaborative fieldwork project at multiple sites on the island of Puerto Rico. Steward's resulting ethnography, *The People of Puerto Rico* (1956), marked the beginning of a significant anthropological turn away from studies of seemingly isolated, small-scale, nonindustrial societies toward studies that examined the integration of local communities into a modern world system. In particular, the new focus explored the impact of colonialism and the spread of capitalism on local people. Mintz, in *Sweetness and Power* (1985), later expanded his fieldwork interests in Puerto Rican sugar production to consider the intersections of local histories and local production of sugar with global flows of colonialism and capitalism. Wolf, in *Europe and the People Without History* (1982), continued a lifetime commitment to reassert forgotten local histories—or the stories of people ignored by history—into the story of the modern world economic system.

Annette Weiner: Feminism and Reflexivity. In the 1980s, anthropologist Annette Weiner retraced Malinowski's footsteps to conduct a new study of the Trobriand Islands sixty years later. Weiner quickly noticed aspects of Trobriand culture that had not surfaced in Malinowski's writings. In particular, she took careful note of the substantial role women played in the island economy. Whereas Malinowski had focused attention on the elaborate male-dominated system of economic exchange among islands, Weiner found that women had equally important economic roles and equally valuable accumulations of wealth.

In the course of her fieldwork, Weiner came to believe that Malinowski's conclusions were not necessarily wrong but were incomplete. By the time of Weiner's study (1988), anthropologists were carefully considering the need for **reflexivity** in conducting fieldwork—that is, a critical self-examination of the role of the anthropologist and an awareness that who one is affects what one finds out. Malinowski's age and gender influenced what he saw and what others were comfortable telling him. By the 1980s, feminist anthropologists such as Weiner and Kathleen Gough (1971), who revisited Evans-Pritchard's work with the Nuer, were pushing anthropologists to be more critically aware of how their own position in relationship to those they studied affected their scope of vision.

reflexivity
A critical self-examination of the role the anthropologist plays and an awareness that one's identity affects one's fieldwork and theoretical analyses.

Barbara Myerhoff: A Turn to Home. Barbara Myerhoff's first book, *Peyote Hunt* (1974), traces the pilgrimage of the Huichol Indians across the Sierra Madre of Mexico as they retell, reclaim, and reinvigorate their religious myths, rituals, and symbols. In her second book, *Number Our Days* (1978), Myerhoff turns her attention closer to home. Her fieldwork focuses on the struggles of older Jewish immigrants in a Southern California community and the Aliyah Senior Citizens' Center through which they create and remember ritual life and community as a means of keeping control of their daily activities and faculties as they age. Their words pour off the pages of her book as she allows them to tell their life stories. Myerhoff becomes a character in her own book, tracing her interactions and engagements with the members of the center and reflecting poignantly on the process of self-reflection and transformation that she experiences as a younger Jewish woman studying a community of older Jews.

Number Our Days marks a turn in anthropology from the study of the "other" to the study of the self—what Victor Turner calls in his foreword to Myerhoff's book "being thrice-born." The first birth is in our own culture. The second birth

Anthropologist Barbara Myerhoff with two members of the Aliyah Senior Citizens' Center in Southern California, the focus of her book *Number Our Days*.

immerses the anthropologist in the depths of another culture through fieldwork. Finally, the return home is like a third birth as the anthropologist rediscovers his or her own culture, now strange and unfamiliar in a global context.

ENGAGED ANTHROPOLOGY

Over the past thirty years, an increasing number of anthropologists, including Nancy Scheper-Hughes, whose work bookends this chapter, have identified their work as **engaged anthropology**. Engaged anthropologists argue that in a world of conflict and inequality, social scientists must develop an active, politically committed and morally engaged practice to address concrete local and global problems. Engaged anthropology is characterized by a commitment not only to revealing and critiquing but also to confronting systems of power and inequality. Design, implementation, and analysis of research involve close collaboration with colleagues and co-researchers in the community. Advocacy and activism with local communities on matters of mutual concern are central tenets of engaged anthropology (Scheper-Hughes 1995; Speed 2006).

Engagement is not new to anthropology. As early as 1870, John W. Powell, the first director of the U.S. Bureau of Ethnology and Geologic Survey, testified before Congress about the genocide of Native Americans following the westward expansion and construction of the railroads. African American anthropologist, novelist, journalist, playwright, and activist Zora Neale Hurston (1891–1960) vividly illuminated the culture and folklore of the early twentieth-century African American diaspora (1935, 1938; McClaurin 2007). Beatrice Medicine (1924–2005), Native American anthropologist, long advocated for the rights of women, children, Native Americans, and gay, lesbian, and transgender people. In recent decades, this focus on engagement, advocacy, and activism, also influenced

engaged anthropology

Applying the research strategies and analytical perspectives of anthropology to address concrete challenges facing local communities and the world at large.

by the work of Boas and Meads, has taken an increasingly central role in anthropologists' research strategies (Low and Merry 2010).

How Do Anthropologists Get Started Conducting Fieldwork?

Today cultural anthropologists call on a set of techniques designed to assess the complexity of human interactions and social organizations. You probably use some variation of these techniques as you go about daily life and make decisions for yourself and others. For a moment, imagine yourself doing fieldwork with Nancy Scheper-Hughes in the Brazilian shantytown of Alto do Cruzeiro. How would you prepare yourself? What strategies would you use? How would you analyze your data? What equipment would you need to conduct your research?

PREPARATION

Prior to beginning fieldwork, anthropologists go through an intense process of preparation, carefully assembling an **anthropologist's toolkit**: all the information, perspectives, strategies, and even equipment that may be needed. We start by reading everything we can find about our research site and the particular issues we will be examining. This *literature review* provides a crucial background for the experiences to come. Following Malinowski's recommendation, anthropologists also learn the language of their field site. The ability to speak the local language eliminates the need to work through interpreters and allows us to participate in the community's everyday activities and conversations, which richly reflect local culture.

Before going to the field, anthropologists search out possible contacts: other scholars who have worked there, community leaders, government officials, perhaps even a host family. A specific research question or problem is defined and a research design created. Grant applications are submitted to seek financial support for the research. Permission to conduct the study is sought ahead of time from the local community and, where necessary, from appropriate government agencies. Protocols are developed to protect those who will be the focus of research. Anthropologists attend to many of these logistical matters following a preliminary visit to the intended field site before fully engaging in the fieldwork process.

Finally, we assemble all the equipment needed to conduct our research. What tools would Nancy Scheper-Hughes have needed to conduct her research on a daily basis in Brazil? Today this aspect of your anthropologist's toolkit—most

anthropologist's toolkit
The tools needed to conduct fieldwork, including information, perspectives, strategies and even equipment.

likely a backpack—might include a notebook, pens, camera, voice recorder, maps, cell phone, batteries and chargers, dictionary, watch, and identification.

STRATEGIES

Once in the field, anthropologists apply a variety of research strategies for gathering quantitative and qualitative data. **Quantitative data** include statistical information about a community—data that can be measured and compared, including details of population demographics and economic activity. **Qualitative data** include information that cannot be counted but may be even more significant for understanding the dynamics of a community. Qualitative data consist of personal stories and interviews, life histories, and general observations about daily life drawn from participant observation. Qualitative data enable the ethnographer to connect the dots and answer the questions of why people behave in certain ways or organize their lives in particular patterns.

Central to a cultural anthropologist's research is participant observation. By participating in our subjects' daily activities, we experience their lives from the perspective of an insider. Through participant observation over time, we establish *rapport*—relationships of trust and familiarity with members of the community we study. The deepening of that rapport through intense engagement enables the anthropologist to move from being an outsider toward being an insider. Over time in a community, anthropologists seek out people who will be our advisors, teachers, and guides—sometimes called **key informants** or cultural consultants. Key informants may suggest issues to explore, introduce community members to interview, provide feedback on research insights, and warn against cultural miscues.

Another key research method is the *interview*. Anthropologists are constantly conducting interviews while in the field. Some interviews are very informal, essentially involving a form of data gathering through everyday conversation. Other interviews are highly structured, closely following a set of questions. Semi-structured interviews use those questions as a framework but leave room for the interviewee to guide the conversation. One particular form of interview, a **life history**, traces the life story of a key informant as a means of understanding change over time in that person's life and illuminating the interlocking network of relationships in the community. Life histories provide insights into the frameworks of meaning that individuals build around their life experiences. **Surveys** can also be developed and administered to gather quantitative data and reach a broader sample of participants around key issues, but rarely do they substitute for participant observation and face-to-face interviews as the anthropologist's primary strategy for data collection.

Anthropologists also map human relations. **Kinship analysis** enables us to explore the interlocking relationships of power built on family and marriage (see

quantitative data

Statistical information about a community that can be measured and compared.

qualitative data

Descriptive data drawn from nonstatistical sources, including personal stories, interviews, life histories, and participant observation.

key informant

A community member who advises the anthropologist on community issues, provides feedback, and warns against cultural miscues. Also called *cultural consultant.*

life history

A form of interview that traces the biography of a person over time, examining changes in the person's life and illuminating the interlocking network of relationships in the community.

survey

An information-gathering tool for quantitative data analysis.

kinship analysis

A fieldwork strategy of examining interlocking relationships of power built on marriage and family ties.

Chapter 9). In more urban areas where family networks are diffuse, a **social network analysis** may prove illuminating. One of the simplest ways to analyze a social network is to identify who people turn to in times of need.

Central to our data-gathering strategy, anthropologists write detailed **field notes** of our observations and reflections. These field notes take various forms. Some are elaborate descriptions of people, places, events, sounds, and smells. Others are reflections on patterns and themes that emerge, questions to be asked, and issues to be pursued. Some field notes are personal reflections on the experience of doing fieldwork—how it feels physically and emotionally to be engaged in the process. Although the rigorous recording of field notes may sometimes seem tedious, the collection of data over time allows the anthropologist to revisit details of earlier experiences, to compare information and impressions over time, and to analyze changes, trends, patterns, and themes.

Sophisticated computer programs can assist in the organization and categorization of data about people, places, and institutions. But in the final analysis, the ability to recognize key themes and patterns relies on the instincts and insights of the ethnographer.

MAPPING

Often one of the first steps an anthropologist takes upon entering a new community is to map the surroundings. **Mapping** takes many forms and produces many different products. While walking the streets of the field site, the ethnographer develops a spatial awareness of where people live, work, worship, play, and eat, and of the space through which they move. After all, human culture exists in real physical space. And culture shapes the way space is constructed and used. Likewise, physical surroundings influence human culture, shaping the boundaries of behavior and imagination. Careful observation and description, recorded in maps and field notes, provide the material for deeper analysis of these community dynamics.

Urban ethnographers describe the power of the **built environment** to shape human life. Most humans live in a built environment, not one made up solely or primarily of nature. By focusing on the built environment—what we have built around us—scholars can analyze the intentional development of human settlements, neighborhoods, towns, and cities. Growth of the built environment is rarely random. Rather, it is guided by political and economic choices that determine funding for roads, public transportation, parks, schools, lighting, sewers, water systems, electrical grids, hospitals, police and fire stations, and other public services and infrastructure. Local governments establish and enforce tax and zoning regulations to control the construction of buildings and approved uses. Mapping the components of this built environment may shed light on key dynamics of power and influence in a community.

social network analysis

A method for examining relationships in a community, often conducted by identifying whom people turn to in times of need.

field notes

The anthropologist's written observations and reflections on places, practices, events, and interviews.

mapping

The analysis of the physical and/or geographic space where fieldwork is being conducted.

built environment

The intentionally designed features of human settlement, including buildings, transportation and public service infrastructure, and public spaces.

Anthropologists turn to quantitative data to map who is present in a community, including characteristics such as age, gender, family type, and employment status. These demographic data may be available through the local or national census, or the anthropologist may choose to gather the data directly by surveying the community if the sample size is manageable. To map historical change over time in an area and discern its causes, anthropologists also turn to archives, newspaper databases, minutes and records of local organizations, historical photos, and personal descriptions, in addition to census data.

Mapping today may be aided by online tools such as satellite imagery, geographic information system (GIS) devices and data, online archives, and electronic databases. All can be extremely helpful in establishing location, orientation, and, in the case of photo archives, changes over time. On their own, however, these tools do not provide the deep immersion sought by anthropologists conducting fieldwork. Instead, anthropologists place primary emphasis on careful, firsthand observation and documentation of physical space as a valuable strategy for understanding the day-to-day dynamics of cultural life.

SKILLS AND PERSPECTIVES

Successful fieldwork requires a unique set of skills and perspectives that are hard to teach in the classroom. Ethnographers must begin with open-mindedness about the people and places they study. We must be wary of any prejudices we might have formed before our arrival, and we must be reluctant to judge once we are in the field. Boas's notion of cultural relativism is an essential starting point: Can we see the world through the eyes of those we are studying? Can we understand their systems of meaning and internal logic? The tradition of anthropology suggests that cultural relativism must be the starting point if we are to accurately hear and retell the stories of others.

A successful ethnographer must also be a skilled listener. We spend a lot of time in conversation, but much of that time involves listening, not talking. The ability to ask good questions and listen carefully to the responses is essential. A skilled listener hears both what is said and what is not said—something we refer to as zeros or silences. **Zeros** are the elements of a story or a picture that are not told or seen—key details omitted from the conversation or key people absent from the room. Zeros offer insights into issues and topics that may be too sensitive to discuss or display publicly.

A good ethnographer must be patient, flexible, and open to the unexpected. Sometimes sitting still in one place is the best research strategy because it offers opportunities to observe and experience unplanned events and unexpected people. For instance, I have a favorite tea shop in one Chinese village where I like to sit and wait to see what happens. The overscheduled fieldworker can easily miss the "mundane imponderabilia" that constitute the richness of everyday life.

zeros
Elements of a story or a picture that are not told or seen and yet offer key insights into issues that might be too sensitive to discuss or display publicly.

At times the most important, illuminating conversations and interviews are not planned ahead of time. Patience and a commitment to conduct research over an extended period allow the ethnographic experience to come to us on its own terms, not on the schedule we assign to it. This is one of the significant differences between anthropology and journalism. It is also a hard lesson to learn and a hard skill to develop.

A final perspective essential for a successful ethnographer is openness to the possibility of **mutual transformation** in the fieldwork process. This is risky business because it exposes the personal component of anthropological research. It is clear that by participating in fieldwork, anthropologists alter—in ways large and small—the character of the community being studied. But if you ask them about their fieldwork experience, they will acknowledge that in the process they themselves become transformed on a very personal level—their self-understanding, their empathy for others, their worldviews. The practice of participant observation over time entails building deep relationships with people from another culture and directly engages the ethnographer in the life of the community.

Nancy Scheper-Hughes could not have returned unchanged by her research experience. The people of Alto do Cruzeiro would not let her simply observe their lives; they made her work with them to create a neighborhood organization to address community problems. Indeed, the potential for the fieldworker to affect the local community is very great. So is the potential for the people being studied to transform the fieldworker.

mutual transformation
The potential for both the anthropologist and the members of the community being studied to be transformed by the interactions of fieldwork.

ANALYSIS

As the fieldwork experience proceeds, anthropologists regularly reflect on and analyze the trends, issues, themes, and patterns that emerge from their carefully collected data. One framework for analysis that we will examine in this book is power: Who has it? How do they get it and keep it? Who uses it, and why? Where is the money, and who controls it? The anthropologist Eric Wolf thought of culture as a mechanism for facilitating relationships of power—among families, between genders, and among religions, classes, and political entities (1999). Good ethnographers constantly assess the relations of power in the communities they study.

Whereas earlier anthropologists such as Evans-Pritchard focused narrowly on the local culture being studied, today's anthropologists explore and analyze global connections as well—relationships between the local community and the global processes that affect it. For example, in the 2005 film *Mardi Gras: Made in China*, the ethnographic filmmakers David Redmon and Ashley Sabin trace the connection between (1) the beads used in New Orleans Mardi Gras festivities to entice women to bare their breasts, and (2) the sweatshop factories in China where the beads are made by young teenage girls who work twelve-hour days, six

emic

An approach to gathering data that investigates how local people think and how they understand the world.

etic

Description of local behavior and beliefs from the anthropologist's perspective in ways that can be compared across cultures.

ethnology

The analysis and comparison of ethnographic data across cultures.

days a week. As globalization intensifies in the twenty-first century, anthropologists who conduct fieldwork in local communities are paying increasing attention to these kinds of local-global links.

Ethnographers also submit their local data and analysis to cross-cultural comparisons. We endeavor to begin from an **emic** perspective—that is, understanding the local community on its own terms. But the anthropological commitment to understanding human diversity and the complexity of human cultures also requires taking an **etic** perspective—viewing the local community from the anthropologist's perspective as an outsider. This provides a foundation for comparison with other relevant case studies. The overarching process of comparison and assessment, called **ethnology**, uses the wealth of anthropological studies to compare the activities, trends, and patterns of power across cultures. The process enables us to better see what is unique in a particular context and how it contributes to identifying larger patterns of cultural beliefs and practices. Perhaps the largest effort to facilitate worldwide comparative studies is the Human Relations Area Files at Yale University (http://hraf.yale.edu/), which has been building a database of ethnographic material since 1949 to encourage cross-cultural analysis.

How Do Anthropologists Write Ethnography?

After gathering data through fieldwork, anthropologists must decide how to tell the stories of the people they study. Although ethnographic films are a vibrant part of our field, most anthropologists make their contributions through ethnographic writing—either articles or books. The art of ethnographic writing has been a particularly hot topic within anthropology for the past twenty-five years, and both style and content have changed dramatically since Malinowski and Evans-Pritchard published their books in the early twentieth century.

Ethnography has changed as anthropology has changed. More women and people of color are writing, bringing their unique perspectives into the anthropological discourse. More people from non-Western countries are writing, challenging the position of Western writers as unquestioned authorities on other cultures. And with better communication systems, people are reading what we write about them, even when we write it halfway around the world. This has had a profound effect on the conversations between author and subject and on the ethnographer's final product.

It is unavoidable that what we write will in some way provide only a limited view of the lives of those we study. The process of collecting, organizing, and analyzing our data presumes not only that we present facts but also that we choose which facts to present, which people to highlight, and which stories to tell. As authors, we have the power to interpret the people and their experiences to our audience. This is an awesome and sometimes overwhelming responsibility, which often leaves the ethnographer at a loss for how to proceed. In researching my book *God in Chinatown*, for instance, I conducted more than one hundred interviews, each lasting one hour or more. The process of selecting certain stories and specific quotations was arduous.

POLYVOCALITY

Changes in ethnographic fieldwork and writing over recent decades have sought to make the process more participatory and transparent. Today most ethnographic projects involve people from the community in the research process and include their voices more directly in the written product.

Polyvocality—the use of many voices in ethnographic writing—allows the reader to hear directly from the people in the study and, by bringing their stories to life, makes them more vibrant and available to the reader. Anthropologists also increase polyvocality in their research by inviting key informants to help design the research, including interview and survey questions. Others may be invited to read sections of the manuscript as it is being drafted. In contemporary ethnographic writing, the author's voice also comes out more clearly as ethnographies have moved from the style of Evans-Pritchard (1940) toward that of Geertz (1973a)—from being a scientific report toward being thick description and an interpretation of what is observed.

polyvocality
The practice of using many different voices in ethnographic writing and research question development, allowing the reader to hear more directly from the people in the study.

REFLEXIVITY

In recent years, the practice of reflexivity—self-reflection on the experience of doing fieldwork—has become more prevalent in written ethnographies. Contemporary writers make an effort to reveal their own position in relationship to their study so that readers can assess what biases, strengths, or handicaps the author may have. The ethnographer's age, gender, race/ethnicity, nationality, sexuality, and religious background may have a direct impact on the ease with which he or she establishes rapport or gains access to the research community and on the successful analysis of his or her findings. A careful ethnographer must address these issues in the research design and implementation and may choose to reflect on them in the written report.

ETHNOGRAPHIC AUTHORITY

Ultimately, the ethnographer must wrestle with the question of ethnographic authority: What right does he or she have to present certain material, make certain claims, and draw certain conclusions? That authority is not automatically given, so writers make efforts, often early on in the ethnography, to establish their credentials and identify the grounds on which readers should trust them and the decisions they made during fieldwork and writing. These attempts to establish ethnographic authority include discussions of the length of time engaged in the study, language skills, special training and preparation, research design and implementation, and the quality of the relationship with subjects in the study. The quality and persuasiveness of the writing can also be significant in establishing the ethnographer's credibility. The inclusion of direct quotes can confirm the author's conclusions, provide more direct access to the fieldworker's data, and enable the reader to better assess the author's conclusions.

What Moral and Ethical Concerns Guide Anthropologists in Their Research and Writing?

Anthropologists often face moral and ethical dilemmas while conducting fieldwork. These dilemmas require us to make choices that may affect the quality of our research and the people we study. Indeed, the moral and ethical implications of anthropological research and writing are of deep concern within the discipline and have been particularly hot topics at various times in its history. As a result, the American Anthropological Association (AAA) has developed an extensive set of ethical guidelines, which you can view at www.aaanet.org.

DO NO HARM

At the core of our ethics code is the mandate to do no harm. Even though as anthropologists we seek to contribute to general human knowledge, and perhaps shed light on a specific cultural, economic, or political problem, we must not do so at the expense of the people we study. In fact, this issue spurred the creation of the AAA's code of ethics. The organization's website presents a great variety of advice about the anthropologist's responsibility to the people being studied.

Several key examples in the history of anthropology demonstrate the importance of the "Do no harm" mandate. In the 1960s and 1970s, anthropologists came under heavy criticism for their role in colonialism, particularly for intentionally and unintentionally providing information on local cultures to colonial administrators and military agents. After World War II, anthropology as a discipline was criticized for aiding the European colonial encounter, assisting colonial administrators by providing detailed descriptions and analysis of local populations, many of which were actively engaged in struggles against colonial rule. Anthropology was criticized for helping to create an image of colonial subjects as unable to govern themselves and in need of Western guidance and rule (Asad 1973). During the Vietnam War in the 1960s, some anthropologists were criticized for collaborating with the U.S. military occupation and counterinsurgency efforts. In the 1970s, the AAA experienced internal political turmoil as it addressed accusations of covert research conducted in Southeast Asia by anthropologists (Petersen 2015; Price 2004; Wakin 1992; Wolf and Jorgensen 1970).

More recently, the ethical practices of two American researchers, anthropologist Napolean Chagnon and geneticist/physician James Neel, who worked among Brazil's indigenous Yanomami people (Chagnon 1968) in the 1960s and following, have come under question. In his book *Darkness in El Dorado* (2000), journalist Patrick Tierney claimed, among other things, that Chagnon and Neel compromised their subjects' health to see how unprotected indigenous populations would respond to the introduction of infectious disease. Later investigations did not support Tierney's most serious charges, and the original findings of the AAA against Chagnon and Neel were rescinded. The controversy, however,

The relationship of anthropology to colonialism and war has been complicated. During the Vietnam War, for instance, some anthropologists were criticized for collaborating with the U.S. military occupation and counterinsurgency efforts. *(left)* An American soldier in rural Vietnam, 1967. Recently, the controversy continued as the U.S. military's Human Terrain Systems program (2007–2014) recruited anthropologists *(right)* to help troops understand local culture and make better decisions in the field.

stimulated a significant debate within anthropology about the code of ethics expected of all members.

Recently the U.S. military has actively recruited anthropologists for service as cross-cultural experts in Iraq and Afghanistan, renewing impassioned debates within the discipline about the proper role of anthropologists in military and covert operations. Through the Human Terrain Systems program, between 2007 and 2014 the U.S. military recruited, trained, and deployed anthropologists to be embedded with combat units and to advise military commanders on building local community relationships. Though this program has ended, a similarly controversial project, the Minerva Initiative of the U.S. Department of Defense that funds social science research of benefit to U.S. military planning and operations, has raised concerns among anthropologists (Gusterson 2008). The role of anthropologists in military-sponsored "nation building" projects has been supported by some (McFate 2005) but criticized by many others, who have warned of the "weaponizing of anthropology"—turning anthropological research strategies and knowledge into a tool of war (Price 2011).

OBTAIN INFORMED CONSENT

One of the key principles for protecting research subjects involves obtaining **informed consent**. It is imperative that those whom we study agree to participate in the project. To do so, they must understand clearly what the project involves and the fact that they have the right to refuse to participate. After all, anthropological research is not undercover investigation using covert means and deception. The anthropologist's hallmark research strategy is participant observation, which requires establishing rapport—that is, building relationships of trust over time. To develop rapport, the subjects of our studies must be clearly informed about the goals and scope of our projects and must willingly consent to being a part of them.

U.S. federal regulations protect human subjects involved in any research, and proposals to conduct research on humans, including anthropological research, must be reviewed by the sponsoring organization. Such regulations were originally designed to cover medical research, but anthropologists—whether students or professionals—now participate in these institutional reviews before conducting research.

ENSURE ANONYMITY

Anthropologists take precautions to ensure the privacy and safety of the people they study by providing anonymity in research notes and in publications. We frequently change the names and disguise the identities of individuals or, at times, whole communities. For example, Nancy Scheper-Hughes disguises the identities of people and places in Brazil to protect the community and individuals she

informed consent

A key strategy for protecting those being studied by ensuring that they are fully informed of the goals of the project and have clearly indicated their consent to participate.

worked with (for example, "the market town that I call Bom Jesus da Mata"). **Anonymity** provides protection for the people in our studies who may be quite vulnerable and whose lives we describe in intimate detail. This consideration becomes particularly important and sometimes controversial in situations in which research involves illegal activities—for instance, Claire Sterk's ethnography about prostitution (2000) or Philippe Bourgois's work with drug dealers in New York City (2003).

anonymity

Protecting the identities of the people involved in a study by changing or omitting their names or other identifying characteristics.

How Are Fieldwork Strategies Changing in Response to Globalization?

The increased movement of people, information, money, and goods associated with globalization has transformed ethnographic fieldwork in terms of both its process and its content.

CHANGES IN PROCESS

Changes in communication and transportation have altered the ongoing relationship between the anthropologist and the community being studied. Global communication allows the fieldworker and the community to maintain contact long after the anthropologist has left the field, facilitating a flow of data, discussions, and interpretation that in the past would have been very difficult to continue. The expansion of global transportation networks further increases the opportunities for personal interactions between an anthropologist and someone from the researched community outside the original research setting.

CHANGES IN CONTENT

Globalization has also deeply affected fieldwork content. No longer can an anthropologist study a local community in isolation from global processes. As even the most remote areas are affected by intensifying globalization—whether through media, tourism, investment, migration, or global warming—ethnographers are increasingly integrating the local with the global in their studies. In some cases, particularly in studies of migration, ethnographic fieldwork is now multi-sited, encompassing research in two or more locations to more fully represent the scope of the issue under study.

Nancy Scheper-Hughes's career reflects many recent changes in ethnographic fieldwork. Her earliest research, introduced in the chapter opener, focused on local life in the Brazilian shantytown Alto do Cruzeiro. She has

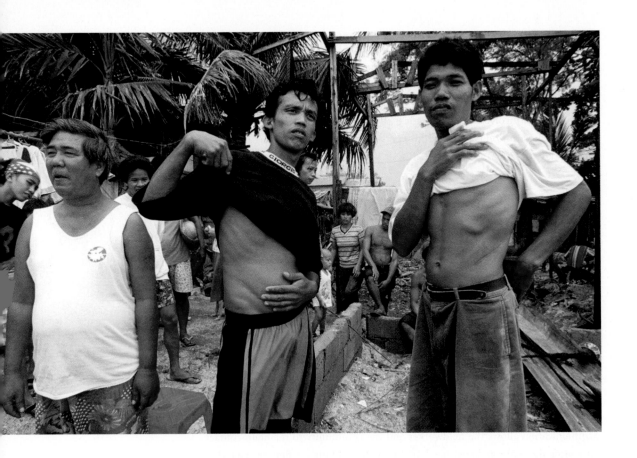

A middleman and two young Filipino men with scars; each of the two men has sold a kidney as part of the global trade in human organs.

carefully monitored changes in the community in the ensuing years, including dramatic recent improvements in infant mortality rates stemming from Brazilian economic growth combined with direct government promotion of local health care services (Scheper-Hughes 2013).

Scheper-Hughes's other recent work places Alto do Cruzeiro in the middle of an illicit global trade in harvested human organs (Scheper-Hughes 2002). While she continues to explore the richness of local life in Brazil, she has expanded her scope to examine how the experiences of the poor in one community are mirrored in the lives of poor people in many other countries and are linked by a gruesome global trade driven by demand from the world's economic elite. Scheper-Hughes first began hearing rumors while working in northeast Brazil, rumors of the abduction and murder of poor children, whose bodies—minus heart, lungs, liver, kidneys, and eyes—would later be found on roadsides, in sugarcane fields, or in hospital Dumpsters. Later, as she began writing articles about these organ-stealing rumors, other anthropologists reported similar stories of organ theft in Central and South America, India, Korea, Eastern Europe, and many parts of Africa.

Reflecting on the meaning of these stories, Scheper-Hughes writes, "To the anthropologist . . . working closely with the urban poor, the rumors spoke to the ontological insecurity of people 'to whom almost anything could be done.' They reflected everyday threats to bodily security, urban violence, police terror, social anarchy, theft, loss, and fragmentation. Many of the poor imagined, with some reason as it turns out, that autopsies were performed to harvest usable tissues and body parts from those whose bodies had reverted to the state" (Scheper-Hughes 2002, 36).

As an engaged medical anthropologist, Scheper-Hughes has spent countless hours investigating the extensive illegal international trade in smuggled human organs. Contemporary globalization, especially the time-space compression of transportation and communication, enables trafficking networks to spread across national boundaries and around the world. These same cornerstones of globalization have allowed Scheper-Hughes and her organization, Organs Watch, based at the University of California, to develop an extensive global network of anthropologists, human rights activists, transplant surgeons, journalists, and government agencies that have collaborated to address issues of human organ trafficking in India, Pakistan, Israel, South Africa, Turkey, Moldova, Brazil, the Philippines, and the United States.

As a member of two World Health Organization panels on transplant trafficking and transplant safety, Scheper-Hughes has seen firsthand the global search for kidneys: the often-poor kidney sellers; the kidney hunters who track them down; and the kidney buyers willing to cross borders, break laws, and pay as much as $150,000 in advance to the organ brokers for a chance at a new kidney and a new life. In 2009 the U.S. Federal Bureau of Investigation arrested a Brooklyn rabbi who had been arranging kidney sales, highlighting the deep integration of illegal international organ trafficking into developed-country markets where, for example, over 100,000 Americans linger on a kidney waiting list, struggling through dialysis to stay alive, and where the wait times for a donor in some parts of the country are as long as nine years.

The trajectory of Scheper-Hughes's career from fieldwork in a small favela in Brazil to fieldwork in international organ-trafficking networks reflects many of the transformations shaping anthropological fieldwork over the last forty years. No local community can be viewed as isolated. Anthropologists must consider each local fieldwork site in light of the myriad ways in which local dynamics link to the world beyond. Today fieldwork includes attention to global flows, networks, and processes as anthropologists trace patterns across national and cultural boundaries while keeping one foot grounded in the lives of people in local communities.

Toolkit

Thinking Like an Anthropologist:
Applying Aspects of Fieldwork to Your Own Life

You don't have to go to Brazil to use the skills of an anthropologist. Maybe you will be inspired by this book—or by a language you study, a professor whose class you take, or a new friend you meet—to explore a culture in another part of the world. Or maybe you will apply these skills nearer to home. In Chapter 1 you were asked to begin seeing yourself as a budding anthropologist, one who is already working hard to understand the complicated, globalizing world and how you fit into it. Fieldwork skills are the key to navigating what lies ahead of you.

As you think back to the fieldwork of Nancy Scheper-Hughes, remember the questions we asked at the beginning of the chapter:

- **What is unique about ethnographic fieldwork, and why do anthropologists conduct this kind of research?**
- **How did the idea of fieldwork develop?**
- **How do anthropologists get started conducting fieldwork?**
- **How do anthropologists write ethnography?**
- **What moral and ethical concerns guide anthropologists in their research and writing?**
- **How are fieldwork strategies changing in response to globalization?**

Consider how the concepts we have discussed can be applied not only by a professional anthropologist but also by each one of us in our daily lives.

You already use many of the strategies, skills, and perspectives of ethnographic fieldwork to navigate your daily journey through life. Whether in your family, your workplace, or your school, you have to understand the people with whom you interact. You participate and observe, establish rapport, listen, interview, gather life histories, and map out family and social networks. If you keep a journal or diary, you have already started taking field notes about the people and cultural patterns around you. You are constantly assessing who has power, how they got it, and how they use it. While you may already use many of these tools, the goal of this chapter has been to show the rigor with which they can be applied if you take fieldwork seriously and to enable you to apply them in a more systematic and self-conscious way in your daily life.

Key Terms

ethnographic fieldwork (p. 63)

salvage ethnography (p. 69)

cultural relativism (p. 69)

participant observation (p. 70)

reflexivity (p. 73)

engaged anthropology (p. 74)

anthropologist's toolkit (p. 75)

quantitative data (p. 76)

qualitative data (p. 76)

key informant (p. 76)

life history (p. 76)

survey (p. 76)

kinship analysis (p. 76)

social network analysis (p. 77)

field notes (p. 77)

mapping (p. 77)

built environment (p. 77)

zeros (p. 78)

mutual transformation (p. 79)

emic (p. 80)

etic (p. 80)

ethnology (p. 80)

polyvocality (p. 81)

informed consent (p. 84)

anonymity (p. 85)

Chapter 4
Language

We have a country where to assimilate, you have to speak English.... We have to have assimilation to have a country.... This is a country where we speak English, not Spanish.

—Presidential candidate Donald J. Trump in GOP debate, September 16, 2015

In April 2010, the state of Arizona passed a law mandating police to arrest anyone who gives a reasonable suspicion of being an undocumented immigrant. If that person cannot prove his or her legal status, he or she must be detained immediately. The law treats a very contentious issue. Arizona lawmakers argue that the law responds to the federal government's failure to monitor borders and protect U.S. citizens from foreigners who they fear will take their jobs and endanger their neighborhoods. Civil rights activists, however, ask how police will determine "a reasonable suspicion of being undocumented." They fear that law enforcement officers will rely on how the person looks (skin color), dresses, or speaks. Will someone who

---

Could language use have marked you with "a reasonable suspicion of being undocumented" under a 2010 Arizona law?

speaks Spanish or who speaks English with a Spanish accent be more likely to be arrested and detained? Is language an effective screen for legal status or citizenship?

Debates about language have been raging in the United States over the past twenty years. Thirty-one states have passed English-only laws limiting classroom instruction, driver's license exams, road signs, and even health warnings to one language. The U.S. House of Representatives has passed legislation several times declaring English to be the national language of the United States, although these bills have never been signed into law. The United States, historically, has been a country of many languages: Spanish, French, Dutch, German, Italian, Chinese, not to mention hundreds of Native American languages and hundreds of others spoken by contemporary immigrants. Spanish has been spoken in what is now the U.S. South and Southwest since the 1500s, when the Spanish conquistadors Francisco Vázquez de Coronado and Hernando Cortéz explored and colonized the area on behalf of the Spanish Crown. How has language come to be such a hot-button issue in the United States today?

Nearly seven thousand languages are currently in use in the world. Through linguistic anthropology, one of the four fields of anthropology, we explore not only the details of a language's vocabulary and grammar but also the role of language in people's lives—both as individuals and as communities. Languages are not abstract concepts with ideal forms perfectly displayed in a dictionary or a textbook. Languages are dynamic and alive. Communication is a social act. Words are part of actions. We call a friend, text a classmate, tell a story, say a prayer, ask a favor. Human language uses an infinite number of forms to communicate a vast array of information. We communicate through poetry, prose, gestures, signs, touch, text messaging—even anthropology textbooks. Not only can we communicate content in great detail, but we also have the wondrous capacity to share the content of our imaginations, our anger, fear, joy, and the deepest longings of our souls.

Humans are born with the ability to learn language—not a particular language, but whatever one they are exposed to as they grow up. Exactly what we learn and the context in which we learn it vary widely. Languages change and grow, constantly adapting to the needs and circumstances of the people who speak them. Although the number of languages shrinks every year under the pressures of globalization, the remarkable diversity of human language reflects humans' dramatically different ways of perceiving, thinking about, and engaging with the world. Because languages are deeply embedded in culture—languages *are* culture—they also become arenas where norms and values are created, enforced, and contested, where group identity is negotiated, and where systems of power and status are taught and challenged.

In this chapter we will consider how anthropologists study human language and communication. In particular, we will ask:

- **What is language and where does it come from?**
- **How does language shape our ways of thinking?**
- **How do systems of power intersect with language and communication?**
- **What are the effects of globalization on language?**

By the end of the chapter you will have a better understanding of how language works, have the conceptual tools to analyze the role of language in your personal life and within your language community, and comprehend the forces that will shape language and communication in our increasingly global future.

What Is Language and Where Does It Come From?

Language is a system of communication that uses symbols—such as words, sounds, and gestures—organized according to certain rules, to convey any kind of information. All animals communicate in some fashion, often relying on a *call system* of sounds and gestures that are prompted by environmental stimuli. Ants share information through chemical trails and pheromones; bees dance to communicate distance and direction to flower petals and nectar. Dogs growl or bark to express hostility or warning. And a border collie named Betsy, featured on the cover of *National Geographic* magazine, could recognize more than 340 distinct words and commands (Morrell 2008). Dolphins produce complicated vocal signals—clicks, whistles, squeaks, trills. Whales have been found to "sing"—to create a vocalization that appears to have a unique tune or accent for each clan or pod of whales.

Although these are all examples of communication—providing information by a sender to a receiver—they are not symbolic language as humans use it. In comparison, human language is a complex system that involves the combination of many small, meaningful elements into larger syllables, words, and sentences following certain rules but with infinite variations. Human language involves sounds and gestures along with myriad symbols that have deep historical and cultural meaning. It is remarkably flexible and creative, rapidly adapting to changes in human life and the environment.

THE ORIGINS OF HUMAN LANGUAGE

In searching for the evolutionary origins of human language, anthropologists, particularly primatologists, have investigated language use and communication

language

A system of communication organized by rules that uses symbols such as words, sounds, and gestures to convey information.

All animals communicate in some fashion. A border collie named Betsy could recognize more than 340 distinct words and commands.

Do nonhuman primates have the capacity to create human language? Koko, a gorilla, with Francine Patterson, learned over 400 signs in sign language.

among our nearest primate relatives—chimpanzees, orangutans, and other great apes—with some surprising results. In their natural habitats, primates produce an astonishing array of vocalizations to communicate information about food, sex, and potential predators. These calls are passed along genetically through the generations. Nonhuman primates lack the physical apparatus to create human sounds and human speech. Specifically, their ability to manipulate their vocal cords, tongue, and lips is far more limited than that of humans. But do they have the mental capacity to create human language? Scholars have conducted a set of landmark studies to explore this question of nonhuman primate language capabilities.

Chantek, an orangutan, was raised much like a human child from nine months of age by anthropologist Lyn Miles at the University of Tennessee at Chattanooga. Now living at Zoo Atlanta in a special habitat, Chantek has mastered several hundred signs and can also understand some spoken English. Reports on the language development of Chantek and other primates suggest that they have the ability to move beyond rote memorization of certain signs and indicate a more humanlike capacity to lie, swear, tell jokes, invent new words by combining signs, and even try to teach language to others (Fouts 1997; Miles 1993).

Scholars disagree about the final implications of research on nonhuman primate language capacity. Some have suggested that although this capacity is not as complex as human language, these nonhuman primates can develop language skills at the level of a two- or three-year-old human child (Miles 1993). Others argue that their behavior is mostly imitative—imitating their caregivers rather than using language creatively (Sebeok and Umiker-Sebeok 1980; Terrace et al. 1979). Certainly chimpanzees, gorillas, and orangutans can master rudimentary language signs and can even, at times, exhibit key aspects of human language skills. Their language use reflects *productivity*, meaning that they can use known words to invent new word combinations. Their language can also exhibit *displacement*—that is, the ability to use words to refer to objects not immediately present or events happening in the past or future. But, fundamentally, these primates do not use language in the human sense. In their natural habitats, they do not create and use basic language elements. They cannot achieve the extremely complex human language system that is perhaps the most distinct aspect of human culture and that enables us to store and pass on to succeeding generations huge quantities of information not embedded in our genes.

If our most immediate primate relatives do not approach the physical or mental language capacity of humans, then how did human language capacity evolve? Recent genetic information and archaeological evidence provide strong clues. Let's consider the genetic information first. Around 1990, a family in Britain (now known only as KE to protect their privacy) was discovered to have a rare mutation of the *FOXP2* gene. The same variant of *FOXP2* is found in chimpanzees. More than half of the members of the KE family inherited severe speech problems that made them unintelligible even to their own relatives (Trivedi 2001). Not only were affected family members unable to physically form words because of a limited ability to make fine lip and tongue movements, but cognitive differences also led them to have difficulty in recognizing and using grammar. As children, these family members were taught to use certain hand gestures to compensate. Genetic analysis indicates that the presence of the particular *FOXP2* gene variant may be crucial for activating and inactivating key human speech capacities, an evolutionary development that appears to be essential to human speech. Such analysis also traces the emergence of human language to within the past 150,000 years.

Archaeological evidence provides further clues to the origins of human language. Fossilized brain casts from archaic *Homo sapiens* known as Neandertals (who lived from about 130,000 to about 30,000 years ago) and even earlier *Homo* species reveal the neurological and anatomical features necessary for speech. Our early human ancestors' capacity to cooperate in hunting and tool making also suggests that some language ability may have existed over two million years ago, before the evolution of *Homo sapiens*. Cultural evidence supporting extensive language use by modern humans appears around 50,000 years ago, including art, tool making, and other technologies that required language to facilitate their transmission from generation to generation. Language as it has developed among modern humans would have enhanced the capacity for group cooperation and the transmission of cultural knowledge; in this way, it conferred a significant advantage in adapting to less hospitable natural environments and increasing the potential for survival.

DESCRIPTIVE LINGUISTICS

Language is a system of symbols. It is a system of otherwise meaningless sounds, marks (writing), and gestures that are made meaningful by a group of people through the collective history and tradition of their culture. Think of the English word *pig*. Say it out loud. Now create a mental image of a pig. Why do those three letters and that particular sound represent a pig? They don't look like a pig or sound like any of the noises that a pig makes. But when you say the word, an image is transferred from your brain into sound, which travels through the air into another person's ears and to that person's brain, where an image appears that is similar to yours—if not precisely the same. **Descriptive linguistics** is the study of the construction of those sounds, their meanings, and their combination into forms that communicate meaning. Linguistic anthropologists focus on describing language as it is used and not on prescribing how people should use it.

descriptive linguistics
The study of the sounds, symbols, and gestures of a language, and their combination into forms that communicate meaning.

phonemes

The smallest units of sound that can make a difference in meaning.

phonology

The study of what sounds exist and which ones are important in a particular language.

morphemes

The smallest units of sound that carry meaning on their own.

morphology

The study of patterns and rules of how sounds combine to make morphemes.

syntax

The specific patterns and rules for combining morphemes to construct phrases and sentences.

grammar

The combined set of observations about the rules governing the formation of morphemes and syntax that guide language use.

kinesics

The study of the relationship between body movements and communication.

paralanguage

An extensive set of noises (such as laughs, cries, sighs, and yells) and tones of voice that convey significant information about the speaker.

Through descriptive linguistics, anthropologists work to describe the elements and rules of a particular language. Imagine that you went to conduct linguistic research in a village in the mountains of the Philippines where the residents had no writing system for their local language. Your task might be to learn that oral language and to create a system for representing it in writing, perhaps using the International Phonic Alphabet. Where would you begin? After identifying a person or a few people from the village who would be your teachers, perhaps you would work your way from the most simple aspects of the language to the most complex. A language has a limited number of **phonemes**—the smallest units of sound that can make a difference in meaning. For instance, the English letters *b* and *p* sound very similar, but they make a significant difference in meaning. If you failed to carefully distinguish the different phoneme use in the village where you were working, you might mistakenly switch one for the other in a word followed by the sound *ig* when describing your host's home. In that case, you would end up with *pig* instead of *big*. The study of what sounds exist and which ones are important in a particular language is called **phonology**.

Extending your linguistic analysis, you would know that **morphemes** are the smallest units of sound that carry meaning on their own. (Phonemes, in contrast, have no meaning of their own.) So, for instance, the morphemes *cow* and *horse* can convey meaning without needing additional sounds. The study of the patterns and rules of how sounds combine to make morphemes is called **morphology**. In human languages, we combine morphemes to form phrases and sentences, relying on specific patterns and rules called **syntax**. So, following Standard American English syntax, we would place a possessive pronoun before the noun, not afterward. We would say or write *my pig*, not *pig my*—although the latter pattern might be linguistically appropriate in another language. **Grammar** encompasses the combined set of observations about the rules governing the formation of morphemes and syntax that guide language use.

NONVERBAL COMMUNICATION: KINESICS AND PARALANGUAGE

To fully describe and understand another language, the linguist must master more than its spoken and written elements. Human language is accompanied by and embedded in a gesture–call system made up of nonverbal elements that also convey significant amounts of information. These elements include body movements, noises, tone of voice, touch, and proxemics—cultural understandings about the use of space. **Kinesics**, the study of the relationship between body movements and communication, explores all the facial expressions, gestures, and postures that convey messages with or without words. For example, nods, handshakes, bows, and arms folded tightly across the chest all communicate information, although their meanings are not universal; they vary from culture to culture. The thumbs-up and the "okay" hand signals used in North America are considered rude gestures in certain other cultures. North Americans point with their fingers, but Filipinos point with their lips. Have you ever had the experience of making a motion or gesture that someone else misunderstood? If so, what was the cultural context?

Sign language, while involving elaborate and meaningful movements, is not simply a part of the gesture–call system described here. Rather it is considered to be a language itself, expressed visually rather than aurally.

Human language is also accompanied by **paralanguage**—an extensive set of noises (such as laughs, cries, sighs, yells) and tones of voice that convey significant information about the speaker. Paralanguage indicates whether the speaker is (for example) happy, sad, angry, tired, scared, disgusted, or enthusiastic. Try saying the sentence "The exam is on Thursday" using each of these tones of voice. The effect on communication is really quite stunning.

As much as 90 percent of emotional information is communicated through body movements and paralanguage. No wonder that email and text messaging have developed an extensive set of "emoticons" and "emoji"—symbols that indicate the emotional content intended by the sender. Emails and text messaging are beneficial developments in that they allow rapid response over distances great and small in our globalizing world, and they are increasingly used in the business world and personal life. But because they are devoid of the kinesics and paralanguage that play such key roles in face-to-face human communication, they significantly increase the potential for misunderstandings. Do you trust email or text messaging to communicate your most intimate thoughts? Can you remember an instance when they failed to adequately convey your meaning?

Humans have been communicating in writing for thousands of years. (*left*) Ancient Egyptian stele with hieroglyphs, ca. twenty-seventh to twenty-fifth century BCE. (*right*) Rune stone on Adelso Island near Stockholm, Sweden, eleventh century CE.

Did you ever wonder why emoticons and emoji developed in emails and text messages?

How Does Language Shape Our Ways of Thinking?

The power of language to shape human thought and culture has been a hot topic in linguistic anthropology for many generations. Linguistic anthropologists have considered questions such as: Is there an underlying, genetically structured grammar to all languages? Do languages evolve in response to local environments? Do vocabularies and classifications of reality embedded in a language affect the way its speakers think and see the world? In this section we will look at research on the relationships among language, thought, and culture, as well as a culturally specific phenomenon known as *focal vocabulary*.

LANGUAGE, THOUGHT, AND CULTURE

In the nineteenth and twentieth centuries, a number of linguists, including Ferdinand de Saussure and Claude Levi-Strauss, proposed theories of language that assumed an underlying structure to all the world's languages. In the 1950s Noam Chomsky, a linguist and philosopher, suggested that the human brain is hardwired with a basic framework for organizing language that creates a universal grammar—a similar structure in all languages (1957). In Chomsky's view, all humans share a similar language ability and ways of thinking. He felt that this proposition explains our ability to learn other languages and to translate fluidly from one language to another.

Sapir-Whorf hypothesis

The idea that different languages create different ways of thinking.

The work of Edward Sapir and his student Benjamin Lee Whorf—later given the name **Sapir-Whorf hypothesis**—took a different direction, suggesting that different languages create different ways of thinking (Sapir and Swadesh 1946). Their hypothesis proposed that languages establish certain mental categories, or classifications of reality, almost like a grammar for organizing the worldview that shapes peoples' ways of perceiving the world. Whorf's linguistic research with the Hopi, a Native American group in the southwestern United States, suggested that the Hopi language differs from English both in vocabulary and in basic grammatical categories that are key to conceptualizing how the world works. For instance, rather than using separate verb tenses expressing past, present, and future, the Hopi language combines past and present into one. Whorf suggested that this pattern reflects a different conceptualization of time and a unique worldview in which past and present reflect lived reality whereas the future is hypothetical or potential (Carroll 1956).

"Shakespeare in the Bush": A Tiv Interpretation of *Hamlet*.

Laura Bohannan explores the challenges that different vocabulary and conceptualizations of the world pose for translation between languages and cultures.

She relates her discoveries in her article "Shakespeare in the Bush: An American Anthropologist Set Out to Study the Tiv of West Africa and Was Taught the True Meaning of *Hamlet*" (1966). While Bohannan was conducting fieldwork in a small village in Nigeria, Tiv elders asked her to tell them a story from her own culture. She attempted to explain *Hamlet*, one of the classic stories of English literature, but time and again was unable to translate directly from English to Tiv. Words such as *chief* and *leader* hold distinctly different meanings and roles in the two cultures; they do not translate to people with a different cultural worldview. The "dead" in Hamlet do not translate because the Tiv have no concept of ghosts. Instead, they imagined Shakespeare's characters as beset by witchcraft.

As Bohannan attempted to use Tiv words to tell Shakespeare's story, the original meanings of the English words became blurred, and the standard message of *Hamlet* was lost in translation. Bohannan's insights as related in "Shakespeare in the Bush" reveal both the power of our environment to shape our language and the power of our language to shape the way we see the world.

MAP 4.1
Nigeria

THE ROLE OF FOCAL VOCABULARY

Contemporary studies in linguistic anthropology suggest that although the vocabulary and grammar of the language we learn may influence the way we see the world, language does not control or restrict our thinking. Languages are dynamic. They change and adapt as the natural and cultural worlds shift. Humans creatively invent new words and concepts to describe and discuss the changing world as they experience it. Evidence of this adaptability can be found in a language's **lexicon**—all the words for names, ideas, and events that make up a language's dictionary.

Of particular interest to linguistic anthropologists is a language's **focal vocabulary**—that is, words and terminology that develop with particular sophistication to describe the unique cultural realities experienced by a group of people. Thus the Bolivian Aymar Indians have two hundred names for potatoes, reflecting the potato's role as a major source of food in their diet. The Nuer of Sudan, studied by E. E. Evans-Pritchard (1940), relied on cattle in their economy, political system, and kinship structures; thus, they developed more than 400 words to distinguish different types of cattle. In today's globalizing world, a focal vocabulary has emerged to describe and engage in digital communication. Words such as *mouse, modem, download*, and *attachment*—even *email, texting*, and *tweet*—are very recent creations designed to facilitate communication among those working in the digital communication age.

Even the human description of the color spectrum varies across and within cultures, seemingly according to need. Anthropologist Robin Lakoff (2004) examined how color terms in American English have expanded over the last fifty years, being promoted by the fashion and cosmetics industries. An extensive

lexicon
All the words for names, ideas, and events that make up a language's dictionary.

focal vocabulary
The words and terminology that develop with particular sophistication to describe the unique cultural realities experienced by a group of people.

color vocabulary is not uniform among Americans; it varies primarily by gender. Women are far more likely than men, for instance, to be able to distinguish between salmon and peach, teal and turquoise, or cranberry and dusky orange. A similar gender-based focal vocabulary exists in American sports language. Men are far more likely than women to use the common basketball terms such as *back door, box out, zone, dish, reverse layup, in the bonus, in the paint, isolation play, from downtown!,* or *and one!* This highly specialized set of terms and distinctions allows complex communication about complicated human activity but is applicable in extremely limited scenarios.

Clearly, language, including vocabulary, provides categories for recognizing and organizing the world; but language also reflects reality. Language is not rigidly structured or controlling. It is remarkably flexible and fluid, responding to changes in the surrounding culture and enabling us to describe and analyze our world with remarkable specificity.

How Do Systems of Power Intersect with Language and Communication?

Language comes alive when people communicate with one another. But languages are deeply embedded in the patterns of particular cultures. What people actually say and how they say it are intricately connected to the cultural context, to the speakers' social position, and to the larger systems of power within which the language operates. Linguistic anthropologists, especially sociolinguists, study these connections. **Sociolinguistics**, which we will consider in this section, is the study of the ways in which culture shapes language and language shapes culture, particularly the intersection of language with cultural categories and systems of power such as age, race, ethnicity, sexuality, gender, and class (Wardhaugh 2009).

sociolinguistics

The study of the ways culture shapes language and language shapes culture, particularly the intersection of language with cultural categories and systems of power such as age, race, ethnicity, sexuality, gender, and class.

THE "N-WORD"

Words can be very powerful. They can hurt. They can heal. Some do so more than others. Words are also symbols. They can carry profound meanings based on the history of their use in a culture. As we explore the intersection of language and culture, particularly the intersection of language and systems of power, a consideration of the history and contemporary usage of the "N-word" provides rich insights. In U.S. culture, the "N-word" carries such powerful connotations that many people are reluctant to say it out loud or put it in print. Television stations censor it from their broadcasts. Politicians shy away from controversy over its usage. It is so powerful that most people only refer to it as the "N-word."

Nigger has been used as a derogatory term for African Americans throughout much of U.S. history—as a symbol of white power, slavery, and the threat of violence. In the twentieth century, the use of the "N-word" in public discourse was replaced successively by the use of *Negro, colored, black*, and *African American*. In 1962, the U.S. federal government legally changed the offending name on all public properties under its control, replacing it with *Negro* (Severson 2011). The "N-word," however, has not disappeared. It continues to hold tremendous symbolic power as its use invokes the history of racism, inequality, and the threat to make those dangers real in the present.

Despite its sordid history, use of the "N-word" has been revived among African American youth and in hip-hop and rap music. As a result, a debate has raged even within the African American community about its appropriateness. Many older African Americans reject its use because of its long-standing association with U.S. systems of race and racism. In contrast, younger generations often articulate their desire to appropriate the term for their own generation and rob it of its historical power.

My students remind me that some young people today quite commonly use the "N-word" to express friendship and camaraderie, not anger and hostility. At the same time, they recognize distinct rules about this usage—rules that factor in race, gender, age, and status and that attempt to mitigate against the former role of the "N-word" in this country's systems of race and racism. These young people carefully say "nigga," dropping the hard "r" ending, perhaps taking a slight edge off the word's powerful meaning. They only use it among friends. White people rarely address a person of color with the greeting. Boys never call girls "nigga." Girls rarely use it among themselves. Young people never use it in reference to older people. And students never use it in addressing a professor.

Think about how you feel when you hear the "N-word" spoken aloud. Is your reaction affected by your race, gender, age, or status, or by those of the speaker? Do you feel comfortable using the "N-word" in daily speech? If so, where, when, and with whom? If not, what is the source of your discomfort? Is it ever appropriate for a white person to use it in the U.S. cultural context? Sociolinguists study language in this way. They examine the use of language in its specific contexts and the way language shapes and is shaped by other dynamics of power.

LANGUAGE AND GENDER

Ethnic and racial dynamics are not the only sources of tension in communication. Have you ever walked away from a conversation with someone of the opposite sex and thought to yourself, that person has no idea what I'm talking about! You are not alone. Bookstores are full of titles that promise to help you figure it out: *Men Are from Mars, Women Are from Venus* (Gray 1992); *The 5 Love Languages: The Secret to Love That Lasts* (Chapman 2010); *You Just Don't Understand: Women and Men in Conversation* (Tannen 2001). Clearly, women and men are developing different patterns of language use. How and why?

There is no hard evidence that the brains of men and women are wired differently, leading to gender differences in language and other behavior. But linguistic anthropologists have examined the powerful role of culture in shaping language. In this instance, language and gender are intricately intertwined in personal and public conversations, among groups of men or groups of women, and in mixed-sex talk. In particular, linguists use two main theoretical frameworks for analyzing these patterns. The frameworks are sometimes known as the *difference model* and the *dominance model*.

Linguistic anthropologist Deborah Tannen's popular book *You Just Don't Understand: Women and Men in Conversation* (2001) is built on the difference model. Tannen suggests that conversations between men and women are basically a form of cross-cultural communication. Between the ages of five and fifteen, boys and girls grow up in different linguistic worlds. At the time when most children are developing and perfecting their communication skills, boys and girls are operating in largely segregated gender groups. Girls mostly hang out in small groups, indoors in more intimate conversations. Boys tend to play in larger groups, often outdoors, and compete with one another for group status, often through verbal jokes, stories, and challenges. These patterns, according to Tannen, are reinforced in later years through socializing, sports, and work. No wonder that boys and girls have a difficult time communicating with each other when they finally begin to look for relationships. It is as if they have grown up in two different cultures, two different worlds.

But is miscommunication always rooted in misunderstanding? Or are there real, underlying conflicts between the genders that lead to the miscommunication (Cameron 2007)? Other linguistic anthropologists, working from the dominance model, examine how the cultures of communication learned by boys and girls intertwine with gender dynamics throughout the larger culture: at home, school, work, and play, and even through religion. According to these scholars, if gender stratification and hierarchy are prevalent in the larger culture (see Chapter 7), and if men are generally in positions of superiority, then language will reflect men's dominance and may play a key role in enabling it (Lakoff 2004; West 1998).

Did you ever wonder why men and women struggle to communicate with each other? Are their brains wired differently for language, or have they grown up in different social worlds learning different communication skills?

Research on mixed-sex communication over the past thirty years consistently shows that many men adopt linguistic strategies that allow them to establish and maintain dominance in conversation and in social interaction. Men are more likely to use dominant speech acts such as commands, explanations, contradictions, criticisms, challenges, and accusations. Women are more likely to ask, request, agree, support, accommodate, accept, and apologize. Men are more likely to interrupt other speakers to insert their ideas or concerns, express doubts, or offer advice.

Despite stereotypes to the contrary, men also tend to dominate conversations through the amount of talking they do. Men claim more "air time" than women in meetings, seminars, boardrooms, and classrooms—especially in public forums where they see some possibility of maintaining or increasing their power and status. Working from the dominance model of mixed-sex communication, many linguistic anthropologists suggest that language and gender, as reflected in male and female communication patterns, are intricately connected to patterns of stratification in the culture at large (Holmes 1998).

LANGUAGE AND DIALECT

Politics and power can play key roles in how we evaluate a system of communication. For instance, how do we distinguish between a language and a dialect? Is it purely on a linguistic basis? A language is commonly described as a complete system of communication, while a **dialect** is considered a nonstandard variation of a language. Naming something a dialect generally places it in a subordinate relationship to the language. However, from a linguistic anthropologist's perspective, the distinction is not always simple. Human languages vary widely in spoken and written form and in accent, pronunciation, vocabulary, and grammar. Yet, from a linguistic perspective, all languages serve as effective communication tools for the people who speak them.

The categorization and evaluation of certain ways of speaking as a dialect and others as a language can frequently be traced to the exertion of power—political power of the nation, the state, the media, and even the stratification among racial and ethnic groups. Yiddish linguist Max Weinreich reputedly once said that a language is a dialect with an army and a navy. In other words, the elevated status associated with a language derives not from its superior linguistic form or communication capacity, but from its ability to establish—perhaps impose through force, if necessary—a particular form as the norm by which to judge other ways of speaking. A particular language variation or way of speaking may be elevated in a culture as the **prestige language**, associated with wealth, success, education, and power.

French sociologist Pierre Bourdieu proposes that language skills serve as a type of cultural capital—a resource or asset available to language users that can be converted into financial capital, such as wages and benefits. Mastery over it brings a set of resources that enable the individual to be more successful. Bourdieu notes that linguistic standards are established and reinforced by a culture's educational institutions, government, media, and religious organizations. They may be taught in schools, used in national media broadcasts such as radio and television, or selected as a sign of competence in business hiring practices. Other language variations are then judged against the norm of the prestige language, and their speakers—often said to be speaking a dialect—are associated with inferior positions within the culture (Bourdieu 1982, 1984).

LANGUAGE VARIATION IN THE UNITED STATES

As the chapter-opening story illustrates, the United States is home to people speaking nearly 400 languages, including 169 distinct Native American languages whose origins predate European conquest (U.S. Census Bureau 2011). Some 41 million people speak Spanish as their first language, and another 11 million are bilingual (Instituto Cervantes 2015). The 38 million immigrants in the U.S. bring unprecedented language diversity—though 90 percent of the

dialect
A nonstandard variation of a language.

prestige language
A particular language variation or way of speaking that is associated with wealth, success, education, and power.

children of immigrants learn to speak English proficiently (Pew Research Center 2013).

Although globally the English language varies widely in pronunciation, vocabulary, and grammar, in the United States—through national television, radio, and the educational system—the midwestern accent and grammatical usage have become the prestige language variation. This is sometimes called Standard Spoken American English (SSAE), or simply Standard American English (SAE), against which all other variations are judged. As we explored in this chapter's opening story, judgments about language can have consequences well beyond the realm of communication. We turn first to consider issues of cultural context and race as they intersect with Standard American English.

Code Switching in Academia. In cultures with distinct language variations, dialects, and accents, individuals may become skilled at **code switching**— that is, switching back and forth between one variation and another according to cultural context. Code switching takes many forms, as speakers may switch from language to language and from linguistic style to style.

code switching

Switching back and forth between one linguistic variant and another depending on the cultural context.

Educational systems tend to resist acknowledging speech variations as equally effective, instead choosing to promote a prestigious version as inherently better. (For instance, think about the linguistic standards your instructor used to grade your last English paper.) In educational environments, as a result, students, teachers, and administrators all learn to switch frequently from informal to formal styles of speaking and writing as required. Talking with friends in the hallway may assume a very different form than responding to a professor's query in class. Writing a text message or a post on Facebook elicits a distinctly different writing style compared with polishing a research paper for a class assignment.

I recently received the following email from a student who appears to have struggled to understand when to switch codes:

> Hi, how r u? this is xxxx from ur class which is on monday n wednesday @ 9:30. i just wanted to ask u that about the book critique. I know what i as suppose to do in terms of writing about the book however i am lost n not sure wht i should do abt the articles and how u want us to relate it to our paper. I mean am i suppose to write abt the book n then relate it to da article n den offer my own opinion on it? plz let me know how i should b doing dis or if this is how i should be doing it. . . . . . Thank you

While this use of language may serve perfectly well in a text or email with a friend or peer, the failure to code switch in a communication with a professor runs the risk of sending the wrong signals. What evaluations might a professor make of a communication like this one written by a student in text-speak?

African American English: "Spoken Soul". Linguistic anthropologists and other scholars of language have extensively studied one particular form of English that is spoken by millions of African Americans in the United States. At times, this variation has been referred to as Black English, Black English Vernacular, African American Vernacular English, or African American English (AAE). The language habits of African Americans in the U.S. are not homogenous but vary according to region, gender, social class, and age, and not all African Americans speak AAE. Even among those who do, there are significant differences.

African American English is perhaps the most stigmatized variation of Standard American English, mistakenly criticized as broken or flawed English and associated with urban African American youth. But from a linguistic perspective, AAE is a complete, consistent, and logical variation of the English language with a unique history and a distinct and coherent pronunciation, vocabulary, and grammar. Studies by Labov (1972) and other scholars have carefully demonstrated that African American English is not an ungrammatical jumble but a sophisticated linguistic system with clear rules and patterns (Table 4.1).

Scholars disagree about the exact origins of AAE. Some trace its vocabulary and grammar to the West African linguistic roots of enslaved people who were brought forcibly to work in the American colonies. Others trace its heritage to nonstandard English used by poor English immigrants who interacted with African slave workers in the plantation system of the American South. The creole languages—blends between the indigenous language and the colonial language—found in Jamaica, Trinidad, Barbados, and Guyana that developed during and after the slave trade may also have been potential sources for the unique forms that AAE has taken (Green 2002; Rickford and Rickford 2000).

Despite its stigmatization within certain parts of American society and the intense cultural pressure to assimilate to Standard American English, AAE not

TABLE 4.1

Contrasts between Standard American English and African American English

STANDARD ENGLISH	STANDARD ENGLISH CONTRACTION	AFRICAN AMERICAN ENGLISH VERNACULAR
You are ready	You're ready	You ready
He is ready	He's ready	He ready
We are ready	We're ready	We ready
They are ready	They're ready	They ready

Source: William Labov. 1972. *Language in the Inner City: Studies in the Black English Vernacular.* Philadelphia: University of Pennsylvania Press.

Here, the Oakland, California, Task Force on the Education of African American Students presents a resolution on Ebonics in public education, on January 12, 1997.

only has survived and developed but has become a symbol of identity and solidarity for many within the African American community. Rickford and Rickford (2000) document how this "Spoken Soul"—spoken by African Americans of all ages across the United States and closely associated with African American identity and culture—comes alive in the African American community. Indeed, it is vibrant in homes, schools, streets, and churches and on the airwaves. It is representative of a culture, history, and worldview that are distinct from white culture and ways of speaking.

The linguistic status of African American English entered prominently into the U.S. national debate in 1996. At that time, the Oakland Unified School District in California recommended recognizing it, under the name Ebonics— from *ebony* ("black") + *phonics* ("sounds")—as a distinct language and supporting student speakers of AAE as if they were learning Standard American English as a second language in school. In response, critics from across the country warned that the teaching of Ebonics in U.S. public schools would undermine the use of Standard American English, which they considered central to U.S. national identity, unity, and progress.

Under pressure, the Oakland school district revised its plan, but the controversy effectively obscured their efforts to address a local problem with national implications—the struggles of African American children to succeed in school. Today, resistance to recognizing African American English continues, creating negative stereotypes that undermine efforts to understand the unique linguistic character of AAE and the struggles that young AAE speakers may have in educational settings dominated by Standard American English. In fact, the debate about English language diversity and the place of Standard American English in U.S. culture continues through efforts at the local, state, and national levels (Ahearn 2012).

HISTORICAL LINGUISTICS

Historical linguistics is the study of the development of language over time, including its changes and variations. By analyzing vocabulary and linguistic patterns, historical linguists trace the connections between languages and identify their origins. For example, through comparative analysis of vocabulary, syntax, and grammar, we know that Spanish and French historically developed from their parent language, Latin. English, German, Dutch, and Scandinavian languages evolved from an earlier proto-Germanic language. Both Latin and proto-Germanic branched out from an even earlier language called Proto-Indo-European; it was spoken more than 6,000 years ago and also gave birth to the languages spoken today in Greece, India, Iran, and Eastern Europe (Mallory and Adams 2006; McWhorter 2001).

Over thousands of years of adaptation, growth, and change, human language developed more along the lines of a **language continuum** rather than into distinct languages. In a language continuum, people who live near one another speak in a way that is mutually intelligible. The farther one travels, the more the language varies, but it tends to be at least partially mutually intelligible to those living nearby—if not 100 percent, then substantially. Although disrupted to some extent over centuries by migration and the strengthening of nation-states, language continuums still exist in many parts of the world. For instance, a strong language continuum has existed between Italy and France. If you were to walk from village to village beginning at the southern tip of Italy, travel northward, and then head northwest into France, you would find that people at either end of the journey would not be able to communicate with one another—their languages would be mutually unintelligible. But along the journey, the local residents of each village you pass through would be able to understand their neighbors in the nearby villages. Changes would be evident from location to location, but communication would be mutually intelligible.

An extensive language continuum exists in China as well. Though written Chinese is essentially the same throughout the country, there are thousands of local variations of spoken Chinese, most of which are mutually unintelligible. For example, speakers of Mandarin, Cantonese, Shanghainese, Fuzhounese, and Sichuanese cannot understand one another. Linguistically none is considered superior or inferior to another, but they do vary in prestige. Mandarin is the most widely spoken Chinese language variation. Called *Putonghua* ("the common language") or *Guoyu* ("the national language"), Mandarin is based on the local version of Chinese spoken in and around the national capital, Beijing. For centuries,

---

historical linguistics

The study of the development of language over time, including its changes and variations.

language continuum

The idea that variation in languages appears gradually over distance so that groups of people who live near one another speak in a way that is mutually intelligible.

imperial administrators who governed areas across China on behalf of the emperor in Beijing adopted Mandarin, so it became the norm associated with China's economic and political elite. After the Chinese civil war in 1949, the new government established *Putonghua* as the national standard for all media broadcasts as well as for instruction in all schools. As a result, regardless of the local variations of the Chinese language, today everyone learns *Putonghua* as a second language. But this is a political decision, not a statement of its linguistic superiority.

Clearly, languages evolve as human groups use them, adapt them, or surrender them to more prevalent forms. The current age of globalization will provide even more opportunities for languages to meet and either mix or remain largely unchanged. This means that the field of historical linguistics will continue to trace dynamic aspects of language variation and change well into the future.

What Are the Effects of Globalization on Language?

The movement of people throughout human history has played a role in the way that languages change and develop. As people move, elements of vocabulary and grammar are loaned to and imposed on populations that come into contact. Languages are full of loanwords that have been adopted from others. The encounter of linguistic communities occurs with increasing rapidity in the contemporary era of globalization. Still, approximately 7,000 languages resound around the world today (Figure 4.1). A few have hundreds of millions of speakers. Most have a few thousand. However, globalization is consolidating language use among a small group of languages while threatening the extinction of thousands of others (Table 4.2).

DIMINISHING LANGUAGE DIVERSITY

The current pattern of increasing global interconnection threatens to diminish language diversity worldwide. In an earlier era of globalization, colonialism spread English, Spanish, Portuguese, French, Dutch, German, and Russian beyond Europe to people around the globe. Because these former colonial languages provide points of access to the current global economic and political system, many of them continue to expand today. In addition, increasing migration to urban centers often leads speakers of less widely used languages to assimilate and adopt the more widely used language. The more prominent languages—including the former colonial languages and other regional or national languages—dominate global media, including television, radio, print, and digital media. Through this

FIGURE 4.1

World Languages by Country, 2017

The languages of the world are spread across countries in ways that may surprise you. Take a moment to identify the twenty countries with the most language diversity and the country with the least language diversity.

COUNTRY RANKINGS

1 Highest number of spoken languages

(1) (Lowest number of spoken languages)

EACH SQUARE REPRESENTS ONE LANGUAGE

Source: Simons, Gary F. and Charles D. Fennig (eds.). 2017. *Ethnologue: Languages of the World*, 20th ed. Dallas, TX: SIL International. Online version: www.ethnologue.com.

TABLE 4.2
Top Twenty World Languages, 2017

LANGUAGE	NUMBER OF NATIVE SPEAKERS
1. Chinese	1,284 million
2. Spanish	437 million
3. English	372 million
4. Arabic	295 million
5. Hindi	260 million
6. Bengali	242 million
7. Portuguese	219 million
8. Russian	154 million
9. Japanese	128 million
10. Lahnda	119 million
11. Javanese	84.4 million
12. Korean	77.2 million
13. German	76.8 million
14. French	76.1 million
15. Telugu	74.2 million
16. Marathi	71.8 million
17. Turkish	71.1 million
18. Urdu	69.1 million
19. Vietnamese	68.1 million
20. Tamil	68.0 million

Source: Simons, Gary F. and Charles D. Fennig (eds.). 2017. *Ethnologue: Languages of the World*, 20th ed. Dallas, TX: SIL International. Online version: www.ethnologue.com

dominance they are crowding out the less widely used languages and their speakers.

As a result of these dynamics, today the eight most prominent languages are spoken by more than 40 percent of the world's population. The top 90 languages account for 80 percent of humanity. The 4,000 least widely used languages, in total, account for only 0.12 percent of the world's language users (Simons 2017). English has a unique position in the world at the moment, with as many as two billion speakers. Many of these are nonnative speakers who learn English as a second language because of its central role in universities, medicine, computing, entertainment, and intergovernmental relationships. English is currently a prestige language that provides effective access to international economic activity and political engagement.

HASTENING LANGUAGE LOSS

Linguistic anthropologists warn that as many as half of the 7,000 languages in the world today could be lost by the end of the twenty-first century. In 2017, 144 languages had fewer than ten speakers. Another 329 had fewer than one hundred speakers. Together, these 473 languages represent almost 7 percent of the world's languages (Simons 2017). They have very little chance of survival and face almost certain language death. This is the outcome of **language loss**. On average, one language is lost every ten days (Harrison 2007). The most rapid disappearances are in northern Australia, central South America, the Pacific Northwest of North America, and eastern Siberia; this group also includes the Native American languages spoken in Oklahoma and the southwestern United States.

language loss
The extinction of languages that have very few speakers.

Languages develop over time to enable human groups to adapt to a particular environment and to share information that is essential to their local culture. When a language is lost, when it is crowded out by more widely used languages, we lose all of the bodies of information and local knowledge that had been developed—perhaps over thousands of years—by that community. Within a language is embedded rich knowledge about plants, animals, and medicines. Within a language is embedded a particular group's unique way of knowing the world and thinking and talking about human experience.

Language Revitalization. Most languages have never been written down. Does this surprise you? If you are a speaker of one of the more prominent languages, such as English, perhaps it does. As many of the less widely used languages face extinction, some groups are undertaking efforts to preserve them in written form.

Documenting a local language may involve years of work in a detailed and painstaking process that draws on all the basic skills of fieldwork and descriptive linguistics. One of the most extensive efforts to create written records of small languages is the work of a group called the Summer Institute of Linguistics (SIL), which together with its partner, the Wycliffe Bible Translators, trains missionaries in linguistic and anthropological methods and sends them to the field, often to remote areas, to live with a community and create a written language in order to translate the Christian Bible into the local language.

Some linguistic anthropologists consider SIL's work to be controversial. They are concerned that the Christian nature of the project means that certain aspects of local culture—including indigenous religious beliefs, ritual language, songs, and art connected to local religion—are at risk of being ignored and extinguished. Other scholars acknowledge the significant data that would be lost if SIL translators were not doing the detailed work of documenting hundreds of local languages that are threatened with extinction in small communities worldwide. Despite this controversy, SIL has succeeded in producing a widely used compendium of all the world's languages called *Ethnologue*. Although it started with only forty entries in 1951 as a language guide for Christian missionaries, in 2017 *Ethnologue*'s twentieth edition catalogued 7,099 languages (Simons 2017).

Preserving Endangered Languages. Information technology is beginning to transform the ways in which linguistic anthropologists document and preserve endangered languages, creating new opportunities for revitalization. Consider the Native American Lakota language. Its approximately 25,000 speakers live primarily in tribal areas scattered across North and South Dakota, as well as in cities, towns, and rural areas throughout the United States. Their tribally owned lands are in some of the poorest U.S. counties. Few children learn Lakota today, threatening the language with eventual extinction. So the Lakota have placed a high priority on preserving their language and culture and increasing Lakota language use among young people. Linguists have been working to document the Lakota language by collecting and preserving language samples, cultural knowledge, and artifacts. Some have even done intensive immersion in the Lakota language. But limited resources, combined with the geographic dispersion of Lakota speakers, have inhibited these efforts.

In 2009, a small local company, LiveAndTell, built an online digital platform for Lakota language preservation and instruction. Using participatory social media technology similar to that of YouTube and Flickr, LiveAndTell created opportunities for Lakota speakers to collaborate, create, and share digital artifacts. Families wrote family stories and posted photos, audio recordings, videos, and online annotations. School research projects were uploaded to community sites. In these ways, the dispersed Lakota language community has created an online archive of the living language. For instance, one contributor posted a picture of a car and then tagged each part—steering wheel, mirror, tire, and so on—with the Lakota name and an audio file of its pronunciation. Entries like these provide detailed linguistic information that is not available in standard dictionaries and may never come to light in formal oral interviews with professional linguists (Arobba et al. 2010).

Humans are born with the ability to learn language. But exactly what we learn and the context in which we learn it vary widely. Languages change and grow, they are taught, debated, and contested. Humans are constantly adapting language to meet the needs of local communities and global interactions. And while today local languages are under increasing stress, the continuing diversity of human languages provides a vivid portrait of the dramatically different ways humans perceive, consider, and engage the world. As we have seen throughout this chapter, linguistic anthropologists are deeply engaged in the analysis and understanding of the role language plays in human life and in understanding the transitions and changes that are facing the human linguistic landscape in an era of increasing globalization.

Globalization threatens the loss of many smaller local languages, and with them their local knowledge and ways of understanding the world. Ramona Dick is an elder in the Washoe tribe, which is based in Nevada and California. As a child, she refused to be sent to a school where students were required to speak only English.

Toolkit

Thinking Like an Anthropologist:
Language, Immigration, and U.S. Culture

As you encounter the complexities of language in daily life—communicating with a boyfriend or girlfriend, collaborating with classmates from other places, studying abroad, working with people in multinational corporations, debating immigration policy, or understanding gender in classroom dynamics—thinking like an anthropologist can help you better understand your own experiences and those of others. First, take a moment to review the questions we asked at the beginning of this chapter:

- **What is language and where does it come from?**

- **How does language shape our ways of thinking?**

- **How do systems of power intersect with language and communication?**

- **What are the effects of globalization on language?**

In our opening story, we considered how language has entered the immigration debates in Arizona. Now that you have been studying anthropology—and in this chapter, linguistic anthropology—how would you analyze the underlying issues at play in this debate? Why has language become such a hot-button issue in U.S. politics? How is English intertwined with notions of American identity, class, and belonging?

Language use has become symbolic of larger cultural debates. Studies consistently show that the children of immigrants grow up speaking English as their first language, not the language of their parents' country of origin (Portes, Fernandez-Kelly, and Haller 2009). Yet the debate over language instruction in education continues. Along with Arizona's restrictive immigration laws, the Arizona Department of Education has seen a 180-degree turn in its policies for bilingual education programs. Facing a teacher shortage in the 1990s, Arizona recruited thousands of bilingual teachers to lead bilingual classes for the tens of thousands of students who may have grown up speaking Spanish at home. Many of the new teachers were recruited from Latin America, and their first language was Spanish. Then, in 2000, Arizona voters passed a referendum mandating that instruction of nonnative English speakers be in English only. In 2010 the state adopted further policy changes, including new fluency standards for teachers, focusing on pronunciation and writing. Teachers who were unable to meet the new standards were removed from the classrooms of nonnative English speakers (Jordan 2010).

The Arizona education debates reveal the way that language functions as more than a system of symbols that enable people to communicate. Language is also a key cultural arena in which norms are established, values are promoted, and relationships of power are negotiated.

Key Terms

language (p. 93)

descriptive linguistics (p. 95)

phonemes (p. 96)

phonology (p. 96)

morphemes (p. 96)

morphology (p. 96)

syntax (p. 96)

grammar (p. 96)

kinesics (p. 96)

paralanguage (p. 96)

Sapir-Whorf hypothesis (p. 98)

lexicon (p. 99)

focal vocabulary (p. 99)

sociolinguistics (p. 100)

dialect (p. 104)

prestige language (p. 104)

code switching (p. 105)

historical linguistics (p. 108)

language continuum (p. 108)

language loss (p. 112)

Part 2

What lies beneath the surface of any beautiful scene? The project of anthropology includes unmasking the structures of power—the deep complexities of how humans organize themselves in groups. In Part 2 we will explore structures of race, ethnicity, gender, sexuality, kinship, and class in order to help you develop the analytical tools to see more deeply, navigate more carefully, and engage more fully the world around you. Here, women smoke a hookah at a coffee shop in Cairo, Egypt.

Unmasking the Structures of Power

Chapter 5
Race and Racism

On the afternoon of August 9, 2014, twenty-eight-year-old white police officer Darren Wilson shot and killed unarmed eighteen-year-old African American Michael Brown after a 90-second encounter on a street in Ferguson, Missouri. Over the following weeks, growing crowds of demonstrators organized in Ferguson to express their outrage over Michael Brown's shooting and long-simmering grievances of discriminatory treatment at the hands of the Ferguson Police Department and courts. As demonstrations intensified, the police rapidly escalated their response. A nightly curfew was declared. Police in riot gear with gas masks, shields, and batons—backed up by helicopters, floodlights, and armored vehicles with snipers perched atop—fired tear gas, concussion grenades, and rubber bullets to control and disperse crowds. Much of the nation and the world watched in disbelief.

In November of 2014, a local grand jury, after hearing the evidence, chose to not indict Officer Wilson,

How do we make sense of the continuing inequality in the United States that breaks so clearly along lines of race? Here, police in military gear arrest a demonstrator during protests in Ferguson, Missouri, in August 2014.

accepting his statement that he feared for his safety and declaring that he had acted in self-defense. Demonstrations erupted again. In March 2015, after a six-month investigation, the U.S. Department of Justice cleared Officer Wilson of any civil rights violations in the shooting of Michael Brown.

But a second DOJ report on the Ferguson Police Department offered deeper insights into the roots of the racial tension running through the Ferguson uprising (U.S. Department of Justice 2015). The DOJ investigation found that in a town of 21,200 residents, of whom 67 percent were African American, during the previous two years African Americans comprised 85 percent of all traffic stops, 90 percent of all tickets, 93 percent of arrests, and 95 percent of citations for jaywalking or disturbing the peace, violations that hinge significantly on police discretion. When whites were charged for similar discretionary offenses, Ferguson courts dismissed the charges 68 percent more often. Ferguson police used force almost exclusively against blacks and were twice as likely to search a black motorist as a white motorist after a traffic stop even though white motorists were more likely to have drugs or other contraband. The DOJ report unambiguously concluded that the Ferguson Police Department routinely violated the constitutional rights of the town's African American residents. Its findings of racial profiling, discrimination, use of excessive force, and patterns of unlawful conduct confirmed the long-standing complaints of Ferguson residents that, in the most fundamental ways, the criminal justice system worked differently for whites and blacks.

The tragic death of Michael Brown, the events in Ferguson, the torrent of deadly encounters between police and African Americans, and the growth of the Black Lives Matter movement have again pushed race and racism directly into the U.S. national spotlight. Race and racism are incredibly difficult topics of conversation in U.S. culture, whether we are in a classroom, a courtroom, a religious setting, the halls of Congress, the streets of Ferguson, Missouri, or our own local communities. How do we create opportunities to explore ideas of race and the way those ideas shape our lives and culture? In a country that likes to think of itself as color-blind, how do we as anthropologists make sense of the continuing inequality in income, wealth, education, access to health care, police enforcement, and incarceration rates that breaks so clearly along color lines (Shanklin 1998)?

Anthropologists view race as a framework of categories created to divide the human population. Western Europeans originally developed this framework as part of their global expansion beginning in the 1400s (Sanjek 1994). As they encountered, mapped, and colonized people in Africa, Asia, the Pacific, and the Americas, Europeans placed them into an "international hierarchy of races, colors, religions and cultures" (Trouillot 1994, 146). The exact labels and expressions have varied over time and place as colonial powers engaged with local cultures and confronted local resistance. But the underlying project—to stratify people into groups based on assumptions of natural differences in intelligence, attractiveness, capacity for civilization, and fundamental worth in relation to people of European descent—has been remarkably consistent (Mullings 2005a).

As we will explore in this chapter, today anthropologists find no scientific basis for classifications of race. Genetically there is only one race—the human race, with all its apparent diversity. Yet despite consistent efforts over the last century by anthropologists and others to counter the inaccurate belief that races are biologically real, race has remained a powerful framework through which many people see human diversity and through which those in power organize the distribution of privileges and resources. Race—which is scientifically not real—has become culturally real in the pervasive racism found in many parts of the globe, including the United States.

Over the past 500 years, race as a way of organizing the world has been put to destructive use, wreaking an enormous toll on both its victims and its proponents. Race and racism have justified the conquest, enslavement, forced transportation, and economic and political domination of some humans by others. Today race and racism have become so integral to patterns of human relations in many parts of the world that inherited racial categories may seem to be natural, and the inequality built on racism may seem to represent "real" differences among "real" races.

In this chapter we will critique arguments for the existence of discrete biological human groups called "races." We will consider the roots of race and racism in the European colonial past and their expression in various places today. We will examine the construction of race in the United States over the past 400 years and the way race and racism continue to shape U.S. culture. In particular, we will consider the following questions:

- **Do biologically separate races exist?**
- **How is race constructed around the world?**
- **How is race constructed in the United States?**
- **What is racism?**

We will examine **race** as a flawed system of classification, created, and re-created over time, that uses certain physical characteristics (such as skin color, hair texture, eye shape, and eye color) to divide the human population into a few supposedly discrete biological groups and attribute to them unique combinations of physical ability, mental capacity, personality traits, cultural patterns, and capacity for civilization. Drawing on anthropological research, we will see, however, that racial categories have no biological basis. We might even say that races, as a biological concept, do not exist. The danger in this statement about biological race is that it may lead us to the mistaken conclusion that race does not exist. On the contrary, race has very real consequences.

race

A flawed system of classification, with no biological basis, that uses certain physical characteristics to divide the human population into supposedly discrete groups.

Race is a deeply influential system of thinking that affects people and institutions. Over time, imagined categories of race have shaped our cultural institutions—schools, places of worship, media, political parties, economic practices—and have organized the allocation of wealth, power, and privilege at all levels of society. Race has served to create and justify patterns of power and inequality within cultures worldwide, and many people have learned to see those patterns as normal and reasonable. So in this chapter we will also examine **racism**: individuals' thoughts and actions, as well as institutional patterns and policies, that create or reproduce unequal access to power, privilege, resources, and opportunities based on imagined differences among groups (Omi and Winant 1994).

By the end of the chapter you will have the anthropological tools to understand not only the flaws in arguments for biologically discrete races but also the history and current expressions of race and racism globally and in the United States. You will be prepared to apply those tools, if you so choose, to engage in efforts against racism on your college campus, in your community, and throughout the world.

racism

Individuals' thoughts and actions and institutional patterns and policies that create or reproduce unequal access to power, privilege, resources, and opportunities based on imagined differences among groups.

Do Biologically Separate Races Exist?

Many of us were enculturated to believe that "race" refers to distinct physical characteristics that mark individuals as clearly belonging in one group and not in another. However, anthropologists see race very differently. Contemporary studies of human genetics reveal no biologically distinct human groups. We can state this with certainty despite centuries of scientific effort to prove the existence of distinct biological races, and despite widespread popular belief that different races exist. In fact, humans are almost identical, sharing more than 99.9 percent of our DNA. The small differences that do exist are not distributed in any way that would correspond with popular or scientific notions of separate races. Race is not fixed in nature but, as we will explore later in this chapter, is created, perpetuated, and changed by people through individual and collective action.

First, however, let's explore some of the science behind race.

FUZZY BOUNDARIES IN A WELL-INTEGRATED GENE POOL

Some physical anthropologists have compared modern humans to a little village that has grown very quickly. Throughout the short 200,000-year history of modern humans, we have basically been functioning as one enormous, interconnected gene pool, swapping genetic material back and forth (by interbreeding) quite freely within the village. Over the years, our family trees have intersected again and again.

If you trace your own family back for thirty generations—parents to grandparents to great-grandparents, and so on—you will find that in less than a thousand years you have accumulated one billion relatives. So it is not hard to imagine the myriad and unpredictable exchanges of genetic material among that large a group. Now extend your family tree back 100,000 years—the time it has taken for a few small groups of humans to migrate out of Africa and populate the

What can you know about a person's genetic makeup based on her (or his) outward appearance? Variations of skin color or other visible characteristics often associated with race are shaped by less than 0.1 percent of our genetic code. Contrary to certain stereotypes, they do not predict anything else about a person's genetic makeup, physical or mental capabilities, culture, or personality.

entire planet. It is easy to imagine the billions of times this growing population has exchanged genetic material. Such deep integration of the human gene pool means that no clear and absolute genetic lines can be drawn to separate people into distinct, biologically discrete, "racial" populations.

As a result of this gene flow, human variation changes gradually over geographic space in a continuum (what physical anthropologists refer to as a *cline*), not by abrupt shifts or clearly marked groups. Even skin color, perhaps most frequently imagined to demarcate separate races, in fact varies so gradually over geographic space that there are no clear boundaries between one population and another, nor color groupings that distinguish one population from another. If you flew from western Africa to Russia, you would notice distinct variations in physical human form between the population where you boarded the plane and the population where you disembarked. But if you walked from western Africa to Russia, there would never be a point along the way where you would be able to stop and say that the people on one side of the road are of one race and the people on the other side are of a different race.

Perhaps more surprising, a person from western Africa who starts walking east may have more in common genetically with someone at the end of her trek in Russia than she does with a neighbor at home. This seems hard to imagine because we have been encultured to believe that a very small number of traits—including skin color, hair texture, and eye color and shape—can serve to categorize people into distinct groups and predict larger genetic patterns. This is a flawed assumption. The human gene pool continues to be highly integrated. Genetic variations such as skin color, expressed in an individual's external appearance, are only 0.1 percent of that person's genetic code; they do not predict anything else about his or her genetic makeup. People in a particular region of the world whose ancestors inhabited that area for an extended period may have some increased probability of genetic similarity because of the greater probability of swapping genetic material with those geographically closer. But group boundaries are fuzzy and porous. People move and genes flow. Ultimately, group genetic probabilities cannot predict any one individual's genetic makeup.

THE WILD GOOSE CHASE: LINKING PHENOTYPE TO GENOTYPE

genotype

The inherited genetic factors that provide the framework for an organism's physical form.

phenotype

The way genes are expressed in an organism's physical form as a result of genotype interaction with environmental factors.

In considering human physical diversity, physical anthropologists distinguish between genotype and phenotype. **Genotype** refers to the inherited genetic factors that provide a framework for an organism's physical form; these factors constitute the total genetic endowment that the organism, in turn, can pass down to its descendants. In contrast, **phenotype** refers to the way genes are expressed in an organism's physical form (both visible and invisible) as a result of the interaction of genotype with environmental factors, such as nutrition, disease, and stress.

The widespread belief that certain phenotypes such as skin color are linked to physical and mental capabilities, personality types, or cultural patterns is incorrect but deeply ingrained and difficult to reimagine.

As individuals, we may make snap judgments based on phenotypical traits that we erroneously assume indicate a person's "race"; with a quick glance we may think we know something significant about that individual. On the basis of phenotype alone, we may consider someone to be smarter, faster, stronger, safe or dangerous, better at business, better at math, a better dancer or singer, more prone to alcoholism, more artistic, more susceptible to certain diseases, a better lover. You might call this the "White Men Can't Jump" or "Asians Are Better at Math" way of thinking about race and genes. We assume that we can know something significant about a person's genetic makeup just by looking at her phenotype. But can we really tell anything about someone from the way he or she looks?

A relatively small number of genes control the traits frequently used today to distinguish one "race" from another—skin color, eye shape, or hair texture. As a result, in the short history of modern humans these genes have been able to change rapidly in response to the environment. For example, as humans moved out of Africa and across the globe into a wide variety of physical environments, traits such as skin color, shaped by a relatively small cluster of genes, were more susceptible to environmental pressures and adapted more quickly. In contrast, traits such as intelligence, athletic or artistic ability, and social skills appear to be shaped by complex combinations of thousands or tens of thousands of genes, so they have been much less susceptible to environmental pressures. Adaptations in skin color were not accompanied by adaptations in, say, intelligence, musical ability, or physical ability. It is important to note that genetic research consistently shows that the genes that influence skin color, eye shape, or hair texture are not linked to any other genes and cannot predict anything about the rest of a person's underlying genotype (Mukhopadhyay, Henze, and Moses 2007).

Jonathan Marks, a leading physical anthropologist, compares the problem of sorting people into races with the problem children might have in sorting blocks into categories. Imagine that you start with a pile of blocks and ask a group of children to sort them into "large" and "small." They might agree on some—the largest and the smallest. But others in between might be harder to classify. "The fact that the blocks can be sorted into the categories given, however, does not imply that there are two kinds of blocks in the universe, large and small—and that the child has uncovered a transcendent pattern in the sizing of the blocks. It simply means that if categories are given, they can be imposed upon the blocks" (Marks 1995, 159).

What if you asked the children to sort instead by color or to distinguish among wooden, metal, and plastic blocks? What about blocks with smooth sides or grooved sides? The children could sort the blocks into any of these categories.

But if you didn't link the multiple characteristics of the blocks—all the wooden red blocks, or all the grooved plastic blocks—the children would end up with a completely different arrangement of blocks depending on whatever categories they arbitrarily decided to sort for.

The same is true for humans and the concept of race. If you give people a limited range of categories for skin color groups, they will be able to place many people into these categories. Some individuals who lie in the boundaries may be more difficult to categorize. But would this exercise uncover some deep, intrinsic pattern about humans? No, because traits like skin color are not linked to any other particular set of genes and cannot serve to predict anything else about the underlying genotype.

How Is Race Constructed around the World?

Racial categories are human constructs; they are not found in nature. Yet they have become so deeply internalized that they feel natural and provide one of the most powerful frameworks through which we experience the world (Mukhopadhyay, Henze, and Moses 2007). Anthropologists examine race and racism on a global scale and thus from different angles, identifying their similarities and variations and, in the process, revealing the ways those concepts have evolved and might be changed through individual and collective action.

RACE AND THE LEGACY OF COLONIALISM

Contemporary global expressions of race and racism are deeply rooted in the systems of classification that western Europeans created as they expanded their colonial empires into Africa, Asia, the Pacific, and the Americas beginning in the 1400s. **Colonialism** became the centerpiece of European global economic activity, combining economic, military, and political control of people and places to fuel Europe's economic expansion and enhance the European position in the emerging global economy (see Chapter 11). The classification of people based on phenotype, particularly skin color, became the key framework for creating a hierarchy of races—with Europeans at the top—that linked people's looks with assumptions about their intelligence, physical abilities, capacity for culture, and basic worth. Eventually this framework served to justify colonial conquests, the transatlantic slave trade, and the eradication of much of the indigenous population of the Americas (Gregory and Sanjek 1994).

Taking a global perspective, anthropologists often refer to "racisms" in the plural, reflecting the varieties of ways race has been constructed among people in

colonialism

The practice by which a nation-state extends political, economic, and military power beyond its own borders over an extended period of time to secure access to raw materials, cheap labor, and markets in other countries or regions.

different places. Locally, racisms and systems of racial classification are complex frameworks built out of the encounter of colonialism with local cultural patterns, global migration, and specific movements of resistance. While racializing systems around the world may all have their roots in European colonialism, they manifest themselves differently in different places and at different times.

Racial frameworks and systems of racism have changed significantly over the last century. After World War II, colonial-era racist political and legal structures shifted as national liberation movements struggled to end occupations by foreign powers. In addition, in this postcolonial period, anti-racist liberation movements challenged long-term patterns of race and racial discrimination. Notably, the anti-apartheid movement in South Africa resisted dominant white rule, eventually reversing decades of legal structural discrimination and violence. The civil rights movement challenged more than 300 years of race-based inequality in the United States. Today globalization has brought about new experiences of race and racism.

Indeed, in today's global world, flexible accumulation produces new relationships between corporations and workers; the migration of workers within countries and across national borders yields new racial formations; and time-space compression enhances communication tools that can be employed to resist old hierarchies while also perpetuating old racial frameworks on a global scale. Racisms today, though rooted in similar historic realities, are shifting as they intersect with other systems of power, whether those are ethnicity, gender, sexuality, kinship, or class (Mullings 2005a). The exact expression of these constructs varies from culture to culture and place to place, depending on why races were originally invented and how they have been used to establish and maintain hierarchies of power.

Diagram of a slave ship from the Atlantic slave trade.

Class, Gender, and Hundreds of Races in Brazil.
Brazil provides a good location to explore the cultural construction of race and the application of ideas of race to the creation of stratification. The United States and Brazil are today the two largest multiracial countries in the Western Hemisphere, although they have traveled two very different paths in framing racial identities and hierarchies. By the time Brazil outlawed slavery in 1888, the country had the largest African population in the New World. This situation reflected the grim fact that during and after Brazil's time as a colony of Portugal (1500–1815), 40 percent of all Africans in the Atlantic slave trade were brought to Brazil to work on Portuguese plantations and mines. Brazil was the last country in the Americas to outlaw slavery—a full generation after the U.S. Emancipation Proclamation in 1863.

Today Brazilians describe the human physical diversity called "race" in great detail. Although Brazil's system of racial classification is color-coded, its color

MAP 5.1
Brazil

terminology is far more expansive, encompassing hundreds of categories (Freyre 1933; Harris 1964, 1970). Terms include *alva* (pure white), *alva-escuro* (off-white), *alva-rosada* (pinkish white), *branca* (white), *clara* (light), *branca morena* (darkish white), *branca suja* (dirty white), *café* (coffee colored), *café com leite* (coffee with milk), *canela* (cinnamon), *preta* (black), and *pretinha* (lighter black) (Fluehr-Lobban 2006). Race categories follow along a nuanced continuum of appearance rather than a few rigid categories such as those used in the United States.

Brazil's population of Europeans, Africans, and indigenous people has had a long history of interracial mixing. The Portuguese colonial government promoted assimilation and did not bar **miscegenation**—that is, interracial marriage. As a result, many single Portuguese men who settled in Brazil chose to intermarry. Nor has Brazil applied the rule of hypodescent—the "one drop of blood" rule—that in the United States meant that having even one black ancestor out of many could mark an individual as black (see "The Rule of Hypodescent" later in this chapter). As a result, a Brazilian family may include children who are categorized as various shades of white, brown, and black.

Race in Brazil is not solely a function of skin color. In fact, race intersects closely with class—including land ownership, wealth, and education—in determining social status. Because of the power of class, a Brazilian's racial position can be modified by his or her level of affluence. Affluence can shift a Brazilian's racial identity in spite of skin color and other supposedly "racial" markers (Walker 2002).

Some scholars refer to Brazil as a "racial democracy" and extol the nation as an exceptional example of racial harmony (Freyre 1933; Harris 1964; Kottak 2006). Brazil's government abolished the use of racial categories in the 1930s and constitutionally banned racism in 1951. The complex and fluid color classifications—and the absence of political and legal mechanisms to establish and enforce a clear color line between black and white—are seen as a sign of tolerance. In addition, the incorporation of key African cultural practices (including carnival, samba, Candomblé religious practices, capoeira, and specific cuisine) as symbols of the Brazilian nation is often cited as supporting evidence for the racial democracy thesis (Downey 2005).

Other scholars have noted that despite the appearance of racial democracy, inequality exists in almost every area of Brazilian life and is directly linked to color. Darker-skinned Brazilians face higher levels of exclusion and injustice, including a systemic correlation between color and economics. Most of the poor are Afro-Brazilians. Most of the rich are white. Racial democracy may instead be simply a myth that serves as a cornerstone of Brazil's national denial of the existence of racism (Harrison 2002b; Roth-Gordon 2016; Smith 2016).

In *Laughter Out of Place* (2003), anthropologist Donna Goldstein writes about poor working women from the bleak favela (shantytown), ironically named

miscegenation

A demeaning historical term for interracial marriage.

Felicidade Eterna ("eternal happiness"), who support their families as domestic workers in the homes of middle-class Brazilian families in the affluent sections of Rio de Janeiro. Gloria, poor and dark skinned, raising fourteen children, including nine of her own, works as a domestic servant, shopping, cooking, and cleaning. She earns five dollars a day—just enough to feed herself and her family. The pay is off the books, so she has no legal labor protections, no insurance, and no pension. Goldstein links the contemporary culture of domestic work, particularly the employer–domestic servant relationships, to the historic institution of slavery in Brazil. Middle-class families enjoy a kind of learned helplessness similar to that of the slave owner—allowing their workers to do the dirty, manual chores. The employer–domestic servant relationship, like the owner–slave relationship, is characterized by domination, strict rules, and social separation.

How do Brazil's marginalized and oppressed people make sense of their lives—lives overburdened with poverty, violence, and work at the bottom of a global hierarchy of race, class, and gender, yet lives that also display dignity and resilience? Goldstein explores the role of laughter and humor as means to cope with persistent brutality. She particularly notes a humor that recognizes life's absurdities and ironies and provides perspective to a sense of injustice. She recalls, for instance, the awkwardness of "laughter out of place," as domestic workers and employers laugh at different times and for different reasons when they watch the local soap operas that dramatize middle-class Brazilian life. The distinctive life experiences of worker and employer create vastly different viewing experiences, casting the televised dramas and traumas of the Brazilian middle class in sharp contrast to the survival needs of the domestic workers living in the favela—a contrast so absurd as to evoke laughter out of place.

How Is Race Constructed in the United States?

Race is perhaps the most significant means used to mark difference in U.S. culture. References to it can be found on census forms, school applications, and birth certificates, as well as in the media and casual conversation. Race is also a key framework that shapes the allocation of power, privilege, rewards, and status, and it infuses all of our political, economic, religious, recreational, educational, and cultural institutions (Smedley 1993). Yet it is one of the least discussed topics in U.S. culture and one of most difficult to explore, even in anthropology. How do we begin to engage this difficult dialogue?

How can anthropology help make sense of race as you experience it in the classroom, your workplace, your family, and today's rapidly globalizing world?

Because race is not biologically fixed, we must instead examine the process through which race has been—and still is being—constructed in the United States.

RACE AND THE U.S. CENSUS

The U.S. Census, taken every ten years since 1790, provides a fascinating window into the changing conception of "race." The 1850 census had three categories: White, Black, and Mulatto. Mulatto referred to people of mixed race. The 1870 census expanded to five categories to incorporate new immigrants from China and to count the Native American population: White, Black, Mulatto, Chinese, and Indian (Native American). Respondents did not identify their own race; instead, census workers assigned them to a racial category based on their appearance.

By 1940, the census form had eight categories, eliminating the option for mixed race and adding more categories from Asia, including Hindu, a religion: White, Negro, Indian, Chinese, Japanese, Filipino, Hindu, and Korean. The 2010 census form included fourteen separate "race" boxes. Respondents could check one, many, or all of them.

This brief look at changes in the census form provides clear indications that race has been and still is an evolving human construction. The changing race categories do not reflect a change in human genotype or phenotype, but in how the government organizes the diversity of people within its borders. The census construction of race reflects the U.S. government's power to establish certain

What can changes in the U.S. census form tell us about shifting concepts of race? Here, compare parts of the United States Census Questionnaire, 1870, and the United States Census Questionnaire, 2010.

The name of every person whose place of abode on the first day of June, 1870, was in this family.	DESCRIPTION.		
	Age at last birth-day. If under 1 year, give months in fractions, thus, $\frac{2}{12}$.	Sex.—Males (M.), Females (F.)	Color.—White (W.), Black (B.), Mulatto (M.), Chinese (C.), Indian (I.)
3	4	5	6

8. Is Person 1 of Hispanic, Latino, or Spanish origin?

☐ No, not of Hispanic, Latino, or Spanish origin
☐ Yes, Mexican, Mexican Am., Chicano
☐ Yes, Puerto Rican
☐ Yes, Cuban
☐ Yes, another Hispanic, Latino, or Spanish origin — *Print origin, for example, Argentinean, Colombian, Dominican, Nicaraguan, Salvadoran, Spaniard, and so on.* ⟋

[   ]

9. What is Person 1's race? *Mark* ☒ *one or more boxes.*

☐ White
☐ Black, African Am., or Negro
☐ American Indian or Alaska Native — *Print name of enrolled or principal tribe.* ⟋

[   ]

☐ Asian Indian   ☐ Japanese   ☐ Native Hawaiian
☐ Chinese   ☐ Korean   ☐ Guamanian or Chamorro
☐ Filipino   ☐ Vietnamese   ☐ Samoan
☐ Other Asian — *Print race, for example, Hmong, Laotian, Thai, Pakistani, Cambodian, and so on.* ⟋   ☐ Other Pacific Islander — *Print race, for example, Fijian, Tongan, and so on.* ⟋

[   ]

☐ Some other race — *Print race.* ⟋

[   ]

categories and apply those categories to make decisions about government resources.

Borderlands where racial categories are under debate provide a glimpse of the nation's changing racial past and future. For instance, increased immigration from Latin America, Asia, the Pacific Islands, and the Middle East has complicated the census form and discussions about race in the United States. Note the rapid expansion of options in the census for people from Asia.

The position of Hispanics is also in flux. Beginning with the 2000 census, for instance, "Hispanic" was removed from the race question. In effect, Spanish/Hispanic/Latino became a unique ethnic group with its own separate question. Unlike others—for example, Irish, Welsh, Italians, or Greeks—the census form now suggests that Hispanics are the only U.S. ethnic group that could be of any race. It remains to be determined whether U.S. culture will move beyond the underlying black/white dichotomy, or whether the current flux is simply a reorganizing of new immigrants into that dichotomy (Rodriguez 2000).

HISTORY OF U.S. RACIAL CATEGORIES: CONSTRUCTING WHITENESS

The U.S. racial system developed at the intersection of slavery and the European conquest of indigenous people of the North American continent. From its origins, American colonial life was built on the importation of indentured workers from Europe and enslaved people from Africa, along with the expropriation of land from Native Americans. Intensive agricultural work, particularly in the U.S. South, required a reliable and plentiful labor supply. Native Americans suffered quick and brutal extermination in other parts of the Americas through forced labor, violence, and disease, but they largely resisted forced labor in the North American colonies. European indentured laborers were in short supply. So imported enslaved Africans became the preferred workforce. Over 300 years, millions were forcibly transported to the Americas through the transatlantic slave trade.

The unique slave system that emerged relied not only on the legal right of landholders to enslave but also on the widespread acceptance of **white supremacy**—the belief that nonwhites were biologically different, intellectually inferior, and not fully human in a spiritual sense. Reflecting these ideas, the U.S. Census from 1790 to 1860 counted slaves as only three-fifths of a person. Only in 1868 did the Fourteenth Amendment to the U.S. Constitution put an end to this practice. Subsequently, the 1870 census was the first to count all people as whole people.

The term *white* was itself a construction, first appearing in a public document in reference to a separate race only in 1691 in Virginia. Colonial laws created and rigidly regulated **whiteness**, establishing sharp boundaries of who was white and

white supremacy
The belief that whites are biologically different from and superior to people of other races.

whiteness
A culturally constructed concept originating in 1691 Virginia designed to establish clear boundaries of who is white and who is not, a process central to the formation of U.S. racial stratification.

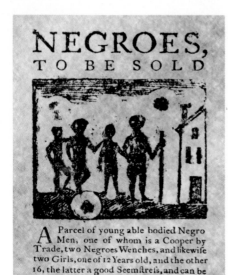

NEGROES,
TO BE SOLD

A Parcel of young able bodied Negro
Men, one of whom is a Cooper by
Trade, two Negroes Wenches, and likewise
two Girls, one of 12 Years old, and the other
16, the latter a good Seemſtreſs, and can be
well recommended.

(*left*) An advertisement for a slave auction, June 23, 1768. (*right*) A slave family picking cotton in the fields near Savannah, Georgia, ca. 1860s.

Jim Crow

Laws implemented after the U.S. Civil War to legally enforce segregation, particularly in the South, after the end of slavery.

who was not. Intermarriage was outlawed—a practice that the U.S. Supreme Court did not overturn until 1967. Mixing was punished by the loss of white status.

Anthropologist Pem Buck's *Worked to the Bone* (2001) documents the ways in which white privilege was invented in early 1700s Virginia to prevent rebellion among poor landless whites who were beginning to join with enslaved African workers against the European economic elite. Elites introduced a set of privileges reserved for whites—the right to own a gun, livestock, and land; the right to obtain freedom at the end of indenture; the right to discipline blacks; and eventually the right to vote. These legal privileges were designed to ensure the cooperation of poor working whites and white indentured servants, who together constituted a majority of the early colonial populations, and to drive a wedge between the European and African laborers who had much in common.

Efforts to eliminate slavery spread rapidly but unevenly after the American Revolution (1775–83), culminating in the Civil War (1861–65) and President Abraham Lincoln's 1863 Emancipation Proclamation. Yet long-established patterns of unequal treatment and entrenched ideas of white racial superiority persisted, providing the foundation for continuing inequality, discrimination, and white dominance. **Jim Crow** segregation laws throughout the South legally enforced the boundaries between whites and blacks in housing, education, voting rights, property ownership, and access to public services such as transportation, bathrooms, and water fountains. Vigilante white-supremacist groups such as the Ku Klux Klan, founded in 1866, emerged to enforce through violence and terror what they considered to be the natural racial order. Especially in the South, lynchings became a widespread means to intimidate blacks, enforce segregation, and ensure behavior that whites considered normal and appropriate. Between 1870 and the 1940s, untold thousands of African American men and women were tortured and brutally murdered (Brundage 1993).

THE RULE OF HYPODESCENT

Imposition of the rule of hypodescent has been key to drawing and maintaining boundaries between the races since the days of slavery, when one single drop of "black blood"—that is, one African ancestor—constituted blackness. *Hypo* literally means "lower." Through **hypodescent** the race of children of mixed marriages is assigned to the lower or subordinate category of the two parents—or, in many cases, the subordinate category of any one of many ancestors.

hypodescent

Sometimes called the "one drop of blood rule"; the assignment of children of racially "mixed" unions to the subordinate group.

Hypodescent rules were enshrined in the laws of many U.S. states and backed by the U.S. Supreme Court. Consider the 1982 court case of Susie Phipps. Born looking "white," Phipps grew up assuming she was white. But when she requested a copy of her birth certificate in 1977, she found herself listed as "colored." A 1970 Louisiana law mandated that a person be designated black if his or her ancestry was even one-thirty-second black—referring to any one of the thirty-two most recent ancestors. Phipps lost a court challenge to this categorization because the state produced evidence that she was three-thirty-seconds black—more than enough to satisfy the 1970 legal standard. Both the Louisiana Supreme Court and the U.S. Supreme Court refused to review the lower court's ruling and allowed the decision to stand (Fluehr-Lobban 2006; Jaynes 1982). Phipps's case reveals the process through which U.S. categories of race have been created and the tortured legal logic employed to assign individuals to particular racial categories. Also on full display are (1) the central role of the state in establishing and maintaining boundaries between the races it has constructed, and (2) the powerful influence of the legacies of slavery and past discrimination on the present (Omi and Winant 1994).

Although hypodescent is no longer enforced in law, it is still widely practiced in U.S. culture. A prominent contemporary example would be U.S. president Barack Obama. His mother was a white woman from Kansas (she was also an anthropologist). His father was a black man from Kenya in East Africa. They met as students in Hawaii, where Obama was born. Though 50 percent of his genes came from his father and 50 percent from his mother, the concept of hypodescent still shapes the way some people regard Obama's race.

RACE AND IMMIGRATION

For four centuries, the boundaries of whiteness in the United States have been carefully guarded, and a group's admission to that category has been rare and difficult. When the nation encountered diverse immigration from Asia and eastern and southern Europe beginning in the nineteenth century, debate raged about where the newcomers fit: Were the Chinese white? Were the Irish, Germans, Greeks, Italians, eastern Europeans, Jews, and Catholics really white, or were they biologically distinct from earlier immigrants from England, France, and the Nordic countries? Where would people from Mexico, Central America, and South America be placed in the U.S. racial framework?

The struggle to guard the boundaries of whiteness in order to protect the power and privileges reserved for whites has been particularly intense at certain times, generating passionate debate and sparking a sentiment of **nativism**—that is, the desire to favor native inhabitants over new immigrants. Nativists in the nineteenth century fought particularly hard to preserve the so-called racial purity of the nation's Anglo-Saxon origins. Riots, violence, discrimination, and anti-immigrant sentiment were commonplace.

nativism

The favoring of certain long-term inhabitants, namely whites, over new immigrants.

Chinese, Irish, and Other Immigrants: What Race? Chinese immigrants first arrived in large numbers in the 1850s to work in California's gold mines, on its farms, and in railroad construction. Because they constituted

the first group of Asians to come to this country, other residents struggled to place them in the U.S. racial hierarchy. European immigrant laborers saw the Chinese as competitors for jobs and branded them the Yellow Peril—a "race" that could not be trusted. Federal and state governments treated the Chinese immigrants ambivalently at best and often with great hostility.

Today most people consider Irish, Italians, Greeks, and eastern Europeans to be white, but none of these groups were received as white when they first came to the United States. They initially faced discrimination, prejudice, and exclusion because they were not Anglo-Saxon Protestants. When the Irish immigrants arrived in the 1840s and 1850s, they were poor, rural, Catholic, landless, and fleeing intense poverty and disease as a result of the Irish potato famine. Thus, they were seen as an inferior race (Ignatiev 1995).

Confronted with increasing immigration and diversity in the nineteenth and early twentieth centuries, the U.S. legal and political systems struggled for consistent definitions of who was white and who was not. Consider the 1923 U.S. Supreme Court case in which Bhagat Singh Thind, an upper-class Sikh immigrant from India, applied for U.S. citizenship. Despite the 1790 U.S. law limiting the right to naturalization (that is, becoming a citizen) to whites, Thind argued that as a part of the original "Aryan" or Caucasian race, he was white. Even though the justices agreed with his claim of Aryan or Caucasian ancestry, the Court found that Thind was not white as used in "common speech, to be

A 1903 cartoon from the magazine *Judge* illustrates anti-immigrant sentiment at the turn of the twentieth century. A tide of newcomers—Riff Raff Immigration—representing the criminal element of other countries washes up on American shores, to the displeasure of Uncle Sam, presenting a "danger" to American ideas and institutions.

interpreted in accordance with the understanding of the common man" (Lopez 2006, 66). Popular anti-immigrant and nativist sentiment had overcome even the pseudoscience of race prevalent at the time.

How exactly did the Irish, the Italians, and the eastern European Jews become "white"? Their increasing numbers, their intermarriage with members of other white groups, and their upward class mobility created conditions for inclusion in the white category. Karen Brodkin's book *How the Jews Became White Folks* (1998) offers additional insights into the whitening process of immigrants after World War II. At that time, the U.S. economy was emerging virtually unscathed from the war's destruction, unlike its competitors in Europe and Japan. And rapid growth in the U.S. economy was supporting an unparalleled expansion of the nation's middle class. Brodkin suggests that an extensive government program to reintegrate soldiers after the war paved the road to upward mobility for many U.S. citizens.

Indeed, the GI Bill of Rights provided a wide array of programs to 16 million soldiers, who were primarily white and male. The benefits included preferential hiring, financial support during the job search, small-business loans, subsidized home mortgages, and educational benefits that included college tuition and living expenses. Newly trained and educated veterans quickly filled the needs of the growing U.S. economy for professionals, technicians, and managers—jobs that offered opportunities for upward mobility and, thus, racial mobility. These educational opportunities, the dramatic rise in home ownership, and the expansion of new corporate jobs dramatically enlarged the U.S. middle class. The simultaneous elevation of living standards and financial assets of both native whites and new European immigrants softened earlier boundaries of whiteness and allowed the status of many immigrants to shift from racially nonwhite to ethnic white.

Middle Easterners. Racial categories continue to be created and contested in the United States today. Where, for example, do people from the Middle East fit? Are Saudis, Iranians, Afghanis, Kurds, Syrians, Turks, and Egyptians "white," African American, or Asian? The shifting characterization of people from the Middle East—especially after the terrorist attacks of September 11, 2001, and the ensuing "war on terror"—reveals newly contested terrain in the race debate and demonstrates how conceptions of race in the United States are constantly changing.

In a study of fourth graders in Brooklyn, New York, after the September 11 attacks, Maria Kromidas (2004) explores the way nine-year-old children engage issues of race, religion, and region to create racial categories, assign certain people (both children and adults) to them, and enforce those boundaries through language, humor, and social interaction.

Using the common U.S. Census categories, the school that Kromidas studied could be described as 28 percent black, 1 percent white, 46 percent Hispanic, and 25 percent Asian. But these four categories do not reveal the diversity of the school and its neighborhood—a diversity that makes the students' formulations of race all the more complicated. Although the students and the surrounding community are predominantly African American and second- and third-generation Latino, a significant part of the population is composed of new immigrants from Nigeria, Bangladesh, Guyana, Jamaica, and the Dominican Republic.

In light of the events of September 11, students in the elementary school seem preoccupied with the potential danger from a perceived enemy—one they see racially as "brown, foreign, strange, and Muslim" (Kromidas 2004, 29). Though the children do not consider their Muslim classmates to be "evil" or "terrorists," they do take note of these classmates' identities as never before. Kromidas ("MK" in the dialogues below) notes in particular the equation of enemies with Indians, Pakistanis, or Afghanis, and eventually all Arabic ("Araback") people. Here we see a racial construction, a lumping together of unrelated people based on a general phenotype—in this case, skin color.

Consider the following small-group student discussions:

EXAMPLE 1

SHERI:	We were talking about who started it first, and if they kill a lot of white people. . . . I mean a lot of people we got to go to war right then.
MK:	Who are they?
SHERI:	The Indians.
MK:	The Indians?
SHERI:	I don't know—that's what I call them.
JONATHAN:	The Pakistans!
MK:	The Pakistans?
SODIQ:	The Afghanistans!
MK:	The Afghanistans?
JOSEPH:	The terrorists.

Later that afternoon:

EXAMPLE 2

SHERI:	I feel sorry for the Afghanistan people.
SUSANNA:	Why do you feel sorry after what they did?
SHERI:	Because they gonna die!
	(*Most of the class breaks up with laughter.*)
LATISHA:	(*standing up*) I feel happy!
	(*laughter*)

LATISHA:	No, no, no . . . because they want to kill our people, they're going to die too. They want to have a party when we die, so we should celebrate! [*referring to news clips of street celebrations in the Middle East after September 11*]
ANUPA:	If they die, it will be better for us.
MK:	Who are they?
ANUPA:	The Araback people.
MARISELA:	The Afghanistans have always hated the Americans. I know because I always watch the news. (Kromidas 2004, 18–19)

These conversations yield some interesting observations. First, the students have taken on images presented in the media and from the conversations of adults around them; second, the students manipulate those images to create patterns of exclusion in their own context. Through their conversations, language groups, social interactions, and friendship networks, the students seek to clarify boundaries and to include and exclude newcomers according to what they see as racial characteristics. In the racial maps of the United States, South-Asian Americans and Arab Americans do not have a clear place. Kromidas suggests that in the classroom, as in U.S. culture at large, the fourth graders of New York City are creating a new racial category and placing people in it. The category is generally defined as not white, not black, but brown; foreign, strange, Muslim, and possibly enemy.

Before September 11, "Middle Eastern" was not considered a separate race in the United States. Officially, the government's Office of Management and Budget includes people of Middle Eastern descent as whites, along with people of European and North African descent. But the **racialization** (that is, giving a racial character) of Middle Easterners in U.S. culture after September 11 suggests a movement away from whiteness as reflected in Kromidas's study of fourth graders in Brooklyn.

racialization

The process of categorizing, differentiating, and attributing a particular racial character to a person or group of people.

What Is Racism?

Having considered the ways concepts of race are constructed in the United States and globally, we now turn to consider the ways ideas of race are used to construct and maintain systems of power that we call racism. Racism draws on the culturally constructed categories of race to rank people as superior or inferior and to differentially allocate access to power, privilege, resources, and opportunities.

TYPES OF RACISM

Racism has multiple aspects that include individual and institutional components as well as the set of ideas—the ideology—that acts like glue to hold them together.

Individual Racism. **Individual racism** is expressed through prejudiced beliefs and discriminatory actions. Being prejudiced involves making negative assumptions about a person's abilities or intentions based on the person's perceived race. Discriminating involves taking negative actions toward a person on the basis of his or her perceived race. Individual racism may be expressed through a lack of respect or through suspicion, scapegoating, and violence ranging from police brutality to hate crimes (Jones 2000). Individual, personally mediated acts of racism may be intentional or unintentional. They may be acts of commission (things that are done) or acts of omission (things that are left undone).

Individual racism can also be expressed through microaggressions. **Microaggressions** refer to common, everyday verbal or behavioral indignities and slights that communicate hostile, derogatory, and negative messages about someone's race, gender, sexual orientation, or religion. Racial microaggressions in the U.S. context include subtle slights, snubs, or insults directed toward people of color, often by whites who are unaware that they have transgressed against someone: clutching a handbag, checking a wallet, locking a car door, changing seats, commenting "You speak English well," or asking "Where do you come from?" These actions and comments may communicate that someone is considered prone to criminality, not to be trusted, is different, or is considered a stranger. Underlying these acts is a hidden cultural curriculum through which people have been taught certain biases associated with race, gender, sexual orientation, or religion which are then acted out intentionally or unintentionally. Research has shown that the cumulative and recurring experience of microaggressions over a lifetime can create intense psychological dilemmas ranging from frustration to depression and rage (Sue 2010, 2015).

Institutional Racism. Racism is more than individual prejudiced beliefs or discriminatory acts. Racism also includes **institutional racism**, sometimes called *structural racism*—patterns by which racial inequality is structured through key cultural institutions, policies, and systems. These include education, health, housing, employment, the legal system (legislatures, courts, and prison systems), law enforcement, and the media. Institutional racism originates in historical events and legal sanctions. But, even when outlawed, it can persist through contemporary patterns of institutional behavior that perpetuate the historical injustices (Cazenave 2011; Feagin and Feagin 2011; Jones 2000; Neubeck and Cazenave 2001).

individual racism
Personal prejudiced beliefs and discriminatory actions based on race.

microaggressions
Common, everyday verbal or behavioral indignities and slights that communicate hostile, derogatory, and negative messages about someone's race, gender, sexual orientation, or religion.

institutional racism
Patterns by which racial inequality is structured through key cultural institutions, policies, and systems.

In the United States, stratification along racial lines is a legacy of discrete historical events that include slavery, Jim Crow legal segregation, expropriation of indigenous lands, and immigration restrictions. Through these legal forms of institutional racism, the political, economic, and educational systems were organized to privilege whiteness. Today, despite the elimination of legal racial discrimination and segregation, patterns of inequality still break along color lines as a result of continuing individual and institutional racism. Such racism is evident in employment rates, income and wealth differentials, home ownership, residential patterns, criminal sentencing patterns, incarceration rates, application of the death penalty, infant mortality, access to health care, life expectancy, investments in public education, college enrollments, and access to the vote (Alexander 2012).

For example, the U.S. educational system has been a site for intense contestation over race and racism. In 1896—three decades after the end of slavery—the Supreme Court ruled in *Plessy v. Ferguson* that state-sponsored segregation, including in public schools, was constitutional as long as the separate facilities for separate races were equal. Across the South, individual white school administrators often refused, on overtly racist grounds, to allow children of color—black, Hispanic, Asian American—entrance to school buildings. But these individual actions alone did not constitute the total system of racism at work. They were systematically supported and enforced by government institutions: local boards of education, legislators, local police with guns and dogs, and court systems—including the U.S. Supreme Court.

Only in 1954 did the Supreme Court reverse itself in the case of *Brown v. Board of Education*, declaring unanimously that state laws establishing separate public schools for black and white students were unconstitutional and that separate educational facilities were inherently unequal. At the time, seventeen states, primarily across the South, required racial segregation. Sixteen prohibited it. Even after the Supreme Court ruling banning segregated schools, the federal government was forced to intervene in states like Mississippi and Arkansas, sending national guard troops to escort students to classes in order to end racist practices and protect student safety.

Contemporary racial disparities in school funding reveal how historical patterns of institutional racism can continue long after discrimination has been declared illegal (Miller and Epstein 2011). In 2003, the New York Court of Appeals, the state's highest court, found a long-standing disparity in state funding of public schools in New York City and suburban areas. New York City public schools, with high proportions of students of color, received an average of $10,469 per student, whereas schools in more affluent, predominantly white New York suburbs received $13,760 per student. The courts ordered New York State to increase its annual education budget by up to $5.6 billion to cover the costs of redressing this inequality while also providing $9.2 billion for capital

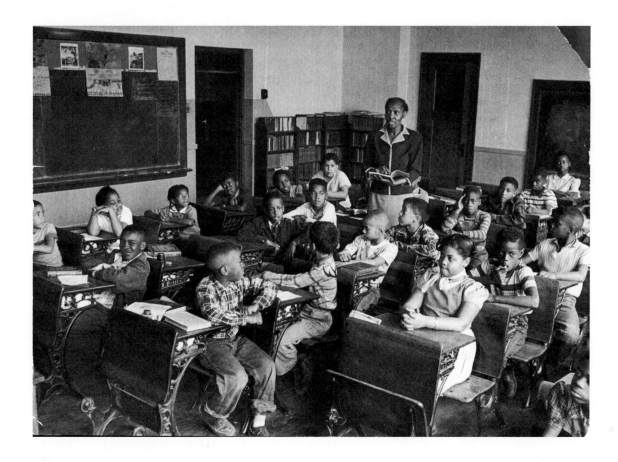

improvement of New York City school buildings. The State of New York has yet to fully comply with these requirements.

Racial Ideology. Racism relies on a third component—a set of popular ideas about race, or a **racial ideology**—that allows the discriminatory behaviors of individuals and institutions to seem reasonable, rational, and normal. Ideas about the superiority of one race over another—shaped and reinforced in the school system, religious institutions, government, and the media—caused people in the United States to believe that slavery was natural, that the European settlers had a God-given right to "civilize" and "tame" the American West, and that segregated schools were a reasonable approach to providing public education. As these ideas became ingrained in day-to-day relationships and institutional patterns of behavior, they ultimately provided the ideological glue that held racial stratification in place.

Today, social scientists note that contemporary racial ideologies are much more subtle, often drawing on core U.S. values of individualism, social mobility, meritocracy, and color blindness to make their case. So, for instance, in his book

A racially segregated classroom in Monroe Elementary School, Topeka, Kansas, March 1953. Students Linda Brown (*front right*) and her sister Terry Lynn (*far left, second row back*), along with their parents, initiated the landmark civil rights lawsuit *Brown v. Board of Education*.

racial ideology

A set of popular ideas about race that allows the discriminatory behaviors of individuals and institutions to seem reasonable, rational, and normal.

Racism without Racists (2010), sociologist Eduardo Bonilla-Silva critiques the contemporary calls in U.S. culture for color blindness—the elimination of race as a consideration in a wide range of institutional processes from college admissions to the reporting of arrests by police. The ideology of color blindness suggests that the best way to end discrimination in the post–civil rights era is to treat individuals as equally as possible without regard to race. Bonilla-Silva warns that while the desire to transcend race by adopting a stance of color blindness appears reasonable and fair, the approach ignores the uneven playing field created by centuries of legal racism in areas such as wealth, property ownership, education, health, and employment. A color-blind ideology, Bonilla-Silva suggests, may actually perpetuate racial inequality by obscuring the historical effects of racism, the continuing legacy of racial discrimination, and the entrenched patterns of institutional behavior that undergird racism today.

In a country like the United States, which prides itself on being a meritocracy (a system that views people as a product of their own efforts and in which equal opportunity is available to all), the continuing existence of racism and skin-color privilege in the twenty-first century is difficult for many people to acknowledge. When the dominant culture celebrates the ideals of individualism and equal access to social mobility, it is ironic that for many people, success depends not only on hard work, intelligence, and creativity but also on the often unrecognized and unearned assets—cultural, political, and economic—that have accrued over hundreds of years of discrimination and unequal opportunity based on race.

RESISTING RACISM

Along with the history of individual and institutional racism, it is important to also acknowledge the long tradition of work against racism that continues today. Anthropologist Steven Gregory's ethnography *Black Corona* (1998) tells the story of the organized political resistance by a predominantly African American community in Corona, Queens, in New York City, when confronted by attitudes and policy expressions of racial discrimination. The African American community in Corona dates back to the 1820s, and it expanded under an influx of middle-class residents from Harlem in the first half of the twentieth century. By the 1970s, however, Corona, like many other urban U.S. communities, began to feel the devastating impact of globalization, particularly flexible accumulation, as New York City's economy deindustrialized. At this time, the city's economy moved from an industrial and manufacturing base to one driven by finance, information, and services (Baker 1995; Harvey 1990). As New York lost thousands of manufacturing jobs and billions of dollars in tax revenue and federal funds, residents of Corona struggled during the transition.

MAP 5.2
Queens, New York City

In the face of drastic government cutbacks to basic community services such as housing, education, and public safety, residents of Corona's LeFrak City—a public housing complex containing 6,000 rental apartments—mobilized to demand sustained public investment in the maintenance and security of the property from their landlord, the City of New York. Confronting stereotypes of the apartment complex as a site of crime, welfare dependency, and family disorganization, African American parents in LeFrak City founded Concerned Community Adults (CCA), a community-based civic association, to engage in neighborhood improvement projects and strengthen relationships with the city's politicians and agencies. The CCA's Youth Forum organized neighborhood young people for social activities and leadership formation; together with the CCA, it worked to improve relations with the local police, who regularly harassed youth in the area. Through community-based action, LeFrak City residents worked with churches, community groups, and informal associations to establish their position as political actors, assert control over the neighborhood's physical condition, and insist on self-definition rather than accept the stereotypes held by surrounding communities and city leaders.

In the early 1990s, the Port Authority of New York and New Jersey—which controls the area's airports, bridges, and port facilities—announced plans to build an elevated light rail train between Manhattan's central business district and LaGuardia Airport that would cut directly through the heart of Corona's African American community. Residents had had extensive negative experiences battling the city over earlier plans to expand LaGuardia, which abuts Corona, that involved the loss of waterfront properties to the construction of runways, highway access, and exposure to the pollution of adjacent Flushing Bay. In its new plan, the Port Authority, representing the City of New York, argued that the city needed improved public transportation between Manhattan and LaGuardia to compete in the global economy and in the burgeoning global financial services industry. The elevated rail line through Corona, the argument went, would be good for the city's economy.

Corona residents warned that construction of this major infrastructure project through their community would not have any local benefit but instead would generate severe environmental consequences, lower the quality of life in the neighborhood, and divide and isolate portions of the community. They demanded that

The history of race in the United States includes a strong tradition of resistance to individual and institutional racism. Here, demonstrators protest against unfair lending practices and mortgage foreclosures.

the rail line be built underground on property already owned by New York City between Corona and the airport that had been carved out to build the Grand Central Parkway years earlier. Local residents formed neighborhood committees and alliances with existing civic organizations, community groups, and churches. They engaged the city's public planning process and established alternative political forums outside the government's control to press for their case. They also created multicultural alliances with concerned groups in neighboring communities. Eventually the Port Authority abandoned the planned elevated train.

Gregory's ethnographic study of Corona's African American community reveals the power of local communities of color to mobilize and engage in political activism. It also demonstrates how such groups can contest the stereotypes of urban black communities and the practices of racial discrimination and exclusion, whether those involve housing, policing, or the environmental and community impacts of public infrastructure projects.

RACE, RACISM, AND WHITENESS

Popular conversations about race and racism tend to focus on the experiences of people of color. Whiteness is typically ignored, perhaps taken for granted. But analyzing race in the United States requires a careful look at whiteness. Anthropologists refer to "white" as an unmarked category—one with tremendous power, but one that typically defies analysis and is rarely discussed. Recent scholarship has been moving whiteness into the mainstream debates about race in the United States (Hargrove 2009; Harrison 1998, 2002a; Hartigan 1999; Marable 2002; Mullings 2005a; Roediger 1992).

Although the events of the U.S. civil rights movement occurred well before most of today's college students were born, the media images of police blocking African Americans from attending white schools, riding in the front of the bus, sitting at department store lunch counters, or drinking from "whites-only" water fountains remain etched in our collective cultural memory. Although the overt signs declaring access for "whites only" have been outlawed and removed, many patterns of interpersonal and institutional behavior have resisted change (McIntosh 1989).

"White Privilege." In her article "White Privilege: Unpacking the Invisible Knapsack" (1989), anthropologist Peggy McIntosh writes of "an invisible package of unearned assets" that are a legacy of generations of racial discrimination. Through these assets, whites have become the beneficiaries of cultural norms, values, mental maps of reality, and institutions. Unearned advantages and unearned power are conferred systematically and differentially on one group over others, whether those benefits lie in health, education, housing, employment, banking and mortgages, or the criminal justice system.

McIntosh articulates an extensive list of these privileges, ranging from the mundane to the profound. They include (1) going shopping without being followed or harassed by store security; (2) using checks, credit cards, or cash and counting on skin color to not work against the appearance of financial responsibility; (3) seeing people of your "race" widely represented in the news, social media, and educational curricula; (4) swearing, dressing in second-hand clothes, or not answering letters or emails without having people attribute these choices to bad morals, poverty, or the illiteracy of your "race"; (5) feeling confident that you have not been singled out by race when a police officer pulls you over or an airport security guard decides to conduct a full-body scan; (6) criticizing the government and its policies without being considered an outsider.

As we have discussed in this chapter, since the early European settlement of North America, the boundaries of whiteness have been carefully constructed and guarded. Today the skin-color privileges associated with whiteness still pass down from generation to generation. They are simply harder to see. Acknowledging this fact enables us to analyze the functioning and effects of race and racism as a complete system.

As McIntosh writes, "For me white privilege has turned out to be an elusive and fugitive subject. The pressure to avoid it is great, for in facing it I must give up the myth of meritocracy. If these things are true, this is not such a free country, one's life is not what one makes it; many doors open for certain people through no virtues of their own" (1989, 12). Moving forward, McIntosh urges students to distinguish between (1) the positive advantages that we wish everyone could have and that we can all work to spread, and (2) the negative types of advantages that, unless challenged and corrected, will always reinforce current racial hierarchies.

Intersections of Race and Class. It is important to note the powerful intersection of race and class. **Intersectionality** provides a framework for analyzing the many factors—especially class and gender—that determine how race is lived and how all three systems of power and stratification build on and shape one another. In *Living with Racism: The Black Middle-Class Experience* (1994), sociologist Joe Feagin and psychologist Melvin Sikes write about middle-class African Americans who, despite their class status, continue to face racial discrimination. Though reflecting a privileged class status in comparison to other African Americans, the class advantages of middle-class African Americans are still limited by racial disadvantage. Because race and class intersect so deeply, improved class status cannot be assumed to bring a decrease in the experience of racial discrimination.

Whiteness is also stratified along deep, intersecting lines of class and region, gender and sexuality so that not all people of European descent benefit equally

intersectionality

An analytic framework for assessing how factors such as race, gender, and class interact to shape individual life chances and societal patterns of stratification.

MAP 5.3
Florida

Anthropologists of race in the United States have studied the often "unmarked" category of whiteness. The privileges of whiteness in the United States are not experienced uniformly but rather are stratified along deep lines of class, region, gender, and sexuality.

from the system of white privilege. In a study of a town she calls Shellcracker Haven, southwest of Gainesville, Florida, anthropologist Jane Gibson (1996) explored the process through which a community of poor whites has been systematically cut off from their local means of making a living. By imposing restrictions on fishing, gaming, and trapping as well as on agricultural activities—all of which benefit large-scale businesses—the Florida state government and its agencies have gradually prevented Shellcracker Haven's residents from making a living on the land or nearby water.

Gibson argues that these policies of disenfranchisement have been rationalized by stereotypes that state authorities promote. Such stereotypes portray the local people as "white trash," "swamp trash," and "crackers"; as dirty, skinny, shoeless, toothless, illiterate, and unintelligent. The stereotypes deflect attention from the skewed distribution of wealth and power and the uneven investments in roads, education, and health care that result from state policies. Poor whites are a subordinated group, distinct from successful middle- and upper-class whites in the state.

Gibson's study reveals that whiteness is not monolithic. Indeed, people who place themselves in this racial group experience a wide range of life chances. Poor whites in the United States comprise a mix of 29.9 million people, both urban and rural, who do not necessarily reflect the advantages of whiteness (U.S. Census Bureau 2013). The worst stereotypes portray poor whites as backward, inbred, lazy, illiterate, and uncultured. Epithets such as "redneck," "hillbilly," and "white trash" distance these whites from the middle-class social norms and economic success stereotypically associated with their whiteness (Hartigan 2005). Although the historical development, regional particularities, and current circumstances vary among groups of poor whites, their poverty and social ostracism mark an extreme end of the U.S. class spectrum. In the current age of globalization, economic restructuring and global competition are further undermining the white privilege for many poor and working-class whites as manufacturing jobs leave the United States.

In this chapter we have begun our work as budding anthropologists to unmask the structures of power, starting with race and racism. We have seen how flawed ideas of "race" serve as a rationale for very real systems of power built around racial stratification both in the United States and around the world. As globalization, particularly global migration, brings cultural systems of meaning and stratification into closer contact, your ability to analyze and engage dynamics of race and racism will prove to be increasingly important. In the following chapters we will consider other systems of power—including ethnicity, gender, sexuality, kinship, and class—and their points of mutual intersection with race.

Toolkit

Thinking Like an Anthropologist:
Shifting Our Perspectives on Race and Racism

As you encounter race and racism in your life—on campus, in the classroom, at the workplace, in the news, or in your family—thinking like an anthropologist can help you to better understand these experiences. As you untangle this knotty problem, remember to think about the big questions we addressed in this chapter:

- **Do biologically separate races exist?**

- **How is race constructed around the world?**

- **How is race constructed in the United States?**

- **What is racism?**

After reading this chapter, you should be better equipped to engage the challenges of race and racism. As you think back on the chapter-opening story about the events in Ferguson, Missouri, how would you apply the ideas of this chapter to assist your analysis and inform your responses?

Race and racism continue to be powerful dynamics in American culture. Following Michael Brown's death in Ferguson, violent encounters between police and African Americans have continued to draw significant attention across the country. Eric Garner was choked to death during an arrest on Staten Island, NY, for selling loose cigarettes. Twelve-year-old Tamir Rice of Cleveland was shot to death in the playground near his home when officers on the scene for just a few seconds mistook his toy gun for a weapon. John Crawford III was killed in an Ohio Walmart after he picked up a BB gun from the shelf. The death of Freddie Gray in police custody sparked weeks of unrest in Baltimore. Alton Sterling, arrested for selling CDs on the sidewalk, was shot while pinned to the ground by police in Baton Rouge, Louisiana. Philando Castile was killed by an officer during a traffic stop outside St. Paul, Minnesota.

At the same time, the events of Ferguson have spurred efforts to address ongoing patterns of racism. The Black Lives Matter social movement launched rallies, marches, die-ins, and disruptions of political candidates, using social media and direct action to bring attention to the deaths of African Americans in encounters with law enforcement, racial profiling, and racial inequality in the U.S. criminal justice system (Bonilla and Rosa 2015). Under intense pressure after the massacre of nine people in the historic African Methodist Episcopal Church in downtown Charleston, the South Carolina legislature voted to remove the Confederate battle flag flying over the Statehouse, 150 years after the end of the Civil War. Students at Missouri University staged demonstrations—supported by the school's football players who threatened to boycott their upcoming games—to demand school administrators address a series of racist incidents on campus.

How can an anthropological approach to the study of race and racism help us analyze and confront these and similar acts of violence? How can we learn a language about race and racism that will allow us to talk and work together across lines of race, gender, sexuality, class, and political perspective to confront the continuing American legacy of racism? As we have seen throughout this chapter, the anthropological study of race examines not only the social construction of race and the establishment of systems of racism but also takes seriously movements against racism that emerge from communities of color and their allies. How can you begin to engage these crucial issues of our time and to apply these anthropological concepts to your life today?

Key Terms

race (p. 121)

racism (p. 122)

genotype (p. 124)

phenotype (p. 124)

colonialism (p. 126)

miscegenation (p. 128)

white supremacy (p. 131)

whiteness (p. 131)

Jim Crow (p. 132)

hypodescent (p. 133)

nativism (p. 134)

racialization (p. 138)

individual racism (p. 139)

microaggressions (p. 139)

institutional racism (p. 139)

racial ideology (p. 141)

intersectionality (p. 145)

Chapter 6
Ethnicity and
Nationalism

When the World Cup soccer tournament opened in
June 2010 in South Africa, teams from thirty-two nations
carried the hopes and dreams of their supporters into the
competition. Soccer stadiums filled up with fans painted
in national colors, draped in national flags, and singing
national songs and anthems. Other fans tuned in to television and radio broadcasts around the world, exulting
and suffering along with the fates of their national teams.
Over three years, 205 teams had battled through 848
matches to reach South Africa—the most extensive global
tournament in history. At the time of the World Cup final,
more than 700 million people gathered worldwide in pubs,
restaurants, and crowded town squares to watch Spain
play the Netherlands. What can we learn about ethnicity
and nationalism from the World Cup?

What can soccer teach us about ethnicity
and nationalism? Here Germany's Jerome
Boateng (left) challenges for the ball against
his half-brother, Ghana's Kevin-Prince
Boateng, during a 2010 World Cup soccer
match in Johannesburg, South Africa.

Jerome Boateng and Kevin-Prince Boateng, two half-brothers born in Germany to a Ghanaian father and German mothers, both played in the World Cup—but for different national teams. Jerome played for Germany, the country of his birth. Kevin-Prince played for the Ghanaian national team, representing the country of his father's birth. What makes someone a member of a certain nation? The simple answer, it seems, should be birth. But in today's age of globalization, nationality is not so simple. The rules of FIFA, the world soccer federation, state that to play for a national team, a player must either be born in that country or have a parent or grandparent from that country. A player can also establish a new nationality by living in a new country for five years. But once a choice of nationality is made, it is irrevocable. As the son of an immigrant from Ghana, but born in Germany, Kevin-Prince could choose his nationality. In the World Cup, we see the complications of identity for children of immigrants and the changing rules of nationality on the international stage.

But what exactly is a nation? When Germany knocked England out of the World Cup, commentators in the United Kingdom lamented the death of the "90-minute nation" (Younge 2010). What did this mean? First, consider that England no longer exists as a separate nation. It is now part of the United Kingdom—along with Scotland, Wales, and Northern Ireland. In fact, the disappearance of England within the United Kingdom is a sore point for many of English descent. Their rival ethnic groups have gained political recognition in recent years. Scotland has a parliament; Wales and Northern Ireland have national assemblies. But politically, England has been subsumed into the United Kingdom.

The soccer pitch is one of the few places where English ethnic identity and nationalism can still be expressed. The game was born in England. In consideration of this, FIFA allows the English to continue fielding a World Cup team even without a nation. When the England team takes the field, English ethnicity and nationalism reemerge. The flag of England's patron saint, St. George, flies high over the prime minister's residence, temporarily replacing the Union Jack. Period costumes emerge on the streets of London. Traditional English songs resound in pubs. Through sports, the nation exists as long as England is playing. But at the end of a 90-minute game, the "90-minute nation" returns to its place within the United Kingdom.

Let's consider another example. Midway through the World Cup, the French national team imploded as the world and the French nation watched. The whole team went on strike, refusing to practice before a crucial match that resulted in a humiliating early exit from the tournament. What had happened? During the competition, a vitriolic rant by one of the team's stars, laced with ethnic comments, set off intense conflicts within the diverse French team—whose racial and ethnic composition reflects the country's colonial past and recent immigration. Indeed, immigration, nationality, and race had been red-hot topics in France long before the 2015 terrorist attacks in Paris. With a long colonial past in Africa and Asia and significant recent immigration from these former colonies, France seethes with conflict over who is really French. Riots have erupted in immigrant neighborhoods (Newman 2015). The national government banned Muslim women from wearing the veil in public. And in response to terror threats, the French government wrestles with how to balance security and privacy concerns of its citizens. Thus one must ask: What does it mean to be "French"? What are the standards for assessing this claim of ethnic and national identity? The difficult French national debates over ethnicity and nationalism were clearly on display and under negotiation at the 2010 World Cup.

The World Cup is more than a series of soccer matches. As anthropologists, we know that sports are more than just a game. Yes, games happen in real time with dirt and sweat, tactics and strategies, wins and losses and ties. But games are also symbolic, both for the players and for their fans. Victory and defeat, disappointment and heroism are wrapped up in a drama larger than life. Sports are a venue for the creation and negotiation of personal and national identity. They are sites of moral education about sportsmanship, leadership, the value of compromise, how to cope with victory and defeat, how to perform masculinity or femininity, and how to work together with diverse people (MacClancy 1996). Wrapped up in an international competition like the World Cup are emotionally fraught matters: national identity and citizenship, the national and ethnic imaginations of people worldwide, the history of colonialism and independence, old rivalries, national pride, the expression of national character, and the negotiation of a people's place on the modern world stage. Moreover, the spectacle of the World Cup illustrates how the promotion of nationalism by the media, corporations, and national leaders has direct benefits for viewership, profit, and political power.

In this chapter we will explore ethnicity and nationalism from an anthropological perspective. In particular, we will ask three key questions:

- **What does "ethnicity" mean to anthropologists?**
- **How and why is ethnicity created, mobilized, and contested?**
- **What is the relationship of ethnicity to the nation?**

After reading this chapter you will have the tools to understand and analyze the role of ethnicity and nationalism in your own life and in communities and countries worldwide.

What Does "Ethnicity" Mean to Anthropologists?

We hear the word *ethnicity* all the time. The press reports on "long-held ethnic conflicts" that shatter the peace in Rwanda, Iraq, India, and the former Yugoslavia. We check boxes on college applications and U.S. census forms to identify our ethnicity or race. We shop in the "ethnic foods" aisle of our super-sized grocery store to find refried beans, soy sauce, pita, and wasabi. Our use of *ethnicity* is not particularly consistent or terribly clear. In recent years in the United States, *ethnicity* has been increasingly substituted for *race* when describing group differences. *Ethnic* is often paired with *minority*, a term signifying a smaller group that differs from the dominant, majority culture in language, food, dress, immigrant history, national origin, or religion. But this usage ignores the ethnic identity of the majority. The same lack of clarity is true for our use of the terms *nation, nationalism,* and *nation-state*, all of which often blur together and at times seem indistinguishable from *ethnicity*.

ETHNICITY AS IDENTITY

Over a lifetime, humans develop complex identities that connect to many people in many ways. We build a sense of relationship, belonging, and shared identity through connections to family, religion, hometown, language, shared history, citizenship, sports, age, gender, sexuality, education, and profession. These powerful identities influence what we eat, who we date, where we work, how we live, and even how we die. **Ethnicity** is one of the most powerful identities that humans develop: It is a sense of connection to a group of people who we believe share a common history, culture, and (sometimes) ancestry and who are distinct

ethnicity

A sense of historical, cultural, and sometimes ancestral connection to a group of people who are imagined to be distinct from those outside the group.

from others outside the group (Ericksen 2010; Jenkins 1996). Ethnicity can be seen as a more expansive version of kinship—the culturally specific creation of relatives—only including a much larger group and extending further in space and time. As we will see in this chapter, the construction of ethnicity, like kinship, is quite complicated, moving well beyond easy equation with biological ancestry. In this chapter we will explore the ways ethnicity may be perceived, felt, and imagined by a group as well as the ways it may be imposed on a group by others.

With the intensification of globalization and the increasing flows of people, goods, and ideas across borders, one might anticipate that the power of ethnicity to frame people's actions and to influence world events would diminish. Instead, ethnicity seems to be flourishing—rising in prominence in both local and global affairs. Why is it so powerful? When threatened or challenged, people often turn to local alliances for support, safety, and protection. Ethnicity is one of the strongest sources of solidarity available.

As the effects of globalization intersect with systems of power at the local level, many people turn to ethnic networks and expressions of ethnic identity to protect their local way of life in the face of intense pressures of homogenization. As we will consider later in this chapter, ethnicity can also serve political purposes on the national and local levels as political elites and other ethno-entrepreneurs may impose or enforce ethnic distinctions or use calls for ethnic solidarity to mobilize support against perceived enemies inside and outside the nation-state. Rather than diminishing in the face of globalization, ethnicity emerges even more powerfully in specific situations of conflict, tension, and opportunity.

CREATING ETHNIC IDENTITY

Anthropologists see ethnicity as a cultural construction, not as a natural formation based on biology or inherent human nature. Fredrik Barth (1969) describes ethnicity as the "social organization of cultural difference"; in other words, people construct a sense of ethnicity as they organize themselves in relation to others whom they perceive as either culturally similar or culturally different. Ethnic identity starts with what people believe about themselves and how others see them. Identity formation begins early and continues throughout our lives. People learn, practice, and teach ethnicity. Anthropologists who study it seek to understand how it is created and reinforced, how boundaries are constructed, how group identity is shaped, and how differences with others are mobilized and perpetuated (Jenkins 2008). Who do you consider to be in your ethnic group? Who belongs to a different group?

Ethnic identity is taught and reinforced in a number of ways. One key method is the creation and telling of **origin myths**. By myth, we do not mean falsehood but rather a story with meaning. In the United States, the "American" origin myth includes stories of historical events—such as the landing of the *Mayflower*, the

origin myth

A story told about the founding and history of a particular group to reinforce a sense of common identity.

In what ways do stories, paintings, and even Thanksgiving turkey floats help create an American ethnic identity? (*left*) A 1914 depiction of the first Thanksgiving at Plymouth, Massachusetts. (*right*) The Tom Turkey float moves through Times Square during the Macy's Thanksgiving Day Parade, in New York City.

ethnic boundary marker
A practice or belief, such as food, clothing, language, shared name, or religion, used to signify who is in a group and who is not.

first Thanksgiving, the Boston Tea Party, the American Revolution, the Civil War, the settling of the West—that are retold to emphasize a shared destiny as well as shared values of freedom, exploration, individualism, and multiculturalism. The American origin myth of the first Thanksgiving is ritually enacted each year with a national holiday. Schoolchildren produce dramas and artwork based on textbook stories. Families gather to feast, usually eating certain traditional foods. Nationally televised parades and sporting events add to the ritual's celebratory character. However, origin myths—like all elements of culture—are continuously promoted, revised, and negotiated. For example, recent years have seen more open discussion of the brutal conquest of Native Americans (Deloria 1969) and, in books such as Howard Zinn's *A People's History of the United States* (2005), more challenges to classic textbook representations of the American origin myth.

People create and promote certain **ethnic boundary markers** in an attempt to signify who is in the group and who is not. These may include a collective name; shared cultural practices such as food, clothing, and architecture; a belief in common history and ancestors; association with a particular territory; a shared language or religion; and an imagination of shared physical characteristics. But ethnic boundaries are usually not clearly fixed and defined. Our social worlds rarely have distinct groups with clear boundaries. Not everyone imagined to be inside the group is the same; not everyone imagined to be outside the group is noticeably different. No group is completely homogeneous. Boundaries between groups can be quite porous. People move between groups through marriage, migration, and adoption. Identity, including ethnic identity, can be fluid and flexible, reflecting shifting alliances and strength over time and according to need. Groups may vanish in situations of war or violence. New ethnic groups may come into existence when part of an existing group splits off or two groups form a new one (Ericksen 2010).

Because ethnicity is not biologically fixed, self-identification with a particular ethnic group can change according to one's social location. This occurs through a process called **situational negotiation of identity**. For example, Kevin-Prince Boateng in our chapter-opening story could have chosen to be German, German-Ghanaian, Ghanaian, African, Afro-European, or perhaps even a member of his father's local ethnic group in Ghana. At points during his life he may choose to identify himself with any of these, depending on the situation. Have you ever had the experience of identifying with a different aspect of your identity as you moved between groups or locations?

situational negotiation of identity

An individual's self-identification with a particular group that can shift according to social location.

Constructing Indian Identity in the United States.
The immigration experience profoundly affects ethnicity and ethnic identification. New immigrants reshape their home-country ethnic identification to build alliances and solidarity in their new host country. In her book *From the Ganges to the Hudson* (1995), anthropologist Johanna Lessinger explores the process by which a new Indian ethnic identity is created and publicly demonstrated through consumption, public festivals, and Indian immigrant media. Indian immigrants arrive in New York from all corners of their homeland, speaking different languages, following diverse cultural practices and religions, and reflecting class and caste stratifications. In India, a country of more than 1.2 billion people, these individuals would identify themselves as representing different ethnicities shaped by geography, language, food, and cultural practices. But after arriving in New York as immigrants from India, they all begin the process of becoming Indian American.

MAP 6.1
New York/India

New York City's Little India, a bustling shopping district in Jackson Heights, Queens, has become the symbolic center of Indian immigrant life and a key to the construction of Indian ethnic identity in the United States. Vibrant with the sights, sounds, and smells of India, the streets are lined with Indian grocery and spice shops, restaurants, clothing and jewelry stores, travel agencies, music and video distributors, and electronics stores. Indian immigrants come from all parts of New York City and the metropolitan region to walk the streets of Little India and shop, eat, and take in the many symbols of "home."

Here Indian immigrants have created a wide-ranging ethnic infrastructure that supports and promotes the construction of a unified Indian ethnic identity in their new homeland. The infrastructure includes ethnic associations, religious temples, cultural societies, newspapers, television programming, and major public festivals. One of the largest festivals is the India Day Parade held in late August to mark India's nationhood and independence from British colonialism. Like the dozens of ethnic parade celebrations in New York each year, Indian immigrant community organizations, businessowners, and hometown associations sponsor marching bands, singers, dancers, banners, and a vast array of colorful floats. Holding a public festival like the India Day Parade is a powerful way to stake a claim to a place in the multiethnic mosaic that is New York—to send a clear

The India Day Parade in New York City helps to construct an Indian American identity in the United States.

signal to all New Yorkers, including the political establishment, that Indians are here, are organized, and want to be taken seriously.

Ethnic boundaries are often fluid, messy, and contested. For example, exactly who is Indian American? For over fifteen years, until 2010, the South Asian Lesbian and Gay Alliance (SALGA) requested permission to march in the India Day Parade, only to be denied by parade organizers. Members of SALGA held demonstrations each year along the parade route, holding signs that read, "We are also Indians!" Despite the parade organizers' desire to build a broad-based Indian American identity and coalition, they were willing to declare SALGA not Indian enough to participate in the event. In this situation, sexuality became a more powerful boundary marker than country of origin. The rift over the India Day Parade became a very public and symbolic representation of the contestation of ethnic boundary markers—a struggle that reveals deep disagreements among Indian immigrants and many of their children—and the debate involved in defining who is Indian in the United States.

How and Why Is Ethnicity Created, Mobilized, and Contested?

For many of the world's people, ethnicity is not a pressing matter in daily life. But it can be activated when power relationships undergo negotiation in a community or a nation. Then people call on shared ideas of ethnicity to rally others to participate in their causes, whether those causes involve ensuring self-protection, building alliances, constructing economic networks, or establishing a country. Ethnicity can also be activated by charismatic entrepreneurs of ethnicity who seek support from co-ethnics in their fight for political, economic, or military power against real or perceived enemies. The sections that follow illustrate how ethnicity can be harnessed for either harmful or beneficial outcomes.

ETHNICITY AS A SOURCE OF CONFLICT

Anthropologists explore the complex ways culture can be invented, transformed into ethnicity, and mobilized in situations of ethnic conflict (Eller 1999). The anthropological study of ethnic conflict requires an open-mindedness to new ideas of how ethnicity is formed and how it works—ideas that may be at odds with our everyday usage of the terms *ethnicity* and *ethnic groups*. Rogers Brubaker, in his book *Ethnicity without Groups* (2004), warns against "groupism" when studying ethnicity. Anthropologists may anticipate that we will work with clearly defined groups having fixed boundaries and homogenous membership who will act in a unified fashion. But this is not what we find on the ground as we explore ethnicity on the local level. Ethnicity is much more complicated, involving people with many perspectives, disagreements, and at times competing loyalties. The strong bonds of ethnicity that we associate with ethnic groups may wax and wane.

Why do the power and intensity of ethnicity harden and crystallize at certain times into ethnic conflict? As in the cases of Rwanda and the former Yugoslavia that follow, Brubaker encourages paying attention to ethnic group–making projects. Such projects occur when **identity entrepreneurs**—political, military, and religious leaders—promote a worldview through the lens of ethnicity. They use war, propaganda, and state power to mobilize people against those whom they perceive as a danger. Ethnicity may not actually be the problem. Rather, the struggle for wealth and power uses the convenient narrative of ethnic difference to galvanize a population to collective action. Once the wedge of ethnic difference has been driven into a population and used to achieve power, it can be self-perpetuating and extremely difficult to break. In these instances, ethnic conflict may intensify into violent acts, including **genocide**—the deliberate and systematic destruction of an ethnic or religious group (Eller 1999; Ericksen 2010; Scheper-Hughes and Bourgois 2004).

identity entrepreneurs

Political, military, or religious leaders who promote a worldview through the lens of ethnicity and use war, propaganda, and state power to mobilize people against those whom they perceive as a danger.

genocide

The deliberate and systematic destruction of an ethnic or religious group.

Mobilizing Ethnic Differences in Rwanda. In 1994, the East African country of Rwanda was shattered by a horrific genocide involving two main groups, Hutu and Tutsi. Over a few months, as many as one million Tutsi and an unknown number of moderate Hutus died in a slaughter perpetrated by extremist Hutu death squads. In a country of only seven million people before the genocide, where Hutu made up 85 percent of the population and Tutsi 15 percent, how did this tragic genocide occur? How did Tutsi and Hutu, who have lived together in the region for generations and centuries, come to perceive such clear differences between them and choose to act on those differences in such violent ways?

Before German and Belgian colonial rule in the early twentieth century, Hutu and Tutsi were distinguished mainly by occupation and social status. Hutu were primarily farmers; Tutsi were cattle owners. The two groups share a common language and religious affiliations. Intermarriage has been quite common. Children of mixed marriages inherited their fathers' identity. Although Tutsi were later stereotyped as taller and thinner than Hutu, it is not possible to distinguish between members of the two groups by looks alone.

In a common colonial practice used in countries worldwide, colonial governments chose one native group to serve as educated and privileged intermediaries between the local population and the colonial administration. The Belgian colonial government (1919–62) elevated Tutsi to the most influential positions in Rwandan society, to the exclusion of Hutu leaders. In an attempt to rationalize its prejudicial behavior, in the 1920s the Belgian colonial government hired scientists to measure Hutu and Tutsi anatomy—including skull size—so as to physically differentiate between the two groups. These flawed studies, based on the pseudoscience of eugenics that developed in Europe and the United States, declared that Tutsi were taller, bigger brained, and lighter skinned—closer in physical form to Europeans and thus "naturally" suited to the role assigned to them by the Belgian colonial government.

To maintain and enforce this segregation, in 1933 the Belgian colonial government established a national identity card that included the category "ethnicity." Even after independence in 1962, Rwandan officials continued to use the identity card, forcing all citizens to be labeled as Hutu, Tutsi, Twa (a small minority population), or naturalized (born outside Rwanda). The cards were discontinued only in 1996 after the genocide.

Many Hutu resented the Belgians' decision to elevate Tutsi to power in the colonial government. Periodic protests in the early years of colonial occupation were followed by a major uprising against Tutsi elites in 1956. In 1959, the Hutu seized power and forced many Tutsi into exile in neighboring countries. At independence in 1962, the Hutu consolidated full power and implemented repressive policies toward the Tutsi. A full-blown civil war erupted in 1990. Subsequently, a 1993 United Nations–backed cease-fire collapsed when the plane of the Rwandan president, a Hutu, was shot down in April 1994.

What followed was an extensive genocide campaign by Hutu extremists who blamed Tutsi for the death of their president. Rwandan radio broadcast instructions to kill all Tutsi, including spouses and family members, as well as any Hutu

MAP 6.2
Rwanda

moderates who were unwilling to cooperate. Hutu civilian death squads implemented the "Hutu Power" genocide program, a deliberate and seemingly long-planned extermination of Tutsi. Tutsi and moderate Hutu were killed largely by hand with machetes and clubs after local officials gathered them up into schools and churches. Hutu death squads used the Rwandan identity cards to identify Tutsi victims for extermination.

Rwandan identity cards listing each citizen's ethnic identity were discontinued only in 1996 after the genocide of as many as one million Tutsi.

What role did ethnicity play in the Rwandan genocide? Western press and government reports referred to the extermination as "tribal violence," the result of "ancient ethnic hatreds" and a failed nation-state. However, we can see how colonial European policies constructed and enforced notions of difference between Hutu and Tutsi—including notions of physical and mental difference—that were not deep-rooted historical patterns but that nonetheless later served to rationalize genocide (Mamdani 2002). Indeed, the twentieth-century history of Rwanda reveals the ways in which local ethnic relationships can be broken down and reconstituted in long-lasting ways by a foreign superpower that uses ethnicity as a weapon to divide and rule and how those new patterns of ethnicity can be mobilized to fuel a struggle for economic, political, and military power (Eller 1999).

MAP 6.3
Tanzania

Remaking Identity: Hutu Refugees in Tanzania. In neighboring
Burundi, where Tutsi outnumber Hutu, a series of massacres in the 1970s led to
the exodus of many Hutu refugees to Tanzania. Anthropologist Liisa Malkki's
ethnography *Purity and Exile: Violence, Memory and National Cosmology among
Hutu Refugees in Tanzania* (1995) focuses on the lives of Hutu refugees in a
remote resettlement camp and their experiences of atrocity, displacement, and
exile. Through a year of fieldwork, Malkki collected dozens of life histories,
which she calls mythico-histories—stories through which refugees worked to
remake sense of their past, present, and future.

Through these mythico-histories Hutu refugees reimagined their conceptions of community, history, and ethnic identity often in stark contrast to
both Tutsi accounts of the conflict and Western accounts of the colonial history in Rwanda and Burundi. Hutus instead told of how their essential nature
had emerged through the experience of atrocity and exile. Rather than victims
and outcasts, their stories told of a distinct Hutu people with a long history as
Burundians while the Tutsi were foreign usurpers. In their narrative, the trials of
dispossession and dislocation prepared their "nation in exile" for a restoration to
Burundi. To reinforce this sense of Hutu identity, refugees held to certain purity
practices while in exile—discouraging intermarriage, preserving their language,
and acquiring official recognition as refugees rather than blending into the surrounding Tanzanian community.

By recounting the Hutu refugee mythico-histories, Malkki sheds light on the
dilemmas of displaced people in a world that assumes the nation-state is the natural frame for viewing ethnicity and ethnic identity. In the process, she captures
the creative strategies displaced people deploy to sustain themselves and imagine
a better future. When considering the intersections of ethnicity, ethnic conflict,
and the nation-state, Malkki urges us to move beyond easy explanations of contemporary conflicts as inevitable or natural outcomes of ancient tribal hatreds.
Instead, Malkki's work pushes us to see the complex histories and processes of
identity making that are often obscured by labels like "refugee" and "ethnic conflict" (Haugerud 1998; Malkki 1995; Roseberry 1997).

MAP 6.4
Bosnia

Orchestrating Ethnic Conflict in the Former Yugoslavia. The
disintegration of the former Yugoslavia in the late 1980s and early 1990s led to
a devastating civil war that harnessed ethnicity as a powerful weapon of conflict
and hatred. The war began in 1992 among Catholic Croats, Orthodox Christian
Serbs, and Bosnian Muslims as national political leaders scrambled for control
over land and power. The region is one of the most ethnically diverse in the
world, and the area's national boundaries have shifted constantly over the past
150 years. But in direct contrast to journalistic accounts of the 1992–1995 war,
which traced its origins to ancient ethnic hatreds that condemned the country's

people to an endless cycle of violence, Norwegian anthropologist Tone Bringa has offered a different perspective. In her ethnography *Being Muslim the Bosnian Way* (1995), she declares, "The war was not created by those villagers. . . . The war has been orchestrated from places where the people I lived and worked among were not represented and where their voices were not heard" (5).

Beginning in 1987, Bringa conducted fieldwork in a diverse, Muslim-Catholic village in central Bosnia. She carefully describes the integrated social structures of daily village life—including the role of women, religion, and the family—and pays particular attention to the way Muslims practiced their faith. Bringa did not find a village populated with people who had always hated one another. They spoke the same language, went to school together, traded in the same local market, and shared village life as friends and neighbors. Bringa pointedly notes that despite the usual tensions any small community would face, these people of different faiths had lived together peacefully for 500 years.

Significant change occurred in the community during the short time of Bringa's fieldwork. When she began her research, local Muslims based their identity on differences in religious practices from those of their Catholic neighbors. The emphasis was on practices such as scheduling of worship, prayer, and holiday celebrations, not on religious beliefs and convictions. However, these perceptions of self and others changed as war broke out and state leaders imposed new ethnic and cultural policies. Gradually, local Muslims were forced to identify less with their local community and more with the religious beliefs of other Bosnian Muslims, and they had to turn to the outside Muslim world as a source of solidarity and support.

When Bringa returned to the village in the spring of 1993—revealed in riveting scenes from her documentary film *Bosnia: We Are All Neighbors* (1993)—to her horror she found that almost every Muslim home had been destroyed by Croat forces, with assistance from local Croat men of the village. All 400 Muslims in the village (two-thirds of its population) had fled, been killed, or been placed in concentration camps. **Ethnic cleansing**—efforts of one ethnic or religious group to remove or destroy another group in a particular geographic area—had shattered the dynamic and peaceful fabric of village life that Bringa recalled from only a few years earlier. As she writes in the preface to her book, "My anthropological training had not prepared me to deal with the very rapid and total disintegration of the community. . . . [T]his war has made sense neither to the anthropologist nor to the people who taught her about their way

Bosnian Muslim women comfort one another near coffins of family members, victims of "ethnic cleansing," exhumed from a nearby mass grave.

ethnic cleansing

Efforts by representatives of one ethnic or religious group to remove or destroy another group in a particular geographic area.

Each year, half a million tourists visit the Dai Minority Park in China's southwestern Yunnan Province. This is one of many ethno-parks owned and operated by members of China's Han majority (96 percent of the population), who market the nation's fifty-five ethnic minorities to a primarily middle-class Han clientele (Chio 2014). Here, tourists can live in Dai-style houses, eat ethnic meals, and participate in reenactments of ritual celebrations such as the water festival, pictured here, originally an annual three-day festival but now performed every day for the entertainment of visitors. How might ethno–theme parks benefit the Chinese government's goal of national unity? How do you think they affect the local communities?

of life" (Bringa 1995, xviii). Her second documentary, *Returning Home: Revival of a Bosnian Village* (Bringa and Loizos 2002), examines the return of some of the Muslim refugees and the attempt to reconstruct the village life that was destroyed during the civil war. In Bringa's account of Bosnian village life we can see the vulnerability of local ethnic identities to manipulation by outside political and military forces (Coles 2007; Eller 1999).

ETHNICITY AS A SOURCE OF OPPORTUNITY

Ethnicity is not only mobilized to rally support in times of conflict. Ethnicity can also be mobilized to create opportunities, including engagement in everyday economics. Today ethnicity is being packaged and produced for a multibillion-dollar market: food, clothing, music, fashion, and cultural artifacts. People eat at ethnic restaurants, buy ethnic music, and decorate their homes and offices with ethnic furnishings. Perhaps you have some "ethnic" items in your dorm room or at home. John and Jean Comaroff, in their book *Ethnicity, Inc.* (2009), examine how the purposeful creation of ethnicity facilitates big business. The Comaroffs pay particular attention to the way ethnically defined populations are branding themselves and becoming ethno-corporations in order to capitalize on their ethnicity. Ethno–theme parks, cultural villages, and ecotourism all promote the ethnic experience to attract investors and customers (Chio 2014; Nelson 1999). These are just a few pieces of the "Ethnicity, Inc." puzzle. (In contrast, for an example of a majority group's marketing of minority theme parks, see the group of images on the previous page.)

Bafokeng, Inc., in South Africa.

For a another look at ethnicity being mobilized for economic benefits, the story of one group in South Africa is remarkable for its corporate success. The Bafokeng, a Tswana nation in South Africa's North West province, trace their history in the area to the twelfth century. Between 1840 and the mid-1860s, their land was taken by white colonial settlers. Thereafter the Bafokeng, who could not own land under the new regime, went to work as laborers on the farms that had once been theirs; later they toiled in diamond mines to the south. Ultimately, though, to recover their land, the Bafokeng decided to try to buy it back. Pooling portions of their wage labor under the auspices of the Tswana king, and with a white German missionary serving as their proxy, the Bafokeng began a long-term strategy to repurchase their farms. Eventually, they reacquired thirty-three farms by the early twentieth century. To protect their land rights, the natives registered these farms under the name of the Royal Bafokeng Nation, Inc.—a private, corporate owner—not in the names of individuals.

MAP 6.5
South Africa

Tensions rose dramatically when, in 1924, surveyors discovered that the Merensky Reef geologic formation that lay directly under Bafokeng land was the world's largest source of platinum metals and held significant deposits of chromite and graphite as well. Battles with the state and corporations over mining rights continued until the 1960s, when a deal was reached with a private company to provide the Bafokeng with royalties on all minerals extracted from their land. Once again, the Bafokeng placed their revenues into a communal trust.

Over time, the Royal Bafokeng Nation (RBN) has become a wealthy $3.4 billion corporate conglomerate with an extensive web of investments and holdings—including mining and construction companies, investment companies, and even a premier soccer team—in South Africa and beyond. At home, it has invested heavily in jobs programs by establishing mid-size companies such as Bafokeng Civil Works, Bafokeng Brick and Tile, Bafokeng Chrome, Bafokeng

Bakery, and a Bafokeng shopping center. The RBN has also invested in infrastructure such as roads, bridges, reservoirs, electricity, schools, and health clinics, and it has established a fund for Bafokeng individuals who are pursuing professional training or higher education. The ethnic group has become an ethno-enterprise—built, branded, packaged, and advertised on the Bafokeng ethnic name and identity.

Many scholars, politicians, and economists expected the RBN to wither away in the face of globalization, modernity, and the homogenizing influence of the capitalist economy. However, the RBN ethno-corporation provides a remarkable example of the ways in which ethnicity can be mobilized by stakeholders in identity-based businesses to create alternative strategies for survival and success in the global marketplace.

Despite their corporate success, all is not well within the Bafokeng nation itself. Questions regularly arise about who benefits from this version of "Ethnicity, Inc." Individual Bafokeng do not own shares in RBN, Inc. Its money is not distributed among members but is reinvested in the corporation. Despite investments in job programs, infrastructure, and education in the homeland, recent studies show that the Bafokeng have a 39 percent unemployment rate, 95 percent use pit latrines for toilets, and less than 13 percent have electricity. With extreme poverty rates, some observers refer to the Bafokeng as "a rich nation of poor people" (Comaroff and Comaroff 2009, 109). How would you assess the effectiveness of this mobilization of ethnicity by the Bafokeng?

ASSIMILATION VERSUS MULTICULTURALISM: ETHNIC INTERACTION IN THE UNITED STATES

The United States has an extremely complicated history of dealing with people of different geographic origins, religions, skin colors, and ethnic backgrounds. The relationship of "ethnic" and "American" (as applied to the United States) remains controversial today. From the outset, immigration from various regions in Europe, the enslavement and forced migration of Africans, and the conquest of Native American peoples made the United States one of the most ethnically diverse countries in the world. But these diverse groups and additional waves of immigrants over the past 200 years have experienced extremely different paths to incorporation into U.S. culture. In fact, these paths have often followed color lines that divide people of lighter and darker complexions.

melting pot

A metaphor used to describe the process of immigrant assimilation into U.S. dominant culture.

assimilation

The process through which minorities accept the patterns and norms of the dominant culture and cease to exist as separate groups.

Scholars have often used the **melting pot** metaphor to describe the standard path into U.S. culture. In the melting pot, minorities adopt the patterns and norms of the dominant culture and eventually cease to exist as separate groups—a process scholars call **assimilation**. Eventually all cooked in the same pot, diverse groups become assimilated into one big stew. According to this metaphor, tens of millions of European immigrants from dozens of countries with myriad languages, cultures, and religious practices have been transformed into ethnic whites through marriage, work, education, and the use of English.

But in reality the melting pot has never been completely successful in the United States, even for people of European descent. The creation of whiteness, as we saw in Chapter 5, was often contentious and difficult, marked by intense rivalries and violence. Nathan Glazer and Daniel Patrick Moynihan's landmark study *Beyond the Melting Pot* (1970) found a failure to reach complete assimilation among European immigrants and their descendants as late as the third generation. And many scholars suggest that the melting pot metaphor never meaningfully represented the experiences of Native Americans and people of African descent.

The incredibly diverse flows of immigration to the United States since 1965 have made earlier familiar categories increasingly inadequate to capture the rapidly shifting ethnic character of the nation's population today. For many Africans, Native Americans, Latinos, and Asian immigrants, the United States has been resistant to their assimilation into the dominant culture, regardless of their educational level or socioeconomic status. Yet, as discussed in Chapters 5 and 11 (on race and the global economy, respectively), immigrants and their children are creating new ethnic identities and new ways of becoming American. Today a multiculturalist narrative competes with the melting pot metaphor to represent the role of ethnicity in U.S. culture. **Multiculturalism** refers to the process through which new immigrants and their children enculturate into the dominant national culture and yet retain an ethnic culture. In multiculturalism, both identities may be held at the same time.

Tensions over which model will be dominant in the U.S. ethnicity story—assimilation or multiculturalism—are constantly rising to the surface. For example, attempts to establish English as the official language of towns, states, and even the U.S. federal government can be seen as (1) an effort to mandate language assimilation into the melting pot, and (2) a reassertion of the dominant culture's centrality against the rising trend toward multiculturalism (Rumbaut and Portes 2001).

multiculturalism

A pattern of ethnic relations in which new immigrants and their children enculturate into the dominant national culture and yet retain an ethnic culture.

What Is the Relationship of Ethnicity to the Nation?

state

An autonomous regional structure of political, economic, and military rule with a central government authorized to make laws and use force to maintain order and defend its territory.

Almost all people today imagine themselves as part of a nation-state. But this has not always been the case. **States**—regional structures of political, economic, and military rule—have existed for thousands of years, beginning in the regions now known as modern-day Iraq, China, and India. But the nation-state is a

nation-state

A political entity, located within a geographic territory with enforced borders, where the population shares a sense of culture, ancestry, and destiny as a people.

citizenship

Legal membership in a nation-state.

nation

A term once used to describe a group of people who shared a place of origin; now used interchangeably with *nation-state*.

nationalism

The desire of an ethnic community to create and/or maintain a nation-state.

imagined community

The invented sense of connection and shared traditions that underlies identification with a particular ethnic group or nation whose members likely will never all meet.

MAP 6.6

France

relatively new development. The term signifies more than a geographic territory with borders enforced by a central government. **Nation-state** assumes a distinct political entity whose population shares a sense of culture, ancestry, and destiny as a people. **Citizenship** refers to legal membership in a nation-state. Though the term **nation** once was used to describe a group of people who shared a place of origin, today the word *nation* is often used interchangeably with *nation-state*. **Nationalism** emerges when a sense of ethnic community combines with a desire to create and maintain a nation-state in a location where that sense of common destiny can be lived out (Gellner 1983; Hearn 2006; Wolf 2001).

IMAGINED COMMUNITIES AND INVENTED TRADITIONS

Across the world over the past 200 years, people have shifted their primary associations and identifications from family, village, town, and city to an almost universal identification with a nation or the desire to create a nation. Yet despite our contemporary assumptions that identification with an ethnic group or a nation has deep history, anthropological research reveals that most ethnic groups and nations are recent historical creations, our connection to people within these groups are recently imagined, and our shared traditions are recently invented.

Political Scientist Benedict Anderson (1983) conceived of the nation as an **imagined community**. He called it "imagined" because almost all of the people within it have never met and most likely will never meet. They may be separated by sharp divisions of class, politics, or religion and yet imagine themselves to have a common heritage and collective responsibility to one another and their nation. This sense of membership in an imagined national community can be strong enough to lead people into battle to protect their shared interests.

Anderson traces the imagined communities in Europe to the development of print communication in the capitalist economies that emerged in the eighteenth and nineteenth centuries. As people shared communication and information through newspapers and books published in a common language, Anderson suggests, they began to define themselves—to imagine themselves—as part of the same nation, the same community. Anderson's conception of imagined communities has become an essential analytical tool for thinking about nations and nationalisms.

Historians Eric Hobsbawm and Terence Ranger (1983) suggest that nations are not ancient configurations but instead are recent constructions with invented traditions. Nations may evoke a sense of deep history and inspire a broad sense of unity, but they are, in fact, relatively new. For example, we imagine the French nation-state to have a deep and unitary history, but prior to the 1800s the French were a scattered collection of urban and rural people who spoke different languages, celebrated different holidays and festivals, practiced different religions, and held primary loyalty not to the French state but to their city, town, village, or

French classroom, 1829. What role can education play in creating a sense of common nationality?

extended family. It was two national infrastructure projects, launched in the early 1800s, that ultimately played key roles in inventing a French nation.

What did these infrastructure projects involve? First, a new education system was introduced on a national scale. Its textbooks promoted a shared sense of French history, and perhaps most important, all schools used the Paris dialect of French as the medium of instruction. This created a standard national language—a lingua franca—that facilitated communication among the population. Second, the construction of an extensive network of roads and railways integrated rural areas into a national market economy. This new transportation infrastructure promoted the rapid flow of goods between agricultural and industrial sectors and allowed the regular movement of workers between countryside and city, thereby providing a national labor pool for France's growing economy. These national infrastructure projects proved crucial to transforming the diverse people living within the territorial boundaries of what is now modern-day France into a French people with a common sense of identity, history, language, and tradition (Weber 1976).

Globalization and Transnational Citizenship in Eritrea. Today, globalization is reshaping the ways nation-states operate and are experienced within and beyond their borders. For example, Victoria Bernal's ethnography *Nation as Network* (2014) explores the recent history of Eritrea, a small multi-ethnic nation in the Horn of Africa, and the ways Eritrean out-migration in recent decades has combined with new media technologies to transform notions of the nation-state and citizenship.

MAP 6.7
Eritrea

War and violence have been constant factors for Eritreans in recent decades, from the country's struggle for independence to ensuing border wars with neighboring states. The country's citizens have faced increasing militarization and repression by the Eritrean state.

As a result, tens of thousands of Eritreans have chosen to move abroad in search of economic opportunities and political stability. Scattered over many countries and continents, they have formed what immigration scholars call a **diaspora**—an extensive network of Eritreans living outside their ancestral homeland yet maintaining emotional and material ties to home—through which they continue to participate passionately in Eritrean politics and economic life. They send money to family members back home. They make investments. And through a dynamic network of websites, blogs, and other social media, they connect with one another, debate Eritrean politics, mobilize actions and campaigns, and communicate their political views to the Eritrean state, nongovernmental organizations, and human rights groups. Eritrean political and economic elites actively cultivate the diaspora's involvement and rely on their financial contributions to support Eritrea's welfare and warfare.

Bernal documents the ways new communication technologies create new opportunities to experiment with political expression, including dissent and other activities that would not be safe in Eritrea itself. The online presence of Eritreans in diaspora creates an alternative public sphere in which to challenge Eritrea's authoritarian government, question the mainstream media narratives, and undermine practices of secrecy and censorship. In the process, this transnational network of Eritreans in diaspora participates in building Eritrea as a nation—both in the struggle over Eritrean economic and political priorities and in the making and remaking of the conceptual boundaries of the Eritrean state, Eritrean citizenship, and Eritrean identity (Bernal 2014; Ivana 2015).

diaspora
A group of people living outside their ancestral homeland yet maintaining emotional and material ties to home.

ANTI-COLONIALISM AND NATIONALISM

At times, efforts to imagine a national identity among a diverse group of people gain strength through the need—perceived or real—to join together against the threat of a common enemy. The outsiders—"others" who do not belong to the group—may be stereotyped along lines of religion, race, language, ethnicity, or political beliefs. War is the most dramatic strategy for evoking nationalism and mobilizing a population for the project of nation building.

Through their colonial conquests over more than 400 years, the emerging nation-states of Europe, and later Japan in Asia, redrew the political borders of much of the world to suit their own economic and political interests. In the search for raw materials, cheap labor, and markets for their expanding economies, they mapped out territorial boundaries without regard to local ethnic, political, economic, or religious realities (see Chapter 11 on the global economy).

In the process, colonial activity disrupted long-established and complex local and regional social, economic, and political relationships. Colonialism had a particularly negative impact on indigenous people around the world who faced forced labor, relocations, forced assimilation, violence, and genocide (Maybury-Lewis 2002).

The destruction of European and Japanese economies during World War II (1939–45) weakened the colonial powers' ability to control their colonies. As a result, national independence movements that had been gaining strength in colonies throughout Asia, Africa, the Middle East, Latin America, and the Caribbean before World War II and had developed military capabilities and guerrilla fighting tactics during the war were strongly positioned to turn their efforts toward liberating their countries from the colonial occupiers. The anti-colonialist efforts led to a rise of nationalism in former colonies as disparate populations banded together to reassert local control (Césaire 1955; Fanon 1961).

THE CHALLENGES OF DEVELOPING A SENSE OF NATIONHOOD

Of the nearly two hundred nation-states in the world today, fewer than one-third existed in their current form 40 years ago. Dozens of states were created after World War II as nationalist movements won independence from colonial powers in Asia, the Middle East, and Africa. Dozens more were created in Central Asia and Eastern Europe following the collapse of the former Soviet Union and the breakdown of previously socialist states in the 1990s. Only a handful of the nation-states that exist today date back to the nineteenth century, and almost none have existed for more than 200 years, certainly not in their present form. As a result, by the end of the colonial era few of the newly formed countries had homogeneous populations. Most now encompassed multiple ethnicities and identities within state borders that previously had not existed. Such disparities caused thorny problems for nationalist movements and for the nation-states that formed after independence (Robbins 2013). The following case study from Iraq explores the challenges experienced by emerging nations in the postcolonial period and will expand your understanding of the intersection of nation, nationalism, nation building, and the modern nation-state. Can you identify in this example the key concepts introduced in this chapter?

Are There Any Iraqis in Iraq? Since the U.S. invasion and occupation of Iraq in 2003, news reports have featured stories of ethnic violence among Sunni, Shia, and Kurds—violence that the media portrays as the true obstacle to democracy and peace. The front pages of newspapers and the leads on evening news tell stories of seemingly endless and senseless suicide bombings, roadside explosives, armed militias, kidnappings, assassinations, and warfare. Elections are

MAP 6.8
Iraq

held, but the elected officials, torn by intense ethnic, religious, and political differences, are unable to form a functioning government. In the same way that the Western press typically reports what it describes as ethnic conflicts around the world—whether in Rwanda, Sudan, Sri Lanka, India, or the former Yugoslavia—deep and long-standing ethnic and religious cleavages in Iraq are blamed for an environment in which civil war and government collapse are almost inevitable. The same narrative has been used to explain Iraq's inability to protect its borders and defend its citizens against the invading forces of ISIL (the Islamic State in Iraq and the Levant—sometimes called ISIS), which, beginning in 2014, occupied the key western Iraqi cities of Fallujah, Mosul, Tikrit, and other territories.

Why, after so many years of nation building with U.S. economic and military support, have the Iraqi people been unable to form a strong government and military and stop the violence? Aren't there any Iraqis in Iraq—people who would put the country first, ahead of other ethnic or religious differences?

Iraq does not have an ancient history as a nation. Although cities such as Baghdad have an ancient history in the region of Mesopotamia, sometimes called the "cradle of civilization," the country of Iraq did not exist before World War I. Even then, Iraq was not formed through local initiative. A secret treaty between France and Great Britain (the Sykes-Picot Agreement), signed during World War I, carved up their opponent, the Ottoman Empire, to form many of the countries we find in the Middle East today. The two European powers, with Russia's consent, drew national borders—including those of present-day Iraq—to meet their needs for economic access, trade routes, and political control. The powers mapped out these borders with little regard for the history, politics, religions, and ethnic makeup of the local populations.

With a mandate from the new League of Nations in 1920, the British established a monarchical government in the new state of Iraq and recruited and empowered leaders from the minority Sunni population to run the government. Members of the Shia and Kurd populations, excluded from leadership roles in the government, actively fought for independence from British colonial occupation. Britain subsequently granted full independence to Iraq in 1932 (with the exception of another brief military occupation during World War II), but the Sunni minority retained control of the government until the fall of Saddam Hussein in 2003.

After the U.S. military occupied Iraq in 2003, the people of Iraq inherited a collapsed state structure and confronted the prospects of "nation building" in a country under foreign occupation that had experienced decades of state-sponsored violence. Yet media representations of Iraq consistently traced its problems to the roots of ethnic conflict. Social scientists from many fields question these simple storylines that portray deep ethnic and religious hatreds as the cause of Iraq's current difficulties (Ericksen 2010). Ethnicity, they warn, should never be seen that simply or monolithically. A more careful examination may find that (1) ethnic and religious lines are not drawn so clearly, and (2) other identities based on factors such as region, family, and class—even international relations—may also play key roles in the unfolding of events. With a weak state unable to provide security to its population, people turn to other strategies for mobilizing support, safety, and the means for achieving a livelihood (Eller 1999).

As globalization creates flows of people, ideas, goods, and images across borders and builds linkages among local communities worldwide, we might anticipate that ethnicity and nationalism—which are associated with local and national identities—would have less capacity to shape people's lives and influence the way people make decisions. Instead, in many parts of the world we see an intensification of ethnic and national identities and related conflicts. Understanding the processes through which ethnicity and nationalism are imagined and mobilized and their traditions are invented, often over relatively short periods, can provide a set of tools for analyzing the role of ethnicity in our world today.

Toolkit

Thinking Like an Anthropologist:
Who Is an American?

In the opening story of the World Cup—one of the most global of all sporting events—and in the ethnographic examples throughout the chapter, we have seen how ethnic identity and nationalism continue to be imagined, built, nurtured, taught, learned, promoted, negotiated, and contested. And we have explored an anthropological perspective on three questions that connect the concepts of ethnicity and nationalism:

- **What does "ethnicity" mean to anthropologists?**
- **How and why is ethnicity created, mobilized, and contested?**
- **What is the relationship of ethnicity to the nation?**

Few of us are aware of the role of ethnicity and nationalism in our lives or how our culture works to promote them. As you learn to think like an anthropologist yourself, can you begin to see the process of ethnic identity construction at work in your own life and in the major debates of the culture that surrounds you? Consider these recent debates about who is and who is not an American:

- Despite an official birth certificate and other clear evidence that former President Obama was born in the state of Hawaii on August 4, 1961, more than 20 percent of Americans surveyed in a September 2015 poll by CNN/ ORG claimed that he is not a U.S. citizen, and 29 percent believed President Obama is a Muslim, despite repeated professions of his Christian faith (CNN/ ORC International 2015). How is that possible?

- Some leading politicians want to change the Fourteenth Amendment of the U.S. Constitution. The amendment was passed after the Civil War to protect African Americans by ensuring that anyone born in the United States is granted full rights of citizenship. "Anchor babies," children born in the United States to Hispanic parents who are undocumented immigrants, are the target of these recent suggested changes to the Constitution. Some people fear that these babies are being "dropped as an anchor" so their parents can become citizens when their child attains the age of twenty-one. Do you think the U.S. Constitution should be amended to address this issue?

Or is this debate simply a substitute for a larger struggle over who belongs to U.S. culture and who does not? How should a child's nationality and citizenship be defined?

• In 2015–2016 leading presidential candidates evoked notions of ethnicity, nationalism and citizenship to rally voters, suggesting that Muslims should be required to register with the federal government; that 10–15 million undocumented immigrants living in the U.S., including children who accompanied them and who have grown up in the U.S., should be deported; that Muslim mosques should be placed under surveillance; and that the U.S. should only accept Syrian refugees if they are Christian. What role do ethno-political entrepreneurs play in attempts to define immigrants and Muslims in particular as ethnic outsiders in the United States?

After reading this chapter, you should be better prepared with the anthropological tools to understand the ways ethnicity and nationalism work in your life and in your imagined communities—whether they are built around family, religion, hometown, ethnic group, or nation-state.

Key Terms

ethnicity (p. 154)

origin myth (p. 155)

ethnic boundary marker (p. 156)

situational negotiation of identity (p. 157)

identity entrepreneurs (p. 159)

genocide (p. 159)

ethnic cleansing (p. 163)

melting pot (p. 166)

assimilation (p. 166)

multiculturalism (p. 167)

state (p. 167)

nation-state (p. 168)

citizenship (p. 168)

nation (p. 168)

nationalism (p. 168)

imagined community (p. 168)

diaspora (p. 170)

Chapter 7
Gender

On Friday, August 21, 2015, Captain Kristen Griest and First Lieutenant Shaye Haver became the first women to complete the United States Army's elite Ranger School at Fort Benning, Georgia. Both had previously graduated from the prestigious United States Military Academy at West Point, after which Griest deployed to Afghanistan in the military police and Haver served as an Apache attack helicopter pilot based at Fort Carson in Colorado. The Rangers' grueling 62-day leadership course tests soldiers' physical and mental ability to overcome fatigue, hunger, and stress while leading small-unit combat operations in adverse situations. Of the 19 women and 381 men who began the training, only 2 women and 94 men finished.

Though awarded the coveted black-and-gold Ranger tab, neither Griest nor Haver was eligible to join the elite 75th Ranger Regiment. U.S. military rules still barred women from direct combat roles, including service in the infantry, armored divisions, and special operations units like the Army Rangers.

Why are women underrepresented in the U.S. military? Here, Captain Kristen Griest, center, trains at the Army Ranger School, an elite U.S. military program for special operations forces.

Rather than highlighting an isolated incident, Griest and Haver's story illuminates deep tensions at the intersection of gender and power in the U.S. military and other U.S. cultural institutions. Fifteen percent of 1.4 million active-duty U.S. military personnel are women, and the number continues to increase. (Globally, women make up a significant portion of the military in many countries, including Israel (33 percent), China (25 percent), France (15 percent), South Africa (26 percent) and Eritrea (30 percent)). The U.S. military has a reputation for leadership in creating integrated forces, including the integration of African Americans after World War II and more recently the inclusion of gay men and lesbians in 2011. Issues of gender, however—including the appropriate role of women in combat, the scarcity of women in senior leadership, the high incidence of sexual assaults and the question of whether young women, like their male counterparts, should be required to register for the draft—still roil its ranks.

On December 3, 2015, three months after Griest and Haver graduated, Defense Secretary Ash Carter announced that all military positions, including combat positions, would be open to women. They would be allowed to drive tanks, fire mortars, lead infantry soldiers into combat, and engage in special operations. But what had really changed about women and men that brought about this policy shift?

Questions of gender—that is, the characteristics associated with being a woman or man in a particular culture and the ways those characteristics intersect with dynamics of power—are central to the practice of anthropology. Since the pioneering work of Margaret Mead challenged U.S. cultural assumptions about human sexuality and gender roles (see Chapter 3), anthropologists, especially feminist anthropologists, have been at the forefront of attempts to use the tools and analysis of anthropology to analyze the role of gender in crucial contemporary debates, social movements, and political struggles. Over the last forty years, **gender studies**—research into understanding who we are as men and women—has become one of the most significant subfields of anthropology. Indeed, anthropologists consider the ways in which gender is constructed to be a central element in every aspect of human culture, including sexuality, health, family, religion, economics, politics, sports, and individual identity formation.

As we have seen throughout this book, people create diverse cultures with fluid categories to define complex aspects of the human experience. The same holds true for gender. Even biological sex is far more fluid and complex than people are taught. As we will see later in this chapter, nature creates diversity, not rigid categories. As globalization transforms gender roles and gender relations on both the local level and a global scale, anthropologists play an essential role in mapping the changing gender terrain of the modern world. In this chapter we will explore these issues in more detail:

- **Are men and women born or made?**
- **Are there more than two sexes?**

gender studies

Research into masculinity and femininity as flexible, complex, and historically and culturally constructed categories.

- How do anthropologists explore the relationship between gender and power?

- How is globalization transforming gender roles and stratification?

By the end of this chapter you will be better prepared to understand the roles that sex and gender play in the culture around you, including in the classroom, in the family, in the workplace, in places of worship, and at the ballot box. You will also be able to apply anthropological insights into gender issues as they emerge in your own life—insights that will serve you well as boyfriend or girlfriend, spouse, parent, student, teacher, worker, manager, and community leader in our increasingly global world.

Are Men and Women Born or Made?

"That's just the way guys are," some women sigh when a man says or does some stereotypical "man" thing. "Women!" a man may exclaim, hands in the air, as if all the other guys in the room know exactly what he means. But what *do* they mean? Is there some essential male or female nature that differentially shapes the personalities, emotions, patterns of personal relationships, career choices, leadership styles, and economic and political engagements of women and men?

DISTINGUISHING BETWEEN SEX AND GENDER

Much of what we stereotypically consider to be "natural" male or female behavior—driven by biology—might turn out, upon more careful inspection, to be imposed by cultural expectations of how men and women should behave. To help explore the relationship between the biological and cultural aspects of being men and women, anthropologists distinguish between sex and gender. **Sex**, from an anthropological viewpoint, refers to the observable physical differences between male and female human beings, especially the biological differences related to human reproduction. **Gender** is composed of the expectations of thought and behavior that each culture assigns to people of different sexes.

Historically, biological science has tended to create distinct mental maps of reality for male and female anatomy. Three primary factors have generally been considered in determining biological sex: (1) genitalia, (2) gonads (testes and ovaries, which produce different hormones), and (3) chromosome patterns (women have two X chromosomes; men have one X and one Y). Within this context, human males and females are said to display **sexual dimorphism**—that is, they differ physically in primary sexual characteristics as well as in secondary

sex

The observable physical differences between male and female, especially biological differences related to human reproduction.

gender

The expectations of thought and behavior that each culture assigns to people of different sexes.

sexual dimorphism

The phenotypic differences between males and females of the same species.

sexual characteristics such as breast size, hair distribution, and pitch of voice. Men and women on average also differ in weight, height, and strength. An average man is heavier, taller, and stronger than an average woman. Women on average have more long-term physical endurance and live longer.

But sexual dimorphism among humans is far from absolute. In fact, human male and female bodies are much more similar than different. In comparison to other animal species, human sexual dimorphism, particularly with regard to body size and voice timbre, is relatively modest (Fedigan 1982). On average, human males (U.S. average, 190 pounds) weigh about 15 percent more than females (U.S. average, 163 pounds) (Ogden et al. 2004). In comparison, male gorillas on average are double the size of female gorillas (Cawthon Lang 2005). Many biological characteristics associated with human sexual dimorphism fall along a continuum—a range—in which men and women overlap significantly. Not all men are taller than all women, though many are. Not all women live longer than all men, though most do. And as we will see later in this chapter, even primary characteristics of biological sex do not always fit into the two assumed categories of male and female.

In popular conversations, emphasis is often placed on the role of biology in shaping gender identities and behaviors. Research consistently reveals, however, that biology and culture closely intertwine. Culture, for instance, constantly shapes and reshapes our bodies throughout our lives, whether through nutrition, exercise, stress, exposure to disease, or social stimulation. Our bodies are designed to respond to our environments and life experiences. Our DNA, for instance, can be turned on and off by environmental factors. Our brains are constantly reshaped by the stimuli they receive. Even our hormone production is closely tied to the experiences we have with others. Testosterone levels rise and fall in response to what is going on around us. Studies have even shown that if fathers are actively involved with the children, their bodies respond in ways to help them be good dads (Kuzawa et al. 2009; Muller et al. 2009; Wade and Ferree 2015).

Cross-cultural anthropological research challenges the assumed links between biology and behavior. Knowing a person's biological sex does not enable us to predict what roles that person will play in a given culture. In some cultures, people with two X chromosomes do most of the cooking, farming, public speaking, and ritual activity; in others, people with one X and one Y chromosome fill those roles. Alternatively, the tasks may be done by both but stratified by power and prestige. In many Western cultures, for instance, both XX and XY cook. But women tend to cook in the home, while men predominate as restaurant chefs. Clearly, this is not a biologically driven division of labor. What could be the cultural reasons?

Even roles stereotypically associated with male strength and aggression do not fit an assumed binary gender division. Women do heavy labor—like the women of Plachimada in this book's opening chapter who rise early to carry

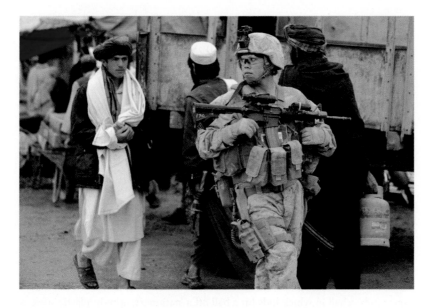

water drums miles from the well to their homes. In addition, the predominance of men in violence and warfare is shifting as militaries in many parts of the world rely on women soldiers to fly remote-controlled predator drones, launch missiles, and engage in firefights on the front lines of battle. Because biology cannot predict the roles that men and women play in a given culture, anthropologists consider how gender is constructed culture by culture, and they explore the implications of those constructions for the men and women in each context.

THE CULTURAL CONSTRUCTION OF GENDER

Humans are born with biological sex, but we learn to be women and men. From the moment of birth we begin to learn culture, including how to walk, talk, eat, dress, think, practice religion, raise children, respond to violence, and express our emotions like a man or a woman (Mauss 1979). We learn what kinds of behavior are perceived as masculine or feminine. Thus, anthropologists refer to the **cultural construction of gender**.

Family, friends, the media, doctors, educational institutions, religious communities, sports, and law all enculturate us with a sense of gender that becomes normative and seems natural. For example, parents "do gender" with their children. They assign them boy or girl names; dress them in appropriately gendered clothing, colors, and jewelry; and give them the "right" haircuts. Parents even speak to their children in gendered tones of voice. As we see gender being performed all around us, we learn to perform it in our turn. In these ways gender is taught, learned, performed, and policed.

cultural construction of gender

The ways humans learn to behave as a man or woman and to recognize behaviors as masculine or feminine within their cultural context.

Over a lifetime, gender becomes a powerful, and mostly invisible, framework that shapes the way we see ourselves and others (Bern 1981, 1983). Our relationships with others become an elaborate gendered dance of playing, dating, mating, parenting, and loving that reinforces our learned ideas of **masculinity** and **femininity** and establishes differing roles and expectations. Gender is also a potent cultural system through which we organize our collective lives, not necessarily on the basis of merit or skill but on the constructed categories of what it means to be a man or a woman (Bonvillain 2007; Brettell and Sargent 2009; Lorber 1994; Rubin 1975).

Teaching Gender in the United States: Boys, Girls, and Youth Sports.

Sports is a key cultural arena in which individuals learn gender roles. A study of young boys and girls playing co-ed T-ball provides insights into how gender in the United States is subtly and not-so-subtly taught, learned, and enforced through youth sports (Landers and Fine 1996). T-ball is the precursor to baseball in which kids hit a ball off a stationary, upright plastic stick (a tee) rather than a ball thrown from a pitcher.

Landers and Fine found that T-ball coaches established a hierarchy of opportunity, training, and encouragement that favored boys over girls. Boys consistently received more playing time than girls, played positions (such as shortstop or first base) that provided more opportunities to touch the ball and develop their skills, and had more opportunities to practice hitting the ball at the plate. Boys frequently received coaching advice, while girls' mistakes went uncorrected. Parents and other players supported this hierarchy of training and opportunity and, along with the coaches, offered less or more encouragement along gender lines. For example, boys received more words of praise for their successes. These hierarchies were apparent not only between boys and girls, but within gendered groups as well. Among the boys, praise and opportunity were unequally distributed: Those who were already stronger, faster, better coordinated, or more advanced in baseball skills were favored over those who were not as advanced. Moving beyond the T-ball experience, the researchers noted that ideal forms of masculinity and manliness are taught, learned, and enforced on the baseball field as well, promoting aggressiveness, assertiveness, competitiveness, physical strength and skill, and a drive to succeed and win (Landers and Fine 1996).

Did you ever participate in youth sports, either in the United States or in another country? If so, what was your experience like? Did your parents sign you up for certain sports—basketball, soccer, lacrosse, football, wrestling, ice hockey, dance, gymnastics, figure skating, cheerleading? If so, what role might their ideas of gender have played in their choice? Landers and Fine's study suggests that attributes stereotypically associated with boys such as athleticism, assertiveness, aggression, strength, and competitiveness are actively constructed along gender lines through a wide variety of youth sports. In considering their study, can you see the ramifications of such gender training on individuals' attitudes and behaviors as they become adults with responsible roles in family, work, and politics?

While recognizing the physical differences between men and women—modest as they are when considering the diversity of the whole human population—how do we factor in the role of culture in something like sports and athleticism? Gender enculturation in sports and physical play begins early and happens in varied settings. I remember taking my toddler son to the playground and watching as other parents encouraged their little boys to run, climb, and jump while urging their little girls to play nicely in the sandbox. Starting in everyday settings like this, perhaps we can begin to imagine the cumulative effects of parental expectations, peer pressure, and media images on girls' motivation to engage in intense physical activity and competition (or boy's willingness to express emotions, play with dolls, or take care of younger siblings). As a result, sports may reflect less about real physical differences in speed, endurance, and strength and more about how a given culture constructs and maintains gender and sex norms. Perhaps becoming a world-class athlete depends more on opportunity, encouragement, coaching, nutrition, training facilities, and wealth than on being a man or a woman.

Today, as training and opportunities increase, women are closing the performance gap with men in many sports. The gap between male and female marathon winners, for instance, has rapidly closed to less than 10 minutes, and women are improving their times faster than men. But the persistence of inequality throughout sports culture precludes an accurate comparison between women and men athletes at the current time (Wade and Ferree 2015).

Constructing Masculinity in a U.S. High School. Since the 1970s, gender studies have focused primarily on women. Recent studies, however, have begun to explore the gender construction of male identity as well as the broader construction of masculinity. The ethnography described here touches on several key aspects of this complex process.

C. J. Pascoe's ethnography *Dude, You're a Fag* (2007) explores the construction of gender—and particularly masculinity—in a suburban, working-class, racially diverse high school in north-central California. Calling someone a fag, what Pascoe calls "fag discourse," occurred almost exclusively among white male students in a daily banter of teasing, bullying, and harassment. Basing her conclusions on interviews with students, Pascoe found that calling someone a fag was not about whether someone was or was not gay; instead, it was directed at guys who danced like girls, cared about their clothing, seemed too emotional, or did something incompetent. In other words, white male students directed the epithet at other males who were not considered sufficiently masculine. Gay guys were tolerated as long as they were not effeminate, as long as they could throw a football around. Among the teenagers in Pascoe's study, fag discourse became a powerful tool for enforcing the boundaries of masculinity—a disciplinary mechanism for making sure "boys are boys" through the fear of abuse or violence.

Moreover, Pascoe points out that masculinity is not always associated with men. Girls can act masculine as well. She describes a group of "masculine" girls who play on the girls' basketball team and "perform masculinity" by the way they dress, display their sexuality, and dominate public spaces around the school. Jessie, a lesbian, is also president of the student council and homecoming queen. Her popularity appears to be related to her performance of masculinity. In these contexts, masculinity and dominance are linked to women's bodies, not to men's. Pascoe thus points out the ways in which both guys and girls can perform masculinity and girls can adopt masculinity to gain status (Bridges 2007; Calderwood 2008; Wilkins 2008).

THE PERFORMANCE OF GENDER

gender performance

The way gender identity is expressed through action.

Recently, anthropologists have moved from focusing on gender roles toward examining **gender performance**. Gender roles can mistakenly be seen as reflecting stable, fixed identities that fall in one of two opposite extremes—male or female. But anthropologists increasingly see gender as a continuum of behaviors that range between masculine and feminine. Rather than being something fixed in the psyche, gender is an identity that is expressed through action (Butler 1990).

My students, when identifying stereotypical masculine and feminine characteristics, often create something similar to the following list:

- *Masculine*: aggressive, physical, tough, competitive, sports oriented, testosterone driven, strong, unemotional

- *Feminine*: gentle, kind, loving, nurturing, smart, persuasive, talkative, enticing, emotional

But we know that both women and men can display any of these characteristics. And any individual may display various characteristics at different times depending on the setting. A man may perform his masculinity—his gender—differently when watching football with his buddies than while out on a date.

Indeed, people regularly make choices—conscious and unconscious—about how they will express their gender identity, for whom, and in what context. This is why we say that gender is performed. A man may drive a truck to make a living but also gently change his baby's diapers and take her in a stroller to play in the park. A woman may enjoy sewing dresses for her daughters but also dominate boardroom discussions as CEO of a company.

Machismo in Mexico. The construction of masculinity does not necessarily yield a rigid result, as the following study reveals. In *The Meanings of Macho* (2007), Matthew Gutmann examines what it means to be a man, *ser hombre*, for the men and women of a small neighborhood in Mexico City. Common understandings of *machismo* as the concept has spread around the world feature stereotypes of self-centered, sexist, tough guys. When macho is applied to men in Latin America, especially working-class Mexican men, these stereotypes can also include insinuations of violence, drug use, infidelity, and gambling. However, Gutmann's research in a working-class community reveals a complex male world of fathers, husbands, friends, and lovers that does not fit the common stereotypes.

For the men whom Gutmann studied, machismo and masculinity constitute a shifting landscape. What it means to be a man (or a woman) in the community can depend on the particular man or woman or the particular circumstance. One of Gutmann's key informants, the elderly Don Timo, rails against effeminate

MAP 7.1
Mexico City

What does it mean to be macho? A couple and their baby on a stroll in Mexico City.

men but has himself crossed stereotypical gender boundaries by actively helping to raise his children. Two other informants, Tono and Gabriel, who are tough young men, argue about a father's proper role in buying children's Christmas presents. These examples illustrate the fluidity of male identity in the population that Gutmann studied.

Ultimately, Guttmann discovered such complex male identities that he found it impossible to use any simple formula to describe a typical Mexican man, a Mexican urban working-class man, or a macho Mexican. Instead he found the men in the community he studied to be working out their roles together with women, debating and deciding about household chores, child rearing, sex, the use of money, work outside the home, and the use of alcohol (Limon 1997; Parker 1999). How do these processes take place in your own family?

Viewing gender as performance enables us to broaden our thinking beyond easy dichotomies and universal characteristics of "man" and "woman." Anthropological research suggests that rather than looking for some essential male or female nature rooted in biology that shapes everything from personality to economic activity, a more fruitful exploration must consider both the ways biology and culture shape one another and the ways in which ideas of gender are constructed and performed in response to each culture's gender norms and expectations. In so doing, gender can be seen less as a naturally limiting framework and more as a set of fluid constructs that can be changed over time. By taking this approach, we can more easily see that stratification based on gender is not fixed and natural; rather, it emerges as a result of decisions to arrange access to power, privilege, and resources in particular ways.

Are There More Than Two Sexes?

As our earlier discussion of sexual dimorphism indicated, primary characteristics of biological sex do not always fit neatly into the two assumed categories of male and female. Moreover, even when we can identify a person's biological sex, we cannot predict what roles that person will play in a given culture. The sections that follow make these points abundantly clear.

A THEORY OF FIVE SEXES

Biologist Anne Fausto-Sterling (1993) has proposed a theory that sheds light on the issue of fluidity versus rigidity in conceptualizing categories of biological sex and how they relate to gender identity. In her article "The Five Sexes: Why Male and Female Are Not Enough," Fausto-Sterling describes the middle ground between these two absolute categories. This middle ground encompasses a diversity of physical expressions along the continuum between male and female that are described as **intersex**.

A review of medical data from 1955 to 2000 suggests that "approximately 1.7% of all live births do not conform to [the] ideal of absolute sex chromosome, gonadal, genital and hormonal dimorphism" (Blackless et al. 2000, 151). Using these statistics, we may estimate that millions of people are born with some combination of male and female genitalia, gonads, and chromosomes. Some have a balance of female and male sexual characteristics—for instance, one testis and one ovary. Others have female genitalia but testes rather than ovaries. Still others have male genitalia with ovaries rather than testes.

Most Western societies ignore the existence of middle sexes. More commonly, they legally require a determination between male and female at birth. Furthermore, since the 1960s, Western medicine has taken the extreme steps of attempting to "manage" intersexuality through surgery and hormonal treatments. According to the 2000 American Academy of Pediatrics policy statement on intersex surgery, "the birth of a child with ambiguous genitalia constitutes a social emergency" (American Academy of Pediatrics 2000, 138). Medical procedures—most performed before a child comes of age and can decide for him- or herself—aim to return intersex infants to the cultural norm for heterosexual males and females, although about 90 percent of the surgeries make ambiguous male anatomy into female. Decisions are often based on the size of the penis: The smaller the phallus, the more likely the surgery will reassign the person as female. These interventions represent what French social scientist Michel Foucault ([1976] 1990) has referred to as *biopower*—the power of the state to regulate the body—in this case through control of biological sex characteristics to meet a cultural need for clear distinctions between the sexes.

These medical interventions have faced increasing criticism both within the medical profession and among advocacy and support groups such as the Intersex Society of North America (www.isna.org), the AIS-DSD support group (www.aisdsd.org), and InterACT: Advocates for Intersex Youth (www.interact advocates.org). Such groups have worked to educate the public and the medical community about the experiences of intersex people, particularly about their right to control decisions about their sexual and gender identities. In 2006, *Pediatrics*, the journal of the American Academy of Pediatrics, published new guidelines that urge practicing greater patient-centered care, avoiding "elective" surgery until the person is old enough to make his or her own decision, and eliminating misleading and outdated language (such as *hermaphrodite*) that distracts from treating the whole person.

The presence of middle sexes suggests that we must reconceptualize one of our most rigid mental maps of reality—the one separating male and female. In the process, perhaps we will recognize that just as gender is culturally

intersex

The state of being born with a combination of male and female genitalia, gonads, and/or chromosomes.

Hindu religious myth, art, and ritual acknowledge alternative gender constructions like this depiction of Ardhanari, an androgynous deity composed of Shiva and his consort Shakti.

transgender
A gender identity or performance that does not fit with cultural norms related to one's assigned sex at birth.

constructed, even our ideas of human biology have been culturally constructed as well. Acknowledgment of a diversity of physical expressions along the continuum between male and female may, in turn, allow for a less dualistic and more holistic approach to understanding the complex relationship between biology and gender (Davis 2015).

ALTERNATE SEXES, ALTERNATE GENDERS

Cross-cultural studies show that not every culture fixes sexuality and gender in two distinct categories. Many cultures allow room for diversity. For example, even though India's dominant system for mapping sex and gender strongly emphasizes two opposite but complementary roles (male and female), Indian culture also recognizes many alternative constructions. Hindu religion acknowledges these variations in myth, art, and ritual. Hindu myths feature androgynous and intersex figures, and Hindu art depicts a blending of sexes and genders, including males with wombs, breasts, or pregnant bellies. In terms of Hindu ritual, the following discussion explores the role of one alternative group, known as *hijras*, in expressing gender diversity in India.

The Role of *Hijras* in Hindu Ritual. *Hijras* are religious followers of the Hindu Mother Goddess, Bahuchara Mata, who is often depicted and described as transgender. (The term **transgender** refers to individuals whose gender identities or performances do not fit with cultural norms related to their assigned sex at birth.) Most *hijras* are born as men, though some may be intersex. In *Neither Man nor Woman: The Hijras of India* (1998) and subsequent writing, Serena Nanda has analyzed these individuals and their role in demonstrating gender diversity.

Through ritual initiation and, for some, extensive ritual surgery to remove penis and testicles (an operation now outlawed in India), *hijras* become an alternative sex and gender. Culturally they are viewed as neither man nor woman, although they tend to adopt many characteristics of the woman's role. They dress, walk, and talk like women and may have sex with men. Because of their transgression of cultural and religious boundaries, they are at once both feared and revered. Many live in *hijra* religious communities on the margins of Hindu society. *Hijras* often face extreme discrimination in employment, housing, health, and education. Many support themselves through begging, ritual performances, and sex work. Violence against them is not uncommon, particularly against *hijra* sex workers.

At the same time, *hijras* are revered as auspicious and powerful ritual figures. They perform at weddings and at birth celebrations—particularly at the birth of a son. Not only do they bless the child and family, they also entertain the celebrants and guests with burlesque and sexually suggestive songs, dance, and comedy. Their life in the middle ground between strong cultural norms of male and female contributes to their ritual power (Nanda 1998). These insights underscore the potential for more complex understandings of sex and gender that move beyond assumptions of two discrete categories of male and female, masculine and feminine.

Two-Spirits in Native North American Cultures.

According to accounts written over the past one hundred years, many Native North American cultures have had traditions of gender diversity. Such traditions have allowed a gender alternative described in the older anthropological literature as *berdache* and now more commonly referred to as Two-Spirits (Roscoe 1991; Williams 1992). Some of these transgender men and women adopted roles and behaviors of the opposite gender. In certain cases, people considered them to have both feminine and masculine spirits. Often they were considered to have supernatural powers and thus held special privileges in the community.

In recent years the term *berdache*, introduced by French colonialists, has fallen into disrepute among scholars and activists. Since 1990 the term *Two-Spirits*, a direct borrowing from the Ojibwa language, has risen in popular and scholarly usage after being proposed by participants in the Third Native American/ First Nations Gay and Lesbian Conference in Winnepeg, Canada. No common term exists across Native cultures for alternative gender patterns, nor are the historical or contemporary practices indicated by these terms by any means uniform. Instead, many different terms have served to represent local expressions of alternative gender and sexuality among Native Americans—for example, *winkte* (Sioux), *kwido* (Tewa), and *nadleeh* (Navajo) (Jacobs 1997).

Current studies of sex and gender diversity in contemporary Native American communities attempt to de-romanticize the accounts offered by

Steven Barrios (*left*), a leader of Montana's Two Spirit Society, works to eliminate homophobia among Native Americans. Caitlyn Jenner (*right*), a transgender woman, was a public figure for four decades as Bruce Jenner, Olympic decathlon champion and reality show personality. Her public transition from male-identified to female-identified has brought increased visibility to the often difficult and violent experiences of transgender women and men and other gender noncomforming people in the United States.

earlier anthropologists, historians, and other social scientists of a tolerant Native American life for those who were not heterosexual. These idealized views do not match the experiences of many gay, lesbian, transgender, transsexual, or Two-Spirit Native Americans today who have experienced homophobia rather than acceptance both within and beyond their Native American communities (Jacobs 1997).

How Do Anthropologists Explore the Relationship between Gender and Power?

Although gender may often be regarded as affecting individuals on a personal basis—for instance, how you negotiate relationships with people you date, study with, or work for—anthropologists also explore how gender structures relationships of power that have far-reaching effects. Understanding these processes becomes increasingly important as individuals and cultures experience heightened interaction in today's global age (Mascia-Lees 2009).

In September 2015, the United Nations announced the establishment of its fifteen-year Sustainable Development Goals, including its Goal 5: Achieve Gender Equality and Empower all Women and Girls (United Nations 2015b). Within this goal the signatory nations committed to:

- End all forms of discrimination against women and girls.
- Eliminate violence against all women and girls, including trafficking and sexual and other types of exploitation.
- Eliminate child, early, and forced marriage and female genital mutilation.
- Recognize and value unpaid care and domestic work.
- Ensure equal opportunities for women's leadership at all levels of public decision making.
- Ensure universal access to sexual and reproductive health and reproductive rights.
- Undertake reforms to give women equal rights to economic resources.
- Enhance the use of information and communications technology to empower women.
- Adopt and strengthen policies and legislation for gender equality and empowerment of all women and girls.

A quick look at some statistics reveals the current contours of women's struggles worldwide: Sixty percent of the world's poorest people are women and girls. Over half of all children unable to attend school are girls. The chance of dying because of pregnancy in sub-Saharan Africa is 1 in 196, but in the developed world it is only 1 in 6,250. Young women ages fifteen to twenty-five are being infected with HIV/AIDS three times faster than men in the same age group. Women are disproportionally affected by environmental degradation. And less than 22 percent of the world's parliamentarians are women (United Nations Development Programme 2015). It is not hard to conclude from these facts that gender plays a key role in power relationships on many levels and in many arenas.

REVISITING EARLY RESEARCH ON MALE DOMINANCE

As gender studies emerged in anthropology in the 1970s, one of the first targets of research was the apparent universality of male dominance across cultures. In searching for an explanation for what appeared to be women's universally low status, anthropologist Sherri Ortner (1974) proposed the existence of a pervasive, symbolic association of women with nature and men with culture (which was more highly valued). Ortner argued that the biological functions of reproduction, breast-feeding, and child rearing associated women with nature and placed them at a consistent disadvantage in negotiating relationships of power.

At the same time, Michelle Rosaldo (1974) saw the gender roles of men and women across cultures as being split between public and private spheres. Women, constrained by their role in reproduction, were confined to the private, or domestic, sphere—including the home, family, and childbearing. Men tended to dominate the public sphere—politics, economic exchange, and religious ritual. Because wealth and social status accrued to activities in the public sphere, men gained and maintained more power, privilege, and prestige than women did. Some scholars speculated that these patterns were rooted in the human evolutionary past—a proposition we will challenge later in this chapter. Others suggested that they might derive from men's superior physical strength (see also Chodorow 1974).

As scholars looked more carefully at women's lives in particular cultures, however, the picture became even more complicated. Previous assumptions about universal male dominance, including the gendered division of labor and uniformly separate spheres of activity and power, were revealed to be historically inaccurate, overly simplistic in their reading of contemporary cultures, and prone to overlook the specific contexts of stratification and inequality (Leacock 1981). This was true not only for women's lives but for men's as well, where wealth,

In contrast to Malinowski's earlier study (1922), why did feminist anthropologist Annette Weiner's research (1976) find Trobriand Island women engaged in significant economic activity, including the elaborate exchange of banana leaf bundles and banana fiber skirts (*left*), as well as participation in the yam harvest festival (*right*)?

MAP 7.2
Trobriand Islands

power, and prestige were stratified both within and between gender groups (Quinn 1977; Rosaldo 1980).

Feminist scholars also began to revisit earlier anthropological research. Perhaps not surprisingly, these scholars discovered the significant role of women in cultures that earlier anthropologists had reported to be uniformly dominated by men. In one important reconsideration of a classic anthropological text, Annette Weiner (1976) revisited Bronislaw Malinowski's (1922) research on the Trobriand Islands, an archipelago of coral atolls just east of Papua New Guinea in the South Pacific. When Weiner reexamined the economic practices of the Trobriand Islands in the 1970s with an eye to the role of gender in shaping economic activity, she found that Malinowski's research was incomplete. Women in fact engaged in an elaborate economic activity that Malinowski had failed to recognize.

The emerging anthropological scholarship of gender in the 1970s provided new tools for Weiner to overcome gender blindness and, instead, see the fullness of Trobriand culture. She wrote:

> Any study that does not include the role of women—as seen by women—as part of the way the society is structured remains only a partial study of that society. Whether women are publicly valued or privately secluded, whether they control politics, a range of economic commodities, or merely magic spells, they function within that society, not as objects, but as individuals with some measure of control. (Weiner 1976, 228)

Weiner's example and admonition resonate throughout anthropology today.

GENDER STEREOTYPES, GENDER IDEOLOGY, AND GENDER STRATIFICATION

The emphasis in gender studies on the cultural construction of gender challenges anthropologists to explore the dynamics of specific cultures to understand what processes serve to construct gender in each society. Today anthropologists are asking questions like these: What are the processes that create **gender stratification**—an unequal distribution of power in which gender shapes who has access to a group's resources, opportunities, rights, and privileges? What are the gender stereotypes and gender ideologies that support a gendered system of power (Brodkin 2007)?

Gender stereotypes are widely held and powerful, preconceived notions about the attributes of, differences between, and proper roles for women and men in a culture. Men, for instance, may be stereotyped as more aggressive, whereas women might be seen as more nurturing. These stereotypes create important assumptions about what men and women might expect from one another. **Gender ideology** is a set of cultural ideas—usually stereotypical—about men's and women's essential character, capabilities, and value that consciously or unconsciously promote and justify gender stratification. Gender stereotypes and ideologies vary from culture to culture, though their effects may appear similar when viewed through a global lens.

We now consider two examples of the ways in which gender ideologies have influenced thinking in U.S. culture.

The Egg and the Sperm.

The Egg and the Sperm. Emily Martin (1991) has explored the ways in which cultural ideas about gender—that is, gender ideologies—have influenced the way biologists have understood, described, and taught about human reproduction. In particular, Martin discusses what she calls the fairy tale of the egg and the sperm. By examining the most widely used college biology textbooks at the time of her research, Martin found that the distinct roles of eggs and sperm were described in stereotypical ways, even if those descriptions did not match up with more recent scientific findings.

The textbooks described the aggressive sperm as being propelled by strongly beating tails searching for the egg in competition with fellow ejaculates attacking and penetrating the protective barriers of the egg to fertilize the passive, waiting, receiving egg.

Yet Martin cites biology research that reveals a very different dynamic. The tail of the sperm actually beats quite weakly and does not propel the sperm forward. Instead the tail serves only to move the head from side to side enough to keep it from getting stuck on all surfaces except the egg. When the egg and the sperm do connect, the sperm is not the assertive aggressor. Rather, adhesive molecules on both create a chemical bond that keeps them attached. Then the sperm and egg work in tandem. The sperm secretes a dissolving fluid that allows it to move toward the egg's nucleus. At the same time, the egg draws the sperm in

gender stratification

An unequal distribution of power in which gender shapes who has access to a group's resources, opportunities, rights, and privileges.

gender stereotypes

Widely held preconceived notions about the attributes of, differences between, and proper roles for men and women in a culture.

gender ideology

A set of cultural ideas, usually stereotypical, about the essential character of different genders that functions to promote and justify gender stratification.

Are the stories you have been told about the meeting of the sperm (blue) and egg drawn from biological research or cultural gender stereotypes?

and actually moves its own nucleus to meet the sperm and better enable fertilization. Thus, rather than displaying active and passive roles, the egg and the sperm appear to be mutually active partners in an egalitarian relationship.

According to Martin, writing in the early 1990s, images of the egg and sperm found in popular and scientific writing have been commonly based on cultural stereotypes of male and female. Moreover, the scientific language of biology has promoted these gender stereotypes. Men are considered more active, vigorous, adventurous, and important than women, who are seen as passive, receptive, nurturing, and less valuable and significant. Martin warns that by reading stereotypical feminine and masculine behavior into our accounts of eggs and sperm, we enshrine these gender roles in nature—we make them seem natural. In turn, when this narrative becomes a common description of nature, it reinforces culturally constructed gender patterns, roles, and hierarchies. It is possible to express the effect of such a process of misinformation in this (mistaken) way: "Of course those characteristics of men and women are natural and normal—they show up at the very beginning with the behavior of the sperm and the egg!"

Martin also warns of the social risks of attributing human personalities to eggs and sperm—for instance, describing them like a human couple engaged in deliberate human activity to make a baby. U.S. culture continues to debate when "life" begins—at fertilization, at viability, or at birth. Describing the egg and sperm as engaged in intentional action—a key criterion for personhood—risks opening the door to more scrutiny of pregnant women and restriction of their health choices, from amniocentesis to abortion to fetal surgeries.

Man the Hunter, Woman the Gatherer. Another familiar story that lies at the heart of U.S. gender ideologies is the tale of Man the Hunter, Woman the Gatherer. This fiction is frequently invoked to explain contemporary differences in gender roles by referencing the effects of human evolution. In our deep past, the story goes, human males—being larger and stronger than females—hunted to sustain themselves, their sexual partners, and their offspring (Lee and Devore 1968). Hunting required aggression, inventiveness, dominant behavior, male bonding, mobility, time away from the home, and less time with offspring—all patterns that we imagine have become hardwired into the human brain or imprinted on the human DNA. The ancient pleasure of killing animals supposedly shaped the human male psyche for aggression and violence and continues to drive men today. Women, in contrast, were gatherers (Dahlberg 1981). They collected fruits, seeds, and nuts and were more sedentary, home oriented, child centered, nurturing, cooperative, talkative, and passive.

This story, closely associated today with the field of evolutionary psychology, underlies much contemporary thinking about the origins and "naturalness" of gender relations. Contemporary gender roles, division of labor, and stratification of power, resources, rights, and privileges are assumed to have emerged directly

Ancient petroglyphs (rock carvings) discovered in the mountains north of the Saudi Arabian city of Hael appear to depict a hunting party. Were they men, as the hunter-gatherer stereotype would suggest?

from physical or mental differences that developed during human evolution. So, for instance, because early human males were hunters two million years ago, today modern human men prefer to go off to work, compete in the marketplace, and leave child rearing and housecleaning to the women. Quite simple, really—or is it?

Despite the popularity of this scenario in explaining contemporary male and female behavior, anthropological evidence does not support it. Yes, food foraging—hunting, scavenging, and gathering—was our ancestors' primary survival strategy for millions of years before the introduction of agriculture 10,000 years ago. Hundreds of thousands of people still live in societies where food foraging is a significant means of making a living. But no contemporary foraging societies or nonhuman primate groups display the division of labor described in the Man the Hunter, Woman the Gatherer story. In known foraging societies, women are not sedentary or passive members of the group (Stange 1997).

Though men appear to have done 70 percent of the hunting, it is not even clear that hunting was the foundational activity of early human groups. In fact, human patterns of group interaction more likely developed through the gathering and sharing of plant and seed resources. Archaeological evidence reveals that early hominid teeth were adapted to an omnivorous diet—most likely of plants, seeds, and meat, depending on what food was available in a particular season or area. Hunting would have contributed to this foundation when available, rather than the reverse. Meat may have been a part of the diet, but there is no conclusive evidence that our earliest human ancestors hunted prey themselves. Just as likely, they scavenged meat left behind by other predators (Fedigan 1986).

Anthropologists find no evidence to prove the existence of historical patterns of male dominance, including the protection of dependent women and children. Instead contemporary food-foraging cultures and the archaeological record on gender roles reveal a highly flexible division of labor that enabled human groups to quickly adapt to changing conditions. In fact, a flexibility of roles rather than a clear division of labor may more properly define the key characteristic of male-female relationships over human evolutionary history. Based on the evidence currently available, Man the Hunter, Woman the Gatherer—much like Martin's description of the fairy tale of the egg and the sperm—appears to be a modern-day cultural myth about gender projected back onto human evolutionary history that serves to imbue contemporary gender patterns with an appearance of inevitability and "naturalness" (Fedigan 1986).

Despite the archaeological, physical, and cultural evidence that anthropologists have accumulated to debunk the Man the Hunter, Woman the Gatherer myth, it is still a daunting task to shake free of the popular idea in U.S. culture that men and women have some essential—and essentially different—nature that was shaped in our deep past. The stereotypical "boys will be boys" and "that's just a girl thing" approach to gender differences has become a powerful gender ideology, deeply ingrained in the day-to-day conversations, expectations, relationships, work patterns, pay packages, promotions, and political activities of contemporary life.

Perhaps it is simpler to believe that our genetic blueprint predetermines who we are as men and women. Perhaps this belief in the inevitability of gendered cultural patterns makes us feel better about the gender inequality structured into our cultural practices and institutions. Why try to change what is "inevitable and natural"? But if these cultural ways of thinking about gender mask the essential changeability of gender, then the burden lies more heavily on the individual, the community, and the body politic to challenge patterns of power, privilege, and prestige drawn along gender lines.

CHALLENGING GENDER IDEOLOGIES AND STRATIFICATION

Women challenge and resist gender stereotypes, ideologies, inequalities, and violence directly and indirectly through creative local strategies, often building movements from the bottom up. Although lacking the global media attention or global solidarity afforded to international social movements, these local initiatives begin with women's culture-specific experiences (Abu-Lughod 2000). The following example provides a dramatic illustration of women challenging gender ideology, stratification, and violence.

MAP 7.3
El Salvador

Mothers of "The Disappeared" in El Salvador. Between 1977 and 1992, the Central American country of El Salvador was torn by a brutal civil war. Threatened by calls for economic equality and political openness, the government unleashed military and military-related death squads in a campaign of violence and terror that targeted students, peasants, union leaders, and anyone else critical of its policies. All who expressed opposition to government policies were labeled subversive and subject to reprisal.

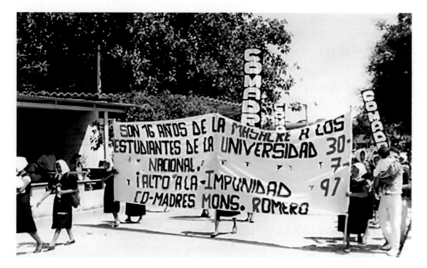

The Mothers of "The Disappeared" march in El Salvador to protest the military's practices of assassination, imprisonment, torture, rape, and "disappearance."

Over the course of the civil war the military assassinated, imprisoned, tortured, raped, and "disappeared" tens of thousands of El Salvadorans. One in every one hundred was murdered or disappeared. The late 1970s were marked by particularly violent campaigns. Every morning, residents of the capital city awoke to the sight of dead bodies—visibly tortured—left lying in the streets or dumped on the outskirts of town by the death squads. Many were disappeared—that is, detained and never seen again.

The grassroots women's organization CO-MADRES (The Committee of Mothers and Relatives of Political Prisoners, Disappeared, and Assassinated of El Salvador) emerged against this backdrop. The committee was one of a number of "motherist" groups across Central America in which the mothers of victims mobilized for human rights and against violence. Originally founded in 1977 by nine mothers, CO-MADRES quickly grew to include teachers, workers, students, lawyers, housewives, and shopkeepers—still mostly mothers, but with a few fathers as well. CO-MADRES became one of the first groups in El Salvador to challenge the brutal actions of the government and the military.

Initially, the women of CO-MADRES focused on demanding information from government, military, and paramilitary groups about family members who had been incarcerated, assassinated, or disappeared. The women occupied government buildings, demonstrated in public parks and plazas, and held hunger strikes to exert pressure on the state. Searching for their missing relatives, they demanded access to prisons and prisoner lists, uncovered clandestine cemeteries, and formed alliances with international human rights groups to publicize the El Salvadoran government's atrocities.

As they became better organized, the women of CO-MADRES began to participate in movements for greater democratization, particularly demanding the inclusion of women at all levels of El Salvador's political decision-making bodies. Eventually, along with other feminist movements emerging globally, CO-MADRES began to address concerns about the prevalence of gender-based violence and rape and the absence of sex education and sexual autonomy for women in El Salvador.

CO-MADRES continued to work throughout the period of the El Salvadoran civil war despite attacks on the organization and its leaders by the government and its allies. CO-MADRES offices were bombed on multiple occasions. A majority of active CO-MADRES members and all of its leaders were detained, tortured, and raped: forty-eight were detained, five assassinated, and three disappeared. In El Salvador, rape became a common experience for the women activists of CO-MADRES and for urban and rural Salvadoran women, whether they participated in a social movement or not.

CO-MADRES activist Alicia Panameno de Garcia, in an interview with anthropologist Lynn Stephen, shared how rape had become a widely used weapon of state-sponsored torture and how psychologically difficult it was to talk about it openly, even with other women victims:

ALICIA: Rape was one of those things we didn't really think about. We weren't really prepared for it happening to us. We didn't think that the military would systematically be using these practices. So the first few women were detained and they were raped and because we are taught that women are supposed to be pure, they didn't talk about that. They didn't say, "They did this to me."

L.S: They didn't talk about it?

ALICIA: Yes. But little by little we discovered it. The women started talking about it. They had to because it had consequences for their health. They needed medical assistance and when we would give people medical aid we started discovering that every one of the women had been raped. (Stephen 1995, 818)

Over time, the CO-MADRES members found that detained men were also being raped as part of their torture. The men were even more reluctant to talk about it than the women.

Eventually, CO-MADRES created a space for women to publicly discuss their experiences, to bring the sexual brutality of the military out into the open, and to talk about their fears—particularly that their husbands would abandon them. Working with other human rights organizations, the group began a process to hold the state accountable for these violations and call into question discriminatory legal codes that provided no rights to rape victims.

The story of CO-MADRES is just one example of the determined, creative, and often risk-filled efforts that women undertake across the globe to address gendered expressions of inequality, stratification, and violence. In an evolving response to their experiences in the midst of El Salvador's civil war, the women of CO-MADRES created a social movement that integrated traditional cultural expressions of femininity—ideas of motherhood, child rearing, and sacrifice for one's children—with direct confrontation of military death squads and government authorities as they demanded equality for women and sought to protect their families and their communities (Martin 1999; Molyneux 1999; Stephen 1995).

How Is Globalization Transforming Gender Roles and Stratification?

Beginning in the 1980s, anthropologists turned their attention to the impact of globalization on women and gender dynamics in local economies. Flexible accumulation—relocation of the production process both through offshoring factories and outsourcing jobs—has spurred increasing migration of women from rural areas to work in urban, coastal, export-oriented factories established by foreign corporations searching for cheap labor, low taxes, and few environmental regulations. As both local and national economies have continued to undergo rapid transitions, these women have had to negotiate between traditional gender expectations and the pressure to engage in wage labor to support themselves and their families (Mills 2003).

IMPACTS ON WOMEN IN THE LABOR FORCE

Working women in various parts of the globe have experienced similar challenges at the volatile intersection of globalization and local realities (Fernandez-Kelly 1983; Mills 2003; Ong 1987; Safa 1995).

Carla Freeman's *High Tech and High Heels in the Global Economy* (2000) explores the gendered production processes in export factories on the Caribbean island of Barbados. Women work in the *informatics* industry: They do computer data entry of airline tickets and insurance claims, and they key in manuscripts for everything from romance novels to academic journals. Instead of toiling in garment or electronics sweatshops, these women enjoy working in cool, air-conditioned, modern offices. Freeman asks whether the comfortable conditions in the data-processing factories establish an improved position in the global economy for Barbadian women, or whether this new factory formation is simply another expression of women's exploitation through flexible accumulation.

Key distinctions separate the Barbadian informatics workers from women working in export-processing factories in other countries. They enjoy improved work conditions. As wives, mothers, and heads of households, rather than young, single, temporary sweatshop workers, they have won concessions from the company that

MAP 7.4
Barbados

include transportation, higher levels of job security, and more flexible work hours to care for their families. Freeman labels these women "pink-collar" workers because they fall between the blue-collar work done on the sweatshop factory floor and the white-collar work carried out in the higher-wage environment of the front office.

Despite the improved working conditions and social status for Barbadian women working in informatics, the company owners strive to extract maximum efficiency from them. Supervisors walk the floor and observe through glass windows to ensure continual surveillance. Managers calculate the keystrokes of each computer terminal. Wages are no higher than those of the typical sweatshop worker and in some cases are lower. The skills of data entry are not transferable to higher-wage clerical work. Women often need to take on additional work sewing, selling in the market, or working in beauty salons to support their families.

Freeman explores the ways in which the Barbadian women express their agency in the face of the informatics factory controls. These women use their status working with computers in air-conditioned offices to negotiate a different class status in the local community. They use clothing to fashion their local identities as well. Indeed, the women workers are preoccupied with fashion: They wear colorful, tailored skirt-suits with jewelry, high heels, and the latest hairstyles. With their clothes, these women perform a professional and modern gender identity that enhances their local reputations and distinguishes them from other low-wage workers in garment and textile factories.

Freeman's research adds to scholarly findings that women factory workers are not simply victims of the exploitative practices of flexible accumulation. Instead, by engaging these capitalist practices directly, women assert their own desires and goals in ways that transform the interaction between the local and the global (England 2002; Richman 2001).

Globalization is reshaping the lives of working women as corporations search the world for cheap labor, low taxes, and fewer environmental restrictions. But are women reshaping globalization? Here, women labor in an international call center in Barbados.

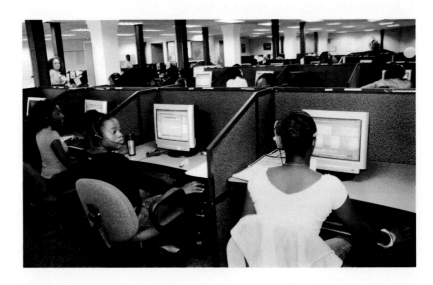

GENDERED PATTERNS OF GLOBAL MIGRATION

Globalization spurs the migration of women within and between countries seeking to support themselves and their families. Tens of millions of women each year leave their homes and travel to urban areas to seek jobs in cities and export-processing factories in their own countries. Millions more leave developing countries in search of work abroad to support their families back home. As an alternative to finding jobs in export-processing factories, many women immigrants work as nannies, cleaning ladies, maids, or home health aides, filling the shortage of what is known as "care work" in wealthier countries. (Ehrenreich and Hochschild 2004; Hondagneu-Sotelo 2001).

Pei-chia Lan's (2006) study of Filipino and Indonesian care workers laboring for newly rich families in Taiwan reveals the ways women—both employers and workers, madams and maids—create new flows of global migration that destabilize traditional gendered and patriarchal roles in surprising ways.

As Taiwan's economy has expanded, first-generation Taiwanese career women, many from newly middle-class, dual-income families, have opted to meet their traditional filial and patriarchal family obligations as mother, wife, and daughter-in-law by hiring transnational migrant women domestic workers to do what was expected of their mothers in previous generations. The care work of Filipino and Indonesian women—allows them to move into the male workforce while still satisfying traditional expectations of womanhood.

MAP 7.5
Taiwan, the
Philippines, and
Indonesia

In contrast, Filipino and Indonesian women convert their transnational migration and domestic labor into remittances that provide the major source of support for families at home. In the process, they assert new status roles as primary breadwinner, though their absence—often for years at a time—severely limits their ability to fulfill more traditional roles of mother, wife, and daughter. Lan calls these immigrant domestic workers "global Cinderellas"—women who dream of escaping poverty and finding freedom through care work abroad, yet whose emancipation is built upon oppression and exploitation within their employer's home.

Anthropologists, whether studying gender, sexuality, kinship, race, ethnicity, religion, or any other cultural construct, seek to understand the rich diversity of human bodies and human lives, both past and present, to unlock the presuppositions that reside in mental maps of reality. As we analyze gender, we strive to unmask the structures of power that create unequal opportunities and unequal access to rights and resources along gender lines. These inequalities are far from natural, essential aspects of human life and human community. Rather, they are cultural constructs established in specific historical moments and cultural contexts. Through a careful analysis and exposure of gender as a culturally constructed system of power—not fixed and natural patterns of human relationship—anthropologists hope to participate in opening possibilities for all humans to live to their full potential.

Toolkit

Thinking Like an Anthropologist:
Broadening Your View of the Cultural Construction of Gender

In the chapter opener, we considered the intersection of gender and power in the U.S. military reflected in the experience of Captain Kristen Griest and Lieutenant Shaye Haver, the first women to complete the United States Army Ranger School. Their story illuminates larger dynamics at work throughout the U.S. military and other cultural institutions as expectations of the roles of men and women, the performances of femininity and masculinity, and stratification along the lines of gender undergo dramatic shifts and changes. The December 2015 opening of combat roles to women did not resolve these tensions in the military. Despite dramatic increases in the number of women serving in the U.S. military and the opening of most military jobs to women, over the past few years the military has been engulfed in a major scandal at the intersection of gender and power. According to a 2014 study by the Rand Corporation commissioned by the U.S. military, as many as 5 percent of active-duty women have been sexually assaulted, as have 1 percent of men. The study also found that women soldiers are so reluctant to report these crimes that only 25 percent of these cases come to light and 62 percent of women who do report sexual assaults say they face retaliation within their units for doing so. Others assume that the military justice system, in which commanding officers, primarily men, decide whether cases should go to a court-martial, will not treat them fairly. Eventually, the report found, 90 percent of assault victims are involuntarily discharged.

Why is this kind of gender-based violence so prevalent in the U.S. military or anywhere in U.S. culture? What are the underlying assumptions about gender—what it means to be a man or woman, boy or girl, masculine or feminine—that lead to power being exercised in these destructive ways? And why does such a powerful institution allow it to continue?

As you reflect on these issues, consider how the big questions that have organized this chapter may help you analyze the situation more deeply:

- **Are men and women born or made?**

- **Are there more than two sexes?**

- How do anthropologists explore the relationship between gender and power?

- How is globalization transforming gender roles and stratification?

Anthropologists consider gender to be a central element in every aspect of human culture, including education, the workplace, sexuality, health, family, religion, politics, sports, and individual identity formation. Throughout this chapter we have explored how anthropologists examine the complex role of gender in crucial contemporary debates, social movements, and political struggles around the world.

Having read this chapter, are you able to take a fresh look at gender in your own life? Perhaps you can begin to see how unique cultural expectations of femininity and masculinity have shaped your ways of thinking and behaving—your interactions with family, friends, romantic interests, classmates, and coworkers. Perhaps you can see how culturally constructed notions of gender have been replicated in patterns of inequality in cultural institutions ranging from education to the workplace. And perhaps you can imagine how stereotypes and gender ideologies like the sperm and the egg or Man the Hunter, Woman the Gatherer provide the rationale for maintaining patterns of inequality and stratification. Try to go through the next week with these tools in your anthropological toolkit and see how your view of the world, particularly the gendered world, might be transformed.

Key Terms

gender studies (p. 178)

sex (p. 179)

gender (p. 179)

sexual dimorphism (p. 179)

cultural construction of gender (p. 181)

masculinity (p. 182)

femininity (p. 182)

gender performance (p. 184)

intersex (p. 187)

transgender (p. 188)

gender stratification (p. 193)

gender stereotypes (p. 193)

gender ideology (p. 193)

Chapter 8
Sexuality

At Columbia University's graduation ceremony in May 2015, Emma Sulkowicz lugged a 50-pound, dark blue, extra-long twin mattress across the platform to receive her diploma. Carrying the mattress—the kind Columbia uses in its dorms—was the final act of a nine-month-long senior project for her visual arts degree called "Carry That Weight," designed to protest the university's refusal to expel the male student she accused of raping her in her dorm room. She carried the mattress with her wherever she went on campus all year. By her own rules she was not allowed to ask for help carrying it, though she was allowed to accept help when offered. The *New York Times* art critic Roberta Smith (2014) described the performance as "a woman with a mattress, refusing to keep her violation private, carrying with her a stark reminder of where it took place."

Following Sulkowicz's lead, in October 2014 Columbia students carried twenty-eight mattresses onto campus, one for each of the plaintiffs who had filed a federal

Emma Sulkowicz, a Columbia University student, carried a mattress across campus for nine months to protest the university's lack of action after she reported being raped during her sophomore year.

Title IX complaint alleging that the university discouraged students from reporting sexual assault, that sanctions were too lenient, and that perpetrators were not removed from campus, leaving survivors to encounter their attackers in dormitories and classrooms. The students were fined $471 to clean up the mattresses left outside the president's home. By November, a group called Carry That Weight organized a national day of action during which students carried mattresses on 130 campuses, joining an increasingly effective anti-rape movement that is working to shatter the silence about widespread sexual assaults and demand that colleges and universities provide safe campus environments.

Surveys reveal that as many as one in five women will experience some form of assault while a college student (Fisher, Daigle, and Cullen 2010; Sanday 1990). In response, college administrations are scrambling to address the crisis, under mandate by Title IX of the Education Amendments of 1972 to ensure gender equality in federally funded institutions. In September 2014 the University of California instituted an affirmative consent policy for sexual encounters between students on all of its campuses. Such policies, originally pioneered by Antioch College in Ohio in the early 1990s, require more explicit communication between sexual partners, including a clear "yes" at every step of the encounter. This shift in the standards of consent from "no means no" to "only yes means yes" has now been adopted at over 1,400 institutions of higher education in the United States, reflecting a growing effort to bring the resources of educational institutions to bear on the troubled intersection of sexuality and power in American culture.

What are your own experiences of the intersection of sexuality and power? Have you heard stories like Emma Sulkowicz's on your own college campus? Sexuality is a profound aspect of human life, one that stirs intense emotions, deep anxieties, and rigorous debate. The U.S. population holds widely varying views of where sexuality originates, what constitutes appropriate expressions of sexuality, and what its fundamental purpose is. It is fair to say that our cultural norms and mental maps of reality are in great flux, and have been for several generations, in response to theological shifts, medical advances, and powerful social movements promoting the equality of women and gay, lesbian, bisexual, transgender, and queer individuals.

Sexuality involves more than personal choices about who our sexual partners are and what we do with them. It is also a cultural arena within which our desires are expressed, socialized, and even thwarted. And it is an arena in which people debate ideas of what is moral, appropriate, and "natural" and use those ideas to create unequal access to society's power, privileges, and resources. Indeed, conflicts about sexuality often reveal the intersections of multiple systems of power, including those based on gender, religion, race, class, and kinship.

Anthropologists have a long but uneven history of studying human sexuality. Bronislaw Malinowski (1927, 1929) and Margaret Mead (1928, 1935), like other early anthropologists writing in the 1920s and 1930s, considered human sexuality a key to understanding the cultures they studied, so they wrote extensively about their research findings of sexuality across cultures. Mead's work with young people in the islands of the western Pacific challenged the assumption that U.S. attitudes about gender roles and expressions of sexuality were universal traits immutably fixed in human nature. Rather, anthropological research began to reveal the vast scope and diversity of human sexuality across time and space and the broad arc of potential human sexual expression.

After World War II, however, anthropological interest turned away from explicit attention to sexuality and focused instead on related issues of marriage, kinship, and the family. Since the mid-1980s, sexuality has reemerged as a key concern in anthropology, paralleling a rise of interest in the wider academic community spurred by the successes of the U.S. women's movement and; the emergence of gay and lesbian studies in the 1980s (Weston 1993) and queer theory in the 1990s (Boellstorff 2007; Boellstorff and Howe 2015; Weiss 2011). Recently, anthropological scholarship has more intently considered the diverse expressions of sexuality in cultures worldwide, including Western cultures and the ways those expressions are being shaped by the intersection of local practices and globalization.

In this chapter we will examine the extensive body of work that anthropologists have compiled primarily in this latter period. In particular, we will consider the following questions:

- **What is sexuality and where does it come from?**
- **What is the scope of human sexuality when seen in a global perspective?**
- **How has sexuality been constructed in the United States?**
- **How is sexuality an arena for working out relations of power?**
- **How does globalization influence local expressions of sexuality?**

Despite all the sexuality in the air, especially in the media, Americans often struggle to find a common language with which to discuss it (whether in their personal lives, their families, their communities, the political arena, or the classroom) and often lack the theoretical and analytical frameworks to add depth to emotionally heated conversations. By the end of this chapter you should have a broader understanding of the vast diversity of human sexuality across cultures. You should be able to discuss the role of nature and culture in shaping human sexuality. Furthermore, you should be able to recognize how norms of sexuality are created and used to organize the way cultures work. And you should be able to incorporate anthropological insights as you seek to better understand the role of sexuality in your own life and in your relations with others.

Sexuality is all around us in U.S. culture. Here, a Calvin Klein billboard uses sexuality to sell underwear. Where have you encountered sexuality today?

What Is Sexuality and Where Does It Come From?

Text three friends and ask them to define sexuality. You will most likely get three very different responses. Perhaps this is not surprising in a culture where sexuality is omnipresent but rarely discussed carefully. In 1998, U.S. president Bill Clinton famously said of his liaison with White House intern Monica Lewinsky, "I did not have sexual relations with that woman." He chose those words presumably because he and Lewinsky had not had intercourse. But did they have sex? Such careful word choice by a sitting president giving testimony under oath reveals the challenges of defining behavior that is not only a physiological process but also a cultural construction whose meaning can vary widely.

Consider the following data. A survey of college students in a large midwestern university, with results published in 2006, asked: "Would you say you 'had sex' with someone if the most intimate behavior you engaged in was . . . ?" The survey results showed that even college students do not agree about what "having sex" means. Kissing (2 percent) and petting (3 percent) clearly did not constitute having sex for almost all respondents. Oral "sex" (40 percent) constituted sex for many but not most. For 20 percent of respondents, anal penetration did not constitute having sex. Fully 99.5 percent of respondents indicated that vaginal intercourse did constitute having sex (Sanders and Reinisch 2006). As this study makes evident, even within one population group—college students at one university—there is disagreement over the meaning of the most physical aspects of sexual relations.

For the purposes of this chapter, we will define sexuality from two key perspectives. First, **sexuality** is the complex range of desires, beliefs, and behaviors that are related to erotic physical contact, intimacy, and pleasure. Second, sexuality is the cultural arena within which people debate ideas of what kinds of physical desires and behaviors are morally right, appropriate, and "natural" and use those ideas to create unequal access to status, power, privileges, and resources.

THE INTERSECTION OF SEXUALITY AND BIOLOGY

Clearly, biology plays a key role in shaping sexuality, for sexuality includes distinct physiological processes. But how much of human sexuality is shaped by our nature? As we will see, exactly how our genetic inheritance shapes our desires, attractions, identities, practices, and beliefs is quite complicated and subject to heated debate.

People sometimes think that sexuality is the most "natural" thing in the world. After all, every species must reproduce or face extinction, right? Therefore, many assume that the sexual instincts and behaviors of other animals provide an indication of the natural state of human sexuality unencumbered by the overlays of culture.

Yet research reveals that human sexuality is actually a distinct outlier in the animal kingdom. In his article "The Animal with the Weirdest Sex Life" (1997), scientist and author Jared Diamond suggested that human sexuality is completely abnormal by the standards of the world's estimated 8.7 million animal species and 5,400 mammal species. Diamond identified many ways in which humans differ from most other mammals, including the following examples:

- Most other mammals live individually, not in pairs, and meet only to have sex. They do not raise children together, and usually the males do not recognize their offspring or provide paternal care. In contrast, most humans engage in long-term sexual partnerships and often co-parent the couple's joint offspring.

- Most mammals engage in public sex, whereas humans, as a rule, have sex in private.

- Most mammals have sex only when the females of the species ovulate, at which time they advertise their fertility through visual signals, smells, sounds, and other changes in their behavior. Human women, however, may be receptive to sex not only during ovulation but also at other times during their menstrual cycle.

- Humans are one of the few species to have sex face to face.

- Possibly most intriguing, humans, dolphins, and bonobos—a variety of ape—are the only mammals that have sex for fun rather than exclusively for reproduction. In fact, in contemporary U.S. culture, humans seem to do it mostly for fun.

By the standards of most mammals (including great apes, to whom we are most closely related), we humans are the sexual outliers. Despite the common

Bonobos, dolphins, and humans are the only mammals that have sex for fun rather than exclusively for procreation.

belief that clues to the essentials of human sex drives and behaviors may be found in "nature," Diamond makes clear that humans have developed a sex life that lies far outside the natural framework of that of our mammal relatives. If other animals' sex lives do not provide clues to the roots of our sexuality, what can human biology tell us about the genetic and hormonal roots of sexual desire and sexual behavior?

One school of thought, which draws heavily on evolutionary psychology, focuses on the ways in which human evolution has created biological drives that are embedded in the genes that shape the human brain and control the body's hormones. These drives work automatically—instinctively—to ensure the reproduction of the species. Human sexuality is thought to rely heavily on the expression of these biological drives.

Physical anthropologist Helen Fisher draws upon many of these ideas to explore the complex biological roots of human sexuality in her book *Why We Love: The Nature and Chemistry of Romantic Love* (2004), particularly the relationship of body chemistry to human sensations of love. Fisher suggests that through evolution humans have developed a set of neurochemicals that drive an "evolutionary trajectory of loving" (93). These neurochemicals guide us through three distinct phases of falling in love: finding the right sexual partner, building a relationship, and forming an emotional attachment that will last long enough to raise a child. First, testosterone—found in both women and men—triggers the sense of excitement, desire, arousal, and craving for sexual gratification that we call "lust." Then our bodies release the stimulant dopamine, and possibly norepinephrine and serotonin, to promote the feelings of romance that develop as relationships deepen. Eventually the hormones oxytocin and vasopressin generate the feelings of calm and security that are associated with a long-term partnership; Fisher calls these feelings "attachment." These phases, she suggests, are built into our biological systems to ensure the reproduction of the human species, and they play key roles in shaping human sexuality.

Genetic science, despite remarkable developments that include the ability to map the human genome (the whole human genetic structure), still has limitations as a predictor of individual human behavior, including sexual behavior. Yes, the frequency of certain behaviors in the human population may suggest an underlying biological component. But it is extremely difficult to directly trace links between specific genes and specific behaviors. So, for instance, despite widespread popular discussion of the topic, geneticists have not been able to identify a "straight" gene or a "gay" gene or any cluster of genes that determines sexual orientation.

Furthermore, we know that genes do not work in isolation from their surroundings. As discussed in Chapter 2, humans are a biocultural species, shaped by the interaction of genes, environment, and culture. Our bodies and minds, which are not fully formed at birth, bear the imprint of this interaction. Beginning in the womb, our genes interact with the nutrients, sounds, emotions, and diseases that surround and infuse us. The exact effects of the interaction of biology, culture, and environment are extremely difficult to measure, and this is particularly true in relationship to complex human sexual desires and behaviors.

Even within the parameters of Fisher's study, we cannot predict a particular man's level of sexual desire for a particular partner by measuring his level of testosterone. Attraction, desire, and even lack of interest are not only biologically driven but also triggered by a vast array of cultural factors—including responses to the potential partner's age, religion, class, race, education, and employment prospects—or previous positive or negative experiences that may shape the body's physiological response to certain stimuli. So, although biology clearly plays a role in human sexuality, exactly how it manifests itself in each individual and how it interacts with the environment and culture is not as clear as many popular descriptions of sexuality suggest.

SEXUALITY AND CULTURE

A second school of thought, one we will consider in more detail throughout the rest of this chapter, focuses on the ways in which the people, events, and physical and cultural environments around us shape—or construct—our sexual desires and behaviors. These feelings and actions may have roots in human evolution, but they are shaped by our experiences and surroundings. So, for instance, humans are enculturated from birth to channel sexual feelings and desires into a limited number of acceptable expressions. Culture shapes what people think is natural, normal, and even possible. Parents, family, friends, doctors, religious communities, sex education classes, the media, and many other individual and institutional actors all play a role in shaping the way we imagine and express our sexuality and what those expressions mean to others. Thus, culture both guides and limits, encourages and thwarts our sexual desires and imaginations.

Constructionists also trace the ways in which, through culture, human groups arrange the diversity of human sexuality into a limited number of categories that are imagined to be discrete (such as homosexual and heterosexual, gay and straight), thereby masking the actual diversity and fluidity of human expressions of sexuality. Where an individual is assigned within these categories has direct consequences for his or her life chances. The meaning certain sexual desires and behaviors acquire in a particular culture has the potential to affect access to social networks, social benefits, jobs, health care, and other resources and to make people vulnerable to discrimination, marginalization, and violence (Harding 1998; Ore 2010).

How do people, events, and the cultural environment around us shape our sexual desires and behaviors? (*clockwise from top left*) Advertisements featuring sex and love; (*right*) plaintiff "Jim" Obergefell speaks on June 26, 2015, after U.S. Supreme Court rules same-sex couples have a constitutional right to marry; (*bottom left*) a sex education class at Kealing Junior High School, Austin, Texas.

It is important to note that the perspectives of evolutionary biology and cultural constructionism discussed in this section need not be mutually exclusive. Rather, they reflect different research emphases into the roots and contemporary expressions of human sexuality.

What Is the Scope of Human Sexuality When Seen in a Global Perspective?

A look at human sexuality over time and across cultures reveals significant diversity in (1) how, where, when, and with whom humans have sex, and (2) what certain sexual behaviors mean. This diversity challenges Western culture-bound notions and suggests alternative options for reinterpreting assumed cultural categories of sexuality. The discussions that follow offer examples of alternative constructions of sexuality in Suriname, Nicaragua, and Japan.

SAME-GENDER "*MATI* WORK" IN SURINAME

In the *Politics of Passion* (2006), cultural anthropologist Gloria Wekker explores the lives of black, working-class Creole women in the port city of Paramaribo, Suriname, a former Dutch colony on the northern coast of South America. Writing about the sexual choices Surinamese women make, Wekker (like Roger Lancaster and Anne Allison in the studies described below) challenges the dominant thinking about sexual identity in Western scholarship and social movements by describing a much more flexible and inclusive approach specific to the local Paramaribo context.

Wekker's study focuses on *mati*—women who form intimate spiritual, emotional, and sexual relationships with other women. Wekker estimates that three out of four working-class black women in Paramaribo engage in "*mati* work" at some point in their lives, establishing relationships of mutual support, obligation, and responsibility with other women—sometimes living in the same household, sometimes separately, and often sharing in child rearing. In contrast to Western notions of fixed, "either/or" sexual identities, *mati* may engage in sexual relationships with both women and men—sometimes simultaneously, sometimes consecutively. Their relationships with men may center on having children or receiving economic support, but frequently *mati* choose a "visiting" relationship rather than marriage in order to maintain their independence.

Born in Suriname and trained as an anthropologist in the United States and the Netherlands, Wekker also writes about the transfer of *mati* work to the Netherlands. In recent decades, young Surinamese women have emigrated from the former colony to its former colonizer in search of economic opportunities.

MAP 8.1
Suriname

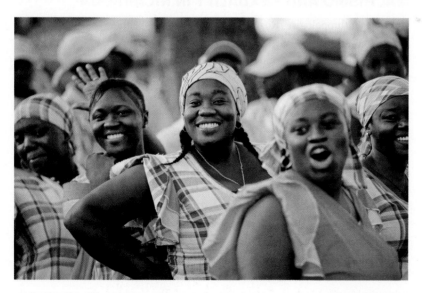

Women join a parade in the port city of Paramaribo, Suriname, on the northern coast of South America.

There, *mati* work has often developed in relationships between young immigrants and older black women of Surinamese parentage who have established Dutch citizenship. Wekker describes these relationships as often fraught with complicated power dynamics involving differential age, class, and citizenship status. Yet she notes that this *mati* work does not parallel European ideas of lesbianism.

Wekker argues that Western scholarship mistakenly links all sexual acts between individuals of the same gender to a notion of "homosexual identity"—a permanent, stable, fixed sexual core or essence, whether inborn or learned, that is counterposed to an equally fixed and opposite heterosexual identity. In the Western framework, a person is "either/or." The *mati* of Paramaribo, Wekker argues, approach their sexual choices very differently, regarding sexuality as flexible behavior rather than fixed identity. Their behavior is dynamic, malleable, and inclusive—"both/and"—rather than exclusive.

Wekker urges students of sexuality to not impose Western views about sexuality—what she considers "Western folk knowledge"—on the rest of the world but to understand sexuality in its local reality. Rather than thinking of one uniform expression of same-gender sexual behavior, she recommends focusing attention on the variation of people's behaviors. Furthermore, thinking cross-culturally, she argues that we must recognize that the identical physical sexual acts between same-gendered people may be understood in multiple ways and have vastly different social significance in different cultures and historical periods (Wekker 1999, 2006; Brown 2007; Stone 2007).

MACHISMO AND SEXUALITY IN NICARAGUA

MAP 8.2
Nicaragua

Cultural anthropologist Roger Lancaster explores similar themes in *Life Is Hard: Machismo, Danger, and the Intimacy of Power in Nicaragua* (1994), in which he considers expressions of sexuality in a working-class neighborhood in Managua, Nicaragua, during the 1980s. In particular, he examined the concept of machismo—which can be defined as a strong, sometimes exaggerated performance of masculinity. This concept, which Lancaster sees as central to the Nicaraguan national imagination, shapes relationships not only between men and women but also between men and other men. Machismo creates a strong contrast between aggression and passivity. "Real" men—masculine men—are aggressive. But a real man's macho status is always at risk. Machismo must be constantly performed to retain one's social status.

Lancaster was particularly intrigued by the way machismo affects the sexual relations between men. Generally, in U.S. culture, any man who engages in a same-gender sexual behavior is considered gay. But in the Nicaraguan community that Lancaster studied, only the men who passively receive anal intercourse are pejoratively called *cochon*—"queer, faggot, gay." The *machista*, the penetrator, is still considered a manly man—an *hombre-hombres*—under the rules of machismo. For it is the *machista*'s role to achieve sexual conquest whenever possible with whoever is available. The active partner acts out machismo, enhancing his status by dominating a weaker person. Among Nicaraguan men, the intersection of sexuality and power creates a culturally constructed system of arbitrary and unequal value for male bodies in which machismo privileges the aggressive, assertive *machista* penetrator over the passive, receptive, penetrated *cochon*.

Lancaster points out that in Nicaragua the same acts that in the United States would be seen to reveal one's "essential" homosexuality—desire for and sexual activity with someone of the same sex—are interpreted differently. In fact, active, aggressive men enhance their masculinity and macho status even if they engage in same-gender sexual activity (Lewin 1995; Pérez-Alemán 1994; Rouse 1994).

SEXUALITY AND PLEASURE IN CORPORATE JAPAN

In Tokyo's fashionable Roppongi district, elegant hostess bars attract groups of white-collar "salary men" for evenings of high-priced entertainment organized and paid for by their employers at elite Japanese corporations (who may spend up to 5 percent of company budgets on entertainment). These are not sex clubs. But they are still part of the commercialized sex industry—only selling the idea of sex, not physical sex. In her ethnography *Nightwork: Sexuality, Pleasure, and Corporate Masculinity in a Tokyo Hostess Club* (1994), anthropologist Anne Allison draws on four months of fieldwork in one club to explore the relationship between sexuality, masculinity, and Japan's capitalist corporate culture. At the clubs, hostesses serve as the focal point of the party. They pour drinks, light cigarettes, flatter, and banter to enhance the clients' pleasure. Discussion of the hostess is also a central feature of the party, as men engage in sexual banter and innuendo about her personal and physical attributes, especially her breasts.

MAP 8.3
Tokyo

Despite the highly charged sexual atmosphere at the club, Allison suggests that corporate trips to hostess clubs are not primarily about sex. Rather, gathering in these spaces, outside the office and outside the home and family life, is about stimulating and channeling these men's sexual desire to strengthen corporate culture and office relationships. All the talk about breasts is not about heterosexuality but about building homosocial relationships with other men. Sexual innuendo transforms women hostesses into sexual objects—a status seemingly all men agree about—and turns men's laughter and banter into a unifying process of male identity construction and bonding. Ideally, difference and discord in the workday can be dissolved into sexual conversation after hours. Allison suggests that in the highly ritualized expression of male dominance and male privilege performed in the hostess bars, the service purchased is not the eroticization of the woman but the eroticization of a man. The hostess does not deliver a sex act but through her banter, service, and submissive role instead projects an image of the potent and pleasing man who is powerful and desirable. Ultimately this nightwork fosters a particular form of masculinity—corporate masculinity—that serves the interests of contemporary Japanese businesses by channeling men's sexuality and desire into work (Curtis 1996; Davidson 1997; Ogasawara 1995).

The studies in Suriname, Nicaragua, and Japan are representative of the vast array of cross-cultural research that cumulatively has been called the "ethnocartography of human sexuality" (Weston 1993), mapping the global scope of diverse human sexual beliefs and behaviors. This ethnocartography marks a period in the anthropology of sexuality that built on the premises that (1) cross-cultural attention to the practices and beliefs of others can yield a deeper analysis of one's own culture, and (2) awareness of the broad panorama of human life offers opportunities for reexamining what seems normal and natural in one's own cultural practices. After reading about these studies, in what ways are you challenged to rethink your own conceptions of human sexuality?

How Has Sexuality Been Constructed in the United States?

In many of the studies discussed throughout this chapter, we see expressions of sexuality that do not fit the dominant Western model that limits discussion to two categories: **heterosexuality**, or attraction to and sexual relations between individuals of the opposite sex; and **homosexuality**, or attraction to and sexual relations with members of the same sex. At times in Western cultures this heterosexual-homosexual binary may be supplemented by discussions of **bisexuality**, or attraction to and sexual relations with members of both sexes, and **asexuality**, or lack of erotic attraction to others of either sex. But these latter categories are less frequently discussed. As we will see, historical and cross-cultural research suggests that the dual-category system of heterosexuality and homosexuality has a uniquely Western cultural history.

THE INVENTION OF HETEROSEXUALITY

Popular conversations about sexuality in the United States often focus on same-gender sexuality. This may not come as a surprise. As discussed in Chapter 5, contemporary conversations about race tend to center on the experiences of being black, Hispanic, or Asian and avoid discussing being white, even though whiteness is the central racial category around which all others have been organized. Likewise, in popular discussions and academic studies of sexuality, talk of different-gender eroticism (heterosexuality) is often overwhelmed by

heterosexuality
Attraction to and sexual relations between individuals of the opposite sex.

homosexuality
Attraction to and sexual relations between individuals of the same sex.

bisexuality
Attraction to and sexual relations with members of both sexes.

asexuality
A lack of erotic attraction to others.

discussions of same-gender eroticism (homosexuality). This emphasis has left heterosexuality largely forgotten and unmarked. In recent years, the anthropology of sexuality has worked to shift scholarly attention to focus on the norm (heterosexuality) and the process by which the particular expression of heterosexuality prevalent in U.S. culture today became the norm (D'Emilio and Freedman 1998).

Historian Jonathan Katz (2007) argues that heterosexuality as it is practiced and understood in contemporary U.S. culture is a fairly recent invention. The respected *Oxford English Dictionary Supplement* lists the first U.S. usage of the term in 1892. Because words provide clues to cultural concepts, Katz suggests that the lack of earlier citations in popular or scientific venues in the United States indicates that heterosexuality had not achieved widespread cultural currency in the nineteenth century.

Does this mean that women and men in the United States were not engaging in opposite-gender sexual activity prior to the invention of this word? Katz suggests instead that heterosexuality as we think of it is not the same as reproductive intercourse between a man and a woman. Instead what we call "heterosexuality" today is a particular arrangement between the sexes that although not excluding reproductive intercourse, also involves ideas about the practice and purpose of sex that have not always been socially authorized. So, for instance, the early references to heterosexuality often referred to it as a perversion of the natural order because of its association with sex for pleasure rather than for procreation. The nineteenth-century Victorian ideal of sexuality, heavily influenced by Christian teachings, considered sex to be for procreation alone. Sex for pleasure represented a danger to the purposes of God. Masturbation—clearly nonprocreative—was considered a life-threatening, depleting form of self-abuse.

Only in 1892 did the translation of German psychiatrist Richard von Krafft-Ebing's influential work *Psychopathia Sexualis* first introduce to the U.S. scene the modern sense of "heterosexuality" as erotic feelings for the opposite sex and "homosexuality" as erotic feelings for the same sex. This marked a significant shift in the scientific community, supported by a growing number of medical doctors, toward the new idea of sexuality for pleasure rather than exclusively for procreation. The rapidly expanding number of newspapers, books, plays, films, restaurants, bars, and baths associated with the rising consumer culture in the early twentieth century reinforced the gradual shift toward the sex-for-pleasure concept.

Sexology. A scientific study of sexuality, called *sexology*, began to emerge in the United States in the late nineteenth century. These studies played a central role in the establishment of heterosexuality as the dominant erotic ideal and

Studies by sexologist Dr. Alfred C. Kinsey (*right*), pictured with his research staff in 1953, challenged common assumptions about U.S. sexual practices.

in the gradual process of dividing the U.S. population into distinct heterosexual and homosexual groups. In the twentieth century, studies led by Alfred Kinsey, Shere Hite, and William Masters and Virginia Johnson used interviews, questionnaires, observation, and participation to explore the sexual lives of thousands of primarily white U.S. residents. Their studies produced surprising results. Kinsey and later sexologists found that human sexuality did not fit into simplistic categories. Same-gendered attraction, fantasies, and experiences were much more common than previously thought. Furthermore, sexual behaviors could shift over the course of a lifetime, spanning both heterosexual and homosexual activity. Rather than finding a sharp dichotomy between heterosexuality and homosexuality, research revealed diversity, flexibility, and fluidity, along a continuum of sexual behavior (Hubbard 1990; Kinsey, Pomeroy, and Martin 1948).

Despite their arguments for the recognition of diversity and fluidity in human sexual behavior, sexology studies contributed to the establishment of heterosexuality as the dominant erotic ideal in U.S. culture and reinforced the emerging popular and scientific consensus that because it was the sex most people were having, heterosexuality was the functional norm for human sexuality (Hubbard 1990; Katz 2007).

Over the course of a century, heterosexuality gradually came to be seen as the norm—the presumed "natural" state—against which to judge all other expressions of sexuality. Today cultural notions of sexuality are in flux, yet a particular version of heterosexuality continues to be constructed and contested.

Within this context, we now consider the role of weddings in shaping contemporary conceptions of human sexuality in the United States.

"WHITE WEDDINGS"

White Weddings: Romancing Heterosexuality in Popular Culture (2008), a study by sociologist Chrys Ingraham, is not a book about wedding ceremonies. It is about wedding culture and what the author calls the "wedding industry"—the vast network of commercial activities and social institutions that market 2.1 million weddings a year in the United States. The wedding industry and the wedding culture, Ingraham argues, provide insights into how U.S. culture gives meaning to marriage and, in the process, constructs contemporary understandings of heterosexuality.

Constructing Heterosexuality. It's hard to turn on the television, log on to the Internet, or check out at the local grocery store without encountering some reminder of U.S. society's fascination with weddings. Bridal magazines, popular tabloids, television shows, and commercials in every medium saturate the culture with images of a spectacle of excess that will, they promise, lead to everyone's fairy-tale ending of "happily ever after." Wedding consultants push wedding announcements, bridal showers, wedding halls, floral arrangements, diamond rings, rehearsal dinners, receptions, gifts and favors, caterers, photographers, bands, limousines, and glamorous honeymoons to romantic destinations. Wedding registries orchestrate the delivery of just the right gifts of kitchenware, china, household furnishings, and every appliance imaginable. The average bridal gown (mostly made in Third World garment shops by women who will never have a white wedding), including alterations, headpiece, and veil, will cost $1,357 (2014 figures). The average U.S. couple will spend more than $31,213 (in 2014) on their "big day." Altogether, the annual $80 billion wedding industry wields enormous social and economic power.

Ingraham reminds her readers that brides are not born. They are made. Every girl in U.S. culture, almost from birth, is bombarded with cultural symbols and messages about what it will take to have her very own white wedding. Barbie dolls and other toy-industry favorites model the perfect bride, complete with accessories (including Ken?) for the perfect white wedding. Disney movies, feature films, and television shows celebrate weddings as key life moments (and central plot devices) and essential cultural symbols. Every broadcast season features a spate of elaborate made-for-television weddings, especially on shows struggling in the ratings.

From childhood, girls are tutored in preparation for the "you may kiss the bride" moment, learning to apply makeup, wear high heels, send valentines, go on dates, and select a prom dress. Boys learn to buy flowers and corsages, wear

What is your idea of a perfect wedding? Here, a woman adjusts a bridal gown at a wedding fair in Bucharest, Romania, where the wedding industry has grown despite an economic crisis.

tuxedos, pay for dates, lead during the first dance, buy an engagement ring, and initiate sex. But no matter where you think human sexuality originates, it is clear that these behaviors do not occur in nature. They are constructed in culture. The wedding industry and wedding culture—the romantic idealization of the wedding ritual—enculturate boys and girls, men and women, about what to do, when, and with whom, in order to lead up to that perfect day. Weddings, Ingraham suggests, and the elaborate rituals that lead up to them over a lifetime, are not only exuberant public celebrations of romantic love. Weddings are also key cultural institutions through which we learn what it means to be heterosexual.

Inequality and Unequal Access. What do weddings tell us about the construction of heterosexuality in U.S. culture? Building on recent feminist scholarship, Ingraham suggests that white weddings, and the marriages that result, offer insights into the gendered power dynamics embedded in the normative patterns of heterosexuality that have developed since the late nineteenth century. These power dynamics disadvantage women while being largely obscured by the idealism and romance that U.S. culture wraps around these institutions. Historically, the institution of heterosexual marriage included legal stipulations that effectively made women the economic and sexual property of their husbands. This assumption continues to be ritualized in contemporary U.S. weddings by the father "giving away" the bride to her soon-to-be husband, exchanging the woman between two men.

Today patterns of inequality are not legally sanctioned but still significant. In the home the gendered division of labor means that frequently the woman carries a double workload as a wage earner while simultaneously bearing primary responsibility for domestic work and child rearing. In the workplace, usually still dominated by male leadership, women receive unequal pay for equal work, are promoted less often than men, and are targets of sexual harassment.

Ingraham selected the book title *White Weddings* to highlight the issues of class and race that also are embedded in the workings of the wedding industry and the fairy tale of the wedding ritual. White weddings are not available to all. The women sewing wedding dresses, the young men mining diamonds, and the staff serving dinner on the Caribbean honeymoon island cannot afford a white wedding. Nor does the industry depict a diverse population in its advertising, insinuating that white weddings are primarily for white folks. Actually, most Americans cannot afford the average U.S. wedding; they incur significant debt for the ceremony and the honeymoon to launch their marriage.

Today U.S. marraige patterns—and relationship patterns more generally—are shifting rapidly. Placed in historical perspective and in light of our anthropological perspectives on the fluidity and malleability of human sexuality, perhaps we can view these shifts not as some new and surprising contestation of age-old "natural" patterns of sexuality, but as the most recent rethinking of human sexuality in U.S. culture. If so, we might then be better prepared to analyze the underlying intersections of sexuality and power in our own personal and political lives.

How are contemporary understandings of sexuality being shaped by the highly symbolic ritual of marriage? Here, a couple exchanges rings at their wedding ceremony.

How Is Sexuality an Arena for Working Out Relations of Power?

As we have noted, sexuality is more than an expression of individual desires and identities. French philosopher and social scientist Michel Foucault (1978) described sexuality as "an especially dense transfer point for relations of power." By this he meant that in every culture, sexuality—like race, ethnicity, class, and gender—is also an arena in which appropriate behavior is defined, relations of power are worked out, and inequality and stratification are created, enforced, and contested.

Indeed, cultural institutions ranging from governments to religious bodies attempt to regulate many aspects of sexuality. These aspects include marriage and divorce; monogamy and polygamy; age of consent; definition of incest; reproductive rights; the rights of gay men, lesbians, bisexuals, and transgender persons; pornography; and prostitution. A consideration of "who is allowed to do what with whom and when" exposes the intersections of sexuality and power in a culture. Attention to intersectionality—the way systems of power interconnect to affect individual lives and group experiences—offers a fundamental shift in the way social scientists study inequality and stratification, including the way we think about sexuality. In this section we consider case studies that reflect on these intersections.

INTERSECTIONS OF RACE AND SEXUALITY FOR BLACK GAY WOMEN

Mignon Moore's study *Invisible Families* (2011) explores the impact of the intersection of race and sexuality on the identities, relationships, and families of black gay women in the United States. Moore notes that, historically, race has framed black women's political, economic, and religious identities (see also Dill 1983; Higgenbotham 1992). And whereas many middle-class white lesbian couples experience sexuality as the primary framework that shapes their identity, many in the black lesbian community (including African American, Afro-Caribbean, and African immigrant women) find that race—perhaps as much as, if not more than, sexuality—is the primary framework that shapes their identity.

In an interview with Moore, Zoe Ferron (a pseudonym), an African American woman born in 1960 in Brooklyn, New York, reflected on how the identities of race, gender, and sexuality described her:

> If I had to number them one, two, three? Probably Black and lesbian—real close, to be honest with you. I don't know which would come up as one. Probably Black. Woman last. . . . Because that is just

what it is. People see your Blackness, and the world has affected me by my Blackness since the very inception of my life. . . . My sexuality is something that developed later on, or I became aware of later on, [because] I think *it's always been what it's been*, but I think that it was just something that developed in my psyche. But being Black is something that I've always had to deal with: racism since day one and recognizing how to navigate through this world as a Black person, and even as a Black woman. (Moore 2012, 33)

The intersection of race and sexuality becomes particularly meaningful as black gay women participate in black or gay communities that define themselves around just one of these statuses.

Moore notes that prior to the 1980s, gay sexuality in racial minority communities was rarely articulated in public settings. And only infrequently was it recognized as a component of the community's larger experiences of discrimination and struggle. Instead, openly gay sexuality was perceived to flout notions of "respectability"—virtue, modesty, discipline, responsibility—that had developed within the black middle class and that its leadership promoted as important tools to combat racist stereotypes in the workplace, political arena, and family life (Shaw 1996; Wolcott 2001). Moore points to a strong reluctance during that period by gay blacks to challenge community expectations about respectability by creating families together.

In the intervening years, same-gender sexuality has become an increasingly public issue in U.S. culture through prominent debates about same-sex marriage, the rights of gay men and lesbian women to adopt children, and the rights of lesbians and gay men to serve openly in the military. At the same time, recognition of same-sex relationships and families has increased in the black community, and black political and religious leaders have begun to address issues related to gay sexuality as matters of civil rights and fairness. Relationships once hidden from families and communities have gradually moved into the public sphere, where the participants can be celebrated as gay women and men and can openly form unions and raise families.

How do the women in Moore's study navigate the black middle-class politics of respectability in order to both live their sexuality openly and maintain strong community connections? Moore suggests that by risking the disruption of this particular version of respectability, black women who live openly as lesbians—forming families, getting married, becoming mothers, and raising children—offer an alternative manifestation of respectability at the intersection of sexuality and race.

Can you see how the intersection of race and sexuality may differentially affect one's life choices and opportunities? In your own life, how is your sexuality shaped by its intersection with other systems of power—perhaps age, gender, race, class, or religion?

SEX, DISABILITY, AND SOCIAL JUSTICE IN DENMARK AND SWEDEN

MAP 8.4
Denmark and Sweden

Anthropologists Don Kulick and Jens Rydstrom explore the intersections of state power and sexuality in their book, *Loneliness and Its Opposite: Sex, Disability, and the Ethics of Engagement* (2015), focusing on the constraints and potential for sexuality for severely disabled people in Denmark and Sweden. In recent decades the disability rights movement has successfully advocated for access to physical spaces, jobs, social services, and other public arenas where people with disabilities have commonly faced discrimination and marginalization. But the more private realm of the erotic lives of people with disabilities has more often than not been ignored or viewed with discomfort or anxiety. Should a person with severe disabilities hope to have a meaningful sex life? And how can that be possible for someone who needs assistance to perform most basic life activities such as eating, bathing, and going to the bathroom?

Denmark and Sweden are two liberal welfare states with similar cultural histories, considered to be sexually progressive and at the forefront of the global movement for disability rights. Both countries commit significant portions of their budgets to social services (30 percent) and provide disability pensions, housing in group homes, or personal assistance to those who desire to live independently. But these countries take distinctly different approaches to the erotic lives of people with disabilities. In Denmark their sexuality is acknowledged, discussed, and

"I want a family—a marriage, children, the whole thing. 'Family' is happy is strong." So says Nick Hogan of Australia, one of an estimated seven million people around the world with Down Syndrome. What can we do to support people with disabilities as they form attachments with other people, including attachments that involve sexual pleasure and love?

facilitated. In Sweden, as in the overwhelming majority of countries around the world, the erotic lives of people with disabilities are denied, repressed, and discouraged. Their desires for sexual pleasure are ignored. These adults with disabilities are commonly treated as children whose erotic desires and sexual behaviors are seen as inappropriate or even dangerous to their own well-being.

Kulick and Rydstrom's study focuses specifically on severely disabled people, including those with intellectual and physical disabilities, limited mobility in their limbs, and limited verbal language abilities who live in group homes. In Sweden staff are trained to discourage the erotic lives of their residents, to never "wake the sleeping bear"—meaning to avoid all mention of sexuality—and to shut down erotic feelings when they do arise. In stark contrast, the group homes in Denmark promote welcoming attitudes and affirmative policies regarding sex. Denmark supports a network of advocates, sexual advisors, social workers, medical professionals, educators, and counselors who work toward recognizing and facilitating the sexual desires and practices of people with disabilities. The government sponsors an eighteen-month training course to become a sexual advisor. An elaborate set of national *Guidelines about Sexuality—Regardless of Handicap* discusses how these advisors can support people with disabilities to engage in activities such as having sex with a partner, masturbation, or purchasing sexual services from a sex worker.

Ultimately, Kulick and Rydstrom are most interested in the impact of state policies on the lives of women and men with disabilities and their potential to develop, explore, and thrive as sexual human beings. Kulick and Rydstrom frame this as an ethical question—a matter of social justice. While few would oppose accessibility to public spaces, social services, and jobs for people with disabilities (though funds to realize those goals are often in short supply), sex is often another matter completely. But what can we do to support people with disabilities as they form attachments with other people, including attachments that involve sexual pleasure and love? And how can we foster the circumstances that allow each individual to realize a life of human dignity? This, Kulick and Rydstrom argue, is the true measure of a just society.

How Does Globalization Influence Local Expressions of Sexuality?

Globalization has significantly influenced local expressions of sexuality, and this effect is evident in many arenas. For example, time-space compression (see Chapter 1) is facilitating the movement of people—particularly men—within countries and across national borders in search of sexual pleasure. In addition, disruptions of local economies are pushing women to find wage labor to support themselves and their families. And international campaigns for gay and lesbian rights, often initiated in Western countries, are shaping a global conversation about sexuality and the human rights of sexual minorities worldwide. At the same time, groups opposing gay and lesbian sexuality are promoting their own agendas on a global platform. These transformations suggest that individual expressions of sexuality and local understandings of sexuality are undergoing dramatic shifts as they intersect with economic policies, immigration practices, and political movements at the national, regional, and international levels influenced by processes of globalization (see Curtis 2009).

SEXUALITY, LANGUAGE, AND THE EFFECTS OF GLOBALIZATION IN NIGERIA

The tendency of globalization to intensify connections across national boundaries may generate opportunities for greater cooperation on issues of mutual concern affecting people in disparate parts of the world. But this capacity to bridge barriers also has the potential to homogenize—to shape global discourses that blur distinctions and smooth over differences—in a way that may put local indigenous expressions at risk.

In *Allah Made Us: Sexual Outlaws in an Islamic African City* (2009), linguistic anthropologist Rudolf Gaudio presents an ethnographic study of the language practices of *'yan daudu*, feminine men in the northern Nigerian (Hausa-speaking) city of Kano. *'Yan daudu* are one group of *masu harka*, a code term for "people who do the deed"—that is, men who have sex with other men. *'Yan daudu* are men who act like women: They cook, serve food, sing, dance, or work as prostitutes. Over the years, their role has been publicly recognized in northern

MAP 8.5
Nigeria

Nigerian culture. But with the introduction of strict Islamic sharia law, which forbids same-gender sexuality, in recent years, *'yan daudu* have faced increased persecution, harassment, and marginalization because of their gender and sexual nonconformity. As international campaigns for gay rights intersect with Nigerian culture, the resulting conversations risk drawing local expressions of human sexuality into a national and international debate that links them to so-called Western decadence and new forms of colonialism considered unacceptable by the Nigerian government.

Unlike most Western conceptions of sexuality, *masu harka* and *'yan daudu* do not see homosexual behavior as incompatible with marrying women, forming families, and having children. Nor do they necessarily consider their sexuality incompatible with their Muslim faith. Gaudio met many who are observant Muslims and some who have taken the *hajj,* a pilgrimage to the Muslim holy city of Mecca that is required of every believer who can manage the journey. For some of these men, the pilgrimage to Mecca may enable them to establish status and respectability in the international arena that they could not achieve on their own at home, where many other Nigerians consider them to be outlaws and deviants.

Globalization's Homogenizing Influence. *'Yan daudu* sexual practices in northern Nigeria are complicated by the effects of globalization. Most African countries achieved their independence from European colonial powers in the 1960s and 1970s, and memories of those incursions are still fresh in Africans' collective memory. Moreover, the awareness of new forms of economic, military, political, and cultural domination that have emerged since the end of colonialism are ever present. Like many Africans, many Nigerians regard homosexuality as part of the wave of Western influences that have been flooding their country and continent for well more than a hundred years.

Most national governments in Africa do not consider the practice of homosexuality as authentically African—certainly not the way homosexuality is framed in international scholarly and activist discourse. These governments see the push for recognizing gay sexual rights as a human right as simply a new front of Western imperial domination. One exception to this perspective is South Africa, where gay rights were included in the new constitution of 1994.

Gaudio's ethnography of *masu harka* shows diverse expressions of sexuality on the local level. The presence of *'yan daudu,* for example, challenges the notion that Africa is devoid of indigenous sexual minorities. But the emergence of an international movement for gay rights threatens to undermine the diversity of local expressions of human sexuality. Gaudio notes that Western scholars and international activists often presume that the international movement's categories can be applied with relative ease from one linguistic and cultural setting to another. However, forcing the conversation into restrictive, binary categories of heterosexuality and homosexuality endangers the continued existence of local sexual expression by placing those indigenous expressions into a debate about foreign influence, imperialism, and so-called Western decadence.

The emerging anti-gay rhetoric unifies Muslim fundamentalist, Christian orthodox, and evangelical groups. It threatens to close off the possibility of recognizing the diversity of sexual desires, practices, and identities of individuals and local communities that may have previously operated outside the Western-oriented, homosexual-heterosexual framework. In so doing, it reveals the power of globalization to introduce narrower, homogenizing perspectives on the many and varied expressions of human sexuality found in cultures around the globe (Gaudio 2009; Harris 2009; Leap 2010).

In this chapter we have considered the vast scope and diversity of human sexuality across cultures, time, and space. The sexual dimensions of human diversity in turn challenge us to expand our imaginations about the potential for human sexuality available to us. But as we have seen throughout this chapter, human sexuality is more than the personal choices we make about our sexual partners and how we express our erotic desires. The anthropological lens and a global perspective have enabled us to see that sexuality is a complex relationship between individuals as well as between individuals and the larger culture. We have examined how elements of human sexuality are culturally constructed—formed in relationship to particular people, cultural norms, and expectations. Rather than representing sharply drawn, fixed, and oppositional identities representing two discrete categories, sexuality is diverse, flexible, and fluid.

But we have also seen that the construction of human sexuality—how it is perceived and valued—is a highly contested process. Debates rage and decisions are made about human sexuality that affect people's life chances and access to power, privileges, rights, and resources. Certain rights or benefits may be granted or restricted based on assumptions about sexual preferences or sexual behavior. Given this reality, within anthropology sexuality has become a key cultural location for analyzing, understanding, and contesting stratification and inequality, including the ways sexuality intersects with other systems of power, such as race, gender, ethnicity, nationality, religion, kinship, and class.

Toolkit

Thinking Like an Anthropologist:
Sexuality in Your Life

Sexuality is all around us. Turn on the television, search the Internet, check out at the grocery store, or drive down an interstate highway, and you will find sexuality all around you in reality shows, websites, magazines, and billboard advertisements. At times in U.S. culture, the presence of sexuality is so pervasive as to be overwhelming. In such an environment, how do you begin to make sense of what sexuality means for you on a personal level and for U.S. culture on a political level?

Remember to consider the big questions that have organized this chapter:

- **What is sexuality and where does it come from?**
- **What is the scope of human sexuality when seen in a global perspective?**
- **How has sexuality been constructed in the United States?**
- **How is sexuality an arena for working out relations of power?**
- **How does globalization influence local expressions of sexuality?**

Think again about the story that opens this chapter. In what ways do sexuality and power intersect on your college campus? If, as anthropologist Eric Wolf argues (see Chapter 2), every relationship is embedded in complex dynamics of power, how do you navigate intersections of sexuality with gender, age, class, race, or religion? Has your college or university created opportunities to discuss matters of sexuality?

Certainly, attention to sexual violence on college campuses has increased. Terms such as *date rape* and *domestic violence* have become part of the national conversation, and many colleges and universities have implemented policies on sexual harassment and sexual conduct. Still, many women experience sexual harassment, violence, and rape while in college (Fisher, Daigle, and Cullen 2010; Sanday 1990). While these policies attempt to address extreme expressions of the intersection of power with sexuality, conversations about sexuality can be far more wide-ranging.

Until recently, most sexual offense policies have started with the assumption that "*No* means *no.*" Most legal definitions of rape have assumed that if a woman does not consent or is incapable of consent for any reason, then any sexual activity with her is considered rape. But more recently, affirmative consent policies have been developed that require consent to be an ongoing process and verbal consent to be obtained with each new level of physical intimacy.

An affirmative consent policy requires a dramatic shift in thinking about intimate sexual encounters. It also commands a new attention to shifting the power dynamics that underlie current patterns of gender and sexuality in the culture at large. Imagine if all forms of coercion—physical and psychological coercion; the pressure of norms, obligations, and expectations; and the fear of ridicule or abandonment—were removed from the equation, enabling people to engage in sexual intimacy only when they really wanted to. What if "yes" really meant "yes" (Friedman and Valenti 2008)?

Although anthropology may not be able to help you decide whom to date or when to do what and where, it does offer a set of tools—perspectives and insights—that may help you think more clearly about what it all means, what the cultural frameworks are within which you negotiate your desires and decisions, and what your full range of options may be when you consider your sexuality within a global perspective. Questions of sexuality run deep in U.S. cultural conversations. Having thought through key issues of sexuality from an anthropological perspective, are you better prepared to engage in the debates and advance the conversation?

Key Terms

sexuality (p. 208)

heterosexuality (p. 216)

homosexuality (p. 216)

bisexuality (p. 216)

asexuality (p. 216)

ONE FAMILY. NO APOLOGIES.

AN AMAZON ORIGINAL SERIES

TRANSPARENT

Chapter 9
Kinship, Family, and Marriage

In season one of the Amazon television series *Transparent*, Mort, a retired professor of political science, who is transitioning to Maura, walks in on his daughter Amy—wife of Len and mother of two children—making out with Tammy, her ex-college girlfriend, now married to her second wife and raising a child in that relationship. Maura comes out to her daughter and says that after years of dressing up as a man she is finally able to be who she has known herself to be since the age of five. The series follows the stories of this family as Maura comes out to her children, ex-wife (who is caring for a second husband with Alzheimer's), and grandchildren and builds a new set of supportive relationships with people taking the same journey. The children wrestle with learning that the person they knew as their father is transgender and navigate their own complicated journeys toward creating family and meaningful relationships.

Who is family? The success of the television series *Transparent* reveals a growing openness to shifting American notions of family—what anthropologists call kinship.

Though created by Jill Soloway as a television comedy-drama, *Transparent* is inspired by the story of her father, who came out as transgender just a few years ago, and offers a reflection on the shifting notion of family in the twenty-first–century United States. The show's critical and financial success reveals a growing willingness to engage the emerging new configurations of the relationships we sometimes call "family" and that anthropologists have explored under the category of *kinship*. Who is "related" to whom? Who decides? Is kinship biological or chosen? Who actually constitutes a family?

Humans live in groups. As a species, we rarely live alone or in isolation. Kinship is perhaps the most effective strategy humans have developed to form stable, reliable, separate, and deeply connected groups that can last over time and through generations.

kinship

The system of meaning and power that cultures create to determine who is related to whom and to define their mutual expectations, rights, and responsibilities.

Kinship is the system of meaning and power created to determine who is related to whom and to define their mutual expectations, rights, and responsibilities. Of course, humans also form groups through work, religion, education, and politics. But none compare to the power of families and kinship networks to provide support and nurture, ensure reproduction of the next generation, protect group assets, and influence social, economic, and political systems.

Kinship groups are often assumed by many in Western cultures to have a biological basis and to arise around the **nuclear family** of mother, father, and children. But when we examine these assumptions in a cross-cultural context, they show themselves to be a Euro-American ideal that not even those cultures have realized. Kinship groups come in a variety of shapes and sizes: We trace our connections through biological ancestors. We create kinship relations through marriage and remarriage. We adopt. We foster. We choose families of people who care about us. Sometimes we even imagine everyone in our nation to be part of one big, related, kinship community.

nuclear family

The kinship unit of mother, father, and children.

In the twenty-first century, we are vividly aware of new forms of family life as kinship relations shift, closing off familiar patterns and opening up new ones. The image of a family with mother, father, and two kids gathered around the dining room table every evening for a home-cooked meal and conversation may be familiar as a cultural icon, but for many people the experience of family is more complicated as families are made, taken apart, reconstructed, and blended. Gay and lesbian couples and their families are achieving increased acceptance and official recognition. New reproductive technologies—including artificial insemination, in vitro fertilization, and surrogacy—continue to stretch our ideas of kinship and families by showing how human culture, through science and technology, is shaping biological relationships.

Although the term *kinship* may be unfamiliar to you, the subject material is not. Through kinship studies, anthropologists examine the deepest and most complicated aspects of our everyday lives—our relationships with people closest to us, including our mothers, fathers, brothers, sisters, grandparents, cousins, husbands, wives, partners, and children. These are the people we live with, eat with, count on for support, and promise to take care of when they are in need. We pour our emotions, creative energy, hopes, and dreams into these relationships. Many of the most emotionally vibrant moments of our lives—from joy and love to anger and pain—occur at the intersection of individual and family life: birthdays, holiday celebrations, shared meals, weddings, illnesses, and funerals. Through kinship, we see our lives as part of a continuum. We look back to see the history of the people we come from, and we look ahead to imagine the relatives and families yet to be.

At the same time, kinship is deeply intertwined with forces beyond the everyday activities of family and home. In our families, we also learn basic patterns of human behavior—how to treat one another, how to act in groups, how to navigate differences of age, gender, ethnicity, and sexuality. This enculturation shapes our lives outside the household, including the ways we think about gender roles, the division of labor, religious practices, warfare, politics, migration, and nationalism. Because cultural norms, values, and social structures can always be changed, kinship and family also become places of contestation, experimentation, and change that reflect and shape debates within the larger culture.

The study of kinship is one of anthropology's unique innovations for thinking about how culture works. In this chapter, we will explore the following questions about kinship:

- **How are we related to one another?**
- **Are biology and marriage the only basis for kinship?**
- **How are ideas of kinship linked to the nation-state?**
- **How is kinship changing in the modern world?**

We will examine the many strategies people use to form kinship groups, and we will consider the implications of kinship's changing expressions in the twenty-first century. By the end of the chapter you should be ready to interpret your own family tree—not just by creating a list of relatives, but also by considering how those ties are formed and the role that kin play in shaping who you are as an individual and as a member of society. You will also be prepared to understand and analyze the ways debates about kinship shape important aspects of our individual and collective lives locally, nationally, and globally.

How Are We Related to One Another?

Who are you related to? All humans are closely related genetically, sharing more than 99.9 percent of our DNA. Despite this close biological "kinship" among all humans, closer to home we tend to organize our personal relationships more specifically through systems of common biological descent, marriage, love, and choice. As you will discover throughout this chapter, cultures have a variety of ways of organizing kinship relationships. Some will be familiar to you, and others will not. All are equally valid.

DESCENT

One way that humans construct kinship groups is by tracking genealogical descent. In **descent groups**, primary relationships are with certain consanguineal relatives (what U.S. culture refers to as "blood" relatives). These would include your mother, father, sister, brother, grandparents, children, and grandchildren, as well as your uncles and aunts who are your parents' siblings—but not your uncles and aunts who are married to your parents' siblings. Descent groups are often imagined as long chains of connections from parent to child that reach back through many generations to a common ancestor or group of ancestors and forward to imagined future generations.

Early anthropological studies through the mid-twentieth century assumed the descent group to be central to the social structure of most nonindustrial cultures outside Europe and North America (Evans-Pritchard 1951; Fortes 1949; Malinowski 1929, 1930; Radcliffe-Brown 1950). Anthropologists of that period expected to find extended descent groups that stretched back over many generations and worked together. Such groups were considered key to understanding each culture's economic, political, and religious dynamics because of the way kinship underlies large social networks extending beyond the immediate family into all aspects of cultural life. We will consider one classic example, the Nuer, in the following section.

In contrast, most European and North American cultures do not use descent to organize social groups. Although we may keep track of our ancestors over a few generations, we do so bilaterally—through both the mother's and the father's relatives—and generally we have not constructed large social networks based on kinship connections. In the United States, perhaps the Rockefeller, Kennedy, and Bush families might loosely qualify as descent groups. They stretch back over a few generations, tracing roots to a much more recent common ancestor (either John D. Rockefeller, Joseph Kennedy, or Prescott Bush); and although now subdivided into smaller segments, they still maintain strong enough connections to

descent group

A kinship group in which primary relationships are traced through certain consanguineous ("blood") relatives.

lineage

A type of descent group that traces genealogical connection through generations by linking persons to a founding ancestor.

clan

A type of descent group based on a claim to a founding ancestor but lacking genealogical documentation.

function together at times on common economic, social, political, or ritual activities and projects. But such descent groups are extremely rare in North America.

Anthropologists distinguish two types of descent groups: lineages and clans. **Lineages** can clearly demonstrate genealogical connections through many generations, tracing the family tree to a founding (apical) ancestor. **Clans** likewise claim connection to a founding ancestor, but they do not provide the same genealogical documentation. Descent groups may be *matrilineal*, constructing the group through female ancestors, or *patrilineal*, tracing kinship through male ancestors. Both matrilineal and patrilineal patterns reflect *unilineal* descent because they build kinship groups through either one line or the other. In contrast, *ambilineal* descent groups—including Samoans, Maori, Hawaiians, and others in Southeast Asia and the Pacific—trace kinship through both the mother and the father. This alternative pattern is sometimes called *cognatic* or *bilateral*.

Most people in the world practice patrilineal descent as their primary strategy to track kin group membership. At the same time, most people still build kinship networks bilaterally through both parents, even when tracing descent unilineally. Are you aware of how your own family traces descent?

The Nuer of Southern Sudan. The Nuer people of southern Sudan in northeast Africa constitute a classic representation of the descent group.

What does a descent group look like? (*clockwise from left*) A chief (standing) and his sons, photographed by Bronislaw Malinowski represent the core of a patrilineal descent group in the Trobriand Islands. (*top right*) A Kennedy family portrait, Hyannis, Massachusetts, 1930s, including, seated second from left, future U.S. attorney general Robert Kennedy; center, future U.S. president John F. Kennedy; and second from right, family patriarch Joseph Kennedy Sr. (*bottom right*) A Bush family portrait at the White House, 2005, including, seated from right, Florida Governor Jeb Bush, U.S. President George H. W. Bush, and fourth from right, U.S. President George W. Bush.

MAP 9.1
The Nuer Region of
East Africa

British anthropologist E. E. Evans-Pritchard studied this group in the 1930s (Evans-Pritchard 1951). At the time of his research and until the later part of the twentieth century, the Nuer were primarily a pastoral, cattle-herding people that moved between settlements throughout the year to adapt to rainy and dry seasons. The Nuer constituted a patrilineal descent group: Both boy and girl children were born into the group, but membership could only pass to the next generation through the sons, who inherited membership through their fathers. Nuer clans were *exogamous*—meaning that marriages within the group were not permitted. Large clans were divided into lineages, although lineages were extensive enough to spread over several villages.

Cattle were the center of Nuer economic life. They were owned by men, but they were milked by women as well as by boys who had not yet come of age and been initiated into the descent group. A successful marriage proposal often required the groom to provide cattle in exchange for the bride.

The patrilineal kinship structures of clans and lineages provided the primary structure for Nuer political and economic activity. In the villages, the lineages collectively owned land, fisheries, and pastures. Ceremonial leadership of Nuer group life was organized under sacred ritual leaders, but these individuals did not control the social networks built around kinship and cattle, so they were not the driving force in Nuer culture (Stone 2009).

Searching for Kinship Patterns. As early anthropologists gathered kinship data from cultures worldwide, they developed a limited number of general categories that facilitated comparison. Despite vast geographic distances and language differences, only four primary systems were identified to classify relatives in the parental generation: *lineal, bifurcate merging, generational,* and *bifurcate collateral*. When beginning with the ego's generation (the ego being the central character and starting point in tracing kinship relationships—for example, you in your own family tree), anthropologists found only six different ways of organizing relatives, in which the variation centered on the classification of siblings and cousins. Each of these six were named after a key group in which the pattern occurred: Eskimo, Hawaiian, Sudanese, Omaha, Crow, and Iroquois (Figure 9.1).

Generalized systems of kinship classification can be very useful for identifying and comparing broad patterns of social structure. But anthropologists have found that actual, local kinship patterns do not always match the generalized models. The ways in which human groups trace connections between generations—in other words, how they construct genealogies—can be messy and far from exact. Genealogies are full of gaps, interruptions, disruptions, uncertainties, and imagined or assumed connections. Some groups have extensive genealogies, but even these carefully constructed records may be partly mythical and based on limited recollections or partial history. In contrast, other groups have extremely shallow

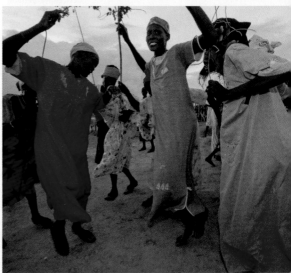

The Nuer, of the Sudan, are a classic representation of a descent group. (*top left*) A Nuer man, his sons, and cattle outside the family homestead, 1930s. (photo by E. E. Evans-Pritchard). (*top right*) A Nuer family homestead, 2007. (*bottom left*) Nuer men leaping (beside Evans-Pritchard's tent) in a dance that often took the form of mock battles between village groups. Dances accompanied marriages and provided courtship opportunities for Nuer youth. (*bottom right*) Nuer women dancing in the bride's family homestead at a contemporary Nuer wedding.

genealogical memories that span only two or three generations. Segments of these descent groups may no longer live together or act together. Other relatives may have been forgotten or excluded from the main line through conflict. Political, economic, and/or military upheaval, colonial interventions, and the establishment of modern nation-states may have disrupted collective memory and records. Or kinship patterns may have changed over time as groups adapted

FIGURE 9.1

Kinship Naming Systems

Early anthropologists identified only six general patterns worldwide for classifying relatives when beginning with the ego's generation: Eskimo, Hawaiian, Sudanese, Omaha, Crow, and Iroquois.

ESKIMO

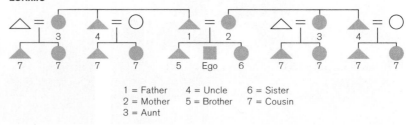

1 = Father   4 = Uncle   6 = Sister
2 = Mother   5 = Brother 7 = Cousin
3 = Aunt

The Eskimo kinship naming system is the most common in Europe and North America. Only members of the nuclear family are given distinct terms. Aunts and uncles are distinguished from parents but not by side of the family. All cousins are lumped together.

HAWAIIAN

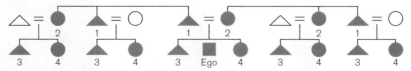

1 = Father and father's brothers 3 = Brothers and male cousins
2 = Mother and mother's sisters 4 = Sisters and female cousins

The Hawaiian system is the least complicated. The nuclear family is deemphasized, and relatives are distinguished only by generation and gender.

SUDANESE

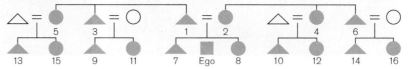

The Sudanese kinship system is the most complex. Each category of relative is given a distinct term based on genealogical distance from ego. There can be eight different cousin terms, all of whom are distinguished from ego's brother and sister.

Source: From Dennis O'Neil, "Kin Naming Systems: Part 1, The Nature of Kinship," http://anthro.palomar.edu/kinship/kinship_5.htm.

to external pressures. As a result, these groups' knowledge of individual ancestors and even whole generations may have been lost.

Once again, the Nuer are an excellent example. Despite representing one of the six key cross-cultural variations in kinship studies (Sudanese), their day-to-day kinship practices did not exactly match the clear patrilineal descent model that might be imagined on a Nuer family tree. Evans-Pritchard determined that

OMAHA

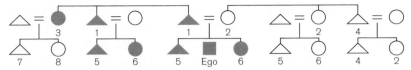

1 = Father and father's brothers
2 = Mother and females on mother's side
3 = Females on father's side
4 = Males on mother's side

5 = Male siblings and parallel cousins
6 = Female siblings and parallel cousins
7 = Male cross cousins
8 = Female cross cousins

The Omaha, Crow, and Iroquois naming systems trace kinship through unilineal descent—either patrilineally or matrilineally—so distinguishing between cousins takes on importance. The Omaha system is typical of kinship patterns traced through patrilineal descent.

CROW

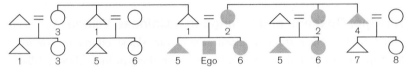

1 = Father and father's brothers
2 = Mother and mother's sisters
3 = Females on father's side
4 = Male on mother's side

5 = Male siblings and parallel cousins
6 = Female siblings and parallel cousins
7 = Male cross cousins
8 = Female cross cousins

The Crow system is typical of kinship patterns traced through matrilineal descent.

IROQUOIS

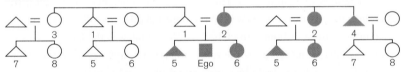

1 = Father and father's brother
2 = Mother and mother's sister
3 = Female on father's side
4 = Male on mother's side

5 = Male parallel cousins
6 = Female parallel cousins
7 = Male cross cousins
8 = Female cross cousins

The Iroquois kinship system can be traced either matrilineally or patrilineally. Note the same term is used for father and father's brother and for mother and mother's sister, reflecting shared membership in lineages.

the Nuer inherited formal group membership through patrilineal descent, but he and Kathleen Gough (1971), who revisited the study a generation later, found that most Nuer individuals continued to trace kinship relations through both parents. These bilateral kinship relationships created by marriage were often just as important as those created through descent. Specifically, while women married into the Nuer descent group and produced children for that group, they also provided their children with close connections to kin on the mother's side, particularly the mother's brother. This pattern often occurs in patrilineal groups.

When Gough revisited Evans-Pritchard's original study, she suggested that local events in the 1930s may have affected Nuer kinship practices at the time. During the time of Evans-Pritchard's research in the 1930s, the Nuer were resisting British colonial occupation of the Sudan. In addition, they were involved in a conquest of the neighboring Dinka ethnic group. Additional intense conflicts existed among Nuer groups. Gough suggests that these tensions, conflicts, and disruptions may have intensified Nuer attention to kinship and marriage patterns as they attempted to reinforce group identity and assimilate outsiders. Gough also suggests that the particular expressions of kinship recorded by Evans-Pritchard may have been adaptations to political and economic conditions rather than an entrenched, changeless kinship norm (Gough 1971; see also Stone 2009).

Kinship, Descent, and Change in a Chinese Village. As Gough found in her Nuer study, political factors can shape efforts to construct kinship—a pattern I also uncovered in my own research in a Chinese village. When I conducted fieldwork in the late 1990s, I thought I had found a classic, Nuer-style patrilineal descent group. Ninety percent of the men in the village had the surname Chen and traced their origins back to the founding Chen—the apical ancestor—who they believed had settled in the area more than 700 years earlier. The village children, boys and girls, were all named Chen. But the Chen daughters were all to be married out to men in neighboring villages. The Chen men were to marry women from the same neighboring villages who would move in with them at home. The Chen family temple was the largest ancestral hall in the village and served as the center for venerating Chen ancestors. Until the 1960s, village lands, including agricultural plots and fisheries, were held in common by the Chen lineage, which acted like a small corporation. Male elders allocated access to the collectively owned village property to the other males in the descent group during an annual lineage meeting.

The village appeared to be a textbook case of a patrilineal Chinese descent group. But kinship is always a bit more complicated and interesting than anthropologists first imagine. In the late 1960s, family and temple ancestral records were destroyed as part of a chaotic and brutal national political movement known as the Cultural Revolution—a modernization campaign promoted by the Chinese government to throw out the old and bring in the new. Only in the 1990s did political and economic conditions improve enough for local villagers to consider reconstructing their lost records. An older village member who had become a university professor in the provincial capital accepted the task of writing and publishing a local village history book called a *zupu* ("gazetteer"). His research included an effort to reconstruct the village genealogy and the Chen line of descent. Funding came from villagers working abroad, particularly in the United States.

MAP 9.2
Fuzhou

When the research was complete, however, the devastating impact of the Cultural Revolution became apparent. Without written records, the reconstructed genealogy relied primarily on oral histories stored in the memories of village elders. Many vividly recalled their parents' and grandparents' generations. Some had heard stories of a few prominent Chen villagers whose earlier travel, business success, or scholarship had made them famous in the villagers' collective memory. Of course, the apical ancestor, his sons, and a few of their immediate descendants had been remembered. Unfortunately, most of the generations prior to 1900 had been left blank. The genealogical details, if they had ever existed, had been destroyed during the Cultural Revolution.

Migration has also challenged the Chen descent group's ability to maintain kinship connections, especially in the context of the current global age. In fact, fully 70 percent of the villagers—most between the ages of eighteen and fifty— have left China since the early 1980s to seek their fortunes in the United States, Japan, South America, Canada, Europe, and the Middle East. Some return to visit their hometown. Most marry and have children in their new host country. According to the rules of the patrilineal descent group, all children born to villagers working abroad still belong in the descent group, and males can pass on that membership to the next generation. But faced with such a massive out-migration and global diaspora of the lineage, how would they keep track as villagers migrated halfway around the world?

New York is the primary international destination for the village's immigrants. There, with the support of village leaders in China, immigrants have created a village hometown association to rebuild and strengthen hometown kinship

Chinese family ancestral hall outside Fuzhou, China, built with money sent by villagers working abroad.

ties. The association enables villagers to reconnect, provide mutual support, share information, and use their kinship networks to improve their immigrant experience. Association leaders also keep track of fellow villagers, their marriages, and their offspring. They report these developments back to the Chen family elders in China for proper recording. Through this process, long-held village strategies for kinship formation and group building are adapting to the challenges of wide-scale international migration, spurred by globalization. Modern communication and transportation technologies are enabling Chinese villagers to innovatively extend their notions of patrilineal descent, both spatially beyond China's national boundary and temporally forward into the future.

Certainly the forces of globalization, including migration and time-space compression, are placing stress on kinship systems worldwide. This is occurring as members of kinship groups relocate temporarily or permanently to nearby factories or jobs in other countries to seek improved economic and educational opportunities or to avoid natural disasters and political upheavals. Although generalized kinship categories developed by an earlier generation of anthropologists have provided insights into broad patterns of kinship, anthropologists who study kinship today confront more fluid kinship patterns maintained through flexibility and creativity.

MARRIAGE AND AFFINAL TIES

affinal relationship
A kinship relationship established through marriage and/or alliance, not through biology or common descent.

A second way humans form kinship groups is through marriage—what anthropologists refer to as **affinal relationships**. Unlike the construction of kinship groups through descent, which links direct genealogical ancestors and descendants, marriage builds kinship ties between two people who are (usually) not immediate biological kin. Marriage also creates a relationship between the spouses' respective kinship groups, called "in-laws" in U.S. culture. The new kinship group created through marriage is linked through affinity and alliance, not through shared biology and common descent.

marriage
A socially recognized relationship that may involve physical and emotional intimacy as well as legal rights to property and inheritance.

Something like marriage exists in every culture, but its exact form and characteristics vary widely—so widely, in fact, that it is difficult to say that any one characteristic is universal. **Marriages** create socially recognized relationships that may involve physical and emotional intimacy, sexual pleasure, reproduction and raising of children, mutual support and companionship, and shared legal rights to property and inheritance. The bond of marriage may also serve to create connection, communication, and alliance between groups.

arranged marriage
Marriage orchestrated by the families of the involved parties.

Marriages take many forms, including arranged marriages and companionate marriages. **Arranged marriages**, orchestrated by the families of the bride and groom, continue to be prominent in many cultures in Asia, the Pacific, the Middle East, and Africa. Arranged marriages are even common among some religious groups in the United States and, in a sense, among some segments of the upper class who send their children to elite private schools to meet future partners and encourage in-group marriage. These traditional marriages ensure the reproduction and continuation of the kinship group and build alliances with other kin groups. Thus the couple's parents may view the economic and political consequences of marriage alliance as being too important to the larger kinship group to be left to the whims of two young people. In this context, marriage becomes a social obligation and a symbol of commitment to the larger group rather than a mechanism for personal satisfaction and fulfillment. Alliance marriages of this sort require extensive negotiation to balance the needs of the group and the intimate personal feelings of the individuals being married. Bonds of affection may develop in an arranged marriage, but this is not the primary goal.

What about Love? Today marriage patterns are changing rapidly. Younger generations are increasingly thinking of love, intimacy, and personal pleasure—not social obligation—as the foundation on which to build families and kinship relations. Love—and what anthropologists call **companionate marriages**, which are built on love—is the ideal to be achieved (Chan 2006; Gregg 2003; Inhorn 1996; Rebhun 1999; Wardlow 2006; Yan 2003).

On a global scale, changing notions of marriage are combining with expanding economic opportunities for women to spur a rapid rise of divorce and marriage dissolution. Melanie Medeiros's (2014) ethnographic study of the small town of Brogodo in the rural interior of Northeast Brazil reveals the local impact of these transformations. Populated by Afro-Brazilian descendants of slaves and plantation workers, Brogodo's economy shrank drastically in the early twentieth century because of the decline of the mining industry, leaving residents to rely primarily on small-scale farming and remittances from relatives in urban areas. When the adjacent area was declared a national park in 1985, however, the growing eco-tourism industry generated better-paying local jobs, particularly for women who were recruited to work as receptionists, waitresses, and housekeepers. Economic opportunities for men were more limited, as tour guide jobs went primarily to bilingual outsiders. Medeiros's fieldwork in Brogodo found that 40 percent of couples in local households surveyed were separated or divorced and that 95 percent of those dissolutions occurred at the request of women. Interviews confirmed that women's increased economic independence, combined with shifting expectations about gender roles and marriage, was driving up the rate of marital dissolution in Brogodo.

Cross-cultural ethnographic research reveals diversity in local expressions of companionate marriage but shows that young people around the world increasingly frame marriage in terms of love, in contrast to the marriage patterns of their parents (Hirsch 2007). Consider for a moment how your own views on marriage compare to those of your parents and grandparents.

companionate marriage
Marriage built on love, intimacy, and personal choice rather than social obligation.

MAP 9.3
Brazil

Monogamy, Polygyny, and Polyandry. Cultural rules, often inscribed in law, may determine who is a legitimate or preferred marriage partner. They may even determine how many people one can marry. Historically, some cultures, such as the Nuer of the Sudan or the Brahmans of Nepal, practiced **polygyny**—several marriages involving one man and two or more women. In a few cultures, including the Nyar of India and the Nyimba of Tibet and Nepal, **polyandry** has been common—marriages between one woman and two or more men. Most marriages in the world demonstrate **monogamy**—marriage (usually) between one man and one woman, though, as of 2017, twenty-two countries also legally recognize same-sex marriages, as we will discuss later in the chapter.

Even where monogamous marriages are the norm, it is common for people to marry more than one person in their lifetime. How does this happen? Marriages may be interrupted by divorce or death. In these cases, individuals who marry again reflect a process called *serial monogamy* in which monogamous marriages follow one after the other.

Incest Taboos. Just as some form of marriage exists in essentially all cultures, likewise all cultures have some form of **incest taboo**, or rules that forbid sexual relations with certain close relatives. Such taboos relate to nuclear family members: parents and children, siblings, and grandparents and grandchildren. Incest taboos also affect marriage patterns. A few historical examples of brother-sister marriage exist: among the Inca of Peru, among certain traditional Hawaiian groups, and among ancient Egyptian royalty (perhaps to preserve family control over wealth and power). But these cases are rare. Incest taboos universally prohibit marriage between siblings and between parents and children. But can a person marry a cousin? Let's explore that question more closely.

Beyond the nuclear family, incest taboos vary from culture to culture. In some contemporary cultures, including parts of China, India, the Middle East, and Africa, *cross-cousins* (children of a mother's brother or father's sister) are preferred marriage partners, but *parallel cousins* (children of a father's brother or a mother's sister) are excluded. Even in the United States, incest rules regarding marriage between cousins vary from state to state. Nineteen states allow *first-cousin* marriages (between the children of two siblings). More distant cousins are not excluded from marriage under U.S. law. No other country in the Western world prohibits first-cousin marriage. Moreover, although it is illegal in the United States to marry a *half-sibling* (a brother or sister with whom one shares a parent), this is not illegal in many other cultures. Can you think of anyone in your family or a friend's family who is married to a cousin?

Even though the incest taboo is universal, its origins are unclear. Some scholars have suggested that the taboo arises from an instinctive horror of sex with immediate family members that developed during our evolutionary history (Hobhouse 1915; Lowie 1920). But studies of primates do not reveal a

---

polygyny

Marriage between one man and two or more women.

polyandry

Marriage between one woman and two or more men.

monogamy

A relationship between only two partners.

incest taboo

Cultural rules that forbid sexual relations with certain close relatives.

consistent incest taboo that humans might have inherited (Rodseth et al. 1991). Furthermore, if this instinctive horror existed, then it seems likely that humans would not need to create taboos to restrict incest.

Other theories have addressed the issue from different perspectives. For example, anthropologist Bronislaw Malinowski (1929) and psychologist Sigmund Freud (1952) both suggested that incest taboos might have developed to protect the family unit from sexual competitiveness and jealousy, which would disrupt cooperation. However, neither scholar could substantiate this claim with historical or contemporary ethnographic data. Another theory suggests that incest taboos arose out of concern that inbreeding would promote biological degeneration and genetically abnormal offspring (Morgan 1877). However, incest taboos predate the development of population science and the understanding of human genetics.

Even using contemporary genetic information, the science does not support the assumptions behind the incest taboo. For instance, incest does not create defective genes. If a harmful trait runs in the family, systematic inbreeding will increase the possibility of the defective gene being passed along and amplified in the gene pool. But long-term systematic inbreeding over many generations has few actual historical human examples. Genetic studies of consanguineous unions (between "blood" relatives) show some increased risk of congenital defects, but only within the studies' margin of error. These risks are actually less than the risk of congenital defects in children whose mothers are over the age of forty; yet this older population is not prohibited from marrying or giving birth (Bennett et al. 2002). Therefore, despite the universal existence of incest taboos, the extent of the taboos varies widely and no consensus exists as to their origins or exact purpose.

Other Marriage Patterns. Beyond explicit incest taboos, all cultures have norms about who is a legitimate or preferred marriage partner. In some groups, including most descent groups, marriage tends to reflect **exogamy**, meaning marriage to someone outside the group. Other groups practice **endogamy**, requiring marriage inside the group. Although kin group exogamy is more prevalent, endogamy exists in numerous cultures. It is practiced, for example, within the Indian caste system and within whole ethnic groups, as evidenced by both historical and contemporary U.S. marriage patterns.

In the United States, we practice *kindred exogamy*: We avoid, either by force of law or by power of tradition, marriage with certain relatives. At the same time, we also follow clear patterns of class, race, and religious endogamy. Indeed, most marriages occur between people of the same economic class, of the same religious tradition, and within the same "race" (U.S. Census Bureau 2010). As noted in Chapter 2, interracial marriages were outlawed for most of U.S. history, and only in 1967 did the U.S. Supreme Court rule that anti-miscegenation laws are unconstitutional. Although interracial marriage is legal today, intense patterns of racial endogamy continue.

exogamy
Marriage to someone outside the kinship group.

endogamy
Marriage to someone within the kinship group.

While interracial relationships are legal in the United States today, intense patterns of racial endogamy (marriage within the same group) continue. Here, (*left*) Mildred and Richard Loving embrace at a press conference the day after the U.S. Supreme Court ruled in their favor, June 13, 1967, in *Loving v. Virginia*, overturning Virginia's laws banning interracial marriage. And (*photo right*) John Lawrence (*left*) and Tyron Garner (*right*) attend a press conference in Houston, June 26, 2003, after the U.S. Supreme Court in *Lawrence v. Texas* struck down the Texas ban on gay sex as an unconstitutional violation of privacy.

Most monogamous marriages occur between one man and one woman, but there are important exceptions, including female marriage among the Nuer of the Sudan and the Nandi of Kenya. Today same-sex marriage has gained increasing acceptance globally, being recognized in the Netherlands (2001), Belgium (2003), Spain (2005), South Africa (2006), Norway (2009), Sweden (2009), Argentina (2010), Iceland (2010), Portugal (2010), Denmark (2012), France (2013), Brazil (2013), Uruguay (2013), New Zealand (2013), the United Kingdom (2014), Luxemborg (2015), Ireland (2015), Greenland (2016), Colombia (2016), and Finland (2017). In North America, Canada legalized same-sex marriages in 2005. In the United States, as of June 2015 same-sex marriages are legal in all fifty states and Washington, D.C.

Whether arranged or not, and whether monogamous, polygynous, or polyandrous, same or opposite gender, marriages may be accompanied by an exchange of gifts—most commonly, bridewealth and dowry—used to formalize and legalize the relationship. Though most contemporary Western cultures view marriage as an individual matter entered into by a couple who are romantically in love, in many non-Western cultures marriages focus on the establishment of strategic alliances, relationships, and obligations between groups—namely, the bride's kin and the groom's kin. Bridewealth and dowry gifts formalize and legalize marriages and establish the relationship between these groups.

Bridewealth—common in many parts of the Middle East and Africa, where it often involves the exchange of cattle, cash, or other goods—is a gift from the groom and his kin to the bride's kin. Often thought of as a means to compensate her family for the loss of the bride, bridewealth agreements also establish reciprocal

bridewealth

The gift of goods or money from the groom's family to the bride's family as part of the marriage process.

rights and obligations of the husband and wife, give legitimacy to their children, and assign the children to the husband's family. Even with the exchange of bride-wealth, though, marriages may not always remain stable. Incompatibility, infertility, and infidelity can threaten the marriage agreement and trigger a return of the bridewealth. In this way, bridewealth can stabilize the marriage by establishing a vested interest for both extended families in the marriage's success (Stone 2009).

Through a **dowry**, the bride's family gives gifts to the husband's family at marriage. Common in India, a dowry may be part of a woman's family inheritance that the woman and her new husband can use to establish their household. In many cases, dowries may be seen as compensation to a husband and his family for taking on the responsibility of a wife, perhaps because of women's relatively low status in India or because upper-class and upper-caste women are not supposed to work. Today gifts often include personal and household items. Compulsory dowries are no longer legal in India (since 1961). But dowries are still quite common as part of the public process of transferring rights and legitimizing alliances. In some unfortunate instances where the dowry is considered insufficient, the bride may become the victim of domestic violence. In extreme cases this may lead to the murder or suicide of the bride, sometimes through bride burning or self-immolation. Such practices have come under severe criticism and are the target of human rights campaigns by groups inside India and in the international community that are committed to protecting the rights and lives of Indian women (Stone 2009).

dowry
The gift of goods or money from the bride's family to the groom's family as part of the marriage process.

Are Biology and Marriage the Only Basis for Kinship?

Cross-cultural ethnographic research reveals diverse strategies for constructing kinship ties that do not require direct biological connection or marriage alliances. As you will see, the range of strategies underscores the fluid, socially constructed aspect of kinship in many cultures.

HOUSES, HEARTHS, AND KINSHIP: THE LANGKAWI OF MALAYSIA

Among Malay villagers on the island of Langkawi, studied by Janet Carsten in the 1990s, kinship is not only given at birth but also is acquired throughout life (Carsten 1997). The Langkawi house and its hearth—where people gather to cook and eat—serve as places to construct kinship. In particular, Langkawi kinship is acquired through co-residence and co-feeding. In the local thinking, "blood" and other bodily substances are formed by eating food cooked at home. Other bodily

MAP 9.4
Langkawi

Among the Langkawi in Malaysia, kinship is created by sharing meals prepared in the family hearth and living together in the same house. (*left*) Langkawi children eat together near the family kitchen. (*right*) A Langkawi child and her maternal great-grandmother sit together, becoming kin, on a house ladder.

substances, explicitly breast milk and semen, are regarded as forms of blood. Thus, a husband and wife gradually become more similar by living and eating together. Sisters and brothers have the closest kinship relationship in childhood because they grow up in the same household eating the same food; but as they marry and move out of the shared home, their "blood" becomes less similar.

The Malay ideal is to marry someone close in terms of genealogy, geography, social status, or disposition. But perhaps because of the Langkawis' history of mobility, as well as the arrival of settlers in their outlying region of the Malay state, local notions of kinship have allowed new people to become close kin by living and eating together. For example, many children in the community have grown up spending significant time in homes with adults other than their birth parents. This fostering has been common for nieces, nephews, grandchildren, and others who are welcomed into the foster family and treated on an equal basis with those born into the family.

In addition, Langkawi understandings of fostering have often included expressions of hospitality in the community, whether one is a short-term or long-term visitor, a visiting student, or a distant relative. Villagers assume that all those who live together and eat together, regardless of their backgrounds, gradually come to resemble one another physically. The ideal guest—successfully fostered—stays for a long time, becomes part of the community, marries a local person, and raises children. In this way, the individual fully enters the kin group. This flexible process has built kinship relations that do not require the connection of biology or marriage. Instead, "[h]ouses and their hearths are the sites of the production of kinship" (Carsten 1997, 128; Carsten 2004; Peletz 1999; Stone 2009).

CREATING KIN TO SURVIVE POVERTY: BLACK NETWORKS NEAR CHICAGO, ILLINOIS

Kinship can even be a means to survive poverty, as Carol Stack's *All Our Kin: Strategies for Survival in a Black Community* (1974) demonstrates. This ethnography is a classic in anthropological kinship studies. Through deep involvement in an impoverished urban African American community called the Flats in a town outside Chicago, Stack uncovered residents' complex survival strategies based on extended kinship networks.

Although the federal government's 1965 Moynihan Report "The Negro Family: The Case for National Action" had branded the black family as disorganized, dysfunctional, and lost in a culture of poverty of its own making (see Chapter 10), Stack found otherwise. She uncovered a dynamic set of kinship networks based on mutual reciprocity through which residents managed to survive conditions of intense structural poverty and long-term unemployment.

These kinship networks included biological kin and *fictive kin*—those who became kin. They stretched among households and across generations, extending to include all those willing to participate in a system of mutual support. Members provided child care. They loaned money to others in need. They took in children who needed a foster home for a while. They borrowed clothes. They exchanged all kinds of things when asked. They cared for one another's sick or aging family members. Despite survival odds stacked against them in a community with few jobs, dilapidated housing, and chronic poverty, residents of the Flats succeeded in building lifelines for survival through their extended kinship networks (McAdoo 2000; Taylor 2000).

MAP 9.5
Chicago

How Are Ideas of Kinship Linked to the Nation-State?

References to the nation often invoke metaphors of homeland, motherland, fatherland, and ancestral home. These concepts consolidate political force and build a sense of common nationality and ethnicity. Indeed, Benedict Anderson, in *Imagined Communities* (1983), marvels at the ability of nation-states to inspire a common national or ethnic identity among people who have never met, most likely never will meet, and have little in common socially, politically, or economically. Yet many people feel so connected to their country that they are even willing to die for it. How does this idea of the "nation" gain such emotional power? Janet Carsten (2004) suggests that nationalism draws heavily on ideas of kinship and family to create a sense of connection among very different people.

Like membership in many families, citizenship in the nation generally derives from birth and biology. Citizenship may be conveyed through direct descent from a current citizen. Another key pathway to membership in some nations, available to immigrants and other outsiders, like membership in many other families, is through marriage. Over time, members of the nation come to see themselves as part of an extended family that shares a common ancestry and a deep biological connection. As the boundaries blur among kinship, nationalism, and even religion, these powerful metaphors shape our actions and experiences (Carsten 2004).

REPRODUCING JEWS: ISSUES OF ARTIFICIAL INSEMINATION IN ISRAEL

MAP 9.6
Israel

In Israel, we can see how women serve as key players in defining and maintaining kinship connections. Susan Kahn's (2000) ethnography *Reproducing Jews: A Cultural Account of Assisted Conception in Israel* provides a dramatic contemporary example of the powerful intersection among reproduction, kinship, religion, and the state. For historical and religious reasons, Jewish women in Israel feel great pressure to reproduce the family and the nation. Israel's national health policies heavily favor increased reproduction. The national health insurance, for instance, subsidizes all assisted reproductive technologies. It does not promote family planning services to prevent pregnancy. Today the country has more fertility clinics per person than any other nation in the world, and it was the first to legalize surrogate motherhood.

Kahn's study examines a small but growing group of single Jewish mothers who are giving birth through artificial insemination. Because Jewishness passes down matrilineally from mother to child, what happens when a child is conceived through assisted reproductive technologies? These matters are of vital importance to the reproduction of Judaism and the state of Israel and, thus, are subject to intense debate by Jewish rabbis and Israeli state policymakers alike. Some scenarios are straightforward. For instance, in the eyes of the Israeli state any offspring conceived through artificial insemination and born to unmarried Jewish women are legitimate citizens. The line of descent and religious inheritance through the mother is clear. As evidence, the state provides these unmarried mothers with a wide range of support, including housing, child care, and tax breaks.

But other scenarios spur complex disagreements about religion and nationality. What is the effect on citizenship and religious identity when non-Jewish men donate sperm to Jewish women? Who is considered to be the father—the sperm donor or the mother's husband? When Jewish women carry to term eggs from non-Jewish women, who is considered to be the mother—the donor of the egg or the woman who carries the egg to term? The situation is equally complicated if a non-Jewish surrogate mother carries the embryo of a Jewish woman that was fertilized by a Jewish man through in vitro fertilization.

Much is at stake in these arguments for the Jewish religion and for the state of Israel. The decision about kinship in these cases of assisted reproductive technologies intersects with heated debates about how Judaism is reproduced and how Israel is populated. In fact, the decision has implications not only for the Jewish religion but also for notions of ethnic and national belonging and for the pathways to legal citizenship in the state of Israel (Feldman 2001; Finkler 2002; Nahman 2002; Stone 2009).

How Is Kinship Changing in the Modern World?

Kinship patterns are rapidly changing around the world in response to cultural shifts, changing gender roles, new imaginations of marriage, technological advances, and processes of globalization.

THE NUCLEAR FAMILY: THE IDEAL VERSUS THE REALITY

The nuclear family concept acquired a particular history in Western industrialized cultures. This occurred as families adapted to an economic system that required increased mobility to follow job opportunities wherever they might lead. Though people are born into a **family of orientation** (in which they grow up and develop life skills), when they reach adulthood they are expected to detach from their nuclear family of orientation, choose a mate, and construct

family of orientation
The family group in which one is born, grows up, and develops life skills.

FIGURE 9.2
U.S. Households by Type, 1970–2010

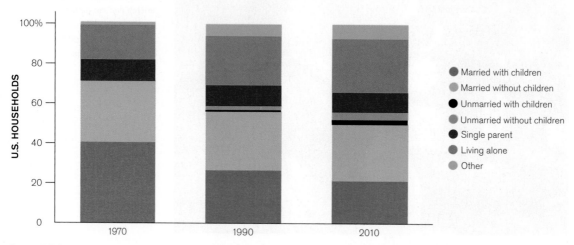

Source: U.S. Census Bureau. 2014. "Families and Living Arrangements." http://www.census.gov/hhes/families/data/families.html.

family of procreation

The family group created when one reproduces and within which one rears children.

a new nuclear **family of procreation** (in which they reproduce and raise their own children). These "detachable" nuclear family units are extremely well adapted to a culture that prioritizes economic success, independence, and mobility over geographic stability and intergenerational continuity. In many ways, this view of the nuclear family has become entrenched as the standard against which to judge other family forms (Schneider 1980).

Historical studies suggest that the place of the nuclear family as the cornerstone of U.S. culture may be more myth than reality (Coontz 1988, 1992). Although the nuclear family came into prominence during a unique period of economic expansion after World War II, before that time it had not played a major role in the kinship history of the United States. The idealized nuclear family of the twentieth century did not exist for the early colonists and only emerged as a result of industrialization in the nineteenth century. Even at its height in the mid-twentieth century, participation in the nuclear family model was far from universal. It was limited to a minority of Americans, particularly those in the white middle class (Carsten 2004; Coontz 1988, 1992; Stone 2009).

Current kinship patterns in the United States are changing rapidly, just as they are in many other parts of the world. In a wide variety of newly constructed family forms and kinship networks, biology is becoming less central and personal choice is becoming more important (Figure 9.2). Families are creatively renegotiating kinship after divorce. Blended families are constructing new relationships to include step-parents, step-children, step-siblings, multiple sets of grandparents, and extended households of former spouses. Unmarried couples are living together. Same-sex couples are having or adopting children. Families are supplementing biological connections and affinal marriage connections with alternative family forms based on friendship, respect, and mutual support. New reproductive technologies are yielding families of choice through in vitro fertilization, artificial insemination, and surrogacy. These patterns cut across all social classes and ethnic groups and reflect new residential and interpersonal relationships that contrast sharply with the imagined privacy and separation associated with the nuclear family ideal.

CHOSEN FAMILIES

Kath Weston's (1991) ethnographic study of the construction of gay and lesbian families in San Francisco in the 1980s, *Families We Choose*, provides an example of creating kinship through choice. For many gay men and lesbians, "coming out" is a uniquely traumatic experience, especially when the revelation of one's sexuality and life choices generates hostility from close friends and family. When parents, siblings, and other close relatives cut off the kinship ties that U.S. culture suggests should be permanent and enduring, gay men and lesbians have turned to chosen families instead.

Not surprisingly, chosen families come in many shapes and sizes. Gay and straight friends, biological children, children adopted formally and informally, and former lovers all can become kin. Close friends can become family. Support networks and caregivers can take the place of biological kin and become kin themselves. Weston finds this to be a particularly common experience for those who provide care through intense illness, such as AIDS. Love, compassion, and the hard work of care over time make kinship very real in chosen families. This is a crucial development, especially when biological kin ties are inadequate or have failed completely.

Weston's study reminds us not to assume that the natural characteristics of biological kinship ties are better than the actual behavior of chosen families. In the absence of functional, biologically related families, Weston points out, chosen families take on the characteristics of stability, continuity, endurance, and permanence to become "real." Yet while these families become real in many ways, they may not be recognized under the law or provide a range of state-regulated rights—from hospital visitation to inheritance (Bolin 1992; Lewin 1992).

THE IMPACT OF ASSISTED REPRODUCTIVE TECHNOLOGIES

Discussions of new technologies that assist in human reproduction have filled the popular media, religious publications, courtrooms, and legislative halls of government. Such technologies include sperm and egg donation, in vitro fertilization, surrogacy, and cloning. Their emergence raises questions about the rights

Increasingly people are creating kinship through choice. Here, a gay couple in Chengdu, China, share their home with their adopted son, daughter-in-law, and grandson.

of parents and of children born with this assistance, as well as the impact of these innovations on our ideas and experience of kinship and family. Culture, in the form of medical technology, is now shaping biology. The long-term implications for kinship are unclear but deserve consideration (Franklin 1997).

Reproductive technologies are not new. Most, if not all, cultures have had techniques for promoting or preventing conception or enabling or terminating pregnancy. These have included fertility enhancements, contraceptives, abortion, and cesarean surgeries. Over the last thirty years, technological developments have opened new avenues for scientific intervention in the reproductive process and the formation of kinship. DNA testing can now determine the identity of a child's father with remarkable certainty, erasing uncertainty about paternity. Medical tests can now identify the sex of unborn children, a practice that has become problematic in parts of India and China where a strong cultural preference for male children has led to early termination of many female fetuses (Davis-Floyd & Dumit 1997). Across the globe, when reproductive technologies become increasingly specialized, the implications for cultural constructs such as family and kinship become progressively more complex.

FAMILIES OF SAME-SEX PARTNERS

Gay and lesbian couples are not new in U.S. culture, but recently they have become more open about their sexual orientation and their relationships. At the same time, many other people are having an increasingly open discussion about gay men, lesbians, and same-sex marriage. Television shows and movies routinely include gay characters. Celebrities like Elton John, Jillian Michaels, and Neil Patrick Harris raise children with their same-sex partners. The United Methodist Church ordained its first openly gay bishop, Karen Oliveto, in 2016. And when a high school in Louisiana canceled its senior prom in 2010 rather than allow a graduating student to bring her girlfriend as her date, a group of parents organized an alternative prom so the girls could attend. These examples demonstrate a growing recognition of same-sex relationships in numerous U.S. cultural arenas.

However, the cultural debate about homosexuality and same-sex marriage in the United States is intense and by no means settled. Within the debate we can see the contestation of cultural norms and values. Opponents raise concerns that these alternative kinship patterns will cause the breakdown of the traditional family and that the acceptance of homosexuality will lead to social disorder.

Drawing on generations of cross-cultural research on kinship, marriage, and the family, in 2004 the American Anthropological Association issued the following statement:

> The results of more than a century of anthropological research on households, kinship relationships, and families, across cultures and through time, provide no support whatsoever for the view that

Julia Troxler (*right*) and new spouse Barbara Schwartz (*center*) celebrate their wedding in Atlanta, Georgia, in 2015, just hours after the U.S. Supreme Court ruled same-sex marriage a constitutional right.

either civilization or viable social orders depend upon marriage as an exclusively heterosexual institution. Rather, anthropological research supports the conclusion that a vast array of family types, including families built upon same-sex partnerships, can contribute to stable and humane societies. (American Anthropological Association 2004)

From an anthropological perspective, these discussions about same-sex marriage illustrate the changing patterns of kinship in the United States. Looking cross-culturally, we see that there is no single definition of marriage, but many. As anthropologist Linda Stone notes, "From a global, cross-cultural perspective, those who seek same-sex marriage are not trying to redefine marriage, but merely to define it for themselves, in their own interests, as people around the world have always done" (2009, 271).

Today, changes in the nuclear family, the rise of families of choice, the increase of same-sex marriages, and advances in assisted reproductive technologies are reshaping views of kinship and family in the United States and globally. These changes do not necessarily indicate an improvement or decline of family life or moral values. However, they do reveal a shift of kinship patterns away from a biologically defined, nuclear family model toward other models based on choice, flexibility, and fluidity (Coontz 1992; Stone 2009).

While debates will continue over changing patterns of marriage and family, from an anthropological perspective one point is undeniable: Marriage, family, and kinship are cultural constructs, and as such they are subject to change. You are certain to see even more change in these arenas during your lifetime.

Toolkit

Thinking Like an Anthropologist
Kinship in Personal and Global Perspective

We experience kinship all the time, although we may not use that term to describe it. Kinship is close to home, for it comes alive in the people we live with, eat with, play with. It is vital as we experience the most dramatic periods of our personal lives. You will continue to make kinship and family relationships—perhaps through marriage, having children, and choosing close friends who ultimately become family. Thinking like an anthropologist can help you to better understand these experiences. And in today's globally interconnected world, having an understanding of the vast diversity of kinship patterns may help you navigate relationships with classmates, friends, family, and colleagues. As you do so, keep in mind the questions that have guided our discussion in this chapter:

- **How are we related to one another?**
- **Are biology and marriage the only basis for kinship?**
- **How are ideas of kinship linked to the nation-state?**
- **How is kinship changing in the modern world?**

In thinking about the complex family relationships described in the chapter opener, how can we apply this chapter's ideas to better understand their situation and, more generally, any future changes in the constructs of kin and family? Who is related to whom? Who decides? Is kinship primarily biological, or can family be chosen? Who constitutes your own family? As you traced your family tree, did you see that kinship is not only about creating a list of relatives but also about understanding the many ways those ties are formed and the role that kin play in shaping you as an individual and as a member of society? These tools of anthropological analysis will become increasingly important to you as you engage changing concepts of kinship in cultures across the globe during the twenty-first century.

Key Terms

Chapter 10
Class and Inequality

In January 2016, National Guard troops deployed to Flint, Michigan, distributing bottled water to residents who for nearly two years had unsafe water flowing out of their taps. In April 2014, the emergency manager appointed by Michigan's governor to tackle Flint's fiscal crisis had switched the source of drinking water from Lake Huron to the highly corrosive and historically polluted Flint River. The city's failure to implement corrosion control measures then caused lead to leach out of aging water pipes into residents' drinking water.

Widespread complaints and public protests of foul smelling orange-brown water, rashes, hair loss, abdominal pains, and other health problems were dismissed by city and state officials who offered assurances that the water was safe to drink. It was not.

Only when a Flint pediatrician, Dr. Mona Hanna-Attisha, and researchers from Virginia Tech in September 2015 reported widespread incidents of children testing positive for elevated lead levels did officials begin to

Labor and community activists call for Michigan Governor Rick Snyder to resign over the Flint water contamination crisis.

react, and then only after more weeks of denial. Lead is a known neurotoxin, and lead poisoning can severely affect children's physical and mental development. Its effects are irreversible.

Under mounting pressure, in October 2015 officials returned Flint's water supply to its Lake Huron source. But using bottled water for drinking, cooking, and bathing has become a daily routine for Flint residents in a city with a severely damaged water system. The long-term effects of Flint's public health emergency are unknown.

How could such a water crisis—more often associated with megacities in the global South—have been created in one of the wealthiest countries in the world? What made Flint particularly vulnerable?

Flint, about an hour's drive north of Detroit, was once a prosperous working-class city at the center of the Industrial Revolution. Birthplace of General Motors and the United Automobile Workers union, its population peaked at almost 200,000 in 1960, and as late as 1978 GM employed nearly 80,000 residents. But over the next forty years Flint was gutted by deindustrialization and flexible accumulation as GM relocated jobs overseas in search of cheaper wages, fewer environmental restrictions, lower taxes, and greater profits. Today Flint is one of the country's poorest cities. Its majority African American population has dropped to under 100,000, and fewer than 8,000 GM jobs remain. The city's poverty rate is over 40 percent and its median household income is $24,679.

MAP 10.1
Flint

As anthropologists have long noted (Wittfogel 1957), the circulation of water is not a strictly natural process involving oceans, lakes, streams, evaporation, clouds, and rain. Increasingly, the circulation of water intersects with human systems of power to become a *hydro-social process*. Nature intersects with dams, canals, irrigation systems, pipes, pumps, faucets, drains, and sewers. Technicians manage its circulation. Politicians allocate resources for its infrastructure. On a global scale, the distribution of water reveals the distribution of social power along intersecting lines of class, race, gender, and age (Harvey 1996, 2003). Who has access to it, controls its flow, and organizes its distribution? According to the United Nations and the World Health Organization, 663 million people in the world lack access to safe drinking water, 1.8 billion people use a water source contaminated by fecal matter, and each year 340,000 children die from related diseases (World Health Organization, 2015). In Flint, the hydro-social process led to the poisoning of the city's water supply.

The water crisis in Flint offers particular insights into the complicated workings of class and inequality in U.S. culture. Of all the systems of stratification and power, class may be the most difficult to see clearly and discuss openly. In previous chapters we have considered stratification along lines of race, ethnicity, gender, and sexuality. In this chapter we will explore the systems of class and inequality that exist in the United States and elsewhere: how they are

Flint resident and community activist LeeAnne Walters shows polluted water samples from her home in January 2015, ten months before officials publicly acknowledged the city-wide problem. How has class intersected with race, gender, and age to bring about this crisis?

constructed, how class intersects with race and gender, and how inequality affects individuals' life chances.

By **class** we refer to a system of power based on wealth, income, and status that creates an unequal distribution of the society's resources—usually moving wealth steadily upward into the hands of an elite. Systems of class stratify individuals' life chances and affect their possibilities for upward social mobility.

In this chapter we will consider the following questions:

- Is inequality a natural part of human culture?
- How do anthropologists analyze class and inequality?
- How are class and inequality constructed?
- What makes class and inequality largely invisible?
- What are the effects of global inequality?

By the end of the chapter, you will understand how systems of class work and how they affect your life chances and those of others. You may also be motivated to engage in efforts to change systems of inequality if you so choose.

class

A system of power based on wealth, income, and status that creates an unequal distribution of a society's resources.

Is Inequality a Natural Part of Human Culture?

Inequality exists in every contemporary culture, though it may be organized in very different ways. Each society develops its own patterns of stratification that differentiate people into groups or classes. Such categories serve as the basis for unequal access to wealth, power, resources, privileges, and status. As discussed in earlier chapters, these systems of power and stratification may include race, ethnicity, gender, and sexuality. In addition, systems of social class create and sustain patterns of inequality, structuring the relationships between rich and poor, between the privileged and the less well off. But are stratification and inequality intrinsic to human culture?

EGALITARIAN SOCIETIES

As we will consider further in Chapter 11, for thousands of years, until the development of agriculture approximately 10,000 years ago, the primary human economic and social structure was hunting and gathering. This type of structure has promoted **egalitarian societies** based on the sharing of resources to ensure group success with a relative absence of hierarchy and violence within or among groups. Most modern humans who have ever lived have been hunter-gatherers.

Archaeological evidence suggests that human evolutionary success relied on cooperation and the sharing of food, child rearing, and hunting-and-gathering responsibilities, not on hierarchy, violence, and aggression. After all, building a system of **reciprocity** in which group members equally share the bounty of the moment has long-term benefits for sustaining the group. Members can then expect the generosity to be reciprocated (Knauft 1991). Although contemporary economic relations tend to be organized around the exchange of money for services, patterns of reciprocity still exist. You may take class notes for someone who returns the favor—reciprocates—at a later date. You may give someone a ride or walk their dog or share your lunch with the understanding that at some point in the future your favor will be reciprocated. In these instances, members of our extended "group"

egalitarian society

A group based on the sharing of resources to ensure success with a relative absence of hierarchy and violence.

reciprocity

The exchange of resources, goods, and services among people of relatively equal status; meant to create and reinforce social ties.

Reciprocity in action: an Amish community gathers to raise a barn.

share their resources of time, food, or other amenities for the long-term benefit of sustaining the group. (See Chapter 11 for a longer discussion of reciprocity.)

Anthropologists have studied egalitarian societies among contemporary hunter-gatherer groups such as the Ju/Hoansi of Africa's Kalahari region (Lee 2003), as well as the Canadian Inuit and the Hadza of Tanzania (Marlowe 2010), among many others. Efforts to establish more egalitarian systems of economic and social relations have also occurred within highly stratified societies. The Amish (Hostetler 1993) and Hutterite (Hostetler 1997) communities in the United States are good examples on a small scale.

RANKED SOCIETIES

Anthropologists also recognize **ranked societies,** in which wealth is not stratified but prestige and status are. In these societies, positions of high prestige—such as chief—are largely hereditary. Because only certain individuals can occupy these positions, the social rank of the society is set regardless of the skills, wisdom, or efforts of other members.

ranked society
A group in which wealth is not stratified but prestige and status are.

Chiefs usually do not accumulate great wealth, despite their high prestige. In fact, their lifestyle and standard of living may not vary significantly from those of any other member of the group. Group members offer gifts of tribute to the chief, but these are not kept and hoarded. Instead, the chief redistributes the tribute to group members. This act of gift giving—a form of **redistribution**—ensures his or her prestige while also preserving the well-being of all group members. The chief's rank and status are reinforced not through accumulation of wealth but through reciprocity and generosity (Petersen 2009).

redistribution
A form of exchange in which accumulated wealth is collected from the members of the group and reallocated in a different pattern.

One redistribution ceremony famous in the field of anthropology is the **potlatch** practiced among the Kwakiutl of the Pacific Northwest. Among this Native American group, the chief would establish and reestablish claims to prestige and status by holding an elaborate feast and gift-giving ceremony—a potlatch. He would give guests all of his personal possessions, including supplies of food, cooking pots, blankets, weapons, and even boats. What was not given away might be destroyed as a sign of the chief's great capacity. The more elaborate the gift giving, the more status and rank the chief gained in the community. The chief's generosity also applied pressure on his guests to reciprocate in like manner, or even more elaborately in a later ceremony (Boas 1966). In a practical sense, the potlatch served to distribute key community resources of food and clothing broadly among group members. As a ritual ceremony, it represented a tradition among the Kwakiutl and other ranked societies in which social status is established not by wealth and power, but by the prestige earned via one's capacity for generosity (Boas 1966).

potlatch
Elaborate redistribution ceremony practiced among the Kwakiutl of the Pacific Northwest.

Contemporary patterns of cooperation, sharing, collaboration, and reciprocity draw on patterns of behavior central to human evolutionary success over

Women of the Makah Nation on the U.S. Pacific Northwest coast prepare salmon steaks for a potlatch, a communitywide redistribution ceremony and feast.

millions of years. In contrast, social patterns of entrenched hierarchy and stratification emerged much more recently in the human story.

The extreme stratification in today's world is a fairly recent development. Anthropologists trace its roots to the rise of intensive agriculture and populous market towns, where relatively small groups of elite merchants and landholders were able to accumulate wealth. Stratification and inequality became more pronounced in industrialized capitalist economies over recent centuries, and this uneven development appears to be accelerating under the forces of globalization, further concentrating wealth in the hands of the few (Stiglitz 2012).

How Do Anthropologists Analyze Class and Inequality?

We turn now to consider four key theorists of class and inequality. European social philosophers Karl Marx and Max Weber, writing in the nineteenth and early twentieth centuries in the context of the Industrial Revolution, are separated by a century from French sociologist Pierre Bourdieu and U.S. anthropologist Leith Mullings, whose late-twentieth-century writings are based in the context of a much more complicated and advanced capitalist economic system.

THEORIES OF CLASS

Each theorist discussed here has responded to the unique social and economic challenges of his or her time and offers key analytical insights that allow anthropologists today to more deeply investigate the realities of class and inequality. As you read about each theorist, consider how you might apply their key concepts to understanding the social class relationships and inequality in our opening story about the Flint water crisis.

Karl Marx: Bourgeoisie and Proletariat. Karl Marx (1801–1882),

perhaps the most widely read theorist of class, wrote against a background of economic change and social upheaval. During the nineteenth century, rapid economic changes and new government policies brought massive social upheaval and dislocation to western Europe. As the Industrial Revolution swept through the area, government policies restricted poor rural families' use of common village lands. Deprived of access to land they had depended on for farming, grazing, and gathering, rural people migrated to urban centers to seek jobs in the expanding industrial factories.

Marx's analysis of the increasing inequalities in the emerging capitalist economy of nineteenth-century Europe distinguished between two distinct classes of people. The **bourgeoisie**, or capitalist class, owned the **means of production**—the factories, machines, tools, raw materials, land, and financial capital needed to make things. The **proletariat**, or working class, lacked land to grow their own food, tools to make their own products, and capital to build workshops or factories. Unable to make their own living, they sold their work—their labor—to capitalists in return for wages.

Marx identified labor as the key source of value and profit in the marketplace. Owners sought to constantly increase their income by forcing workers to toil faster, longer, and for lower wages, thereby reducing the cost of production and increasing the difference between the production cost and the sale price. The surplus value created by the workers could then become profit for the owner. In this relationship, capitalists increased their wealth by extracting the surplus labor value from workers. Recognition of these two fundamentally different positions within the economy—two different classes—was essential to Marx's understanding of power relations in a culture.

Today anthropologists apply Marx's ideas to analyze class and power in contemporary society while acknowledging that capitalism has grown much more complex since Marx's time. Intense competition has grown among capitalists, notably between those in the manufacturing and financial sectors. Small-business

bourgeoisie
Marxist term for the capitalist class that owns the means of production.

means of production
The factories, machines, tools, raw materials, land, and financial capital needed to make things.

proletariat
Marxist term for the class of laborers who own only their labor.

Can you apply Marx's understanding of class to a fast-food restaurant? The median full-time salary for a fast food worker is $16,278 with no benefits. The store manager, who makes closer to $40,000 annually plus benefits, serves the owner by ensuring that the most surplus labor value possible can be extracted from the workers (PayScale 2015).

owners and farmers now own the means of production, technically making them part of Marx's bourgeoisie, but they do not possess the same access to capital as others in that class. The working class—the proletariat—is divided, with conflicts along lines of race, gender, and ethnicity. Moreover, increasing global circulation of capital is drawing local cultures and communities into class-based relationships that were not present even a generation ago.

Many contemporary social scientists recognize a middle class of professionals and managers (white-collar workers) that has emerged between capitalists and the working class (blue-collar workers). But others who take a more strict Marxist view of class argue that professionals and managers are still members of the proletariat (Buck 2009; Durrenberger and Erem 2010). They may have more power in the workplace and substantially higher incomes, but they still sell their labor to the bourgeoisie. These managers, government officials, military, police, and even college professors receive special privileges from the bourgeoisie. But it is worth the price to gain the cooperation of this middle class in organizing, educating, and controlling the working class, thereby maximizing the extraction of profits by the capitalist class.

Along with Friedrich Engels, Marx wrote the *Communist Manifesto* (1848) as a political pamphlet urging workers to recognize their exploited class position and to unite in order to change the relations between proletariat and bourgeoisie emerging in the capitalist system. Marx noted, however, the extreme difficulty for workers to develop a class consciousness—a political awareness of their common position in the economy that would allow them to unite to change the system. Why? Because their continuous struggle simply to make ends meet, as well as the creative means used by the bourgeoisie to keep the proletariat divided, works against a unified challenge to the stratification of society.

Max Weber: Prestige and Life Chances. Max Weber (1864–1920), like Marx, wrote against the backdrop of economic and social upheavals in western Europe caused by the expansion of capitalism during the Industrial Revolution. In analyzing the emerging structures of stratification, Weber added consideration of power and prestige to Marx's concern for economic stratification of wealth and income. By **prestige**, Weber referred to the reputation, influence, and deference bestowed on certain people because of their membership in certain groups (Weber [1920] 1946). Thus, certain occupations may hold higher or lower prestige in a culture—for instance, physicians and farm workers. Prestige, like wealth and income, can affect life chances. Prestige rankings affect the way individuals are treated in social situations, their access to influential social networks, and their access to people of wealth and power.

Weber saw classes as groups of people for whom similar sets of factors determine their life chances. By **life chances**, Weber referred to the opportunities that individuals have to improve their quality of life and realize their life goals. Life chances are determined by access not only to financial resources but also to social resources such as education, health care, food, clothing, and shelter. Class position—relative wealth, power, and prestige—determines access to these resources. According to Weber, members of a class share common life chances, experiences, and access to resources, as well as similar exposure and vulnerability to other systems of stratification. For Weber, however, class stratification doesn't just happen. Instead, he suggests that the state holds the monopoly on the legitimate use of force, and class-based societies and elite control of the means of production would not be possible without the exercise of state power through police, tax collectors, and even the military.

prestige
The reputation, influence, and deference bestowed on certain people because of their membership in certain groups.

life chances
An individual's opportunities to improve quality of life and realize life goals.

Pierre Bourdieu: Education and Social Reproduction.

Pierre Bourdieu (1930–2002) studied the French educational system to understand the relationship among class, culture, and power ([1970] 1990). Throughout much of the world, education is considered the key to upward social mobility within stratified societies. **Social mobility** refers to one's change of class position—upward or downward—in stratified societies. Theoretically, the *meritocracy* of education—whereby students are deemed successful on the basis of their individual talent and motivation—should provide all students an equal opportunity. Instead, Bourdieu's research uncovered a phenomenon of **social reproduction** in the schools: Rather than providing opportunities for social class mobility, the educational system helped reproduce the social relations that already exist by passing class position from generation to generation in a family.

What factors in schools work against the meritocratic idea and instead serve to limit a person's life chances? First, a family's economic circumstances make a difference. But Bourdieu identified two additional key factors: *habitus* and cultural capital.

social mobility
The movement of one's class position, upward or downward, in stratified societies.

social reproduction
The phenomenon whereby social and class relations of prestige or lack of prestige are passed from one generation to the next.

habitus

Bourdieu's term to describe the self-perceptions, sensibilities, and tastes developed in response to external influences over a lifetime that shape one's conceptions of the world and where one fits in it.

Bourdieu described *habitus* as the dispositions, self-perceptions, sensibilities, and tastes developed in response to external influences over a lifetime that shape one's conceptions of the world and where one fits into it. *Habitus* is taught and learned from an early age and is culturally reinforced through family, education, religion, socioeconomic status, and the media. It is not fixed or predetermined, but it is so deeply enculturated and embedded that it becomes an almost instinctive sense of one's potential. *Habitus* emerges among a class of people as a set of common perceptions that shape expectations and aspirations and guide the individual in assessing his or her life chances and the potential for social mobility. Life decisions—for instance, the choice of college education or career—are made on the basis of the individual's *habitus*.

Cultural capital is another key to the social reproduction of class. Bourdieu defined **cultural capital** as the knowledge, habits, and tastes learned from parents and family that individuals can use to gain access to scarce and valuable resources of society. For example, family wealth can create cultural capital for children. With enough money, parents can provide their children with opportunities to travel abroad, learn multiple languages, take music lessons, join sports clubs, go to concerts and museums, have enriching summer experiences, and build social networks with others who have similar opportunities. The less wealthy may pass along existing cultural capital through inexpensive activities like reading, while others may divert additional financial resources toward cultural-capital-building activities for their children. These opportunities build the social skills, networks, and sense of power and confidence that are essential for shaping class position and identity in stratified societies. Family wealth enables children to perpetuate cultural capital, including high motivation and a sense of possibilities that are crucial for academic success. Schools reward cultural capital. In the process, schools reproduce social class advantage.

cultural capital

The knowledge, habits, and tastes learned from parents and family that individuals can use to gain access to scarce and valuable resources in society.

The U.S. public school system is heavily influenced by cultural capital. From an early age, students are split into separate tracks based on standardized test performance and teacher evaluations. Around sixth grade, for example, students are separated into the mathematics track that will lead either to Advanced Placement Calculus their senior year in high school or to remedial or regular math. Selective colleges often screen positively for applicants with AP Calculus credits. As a result, decisions made in sixth grade affect students' college possibilities. Did you know this? Some people with cultural capital do know. A study of middle-school math groups in Boston public schools revealed the way mathematics tracking tends to reproduce class in the classroom. Of the students in the accelerated math track, 56 percent had fathers with a doctorate or other professional degree, and 33 percent had fathers with a master's degree. Just 5.6 percent had fathers with only a high school degree. Of the students in remedial math, 48 percent had fathers with a high school diploma or less (Useem 1992).

Leith Mullings: Intersectionality among Race, Gender, and Class.

In recent years, Leith Mullings's work on intersectionality has led anthropologists to reexamine class by analyzing the deep connections among class, race, and gender. Building on the field's long history of holistic ethnographic studies of local communities, Mullings offers an intersectional approach: She asserts that class, in the United States and many other areas, cannot be studied in isolation but, instead, must be considered together with race and gender as interlocking systems of power. **Intersectionality** provides a framework for analyzing the many factors—especially race and gender—that determine how class is lived and how all three systems of power and stratification build on and shape one another.

In the 1990s Mullings led a study, The Harlem Birth Right Project, on the impact of class, race, and gender on women's health and infant mortality. The study focused on central Harlem, at that time a vibrant, primarily African American community in northern Manhattan, New York City (Mullings 2005b; Mullings and Wali 2001). Of particular concern, infant mortality rates in Harlem were twice the rate of New York City's overall. Previous studies (e.g., Schoendorf, Hogue, and Kleinman 1992) had demonstrated that at all class levels African American women in the United States have more problematic birth outcomes than white women of similar class. Even college-educated African American women experienced infant mortality at twice the rate of college-educated white women. This observation suggested that factors other than education and social status were at work.

Mullings's research team gathered data through participant observation in community organizations and other sites in Harlem, as well as through surveys, in-depth interviews, and life histories with pregnant women and women with

intersectionality
An analytic framework for assessing how factors such as race, gender, and class interact to shape individual life chances and societal patterns of stratification.

MAP 10.2
Harlem, New York City

children. On the basis of their data, the team examined how the underlying conditions of housing, employment, child care, and environmental factors, as well as the quality of public spaces, parks, and even grocery and retail stores, might affect the health outcomes being reported in Harlem, where both working-class and middle-class women lived. Since the early 1990s, Harlem has been hard hit by dramatic changes in New York City's economy. Manufacturing jobs with middle-class wages have been lost to flexible accumulation (see Chapters 1 and 11), as New York City–based companies relocate production overseas. Meanwhile, job growth in the metropolitan area has occurred in the high-wage financial sector and in the low-wage service sector. Throughout the 1990s, government social services were cut back while public housing and transportation were allowed to deteriorate.

The effects on working-class and middle-class women in Mullings's study were notable, with increased physical and mental stress, especially for pregnant women. For working-class women, inadequate, overpriced, and poorly maintained private and public housing forced many mothers and their children to be constantly on the move, searching for affordable housing and sharing living spaces with friends and relatives to make ends meet. The need to regularly fight for needed repairs drained time and energy from hardworking women holding multiple low-wage jobs while juggling work and child care. A shortage of steady, well-paying jobs meant that women had very little income security or benefits, so they often pieced together a living from multiple sources. Middle-class women, many of whom were employed in the public sector, were also increasingly subject to layoffs as local governments downsized. The study also found that heavy pollution in the Harlem area, including airborne pollutants from a sewage treatment plant and six bus depots, contributed to elevating the child asthma rate to four times the national average (Mullings 2005b; Mullings and Wali 2001).

The Harlem Birth Right Project illustrates a powerful application of the intersectional approach to understanding class and inequality. It reveals how inequality of resources (class), institutional racism, and gender discrimination combine to affect opportunities for employment, housing, and health care in the Harlem community. It also shows how these factors link to elevated health problems and infant mortality.

Mullings points out the many forms of collaboration that women in Harlem use to resist these structures of inequality and survive in their chosen community. Calling this the *Sojourner syndrome*, she links the agency of contemporary African American women to the life story of Sojourner Truth. Truth was born into slavery in the late 1790s and was emancipated in 1827 after experiencing physical abuse and rape and watching many of her children be sold away from her. Subsequently she became an itinerant preacher for the abolition of slavery, building coalitions with white abolitionists and later participating in the early

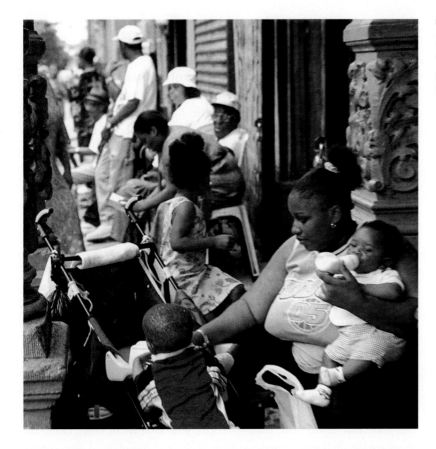

Mother and children, Harlem, New York. How do class, race, and gender intersect to affect people's life chances?

women's rights movement. The stories of the women in Harlem today, like Sojourner Truth's, reflect the determination and creativity required to overcome interlocking constraints of racism, sexism, and class inequality.

How Are Class and Inequality Constructed?

The United States' national myth tells of a "classless" society with open access to upward social mobility for those who are hardworking and talented, including the potential to rise from rags to riches in a single generation. This is the cultural story we tell, but is it reality? In fact, in the United States one's life chances are heavily influenced by the class position of one's family—the financial and cultural resources passed from generation to generation. What are the chances that a child affected by lead poisoning in Flint will someday grow up to be the president of General Motors or governor of the state of Michigan?

ETHNOGRAPHIC STUDIES OF CLASS IN THE UNITED STATES

Anthropologists have studied the construction of class and its effects across the spectrum of U.S. culture—in rural, urban, and suburban settings and in relationship to race and gender. Ethnographic studies like those presented here explore class and income inequality in local contexts and their impact on the life chances of real people in local communities.

MAP 10.3
Kentucky

Poor Whites in Rural Kentucky. In *Worked to the Bone: Race, Class, Power, and Privilege in Kentucky* (2001), anthropologist Pem Davidson Buck provides a dynamic introduction to intersectionality. She analyzes the intersections of class, race, and gender through the history of the poor white population in two rural Kentucky counties. Here, the privileges often associated with whiteness in the United States have been severely limited by class. Buck traces the development of an economic system built on tobacco cultivation, coal mining, and manufacturing that has created a class hierarchy in which "sweat is made to trickle up" (13). In other words (reflecting Marx's theory), the surplus value of workers' labor drains upward into the hands of successive layers of elites.

According to Buck, numerous historical events and processes contributed to this development. The construction of race in Kentucky through slavery, sharecropping, and Jim Crow legislation served to persuade European laborers that they should value their whiteness and attach their primary identities with the white elite rather than build solidarity with laborers of other races. The dispossession of Native Americans from their land consolidated elite control over the territory's natural resources. Later, poor and working-class whites were enticed by the elites with promises of white privilege to view all newcomer groups (such as Jews, Catholics, Irish, and later immigrants) with suspicion as outsiders, ethnic "others," and "white trash," rather than as potential allies in the struggle for fair value, wages, and compensation for their work.

Buck writes about life in central Kentucky from a personal perspective. She and her husband bought land in the rolling farm country, choosing to not pursue careers but to try to live off of the land. They grew food in their garden, raised goats and dairy calves, and took various jobs shoveling corn or stripping tobacco on a large farm to make ends meet. Her husband eventually took a job with a plumbing and heating supply company, and later they started a small plumbing and heating business of their own. All told, they spent twelve years living under the poverty line and producing most of their own food. Reflecting on her time in central Kentucky, Buck writes:

> It was while fixing plumbing leaks, lying on my back under kitchen counters, soldering pipes while wedged between bottles of cleaning

Miners in Hazard, Kentucky, sit in a "break car" that will carry them down a coal mine shaft for their daily work shift. How does their sweat "trickle up"?

fluids, that I learned about the view from under the sink. I often found myself in fairly wealthy homes, looking up from under the sink at the lady of the house and thinking about her life. She had furniture I could not afford, dressed her children from stores I never entered, and complained about leaking plumbing at a time when what few pipes we had in our own house froze and burst with remarkable regularity. (Buck 2001, 2)

It is this view "from under the sink" that Buck brings to her analysis—the view of the farmhands, handymen, factory workers, and students struggling to make ends meet despite endless hours of back-breaking work. It is the view of people who see clearly how their sweat trickles up to enhance the lives and economic success of others who are already better off.

Buck places Kentucky's economic development within the context of national economic trends and the global economy. Whiteness has been a continuously evolving smokescreen, she claims, adjusted and readjusted to the changing needs of the elites as the drainage system has been reorganized:

We are presently in . . . a period of intense competition, this time between elites around the world struggling to control the global economy. The consequences of that struggle are now filtering into the middle class, although they have been affecting people lower in the drainage system since the late 1970s. Whiteness no longer provides protection from the consequences of policies that make larger and larger portions of the United States into a Third World labor force. Nor does middle-class status provide complete protection. (221–22)

Through her analysis, Buck—who drew on her own middle-class cultural capital to escape poverty—draws connections between class and race in U.S. culture. The construction of class, as she chronicles in her reflections on her community in central Kentucky, has relied on a complex manufacturing of what it means to be white. But as the local economy of the rural United States becomes further integrated into the global economy, and as the sweat of local workers trickles further and further up, even the privileges of whiteness are not enough to protect those who live at or below the poverty line and whose fingers are already "worked to the bone."

Wealth, Inequality, and Wall Street. Although many anthropologists study the most marginalized members of a culture, a number of research projects have "studied up" (Nader 1972; Savage and Williams 2008): They have investigated power elites and cultural decision makers ranging from elite scientists (Gusterson 1996) and Wall Street executives (Tett 2010) to government officials (Brash 2011). In *Liquidated: An Ethnography of Wall Street* (2009), anthropologist Karen Ho relates how she went to work in a Wall Street investment bank to understand the inner workings of Wall Street in the 1990s during one of its biggest boom periods. Why, she asks, in a time of record corporate profits and soaring stock prices, do we see rapid downsizing, layoffs, and dismantling of the social safety net? She focuses on the surprising fact that when corporations lay off workers and downsize, not only do the companies' stock prices go up but the stock values of the investment banks go up as well.

Ho points to a transformation of the corporate culture of Wall Street: The desire for profits is not new; what is new, she finds, is a disconnect between what is considered best for the corporation and what is best for most of its employees. Today employees seldom benefit from corporate success. Instead, the benefits go to stockholders. Ho suggests that a "new cultural code for doing business" on Wall Street—characterized by a relentless search for unending profits and combined with government deregulation of the financial services industry—rewards efforts to make money, not to make goods and services. Witness in recent years the willingness of commercial banks and investment houses to bundle and resell so-called toxic assets, exposed in the book and feature film *The Big Short* and the documentary *The Inside Job*, including the high-risk mortgages that played a key role in the 2008 market meltdown and Wall Street collapse. Ho claims that Wall Street participated in its own dismantling through mergers and liquidations within the financial community itself as large companies consumed smaller

What is the corporate culture of Wall Street investment banks? Did it contribute to the 2008 financial crash?

ones, downsized, and laid off employees to maximize their own stock values. Ho regards the collapse of Wall Street banks and investment houses in 2008 not so much as a surprise or anomaly, but as a predictable result of Wall Street culture, values, and workplace models.

Despite the U.S. national myth of a classless society, quantitative and qualitative research studies expose the depth of inequality and stratification as well as the obstacles to social mobility. Although class stratification is not new, historical research suggests it is also not inevitable. By examining both statistical and ethnographic material, anthropologists seek to reopen a conversation about the roots of inequality—the obstacles to greater opportunity, social mobility, and improved life chances in a culture that is reluctant to discuss class.

A LOOK AT THE NUMBERS

Economic statistics provide a sobering picture of inequality in the United States today. They also reveal the increasing concentration of income and wealth at the top rungs of the class ladder. In reviewing statistics related to class, we examine both income and wealth.

Income. **Income** is what people earn from work, plus dividends and interest on investments along with rents and royalties. (A *dividend* is a payment by a corporation to its shareholders of a portion of corporate profits. *Interest* is a fee paid for the use of borrowed money—for example, interest paid on a bank savings account. *Rent* refers to payment to an owner as compensation for the use of land, a building, an apartment, property, or equipment. *Royalties* are income based on a percentage of the revenue from the sale of a patent, book, or theatrical work paid to the inventor or author.) Table 10.1 shows a breakdown of average household

income

What people earn from work, plus dividends and interest on investments, along with rents and royalties.

TABLE 10.1

Income Disparities in the United States

a) Average U.S. Household Income by Percentage of the Population, 2015

PERCENTAGE OF U.S. POPULATION	HOUSEHOLD INCOME RANGE
Top 5%	Above $214,462
Top 20%	Above $117,002
Second 20%	$72,002–$117,002
Middle 20%	$43,512–$72,001
Fourth 20%	$22,801–$43,511
Bottom 20%	Less than $22,800

b) Distribution of Total U.S. Household Income, 1967 Versus 2015

	TOP 5% OF POPULATION	TOP 20% OF POPULATION	BOTTOM 40% OF POPULATION	BOTTOM 20% OF POPULATION
1967	16.3%	43%	15%	4.1%
2015	21.9%	51.1%	11.3%	3.1%

Source: U.S. Census Bureau, 2016. Historical Income Tables: Income Inequality, Tables H-1 and H-2 All Races. www.census.gov.

income in the United States for 2015. Do you know where your family fits in the national income range?

Income patterns reveal the way power is distributed in a society. As Table 10.1b illustrates, income distribution among the U.S. population shows a heavy concentration at the top. These gaps have widened substantially over the past four decades. Furthermore, the gap between people at the top end of the income scale and the average worker has dramatically increased over the past five decades.

Wealth. Wealth is another key indicator of the distribution of power in a society. By **wealth** we mean the total value of what someone owns—including stocks, bonds, and real estate—minus any debt, such as a mortgage or credit card debt. If wealth were evenly distributed, every U.S. household would have had $498,800 in 2010 (Board of Governors of the Federal Reserve System 2012). But wealth is not evenly distributed.

Wealth is even more unevenly distributed than income, and the widening gap has multiple causes. First, shifts in the U.S. tax code have lowered the top tax rate from 91 percent in the years from 1950 to 1963, to 39.6 percent beginning in 2014, allowing the wealthy to retain far more of their income (Tax Policy Center 2015). Second, wages for most U.S. families have stagnated since the early 1970s. Moreover, credit card, education, and mortgage debt have skyrocketed.

wealth

The total value of what someone owns, minus any debt.

Despite our society's cultural images of the United States as a nation of stockholders, Wall Street as a democratizing institution, and the stock market as a place of economic empowerment, the actual distribution of stocks in the U.S. population tells another story. The top 1 percent of all U.S. households own 38.3 percent of all stocks. The top 10 percent own roughly 81 percent. Fully 50 percent of U.S. households own no stocks. Even among those who do hold stocks, most own them through pension and retirement funds, where they are not accessible for general use.

In another surprising statistic about the transfer of wealth from generation to generation, only 1.6 percent of Americans receive $100,000 or more in inheritance. Another 1.1 percent receives $50,000 to $100,000. Ninety-two percent of the population receives no inheritance whatsoever (Domhoff 2012).

Wealth is also stratified by race. Reflecting the devastating long-term effects of slavery and Jim Crow segregation on the African American community, as well as the difficult immigration experiences of most of the U.S. Hispanic population, white households have accumulated fifteen times the net worth of black and Hispanic households.

Most Americans struggle to identify the distribution of income and wealth in the United States and to locate their position within it (Norton and Ariely 2011). After reviewing the quantitative data on income and wealth stratification in the United States, can you identify pieces of information that were particularly surprising to you? Does the statistical picture correspond with the picture of U.S. society that you imagined? Do you have a clearer sense of where you and your family currently stand?

THE ROOTS OF POVERTY

Why do people live in poverty in the United States—one of the wealthiest countries in the world? The actual roots of poverty—part of the same system that creates wealth—must be clearly understood if the experience of poverty is to be eliminated or ameliorated.

A 2015 report of the U.S. Census Bureau found 43.1 million people—13.5 percent of the U.S. population—living in poverty (U.S. Census Bureau 2016). The 48.8 million people living in poverty in 2012 was the largest number in the fifty-five years that poverty statistics have been tracked. Just over twenty percent of U.S. children live in poverty. The 2016 U.S. government's poverty line for single adults stood at $11,880 in pretax income and $24,300 for a family of four. How could a family of four (or two or three for that matter) eat, pay rent, keep heat, water, and electricity turned on, have clean clothes, and care for even the most rudimentary dental or health needs on $506 per family member per month? The U.S. poverty line calculations, developed in 1964, are widely considered to be unrealistic in today's economy; instead, most scholars calculate a

FIGURE 10.1

Percentage of People in Poverty within Racial Groups, 2015

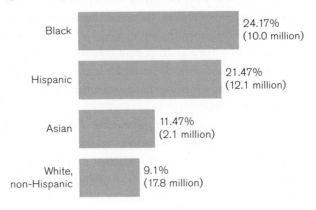

Black 24.17% (10.0 million)

Hispanic 21.47% (12.1 million)

Asian 11.47% (2.1 million)

White, non-Hispanic 9.1% (17.8 million)

Source: U.S. Census Bureau, 2016. Income and Poverty in the United States, 2015. Table 3. www.census.gov.

poverty line at 50 percent higher to be a more useful representation of people's standard of living.

Poverty rates vary by race (Figure 10.1). Our discussions of the history and contemporary expressions of race and racism in the United States in Chapter 5 helped shed light on these disparities. Despite prevalent media representations of inner-city poverty among communities of color, it is important to note that the largest group of the nation's poor are white and live in rural and suburban areas, as represented in the work of Pem Buck.

Anthropologists and other social scientists have articulated numerous theories to explain poverty's origins and persistence. In the United States, two key theories have focused on poverty as pathology and poverty as a structural economic problem.

THE "CULTURE OF POVERTY": POVERTY AS PATHOLOGY

Theories of poverty as pathology trace ongoing poverty to the personal failings of the individual, family, or community. Such theories—which most anthropologists reject—see these failings as stemming from a combination of dysfunctional behaviors, attitudes, and values that make and keep poor people poor. Anthropologist Oscar Lewis called this a "culture of poverty." His research in Mexico (1959) and the United States (1966) suggested that certain ways of thinking and feeling lead to the perpetuation of poverty among the poor. Lewis argued that children growing up poor in a highly class-stratified economic system were particularly vulnerable to developing feelings of marginality, helplessness, and dependency that would shape their value system, worldviews, aspirations, and character and make it difficult for them to escape poverty.

Lewis's research and theory of a culture of poverty became attractive to policymakers in the United States. Although many scholars, including anthropologists, discredited this theory on the grounds that it blamed the victims of poverty for structural problems beyond their control, the theory formed the basis of key social policies during the latter part of the twentieth century (Wilson 1987).

POVERTY AS A STRUCTURAL ECONOMIC PROBLEM

Many anthropologists have critiqued the "culture of poverty" theory, beginning with a series of essays edited by Eleanor Burke Leacock (1971), and have proposed instead that poverty is a structural economic problem. If there are no jobs, inadequate education and health care, and systematic failure to invest in the infrastructure of impoverished neighborhoods and communities, then poverty cannot be changed by changing attitudes and values. What are often considered to be characteristics of a culture of poverty are actually characteristics of poverty itself; they have nothing to do with the attitudes, values, and life choices of those forced to live in poverty. As discussed earlier, Leith Mullings (2005b) and others have challenged the depiction of a complacent and ghettoized underclass by pointing to the resilient and determined efforts made by the poor to overcome the dire economic, social, and political conditions that they face.

Anthropologists Judith Goode and Jeff Maskovsky (2001) challenge the culture of poverty argument by questioning its focus on poor communities as isolated spheres. Instead, they trace the roots of contemporary poverty in the United States to the impact of global economic processes on the nation's economy, particularly the effects of flexible accumulation and uneven development. The growth of globalization and the expansion of global capitalism, they argue, have launched an economic restructuring in which corporations ship high-paying, blue-collar manufacturing jobs overseas in search of cheaper labor,

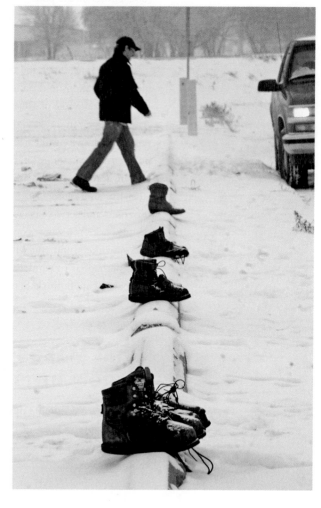

How is flexible accumulation shaping U.S. inequality? Laid-off factory workers of the closed Doosan Bobcat plant, Bismarck, North Dakota, symbolically leave behind steel-toed work boots in the parking lot as they exit the plant for the final time.

lower taxes, and fewer environmental restrictions. The U.S. workforce has become more polarized between highly educated, well-paid professionals and managers and undereducated workers who struggle with low pay, no benefits, and little job security. U.S. government policies and programs designed to regulate the economy, protect the most vulnerable, and provide opportunities for social mobility have been reduced, including public education, housing, and investment in infrastructure—roads, bridges, water systems, and power grids.

Goode and Maskovsky warn that as poverty and inequality grow, those most deeply affected—including the one in five U.S. children who live in poverty (U.S. Census Bureau 2016)—remain largely hidden and disappear from national awareness. In response, they encourage a new awareness of the many ways in which poor people engage in collective and individual strategies to survive. They call for anthropologists to engage in ethnographic research that contributes to the grassroots efforts of the poor (Anglin 2002; Checker 2005; Dudley 2000; Goldstein 2016; Speed 2007). In addition, they call for adequate public investment in affordable housing, health care, education, and nutrition programs to create a framework whereby individual initiative can more readily lead to upward mobility.

Discussions about the root causes of poverty continue today in both popular conversations and policy circles. Intense debate continues, for instance, on the appropriate role of government in addressing problems of persistent poverty. Arguments often draw on the distinction between seeing its roots in a culture of poverty or in a long-term structural problem of exclusion built into government policies and economic practices. Can poverty be addressed through improved housing, provision of health care, education, and the creation of living-wage jobs (the structural causes), or must perceived patterns of dependency on government programs and services be addressed to confront an underlying culture that holds people back? You will encounter these questions in conversations with classmates and coworkers, and you will influence these debates at different points in your life—perhaps as you undertake community service as a college student or later as you participate in the U.S. political process.

What Makes Class and Inequality Largely Invisible?

The review of economic data in this chapter has revealed the existence of class and inequality in U.S. society as well as the disturbing reality that inequality is increasing. Even with the statistical evidence of class in America, attention to this pattern of stratification historically has been minimal and inequality remains largely invisible. Why?

The role of class is rarely discussed but is present virtually everywhere in U.S. society, as is the attempt to "consume" class. In *Consuming the Romantic Utopia: Love and Cultural Contradictions of Capitalism* (1997), sociologist Eva Illouz suggests that even love and romance are shaped by class—both by financial capital and by cultural capital. As a college student, you experience this tension all the time. Dating is expensive. Romance takes time and money. How do you show you are in love? The rituals of love—the acts that are expected to show affection and cultivate romance—depend on the ability to shop and buy. You need the right clothes, haircut, makeup, perfume or cologne, shoes, birth control. You need a gym membership to stay fit or diet pills to stay skinny. The rituals of romance, including food, drinks, movies, gifts, and travel, all require money. A romantic dinner out is expensive.

Class even shapes our choice of romantic partners. We often think of love as a spontaneous act of emotion, good chemistry—a matter of the heart. But why do we feel that connection? Research shows that people are likely to marry someone of their own race (see Chapter 2). Discounting Hollywood movies, how likely is it that you would marry someone outside your class? Finding someone of a similar background who has the same cultural capital and knows the same language and symbols of romance strongly influences our choices of romantic partners. What has your own experience been in this regard?

CONSUMER CULTURE

Consumer culture is a key factor in masking class in the United States. Despite falling incomes over the past thirty years, many families have been able to pay for necessities and maintain at least the experience of a middle-class lifestyle. They accomplish this by working more (especially women, who have entered the workforce in increasing numbers), borrowing money in mortgages against the value of their homes, running up credit card debt, and taking out more student loans to pay for their own or their children's college education.

Though income and wealth have not increased for the vast majority of the nation's population, people have been able to consume as if they were upwardly mobile—at least until the collapse of the housing bubble in 2007 and the meltdown of financial markets beginning in late 2008. At that point, banks began to foreclose on homes that were no longer worth as much as the owners had borrowed against them. Credit card interest rates skyrocketed, and credit lines were reduced. Still, total credit card debt in 2016 was $762 billion (Board of Governors of the Federal Reserve System 2016a), a sign of the extent to which the population continues to consume as if it were middle and upper class even when annual income does not support this lifestyle. Fully 56 percent of U.S. households carried a balance on their credit cards, with an average of over $16,000 per indebted household in 2016. Perhaps more surprising, in 2010 student loan debt surpassed total credit card debt for the first time, climbing to $1.3 trillion in 2016 and revealing the shifting burden of educational expenses into long-term debt (FinAid 2016). Total mortgage debt in 2015 stood at a staggering $13.8 trillion (Board of Governors of the Federal Reserve System 2016b). These sobering statistics reveal the ways consumer spending has been supported by mortgage, credit card, and education debt, thereby masking the growing inequalities of income and wealth in the United States (Williams 2004).

If class is so pervasive, why is it seemingly so invisible and discussed so seldom?

As you develop your skills as a budding anthropologist, clearly seeing the outlines of class and its effects on you and the people around you may require extra effort. Media—from movies to television to the press—largely ignore the existence of the poor and working class and the gaps between wealth and poverty. Consumption patterns, fueled by deep indebtedness through credit cards, home mortgages, and educational loans, mask class differences at least on the level of acquisition of consumer goods. Perhaps this cultural tendency to mask class and inequality—to make them invisible—is one reason that the abrupt rise of the Occupy Wall Street movement in the fall of 2011, with its class-revealing slogan "We Are the 99%," surprised many people. But perhaps the same tendency to make class invisible explains why the movement fell so quickly from the media's public eye once protesters were removed by police from the spaces they physically occupied in parks and town squares. Their removal continues a long historical pattern of crackdowns against labor unions, anti-war demonstrators, civil rights protesters—even against residents of Ferguson, Missouri, after the shooting of Michael Brown—as the state, as Weber pointed out, reserves the monopoly on the use of force in order to keep the class structure in place. In a time of increasing inequality in the United States and around the world, a careful consideration and analysis of class will prove to be a crucial tool in your toolkit as you attempt to understand the complexities of the global world in which you live.

What Are the Effects of Global Inequality?

Globalization has produced unprecedented opportunities for the creation of wealth, but it has also produced widespread poverty. This uneven development is a central characteristic of the global capitalist system. Because it affects every corner of the world, it will be increasingly important for you as a global citizen to understand its impact.

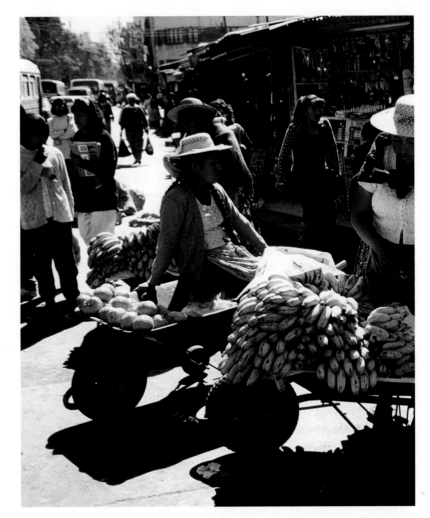

The informal economy—small-scale, underground, and sometimes illegal—has become the primary economic activity in many poor countries. Here, street vendors and stall vendors compete for customers at the sprawling Cancha outdoor market in downtown Cochabamba, Bolivia.

STREET VENDORS IN THE GLOBAL ECONOMY

Anthropologist Daniel Goldstein (2016) explores the contours of class and inequality in his study of street vendors in the enormous Cancha outdoor market in Cochabamba, Bolivia. Today's global economic transformations have led to historic levels of poverty in the world's poorest cities as rural dwellers move to urban areas in search of jobs and security for themselves and their families. Goldstein's ethnographic research focuses specifically on vulnerable street vendors and their small-scale commercial activities—what scholars call the informal economy, the underground, and sometimes illegal, system of buying and selling that parallels the official economy.

In the bright, colorful, and dynamic Cancha marketplace, thousands of long-term merchants, known as *fijos*, sell their wares from narrow stalls in the market's

MAP 10.4
Cochabamba

central pavilion. At the same time, thousands of street vendors, locally known as *ambulantes*, rove the surrounding, traffic-clogged streets and packed sidewalks, alleyways, and passageways hawking food, drink, watches, radios, DVDs, men's briefs, hardware, soap, cosmetics, bananas, rice—any small, portable item that might attract the attention of a local shopper or visiting tourist. Tensions between the groups run high. Their furious competition for sales ensures that. But the *fijos* and *ambulantes* operate on unequal playing fields. For stall vendors, their fixed, permanent, and legal locations at the center of the market provide a more secure position in the local economy. Their stability and legal status create conditions for economic success and the potential for upward economic mobility. The street vendors of the Cancha, in contrast, are harassed by police, insulted by motorists and pedestrians, and preyed upon by shoplifters and muggers. State laws explicitly prohibit them from selling on the street.

Goldstein argues that the marked growth of informal urban economic activity worldwide is produced not by the informal workers themselves, but by the way economic and political conditions are created and regulated by the state. What may appear to the outsider as chaotic, disorderly, even criminal and dangerous, is not random at all. Rather, the state and its representatives create and benefit directly from the conditions of informality and illegality that turn urban small-scale entrepreneurs into criminals. Inconsistently enforced laws and regulations applied to the urban poor—an increasingly common pattern in the contemporary global economy—only increase workers' experience of uncertainty, insecurity, and vulnerability.

Despite the chaos and disorder built into the informal activity in the Cancha, Goldstein's ethnography reveals the determined efforts of street vendors—poor urban small business people—to scrabble together a living against the odds in the only way available to them—as precarious owners of the streets and sidewalks of the informal city.

CLASS AND THE CIRCULATION OF WATER IN MUMBAI, INDIA

Eight thousand miles from Flint, Michigan, poor people in Mumbai, India, also navigate a water crisis affecting the city's most marginalized communities. Sixty percent of Mumbai's 20.5 million people are poor urban settlers evicted from the city center or arriving from rural areas. With no permanent, legally recognized residence, the city's rules provide no legal rights to Mumbai's water. Anthropologist Nikhil Anand (2011a, 2011b, 2012) explores the strategies Mumbai's poor use to stake their claim to a hydraulic citizenship—a right to water—as they seek to make reliable homes for themselves and their families.

Purchasing bottled water as a private commodity is prohibitively expensive. So everyone must access Mumbai's municipal water in some fashion. With

MAP 10.5
Mumbai

limited financial capital, Mumbai settlers mobilize social capital—relationships with friends, employers, clients, siblings, water officials, and fictive kin—to find points of access. They stage protests and write petitions. And they surreptitiously connect to public water mains late at night or early in the morning. Anand tells the story of accompanying a friend to connect to the water supply at 4:30 in the morning, waiting in a long line for his allotted water distribution. In the pre-dawn darkness, Anand's friend—a housekeeper at a luxury downtown hotel—tells a painfully ironic story of his own, recounting a recent request from his manager to turn off the tap of a guest who had left it running when he went out. Anand notes how class structures are made visible as poor Indian laborers travel across the city, passing shanties and luxury buildings, seeing poverty and wealth and remembering having turned off a running hotel tap while standing in line for water. Urban infrastructure plays a key role in establishing these patterns of class stratification and inequality.

Cities are made possible by the circulation of water in city pipes. But what kind of a city? The complex assemblages of water pipes in Mumbai tell a story and enable an analysis of how marginality is created. Mumbai's municipal water system returns a hefty profit to the city, yet its managers and political decision makers are unable to provide a steady and safe supply to its most vulnerable population. What is citizenship if it does not include the right to water? Anand's research offers insights into the creative, persistent, informal, and even illegal strategies Mumbai's poor settlement dwellers use to resist the city's water rules and renegotiate the terms of their hydraulic citizenship.

THINKING GLOBALLY ABOUT INEQUALITY

Statistics reveal the extremes of uneven development described in the ethnographic studies of Cochabamba and Mumbai. For example, in 2016 the world had 1,810 billionaires, up from 937 billionaires in 2010 (Dolan and Kroll 2016); yet, with the exception of China, global poverty has increased over the past twenty years. Today 40 percent of the world's population lives in poverty, defined by the United Nations as income of less than $2.00 per day. Nearly 1 billion people live in extreme poverty, surviving on less than $1.25 each day (United Nations 2015). The U.N. has calculated that if household wealth were divided equally on a global basis, using 2000 data each household would have roughly $20,000. Instead, the report found that 2 percent of the world's population owns more than half of all wealth on the entire planet. The wealthiest 20 percent of the world's population receive 75 percent of the total global income (Davies et al. 2007).

The Gini index developed by the World Bank provides a global picture of inequality by comparing the per capita gross national income—total income produced by the economic activity of a state—of the world's economies. The World Bank classifies countries as high income ($12,476 or more per person), upper middle income ($4,036 to $12,475), lower middle income ($1,026 to $4,035), or low income ($1,025 or less). According to the Gini index, the gap between rich and poor countries has grown in recent years and continues to widen (Figure 10.2). Although the index provides a comparison of country averages, it does not take into account inequality within countries. Even the poorest countries have an elite organized around political, economic, or military power. The richest countries, as we have seen in the United States, have an increasing number of people living in poverty. What does this mean in concrete terms?

Growing global inequality affects the life chances of the world's population on many fronts, including hunger and malnutrition, health, education, vulnerability to climate change, and access to technology. Hunger is indeed a global problem. Although there is enough food in the world to feed everyone, it is unevenly distributed. Every day 870 million people go hungry—one out of every eight—and 200 million children under age five are malnourished (World Food Programme 2013).

Health and mortality are also serious problem areas. Preventable infectious diseases such as malaria, measles, and HIV/AIDS kill millions each year in poor countries. People are more likely to die in infancy in low-income countries—and

FIGURE 10.2
The World by Income, 2017

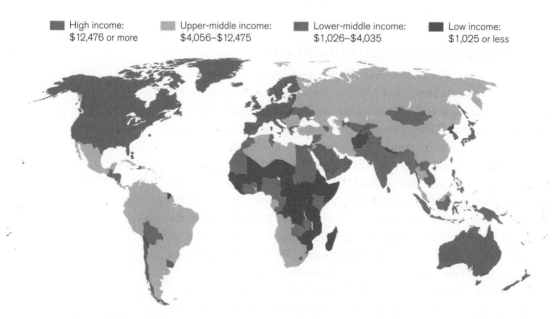

■ High income:
 $12,476 or more

■ Upper-middle income:
 $4,056–$12,475

■ Lower-middle income:
 $1,026–$4,035

■ Low income:
 $1,025 or less

Source: The World Bank. 2017. Country and Lending Groups. data.worldbank.org.

are eleven times more likely to die at birth than in wealthy countries. Moreover, people live longer in high-income countries, averaging a seventy-eight-year life span compared to fifty-eight in low-income countries (World Food Programme 2013).

Access to education, a gateway to economic advancement, is also uneven. Basic literacy varies widely between high- and low-income countries. In addition, the digital divide prevents the majority of the world's inhabitants from participating in technological advances that are transforming the world's economy.

Climate change also affects the rich and poor unequally. Those with financial and political resources can buy safety, living outside areas that are vulnerable to natural disasters. A recent example from the United States underscores this point: Anthropologist Neil Smith (2006), when examining the effects of Hurricane Katrina on the people of New Orleans, called it an "unnatural disaster" because the storm's most severe effects were caused by the government's failure to adequately build and maintain the city's levee system, not by the storm itself. New Orleans residents experienced Katrina's effects unevenly along lines of class as well as race and gender.

Throughout this chapter we have explored the complexity of class stratification and inequality both within the United States and globally. Despite the centrality of class-based stratification in the dynamics of globalization and its powerful effects on individuals' life chances and possibility for social mobility, class arguably remains the most overlooked of the systems of power we have considered in this textbook. Careful attention to the theoretical approaches to class adopted by anthropologists, including ethnographic research and data analysis, will position you to more fully engage issues of income and wealth inequality as you participate in a rapidly globalizing world.

Toolkit

Thinking Like an Anthropologist:
The Dynamics of Class through Water and Beyond

In our chapter-opening story, we began to tease out the dynamics of class through the story of Flint, Michigan's water crisis. Water is essential to human life. Humans need a steady supply of quality water every day. Yet people in Flint, and others around the globe, struggle to gain access to safe and abundant water. What is for many in the United States an afterthought—a drink of water—has become one of the most highly contentious issues of our time. What is too often thought of as a natural process—the circulation of water—has now become a hydro-social process, shaped and determined not only by rainfall and topography but increasingly by infrastructures, technological skills, and political decision makers. And as we have seen in this chapter, in Flint and Mumbai, inequalities in the distribution of water often map directly onto inequalities in class, race, gender, and ethnicity.

Having read this chapter, you are now better prepared to analyze the water crisis in Flint through the lens of class. For underneath the decision to switch water supplies, the orange-brown water, and corroded pipes lies a set of unequal relationships. And these differences—starkly revealed by the health consequences of water management decisions—translate into significantly different access to services, resources, and life chances. Our discussion in this chapter has expanded from Flint's water crisis to explore the following questions:

- Is inequality a natural part of human culture?
- How do anthropologists analyze class and inequality?
- How are class and inequality constructed?
- Why are class and inequality largely invisible?
- What are the effects of global inequality?

As systems of class stratification create widening inequality, your ability to perceive, analyze, and discuss class will become increasingly important. Class affects life chances in almost all realms of culture, including infrastructure, the restaurant industry, universities and other elements of the education system, health care, religious organizations, housing, government services, and many others that you can identify. How do these systems of class and inequality affect your own life chances and those of the people closest to you? As you consider these issues, you may be motivated to engage in efforts to reshape systems of inequality. Certainly, as you prepare for a career in the global economy and a life in this global age, being able to analyze the effects of class and inequality will be an essential tool in your anthropological toolkit.

Key Terms

class (p. 263)

egalitarian society (p. 264)

reciprocity (p. 264)

ranked society (p. 265)

redistribution (p. 265)

potlatch (p. 265)

bourgeoisie (p. 267)

means of production (p. 267)

proletariat (p. 267)

prestige (p. 269)

life chances (p. 269)

social mobility (p. 269)

social reproduction (p. 269)

habitus (p. 270)

cultural capital (p. 270)

intersectionality (p. 271)

income (p. 277)

wealth (p. 278)

Part 3

The world is changing rapidly in the twenty-first century. People are on the move, spurred by changes in the global economy, political systems, communication and transportation infrastructures, and more. At Tongi Station on the outskirts of Dhaka, Bangladesh, hundreds of people sit on the roof of an overcrowded train to travel homeward for Eid al-Fitr, a Muslim festival marking the end of the fasting month of Ramadan.

Change in the Modern World

Chapter 11
The Global Economy

Do you know where your last chocolate bar came from?

Today's global economy is a complex network of exchanges and connections that reach far beyond the candy machine outside your classroom or the store across the street. A piece of chocolate, a cup of coffee, or an iPhone can link the wealthiest resident of a world capital or a student at an elite college to a subsistence farmer in Africa or a factory worker in China. In today's world we are all deeply connected. Let's use the chocolate bar to illustrate this point.

Côte d'Ivoire, West Africa, exports 40 percent of the world's cocoa, which is used to make chocolate. Much of the country is covered in tropical forest, amid which are plantations carved out by farmers using hand tools. Seven million Côte d'Ivoirians make a living farming cocoa and coffee. Although the global price for cocoa—set on the commodities market in New York City—is relatively high, Côte d'Ivoire's farmers see little return for their work. The bulk of the profits go to transnational agricultural

Where does your chocolate come from?
A young man on an eastern Côte d'Ivoire
farm breaks cocoa pods to extract the beans
used to make chocolate.

corporations, such as U.S.-based Cargill and Archer Daniels Midland (ADM) and the Swiss firm Barry Callebaut. These corporations buy cocoa beans and process them into chocolate products to be eaten worldwide. Few local farmers in Côte d'Ivoire have ever eaten a chocolate bar.

In recent years, Côte d'Ivoire has been riven by poverty, civil war, and conflict over cocoa and coffee revenues. In a fiercely contested election in 2010, Alessane Ouattara defeated incumbent Laurent Gbagbo for the presidency. Gbagbo's regime had relied on high taxes on cocoa and coffee farmers to subsidize its excesses and to fund Gbagbo's paramilitary hit squads. The election of Ouattara, a former deputy director of the International Monetary Fund (IMF), gave Côte d'Ivoirians hope of a more secure and prosperous future. But Gbagbo refused to acknowledge his loss in the election and remained ensconced in the presidential palace. By clinging to power and stirring ethnic violence, Gbagbo pushed the country toward civil war.

To undercut Gbagbo's financial base, Ouattara called on international corporations to embargo Côte d'Ivoire's coffee and cocoa exports, claiming that Gbagbo used profits from the sales to fund his armed resistance. Giant U.S. agribusiness corporations eventually pledged to cooperate, but they refused to allow independent inspection of their exports. Many nongovernmental organizations (NGOs) charged that Côte d'Ivoire was circumventing the embargo by shipping its coffee and cocoa overland to neighboring Mali and Burkina Faso, which were reselling the goods to the same corporations.

As fighting between Gbagbo's and Ouattara's supporters escalated in 2011, the French military, returning to its colonial role, stormed the airport outside Abidjian, the country's economic capital and primary port. The French had established a colony in Côte d'Ivoire in 1840 to enter the ivory trade and build coffee and cocoa plantations. Even after Côte d'Ivoire's independence in 1960, however, the French maintained a strong economic and military presence there. In the hopes of limiting violence in the civil war, France joined with the United Nations to create a demilitarized zone stretching across the country. French and U.N. soldiers then isolated the presidential palace, still occupied by the defeated Gbagbo, until forces loyal to new president Ouattara ousted Gbagbo from the residence and arrested him. Despite continuing hostility between supporters of Gbagbo and Ouattara, in 2012 the country's economy began to recover (Monnier 2013; North 2011). In recent years, cocoa production has stabilized, France and China have launched large infrastructure projects, and the International Cocoa Federation is moving its headquarters from London to Abijian. Laurent Gbagbo was tried by the International Criminal Court for crimes against humanity and war crimes.

The conflict in Côte d'Ivoire reveals many of the complex dynamics of today's global economy: (1) the interconnectedness of farmers in rural West Africa with chocolate eaters and coffee drinkers worldwide; (2) the tension-filled

MAP 11.1
Côte d'Ivoire

relationship between nation-states and transnational corporations; (3) the strategic military interventions, often by former colonial powers, that serve to police local political affairs and global economic flows; (4) the power of global financial markets to determine the price of coffee and cocoa, and thus the quality of life of small farmers; and (5) the link between consumers and producers through global commodity chains that have blurred notions of distinct national territories.

To fully understand the modern world economy, we must examine the concept of an economy as well as the historical developments that underlie today's global economy. In this chapter we will explore the following questions:

- **What is an economy, and what is its purpose?**
- **What are the roots of today's global economy?**
- **What are the dominant organizing principles of the global economy today?**
- **How does today's global economy link workers with consumers worldwide?**
- **How is today's global economy reshaping migration?**
- **Is today's global economic system sustainable?**

By the end of the chapter you should be able to analyze the major economic patterns of the contemporary global economy and assess its underlying principles. Armed with this information, you will be better prepared to make choices about your own lifestyle as a consumer and to engage in debates about how to create a sustainable economic system as the growing human population places increasing pressure on Earth's resources.

What Is an Economy, and What Is Its Purpose?

economy

A cultural adaptation to the environment that enables a group of humans to use the available land, resources, and labor to satisfy their needs and to thrive.

At the most basic level, an **economy** is a cultural adaptation to the environment—a set of ideas, activities, and technologies that enable a group of humans to use the available land, resources, and labor to satisfy their basic needs and, if organized well, to thrive. Thus, an economic system is a pattern of relations and institutions that humans construct to help collectively meet the needs of the community. Of course, today the concept of an economy seems much more complicated. But what is an economy at its core?

Anthropologist Yehudi Cohen (1974) refers to an economy as a set of adaptive strategies that humans have used to provide food, water, and shelter to a group of people through the production, distribution, and consumption of foodstuffs and other goods. In the following sections, we will explore the varied ways humans have produced, distributed, and consumed as part of their economic activity.

Cohen suggests five primary adaptive strategies that developed at different times and places: food foraging, pastoralism, horticulture, agriculture, and industrialism. By reviewing these strategies, we begin to understand that the current consumption-based global economy—with its emphasis on industrial production (even in agriculture), consumption, and technology—is only one of many possible variations.

FROM FORAGING TO INDUSTRIAL AGRICULTURE: A BRIEF SURVEY OF FOOD PRODUCTION

Food Foraging. Before the domestication of plants and animals around 10,000 years ago, all humans were **food foragers**. They made their living by hunting, fishing, and gathering nuts, fruit, and root crops; in fact, humans evolved into our current physical form as food foragers. Mobility was key: small, egalitarian groups followed the movement of large animals and the seasonal growth of fruits, vegetables, and nuts to secure their survival. Throughout human history, food foragers have ranged over a remarkable variety of habitats, from the most hospitable to the most extreme.

food foragers

Humans who subsist by hunting, fishing, and gathering plants to eat.

Today fewer than 250,000 people make their primary living from food foraging. Most food foragers now incorporate farming and the domestication of animals. The remaining food foragers often live in the most marginal of Earth's environments—cold places, forests, islands—where other economic activity and other strategies for food production are not sustainable. Recent food foragers include the Inuit (Eskimos) of Canada and Alaska, Native Australian aborigines, and inhabitants of African and South American rainforests (e.g., Lee 1984; Turnbull [1961] 2010).

Pastoralism, Horticulture, and Agriculture.

Cohen identifies three adaptive strategies for food production in nonindustrial societies: pastoralism, horticulture, and agriculture. The earliest evidence of food production can be traced to approximately 11,000 years ago in the region surrounding the Tigris and Euphrates Rivers (the Fertile Crescent) in what is modern-day Iraq. These strategies for food production led to more permanent human settlements that facilitated the development of tools and pottery and the specialization of human trades.

Pastoralism involves the domestication and herding of animals for food production. **Horticulture** is the cultivation of plants for subsistence through a nonintensive use of land and labor. Horticulturalists use simple tools such as sticks and hoes to cultivate small garden plots. Horticulturalists frequently employ *slash and burn agriculture*—also called "swidden farming"—to clear land for cultivation, kill insects that may inhibit crop growth, and produce nutrient-rich ash that serves as fertilizer.

In addition to the Fertile Crescent, early evidence of agricultural activity exists in Pakistan's Indus River Valley, China's Yellow River Valley, and the Nile Valley of Egypt, as well as in Mexico, the American southwest, and the Andes region of South America. **Agriculture** requires an intensive investment in farming and well-orchestrated land-use strategies. Irrigation, fertilizer, draft animals, and machinery such as plows and tractors provide the technology and labor for successful agriculture. Through agriculture, humans produce enough food on permanently cultivated land to satisfy the immediate needs of the community and to create a surplus that can be sold or traded.

pastoralism

A strategy for food production involving the domestication of animals.

horticulture

The cultivation of plants for subsistence through nonintensive use of land and labor.

agriculture

An intensive farming strategy for food production involving permanently cultivated land.

Whereas hunter-gatherer societies tended to be largely egalitarian, the rise of intensive agriculture in nonindustrial cultures led to social stratification. Social distinctions included large landholders, wealthy merchants, and owners of small businesses, as well as peasants and landless tenants working on large farms and estates as wage laborers.

Industrial Agriculture. Recent years have seen the rise of industrial agriculture, which involves a massive mechanization of farming and the mass production of foodstuffs. In fact, in the twentieth century, agricultural production shifted from individual farms and farmers to large corporate-run farms, or agribusinesses, that rely on the intensive use of machinery (such as tractors and combines), irrigation systems, pesticides, and fertilizers.

Despite increased food production, industrial agriculture and agribusinesses have yielded complicated results. For example, chemical fertilizers and pesticides pose dangers to workers and to local water resources. Antibiotics that keep poultry and livestock healthy in industrial production facilities seep into the human food chain. Genetic engineering reduces crop diversity, making crops more susceptible to harsh weather and pests in the long term. Food irradiation poses potential safety and health hazards. Furthermore, as fewer people work in agriculture, displaced rural populations are moving to urban centers in search of wage labor. And the unequal distribution of global food supplies results in farmers and food shortages in portions of the world.

All adaptive strategies are subject to the limitations of the natural environment. **Carrying capacity** is the number of people who can be supported by the

carrying capacity
The number of people who can be supported by the resources of the surrounding region.

A Chinese-owned farm in Angola, southern Africa, produces corn for export to China, a reflection of industrial agriculture in today's global economy.

resources of the surrounding region. The carrying capacity of land for food foragers, pastoralists, horticulturalists, or lower-intensity agriculturalists is more locally limited. But in most cases, farming generates a higher carrying capacity than food foraging because the labor-intensive activity of farming supports more extensive human settlements.

Given the expansion of industrialism, including industrial agriculture, the impact of economic activity has more global consequences today. What is Earth's carrying capacity? Can the planet support our projected population growth and consumption of natural resources? Can our contemporary economy meet current human needs, given the planet's carrying capacity? We will consider these questions as we explore the modern world economic system over the remainder of this chapter.

DISTRIBUTION AND EXCHANGE

All cultures have developed patterns for the distribution and exchange of goods and information produced by their members. In fact, the exchange of goods and ideas appears to be central to the workings of culture, establishing patterns of interaction and obligation among people. Anthropologists recognize three main patterns of exchange: reciprocity, redistribution, and market exchange. All are embedded in the everyday workings of almost every cultural group.

Reciprocity. **Reciprocity** involves an exchange of goods and services among people of relatively equal status. Such exchanges, including gift giving, create and reinforce social ties between givers and receivers, fulfill social obligations, and often raise the prestige of the gift giver. For example, the sharing of food resources, whether in earlier hunter-gatherer groups or among contemporary families, builds a sense of community, fulfills social obligations to the group, and raises the prestige of the provider. Anthropologists identify three types of reciprocity defined by the social distance between exchange partners: generalized reciprocity, balanced reciprocity, and negative reciprocity (Sahlins [1974] 2004; Service 1966).

Generalized reciprocity encompasses exchanges in which the value of what is exchanged is not carefully calculated and the timing or amount of repayment is not predetermined. Generalized reciprocity is common among close kin or close friends, serving as an expression of personal connection while reinforcing family and social networks. You may often experience generalized reciprocity without recognizing it: offering to take someone to the airport without expecting exact or timely reciprocity; borrowing a pen or sheets of paper; offering some of your food to a friend. Likewise, parents provide for their children—food, shelter, education, clothes, protection—without calculating the value or expecting repayment on predetermined terms.

reciprocity

The exchange of resources, goods, and services among people of relatively equal status; meant to create and reinforce social ties.

Balanced reciprocity occurs between people who are more distantly related. This type of exchange includes norms about giving, accepting, and reciprocating. The giver expects the gift to be accepted and then to receive something in return. The recipient has an obligation to accept the gift (or is otherwise considered rude or ungrateful) and reciprocate promptly with a gift of equal value. The goal of exchanges based on balanced reciprocity is to build and maintain social relationships, often beyond the immediate kin group.

Negative reciprocity refers to a pattern of exchange in which the parties seek to receive more than they give, reaping a material advantage through the exchange. Whereas general and balanced reciprocity are based on relationships of trust and familiarity, negative reciprocity occurs among people who are strangers, antagonists, and enemies with opposing interests. Through hard bargaining, cleverness, deception, or cheating, the parties hope to minimize their cost and maximize their return.

Redistribution. **Redistribution** is a form of exchange in which goods are collected from the members of the group and reallocated in a different pattern. Redistribution requires the collected goods to flow through a central location—a chief, a storehouse, or a central government—where it can be sorted, counted, and redistributed. In small-scale societies, redistribution brings prestige to the community leader as food and goods collected from the leader's supporters are reallocated for supporting the general populace or establishing alliances with outside groups. You have experienced redistribution directly if in your family those who work outside the home share their wages with those who do not in order to provide all members with food and shelter. And if you receive a paycheck for a job, your taxes are part of the U.S. government's system of redistribution.

Redistribution may increase or decrease the inequality of wealth and resources within a group. In fact, many cultures have leveling mechanisms—practices and organizations that level out resources within the group. In the United States, for example, as in many other nation-states, redistribution is enacted through local, state, and federal tax codes. The government collects money (more from those with greater resources) and then reallocates and redistributes the nation's wealth to provide services (for example, the military) and infrastructure (for example, roads and bridges). Leveling mechanisms enact a cultural commitment to the collective good that seeks access to safety, health, education, food, and shelter for all group members irrespective of class.

Market Exchange. Finally, today, patterns of distribution and exchange are heavily influenced by economic markets that facilitate the buying and selling of land, natural resources, goods, services, labor, and ideas. Contemporary markets range in size and scope from village markets in India to the New York Stock Exchange on Wall Street. Though some people may **barter**—that is, exchange goods and services,

redistribution

A form of exchange in which accumulated wealth is collected from the members of the group and reallocated in a different pattern.

barter

The exchange of goods and services, one for the other.

one for the other—most contemporary economic transactions are based on an exchange medium, or some form of money. In recent human history, the medium of exchange has varied. Items such as salt, precious stones, shells, livestock, precious metals such as gold or silver, coins, and most recently paper money and digital transfers of money have served to make payments for goods and services.

Long-distance trade routes have connected Asia, the Middle East, Europe, and Africa for over 2,000 years. The Tabula Rogeriana, a map of trade routes through northern Africa, Europe, the Indian Ocean, and much of Asia, was written in Arabic and attributed to the Arab geographer Muhammad al-Idrisi, 1154.

What Are the Roots of Today's Global Economy?

Recent centuries have intensified the integration of all humanity into an interconnected global economy. Economic anthropology—the study of human economic activity and relations—views the world through the lens of movement rather than through the perspective of fixed and discrete groups. The key characteristics of today's global economy are mobility and connection. But not all of these connections have been smooth and easy. Many have been—and still are—contentious and unequal.

EARLY LONG-DISTANCE TRADE ROUTES

More than 2,000 years ago, long-distance trade routes connected Asia, the Middle East, Africa, and Europe in a dynamic international network of economic exchange (Abu-Lughod 1989; Braudel [1979] 1992; Frank 1998; Schneider 1977; Wolf 1982). Movement was slow, but long-distance trade moved luxury items across a vast territory. China led the world in the production and export of silk, porcelain ceramics (china), tea, fruit, drugs, cotton, tobacco, arms and powder, copper and iron products, zinc, and cupronickel (Abu-Lughod 1989; Frank 1998). Before long, Europe's elite were seeking greater access to China's desirable commodities.

By the time Columbus sailed in 1492, Europe's elite needed more than a shorter trade route to Asia to enter the world economy. They needed a way to buy themselves in. Although China wanted or needed very little from the West, Europeans increasingly sought its export commodities. As a result, European trade in Asia created surpluses for China, whose exports constantly surpassed its imports. China demanded payment of all deficits in silver and gold, setting off an intense global competition for these scarce resources.

As a result, acquisition of silver and gold was high on the Europeans' agenda in the Caribbean and the Americas. They systematically plundered the Mayan and Aztec kingdoms as well as the indigenous populations as they conquered the South American continent. Local populations were forced into slave labor to extract precious minerals, as at the lucrative silver mines in Peru. Between 1500 and 1600 the supply of silver in circulation in Europe increased eightfold (Robbins 2013). The gold and silver plundered from the Americas enabled Europeans to buy a seat on the economic train based in Asia. (Frank 1998; Spence 2013).

COLONIALISM

Europe's global economic engagements between 1500 and 1800 relied primarily on extensive maritime trade within the existing global economic system. The American colonies were an important exception. They served as a harbinger of colonial expansion in the rest of the world in the nineteenth and early twentieth centuries. In fact, the European conquest of the New World—the Caribbean and the Americas—launched an era of colonialism that eventually touched every corner of the globe.

colonialism

The practice by which a nation-state extends political, economic, and military power beyond its own borders over an extended period of time to secure access to raw materials, cheap labor, and markets in other countries or regions.

Under **colonialism**, European powers redrew the map of the world and fundamentally reorganized the political and economic balance of power on a global scale. Europeans' advanced military weaponry and strategies, developed through years of continental warfare and naval battles, gave them an advantage that enabled them to dominate others in the colonial era. Beginning in the 1500s, European colonialism played a pivotal role in establishing the framework for today's global economic system.

THE TRIANGLE TRADE

The triangle trade that emerged in the 1500s among Europe, Africa, and the Americas involved an extensive exchange of goods, people, wealth, food, diseases, and ideas that transformed economic, political, and social life on both sides of the Atlantic (Figure 11.1). It also brought western Europeans the resources they needed in order to grow their national economies and expand their role in international trade.

FIGURE 11.1
The Triangle Trade

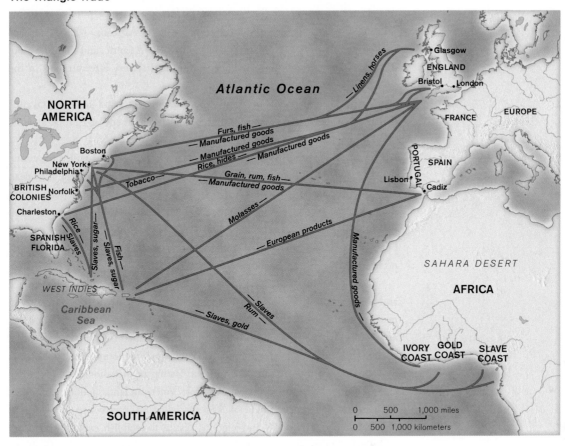

Europeans established a plantation economy in the Caribbean and South America to produce sugar for export to Europe. Columbus had carried sugar to the Caribbean, which, along with Brazil, offered an ideal climate for sugarcane cultivation. But now, plantation production transformed sugar from a luxury item to a key component of the European diet. Sugar also sweetened three other key commodities in the triangle trade—all stimulants (drugs)—coffee, tea, and cocoa (Mintz 1985).

The expansion of sugarcane plantations by the Spanish and Portuguese could not be sustained by the local populations in the Caribbean and South America because they were decimated by European diseases and the grueling conditions of forced labor. So plantation owners turned to the African slave trade to supply their labor needs. Between the sixteenth and eighteenth centuries, millions of Africans were sold into slavery and transported across the Atlantic to work on sugarcane plantations in the Caribbean and South America. Later, rising demand for cotton for England's textile industry required more laborers for cotton plantations in the southern region of what is now the United States. This pressure further stimulated demand for enslaved Africans. Many—perhaps millions—died in the traumatic passage across the Atlantic, and millions more died in inhuman conditions of incarceration and slavery after arriving in the Americas.

The uncompensated labor of enslaved Africans, extracted under brutal conditions, subsidized the economic growth and development of Europe and the American colonies for more than 350 years.

In North America, the fur trade, particularly in beaver pelts, pulled the continent into the global economy. The European demand for fur drove the European expansion deeper into the North American continent. Native American settlement patterns were severely disrupted, as were local agricultural practices and economic activities. Conflicts between the British and French drew indigenous populations into colonial wars. European germs devastated a population that had no immunity to European diseases (Wolf 1982).

The decimation of the indigenous populations in North and South America and the Caribbean (estimated by some scholars to be as many as 15 million people), combined with the forced relocation of millions of Africans and the arrival of millions of European immigrants, transformed the human population of the New World over a period of a few centuries. Furthermore, the large-scale movement of Europeans and Africans had lasting repercussions on their home communities as well. The conquest of Native American lands, genocide of indigenous people, and enslavement of Africans relied on intertwined ideologies of racial supremacy, patriarchy, and religious destiny to establish, expand, and justify a hierarchy of exploitation central to the European colonial enterprise. (Robbins 2013; Trouillot 1994; Wolf 1982).

THE INDUSTRIAL REVOLUTION

The Industrial Revolution in the eighteenth and nineteenth centuries drove the next phase of European colonial activities. As European economies, led by Great Britain, shifted toward machine-based manufacturing, the new industries relied heavily on the raw materials, cheap labor, and open markets of the colonies. At the same time, Europe's expanding cities, combined with growing colonies, provided markets for goods produced in Europe's factories. The huge profits from the transatlantic triangle trade provided the capital infusion necessary to fund Europe's industrial transformation.

Industrial expansion of the capitalist economy created intense competition among European countries for raw materials, cheap labor, and markets. Throughout the nineteenth and early twentieth centuries, Great Britain, France, the Netherlands, Belgium, Russia, and Japan all raced to divide nonindustrial regions of the world into colonies that would secure their economic growth. In the process, European countries redrew the political map of the world—especially in Asia, Africa, and the Middle East—and restructured the global economy to serve their expanding industrial activities.

ANTI-COLONIAL STRUGGLES

Local populations resisted colonialism with mixed success. Independence movements used strategies of rebellion, resistance, and negotiation to achieve their goals. These included nonviolent actions such as those led by Mohandas Ghandi in the Indian struggle against British colonialism, as well as violent uprisings such as those in Algeria. Frequently, external factors such as wars, economic crises, and international pressures aided independence movements by creating conditions for their success.

In the Americas, independence movements on both continents brought changes. The United States declared independence from Great Britain in 1776, eventually winning independence through the Revolutionary War. The people of Haiti, a highly profitable Caribbean French colony known for its sugarcane, coffee, cocoa, indigo, and cotton plantations, declared independence in 1804 and became the first independent former colony to be ruled by people of African descent. In Latin America, Brazil declared independence from Portugal in 1822. By 1825, most of Spain's colonies in South America had achieved independence.

Anticolonial movements blossomed after World War II, often with tragic consequences. Here, Algerian residents do battle against the colonial French military in the film *The Battle of Algiers*, 1965.

Ultimately, World War II created conditions for the success of national independence movements and the collapse of the colonial system. For example, Japanese occupation destroyed much of the European colonial infrastructure in Asia and inspired organized national resistance movements. These forces led efforts toward national independence when the war ended. On a global scale, the war-ravaged economies and political institutions of the European colonial powers could no longer sustain their colonial enterprises, especially in the face of organized resistance movements. Between 1945 and 1990, more than one hundred former colonies gained their independence.

But as we have seen in the opening story about Côte d'Ivoire, and as we will see throughout the remainder of this chapter, despite the formal end of the colonial era, patterns of relationship established under colonialism—from migration and economics to military involvement—continue to influence both former colonies and colonizers.

THE MODERN WORLD ECONOMIC SYSTEM

With the end of the colonial era, many people believed that the former colonies—wealthy in natural resources and freed from colonial control—would see rapid economic growth. But such growth, as well as diminished poverty and the possibility for income equality, has proved to be elusive. Why have patterns of inequality established under colonialism persisted into the current era?

Conflicting Theories. **Modernization theories**, which became popular following World War II, predicted that with the end of colonialism poor countries would follow the same trajectory as the industrialized countries and achieve improved standards of living. Certainly, the rise of industrial capitalism in Europe beginning in the late eighteenth century had spurred spectacular advances in production and a sense of optimism in the possibilities for dramatic material progress—in other words, **development** (Larrain 1989). As decolonization approached, politicians and economists in industrialized nations began to strategize about how to develop the economies of the colonies of Britain, France, Portugal, and other European powers (Leys 1996). The modernization model was assumed to be the key. Progress, modernization, and industrialization would be the natural path of economic development throughout the global capitalist economy, though this process would need nurturing through foreign aid and international investment.

After World War II, policy theorists and planners believed that scientific and technological expertise could help replicate the European and North American style of development across the globe. Through an array of new international aid agencies and financial institutions, such as the World Bank, the IMF, and the U.N., wealthy nations worked with emerging national governments in former

modernization theories

Post–World War II economic theories that predicted that with the end of colonialism, less-developed countries would follow the same trajectory toward modernization as the industrialized countries.

development

Post–World War II strategy of wealthy nations to spur global economic growth, alleviate poverty, and raise living standards through strategic investment in national economies of former colonies.

colonies to develop programs they hoped would stimulate growth, alleviate poverty, and raise living standards. Development projects often emphasized state investment in infrastructure as an engine of economic growth, focusing on the construction of ports, roads, dams, and irrigation systems (Cowen and Shenton 1996; Edelman and Haugerud 2005).

But by the 1960s, scholars began to question the Western development model. Despite the end of colonialism, less-developed countries, even those with rich natural resources, did not experience modernization and economic growth. Many local and national economies remained stagnant or lost ground in the international economy. Many countries took on increasing international debt to keep their economies stable in the postcolonial era.

At this time, **dependency theory** emerged as a critique of modernization theory. Scholars from Latin America, in particular, argued that a new kind of colonialism—neocolonialism—had emerged (Cardoso and Faletto 1969; Frank 1969). Dependency theorists argued that despite the end of colonialism, the underlying economic relations of the modern world system had not changed. These scholars introduced the term **underdevelopment** to suggest that poor countries were not poor because of some fundamental structural flaw (such as inadequate natural resources), but because participation in the global economy left them underdeveloped. The global economy was still structured to extract resources from less-developed countries and transfer them to developed, industrialized countries. Thus, dependency theorists argued, underdeveloped countries should break their dependency on the global economic system and build up and protect their own self-sufficient national economic activities.

Core and Periphery. Immanuel Wallerstein (1974) introduced to these debates a *modern world systems* analysis. Wallerstein characterized the nations within the world economic system as occupying core, semiperiphery, and periphery positions (Figure 11.2). The **core countries**—primarily industrialized former colonial states—dominate the world system, extracting cheap labor and raw materials from periphery countries and sending them to the industrialized core. Finished products, with value added in the manufacturing process, are then returned to markets in the periphery. Core countries control the most lucrative economic processes, including the financial services sectors.

Periphery countries—among the least developed and least powerful nations—serve primarily as sources of raw materials, agricultural products, cheap labor, and markets for the economic activities of the core. Established patterns of economic, political, and military relationship ensure the steady transfer of wealth, natural resources, and human resources from the periphery to core, contributing to underdevelopment. Semiperiphery countries occupy a middle position. They may have developed some industry, draw resources from the periphery, and

dependency theory

A critique of modernization theory arguing that despite the end of colonialism, the underlying economic relations of the modern world economic system had not changed.

underdevelopment

The term used to suggest that poor countries are poor as a result of their relationship to an unbalanced global economic system.

core countries

Industrialized former colonial states that dominate the world economic system.

periphery countries

The least-developed and least-powerful nations; often exploited by the core countries as sources of raw materials, cheap labor, and markets.

FIGURE 11.2
The Core/Periphery Division of the World

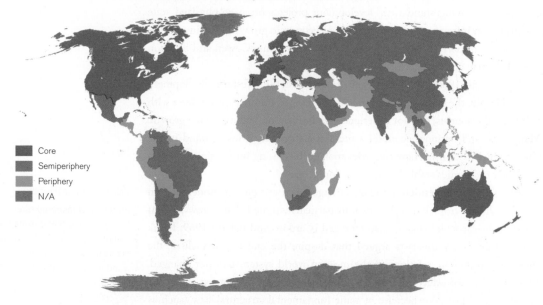

Core
Semiperiphery
Periphery
N/A

export manufactured products to the core and periphery, but they lack the economic and political power of the core.

Core and periphery are not necessarily geographically isolated from one another. Wallerstein suggests that peripheral areas often exist within core countries as pockets of poverty amid generally high standards of living. In the United States, the Appalachian mountain region (see the discussion of Pem Buck's book *Worked to the Bone* in Chapter 10) might be considered a periphery within a core country: It has abundant natural resources of coal, timber, and water but intense poverty, poor education and health care, and limited infrastructure. Core areas also exist within periphery countries. These include urban centers (ports and capital cities), dominated by the economic, military, and political elite, that provide linkages between core countries and the often more rural people in the periphery. Abidjan, Côte d'Ivoire, could be considered a core area within a periphery country, serving to connect rural cocoa farmers and the global chocolate trade.

Over the past forty years, globalization has complicated the neat categories of Wallerstein's theory. Capital, goods, people, and ideas flow less predictably today between a geographically defined core and periphery. But the realities of uneven development and entrenched inequality persist. Over 80 percent of the world's population still live in developing nations decades after the end of colonialism.

FROM FORDISM TO FLEXIBLE ACCUMULATION

Over the past hundred years, the corporation has increasingly challenged the nation-state (which dominated the colonial era) for supremacy in the global economy. We can trace this change through the history of two economic models that dominated the U.S. economy (and beyond) during the twentieth century.

In 1914 Henry Ford, the founder of Ford Motor Company, a U.S. automobile manufacturer, experimented with a new strategy for profit making within the industrializing economy of the United States. Ford is famous for refining the factory assembly line and the division of labor that facilitated efficiency in industrial mass production. Perhaps equally significant, at a time when many U.S. manufacturers were exploiting immigrant workers with low wages and long work hours to maximize profits, Ford introduced a $5, eight-hour workday—a living wage that he hoped would create a worker who was loyal to the company, dependable on the job, and cooperative with management in the grueling, repetitive work environment of the assembly line. Ford also believed that every Ford

Where does your iPhone come from? The journey of an iPhone illustrates Wallerstein's concepts of core, semiperiphery, and periphery. (*clockwise from right*) A worker at a rare earth mine in Inner Mongolia; rare earth elements are vital to the manufacturing of electronics, including iPhones. Factory workers at the Foxconn plant in Shenzhen, south China, where many iPhones, iPads, and other Apple products are made. Footballer Francesco Totti takes a selfie after scoring a goal against S.S. Lazio.

worker should be able to buy a Ford car. He sought to form a new social compact between labor and capital that would benefit his corporation. These were the central aspects of **Fordism**.

Fordism took hold firmly after World War II with growing cooperation among corporations, labor, and government. The latter stepped in to regulate corporate responsibility for worker health and safety and, eventually, environmental impact. An income tax structure with high marginal rates for the very wealthy moderated the growth in income inequality. Wages and benefits, along with corporate profits, rose steadily through a long post-war boom that drove a rapid expansion of the middle class through the early 1970s.

However, industrial economic activity in the late 1960s and 1970s began to shift away from the Fordist model toward what geographer David Harvey (1990) has called "strategies of flexible accumulation" to address shrinking corporate profits brought about by increased global competition and a global recession.

Flexible accumulation refers to the increasingly flexible strategies that corporations use to accumulate profits in an era of globalization. In particular, these strategies include *offshoring* (relocating factories anywhere in the world that provides optimal production, infrastructure, labor, marketing, and political conditions) and *outsourcing* (hiring low-wage laborers in periphery countries to perform jobs previously done in core countries). By so doing, corporations could bypass high production costs, organized labor, and environmental laws in the core industrial cities and core countries.

Under flexible accumulation, corporations—even highly profitable ones—began to eliminate jobs in old core industrial centers such as New York, Chicago, and Detroit. Instead, they opened factories "offshore" in places such as Mexico, the Caribbean, South Korea, and Taiwan. In the 1980s they began to relocate factories to China to take advantage of even lower wages, lower taxes, and weaker

Who answered your last call for tech support? Here, a call center agent in the Philippines talks to a client in the United States, an example of how jobs are being outsourced from core countries to low-wage destinations under flexible accumulation.

environmental restrictions. Recent strikes by Chinese workers demanding higher wages and better working conditions have led some corporations to relocate again, opening new factories in Thailand, Cambodia, Vietnam, and Bangladesh. Over the past forty years, strategies of flexible accumulation have transformed the local factory assembly line into a global assembly line.

What Are the Dominant Organizing Principles of the Global Economy Today?

Flows of capital, goods, and services associated with flexible accumulation have built on old colonial patterns and have made use of advances in transportation and communication technologies (time-space compression). But other forces also help move all people and nations toward one free market with minimal barriers. These forces include powerful international financial institutions, and international and regional trade agreements. Drawing on an economic philosophy called "neoliberalism," these institutions and agreements have created a strong international financial and policy framework, one that promotes an even deeper integration of nations and local communities into the contemporary global economy.

CAPITALISM, ECONOMIC LIBERALISM, AND THE FREE MARKET

The work of the Scottish economist and philosopher Adam Smith (1723–1790) and the British economist John Maynard Keynes (1883–1946) provided key intellectual counterpoints that have shaped economic debates about the functioning of capitalism in modern times. In *The Wealth of Nations* (1776), Adam Smith promoted economic liberalism through his ideas of laissez-faire ("leave it alone") capitalism. In Smith's view, free markets and free trade, being liberated from government intervention, would provide the best conditions for economic growth: They would unleash competition to maximize profits. In contrast, Keynes later argued that capitalism would work best when the government had a role in moderating the excesses of capitalism and ensuring the basic welfare of all citizens (Keynes [1936] 2007).

After World War II, leading Western governments applied Keynesian economic philosophy in rebuilding their war-torn economies and establishing development projects to stimulate growth in former colonies. Keynesian economics began to lose popularity in the 1970s in the wake of a global recession. But today it maintains a role in certain government policies—those that (1) stimulate economic activity through public investment in infrastructure projects and the employment of civil servants while also (2) seeking to regulate the excesses of corporate and financial activities and moderate the most extreme effects of capitalism on the population through the provision of a social safety net and investment in health, education, and housing.

NEOLIBERALISM

Economic liberalism, building on Smith's philosophy, has reemerged since the 1970s as a guiding philosophy for the global economy. This **neoliberalism**, associated with conservative fiscal and political policies in the United States, views the free market—not the state—as the main mechanism for ensuring economic growth. Neoliberal policies focus on promoting free trade on a global scale, eliminating trade barriers, and reducing taxes, tariffs, and most government intervention in the economy. Neoliberalism promotes the privatization of public assets (such as publicly owned utilities and transportation systems) and an overall reduction, if not privatization, of government spending on health, education, and welfare.

Since the 1980s, powerful international financial institutions like the International Monetary Fund (IMF), the World Bank, and the World Trade Organization (WTO) have promoted neoliberal policies, frequently using structural adjustment loans as a key, though controversial, mechanism to address poverty and development in poorer nations. Structural adjustment loans seek to stabilize a country's long-term economic development. They require fiscal austerity measures, a reduced role for the state in the economy, and a restructuring of national trade and tariff policies so as to create freer access to local markets.

Pros and Cons of Neoliberal Policies. Debates continue over the effectiveness of neoliberal policies. In particular, there is skepticism in many countries over the notion that facilitating competition and profit making through free trade, free markets, and privatization promotes improved economic opportunities for most of the world's people. Much of Latin America has repaid debts to the IMF and has rejected neoliberal economic strategies. The World Social Forum, an annual international meeting of social movements and NGOs, explores alternatives to neoliberal economic policies and the negative aspects of globalization.

In Europe, several nations (Greece, Spain, Portugal, and Ireland) have struggled to adapt to mandates for austerity imposed by the IMF and the European Central Bank in return for loans made to stabilize their national economies. Widespread protests by affected workers have threatened the stability of national governing coalitions that agreed to the externally imposed restrictions. Leaders of underdeveloped countries, scholars, and activists have argued that these

What are the most effective strategies for building a healthy economy? Here, protestors in Greece demonstrate against government austerity measures.

policies are the centerpiece of an ever-evolving global economic system that promotes uneven development and ensures that wealthy countries remain wealthy and poor countries remain poor (Krugman 2015; Sachs 2005; Stiglitz 2010).

THE (IN)STABILITY OF THE GLOBAL FINANCIAL MARKETS IN THE TWENTY-FIRST CENTURY

In late 2008 the United States experienced the worst financial collapse in over seventy years. At the center of the crisis was a massive credit bubble created by millions of high-risk mortgages and other complex new financial instruments, including credit default swaps (CDS) and synthetic collateralized debt obligations (CDO)—more generally called credit derivatives. Financial derivatives are essentially contracts based on (derived from) some other asset—commodities, interest rates, credit, foreign exchange rates, equities, and mortgages. In the years leading up to 2008, bankers seeking new investment vehicles for their clients bundled millions of individual mortgages into new financial instruments—derivative contracts—that could themselves be traded, bought, sold, exchanged, and insured. People buying the derivatives were making a bet on the future value of the new asset (Tett 2010).

The U.S. financial collapse of 2008 and its subsequent impact on other countries indicate a significant shift in the global economy. Anthropologists of finance suggest that circulation of capital is now the driving force behind the global expansion of capitalism in the twenty-first century. Accumulated global capital reserves have increasingly been moving away from manufacturing areas toward the creation of financial products and new infrastructures to facilitate their circulation.

Banks have launched corporate finance units and global capital desks and have spun off hedge funds. Financial technicians have been trained, logistical support services have been developed, and new communication technologies—the Internet, microchips, wireless systems, high-speed data transmission, real-time inventory assessments—have been invented that permit instantaneous, around-the-clock global trading. Global capital markets and the firms that service them, based predominately in Europe and the United States, increasingly shape economic and political realities in every part of the world, from corporate board rooms to local economies and national governments (LiPuma and Lee 2004; Zaloom 2006; Ho 2009). As a result, while the total gross domestic product of the global economy was estimated to be $77 trillion in 2014, the face value of derivatives circulating through the global financial markets is now estimated to be between $700 trillion and $1 quadrillion. (Bank for International Settlements 2016).

The debate over neoliberal and Keynesian economic strategies continues to rage in the United States and globally.

Followers of Keynesian economics—often associated with political liberals and moderates—argue for greater regulation of financial markets, increased consumer protections, an expanded health-care safety net, and heavy investment in infrastructure projects to put people back to work. Followers of neoliberalism—primarily associated with political conservatives—seek lower taxes, smaller government, faster debt repayment, and reduced regulation to stimulate economic activity by businesses. Crucial debates continue over efforts to address growing economic inequality, repair crumbling infrastructure, stabilize the future of Social Security, Medicare, and Medicaid, implement the Affordable Care Act (Obamacare), and reduce government support for higher education.

How Does Today's Global Economy Link Workers with Consumers Worldwide?

Through much of recent human history, markets have been places where farmers and craftsmen, traders and consumers exchange products, ideas, information, and news, linking local communities to one another and to communities at greater distances, enabling all to benefit (Polanyi [1944] 2001). Today local markets are more deeply integrated as social and material commodities often flow across national borders (Hannerz 1996). Although **commodity chains**—the hands an item (commodity) passes through between producer and

commodity chains

The hands an item passes through between producer and consumer.

consumer—used to be primarily local, globalization has extended their span across territories and cultures, intensifying the connection between the local and global in ways previously unimaginable (Haugerud, Stone, and Little 2000). Tokyo's Tsukiji Fish Market, the largest fish market in the world today, is a prime example.

TSUKIJI: FISH MARKET AT THE CENTER OF THE WORLD

Standing in the heart of downtown Tokyo, Japan, Tsukiji Fish Market is the center of a massive global trade in seafood and a cultural icon of Japanese cuisine. Each day 60,000 traders gather to auction bluefin tuna from Maine, eel from southern China, octopus from West Africa, salmon from Canada, and shellfish from California; these then make their way into the restaurants, supermarkets, and homes of Japanese people across the country. Tsukiji Fish Market feeds the city's 22 million people and many more throughout Japan. But Tokyo and the Tsukiji Market are also command central for an intricate global trade in seafood.

The Japanese people's desire for sushi and sashimi has established Japan as the world's main market for fresh tuna. And Japanese cultural influence has spurred the consumption of sushi in other countries. At the same time, rising demand in Japan has led to overfishing and the decimation of the local tuna fishery. Forty years of time-space compression have facilitated an extension of the tuna commodity chain to previously unconnected places and people. Advances in transportation and

MAP 11.2
Tokyo

Where does your fish come from? Here, a tuna fish auction at Tsukiji Fish Market, Tokyo, Japan, 2007.

communication—refrigerated trucks and cargo jets traveling international routes, along with cell phones, faxes, and the Internet—have promoted an integrated network of fishermen, buyers, and shippers. The search for the perfect tuna has now expanded to the North Atlantic, the Mediterranean, and Australia.

Anthropologist Theodore Bestor's study (2004) of the transnational tuna trade, particularly in Atlantic bluefin tuna, takes him to coastal Maine and the Mediterranean coast of Spain to reveal a complex view of global markets. The stories of these global commodity chains—what Appadurai (1986) calls tracing the "social life of things"—illustrate how the modern world economic system works. Tsukiji Market and the movement of tuna to it enhance our understandings of Wallerstein's ideas of an integrated, but increasingly complicated, world system. Goods, money, ideas, and even people (or, in this case, tuna) flow from periphery to core. But assumptions of a fixed core and periphery, as well as expectations of a predictable flow of raw materials, are called into question. In the story of tuna and sushi, natural resources flow to consumers at the center of the global market and at the end of the global commodity chain. But in this story Japan is the core. The Atlantic seaboards of North America and Europe are the periphery (Bestor 2001, 2004; Jacobs 2005; Stevens 2005).

How Is Today's Global Economy Reshaping Migration?

Just as globalization has expanded the span of commodity chains, the past thirty years have also seen one of the highest rates of global migration in modern history, not only between countries but within them as well. The powerful effects of globalization have stimulated migration from rural areas to urban areas and from less-developed countries to more-developed countries. At the same time, time-space compression has transformed the migration experience: Rapid transportation and instantaneous communication enable some migrants to travel more cheaply and quickly, and to still stay connected with folks back home, in ways that were impossible for earlier migrant generations. Flexible accumulation also stimulates migration by disrupting local economic, political, and social relationships while linking local communities to global economic processes. In 2015 the United Nations estimated that there were 243 million international migrants, plus hundreds of millions more internal migrants moving within their own national borders (United Nations Department of Economic and Social Affairs, Population Division 2015a). The Chinese government estimates that more than 230 million people migrate internally in that one country alone (Liang 2012).

PUSHES AND PULLS

The decision to migrate and the chosen destination are often shaped by **pushes and pulls**. People are *pushed* to migrate from their home community by poverty, famine, natural disasters, war, ethnic conflict, genocide, disease, or political or religious oppression. Those who are forced to migrate are often termed "refugees." The uneven development in the global economy stimulates much of today's global migration. Frustrated by their inability to achieve life aspirations and meet the needs of their families at home, many people seek opportunities elsewhere (Portes and Rumbaut 2006).

Destinations are not chosen randomly, nor are all destinations equal. When considering migration, people are *pulled* to certain places by job opportunities, higher wages, educational opportunities for themselves and their children, access to health care, or investment opportunities. Family and friends who have already migrated provide encouragement and connections. At the same time, media such as television, music, and film, along with powerful advertising, promote the desire to live a Western middle-class, consumer-oriented lifestyle.

pushes and pulls

The forces that spur migration from the country of origin and draw immigrants to a particular new destination country.

BRIDGES AND BARRIERS

Immigrants also encounter **bridges and barriers** that influence who moves and where they go. Bridges may include family networks, transportation links, government immigration policies, recruitment agencies, and even human smugglers. Barriers range from language difference and geographical distance to tightly regulated borders and expenditures for passports, visas, and transportation.

But why do people migrate? My own research, published in *God in Chinatown: Religion and Survival in New York's Evolving Immigrant Community* (2003), focuses on migrants from towns and villages near Fuzhou in southeastern China. In recent years, these individuals have come in large numbers: first to New York to work in Chinese restaurants, garment shops, nail salons, and construction trades; and now spreading across the United States as they open take-out restaurants and all-you-can-eat buffets. As much as 50–70 percent of the population in many towns and villages has migrated out, and hundreds of thousands of them have come to and through New York City.

Of the more than 1.3 billion people in China, why have people from the Fuzhou City area decided to migrate out of China? And why do so many go to New York City? The conditions are the same for Fuzhounese as they are for many rural people in China—small incomes, difficult farm labor, limited opportunities for upward mobility or education. And the attraction of New York City—in this case, the tremendous need for low-wage workers—exists in many big cities, not only in the United States but also in countries much closer to China.

bridges and barriers

The factors that enable or inhibit migration.

MAP 11.3
Fuzhou City

In the back of a Chinese restaurant in New York City, I interviewed Chen Dawei, age nineteen, who had come from Fuzhou one year earlier and whose story sheds light on the Fuzhounese immigrant experience:

> I didn't really want to go to America. But everyone else my age had already gone. I didn't want to seem stupid. My parents really wanted to send me. They have a little shop on the main street. We aren't poor. But we don't make much money either. Making $1,500 a month as a delivery man for a Chinese restaurant in the United States sounds really good when your family is lucky to make that much in a whole year back home. I really didn't want to go. But people kept calling to say how well they were doing. Both of my uncles were already in the U.S. Lots of people were sending money back home. And people who got green cards would come back and build a nice home for their family.
>
> So my dad arranged with a snakehead (smuggler) to send me to New York. It cost $65,000. We borrowed some from my uncles. And some from friends who had already gone to New York. The rest we borrowed at really high interest. It will probably take me four or five years to pay it all off.

Can you identify the pushes, pulls, bridges, and barriers in Chen Dawei's migration story?

Chinese Restaurants and the Global Economy. The journey of Fuzhounese immigrants does not end in New York and may, in fact, continue to your college dorm or apartment front door. Have you ever wondered why chicken with broccoli is so cheap in your local Chinese restaurant? The answer lies along a street called East Broadway in Chinatown on the Lower East Side of Manhattan. There an entire migration industry draws Chinese immigrants from the rural villages of the Fuzhou area of southeastern China to New York City and sets them on the move again to a Chinese restaurant near you.

Located along East Broadway are a cluster of services that facilitate the movement of Chinese immigrants. Offices for immigration lawyers, English language classes, driving schools, and producers of legitimate and illegitimate documents stand alongside doctors' offices, pharmacies, clothing stores, and gambling parlors. East Broadway's human smugglers help undocumented immigrants make their way across national borders. Phone card sales booths help workers keep in touch with family back in China. MoneyGram and Western Union wire-transfer offices send money back to family members in the home villages. Key to this migration industry are two dozen employment agencies that match newly arrived workers with Chinese restaurants across the country and another dozen long-distance buses that deliver Fuzhounese to those restaurants.

East Broadway, Chinatown, New York, the central business district for new immigrants from Fuzhou, China.

This global flow of Fuzhounese is fraught with frictions. Chinese smugglers charge more than $80,000 to bring a person to the United States, leaving immigrants with huge debts that may take years to repay. Restaurant owners rely on vulnerable, underpaid workers to make their profit margins on inexpensive dishes such as chicken with broccoli. Workers often live and work in the restaurants, putting in twelve- to fourteen-hour days, six or seven days a week. Chinatown buses provide the link that moves workers between out-of-town jobs and the support system of the migration industry along East Broadway. As many as 50,000 individuals are circulating through this Chinese restaurant industry at any given time.

The movement of rural men and women from Chinese villages to the far reaches of the United States illustrates the deep interconnectivity of people in the modern world economic system. The demand for inexpensive Chinese food in Omaha, Nebraska, can pull a young Chinese farmer across an ocean to help fill the demand of a global labor market and pursue her dream of wealth and happiness for herself and her family. That is the story behind your next dish of chicken with broccoli (Guest 2011).

GLOBAL MIGRATION PATTERNS

Globalization has transformed the spatiality of the world economy and has intensified the volume and types of movement occurring within and across political boundaries (Trouillot 2003). But not every country is equally affected by today's global flow of migrants. Some are primarily sending countries; others are primarily receiving countries. Moreover, not all migration occurs across borders. Thus a truly global perspective on migration must include both international and internal migration.

FIGURE 11.3
Contemporary Global Migration Patterns

International migrants, or migrants who cross borders, exist across the globe, but they largely relocate to more-developed countries. Figure 11.3 shows the primary migration flows for receiving and sending countries. **Internal migration** refers to the movement of people within their own national borders. For example, urban-oriented development programs and the establishment of large-scale export processing zones in developing countries have provided the pulls for significant internal migration from rural to urban areas to fill the new labor needs. Women workers, sought after by factory owners in export processing zones, constitute a high proportion of internal migrants.

TYPES OF IMMIGRANTS

Globally, immigration includes people from a wide variety of class backgrounds, ranging from refugees fleeing war or natural disaster, to unskilled workers with little education, to well-educated doctors and elite corporate businesspeople. Immigration scholars often focus on immigrants' economic roles, whether as laborers, professionals, entrepreneurs, or refugees. Although not applicable to every immigrant journey, these categories delineate certain patterns that constitute a general framework for analysis and comparison.

Labor immigrants, like the Fuzhounese, move in search of low-skill and low-wage jobs, filling economic niches that native-born workers will not fill. Labor immigrants constitute the majority of migrants in the world today. They

internal migration

The movement of people within their own national borders.

labor immigrants

Persons who move in search of a low-skill and low-wage job, often filling an economic niche that native-born workers will not fill.

Indonesian women labor migrants return home from working in Saudi Arabia. Excluded from citizenship or permanent residence there, many experience exploitative work conditions.

may be legal or illegal, but they are drawn by employment opportunities that, though limited, provide jobs at higher wages than are available in their home economies.

Professional immigrants are highly trained individuals who move to fill economic niches in middle-class professions marked by shortages in the receiving country. A key component of the professional immigrant category is university students trained in Western-style professions who lack opportunities to implement their training at home. This migration is often referred to as a brain drain, for many of the most highly skilled professionals trained in developing (periphery) countries are enticed by wages and other opportunities to relocate to developed (core) countries.

Entrepreneurial immigrants move to new locations to conduct trade and establish businesses as merchants, restaurateurs, and small shopkeepers in countries worldwide.

A fourth type of immigrant, **refugees**, are people who have been forced to migrate beyond their national borders because of political or religious persecution, armed conflict or other forms of violence, or natural or human-made disasters. The United Nations estimated a total of 19.5 million refugees worldwide in 2014 (United Nations High Commissioner for Refugees 2015).

Although refugee status technically applies to those who seek asylum in another nation, the experiences of *internally displaced persons* can be just as devastating. These migrants' experiences mirror those of international refugees, except they take place in the migrants' own countries.

professional immigrants
Highly trained individuals who move to fill economic niches in a middle-class profession often marked by shortages in the receiving country.

entrepreneurial immigrants
Persons who move to a new location to conduct trade and establish a business.

refugees
Persons who have been forced to move beyond their national borders because of political or religious persecution, armed conflict, or disasters.

Why are an increasing number of U.S. health-care professionals immigrants from India, the Philippines, and the Caribbean? Here, Dr. Saeid Ahmadpour performs a checkup on a baby at a clinic in Cheyenne Wells, Colorado.

In another phenomenon of globalization, time-space compression—notably, advances in communication and transportation—has transformed the migration experience by tying migrants more closely to their families and communities back home. Today, many migrants travel back and forth, send money through Western Union, talk regularly with family and friends by telephone, and share videos and movies. These transnational immigrants actively participate in social, economic, religious, and political spheres across national borders. Contemporary globalization has intensified the webs of interaction, lowered the cost of travel and communication, and speeded up the exchange of people, information, and money, thereby enabling some migrants to enjoy a lifestyle that spans national borders.

Malian Migrants: Reshaping Globalization from the Ground Up. Though international movements of people between continents and across oceans often capture public and scholarly attention, today significant movement occurs between neighboring countries. In *Migrants and Strangers in an African City* (2012), anthropologist Bruce Whitehouse examines the large-scale migrations happening within Africa as people move in response to poverty and uncertainty. Whitehouse focuses on migrants from Mali, a large West African nation of 17 million people. Though landlocked, Mali's position at the center of regional trade networks crisscrossing West and North Africa has a long history. Today Malians, along with hundreds of thousands of other West Africans, increasingly have been on the move. Some have settled in developed Western countries such as France, Spain, and the United States, or in Asian cities such as Dubai, Bangkok, Hong Kong, and Guangzhou. Most, however, have relocated within the African continent—notably to Senegal, Côte d'Ivoire, Burkina Faso, Gabon, Congo, and South Africa.

Whitehouse begins his ethnography with the story of a small town in southern Mali that he calls Togotala. The town lies on an arid plain between desert to the north and forest to the south. The harsh environment brings regular drought and then a three-month rainy season during which torrential downpours threaten to erode the area's fragile soil. With agricultural production being inadequate to meet the immediate needs of the Togotala population, and with no development assistance from the Malian government, the community has a history of producing merchants who enter the regional trade networks in order to send remittances home to support their families and the community at large. The influence of merchant remittances is evident in the larger cinderblock homes that have been constructed in Togotala's central district, a school for children in grades 1 to 9, a water tower run by solar power to pump water to communal faucets throughout the town, a landline phone system, a health clinic, and several modern mosques. These local developments are concrete testimony to Togotala's deep connection to the world beyond its borders, and they hint at the creative individual responses that literally bring home the benefits of the global economy.

MAP 11.4
Mali and Congo

Twice daily, battered buses arrive in Togotala carrying goods and passengers and providing the town's primary link to the outside world. A ride south to Mali's capital, Bamako, connects Togotala's merchants to an extensive transport network through which they can reach more-distant destinations. Whitehouse traces some of Togotala's residents southward to a large Malian community in Brazzaville, capital of the Republic of Congo. A port city of 1.5 million residents on the northern bank of the Congo River, Brazzaville serves as the country's administrative, manufacturing, and financial center. It is also a transfer point for agricultural products, wood, rubber, and other raw materials coming from upriver onto the Congo-Ocean railroad that links Brazzaville to the seaport of Pointe-Noire. French colonialists originally brought West Africans to Brazzaville in the 1800s to serve as soldiers, porters, laborers, and messengers. But West Africans succeeded in creating parallel economic networks of merchants, traders, laborers, blacksmiths, leatherworkers, and traditional storytellers—economic networks that survived the end of colonialism in 1960. Today a large community of Malians, mostly Muslim, work in Brazzaville as importers, shopkeepers, street vendors, entrepreneurs, and merchants in the diamond and jewelry trades.

Despite their long history in Brazzaville, Malians are treated as outsiders and strangers, segregated by language, social organization, and religion. Under these conditions, a strong connection to home enables the migrant Malians to resist

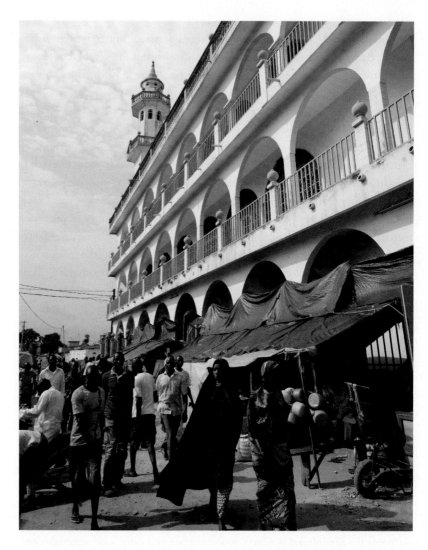

Enterpreneurial immigrants from Mali have built a vibrant community in Brazzaville, Republic of Congo.

the experience of exclusion from key local spaces, whether political, economic, social, or religious. Whitehouse easily portrays why people seek employment outside Togotala. More difficult to understand is why they come back so frequently and continue to be active in Togotala economics, politics, and social life.

From the perspective of Malian life in Brazzaville, the choice to maintain an intense and direct connection to home becomes more understandable. The connection enables them to maintain a sense of place and belonging despite the local marginalization and in the face of increasing mobility and spatial separation from their families and home community.

Migrants, including the merchants of Togotala and other entrepreneurs across Africa, reveal creative individual responses to the intensification of interaction that is occurring worldwide. Actions by migrants such as the Malians in Brazzaville—less powerful people whose stories are often ignored in the grand narrative of globalization—reveal the determined, entrepreneurial strategies that local people employ to bring the benefits of the global economy to their communities and to reshape globalization from the ground up.

Is Today's Global Economic System Sustainable?

Today we have an economic system of astounding complexity. Our economic activity surpasses anything we might have imagined even fifty years ago. The global economy integrates all of the world's people to one extent or another into a global system of exchange. But does it work well for everyone? What are the criteria we might use to assess its effectiveness?

SUCCESSES AND FAILURES

The global economy has achieved remarkable success over the past sixty years. For example, gross national income of the global economy rose from around $1 trillion in 1960 to nearly $77.6 trillion in 2014 (International Monetary Fund 2014). The same period saw a 50 percent increase in school enrollments and a drop in infant mortality rates of more than 60 percent. And life expectancy nearly doubled over the last century, reaching 70 years in 2012 (World Health Organization 2015b).

But the outlook is not all rosy. In 2015 the world had nearly 1 billion people going hungry each day and living in extreme poverty. Over 3 million children under five die of malnutrition each year (United Nations 2015). Clearly, global inequality continues to increase. Is the current trajectory of the global economy sustainable? And what can anthropologists contribute to addressing these questions? (Moran 2006)?

THE HUMAN ECOLOGICAL FOOTPRINT

Since at least the time of the earliest human settlements and the development of farming and pastoralism, humans have had an impact on their local environments. Human impact increased with an expanding population and was accelerated by the Industrial Revolution. Over the past sixty years, we have transformed our relationship with nature, and now our impact is being felt on a planetary scale. Scientists have begun calling this period of Earth's history the Anthropocene to reflect the ways humans are reshaping the physical contours of the planet.

Can Earth sustain the current global economy? Here, demonstrators in the 2014 New York Climate Change March warn that investments in carbon-generating oil companies may backfire and flood Wall Street.

The U.N. estimates that the world population, which was 2.5 billion in 1950, will increase from 7.3 billion in 2015 to 11.2 billion by 2100 (United Nations Department of Economic and Social Affairs, Population Division 2015b). Each day, we add 220,000 people. Each day, human consumption increases while available natural resources decrease. How will we sustain an almost 50 percent increase in global population when current resources are already overused? As this crisis deepens, how will your life be directly affected? What personal and collective strategies can you imagine for addressing the emerging problems?

Accelerating climate change is already evident, and the human contribution to the environmental crisis is clear. Agricultural yields are being affected by rising temperatures and increased greenhouse gases in the atmosphere. Food shortages are increasing despite intensive farm mechanization, chemical fertilizers, and pesticides. Carbon emissions from burning oil and gas are heating the planet and acidifying the oceans. At the 2015 global climate conference in Paris, France, 196 nations endorsed an agreement that acknowledged the need to cut global emissions drastically to hold the overall increase in global temperatures below 2 degrees Celsius (3.6 degrees Fahrenheit). Meeting this goal was recognized as essential to avoid a global ecological catastrophe. Global temperatures have already risen eight-tenths of a degree Celsius, two-thirds since 1975, and humans continue to pour record amounts of carbon into the atmosphere (Kolbert 2014; McKibben 2010, 2012).

The scramble for natural resources—especially freshwater, oil, and coltan (a scarce metal ore used in cell phones and other electronic devices)—pits wealthy nations against poor nations. The ice sheets in the Himalayas that provide drinking water for billions of people in Pakistan, India, Burma, and Indo-China are shrinking from global warming. Underground aquifers that provide freshwater to billions more in China and the Middle East are being depleted faster than nature can replenish them. Environmental trends do not bode well for the global economy using today's technologies.

Humans have a huge ecological footprint. Production, distribution, and consumption have been transformed in the contemporary global economy. And consumerism is driving a dramatic expansion of the human ecological footprint. Studies suggest that as early as 1980 humans began to use more resources than the planet could regenerate. Today, our consumption of the world's resources has stretched above 60 percent over sustainable levels. In other words, at our current rate of consumption, it would take 1.6 Earths to sustain our rate of resource consumption and absorb our pollution using prevailing technologies. By the year 2030, estimates suggest we would need two planets to sustain our economic activity. This is what scientists call "ecological overshoot," which occurs when human demands on nature exceed the planet's ability to provide. The results are depletion of freshwater systems, the buildup of carbon dioxide in the atmosphere, collapsing fisheries in the oceans, and diminishing forest cover (Global Footprint Network 2016).

WORLD ON THE EDGE

Time is short. Scholars in many fields are asking if we have come to the crisis point where our model of economic growth is leading to ecological collapse. Our current economic system risks pushing us closer to the edge. Although most residents of wealthy countries have been shielded from the worst effects of these changes, people in poorer countries, particularly in coastal and low-lying regions, are already hard hit. For example, as we will discuss in Chapter 12, Bangladesh's coastal flood plain has been repeatedly inundated with monsoons, flooding, and devastating erosion. Even the United States is experiencing an increased incidence of droughts, heat waves, and damaging storm fronts.

Perhaps the biggest test of the global economy and its underlying principles will be its sustainability. Can we sustain the current pace of economic growth? Is it within the planet's carrying capacity? Is it reasonable to think that through modernization all people will attain a middle-class lifestyle when we know that if everyone on the planet had the same ecological footprint as an American, the global lifestyle would require five Earths to support?

Toolkit

Thinking Like an Anthropologist: Situating Yourself within the Global Economy

Globalization of the world economy has transformed the way we live. As you analyze the global economy and your connection to it, consider again the questions we raised at the beginning of the chapter:

- **What is an economy, and what is its purpose?**
- **What are the roots of today's global economy?**
- **What are the dominant organizing principles of the global economy today?**
- **How does today's global economy link workers with consumers worldwide?**
- **How is today's global economy reshaping migration?**
- **Is today's global economic system sustainable?**

Our opening story of chocolate in Côte d'Ivoire highlighted both the complexities of the global economy and the connections it facilitates among people, states, and corporations worldwide. Chocolate—like coffee, tea, sugar, a laptop, or a smartphone—reveals both (1) the incredible potential of our globalized economy to create connections, and (2) the unwelcome consequences of globalization that lead to imbalances and inequalities.

We have asked whether the global economy works well. Is it sustainable? How can we ensure the adequate distribution of resources necessary for human life—food, clean water, shelter, and health care? These are questions you will have to answer in your lifetime. And you will answer them by the life choices you make. For, with the continuing intensification of globalization, we are all connected in a web of constraints and opportunities. Your engagement with the global economy may not be constrained by poverty, illiteracy, or violence, but it could be constrained by cultural expectations—for instance, group and peer pressure about what you need to do to fit in, dress well, eat right, and travel from place to place. Do you really have the choice in U.S. culture to not consume? How you address these constraints and opportunities will make a difference.

The good news is that there are many points at which to intervene in the current patterns of the global economy, whether you work to save the forests, recycle, support fair trade, reevaluate your consumption patterns, organize to support the rights of workers around the world, or become an engineer focusing on clean manufacturing or a scientist developing renewable energy sources. Thinking like an anthropologist will help you to analyze your choices in a more informed and responsible way.

Key Terms

economy (p. 298)

food foragers (p. 298)

pastoralism (p. 299)

horticulture (p. 299)

agriculture (p. 299)

carrying capacity (p. 300)

reciprocity (p. 301)

redistribution (p. 302)

barter (p. 302)

colonialism (p. 304)

modernization theories (p. 308)

development (p. 308)

dependency theory (p. 309)

underdevelopment (p. 309)

core countries (p. 309)

periphery countries (p. 309)

Fordism (p. 312)

flexible accumulation (p. 312)

neoliberalism (p. 314)

commodity chains (p. 316)

pushes and pulls (p. 319)

bridges and barriers (p. 319)

internal migration (p. 322)

labor immigrants (p. 322)

professional immigrants (p. 323)

entrepreneurial immigrants (p. 323)

refugees (p. 323)

Chapter 12
Politics and Power

"The Sundarbans is our mother. We won't let it be destroyed."

"We will give our blood and our lives but not the Sundarbans!"

Over 1,000 young people—students, workers, and civil society activists—chanted these words as they marched more than 100 miles over four days in the spring of 2016 from the Bangladesh capital, Dhaka, to the vast Sundarbans tidal forest on the low-lying Bangladesh coast. Their march protested the environmental hazards of constructing two giant coal-fired power plants just a few miles upstream from this World Heritage site. The Sundarbans' mangrove trees, mudflats, and wetlands stretch along the vast coastal delta where the Ganges, Brahmaputra, and Meghna rivers reach the Bay of Bengal and provide protection from frequent storm surges and tidal flooding for 40 million people in southern Bangladesh. Thousands of farmers and fisherfolk call the Sundarbans home, as do

Bangladeshi young people march to protect the Sundarbans coastal forest, home to farmers, fisherfolk, as well as the endangered Royal Bengal tiger. What political activity have you been part of?

endangered Royal Bengal tigers, freshwater river dolphins, and thousands of other indigenous plant and animal species. When climate change is already raising sea levels, why would the government agree to build more fossil fuel plants to spew more pollutants into the air and water of a fragile ecosystem, the protestors asked? And why build them on land already vulnerable to coastal flooding?

The Sundarbans campaign is just one of many ways people around the world today are taking action in an unprecedented global political movement to halt and reverse climate change and global warming.

Just a few months earlier, representatives of 196 nation-states gathered at the United Nations 2015 climate change conference in Paris, France, to discuss plans to limit human-generated greenhouse emissions and global warming. Simultaneously in Paris, thousands of demonstrators and activists from women's groups, indigenous rights organizations, antipoverty coalitions, and environmental movements gathered to pressure national governments to honor their pledges to keep fossil fuels in the ground; to demand that fossil fuel companies be held responsible for environmental damage; and to expand the global movement of local environmental actions to stop global warming and climate change.

In the U.S., students on over 400 campuses have launched campaigns to push for divestment of school endowment funds from fossil fuels. At the University of California, three years of student demonstrations by Fossil Free UC, a group of students, faculty, and alumni, led to the divestment in 2015 of $200 million of shares in companies profiting from coal and tar sands, the largest divestment in the United States to date. In the spring of 2016, six years after the fossil-free movement started at Swarthmore College in Philadelphia and at the same time as the Sundarbans campaign in Bangladesh, student-led divestment actions on campuses included demonstrations, teach-ins, and social media organizing. The dramatic occupation of university administration buildings, presidents' offices, and investment management offices—as well as over sixty student arrests—brought increasing public attention to student political activism and challenges to institutional power.

Power is often described as the ability or potential to bring about change through action or influence—either one's own or that of a group or institution. Indeed, power is embedded in all human relationships, whether that power is openly displayed or carefully avoided—from the most mundane aspects of friendships and family relationships to the myriad ways humans organize institutions and the structural frameworks of whole societies (Wolf 1982).

The presence of politics and relations of power in the ebb and flow of daily life is a central focus of anthropological study. Although uprisings and demonstrations may draw attention to the most public, dramatic, and sometimes violent aspects of politics, anthropologists also consider the multiple local forms of politics—the careful political interactions and activities that occupy much of daily life and are essential in making a community a decent place to live (Gledhill 2000; Kurtz 2001; Lewellen 2003).

Throughout this book we explore power and its intersections with culture. We work to unmask the structures of power built on ideologies of race, gender, ethnicity, and sexuality and the institutions of kinship and religion. We also examine the power dynamics of the world economy and the stratifications of class. In this chapter, we explore power as it is expressed through political systems and processes: the way humans have organized themselves in small groups, the role of the state in national and international politics, and the ability of people (nonstate actors) to engage in politics and exercise power through individual action and social movements outside the direct control of the state. We consider the historical and contemporary approaches that anthropologists have taken toward these crucial issues and the ways in which globalization is shifting the dynamics of power and politics on local and global levels. In particular, we will examine the following questions:

- **How have anthropologists viewed the origins of human political history?**
- **What is the state?**
- **How is globalization affecting the state?**
- **What is the relationship among politics, the state, violence, and war?**
- **How do people mobilize power outside the state's control?**

While reading this chapter, you will analyze many expressions of politics and the ways in which aspects of power are expressed locally and globally today. You will consider how political anthropology can help you think more deeply about your own expressions as a political creature, including the ways you negotiate human relationships on the interpersonal, group, community, national, and global level. You will examine the changing role of the state in local, national, and global affairs and the ways humans mobilize collectively through social movements to challenge the power of the state and the effects of globalization by advocating for social change and human rights. Finally, you will consider an anthropological debate about the roots of violence in human culture. The skills you acquire in this chapter will be valuable additions to your toolkit for living as a political actor and an engaged citizen in today's global world.

How Have Anthropologists Viewed the Origins of Human Political History?

Over the course of history, humans have organized themselves politically by using flexible strategies to help their groups survive and make their communities a better place to live. Our earliest human ancestors appear to have evolved in small, mobile, egalitarian groups of hunter-gatherers. It is in these types of groups that core human characteristics and cultural patterns emerged.

For nearly a century, beginning in the late 1800s, anthropologists studying politics and power focused primarily on the political activities of contemporary hunter-gatherers, pastoralists, and horticulturalists. But beginning in the 1960s, the anthropological gaze shifted to encompass more complex, state-oriented societies and the process by which local settings are politically incorporated into a larger context.

The specialization called *political anthropology* took clear shape after World War II as anthropologists examined the local political systems of Africa (e.g. Fortes and Evans-Pritchard 1940; Turner 1957; Gluckman 1954) as well as the Middle East, and Asia (Barth 1959; Leach 1954) and the indigenous people of the Americas (Redfield 1941; Wallace 1957).

As they undertook these studies of politics in many cultures, anthropologists attempted to create a common language, a typology that would enable them to communicate across cultural areas and compare and contrast their findings (Gledhill 2000; Lewellen 2003). The political anthropologist Elman Service (1962) famously classified the vast and varied world of political systems into four basic types: bands, tribes, chiefdoms, and states. Although infrequently used today, this framework shaped a generation of anthropological thinking about political systems. Service proposed that political systems develop through a natural, evolutionary progression from simple to complex and from less integrated to more integrated, with patterns of leadership evolving from weaker to stronger. Subsequently, when states emerged as the dominant political actors on the world stage, the examination of bands, tribes, and chiefdoms, anthropologists hoped, might provide insights into the origins and fundamental nature of the state.

BANDS

Anthropologists have used the term **band** to describe small, kinship-based groups of food foragers who move over a particular territory while hunting and gathering. Through archaeological evidence and the study of a few remaining band societies, anthropologists have identified key characteristics of band organization and leadership. A band might range in size from twenty to several hundred people depending on the time of year and the group's hunting and ritual cycles. Bands break up and re-form regularly in response to conflicts among members and the formation of new alliances.

Small, close-knit bands served as the primary way of life not only for our human ancestors but also for the entire genus *Homo*, including *Homo habilis*, *Homo erectus*, and early *Homo sapiens*. As a result, evolutionary biologists suggest that life in the band shaped the development of our earliest human characteristics and cultural patterns.

Politically, bands are highly decentralized, with decisions made primarily by consensus. Leaders emerge for a task at hand (organizing the hunt, moving the campsite, negotiating a conflict), with their leadership position resting on their skill, knowledge, generosity toward others, and level of respect within the

band

A small kinship-based group of foragers who hunt and gather for a living over a particular territory.

band. With limited resources to compete for, bands have minimal stratification of wealth and power. But perhaps more important, bands required active cooperation among diverse groups of relatives and nonrelatives in order to successfully adapt to an unpredictable and shifting landscape. In turn, these early patterns may have embedded in humans a tendency toward egalitarian social and political organization rather than hierarchy.

In his book *Hierarchy in the Forest: The Evolution of Egalitarian Behavior* (1999), evolutionary biologist Christopher Boehm explores what life in bands can tell us about whether humans are fundamentally hierarchical or egalitarian. Drawing on ethnographic studies of contemporary and historical hunter-gatherer bands as well as archaeological findings, Boehm argues that the sharing of scarce resources, including food, was for hunter-gatherer bands the most economically efficient—indeed, essential—economic strategy. And this strategy could only be sustained through egalitarianism. Cooperative gathering of foods, coordinated game hunting, and reciprocal sharing went hand in hand with resisting hierarchy and domination as successful adaptations for humans living in hunter-gatherer bands. As a result, over the course of human evolutionary history, hunter-gatherer bands and tribal communities generated an egalitarian ethos that promoted generosity, altruism, and sharing while resisting upstarts, aggression, and egoism.

Despite serving as the predominant economic, social, and political structure over the course of human evolution, by the mid-twentieth century only a few bands of food foragers remained. These groups were living in the most remote areas of the planet: the rain forests of South America, the arctic tundra of North America, and the deserts of Africa and Australia.

TRIBES

The term *tribe* is frequently used in contemporary media when describing conflict among groups within a state. Media coverage of civil wars or internal conflicts—particularly in parts of Africa, the Middle East, Asia, and the Pacific—frequently refers to tribal conflicts, tribal warfare, tribal factions, rifts, and alliances. In these instances, *tribe* is usually a reference to a loosely organized group of people acting together, outside the authority of the state, under unelected leaders and "big men"/"strong men" and drawing on a sense of unity based on a notion of shared ethnicity.

Most popular references to tribes carry connotations of primitive, uncivilized, and violent people who engage in conflict based on "ancient" tribal factions and hatreds. These faulty characterizations reflect the ethnocentric perspectives of observers who operate from inside a state framework. Their characterizations perpetuate the deeply problematic evolutionary assumption that less-complex political organizations are naturally less effective, stable, rational, and civilized.

As originally formulated (Service 1962), the term *tribe* referred to a culturally distinct population, often combining several bands, that imagined itself as one people descended from a common ancestor and organized around villages, kin groups, clans, and lineages. Tribes appear to have emerged between 10,000 and 12,000 years ago as humans began to shift from food foraging to pastoralism and horticulture. Like bands, tribes are largely egalitarian, with a decentralized power structure and consensus decision making. Leaders do emerge, sometimes called "village heads" or "big men" (Sahlins 1971), who garner the support of followers in several villages. But their power is limited. It is built and maintained through the leaders' personal achievements—such as success in war, conflict resolution, group organizing, and generosity of feasts and gifts—rather than awarded through political institutions.

In recent centuries, independent tribal peoples have largely been eliminated; they have been conquered and incorporated into the nation-states that have come to dominate the global political landscape. Today no groups operate totally outside the framework of the state. Even a weak state or a failed state directly influences all those living within its borders. In this context, today we might define a **tribe** more accurately as an indigenous group of people with its own set of loyalties and leaders living to some extent outside the direct control of a centralized, authoritative state. In many cases, current discussions use the term *ethnic group* instead of *tribe* (Ferguson 2011).

CHIEFDOMS

Within Elman Service's evolutionary typology of political systems, the **chiefdom**—an autonomous political unit composed of a number of villages or communities under the permanent control of a paramount chief (Carneiro 1981)—represented a transitional form between the simpler political structures of tribes and the more complex political structures of states. As in bands and tribes, the social relations of the chiefdom were built around extended kinship networks or lineages. The chiefdom might encompass thousands of people spread over many villages.

Unique to chiefdoms, leadership was centralized under a single ruling authority figure—a chief who headed a ranked hierarchy of people, asserted political control over a particular territory, and held the authority to make and enforce decisions. In parts of Polynesia, for instance, chiefs functioned as full-time political specialists, resolving conflicts and organizing collective economic activity. The permanent position of chief endured from generation to generation, often passing through direct descent and inheritance from father to son or through other kinship relationships. Religious rituals and beliefs often served to confirm the chief's authority.

Through feasts and festivals such as the potlatch (see Chapter 10), the chief gathered a portion of the collective bounty of the chiefdom's harvest or hunt and

tribe

Originally viewed as a culturally distinct, multiband population that imagined itself as one people descended from a common ancestor; currently used to describe an indigenous group with its own set of loyalties and leaders living to some extent outside the control of a centralized authoritative state.

chiefdom

An autonomous political unit composed of a number of villages or communities under the permanent control of a paramount chief.

redistributed the communal wealth to the populace, thereby symbolically and practically reinforcing his or her central role among the people. Though group members' access to power and resources depended on their hierarchical relationship to the chief, the process of redistribution served a central role in moderating inequality and limiting conflict within the chiefdom.

PUTTING TYPOLOGIES IN PERSPECTIVE

Though the typology of bands, tribes, chiefdoms, and states provided a basis for cross-cultural comparison, Service's framework has frequently proven too simple to capture the complexity and diversity of political practices and institutions that are reflected in ethnographic studies and the archaeological record. For instance, evidence now clearly suggests that across human history, groups of bands, tribes, and chiefdoms were never as isolated or homogenous as mid-twentieth-century anthropologists proposed. In contrast, today we argue that movement, encounter, exchange, and change have been the hallmarks of human groups, both small and large, throughout human history.

Nor could twentieth-century political systems always be considered trustworthy representations of the human past, recent or distant. Certainly, by the time anthropologists began to enter the field in the late nineteenth century to document and classify people and their political systems, European colonial expansion—including often violent encounters—had transformed peoples and their political structures across the globe. Colonialism, the slave trade, the conquest of indigenous peoples of the Americas, military activity, missionary efforts, and global trade deeply influenced every political arrangement, from the most populous urban setting to the most rural village. It is safe to say that anthropologists have not observed a band, tribe, or chiefdom that has not been influenced by colonialism, the power of the state, and the forces of globalization. And today no political arrangement of band, tribe, or chiefdom can operate outside the pervasive influence of the state.

What Is the State?

state

An autonomous regional structure of political, economic, and military rule with a central government authorized to make laws and use force to maintain order and defend its territory.

As states took on an increasingly central role in shaping the local communities that anthropologists traditionally studied, political anthropologists turned their ethnographic attention to the **state** itself. Today we typically define the state as an autonomous regional structure of political, economic, and military rule with a central government authorized to make laws and use force to maintain order and defend its territory.

Anthropologists link the origins of the state to the rise of agriculture and the emergence of fixed settlements (Carneiro 1978; Tilly 1975; Wittfogel 1957). Some loosely configured states existed as early as 5,000 years ago in Mesopotamia and Egypt, and somewhat later in China, Japan, the Indus Valley (which became parts of modern-day India, Pakistan, and Afghanistan), and portions of the Americas. Throughout most of human history, however, people organized themselves primarily through less centralized, flexible bands, tribes, and chiefdoms.

The global landscape of contemporary states that now dominates local, regional, and international affairs reflects the impact of Western expansion over the past 500 years, particularly European imperial and colonial expansion (see Chapter 11). European colonialists deployed economic, political, and military force to redraw the political borders of much of the world to meet colonial economic needs. In this process, the colonial powers carved states and territories out of geographic areas inhabited by indigenous groups who were previously organized along lines based more on local kinship, political, and economic relations.

Most of the states in the world today did not exist before World War II—certainly not in their current configurations. In fact, few states are older than the United States, which officially formed in 1783. Most gained independence from colonial rule only in the decades immediately following World War II. By 2015, there were 196 independent states in the world.

THE MODERN WESTERN-STYLE STATE

The type of state that has emerged since the sixteenth century, built largely on a Western model and expanded through colonization and globalization, developed with certain unique characteristics (Giddens 1985). Unlike earlier forms of the state, such as China's, which had relatively porous borders and loose administration, modern states feature a central administration designed to penetrate the everyday social life of its citizenry. A standing army asserts control over a carefully defined territory. Administrative, communication, and military infrastructures define and enforce the state's borders. The state, rather than a big man or chief, serves as the source of laws and law enforcement. People of all classes within the bounds of the state acquire an identity as citizens who owe allegiance primarily to the state, not to local networks based on kinship, religion, or ethnicity (Asad 1992).

Externally, modern states compete economically and militarily with other states for resources and territory. Internally, each state seeks to establish a monopoly on the legitimate use of force within a territorial domain (Weber 1919). For example, it enlists citizens' cooperation and pacifies resistance through expanded administrative power in police forces, the judicial system, tax collection, and regulatory regimes (Giddens 1985). It also accomplishes these objectives via surveillance techniques and institutions such as prisons, hospitals, and asylums, through which individuals classified as deviant from the cultural norm are removed from mainstream society and disciplined (Foucault 1977).

One unique contribution of political anthropologists to the study of the state has been a focus on the processes of the state rather than its institutions and structures. Despite the illusion that the state is fixed, cohesive, and coherent, states are in fact constantly being shaped and reshaped by elections, political campaigns, court rulings, creditors, legislation, and executive orders as well as through daily interactions with individuals, communities, nonstate institutions, social movements, and other states. From this perspective, we can see that states are actually quite fluid, contested, and even fragile (Sharma and Gupta 2006).

How does the state become the ultimate authority within a particular territory? Anthropologists suggest that the state becomes real in the imaginations and experiences of people as it is encountered in a particular space. This spatialization of the state (Ferguson and Gupta 2002)—the perception that the state fills a particular space, encompasses all aspects of culture, and stands above all other elements of the society—is produced through mundane bureaucratic state practices. The state is encountered in everyday acts of governance: policing, mail delivery, tax collection, mapping, surveys, issuance of passports, jury duty, voting, notarization, distribution of food to the poor, distribution of pension checks to the elderly. Through these routine and repetitive acts, the state comes to feel all-encompassing and overarching—a dynamic that Ferguson and Gupta call "vertical encompassment." Representations of the state on the television and radio, as well as in the newspapers or movies, all contribute to the construction of the state as concrete and real. These representations reinforce the conception of the state as the primary institutional form through which people experience social relations—family, community, civil society, economic exchange.

ASPECTS OF STATE POWER

The rituals and routines of the state also include overt practices of coercion. In fact, political philosopher Max Weber argued in 1919 that the fundamental characteristic of a state is its ability to establish a monopoly on the legitimate use of force in a particular territorial domain (Parsons 1964). States exert coercive power not only through military and police forces but also through the guarding and regulating of borders, the determining of criteria for citizenship, and the enforcing of discipline through rules, regulations, taxation, and the judicial system.

State power is also established through **hegemony**, which is the ability of a dominant group to create consent and agreement within a population without the use or threat of force (Gramsci 1971). How is this done? As discussed in Chapter 2, cultural institutions of government, media, schools, and religions shape what group members think is normal, natural, and possible, thereby influencing and limiting the scope of human action and interaction. Group members develop a way of seeing the world—a set of beliefs about what is normal and appropriate—that subconsciously limits their life choices and chances. As discussed in Chapter 6, states reinforce this hegemony by promoting intense feelings of nationalism (a sense of shared history, culture, language, destiny, and purpose, often through invented traditions of holidays, parades, national songs, public ceremonies, and historical reenactments) to promote the perception of the state as a unified entity.

The hegemonic aspect of power can make group members discipline their own behavior, believing and acting in certain "normal" ways (often against their own interests), even without threat of punishment for misbehavior (Foucault 1977). Within the hegemony of ideas, some thoughts and actions actually become unthinkable and undoable. Others seem reasonable, necessary, and

hegemony
The ability of a dominant group to create consent and agreement within a population without the use or threat of force.

desirable; these include collective actions for the greater good of the "nation," even going so far as killing and being killed. Some modern states, however, are unable to gain the cooperation of their populace through consent and must resort to coercion. Where do you see this dynamic at work in the world today?

How Is Globalization Affecting the State?

Today globalization presents serious challenges to the state, particularly in terms of flexible accumulation, time-space compression, and expanding migration. The boundaries of the state—its influence and control over internal and external affairs—appear to be shrinking in the face of pressures related to globalization and the neoliberalizing global economy.

INTERNATIONAL NONSTATE ACTORS CHALLENGE STATE SOVEREIGNTY

In a global economy with increasing flows of people, money, goods, and ideas, state borders are becoming more porous. As a result, states are increasingly struggling to control who and what enters and leaves their territories. State sovereignty—the right of the state to maintain self-determination within its borders—is being challenged by powerful international nonstate actors.

As discussed in Chapter 11, international financial institutions such as the World Bank, the International Monetary Fund, and the World Trade Organization, backed by the world's most developed economies, are pressuring states to adopt neoliberal economic policies. These policies include free markets; free trade; the free movement of goods, capital, and ideas; and access to local markets for transnational corporations. Furthermore, to receive development loans from international financial institutions, developing countries are required to privatize state-owned infrastructure such as ports, water systems, utilities, and transportation and to reduce state funding for social services, health care, and education. Neoliberal economists suggest that these changes, while lessening the state's ability to control what flows across its borders, will enhance the state's ability to compete in the global economy.

Economic restructuring promoted by international financial institutions and implemented by the state has yielded a flourishing of civil society. This is evident in the phenomenon of people joining together to form local organizations and movements to protest the social upheaval and uneven development that has accompanied the institution of neoliberal economic policies. These nongovernmental organizations (NGOs), sometimes called **civil society organizations**,

civil society organization

A local nongovernmental organization that challenges state policies and uneven development, and advocates for resources and opportunities for members of its local communities.

have become key players in challenging state policies and in creating space through which activists can work together to access resources and opportunities for their local communities.

CIVIL SOCIETY ORGANIZATIONS GAIN A GLOBAL REACH

One key strategy of civil society organizations—which many states have viewed warily—has been to join forces with transnational movements and networks to transform local problems and conflicts into part of a global project for rights and resources. By linking up with groups outside their national borders, local civil society organizations are able to join forces with other activists, networks, and campaigns, such as Amnesty International, Human Rights Watch, Africa Watch, or World Vision and even international agencies like the United Nations. These linkages enable the civil society organizations to advocate for local environmental concerns, demilitarization, women's rights, LGBT rights, human rights, and indigenous rights—issues that also transcend the borders of the state.

Communication and transportation advances associated with time-space compression—from cell phones to Facebook, Twitter, and YouTube—facilitate the formation of these transnational networks. This process not only promotes the flow of observers, advisors, and participants in meetings and conferences but also stimulates global information flows of on-the-ground developments and organizing strategies. Working together, the international coalitions mobilize international sentiment and bring pressure to bear on nation-states to address problems occurring within their borders. In this way, the coalitions challenge the ultimate claims of state sovereignty over affairs within state borders.

What Is the Relationship among Politics, the State, Violence, and War?

Perhaps no use of power is more troubling and challenging than violence, the "bodily harm that individuals, groups and nations inflict on one another in the course of their conflicts" (Ury 2002, 7). Conflict happens on the playground, in the classroom, in the boardroom, and on the battlefield. As we look globally today, we seem to be experiencing a period during which violent conflict is not sporadic, but permanent—a time of continuous war in one place or another involving extraordinarily sophisticated tools and weaponry (Waterston 2009).

ARE HUMANS NATURALLY VIOLENT OR PEACEFUL?

Underlying many discussions and debates about politics, war, and peace is the question of whether humans are naturally violent or peaceful. Is there something in the human evolutionary past that predisposes modern humans to behave in a particular way when confronted with conflict?

The main arguments can be simplified into three generalizations. First, organized human violence can be seen as a natural expression of the inherent human condition. In this view, human aggression and violence may be attributed to physiological factors such as testosterone, DNA, and neural wiring.

A second conception of violence considers humans to be inherently peaceful. In this view, violence arises through cultural practices and patterns that overwhelm basic human nature. A third scenario places the roots of human violence in between nature and culture. So, for instance, humans may be naturally prone to violence but culturally capable of avoiding it. Or humans may be naturally peaceful and only culturally provoked into forsaking their nature. Or these two alternatives are evenly matched.

Challenging the Myth of Killer Apes and Aggressive Humans.

Some who see contemporary violence as a legacy of our evolutionary past point to a common myth about aggressive primates and killer apes as evidence. If aggression, competition, and violence are part of our primate relatives' evolutionary development, they argue, then these impulses must be deeply ingrained in human nature as well. According to this view, natural levels of aggression, competition, and violence linked to genes and hormones must be generated internally and instinctively released in social relations. Conflict, then, naturally drives individuals farther apart into competing groups.

Physical anthropologist Frans de Waal (2002), reviewing studies of living primate macaques, chimpanzees, and bonobos, points out patterns of behavior that directly challenge this myth. De Waal notes, for instance, that for social animals such as primates, this pattern of conflict and distancing would lead to everyone living alone, yielding an ineffective pattern of social relationships for individuals who rely on social cooperation for survival. In the primate social groups de Waal has reviewed, a far more complicated dynamic emerges in times of conflict. Rather than increased distance, reconciliation occurs on a regular basis. In fact, increased attraction is regularly observed between opponents after fights. Researchers have identified this reconciliation mechanism in twenty-five separate primate groups, revealing powerful inclinations toward reconciliation among individuals who have a great deal to lose if their relationship deteriorates. Among bonobos, a primate group closely related to humans on a genetic level, sex is used to resolve conflicts. Bonobo conflicts and tensions occur in all combinations of female and male. So do reconciliations. Bonobos have a high rate of reconciliation and a low rate of violence.

De Waal suggests that among primates there are various options for resolving conflicts, including avoidance, tolerance, and aggression. These options are used at various times depending on the situation, the partner, and the stakes. According to de Waal, primate studies indicate that "aggression [is] not . . . the product of an inner drive but . . . one of the options that exists when there is a conflict of interest" (24). Ultimately, researchers may find that aggressive primate behavior has a genetic component; but this component does not operate in isolation, nor is it necessarily dominant. Equally natural among primates are mechanisms for cooperation, conflict resolution, rechanneling of aggression, and reconciliation (de Waal 2002).

Are humans naturally violent or peaceful? Despite the myth of killer apes and aggressive humans, primate studies reveal that increased attraction is regularly observed between opponents after a conflict. Here, two female bonobos reconcile after a fight.

Margaret Mead and the Invention of Warfare. Margaret Mead explored the difference between the human instinct for violence and the cultural institution of war in her article "Warfare Is Only an Invention—Not a Biological Necessity," written in 1940, during World War II. She presents ethnographic examples of people who do not go to war to settle disputes, thereby undermining the theory of a universal biological imperative for warfare. She also describes the wide variety of reasons people go to war—not only for land and loot but for prestige and women—that can be satisfied without violence. In the end, Mead comes down firmly on the side of war as a cultural invention. And a bad one at that. What then are we to do about this invention? According to Mead (1940):

> If we despair over the way in which war seems such an ingrained habit of most of the human race, we can take comfort from the fact that a poor invention will usually give place to a better invention. For this, two conditions at least are necessary. The people must recognize the defects of the old invention, and someone must make a new one. (405)

Can your generation invent an alternative to war—a new way to resolve conflicts without violence?

THE STATE AND WAR

Political anthropologists actively explore the complicated cultural processes through which war is invented, learned, and enacted (Besteman 2002; Besteman and Cassanelli 1996; Farmer 2003; Ferguson 2002; Gusterson 1996, 2004; Lutz 2001; Waterston 2009). Over the past 100 years, war has become far more than waging hand-to-hand combat or pulling a trigger at close range—actions that we might associate with aggression driven by hormones. Instead, modern warfare is considerably more premeditated and calculated, relying on computers, satellites, missiles, GPS tracking, and airborne drone strikes.

Today anthropologists study a highly militarized world in which war seems normalized and permanent. Warfare has become one of the most visible of all human political institutions that reveals the state's pursuit of power. As we will see in Carolyn Nordstrom's work later in this chapter, warfare can no longer be viewed as a local military phenomenon. Indeed, modern warfare is embedded in a global system of war making. This fact pushes anthropologists to study the intersection of multiple factors that play a role in constructing warfare as a reasonable means for resolving conflicts. These factors may be as disparate as economic stratification, ethnic identity formation, migration, weapons manufacturing and trade, the imbalance between weak states and strong states, and resource shortages involving oil, water, and land (Nugent and Vincent 2004).

Militarization. A growing body of anthropological literature has focused on **militarization**—the contested social process through which a civil society organizes for the production of military violence (Lutz 2004; see also Bickford 2011; Geyer 1989). Catherine Lutz, an anthropologist of militarization, in *Homefront: A Military City and the American Twentieth Century* (2001), describes how the processes of militarization include not only the production of material objects such as bullets, bombs, tanks, planes, and missiles but also the glorification of war and those who make war, as states seek to shape their national histories and political culture.

Lutz warns that left unchecked, militarization threatens to shape other aspects of cultural institutions to its own ends. For example, it influences research in physics, information technology, and psychology; it affects national budget priorities; it affects discussions and debates about gender and sexuality, race and citizenship, privacy and security; and it limits what can be discussed in the news, online, or in the classroom.

militarization

The contested social process through which a civil society organizes for the production of military violence.

ANTHROPOLOGY ON THE FRONT LINES OF WAR AND GLOBALIZATION

The fact that today's world is rife with conflict presents anthropologists with many opportunities to study current cases of warfare and violence in the context of pressures from globalization. Anthropologist Carolyn Nordstrom's work exemplifies contemporary anthropological contributions to this kind of study. Nordstrom focuses on the real, messy, local experiences of violence, resistance, survival, and creativity in actual communities where war occurs, not in the comfortable offices and remote institutions of military officials and political leaders.

MAP 12.1
Mozambique

At the same time, she turns a spotlight on the complex web of local and foreign interactions and actors that drive war and make warfare a global phenomenon.

Mozambique. Between 1989 and 1996, Nordstrom made multiple visits to war-torn areas of Mozambique, a southeast African country wracked by a fifteen-year civil war after independence from Portugal that claimed a million lives, mostly civilian. To reach rural and forested regions, she traveled with bush pilots making airlifts into war zones. In contrast to typical journalistic war reports, Nordstrom experienced firsthand the low-intensity conflict called "terror warfare," perpetrated by rebel guerrillas and Mozambican government soldiers, that targeted the country's civilian population through military attacks, hunger, and displacement.

These destructive forces of warfare targeted the basic structures of Mozambican community life: hospitals, schools, and government offices, as well as teachers, health-care professionals, religious authorities, and community leaders. By destroying and disrupting the institutions, practices, and key practitioners of local culture, the forces of violence sought to destroy the local population's political will.

In her ethnography of civil war in Mozambique, *A Different Kind of War Story* (1997), Nordstrom recounts the determined creativity that local populations used to combat this terror and violence. In one village heavily targeted and frequently overrun by troops of both armies, most community leaders and service providers had fled as refugees to avoid potential assassination. Most resources and infrastructure had been destroyed. During the first severe attack on the village, however, one remaining health-care practitioner gathered up as many medical supplies as she could carry and hid in the nearby bush until the soldiers left. Though the soldiers knew her name and searched for her, the villagers kept her secret, kept her safe. On the front lines of battle, soldiers passed through the village regularly in subsequent months. Yet the health worker remained, hiding her medical supplies, living a nomadic life on the outskirts of the area, and being protected by the villagers, who continued to carry their ailing members to her for treatment.

These actions by the health worker and the villagers are emblematic of the creativity that Nordstrom's research finds to be the most potent weapon against war—the determination to survive and resist, to continually refashion and reconstruct one's self, community, and world. Nordstrom concludes her ethnography by suggesting that if, as early political philosophers such as Thomas Hobbes proposed, violence is the "natural state" of human affairs when political institutions collapse, then war-torn regions such as Mozambique should be rife with scenes of aggression, acts of self-preservation, and individual attempts at survival in a dog-eat-dog world. Instead Nordstrom consistently found people who resisted

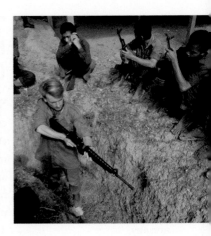

and defeated the political violence of war by attending to the day-to-day matters of their community—sharing food, healing wounds, repairing lives, teaching children, performing rituals, exchanging friendship, rebuilding places, and creatively reconstructing the everyday patterns that constitute a meaningful life (Englund 1999; Honwana 1999; Richards 1999).

A Comparative Study. In a later book, *Shadows of War* (2004), Nordstrom makes the case that standard notions of local wars fought by local actors over local issues are largely fiction. Through a comparative study of war and violence in Mozambique, Sri Lanka, South Africa, and Angola, she instead traces the extensive global networks of individuals and industries that feed and fuel local violence and war. Mercenary soldiers, foreign strategists, arms suppliers, businesspeople, black marketeers, smugglers, humanitarian relief workers, researchers, propagandists, and journalists all circle the globe, moving from one war to the next. Multi-trillion-dollar international financial networks support warfare. Illegal drugs, precious gems, weapons, food supplies, military training manuals, and medicines are products moved by international networks of legitimate and illegitimate businesses and agencies that profit from the business of war.

Thanks to globalization, the business of war now operates on a worldwide scale. It influences both the architects of war, who primarily engage the battle from a distance, and the people who suffer the consequences on a war's front lines. Discussing the local people affected by the business of war, Nordstrom notes that theirs are not the typical war stories recounted in the media. When war is portrayed only through the prism of weapons, soldiers, territory, and strategic interests won or lost, a more significant reality is ignored: the heroic efforts of people on the front lines who resist and maintain life in the face of violence and death (Finnstrom 2005).

With globalization, an extensive network of individuals and industries circles the globe from one war to the next. (*left*) United Nations High Commissioner for Refugees workers distribute blankets to Syrian refugees along the Jordanian-Syrian border, 2012; (*center*) members of the media mark their flak jackets as gunfire rings out near the Tripoli Hotel in Lebanon, 2011; (*right*) an Australian mercenary trains rebel recruits in Myanmar.

How Do People Mobilize Power Outside the State's Control?

Systems of power, including the state, are never absolute. Their dominance is never complete. Even when a culture's dominant groups and institutions are very powerful in terms of their ability to exercise force or to establish control through hegemony, they do not completely dominate people's lives and thinking. Individuals and groups with less power or no power may still contest the established power relationships and structures through political, economic, religious, or military means and challenge and change cultural norms, values, symbols, and institutions. This power is a potential that anthropologists call **agency**.

In such displays of human agency, we see the way culture becomes the realm in which battles over power are waged; where people contest, negotiate, and enforce what is considered normal and what people can say, do, and even think. Because of human agency, cultures do not remain rigid and static. They change.

Efforts to change cultural patterns take various forms, which we will consider further. Human agency may be expressed through individual strategies of resistance, such as the "weapons of the weak" discussed in Chapter 2, collective efforts such as social movements, and alternative institutions to the state such as those based on religion.

SOCIAL MOVEMENTS

Social movements are collective, group actions in response to uneven development, inequality, and injustice that seek to build institutional networks to transform cultural patterns and government policies. Social movements engage in contentious politics, usually outside the mainstream political process, to address specific social issues, although they usually do not seek to overthrow the social order. The study of social movements is interdisciplinary, engaging not only anthropologists but also sociologists, political scientists, and historians (Edelman 2001).

Recently, the anthropological analysis of social movements has focused on the responses of local communities to the forces of globalization. Factors such as the worldwide movement of capital and production through flexible accumulation, the increasing migration within and across national borders, and rapidly increasing yet uneven rates of development have spurred the emergence of social movements as local communities organize to protect their land, environment, human rights, and cultural identities in a changing economic and political context. Simultaneously, time-space compression has facilitated increased communication and cooperation among individuals, social movements, and NGOs, thus creating opportunities for a "globalization from below" (Falk 1993, 39).

agency

The potential power of individuals and groups to contest cultural norms, values, mental maps of reality, symbols, institutions, and structures of power.

social movement

Collective group actions that seek to build institutional networks to transform cultural patterns and government policies.

Activists in Kathmandu, Nepal, demand constitutional protections for "Dalits" who have been systematically marginalized by the region's caste system.

Rural Social Movements. In the last thirty years, rural social movements have drawn anthropologists' attention as farmers engage in creative political struggles to resist the impact of globalization on their land, livelihood, and way of life. As one example, Marc Edelman's *Peasants against Globalization* (1999) examines the activism of the rural poor in Costa Rica, Central America, during the 1980s and 1990s. Edelman recounts a story that reflects the beleaguered experience of rural agricultural workers elsewhere across the globe in recent decades.

MAP 12.2
Costa Rica

Having gained independence from Spain in 1821, Costa Rica is one of the most politically stable countries in the Americas. By the early 1980s, Costa Ricans had built a strong, economically self-sufficient democracy and taken the radical step of abolishing the nation's military in order to invest in programs of national development. Such programs aimed to provide education, health care, tariff protections for local products, and price supports for basic foodstuffs to ensure a basic livelihood for all citizens. The programs also provided government-backed loans to farmers to stabilize agricultural production.

During the mid-1980s, however, Costa Rica was drawn into the civil wars of its neighbors, serving as a key ally of the United States on the Central American peninsula as war and upheaval spread in Nicaragua, Guatemala, and Panama. Simultaneously, a debt crisis affecting most of Latin America shook Costa Rica's economy and spurred rapid inflation. Under the auspices of providing foreign aid to an ally, the U.S.-sponsored Food for Peace program delivered massive quantities of subsidized corn, wheat, and rice—purchased from U.S. farmers—to the Costa Rican market. The subsidized food, however, undercut Costa Rican farm prices, making it increasingly difficult for local farmers to sell their own products at the price needed to break even.

Ultimately, these changes in the Costa Rican food market drove many small-scale farmers out of business, lowered the country's overall food production, and ended its history of food self-sufficiency. Structural adjustment loans offered by the International Monetary Fund and the World Bank to help Costa Rica through the crisis required the government to eliminate price supports, tariff protections, and government-backed loans while drastically reducing investments in health care and education. These measures further deepened the country's crisis.

Edelman retells the stories of local, small-scale farmers—often called "peasants" in the anthropological literature—and their national umbrella group, UPANACIONAL, as they fought these threats to their way of life. The peasants marched, blocked highways, and held street demonstrations. They built alliances with wealthy farmers, lobbied national politicians, and promoted charismatic activist figures into national prominence to speak on their behalf.

The climax of the Costa Rican peasants' collective action and direct pressure tactics came as several dozen farmers and movement leaders occupied government buildings in June 1988. At the conclusion of the standoff, the activists were arrested; however, the negotiated settlement extracted a government commitment

A farmer holds a puppet of Costa Rican president Laura Chinchilla during protests in the capital, San Jose, over new property taxes on agricultural land, 2012.

to provide access to low-interest credit for Costa Rica's rural farmers. This was a significant victory in response to the peasants' demands. Edelman concludes that the Costa Rican peasants may not have stopped the effects of globalization on their nation's rural population, but through collective action they were able to soften the harshest blows (Gudmundson 2001; Welch 2001).

Occupy Wall Street. Anthropologists seek to understand how social movements arise, mobilize, and sustain themselves. Even though conditions of inequality and injustice are widespread in many parts of the world, the activation of movements for social justice occurs in only certain situations. Anthropologists have investigated the material, human, cognitive, technical, and organizational resources necessary for social movements to succeed (McAdam, McCarthy, and Zald 1996). Recent attention has turned to the **framing process** of movements—specifically, how shared meanings and definitions arise to motivate and justify collective action.

Actions by the Occupy Wall Street movement beginning in September 2011 illustrate the role of the framing process. How did Occupy protestors capture the attention of a nation (and beyond) and build a consensus for social action? What factors led to their success?

framing process
The creation of shared meanings and definitions that motivate and justify collective action by social movements.

Occupy Wall Street protestors successfully framed the debate against corporate greed and social inequality with their motto "We Are the 99%." Where else have you heard this framing used?

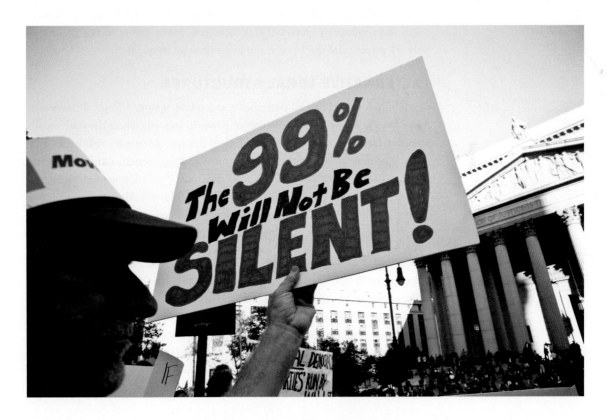

Anthropologist Jeffrey Juris (2012), who studied Occupy Boston, has noted that social media drew a diverse group of people with shared concerns—in this case, economic inequality—into shared physical spaces. Listservs, websites, and collaborative networking tools facilitated new patterns of protest that built on and resonated with more traditional forms.

Another key to Occupy's success rested on framing the movement's cause under the banner "We Are the 99%." With this simple phrase, Occupy Wall Street gradually focused public discourse on questions of the fundamental fairness of the U.S. and global economy in light of rapidly growing conditions of inequality over the past forty years that have steadily transferred wealth from 99 percent to 1 percent of the nation's population. Despite growing calls by political leaders and media critics demanding that Occupy Wall Street activists put forward specific policy proposals to address the problems they were decrying, the movement steadfastly refused. Instead its members focused on the underlying issue of inequality framed in their motto, "We Are the 99%."

Writing in the spring of 2012, Juris noted that Occupy Wall Street had already contributed to a shift in public discourse. The framing process of Occupy has successfully highlighted growing inequality and the influence of financial and corporate interests in the economy and politics. At the same time, Occupy has functioned as a laboratory for the production of alternative forms of democracy and community (Juris 2012). Where have you encountered this framing of the 99 percent and the 1 percent in discussions on inequality?

ALTERNATIVE LEGAL STRUCTURES

In addition to overt social movements and subtle, nonovert forms of resistance, it is possible to challenge structures of power in an arena where the state usually holds clear authority: in matters of the law. But how do people organize alternative legal structures outside the direct control of the modern state? What gives authority and legitimacy to alternative structures if they are not enforceable by the state's coercive power? Legal anthropologist Hussein Ali Agrama spent two years conducting ethnographic research on local courts and councils in Cairo, Egypt, to explore these questions (Agrama 2010, 2012).

Islamic Fatwa Councils in Cairo, Egypt. Agrama compared the operations of two key local sources of legal authority: (1) the Personal Status courts operated by the Egyptian state and (2) the Al Azhar Fatwa Council, independently established in 1935 and one of the oldest and most established centers of Islamic authority. In the busy and crowded Personal Status courts, Egyptians of all walks of life appear before a judge, an official of the state who makes legally binding rulings that draw on the Egyptian Constitution and legal codes that are based on the principles of Islamic Sharia (law). In the equally busy and crowded

Fatwa Council, held in a spacious room located at the main entrance to the Al Azhar mosque, seekers approach Islamic legal scholars and interpreters of Islamic law, or muftis, for religious answers about matters of daily life. The muftis respond freely with legally nonbinding answers to anyone who asks. Their decision is called a "fatwa"—a response to a question about how to live ethically and rightly.

MAP 12.3
Cairo

In comparing these two court systems, Agrama encounters a startling dynamic. Both deal with an overlapping set of issues heavily focused on matters of marriage, sex, divorce, reconciliation, and inheritance. Both draw their decisions from Islamic Sharia, although the Personal Status courts engage Islamic law through the Egyptian Constitution and legal code, whereas the muftis refer directly to Sharia and other Islamic traditions in their fatwas. What interests Agrama is that despite these basic similarities, the petitioners' responses to the authorities' rulings are markedly different. The legally binding judgments of the Personal Status court are generally looked on with great suspicion. People go to great lengths to avoid the consequences of the court's decisions despite the state's ability to coerce obedience to its judgments. In distinct contrast, the Fatwa Council exercises great authority even though seeking decisions from the Council is not obligatory, a fatwa is not legally binding, and once issued, a fatwa does not have to be obeyed. In fact, petitioners can seek more than one fatwa on the same issue if they wish. But Agrama's research finds that petitioners take fatwas very seriously, following the decisions even if they entail great difficulty or unhappiness—this despite no identifiable institutional enforcement mechanism.

What accounts for the differentiation between Personal Status courts and the Fatwa Council? And how does a given fatwa acquire its authority without the threat of coercive force like that which the state makes available to the Personal Status courts? To understand the authority of the fatwa, Agrama explores the complex interactions and expectations between seekers of fatwas and the muftis that issue them. Contrary to popular impressions, fatwas are not merely designed to dispense points of correct doctrine in obedience to prescriptions found in Islamic Sharia. Rather, the mufti seeks to apply Islamic tradition and law to resolve particular problems, identify an effective solution, and point the seeker toward a path forward. The process includes significant perplexities and uncertainties: The fatwa seeker arrives perplexed by his or her life situation, and at least initially the mufti is uncertain about how to respond. In this context, the mufti typically begins by asking for further information in an attempt to fully understand the context and facts as presented. The fatwa seeker approaches the mufti with the hope that he will have the skills to point the way out of the trouble, to offer a way forward—to discern and speak the right words.

Fatwa Council at the Al Azhar
Mosque, Cairo, Egypt.

In the end, both seeker and mufti share a collective responsibility for the success of the fatwa: The mufti must be sure to speak the right words, and the seeker must apply them correctly. Although the consequences of an incorrect fatwa may be most damaging for the seeker during his or her lifetime, the mufti is believed to bear responsibility for the outcome in the hereafter. Ultimately, the fatwa is pronounced in order to put the questioner on the right path forward, to offer direction and facilitate a journey on which the seeker can advance within the range of doctrine toward a Muslim ideal. Agrama suggests that it is careful and personal navigation of these complexities that engenders trust and conveys legitimacy on the muftis and their fatwas.

In the opening story of the Sundarbans march, Paris climate change demonstrations, and U.S. student fossil fuel divestment campaigns, as well as in the ethnographic examples presented throughout this chapter, we have seen the remarkable diversity of strategies that humans use to exercise power through the medium of politics. Although political upheaval in North Africa and the Middle East readily draws the focus of the world media, Agrama's work in Cairo reminds us that human political activity occurs at many different levels during the course of daily life. Whether through the politics of the state, acts of war, social movements, or small-scale resistance that James Scott (1985; see Chapter 2) labeled weapons of the weak, we have considered how anthropologists examine power and politics and the cutting edges of political activism that will continue to draw their interest in the future.

Toolkit

Thinking Like an Anthropologist:
Applying Politics to Daily Life and Beyond

In each chapter of this book, we have investigated how human cultures construct, engage, and negotiate systems of power. We have considered the role of influential ideologies and structures of race, gender, ethnicity, class, kinship, and religion. In this chapter, we have explored how power is expressed and organized through political systems and processes. Politics exist in every human relationship and every community, large or small. People are constantly negotiating the interpersonal and institutional balances of power.

As we saw in the chapter-opening stories, politics is not necessarily separate from daily life. We don't have to run for political office or start an online petition to be involved in politics. At its most basic level, politics encompasses all of the ways we organize ourselves to achieve what we most desire for our community: our family, friends, classmates, fellow citizens, the environment, and fellow inhabitants of planet Earth. As you learn to think like an anthropologist about politics and power, remember the opening questions that we have used to frame our inquiries:

- **How have anthropologists viewed the origins of human political history?**

- **What is the state?**

- **How is globalization affecting the state?**

- **What is the relationship among politics, the state, violence, and war?**

- **How do people mobilize power outside the state's control?**

If, as it appears, humans do not have an overwhelming and uncontrollable biological drive toward aggression and violence, then unlimited avenues open up to explore strategies for addressing problems that confront us today. These strategies include cooperatively engaging the challenging issues of our schools, communities, nations, and world and developing political responses that take into account the unique cultural dynamics of local communities and specific groups.

In this era of globalization, local political action can have global implications. Certainly the challenge of climate change creates opportunities for political action on a global scale. There are no climate-endangering activities anywhere in the world that do not directly affect all of the humans on the planet. But how quickly can activists, investors, civil society groups, and governments coalesce around strategies to address this existential challenge?

As a new generation of social activists around the globe develop social networking and social media strategies for expressing their concerns and attempting to influence the systems of power and politics, the networked nature of these movements also means that you, as a college student, have every possibility of becoming an anthropologist who engages the world.

Key Terms

band (p. 337)

tribe (p. 339)

chiefdom (p. 339)

state (p. 340)

hegemony (p. 343)

civil society organization (p. 344)

militarization (p. 349)

agency (p. 352)

social movement (p. 352)

framing process (p. 355)

Chapter 13
Religion

Entering the United States Capitol to a standing ovation from lawmakers, Pope Francis—dressed in a simple white robe adorned with a silver cross necklace—processed through the assembled senators and representatives before mounting the raised dais to address the joint session of the U.S. Congress. Francis, leader of the world's 1.2 billion Roman Catholics—the world's largest religious denomination—arrived on Capitol Hill in the midst of a U.S. tour that electrified much of the nation in late September 2015.

Since his election as the 266th Pope in March 2013, Francis—formerly known as Jorge Mario Borgoglio, an Argentinian Jesuit and son of Italian immigrants—had revitalized the papacy, rejecting many of the elaborate fineries associated with his position, traveling the world to speak on pressing issues of the day as diverse as the Armenian genocide, the conflict between Israelis and Palestinians, and the atrocities of the Islamic State, and calling for renewed attention to poverty and climate

What is religion? Pope Francis, head of the Roman Catholic Church, addresses a joint session of the U.S. Congress in 2015.

devastation. The Pope's personality, theological openness, and direct actions struck such a chord that both *Rolling Stone* and *The Advocate* featured him on their covers, *Time* magazine and *Vanity Fair* named him Man of the Year, and *Forbes* placed him at the top of a list of the World's 50 Greatest Leaders.

In Washington, some politicians called on the Pope to stick to spiritual matters. The Pope instead continued to integrate theological reflection, social analysis, and calls for action. While some politicians were advocating building a wall on the U.S.–Mexican border, the Pope reminded the assembled leaders that they were all immigrants or descendants of immigrants and had nothing to fear. He advocated protection of life at every stage, including abolishing the death penalty and the reduction of armed conflict. He called for an end to the sale of weapons to people intent on violence, an arms trade driven by "money drenched in blood, often innocent blood." And in a chamber sharply divided on the issue of climate change, the Pope came down clearly on the side of climate science and the need for immediate action.

Only months earlier, in an elaborate reflection on the environment, *Laudato Si'*, the Pope lamented increasing pollution of the planet, global warming, a lack of clean water, loss of biodiversity, and an overall decline in human life and breakdown in society. But he went further, declaring the warming of the planet and expanding global poverty to be symptoms of a greater problem: the developed world's indifference to the destruction of the planet in pursuit of short-term economic gains. The resulting culture of consumerism—a "throwaway culture"—too easily discards unwanted items and unwanted people.

For many, the Pope's bold proclamations seemed out of place for a spiritual leader. But for Pope Francis, the integration of theology, social analysis, and action in addressing the pressing issues facing humanity only continued a long tradition of papal leadership on matters of importance to the church's followers and the world.

Religion plays a central role in human life and human culture. Through the study of religion, anthropologists engage some of the deepest, most difficult, and most enduring human questions—about meaning, difference, power, love, sexuality, mortality, morality, human origins, and kinship. Religion has been a central interest of anthropologists since the beginning of our field (Frazer 1890; Tylor 1871). Research about religious beliefs and practices worldwide has explored an amazing diversity of beliefs, symbols, rituals, myths, institutions, religious experts, groups, deities, and supernatural forces. As you read about diverse religions in this chapter, some beliefs and practices may seem quite familiar. Others may be surprising or unexpected. Many might stretch your basic assumptions of what religion is and does.

Religion offers a rich vein of material for exploring the complexity of human culture, including systems of belief and systems of power. It is perhaps

FIGURE 13.1
Religion in the United States

Extensive public polling in the United States reveals shifts in religious demographics in response to globalization and immigration patterns. In particular, the United States is experiencing a decline in the total percentage of Protestant Christians that parallels a growth in Catholic Christians from Latin America; Muslims from the Middle East, South Asia, and Africa; Orthodox Christians from Eastern Europe and the Middle East; Hindus from India; and Buddhists from China, Southeast Asia, and East Asia.

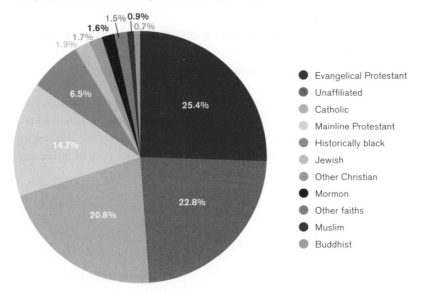

Source: Pew Forum on Religion & Public Life. 2015. "America's Changing Religious Landscape." www.pewforum.org.

the hottest topic in the world today as globalization brings different traditions, beliefs, and practices into contact. In the United States, immigration over the past five decades has transformed the religious landscape (Figure 13.1). Temples, mosques, gurdwaras, and retreat centers now join churches and synagogues in small towns and big cities across the country. College campuses, too, reflect an expanding religious diversity. And while some politicians have called for sweeping bans on Muslim immigrants, at the local level, as people of different religious traditions encounter one another in neighborhoods, schools, and other public institutions, lively debates take place about education, zoning, health care, public security, and civil rights. These encounters create the potential for tension and misunderstanding on school boards, zoning committees, and town and city councils, as well as in civic associations and even college classrooms. But they also offer opportunities for interfaith encounters, learning, and engagement. An anthropological understanding of religion can help you to navigate and engage this changing landscape.

In this chapter, we will consider the anthropological approach to understanding the many groups, beliefs, and practices that are called "religion." In particular, we will examine the following questions:

- **What is religion?**
- **What tools do anthropologists use to understand how religion works?**
- **In what ways is religion both a system of meaning and a system of power?**
- **How is globalization changing religion?**

By the end of the chapter you will be able to investigate and analyze religion using the tools of an anthropologist. You will be better able to understand religion in your own life, in the growing religious pluralism of the United States, and in diverse religious expressions around the world. These skills will be increasingly valuable tools for living and working in the twenty-first century.

What Is Religion?

When anthropologists talk about "religion," what are we really talking about? Since the beginning of the discipline, anthropologists have been attempting to create a universal definition that might apply to all religions' local manifestations. But the vast global diversity of unique local expressions makes defining religion a difficult task. Is there something present in all cultures that we can call "religion"?

SEEKING A WORKING DEFINITION

The unique anthropological approach to religion begins with the everyday religious practices of people in their local communities. Through fieldwork, anthropologists focus on the real religious worlds in which humans experience religion physically and express it through their actions. We may study a religion's history, theology, scriptures, and major figures, but we do so to understand their meaning and significance in the life of a community of people. Religion is not theoretical in people's daily activities. People make sense of the world, reach decisions, and organize their lives on the basis of their religious beliefs. Starting from these beginning principles, anthropologists also explore the myriad ways religion intersects with other systems of power, whether economics, politics, race, gender, or sexuality. And we explore how local religious expressions may be connected to larger religious movements or institutions.

Anthropologists have compiled a vast and diverse set of data on religious beliefs and practices worldwide. But are there any common characteristics that

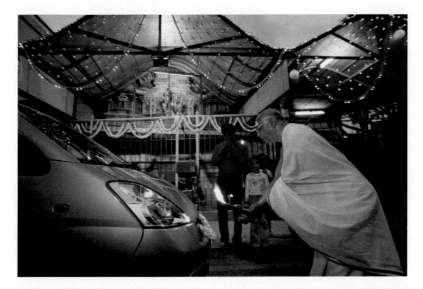

What is religion? At the 600-year-old Prasanna Ganapathy Temple in Bangalore, India, a Hindu priest performs ritual blessings of new cars, auto rickshaws, and motorbikes to bestow divine protections on car and owner.

apply in every situation? In general, we find that all local expressions of religion combine some, but not necessarily all, of the following elements:

- Belief in powers or deities whose abilities transcend those of the natural world and cannot be measured by scientific tools.
- Myths and stories that reflect on the meaning and purpose of life, its origins, and humans' place in the universe.
- Ritual activities that reinforce, recall, instill, and explore collective beliefs.
- Powerful symbols, often used in religious rituals, that represent key aspects of the religion for its followers.
- Specialists who assist the average believer to bridge everyday life experiences and the religion's ideals and supernatural aspects.
- Organizations and institutions that preserve, explore, teach, and implement the religion's key beliefs.
- A community of believers.

As a working definition, we might then say that a **religion** is a set of beliefs and rituals based on a unique vision of how the world ought to be, often focused on a supernatural power and lived out in community. (For an overview of the distribution of adherents to major world religions today, see Figure 13.2. Considering the range of religions shown there, perhaps you can begin to imagine the challenge inherent in creating a working definition to cover such a broad spectrum.)

As social scientists, anthropologists have largely been uninterested in questions of any religion's ultimate truth or falsity. Instead we understand that religious worlds are real, meaningful, and powerful to those who live in them. Our

religion

A set of beliefs and rituals based on a unique vision of how the world ought to be, often focused on a supernatural power and lived out in community.

task is to carefully make those worlds come alive for others by capturing their vivid inner life, sense of moral order, dynamic public expressions, and interactions with other systems of meaning and power—whether those religious expressions occur in a remote Chinese village temple or the most famous Catholic cathedral in Rome (Bowie 2006).

LOCAL EXPRESSIONS AND UNIVERSAL DEFINITIONS

Attention to local religious expressions complicates anthropologists' efforts to create a universal definition of religion. In a religious studies course, you would likely use a textbook that allocates one chapter for each of the largest world religions, including Christianity, Islam, Hinduism, Buddhism, Chinese religion, Sikhism, Judaism, and others. Each chapter might include an overview of the religion's history, theology, scriptures, major figures, and formal institutions. Under such an approach, drawing broad comparisons among the major religions can prove helpful in providing a general picture of the world's most established religious traditions and in understanding each religion's ideal expression. At the same time, it may obscure the creative and flexible ways people actually practice their religion that may diverge from the ideal.

Indeed, local expressions and creative adaptations are often at the heart of anthropological research because they reveal how people make a religious tradition come alive in their own context. Let's consider Islam for a moment. Muslims and non-Muslims alike generally regard Islam as highly uniform wherever it is practiced—as a religion that would consistently manifest its core characteristics and definition regardless of location. For example, all Muslims are expected to follow the Five Pillars of Islam: making a declaration of faith, saying prayers five times a day, performing acts of charity, fasting during the holy month of Ramadan, and undertaking a pilgrimage to Mecca. In addition, all Muslims revere the authority of the Quran and the Prophet Muhammad. But on the local level, Muslims frequently expand these formal borders and develop modes of popular expression that may include distinctive devotional practices, life-cycle rituals, marriage customs, ritual clothing, and forms of veiling.

Awareness of the ways in which Muslim life and religious practice vary locally can offer an important insight to an anthropologist conducting research or to anyone seeking to build relationships across religious boundaries. The examples that follow illustrate the possibilities for local variation within a religious tradition that is often assumed to be universal in its expressions.

A Muslim Saint Shrine. Across India, certain popular expressions of Islam push the boundaries of what many people would consider traditional Islam. One

FIGURE 13.2
Religion in Global Perspective

This chart shows estimated relative distribution of adherents to the major world religions. It is worth noting, however, that few countries collect data on religious beliefs and practices; as discussed in the chapter, local religious expressions may not neatly fit these categories.

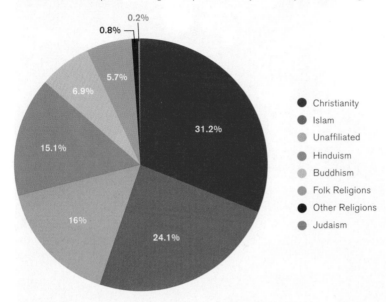

- Christianity
- Islam
- Unaffiliated
- Hinduism
- Buddhism
- Folk Religions
- Other Religions
- Judaism

0.2%
0.8%
5.7%
6.9%
15.1%
31.2%
16%
24.1%

Source: Pew Forum on Religion of Public Life. 2017. "The Changing Global Religious Landscape." www.pewforum.org.

example is Husain Tekri, a Muslim saint shrine, or *dargah*, named in memory of the martyred grandson of the Prophet Muhammad. (A **martyr** is a person who sacrifices his or her life for the sake of his or her religion.) Pilgrims from across northern India come to this shrine to remember Husain Tekri, to venerate the Muslim saints, and to participate in healing rituals. (A **saint** is an individual considered exceptionally close to God who is then exalted after death.) Husain Tekri is part of the religious healing circuit of northern India along which both Hindu and Muslim pilgrims travel as they seek the saint or deity with the specific power to cure their ills.

Pilgrims to Husain Tekri may stay for a day or settle in nearby lodges and remain for days, months, or a year. They come in search of healing from suffering, illness, and financial ruin and for relief from the presence of evil spirits (*haziri*). The main daily ritual activity is the burning and distribution of *loban*—rocklike chunks of incense sold at the shrine and thrown onto red-hot coals eight times a day. As the white smoke of *loban* billows from the braziers, pilgrims—both men and women—are engulfed in the cloud, breathe in the smoke, symbolically consume the *loban*, and absorb its potency. Through pilgrimage and the ritual

martyr

A person who sacrifices his or her life for the sake of his or her religion.

saint

An individual considered exceptionally close to God and who is then exalted after death.

Hindu and Muslim pilgrims at the Husain Tekri shrine in northern India breathe in incense to access the healing powers of the shrine.

consumption of *loban*, pilgrims access the healing powers of the shrine. There, they believe, the power and mercy of the martyred Husain and his family enable them to escape their sick bodies, their mental anguish, and the malevolent spirits possessing them.

Surprisingly, pilgrims to the shrine of Husain Tekri are of many religious backgrounds, not only Muslim but also Hindu, Sikh, and Jain. Seeking healing across religious lines is actually a common occurrence in many parts of India, as pilgrims of various faiths try multiple religious systems to find the most successful means of healing, especially for illnesses beyond the powers of mainstream medicine (Bellamy 2011; Flueckiger 2006).

The example above suggests that what are often considered clearly defined, universally uniform, and consistent world religions actually can be flexible and innovative at the local level. From an anthropological perspective, such local expressions of religion are no less complete, meaningful, or true than those taught in the most elite Muslim madrassa, Buddhist monastery, or Christian school of theology.

What Tools Do Anthropologists Use to Understand How Religion Works?

Anthropologists have developed a set of key insights about how religion works that serve as a toolkit for understanding religion as we experience it in our fieldwork. These concepts may prove useful to you in thinking about religion in your own life and in your community, nation, and the world.

Anthropological theories of religion have been deeply influenced by the ideas of nineteenth- and twentieth-century social scientists Émile Durkheim, Karl Marx, and Max Weber. All three examined the connection between religion and the political and economic upheavals of their time: an Industrial Revolution that spurred massive shifts in land tenure patterns throughout western Europe; large-scale rural-to-urban migration; and high levels of unemployment, poverty, and disease. Through their writing, Durkheim, Marx, and Weber reshaped the study of religion, moving from the theological and cosmological orientation that dominated pre-twentieth-century European and North American thinking to focus on the role of religion in society. These thinkers inspired generations of anthropologists who have expanded and refined their theories.

French sociologist Émile Durkheim.

ÉMILE DURKHEIM: THE SACRED AND THE PROFANE

Émile Durkheim (1858–1917) was a French sociologist who explored ideas of the **sacred** (holy) and the **profane** (unholy), as well as the practical effects of religious **ritual**. His work in these areas has provided key analytical tools for social scientists seeking to understand common elements in different religious movements and the practical application of religious ideas in the social life of religious adherents.

Developing the notion of a fundamental dichotomy between sacred and profane, Durkheim defined religion as "a unified system of beliefs and practices relative to sacred things, that is to say, things set apart and forbidden—beliefs and practices which unite into one single moral community called a Church, all those who adhere to them" ([1912] 1965, 62). Durkheim saw religion as ultimately social—something practiced with others—not private or individual. Through the collective action of religious ritual, group members reaffirm, clarify, and define for one another what is sacred and what is profane. Durkheim's famous study *Elementary Forms of Religious Life* (1912) examined the religious beliefs and practices of indigenous Australians, which he and others believed to be the most primitive culture of the time and, thus, closest to religion's original forms. The indigenous "elementary" religious beliefs and practices, he believed, could reveal the most basic elements of religions and shed light on religion's evolution into present forms.

sacred
Anything that is considered holy.

profane
Anything that is considered unholy.

ritual
An act or series of acts regularly repeated over years or generations that embody the beliefs of a group of people and create a sense of continuity and belonging.

Girls kneeling during the *chisungu*, a coming-of-age initiation ceremony among the Bemba people of Zambia. Have you experienced a coming-of-age ritual or other rite of passage?

As western European societies experienced radical transformations in the late nineteenth and early twentieth centuries, Durkheim turned to the rising problem of *anomie*—an alienation that individuals experience when faced with physical dislocation and the disruption of social networks and group values. He wondered how society would overcome this crisis and reestablish its essential cohesion. Durkheim argued that religion, particularly religious ritual, plays a crucial role in combating anomie and addressing larger social dynamics of alienation and dislocation by creating social solidarity, cohesion, and stability. He saw religion as the glue that holds together society's many different pieces. Through ritual, Durkheim believed, society is able to regenerate its sense of social solidarity and connection. Ritual defines and reinforces collective ideas of the sacred and profane. Thus, through ritual, the community's sense of cosmic order is reaffirmed, its social solidarity is regenerated, and the group's continued survival and growth are ensured.

Durkheim's work has influenced many anthropologists who have explored the role of ritual in religions and in the wider society. As we will see, the focus on how religion is lived out daily and enacted through ritual has become a cornerstone of the anthropological approach to the study of religion.

RELIGION AND RITUAL

Anthropologists of religion have paid particular attention to the role of ritual. They are aware that religion is not so much talked about as it is *performed* in public displays, rites, and rituals—not so much thought about as *danced* and *sung*. Rituals embody the beliefs, passions, and sense of solidarity of a group of people. They make beliefs come alive. When performed repeatedly over years and generations, rituals, as Durkheim suggested, create a sense of continuity and belonging that defines a group and regenerates its sense of solidarity, history, purpose, and meaning.

rite of passage

A category of ritual that enacts a change of status from one life stage to another, either for an individual or for a group.

Rites of Passage. French ethnographer and folklorist Arnold van Gennep (1873–1957) first theorized a category of ritual called **rites of passage** that enacts a change of status from one life stage to another, either for an individual or for a group (van Gennep 1908). Religious rites of passage are life-transition rituals marking moments of intense change, such as birth, coming of age, marriage, and death.

Audrey Richards (1899–1984), a pioneering British woman in early male-dominated British anthropology, observed and recorded one such rite of passage in 1931 among the Bemba people of Zambia, Central Africa. Their elaborate ritual, called the *chisungu*—a coming-of-age ceremony for young teenage women after first menstruation and in preparation for marriage—was danced in eighteen separate ceremonies over one month in a ritual hut and the surrounding bush. Over fifty special *chisungu* songs and forty different pottery emblems were involved. The *chisungu*, exclusively a women's ritual, was performed to provide magical protection to the girl and her family from the physical dangers of puberty and the magical dangers associated with the first act of intercourse in legal marriage. Within the rituals, older women also passed down the songs, sacred stories, sacred teachings, and secret lore of the Bemba womanhood, marking a clear change of status within the tribe from girl to woman (Richards 1956).

Victor Turner (1920–1983) built on Richards's pioneering work to explore why rituals and rites of passage are so powerful across religions and cultures. Drawing on his own research in Africa and on extensive comparison of cross-cultural data, Turner theorized that the power of ritual comes from the drama contained within it, in which the normal structure of social life is symbolically dissolved and reconstituted. He identified three primary stages in all rites of passage. First, the individual experiences *separation*—physically, psychologically, or symbolically—from the normal, day-to-day activities of the group. This may involve going to a special ritual place, wearing special clothing, or performing actions such as shaving one's head. The second stage, **liminality**, involves a period of outsiderhood during which the ritual participant is set apart from normal society, existing on the margins of everyday life. From this position the individual can gain a new perspective on the past, the present, or the future and thereby experience a new relationship to the community. The final ritual stage, *reaggregation* or *reincorporation*, returns the individual to everyday life and reintegrates him or her into the ritual community, transformed by the experience of liminality and endowed with a deeper sense of meaning, purpose, and connection to the larger group (Turner 1969).

Turner believed that all humans experience these rites of passage and that the experiences shape their perceptions of themselves and their community. Through them, he asserted, humans develop **communitas**: a sense of camaraderie, a common vision of what constitutes the good life, and perhaps most important, a commitment to take social action to move toward achieving this vision. Turner felt that the universal practice and experience of ritual reveals at the root of human existence an underlying desire for community and connection. Based on his cross-cultural investigation of the practice of rituals and rites of passage, Turner suggested that at the center of all human relationships there is a deep longing for shared meaning and connection, not a desire for self-preservation or material gain.

Pilgrimage. Turner applied his thinking about rites of passage to the study of religious pilgrimage, which he considered to be a unique form of religious ritual. Pilgrimage rituals, like those to Muslim saint shrines in northern India discussed earlier, exist in religions around the world. In a **pilgrimage**, adherents travel to

MAP 13.1
Zambia

liminality

One stage in a rite of passage during which a ritual participant experiences a period of outsiderhood, set apart from normal society, that is key to achieving a new perspective on the past, future, and current community.

communitas

A sense of camaraderie, a common vision of what constitutes a good life, and a commitment to take social action to move toward achieving this vision that is shaped by the common experience of rites of passage.

pilgrimage

A religious journey to a sacred place as a sign of devotion and in search of transformation and enlightenment.

Pilgrims circumambulate the Kaaba in Al Masjid al-Haram, the most sacred mosque in Islam, during the *hajj*, in Mecca, Saudi Arabia.

sacred places as a sign of devotion and in search of transformation and enlightenment. For example, all Muslims are obliged to perform, if life circumstances allow, the *hajj* pilgrimage to Mecca. Jews, Christians, and Muslims all have pilgrimage sites in Jerusalem. Many Hindus travel to the holy city of Varanasi (Benares) to bathe in the Ganges River. Daoists climb Mount Tai in eastern China. The pilgrimage journey, Turner suggested, involves the same process of separation, liminality, and reincorporation associated with other rites of passage. Similarly, pilgrimage creates a shared sense of communitas among those who undertake the journey, even if years or entire generations separate the pilgrimages.

For Turner (1969), life in society is a process of becoming, not being; it is a process of change. He maintained that rituals, pilgrimages, celebrations, and even theatrical performances facilitate this process and have the potential to initiate and foster change, not only in the individual but in the larger culture as well.

KARL MARX: RELIGION AS "THE OPIATE OF THE MASSES"

Karl Marx (1818–1883) was a German political philosopher. He is primarily known for his *Communist Manifesto* (with Friedrich Engels, 1848) and *Capital* (1867), a radical critique of capitalist economics emerging in western Europe in the nineteenth century (see Chapter 10). However, Marx was also highly critical of the role of religion in society, famously calling religion "the opiate of the masses" (Marx and Engels 1957). What did he mean?

In a time of economic upheaval and intensifying social stratification, Marx warned that religion was like a narcotic: It dulled people's pain so they did not realize how serious the situation was. Religion, Marx argued, played a key role in keeping the proletariat—the working poor—from engaging in the revolutionary social change that he believed was needed to improve their situation.

Marx's statement that religion is "the opiate of the masses" fits within his larger social analysis. He believed that throughout human history, economic realities have formed the foundation of social life and have generated society's primary dynamics, including class stratification and class struggle. He called this economic reality the "base." In his view, the other institutions of culture (including family, government, arts, and religion) arise from and are shaped by economic reality and the deep tensions of economic inequality and class struggle.

The role of these institutions, including religion, according to Marx, is to mask the material conditions and exploitation at the economic base and to contain—or provide a controlled release for—the tensions generated by class difference and class conflict. Religion, which Marx also called "the sigh of the oppressed," could provide to the downtrodden a sense of consolation that the sufferings of this life would end and be rewarded in heaven, thereby offering divine justification for the economic status quo. In Marx's view, religion provides an opiate—a painkiller—to undermine the masses' impulses to resist exploitation and change the social order.

Marx's overall focus on economics and power has pushed anthropologists to consider the relationship between religion and power. Contemporary studies move beyond Marx's idea that religion is merely an illusion that blinds people to economic realities; instead such studies examine how religion can play a complex role in systems of power—both by exercising power through economic resources and the mobilization of religious personnel, and by resisting systems of oppression through alternative ideas, symbols, and resources.

German political philosopher Karl Marx.

Religion and Cultural Materialism.

Anthropologist Marvin Harris (1927–2001) built on Marx's analysis of the base, or infrastructure, and the way in which the material conditions of a society shape its other components. Harris's theory of **cultural materialism** argued that material conditions, including technology and the environment, determine patterns of social organization. In this view, human culture is a response to the practical problems of earthly existence. In *Cows, Pigs, Wars, & Witches* (1974), Harris turned this perspective toward many perplexing questions of why humans behave in certain ways—including why Hindus venerate the cow, Jews and Muslims abstain from eating pork, and some people believe in witches. Harris proposed that these practices might have developed in response to very practical problems as people sought to adapt to the natural environment.

Have you ever wondered why cows are considered sacred in India? Harris approached this question not through personal immersion in the worldviews of

cultural materialism

A theory that argues that material conditions, including technology, determine patterns of social organization, including religious principles.

A sacred cow lies unperturbed and undisturbed in a busy intersection of Varanasi, India. Why is the cow sacred in India?

Indian Hindus, but rather by exploring larger environmental forces—the cultural ecology—that might promote this cultural practice. If you visit India you will find zebu cows—a scrawny, large-humped cattle species found in Africa and Asia—wandering freely about city streets and rural areas. These cows randomly eat food from market stalls, graze on sidewalk shrubs, and defecate indiscriminately. In a country with deep pockets of poverty and malnutrition, why are these cows left to roam and not slaughtered for nutritious, protein-rich dinner beefsteak?

Eating beef is prohibited in Hinduism, as is eating all meat. The cow, in Harris's view, became a symbolic representation of *ahimsa*—the practice of nonviolence and respect for the unity of all life that is key to Hinduism, Buddhism, and Jainism. How this tradition began is unclear, but today the holy mother cow is a symbol of health and abundance, and its image appears throughout Indian culture in media such as posters, movies, and carvings. The symbol also has a literal presence on streets and in fields.

Harris suggests that religious prohibitions protecting the cow have overwhelming practical applications in a culture that relies on agricultural production. Cows, after all, produce calves that grow up to be oxen, which Harris calls the tractor, thresher, and family car of the Indian agricultural system. Without an ox, a family has no way of planting, harvesting, preparing, or transporting its crops. Without an ox, a family loses the capacity to farm and eventually loses its land. Cows also produce vast quantities of dung, almost all of which can be recycled into fertilizer and cooking fuel. Religious dedication to *ahimsa* protects this resource even under the most difficult economic conditions. No matter how hungry the family may be in one season, keeping the cow alive ensures long-term survival.

MAP 13.2
India

For Harris, religiously based practices that appear to function in opposition to sound nutritional practices or economic development strategies may in fact be very rational cultural adaptations to the surrounding ecology. In India, the cow is extraordinarily useful. Its protection, especially during difficult economic times, may be essential to the long-term stability and survival of the Indian people and culture.

Think about any other religion, perhaps one you already have an affiliation with. Can you apply the perspectives of Marvin Harris's cultural materialism to any of its practices and beliefs? Can you begin to imagine how certain material conditions of everyday life may have shaped patterns of religious belief and practice?

MAX WEBER: THE PROTESTANT ETHIC AND SECULARIZATION

Max Weber (1864–1920), a German sociologist, philosopher, and economist, considered religious ideas to be a key for understanding the unique development of societies worldwide and the rise of industrial capitalism, particularly in western Europe. Why, he asked, did this highly rationalized, systematized, and industrial form of capitalism emerge in Europe and not in another part of the world?

Unlike Marx, who considered that economics ultimately shapes society, Weber believed that ideas, including religious ideas, can be equally powerful. His book *Sociology of Religion* (1920) was the first sociological attempt to compare the world's religions. In it, Weber suggested that Asian religious beliefs and ethical systems had stood in the way of capitalist economic growth there and had kept Asian economies from developing along the western European path. China, India, and other cultures had developed aspects of modern capitalism even earlier than western Europe did; but without a certain kind of ideological support, a more advanced capitalism had not evolved in Asia. Weber suggested that economic innovations alone could not explain the different paths.

In *The Protestant Ethic and the Spirit of Capitalism* (1905), Weber suggested that the ascetic values of self-denial and self-discipline that developed in western European Protestantism provided the ethic that was necessary for capitalism to flourish. Certain Protestant sects, including Calvinists, felt that it was important to express their religious beliefs and values in a daily lifestyle of thrift, discipline, and hard work. In these ideas, Weber found evidence of the ethical and psychological framework necessary for the success of industrial capitalism. He did not dismiss the role of economics in shaping the social dynamics of western Europe, but he argued that ideas, including religious ideas, may at times equally influence the economic direction of a society.

Also key to the development of Western capitalism, according to Weber, was an increasing systematization and rationalization of religious ideas. As Western

German sociologist and philosopher Max Weber.

Christianity evolved, this increasing rationality brought a decline of practices based on tradition, ritual, and magic. Weber saw these developments echoed in society at large: Rationalization led to bureaucracies with clear, intellectual, and systematized rules that replaced tradition, sentiment, and charisma as the operating system in social institutions. Weber imagined an evolution of rationalization in religion that led from (1) traditional religion based on magic and led by shamans to (2) charismatic religion based on the persuasive power of prophets such as Buddha, Jesus, and Moses and, finally, to (3) rational religion based on legal codes of conduct, bureaucratic structures, and formally trained religious leaders. He anticipated that this evolutionary process would be almost inevitable. But he warned that as society became more rationalized, it also risked becoming more secular—less religious—and thus losing the very spirit that had driven its success and development.

Scholars have debated Weber's secularization thesis for many years (Asad 1993; Berger 1999; Casanova 1994; Stark and Bainbridge 1985). Certainly in western Europe today, religious identification among native-born residents continues to sink to record lows. In contrast, the United States stands as a striking exception to this pattern in industrialized countries, as religious beliefs and practices remain strong in both the native-born and the immigrant populations. Polls consistently show that nearly 90 percent of the U.S. population believe in God, and about 80 percent identify with a particular religion (Pew Forum on Religion & Public Life 2015). Even the assumed separation of church and state in the United States is far from absolute. Battles continue over the teaching of evolution in the science curriculums of public schools, fans at public high school football games in Texas rise to recite the Christian Lord's Prayer, and crowds at New York's Yankee Stadium stand during the seventh-inning stretch for a moment of silence to remember those serving in the U.S. military and then sing "God Bless America." In these instances, religious sentiments infuse public and political life, and public rituals of civil society take on sacred status (Bellah 1980).

Moreover, widespread revivals of religious ideas, organizations, and movements around the world in the face of increasing modernization—and at times in resistance to the homogenizing influences of globalization and Western culture—provide additional evidence that modernization does not always lead to secularization.

SHAMANISM

shamans

Part-time religious practitioners with special abilities to connect individuals with supernatural powers or beings.

Throughout much of human history, the religious needs of human communities have been served by **shamans**—part-time religious practitioners with special abilities to connect individuals with supernatural powers or beings. More formal religious organizations with trained specialists and elaborate moral rules and ritual practices are fairly recent in human history, spanning 2,000 to 3,000 years at most with the rise of Hinduism, Buddhism, Judaism, Christianity, and Islam. The term *shaman* derives from the name given to healing specialists among the semi-nomadic people of Siberia, but it has since been applied to healers, spiritualists, witches, and witch doctors in cultures worldwide.

Shamans live as part of the local community, participating in daily activities and work, but are called on at times to perform special rituals and ceremonies. They often gain their powers through special training or experience, passing through a journey or test of spirit such as illness, isolation, physical pain, or an emotional ordeal. Through rituals involving prayers, meditation, songs, dance, pain, or drugs, shamans enter a trance, often at will. While entranced, they implore deities and powers to take action or to provide special knowledge and power that may assist individuals or the community at large: healing, medicinal advice, personal guidance, protection from illness or other attack, fortune telling, and control over the weather.

Although the role of the shaman is generally associated with small agricultural or seminomadic societies, shamans today often relocate to contemporary urban settings along with their immigrant communities. A variation of the shaman role also occurs in more formal religious organizations, as trained religious specialists there seek to (1) intervene with their deities on behalf of adherents or (2) assist adherents in practices of prayer and meditation through which they seek healing or guidance.

RELIGION AND MAGIC

Anthropology has a long history of studying cultures where magic is practiced and witches are real. **Magic** involves the use of spells, incantations, words, and actions in an attempt to compel supernatural forces to act in certain ways, whether for good or for evil. Magic is part of cultural practices in every part of the world. And religion, almost everywhere, contains some components of magic.

In *The Golden Bough* (1890), anthropologist James Frazer (1854–1941) distinguishes between imitative magic and contagious magic. **Imitative magic** involves a performance that imitates the desired result, perhaps manipulating a doll or some other representation of the target of magic in the belief that the action will have direct imitative effect. **Contagious magic** centers on the belief that certain materials—perhaps clothing, hair, fingernails, teeth—that have come into contact with one person carry a magical connection that allows power to be transferred from person to person.

In this section we consider the work of E. E. Evans-Pritchard, who sought to understand witchcraft and magic in East Africa; Paul Stoller, who apprenticed with a sorcerer in West Africa; and George Gmelch, who traces the belief in magic in contemporary U.S. society.

magic

The use of spells, incantations, words, and actions in an attempt to compel supernatural forces to act in certain ways, whether for good or for evil.

imitative magic

A ritual performance that achieves efficacy by imitating the desired magical result.

contagious magic

Ritual words or performances that achieve efficacy as certain materials that come into contact with one person carry a magical connection that allows power to be transferred from person to person.

E. E. Evans-Pritchard: Rethinking the Logic of Magic.

E. E. Evans-Pritchard (1902–1973), a British anthropologist who conducted extensive fieldwork in Africa's southern Sudan region, challenged Weber's rationalization thesis that assumed modernization and the rise of science would bring increasing rationality in a culture and its religious practices, thereby leading to a decrease in practices of magic. Instead Evans-Pritchard's research among the tribal Azande people from 1926 to 1930 found that their use of magic was not an irrational expression but a component of a highly organized, rational, and logical system of thought that complemented science in understanding the way the world works.

In *Witchcraft, Oracles and Magic among the Azande* (1937), Evans-Pritchard describes in careful detail the elaborate religious system of the Azande in which magic, witchcraft, and poison oracles are central elements in daily life and conversation. The Azande trace all misfortunes to witchcraft. Their witchcraft does not involve rituals, spells, or medicines. Instead it is a psychic power that may be used consciously or unconsciously by a witch—a woman or a man—to cause misfortunes or death. Witchcraft is inherited from a parent, and a witch's body contains a witchcraft substance (which the Azande described to Evans-Pritchard as an oval, blackish swelling or bag near the liver) that cannot be detected during life but can be found during an autopsy.

MAP 13.3
Azande region, South Sudan

Magic among the Azande, in contrast to witchcraft, is performed consciously through rites, spells, the preparation of herbal medicines, and other magical techniques. Magic has its own power and can be used to combat witchcraft. If people perceive that magic is being deployed against them, they may consult a witch doctor—almost always a man—who will use magic and medicines to try to thwart the work of the witch.

Witchcraft, Oracles and Magic among the Azande is considered one of the outstanding works of anthropology in the twentieth century. It not only stands as an exquisitely detailed ethnography but also provides the basis for rethinking the role of magic in society. Evans-Pritchard challenges the ethnocentric views of Western scholars who dismiss magical practices as irrational and illogical when compared to modern, rational, Western scientific strategies for accumulating knowledge of the external world. He contends instead that Azande ideas that may seem exotic, strange, and irrational to Europeans in actuality formed consistent, comprehensive, and rational systems of thought within the context of the Azande's daily lives and social structures.

Among the Azande, magic explained things that did not make sense otherwise, particularly the experience of misfortune; it provided an alternative theory of causation that supplemented the theory of natural causation. Magic helped explain what could not be explained by scientific study of nature. Evans-Pritchard presented the case of a wooden granary structure that collapsed and

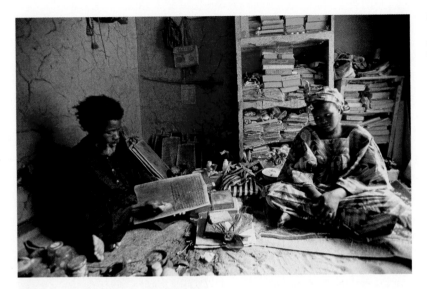

A sorcerer preparing a written tablet for a customer in the Songhay region of Niger.

injured several people seated underneath it. Science could explain how insects had damaged the wood, which led to the collapse. But science could not explain the misfortune of why the people who were injured were sitting in a particular location at a particular time. For the Azande, witchcraft and magic could explain the misfortune.

Evans-Pritchard argued that the Azande saw no contradiction between witchcraft and empirical knowledge. For them, witchcraft and magic provided a rational and intellectually consistent explanation for what science cannot explain. Belief in witchcraft only appears inconsistent and irrational, Evans-Pritchard chided his Western colleagues, when they are arranged like museum objects on a shelf and examined outside the context of daily life.

Paul Stoller: *In Sorcery's Shadow*. In the ethnography *In Sorcery's Shadow* (1987), anthropologist Paul Stoller and his co-author Cherl Olkes extend Evans-Pritchard's commitment to respect and understand others' systems of knowledge, even when they may at first appear irrational, unreasonable, and incomprehensible. Stoller takes Evans-Pritchard's work on magic and sorcery (another term for witchcraft) to a deeper personal level through direct engagement in the beliefs and practices of those he studied.

In the late 1970s Stoller arrived in the Songhay region of the Republic of Niger, West Africa, determined to learn about the role of religion in community life there. Through intensive fieldwork covering five visits over eight years, his deep involvement in a world of magic, spirits, sorcery, and spirit possession prevalent in the Songhay and surrounding regions eventually led him to be initiated as a sorcerer's apprentice. He memorized magical incantations. He ate special foods needed for his initiation. He ingested medicinal powders and wore magical

MAP 13.4
Songhay region, Niger

The success of J. R. R. Tolkien's *Lord of the Rings* trilogy and J. K. Rowling's *Harry Potter* series has revealed a vast appetite in Western culture for magic, witches, and wizards, at least in their fantastical literary and cinematic form.

objects to protect himself from antagonistic sorcerers. And he indirectly participated in an attack of sorcery that temporarily paralyzed the intended victim.

Stoller's fieldwork led him to reflect on the transformative and deeply personal experience of conducting research into people's religious worlds:

> For me, respect means accepting fully beliefs and phenomena which our system of knowledge often holds preposterous. I took my teachers seriously. They *knew* that I used divination in my personal life. They *knew* that I had eaten powders to protect myself. They *knew* I wore objects to demonstrate my respect for the spirits. They *knew* I had an altar in my house over which I recited incantations. They liked the way I carried my knowledge and power and taught me more and more. (1987, 228)

The anthropological commitment to long-term, in-depth participant observation brings many of us into close contact with the beliefs, practices, and emotions of those whom we study, an intimacy that often reveals the vibrant power of religion in their lives that leaves one marked by the encounter.

George Gmelch: Baseball Magic. If reading about the work of Evans-Pritchard and Stoller leaves you relieved that you live in a Western world that relegates belief in magic to children's books and movies, research by anthropologist and former minor league baseball player George Gmelch may surprise you. It turns out that beliefs and practices of magic are not so unfamiliar in U.S. culture.

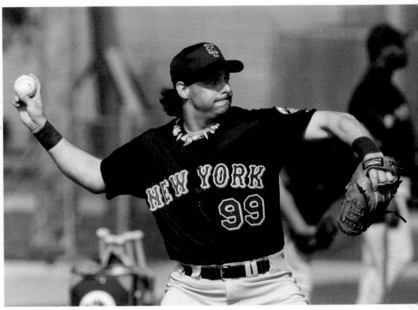

Gmelch's study of baseball in the United States (1992) explores the rituals, taboos, and sacred objects of magic that are in almost constant use. He finds that they reflect the kinds of beliefs and activities that are prevalent in all sports.

Baseball players use charms such as special clothes or jewelry. Moreover, Gmelch found, players believe that good magic is contagious. If it worked before, and if the player uses the same ritual again, perhaps the magical conditions for success can be re-created. Thus players repeat certain actions to help them succeed: Pitchers touch the bill of their cap, wear good-luck charms, or never touch the foul line between home plate and first base when moving between the pitcher's mound and the dugout. Batters wear the same shirt or underwear, or use the same movements over and over again in the batter's box, to capture the magic of previous success.

Magic rituals, taboos, and sacred objects are used constantly in American sports. (*left*) Boston Red Sox designated hitter David Ortiz adjusts his gloves before every swing, drawing on a notion of contagious magic to bring him good luck while batting. (*right*) Former New York Mets reliever Turk Wendell's magical practices included always leaping over the baseline when walking to the mound, brushing his teeth between innings, chewing black licorice while pitching, and wearing a necklace decorated with the teeth of wild animals he had hunted and killed.

In What Ways Is Religion Both a System of Meaning and a System of Power?

Many people in Western cultures think of religion as a system of ideas and beliefs that are primarily a personal matter. In the United States, for instance, doctrines asserting the separation of church and state promote an ideal of the separation of religion from politics. But as we saw in Chapter 2, any analysis of a cultural system that focuses solely on its underlying meanings risks ignoring the ways that power is negotiated within the system and how it engages other systems of power within the culture. This observation applies to our study of religion as well.

RELIGION AND MEANING

Building on the themes of Max Weber's *Protestant Ethic and the Spirit of Capitalism*, anthropologist Clifford Geertz (1926–2006), in his essay "Religion as a Cultural System" (1973b), suggests that religion is essentially a system of ideas surrounding a set of powerful **symbols**. Hindus, for example, consider the cow sacred because by protecting it they symbolically enact the protection of all life. Other widely recognized religious symbols include the cross for Christians, the Torah scroll for Jews, and the holy city of Mecca for Muslims. For Geertz, each symbol has deep meaning and evokes powerful emotions and motivations in the religion's followers. Why?

These symbols acquire significance far beyond the actual material they are made of. Objects made of wood, metal, rock, or paper come to represent influential explanations about what it means to be human and where humans fit in the general order of the universe. Symbols, with their deep pool of meaning, create a sense of order and resist chaos by building and reinforcing a larger worldview—a framework of ideas about what is real, what exists, and what that means.

We can see symbols at work in various religious contexts. For Christians, the bread and wine served at the communion ritual are more than actual bread and wine. They symbolically recall the death and resurrection of Jesus, the power of God to overcome death, and the promise to Jesus's followers of everlasting life beyond the suffering of this world. Communion also recalls the fellowship of all Christian believers who share in the benefits of God's sacrifice, a sense of connection with people around the world. For Jews, the Torah scroll is more than a composite of paper and ink. It represents the holy word of God as revealed through the prophets, the story of a covenant between God and the people of Israel, an agreement that in return for faithfulness God will provide liberation from captivity, the establishment of a nation of people, and abundant life. For Hindus, the cow requires veneration because it represents the Hindu practice of *ahimsa*—nonviolence toward all living things. In a practical sense, this means that no leather may enter the temple and all shoes must remain outside the temple door. Even these acts are symbolic of Hindus' belief that all life is sacred and that attention to this fact will transform the practicing individual and lead to his or her reincarnation as a more sentient being.

symbol
Anything that represents something else.

A Jewish worshiper holds up a Torah scroll to receive a blessing at the Western Wall, Judaism's holiest prayer site, in Jerusalem's Old City. How does an object made of paper and ink become a powerful symbol with deep religious meaning?

RELIGION AND POWER

Anthropologist Talal Asad, in his book *Genealogies of Religion* (1993), criticizes Geertz's explanation of religion. Asad bases his inquiry on questions such as these: How did religious symbols get their power? Who or what gave them their authority? What gives religion the power and authority to have meaning in people's lives? After all, Asad asserts, symbols do not have meaning in and of themselves. He suggests that religion and religious symbols are actually produced through complex historical and social developments in which power and meaning are created, contested, and maintained. What historical processes have given the cross, the Torah, the *hajj*, and the cow their symbolic power? Without understanding these particular **authorizing processes**, Asad claims, we cannot understand what really makes religion work.

Asad argues that most definitions of religion are not universal. Instead, he claims, they are the creations of Western scholars based on western European ideas of what religion is and how it works—in particular, the way Christianity has developed in relationship to the state. Such scholars look for Western ideas of religion in the spiritual and ritual practices of other cultures. Asad warns that these attempts to create a universal definition impede an understanding of religion in other parts of the world. For instance, he suggests that Weber's assumptions that religions become increasingly rationalized as societies modernize and that societies become increasingly secularized as a sharper separation develops between religion and the state are rooted in the way Western Christianity has developed—not in a universal pattern that we can assume exists in religions worldwide.

authorizing process
The complex historical and social developments through which symbols are given power and meaning.

In the case of Islam, religious beliefs and political power are intricately intertwined in many countries, and national governments may seek to impose a version of Islamic religious law, the Sharia, through mechanisms of the state. Asad suggests that in these cases, Western understandings of the essential nature of religion that assume increasing secularization and separation of church and state may lead scholars and casual observers to dismiss other expressions of religion as irrational and backward. Instead, these other religious expressions are simply different—outside the normative definition of religion established in Western scholarship. Asad states that scholars of religion must beware the power of universal definitions to obscure local realities. They must carefully examine local expressions of religion, how those expressions developed over time, and what has given those expressions the power and authority to be so meaningful to believers (Asad 1993).

As you begin to think like an anthropologist of religion, try to examine religious symbols from the perspectives of both Geertz and Asad. As you consider religious symbols in the culture around you—perhaps in your own religious tradition—can you begin to appreciate the power of symbols to evoke intense emotions and motivations that put believers in touch with what feels "really real"? Can you begin to consider the ways in which particular symbols have been constructed, given meaning, and authorized through particular historical and cultural processes?

BLURRING THE BOUNDARIES BETWEEN MEANING AND POWER

The work of both Geertz and Asad has influenced contemporary anthropological research on religion. We now consider a local example of religious activities and organizations in which meaning and power are intertwined and the boundary between religion and other social systems of power is not rigid. As we consider this study, can you begin to see how analyses of both meaning and power are essential in achieving a comprehensive picture of the role of religion in culture?

Religion and Revolution in Mexico. Religion scholar Charlene Floyd's (1996) research on the role of the Catholic Church in a revolutionary movement in the Chiapas region of southern Mexico provides an example of how meaning and power are expressed in religion. Chiapas is one of the poorest states in Mexico, where most children do not finish primary school and many homes have no running water. The people are poor, but the land is rich: It holds large reserves of oil and natural gas, provides most of the country's hydroelectric power, and supports half of its coffee crop. The tension between an impoverished people on the one hand and rich natural resources extracted by Mexico's state and corporations on the other has not always found a smooth resolution.

In the early hours of January 1, 1994, some of the poor people of Chiapas, calling themselves "Zapatistas" (after the Mexican revolutionary Emiliano

MAP 13.5
Chiapas region, Mexico

Catholic bishop Samuel Ruiz of San Cristobal in Chiapas, southern Mexico, and the church's network of *catequistas*, or lay teachers, have been accused by the Mexican government of inciting rebellion.

Zapata), covered their faces with bandanas and ski masks, marched into four Chiapas cities, and declared in a dramatic manifesto, "Today we say enough is enough!" Stunned by the uprising, the Mexican government and the economic leaders of Chiapas quickly accused the Catholic Church of inciting the rebellion. In particular, they blamed one of the bishops of Chiapas, Samuel Ruiz García, and his *catequistas*, or lay teachers. But how could a Catholic bishop and a group of lay teachers be accused of inciting a rebellion? Did they actually do so? In considering these questions, we must explore the Church's role in Mexican society.

Today 90 percent of Mexicans identify themselves as Catholic, a faith that has been a key component of Mexican national identity ever since Spanish colonizers forcibly imported it 500 years ago. In certain periods of Mexican history, religion and politics have been closely aligned. For example, a Catholic priest, Father Miguel Hidalgo y Costilla, is credited with providing the initial spark for the Mexican independence movement in 1810. Calling on the name of Mexico's indigenous saint, the Virgin of Guadalupe, Father Hidalgo challenged his parishioners by asking, "Will you free yourselves?" Despite periods of alignment, Mexican history has seen ongoing tensions between the powerful institution of the Catholic Church (which has been one of Mexico's largest landholders) and the Mexican state. The Church has been involved in political movements in Mexico before, but did it have a role in the 1994 uprising in Chiapas? A quick look at recent Church history may shed light on this question.

In 1959 Pope John XXIII called for a Vatican Council to modernize the Catholic Church. By the end of this conference (1962–65), commonly called Vatican II, the Catholic Church had begun a dramatic revolution in theology and practice. In an attempt to redefine the Church as "the people of God" rather than an institution, Vatican II moved to make local congregations more accessible to the layperson. Congregations were allowed to worship in their own local language rather than Latin. Priests and lay members were encouraged to open the Church as a servant to the poor rather than an ally of the politically powerful.

Bishop Samuel Ruiz García, head of the Diocese of San Cristobal de las Casas in Chiapas, where the Zapatista uprising occurred, attended Vatican II and a subsequent meeting in 1968 of Latin American Catholic leaders. He returned to Mexico determined to implement the new theology of liberation: He would put the Church to work to better the life conditions of the one million primarily indigenous people in his diocese. The diocesan program for training lay teachers (*catequistas*) transformed its curriculum from a primary focus on Church doctrine, scriptures, law, liturgy, and music to include concerns of community life and social needs. By the time of the Zapatista uprising, the *catequistas* had grown from 700 to 8,000. Most were now elected by their local indigenous communities; they were deeply involved not only in traditional Catholic religious education but also in the empowerment of indigenous people in their struggles against poverty. *Catequistas* developed prominent roles as community and political leaders, accompanying their constituents in efforts to eradicate poverty and landlessness in Chiapas and to open the state's political process to greater participation from people at the grassroots.

Were Bishop Ruiz and the *catequistas* responsible for the 1994 Zapatista uprising? No accusations have been proven of a direct role in the Zapatista leadership. But did the theology of liberation, expressing the Catholic Church's desire for the empowerment of indigenous people and the elimination of poverty, provide moral support and practical training to communities engaged in this struggle? If so, then the Catholic Church of Chiapas provides an instructive example for anthropologists of how we must consider the role of religious ideas, symbols, and engagements with other systems of power to understand religion in all its fullness (Floyd 1996).

How Is Globalization Changing Religion?

The forces of globalization—especially migration and time-space compression—are stretching and shaping religions and religious practices. Increasing immigration sometimes means that whole communities—their beliefs, religious architecture, religious leaders, and even their gods—relocate across national boundaries. Travel is broadening the encounters of people of different faiths. At the same time, information about religion is more widely available, and communication technologies enable religious institutions to transform their strategies for cultivating and educating participants. Cities, especially those serving as immigrant gateways, are generally the focal point of this increasing encounter. It is here that new immigrants revitalize older religious institutions and construct new ones, often establishing deep ties to home and sophisticated networks of transnational exchange. For example, throughout the United States, Catholic churches are being rejuvenated as immigration from heavily Catholic countries brings new membership, worship styles, social needs, and political engagements. In response, local Catholic churches and key U.S. Catholic leadership have actively supported the reform of U.S. immigration laws. Indeed, the Church saw as a key human rights issue the reuniting of families across the border and eliminating opportunities for the exploitation of vulnerable, low-wage workers. At the same time, today's immigrants are reshaping the Church's future—just as immigrant waves from Ireland, Germany, and Italy did in the nineteenth century.

How are religious practices crossing national borders in a global age? Every year, Mexican Catholics carry a lit torch and a portrait of Our Lady of Guadalupe from Mexico City to New York, combining religious expression with political advocacy for reform of U.S. immigration laws.

RELOCATING RITUALS AND DEITIES FROM THE HOME COUNTRY

Globalization is transforming the ritual practices of religious communities large and small as congregations adapt to their members' mobility and the lively flow of ideas, information, and money across borders. These dynamics have rapidly spread the religious practices of a small, local, Daoist village temple in rural China to New York and beyond through a network of Chinese restaurants opening across the United States. Today, thanks to globalization, the village temple's adherents and their local god have become international border-crossing immigrants.

Immigrant Chinese Gods. A few years ago, I walked into a little temple just off Canal Street in Manhattan's Chinatown as part of a project to map the Chinese religious communities in New York City (Guest 2003). Women and men, young and old, crowded into the noisy and smoky old storefront space, lighting incense, chatting with old friends, and saying prayers at the altar. Most were from the same small village in southeastern China, outside the provincial capital of Fuzhou. They had opened this temple to continue their religious practices in the United States and to serve as a gathering place for fellow immigrant villagers who lived and worked in and around New York City. Here, immigrants can reconnect with friends and relatives from their hometown, participate in rituals of devotion to their deities, and build networks of fellow devotees they may not have known before arriving in New York.

For a highly transient population, the temple serves as a center for exchanging information about jobs, housing, lawyers, doctors, employment agencies, and more. It operates a revolving loan fund for members to pay off smuggling debts or start up a take-out restaurant. Through the temple, members contribute to building their home temple and support other charitable projects in their home community back in China. Despite the undocumented status of many of these immigrants, the temple provides a way to participate in civic activities and express themselves as contributing members of the community.

I later visited the home village temple in China to learn about village life and local religious traditions. One evening as I prepared to leave, the master of the temple expressed disappointment that I had not been able to meet the temple's spirit medium, a young woman who had a special relationship with the village's local god. He explained that on the first and fifteenth day of each lunar month, the local god possesses her and speaks through her to interpret the villagers' dreams and answer their questions: What name should I give my child? What herbal remedy will cure my ill? Will this woman be a good match for my son? When should I try to be smuggled out of China to the United States? I shared the master's disappointment at this missed opportunity and readily accepted his invitation to return on a future visit.

A year later I did return. The spirit medium, however, was gone. She and her husband, the temple master informed me, had moved to the United States and were now working in a restaurant in a place called "Indiana." I was disappointed again, but I expressed my concern that their departure may have disrupted a key element of temple life. The master then told me this story:

> Actually she still does it—only now it's from Indiana. Our believers
> work in restaurants all over the United States and some are still here
> in China. When they want to ask the advice of the god, they just pick
> up their cell phones and call. The spirit medium keeps careful records
> of their questions and dreams. Then on the first and fifteenth of the
> lunar month, just as always used to happen when she was here, she
> goes into a trance. The god leaves our temple here in China and flies
> to Indiana to possess her. Her husband then asks all the questions
> and writes down the answers. When the possession is over, the god
> returns to our village, and the spirit medium and her husband return
> all the phone calls to report the wisdom of the god.

Perhaps the look on my face and my one raised eyebrow alerted the master to my initial skepticism. "We can feel the god leave here every time," he said. "Really. Why don't you believe that? In America you have lots of Christians who believe the Christian god can be everywhere in the world at the same time. Why can't ours?"

The more I thought about it, the more I wondered why the local god of a village in China couldn't also be in Indiana. As an anthropologist of religion, I was reminded once again that religious practices and beliefs in today's age of globalization continue to be fluid and adaptable. After all, humans are adaptable, and so are their cultural constructions. Religion is a vibrant example of this core anthropological insight.

Anthropology challenges us to understand the beliefs and practices of others from within their own cultural framework. By making the strange familiar, we may then also make the familiar strange. In other words, we may take what seems natural and normal in our own lives and see it through new eyes.

The study of religion often forces anthropologists to address personal issues of identity, belief, and objectivity in ways that many other areas of study do not. Is it possible to fully understand a religion without being a practitioner? Can someone remain objective if he practices the religion he studies? Anthropologists of religion consider these important questions when conducting fieldwork and writing about their experiences. Through any experience of intensive fieldwork we risk challenging, transforming, and possibly shattering our own worldviews even as we risk influencing those of the people we study. These dynamics are particularly volatile in the study of religion.

Toolkit

Thinking Like an Anthropologist: Religion in the Twenty-First Century

After reading this chapter, you should have a deeper understanding of some of the approaches anthropologists take to understanding the role of religion in people's lives and in communities large and small. These insights can serve as a toolkit as you consider expressions of religion in other countries and at home in the United States.

Think again about Pope Francis's address to the U.S. Congress that opened the chapter, and recall the key questions we have asked about religion:

- **What is religion?**
- **What tools do anthropologists use to understand how religion works?**
- **In what ways is religion both a system of meaning and a system of power?**
- **How is globalization changing religion?**

After reading the chapter, can you apply the writings of Durkheim, Marx, Weber, Geertz, and Asad to events in the real world? Can you see concepts of sacred and profane, ritual, rite of passage, communitas, symbol, and power emerge in religious expressions in your own life?

After his visit to the United States, Pope Francis continued his commitment to integrating theological reflection, social analysis and calls to action. In the summer of 2016 alone he lit candles and offered prayers at the World War II era Nazi-run Auschwitz-Birkenau concentration camp; urged the world to never forget the Ottoman genocide of 1.5 million Armenians during and after World War I; warned one million youth at World Youth Day in Poland against consumerism and complacency; and pressed for peace in Syria. While his visits and his words were often highly symbolic, his proclamations reverberated through the powerful institutions of the Catholic Church and its 1.2 billion members worldwide. As the spiritual and political head of the church, what role might Pope Francis's words and actions play in shaping political and economic developments in places around the world? Do you see other religious leaders who exercise both symbolic and material power? Where have religious language and symbols been used to mobilize political action?

Key Terms

religion (p. 367)

martyr (p. 369)

saint (p. 369)

sacred (p. 371)

profane (p. 371)

ritual (p. 371)

rite of passage (p. 372)

liminality (p. 373)

communitas (p. 373)

pilgrimage (p. 373)

cultural materialism (p. 375)

shamans (p. 378)

magic (p. 379)

imitative magic (p. 379)

contagious magic (p. 379)

symbol (p. 384)

authorizing process (p. 385)

Gillette STADIUM

Junior Seau
1969 - 2012

Bank of America

Chapter 14
Health, Illness, and the Body

There is an incredible beauty to American football. Twenty-two men move across the field with precision, intuition, discipline, and creativity—men of immense size yet stunning speed, agility, quickness, and grace. How many years of practice, strength training, weightlifting, running, jumping, and special diets does it take these men to craft bodies so athletic, sharp-minded, healthy, and vibrant?

Americans watch a lot of football. I certainly have—first with my father and then with my son. In 2016, 1,800 players on thirty-two teams generated $13.3 billion in revenue for the National Football League, mostly from television contracts.

The quarterback drops back with the ball. Five linemen form a pocket of protection around him—shoulder to shoulder with teammates, head to head with opponents, hands, arms, feet flying. Five receivers fly downfield,

---

Retired NFL star Junior Seau committed suicide in 2012. An autopsy revealed he was suffering from chronic traumatic encephalopathy, a neurodegenerative brain disease caused by repeated hits to the head. Are our star athletes' bodies healthy?

eyes wide, adrenaline pumping, nimble, savvy, fleet driving quick cuts and sprints. Deep in the pocket, the quarterback lets go a perfect spiral like a rocket down the middle of the field as a racing receiver's body launches into the air at 100 miles an hour, horizontal, arms extended, fingers outstretched—just as the defensive back catapults his body for a perfectly timed collision.

And for a moment everyone holds their breath.

Everyone knows what could happen. Everyone is hoping it doesn't.

At that moment of exquisite gracefulness and athleticism everyone remembers that football is a brutal game and hopes that all the players come out of this encounter alive.

In 2002 Dr. Bennet Omalu, a Nigerian doctor, first diagnosed chronic traumatic encephalopathy (CTE) as the cause of death of fifty-year-old Pittsburgh Steelers championship center Mike Webster. CTE is a degenerative brain disease caused by repeated head injuries that can only be detected after death. Twelve years later, after increasing reports of dementia, Alzheimer's disease, Parkinson's disease, and ALS in retired football players, dozens more CTE cases, and multiple suicides, the National Football League settled a class-action lawsuit brought by 5,000 retired players who accused the league of systematically hiding the dangers of concussions. Actuarial studies suggest 30 percent of NFL players will suffer from Alzheimer's disease or dementia, far above national averages. In 2016, in congressional testimony, an NFL representative admitted for the first time the clear scientific connection between football concussions and CTE.

Tune in again on a Sunday and look closely. The beauty and elegance come through. But between the plays, on the edges of the camera view, just before the cutaway to commercials, you may also see the broken noses, bloodied jerseys, swollen fingers, broken legs, torn ligaments, hanging heads, bandages, braces, crutches, casts, and concussions. Listen more closely for talk of the painkillers, the injections, the dementia, and the tragic suicides.

As we think as anthropologists about health, illness, and notions of the body across cultures, how do we make sense of bodies and health in American sports, and American football in particular? This most successful of U.S. cultural products has transformed play, exercise, and games that build healthy bodies into a multibillion dollar extravaganza in which bodies become entertainment and injuries and long-term health consequences almost invisible. How do we make sense of the NFL's efforts to obscure the scientific data linking football concussions with brain disease or the ways Americans' notions of health, illness, and the body may intersect with concepts of race and class to mask the harsh realities of this game? And why did it take a doctor from Nigeria to see clearly the injuries to bodies and brains in this classic American sport?

Conventional wisdom attributes health and longevity to a combination of "good genes" and good behavioral choices: eating right, not smoking, drinking in moderation, avoiding illegal drugs, exercising, and even flossing. These criteria mesh with core American values of individualism, personal responsibility, and the benefits of hard work and clean living. But are these factors sufficient to explain health and longevity—or the lack of it? Getting sick is a part of life. Everyone experiences colds, fevers, cuts and bruises, perhaps a broken bone. But some people get sick more often than others. Death and dying are part of life; but some people suffer more and die sooner, while others are healthier and live longer. Anthropologists are interested in knowing why.

In this chapter we will explore anthropologists' growing interest in health, illness, and the body. Although these concerns have deep roots in our discipline, the specialization of *medical anthropology* has grown immensely since the 1980s as anthropology's key research strategies—intensive fieldwork, extensive participant observation in local communities, and deep immersion in the daily lives of people and their local problems and experiences—have proven profoundly effective in solving pressing public health problems.

Medical anthropologists use a variety of analytical perspectives to examine the wide range of experiences and practices that humans associate with disease, illness, health, well-being, and the body—both today and in the past. We study the spread of disease and pathogens through the human population (known as epidemiology) by examining the *medical ecology*: the interaction of diseases with the natural environment and human culture. Looking more broadly, medical anthropologists use an *interpretivist approach* to study health systems as systems of meaning: How do humans across cultures make sense of health and illness? How do we think and talk and feel about illness, pain, suffering, birth, and mortality? *Critical medical anthropology* explores the impact of inequality on human health in two important ways. First, it considers how economic and political systems, race, class, gender, and sexuality create and perpetuate unequal access to health care. Second, it examines how health systems themselves are systems of power that promote disparities in health by defining who is sick, who gets treated, and how the treatment is provided.

Medical anthropology's holistic approach to health and illness—examining epidemiology, meaning, and power—assumes that health and illness are more than a result of germs, individual behavior, and genes. Health is also a product of our environment—our access to adequate nutrition, housing, education, and health care and the absence of poverty, violence, and warfare.

In this chapter we will explore the following questions:

- **How does culture shape our ideas of health and illness?**
- **How do different cultural conceptions of the body affect health practices?**
- **How can anthropologists help solve health-care problems?**

- **Why does the distribution of health and illness mirror that of wealth and power?**
- **How is globalization changing the experience of health and illness and the practice of medicine?**

By the end of the chapter you will understand how anthropologists approach the study of health, illness, and the body and how these concepts vary across cultures. You will be able to recognize how your own conceptions of health and illness are a cultural construction. You will be able to critically analyze both the systems of power that shape access to health care and the ways in which health systems create and exacerbate inequalities within and between populations.

How Does Culture Shape Our Ideas of Health and Illness?

What does it mean to be healthy? The World Health Organization proposes that **health** includes not merely the absence of disease and infirmity but complete physical, mental, and social well-being. This is a standard that few people in the world currently attain. Perhaps it is enough to be functionally healthy—not perfectly well, but healthy enough to do what you need to do: get up in the morning, go to school, go to work, reproduce the species. What level of health do you expect, hope for, and strive for? What level of health enables your culture to thrive?

Medical anthropologists have dedicated significant effort to document healing practices and health systems around the globe, from indigenous and tribal communities and urban metropolises to farming communities and groups of migrant workers. In the process, medical anthropologists have identified a vast array of ideas about the causes of health and disease, different notions of the body, and varied cultural strategies to address pain, treat illness, and promote health. One key finding is that these beliefs and practices are intricately intertwined with the way local cultures imagine the world works and the relationship of an individual's body to his or her surroundings.

In assessing how disease and health conditions affect specific populations and how specific cultural groups diagnose, manage, and treat health-related problems, medical anthropologists have found it useful to distinguish between disease, illness, and sickness. A **disease** is a discrete, natural entity that can be clinically identified and treated by a health professional. A disease may be caused genetically or through infection by bacteria, a virus, or parasites. But the bacteria, viruses, or parasites are the same regardless of location or cultural context.

health

The absence of disease and infirmity, as well as the presence of physical, mental, and social well-being.

disease

A discrete natural entity that can be clinically identified and treated by a health professional.

Illness, however, is more than the biological disease. **Illness** is the individual patient's experience of being unwell—the culturally defined understanding of disease. It includes the way he or she feels about it, talks about it, thinks about it, and experiences it within a particular cultural context. Diseases can be observed, measured, and treated by sufferers and healers. But culture gives meaning to disease, shaping the human experience of illness, pain, suffering, dying, and death (Singer and Baer 2007).

Sickness refers to the individual's public expression of illness and disease, including social expectations about how one should behave and how others will respond. Being sick may release the sick person from social obligations like work, school, or parenting. But sickness also requires the patient to perform a certain "sick role" in order to receive the corresponding social support. In American culture this involves showing a clear wish to get well and willingness to cooperate with medial experts (from parents to doctors). If, for instance, you are sick enough to miss class and expect to be released from schoolwork, the social agreement about sickness suggests that you should be resting at home and following a doctor's advice.

People recognize widely different symptoms, illnesses, and causes for health challenges and have developed widely different strategies for achieving and maintaining health. Though the stereotypical Western images of health care often revolve around doctors in white coats, dentists' chairs, hospitals, strong medications, and advanced technology (such as X-rays, MRIs, and CT scans), medical anthropologists have found that these are not the primary points of access to health care for most people in the world. Nor are they even the first point of access for most people in Western countries. Rather, before seeking the assistance of a trained medical professional, people everywhere apply their

Globally, people have created a vast array of healing practices, all intricately intertwined with local cultural understandings of disease, health, illness, and the body. (*right*) A clinical assistant performs an ultrasound sonogram on a pregnant woman. (*left*) An Indian healer provides villagers with ayurvedic medicines.

illness

The individual patient's experience of being unwell.

sickness

An individual's public expression of illness and disease, including social expectations about how one should behave and how others will respond.

personal medical knowledge, their own strategies—often handed down within families or communities—for dealing with disease, illness, pain, and discomfort.

ETHNOMEDICINE

Over the years, medical anthropologists have focused extensive research on **ethnomedicine**. This field involves the comparative study of local systems of health and healing rooted in culturally specific norms and values; it includes the ways in which local cultures create unique strategies for identifying and treating disease and conceptualizing the experience of health, illness, and the physical world.

Early research on ethnomedicine focused primarily on non-Western health systems and emphasized natural healing remedies such as herbs, teas, and massage; reliance on religious ritual in health practices; and the role of locally trained healers such as shamans, spirit mediums, and priests as health-care professionals. The subdiscipline of **ethnopharmacology** emerged from efforts to document and describe the local use of natural substances, such as herbs, powders, teas, and animal products, in healing remedies and practices. But today, as we will see, even Western biomedicine, which emphasizes science and technology in healing but also reflects a particular system of cultural meanings, is considered through the lens of ethnomedicine. Today medical anthropologists use the concept of ethnomedicine to refer to local health systems everywhere (Green 1999; Saillant and Genest 2007).

Healing Practices of Tibetan Buddhism Applied in Northern India. French anthropologist Laurent Pordié (2008) has documented one typical system of ethnomedicine—a variation of Tibetan medicine practiced in the sparsely populated Ladakh region of northern India. Roughly three times the size of Switzerland and straddling the northwestern Himalayas, Ladakh is home to 275,000 villagers, mostly Tibetans, living primarily in remote areas at altitudes up to 5,000 meters (16,400 feet). Their only health care is provided by approximately two hundred *amchis*, traditional healers whose healing practices are deeply rooted in Tibetan Buddhism.

Amchi medicine is based on achieving bodily and spiritual balance between the individual and the surrounding universe. *Amchis* diagnose ailments by asking questions of the patient, examining bodily wastes, and carefully taking the pulse. Recommended treatments include changes in diet and behavior—both social and religious—and the use of natural medicines made from local plants and minerals. Shaped into pills, these remedies are then boiled in water and taken by the patient as an infusion, or drink. Pordié reports that *amchi* treatments are effective for the vast majority of the Ladakhis' health problems, such as respiratory difficulty from the high altitude and smoke in dwellings, hypertension from high-salt diets, and psychological stress. *Amchis* do not perform surgery. Patients who need

An *amchi*, a traditional healer, mixes medicines in his home pharmacy in Ladakh, India.

surgery are transported, if possible, to an urban area to be treated by a doctor trained in Western biological medicine.

Amchi medicine plays a vital role in the survival of Ladakhis. But the *amchis* and their healing practices are under threat from Westernization, militarization, and economic liberalization. For example, the Indian government strongly favors Western biological medicine over traditional ethnomedicine, though it is still unable to provide care to its dispersed rural population. The pervasive presence of the Indian military in response to civil unrest in the bordering Kashmir region inhibits the movement of *amchis* as they gather plants and minerals for natural medicines. In addition, urbanization and modernization, particularly market-oriented economic activity, have increasingly fragmented community life. In the past, *amchi* healers bartered their services for help in plowing, harvesting, and raising livestock. The *amchis* then had time to forage for medicinal plants. But with the penetration of market-oriented economics even into the rural areas, the barter system has been undermined. *Amchis* must now run their therapeutic practices more like businesses, selling medicines and charging for services rather than bartering. Their time to gather medicines has become limited. And with increasing social mobility, the intergenerational transmission of *amchi* skills has been disrupted.

To address this challenge to the *amchi* system, Pordié and a French non-governmental organization, Nomad RSI, have been working with local *amchis*

MAP 14.1
Ladakh

to establish a coordinated system for growing medicinal plants and distributing them among far-flung villages. *Amchis* from across Ladakh now gather annually to share diagnosis and treatment strategies, and a school has been established to train new practitioners.

Although Tibetan medicine struggles in rural areas where it has been practiced for centuries, it is experiencing unprecedented prominence internationally. Pordié's study also considers how the local *amchi* system of healing is entering the global health arena. Over the last thirty years, as more Tibetans migrate abroad and carry their cultural and religious practices with them, Tibetan medicine has been embraced as an "alternative medicine." The international health market, particularly in Europe and North America, has welcomed Tibetan medicine as natural, spiritual, and holistic, drawing as it does from indigenous, traditional practices, Buddhist moral values, and Tibetan ecological worldviews. *Amchis* and their practices of Tibetan medicine have become quite popular. In this era of globalization, a transnational *amchi* is just as authentic as the *amchi* prescribing healing remedies in a remote village in Ladakh.

Medical anthropologists have played a significant role in documenting the diverse forms of treatment and care as well as the complex medical epistemologies (ways of knowing) that have been developed by local cultures across the globe. From the perspective of medical anthropology, all medical systems constitute a form of ethnomedicine because they develop from and are embedded in a particular local cultural reality. And from the perspective of medical anthropology, we might also call all healers ethno-healers, practicing local health knowledge about disease, illness, and health. We now turn to consider why this may be true, whether the healer is an *amchi* or a cardiovascular surgeon.

BIOMEDICINE

Biomedicine is the approach to health that has risen to predominance in many Western cultures. **Biomedicine** seeks to apply the principles of biology and the natural sciences (such as physics and chemistry) to the practice of diagnosing diseases and promoting healing. Individual and institutional practitioners of biomedicine—whether doctors, pharmacies, hospitals, medical schools, or pharmaceutical companies—work to clinically identify discrete natural disease entities that can be diagnosed and treated by biomedically trained health professionals. The term *biomedicine* encompasses many local variations and a wide range of treatment practices. But the use of medication, surgery, and other invasive treatments is characteristic of biomedical healing practices (Baer, Singer, and Susser 2003; Saillant and Genest 2007).

Varieties of biomedicine occur across Western industrialized countries, as we consider later in our discussion of the anthropology of birth. For example, British doctors are far less concerned about elevated blood pressure and cholesterol

biomedicine

A practice, often associated with Western medicine, that seeks to apply the principles of biology and the natural sciences to the practice of diagnosing disease and promoting healing.

counts than their counterparts in the United States. The German health system, which uses far fewer antibiotics than other Western health systems, recognizes two complementary approaches: *schulmedizin* ("school medicine"), which focuses on typical biomedical treatments, and *naturheilkunde* ("nature cure"), which draws on natural remedies. Biomedicine in the United States emphasizes the most extreme treatments—psychotropic drugs, antibiotics, cholesterol and blood pressure medications, C-section births, and hysterectomies (Payer 1996).

Because biomedicine is closely linked with Western economic and political expansion, it has taken hold well beyond its original local cultural boundaries and has increasingly gained an aura of universality, modernity, and progress. But medical anthropologists have been careful to point out the ways in which, like other ethnomedical systems, the epistemology (ways of knowing) and practice of Western biomedicine are rooted in a particular system of knowledge. This system draws heavily on European enlightenment values of rationality, individualism, and progress—values and ideas that are culturally specific and not universally held. The individual body is the focus of treatment. Diagnosis and treatment are based on rational scientific data. And there is a firm conviction that direct intervention through surgery and medications based on scientific facts will positively affect health.

Western biomedicine or alternative medicines? At a biotech company near Berlin, Germany, researchers develop natural remedies to complement biomedical treatments.

ARE THERE OTHER GLOBAL HEALTH SYSTEMS?

Although Western biomedicine is intimately tied to Western culture and its values, anthropologists also acknowledge that with the spread of Western cultural influences, biomedicine has crossed beyond its cultural and regional boundaries to become a global health system now used in a wide array of countries as well as in international health agencies that engage in health promotion globally. But are there health systems other than biomedicine that function on a global level? Earlier in this chapter, we discussed the growing popularity of Tibetan medicine, especially in Europe and North America. Now let's consider Chinese medicine today as one health system with a long history; elaborate theories of health, illness and the body; a global reach; and proven effectiveness (e.g., Farquhar 1986; Scheid 2002; Zhan 2009).

Chinese Medicine Today. In very general terms, Chinese medicine conceptualizes health as a harmonious relationship between Heaven and Earth, which are considered the major forces of the universe. An individual's *qi*—translated as "breath" or "air" and referring to an energy found in all living things—must be balanced and flowing in equilibrium with the rest of the universe for a person to be healthy. Illness occurs when the *qi* is blocked and the flow and balance are disrupted. In traditional Chinese medicine, health-care practices such as acupuncture, *tuina* (therapeutic massage), acupressure, moxibustion (the burning of herbs near the skin), and the consumption of healing herbs and

What are those purple circles on Olympic swimmer Michael Phelps' back and shoulders? Phelps, winner of a record 23 gold medals, is one of a growing number of athletes using the Chinese healing practice of cupping, a technique that places specialized cups on the skin, which, when heated, create suction to stimulate blood flow and healing.

teas promote health by restoring the free flow of *qi* along the body's meridians, or energy pathways (Farquhar 1986; Scheid 2002).

In her book *Other-Worldly: Making Chinese Medicine through Transnational Frames* (2009), medical anthropologist Mei Zhan challenges many of the stereotypes of Chinese medicine, including the idea that it is somehow emblematic of an ancient Chinese culture, regionally limited with fixed healing practices that are the antithesis of, or merely "alternative" to, Western biomedicine. Instead, Zhan argues that Chinese medical practices vary widely even within China. Rather than undergoing a regimented and fixed set of health-care practices, patients participate in a dynamic health-care environment. Patients and doctors carefully negotiate treatments. And no good physician ever writes the same prescription twice, because the treatment must meet the needs of each specific patient (Scheid 2002).

Zhan notes three key historical moments over the past century that have significantly reshaped modern Chinese medicine. First, the early-twentieth-century expansion of Western biomedicine into China influenced the practice of Chinese medicine. Western biomedicine's emphasis on institution building, laboratory research, clinical and teaching practices, and even insurance policies reshaped Chinese medical thinking and practice. Today the everyday world of Chinese medicine includes interactions with biomedical professionals. Patients move back and forth between biomedicine and Chinese medicine.

Second, upon the founding of the People's Republic of China in 1949, the new Chinese government moved to institutionalize traditional Chinese medicine, subsidize research, formalize teaching, and establish a process for professional certification. The government widely promoted traditional Chinese medicine as a low-tech, low-cost approach to preventive care and trained and deployed "barefoot doctors" to promote health care in every rural Chinese community. The government also exported traditional Chinese medicine—including medicines, doctors, and health-promotion strategies—to the developing world, particularly Africa, to establish international ties of solidarity with other developing nations. This move marked a rapid expansion of Chinese medicine beyond China's national borders into the international arena.

Finally, Zhan documents the shift of Chinese medicine beginning in the 1980s from primarily a developing-world medical practice to one with established niches in developed countries. Traditional Chinese medicine has become popular with cosmopolitan consumers in China, North America, and Europe, both as a preventive medicine and as an alternative treatment for illness when biomedicine proves ineffective. The flow of Chinese medical practitioners and Chinese medical knowledge have increased encounters with Chinese medicine, particularly along routes between Asia and Europe and across the Pacific Ocean.

Zhan carefully demonstrates how Chinese medicine—often viewed as an ancient, culturally specific, fixed ethnomedicine "alternative" to Western biomedicine—has been relocated in both time and space to represent a modern, effective, globally respected body of health-care practices (Farquhar 1994; Scheid and MacPherson 2012; Zhan 2009).

Chinese medicine is a globalized health system with its own internal logic for diagnosing disease and promoting healing. (*left*) Chinese diagram of meridians, or energy pathways, indicates potential sites of blockage that can be restored through treatment with acupuncture (*right*), massage, herbs, and teas.

How Do Different Cultural Conceptions of the Body Affect Health Practices?

We live in our bodies. We are embodied beings. Our bodies mediate all of our experiences of living in and encountering the world. But what exactly is a body, and what does the body signify?

Bodies are perceived, known, and understood in various ways by cultures and medical traditions around the world. Anthropological research has challenged the prevalent biomedical notion of the body as an isolated, natural, and universal object. Instead, anthropologists recognize the body as a product of specific environments, cultural experiences, and historical contexts. Culture has shaped the evolution of the human body and shapes individual bodies today. Culture shapes our experience of the world around us, including how we feel and how others feel about us. And health-care systems are a key site of contestation over the management of bodies.

BIOMEDICAL CONCEPTIONS OF THE BODY

Nancy Scheper-Hughes and Margaret Lock (1987) recount a now-famous story of a challenging case that illustrates the powerful influence of cultural values on understanding the body in biomedical healing practices. At a teaching hospital, the case of a woman suffering chronic, debilitating headaches was presented to a lecture hall of 250 medical students. When asked about her ailment, the woman recounted that her alcoholic husband beat her, that she had been virtually house-bound for five years while caring for her ailing and incontinent mother-in-law, and that she worried about her teenage son, who was failing high school. Then one of the medical students raised her hand and asked, "But what is the *real* cause of her headaches?" By this the student meant, What is the real *biomedical* diagnosis— what neurochemical changes in the individual's body created the pain? In the mind of the medical student, the patient's statements were irrelevant to the task of identifying the cause of her pain or determining a treatment. The student's biomedical training, with its focus on the individual body, science, and technology, had not prepared her to recognize that social experiences might produce embodied responses.

THE HUMAN MICROBIOME

Is a typical biomedical notion of the discrete, treatable, individual body really based in science? Recent scientific research suggests that our bodies are not as independent or as self-contained as we have thought. Researchers at the Human Microbiome Project have discovered that the human body, made up of 10 trillion cells, is also host to 100 trillion microbes—microscopic organisms such as bacteria, viruses, and fungi—that live on and within our bodies. Rather than being discrete biological entities, our bodies appear to be more like complex ecosystems (think tropical rain forests), habitats for trillions of different organisms living with us. Thus we can define the **human microbiome** as the complete collection of microorganisms in the body's ecosystem.

human microbiome
The complete collection of microorganisms in the human body's ecosystem.

These microbes are not random hitchhikers, opportunistic parasites, or dangerous outsider enemies of our bodies. They are deeply integrated into the ways our bodies work. Microbes help us digest food, synthesize vitamins, make natural antibiotics, produce natural moisturizer for the skin, guide the immune system, and spur the development of body parts (such as the intestines). Scientists suggest that we have evolved with these microbes as part of our personal ecosystem for promoting health and combating the pathogens that create disease in our bodies. We not only tolerate these microbes, we need them (Helmreich 2009).

Discoveries of the role of microbes in our bodies' experience of health and illness open the door to rethinking one of the central tenets of Western biomedicine—the notion of the discrete individual body—and offer new pathways for the innovative treatment of both common and rare diseases (Zimmer 2010, 2011).

THE BODY AND CHILDBIRTH ACROSS CULTURES

The anthropology of childbirth provides one clear example of the cross-cultural variation of health beliefs and practices and understandings of the body. Anthropologists consider childbirth a bio-social event. Yes, the physiology of childbirth—the biological process—is the same no matter where the birth occurs. But anthropological research shows that cultures around the world have developed unique social and cultural practices and beliefs about pregnancy, delivery, and the treatment of newborns and their mothers that shape the way childbirth is understood and experienced. Different cultures conceptualize birth in different ways, and these shared understandings shape women's experiences. For example, a popular view of birth in the United States sees it as a medical procedure—what Robbie Davis-Floyd (1992) calls the "technocratic birth." In this view, women become patients, seeking the assistance of a medical professional to resolve a dangerous life crisis. Brigitte Jordan and Robbie Davis-Floyd's (1993) study *Birth in Four Cultures* reveals that, in contrast, in Holland birth is perceived as an entirely natural process; in Sweden, as an intensely personal and fulfilling achievement; in Yucatán, Mexico, as a stressful but normal part of life. These differing conceptualizations shape and justify the practices each culture puts into place to support, monitor, and control the birth process. Such practices include the location of the birth, the personnel who attend, the decision-making authority as the birth proceeds, and the expectations of pain and pain management.

Birth practices have changed significantly over the last thirty years and brought about a significant decline in maternal and infant mortality and illness (World Health Organization 2015c). Yet Jordan and Davis-Floyd's 1993 study provides a historical snapshot of ways that cultural practices and beliefs may shape women's experiences of childbirth.

Birth experiences in Yucatán and the United States contrasted sharply. Birth for many Mayan women surveyed in Jordan's study occurred in a small, dimly lit home with a dirt floor, attended by a local midwife using everyday materials, while family life continued around them. Mayan women rested in a hammock, considered the best position for labor, although in the final stages of pushing the women might sit astride a wooden chair turned on its side. The husband and the woman's mother were usually present throughout the entire process. Other women of the extended family, particularly those who had given birth before, might be present as well. During the final stages of labor, the husband and the woman's mother took turns sitting behind the woman, supporting her head and lifting her up toward the ceiling to relieve pressure from the contractions. In a difficult labor, other women would provide emotional and physical support, offering encouragement and participating in "birth talk" by urging, cajoling, and challenging the mother to finish pushing her baby out into the world. There were no drugs and no machines (Jordan and Davis-Floyd 1993).

In contrast, Jordan and Davis-Floyd's study found that into the early 1990s 98 percent of American births occured in a sterile, brightly lit hospital with sophisticated equipment and the attention of highly trained medical professionals who enforced a strict separation of the laboring mother from family and daily life. The father may have been present. Elaborate machinery monitored pregnancy and birth. Sonograms and amniocentesis assessed the health of the fetus during pregnancy, and fetal heart monitors tracked the newborn's heartbeat and stress levels during delivery. Medications were sometimes administered through epidural injections near the spinal cord to deaden the mother's pain. To advance childbirth during a difficult delivery, obstetricians might perform episiotomies, surgically widening the opening to the birth canal.

As recently as 2015, one-third of all babies in the United States were delivered by Caesarean section, a surgical procedure by which the baby is removed directly from the mother's abdomen rather than through the birth canal. This number was an increase from 20.7 percent in 1996 (U.S. Centers for Disease Control and Prevention 2015). This rate of C-sections is among the highest in the world, a fact that raises questions about whether these procedures are performed out of necessity or are influenced by cultural understandings of birth and the institutional pressures that shape health care in hospitals. Rates also vary from region to region in the United States, a reflection of the regional cultural variations in the practice of Western medicine rather than an indication of regional variation in rates of complications.

Can culture shape women's experience of pain during childbirth? Jordan and Davis-Floyd note that some women in every culture give birth without pain. But a certain amount of pain is expected in almost all cultures. What differs from one medical system to another is the way in which that pain is handled. Their study explores the possibility that cultural expectations of pain during childbirth shape the actual experience and display of pain by laboring mothers.

Jordan and Davis-Floyd's study found that the use of pain medication during labor was not consistent across cultures. In the United States, pain medication was administered at the discretion of the medical attendants and was often delayed lest the drugs slow the course of labor. In order to receive medication, a woman had to convince her physician that her pain was severe. This dynamic shaped the woman's experience of childbirth, drawing attention away from the delivery and more toward pain—both the experience of pain and the performance of that pain. Obstetric wards in the United States, as a result of this negotiation between patient and physician, had a relatively high level of noise, anxiety, and vocal despair during the birth process.

In contrast, Jordan and Davis-Floyd (1993) found obstetric wards in Sweden to be characterized by quiet, intense concentration on the process of giving birth. Before labor began, Swedish women were introduced to a variety of pain medicines, their benefits, and side effects. During labor the women themselves made decisions about how much, if any, medication to take and when. Women did not need to convince medical staff of the need for pain medication.

The Dutch viewed birth as an entirely natural process. They administered no pain medication during the normal course of labor, even in many of the same situations that led to the use of pain medication in the United States. The Dutch, like the Maya of Yucatán, were reluctant to interfere with the birth process, waiting for nature to take its course and trusting that women's bodies know best how to handle the process. Birth was not considered a crisis or a medical emergency.

In Yucatán, pain was seen as a natural and expected part of childbirth. It was not frightening. The work of labor was considered a normal part of life. The suffering and pain would pass soon, especially if the mother worked hard. Labor was considered a collective process—an experience shared by the woman's husband, mother, and female family members.

Jordan and Davis-Floyd reflect that the intense experience of childbirth reinforced key Mayan cultural values, particularly local understandings of the importance of hard work, endurance, and tolerance of difficulty. The Maya viewed these values and personal qualities as desirable in childbirth as well as in life. During the stress of childbirth, women display these qualities in the public sphere.

The variation of cultural approaches to labor and childbirth—a common human biological activity—suggests the extent to which cultural concepts of the body, health, illness, and pain may shape every aspect of a medical system.

THE BODY AND DISABILITY

Anthropology's increasing attention to the body has been accompanied by a recent expansion of work on issues of disability—the embodied experiences of people with impairments as shaped by broader forms of social inequality (Ginsburg and Rapp 2013). Disability may include sensory impairments to hearing and sight, limited mobility, epilepsy, autism and psychiatric illness, or chronic pain or dementia related to aging, or it may result from a sudden illness like a heart attack, an accident, or warfare. Anyone can experience impairment and disability, and most people will at some point in their lives. In fact, being "able-bodied" might be considered only a temporary condition. This is a distinctive quality of disabilities when compared to other systems of power and inequality that may affect only certain portions of a population.

Significantly, anthropologists have explored the ways disability is lodged not simply in the body but is socially defined specifically by the often painful and isolating encounters with social and material conditions that "dis-able" and impair people considered to be atypical in a particular culture. So, for instance people restricted to wheelchairs experience their impairment—are "disabled"—differently by the presence or absence of accessibility ramps. Disabilities may interact with other stratified systems of power to create additional vulnerabilities. Poverty, warfare, natural disasters, and unequal access to health care directly affect the experience of disability. Through groundbreaking cross-cultural ethnographic work (Friedner 2015; Nakamura 2006; Ingstad and Whyte 2007; Kohrman 2005; Phillips 2011), anthropologists have also explored how the lived experience of "dis-ability" varies widely within and between cultures. (See Kulick and Rydstrom's study on sexuality and disability in Chapter 8.)

How Can Anthropologists Help Solve Health-Care Problems?

Anthropologists can apply research strategies and key theoretical concepts of our field to solve pressing public health problems, understand the spread of disease, and improve the delivery of health care. In fact, the work of an anthropologist may be just as crucial to explaining and resolving health challenges as that of a physician, epidemiologist, pathologist, or virologist. The following discussion illustrates this point through the groundbreaking efforts of anthropologist Paul Farmer working in Haiti.

CREATING A PUBLIC HEALTH SYSTEM IN RURAL HAITI

When the American Paul Farmer first visited Cange, Haiti, in 1983, the remote village of one hundred families was one of the poorest places in one of the world's poorest countries. Most people in Haiti lived on $1 a day, but residents of Cange lived on less. Along with intense poverty, Farmer found a village overwhelmed by high levels of infant mortality, childhood malnutrition, typhoid, dysentery, HIV/AIDS, and tuberculosis. Many residents were water refugees, having been pushed off their land by the construction of a hydroelectric dam that flooded their valley to provide power to Haiti's cities and irrigation for large landholders and agribusinesses downstream. With the best farmland taken out of production by the dam's reservoir, the surrounding area suffered from widespread deforestation, soil erosion, and terrible health statistics (Farmer 2006).

MAP 14.2
Cange

Farmer's work in Cange, popularized in the best-selling biography *Mountains beyond Mountains* (Kidder 2003), began with the encouragement of a Haitian Anglican priest, Fritz Lafontant, who had been working in the area for years. In 1984, the year after Farmer's first visit to Haiti, he enrolled in Harvard's medical school and doctoral program in anthropology. He believed that anthropology would be essential to addressing the health needs of poor Haitians. The delivery of medicines and medical procedures would not be enough, he felt. Deeper questions would need to be asked: What made the people sick? How could they stay healthy after being treated? The basic approaches of an anthropologist—understanding the local language, norms, values, classifications of reality, and religious beliefs—would help a trained physician to think about health in the broadest possible sense.

How do you create an effective public health system? (*left*) People seeking health care in rural Haiti sleep outside following long journeys from their villages. (*center*) Patients receive direct treatment at a clinic. (*right*) Anthropologist Paul Farmer at the opening of a new teaching and primary care hospital in Mirebalais, north of Haiti's capital.

While at Harvard, Farmer immediately began to apply what he was learning, using the research strategies of anthropology and the professional knowledge of medicine to create a public health system for Cange. Living in the community and speaking the local language, Farmer engaged in a process of listening to the residents' needs and experiences and working with them to identify and treat their public health problems. First he recruited a few villagers to help him conduct a health census. Moving from hut to hut in Cange and two neighboring villages, the census takers identified the breadth of the residents' health problems and established a baseline by which to measure future success. To address the community's needs, Farmer launched Partners in Health, or Zanmi Lasante in the Cange language, with financial support from backers in the United States.

Zanmi Lasante began to create multiple lines of defense to protect the Cange villagers' health. Clean water came first. Because they lived on Haiti's central plateau, the villagers had been climbing down an 800-foot hillside to draw water from the stagnant reservoir created by the hydroelectric dam. Using old plastic jugs and calabash gourds, they had been carrying water back up the hill to their huts, where it sometimes sat uncovered for days. But now Father Lafontant recruited a construction crew from an Episcopal Church diocese in South Carolina to tap into an underground river to provide fresh water to the families at the top of the hill. Thereafter, Farmer and his associates noticed that the incidence of infant deaths began to drop almost immediately.

Sanitation and hygiene came next. Father LaFontant organized the construction of latrines (outdoor toilets) to improve human waste disposal and protect the water supply. He and Farmer raised money to replace the dirt floors and thatched roofs of the residents' crude lean-to homes with tin roofs and cement floors. An expanded village school provided a place to teach children to read and write and a place to teach the community about basic health practices. Malnourished schoolchildren received free meals with dignity. Childhood vaccinations dramatically improved health in the community.

Perhaps most significant, Zanmi Lasante trained local community members as community health workers. Being familiar with the local language, social structure, values, and religious beliefs, the community health workers were able to identify emerging health-care problems, administer vaccinations, and assist people in taking medications. The newly constructed health clinic and hospital of Zanmi Lasante served those who were too sick to be cared for at home. Over time, Zanmi Lasante became one of the largest nongovernmental health-care providers in Haiti, serving an area of 1.2 million people with more than 4,000 doctors, nurses, and community health workers.

Farmer's research and work in Cange explored how anthropology could tackle the day-to-day challenges of health on the ground—nutrition, clean water, prevention of illness, and promotion of health. Public health work could be guided and greatly improved by the strategies and theoretical concerns of anthropology. However, as Farmer notes, to truly make a difference, anthropology must be used not only to analyze and scrutinize a problem but also to turn research into action (Farmer 1985).

Why Does the Distribution of Health and Illness Mirror That of Wealth and Power?

Writing in the late 1800s, Rudolf Virchow, a renowned pathologist considered to be one of the ancestors of medical anthropology, asked why the distribution of health and illness appeared to mirror the distribution of wealth and power. Although anthropology from its inception has focused on concerns of health and illness, in recent years Virchow's question has become central to the critical medical anthropology approach to health and illness. If the distribution of health and illness cannot be explained solely on the basis of genetic vulnerabilities, individual behaviors, and the random spread of pathogens through a population, then what are the root causes of health disparities?

HEALTH TRANSITION AND CRITICAL MEDICAL ANTHROPOLOGY

Over the twentieth century, much of the human population experienced dramatic improvements in health. Life expectancy rose significantly. Infectious diseases (with the exception of HIV) declined as the primary causes of death and were replaced by chronic diseases such as cancer and heart disease and by syndromes such as stroke. Unfortunately, despite improvements in global health statistics, local populations have not experienced the **health transition** equally. Inequalities of health—sometimes extreme—and unequal access to health care persist between local populations and within them.

Although overall human life expectancy increased from 31 years in 1900 to 70.5 in 2015 (from 49.2 in 1900 to 78.9 in 2015 in the United States), extreme differences exist among countries. As Table 14.1 shows, in 2015 Hong Kong ranked first in overall life expectancy at birth at 83.7 years. Swaziland ranked last of 200 countries, with an overall life expectancy at birth of 49.2 years. The United States ranked 42nd.

These statistics raise crucial questions about health disparities that are central to the concerns of critical medical anthropologists. If the United States is the richest and most technologically advanced country in the world, why is its population's average life expectancy shorter than that of people in forty-one other countries? Why is the average life expectancy of the population of Swaziland 30 percent below the global average?

Critical medical anthropology examines health as a system of power. Specifically, it explores the impact of inequality on human health by examining (1) how economic and political systems, race, class, gender, and sexuality create and perpetuate unequal access to health care, and (2) how health systems themselves are systems of power that generate disparities in health by defining who is sick, who gets treated, and how. Critical medical anthropologists look beyond Western biomedicine's traditional focus on individual patients' problems; instead, they analyze patterns of health and illness among entire groups. Critical medical anthropologists search for the origins of these health disparities, the mechanisms that perpetuate them, and strategies for overcoming them (Baer, Singer, and Susser 2003; Budrys 2010).

Patterns of inequality in a culture create patterns of inequality in health care. Health practices and policies in turn create and reinforce patterns of inequality. We might actually say that illness can have social origins in poverty, violence, fear of violence, and discrimination based on race, ethnicity, gender, sexuality, and age. Illness and disease can result from cultural patterns of inequality and the distribution of health-care resources within a population (Schulz and Mullings 2006).

STAFF ATTITUDES AFFECT HEALTH-CARE DELIVERY IN A NEW YORK WOMEN'S CLINIC

Various systems of power—including economics, politics, race, class, gender, and sexuality—shape the distribution and accessibility of health-care resources (Chapman and Berggren 2005). In *Reproducing Race* (2011), legal scholar and anthropologist Khiara Bridges examines the ways in which race, class, and gender intersect to shape the delivery of health care in a women's health clinic at a famous trauma hospital on Manhattan's East Side. This facility provides prenatal,

TABLE 14.1
Global Life Expectancy by Country

Country (state/territory)	Rank	Life Expectancy at Birth (in years)
Hong Kong	1	83.7
Japan	2	83.3
Italy	3	82.8
Switzerland	4	82.7
Singapore	5	82.6
Iceland	6	82.3
Spain	7	82.3
Australia	8	82.1
Israel	9	82.1
Sweden	10	81.9
Netherlands	17	81.3
Germany	21	80.7
United Kingdom	28	80.5
United States	42	78.9
Mexico	56	76.5
China	70	75.4
Egypt	119	70.8
World average		70.5
India	144	67.5
Laos	151	65.5
Papua New Guinea	165	62.3
Haiti	166	62.3
Nigeria	193	52.3
Swaziland	200	49.2

United Nations Department of Economic and Social Affairs, Population Division. 2015. "World Population Prospects, the 2015 Revision." http://esa.un.org/unpd/wpp/

MAP 14.3
New York City

How might dynamics of race, gender, age, and class affect the medical care that patients receive in a hospital, clinic, or doctor's office?

delivery, and postpartum checkups and services to pregnant women who are poor. The women's health clinic of Alpha Hospital (a pseudonym), which also serves as a top-tier teaching hospital, treats an incredibly diverse population of patients, including some whites but mostly people of color. Because of their economic status, all patients qualify for the U.S. federal government's Medicaid program.

In contrast to the patient population, physicians working in Alpha's women's health clinic are predominantly white. Most medical staffers are women of color but of immigrant backgrounds. Tensions exist between these groups. During a year and a half of fieldwork, Bridges documented the stereotypes and prejudices expressed by physicians and medical staff about their patients. In a Medicaid-supported women's health clinic, women of color are already treated in ways that non-Medicaid patients would not be. For example, because the government has categorized Medicaid patients as an "at risk" population whose exceptional health issues require special treatment, these women are subjected to interviews, counseling sessions, intrusive procedures, and invasive examinations that non-Medicaid pregnant women do not undergo. In addition to the exceptional institutional requirements, Bridges raises the possibility that physicians' racial attitudes may contribute to the health disparities experienced by patients who are women of color.

Bridges's research documents a racist oral tradition within the medical profession that features stories and folklore about black women's bodies. One common theme centers on the supposedly unique strength and hardiness of black women and other women of color, who, often referred to as more "primitive" by health workers, were assumed to be able to endure more intense pain and overcome more hardship in medical procedures than other women.

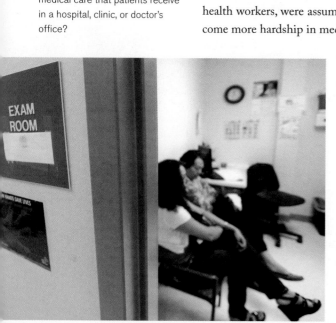

Bridges presents these troubling anecdotes in relationship to statistics that show significant racial disparities in infant and maternal mortality. In the United States, black babies are nearly two and a half times more likely to die as infants than white babies. Black women are three times more likely than white women to die from complications of pregnancy and childbirth. In New York City, they are five times more likely to do so!

Are these women and infants dying because they are poor or because they are black? Bridges suggests that the mortality rates reflect more than poverty. Studies consistently show that racial and ethnic minorities in the United States receive lower-quality health care. But even when ruling out variables such as insurance status, income, age, and severity of medical condition, black women and infants have higher mortality rates than whites with similar profiles.

Bridges notes a deep reluctance within Western medicine to invade physicians' privacy by interrogating their human frailties. Perhaps as a result, the existence of physicians' racism is never addressed in the larger medical literature. But based on the patterns of behavior she observed at Alpha Hospital's women's health clinic, Bridges argues for the need to explore the possibility that physicians' views regarding patients of color may lead to different treatment during pregnancy and childbirth, disparate health outcomes, and higher infant and maternal mortality rates (Bridges 2011; Chapman and Berggren 2005).

How Is Globalization Changing the Experience of Health and Illness and the Practice of Medicine?

The current era of worldwide interconnectedness associated with globalization is bringing profound changes to individuals' experience of health and illness and to the practice of medicine. Various facets of medical migration, as well as global humanitarian efforts and encounters among multiple systems of healing, make today's era of globalization unique.

MEDICAL MIGRATION

Globalization today has launched a new and intensified era of **medical migration**—not only of disease but also of health-care systems, diagnoses, and treatments (Roberts and Scheper-Hughes 2011), with both positive and negative results. Medical treatments and technologies cross national borders as vaccines have been introduced worldwide to treat previously fatal or debilitating illnesses such as polio, tuberculosis, measles, mumps, rubella, tetanus, typhoid, and diphtheria. Antibiotics treat bacterial infections. Pesticides inhibit the spread of disease-carrying insects. At the same time, diseases migrate on a global scale. HIV/AIDS knows no national boundaries. Medical researchers travel with their scientific knowledge and technology in search of subjects for medical research and experimental clinical trials. Images of youth, health, and beauty (as well as consumer products that purport to provide and prolong them) infuse global media.

Medical travelers cross borders in search of cures and therapies for every condition possible, from heart disease to obesity, failed organs, infertility, and sexual dysfunction. Senior citizens travel from the United States to Canada and Mexico to buy lower-priced generic drugs that are unavailable or unaffordable at home. The

medical migration
The movement of diseases, medical treatments, and entire health-care systems, as well as those seeking medical care, across national borders.

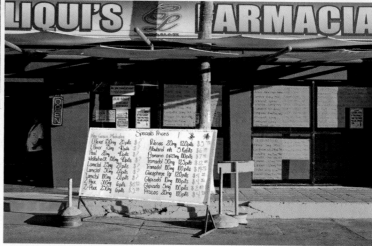

Globalization has spurred many forms of medical migration. (*clockwise from top*) Crowds seek healing at the sacred grotto sanctuary of Our Lady of Lourdes in France. Thousands of Americans cross the border from Arizona to buy prescription drugs at Mexican pharmacies for a fraction of their U.S. cost. A school bus driver, Edna Harsha, from Minnesota, traveled to Bombay, India, for hip replacement surgery.

wealthy travel on tourist visas to impoverished countries to receive organ transplants. The poor travel without documents to wealthy countries to receive basic health care. Religious pilgrims travel to sacred shrines, holy mountains, and healing waters.

MULTIPLE SYSTEMS OF HEALING

The current era of medical migration has spurred the encounter of multiple systems of healing, including ideas of health and illness that overlap and often conflict. The intersection of multiple cultural approaches to healing, called medical pluralism, often creates tensions, especially in the encounter between Western biomedicine and other cultural patterns of health and illness. But the engagement also provides opportunities for additional alternative and complementary choices and medical options to emerge (Lock 1993, 2002).

Colliding Cultures: Hmong Refugees and the U.S. Health-Care System.

Anne Fadiman's *The Spirit Catches You and You Fall Down* (1997) captures the intensity and danger of cross-cultural medical encounters through the story of the Lees, a Hmong refugee family from Laos in Southeast Asia. The Lees settled in the city of Merced in California's agricultural Central Valley in the 1980s. More than 150,000 Hmong refugees fled Laos in the 1970s and 1980s. Many had fought clandestinely with the United States on the losing side of wars in Vietnam and Laos. More than 12,000 Hmong eventually settled in Merced, a city of only 61,000 people.

MAP 14.4
Laos

The Lees' fourteenth child, Lia Lee, was born on July 9, 1982, apparently a healthy, happy baby. But at three months of age, her seizures began. At first, her family comforted her and cared for her at home. Her uncontrollable convulsions on October 24 led the family to Merced Community Medical Center (MCMC), a small county hospital but also a teaching hospital where first-year residents from the University of California–Davis train in family practice. The October 24 visit began a long and painful encounter—a collision—between the Lee family and the U.S. health-care system.

Unbeknownst to the doctors at MCMC, the Lees had already diagnosed Lia's illness as *qaug dab peg*, which translates into English as epilepsy. Familiar with *qaug dab peg* in their own cultural context, the Lees were ambivalent about their daughter's illness. The seizures, they knew, could be dangerous. But among the Hmong, those suffering from *qaug dab peg* were held in high esteem. Many became powerful shamans—traditional healers and community visionaries. The Lees had come to the hospital for their daughter to be healed, but they also wondered about her potentially auspicious future.

Also unbeknownst to the MCMC doctors, the Lees knew what had caused Lia's illness and how to treat it. She suffered from soul loss. Her older sister had allowed the front door of their small home to slam, and the loud noise had scared Lia's soul away. An elaborate ritual of soul-calling conducted by a Hmong shaman could trap the lost soul and return it to Lia's body. But her seizures on that October night were overwhelming, and her parents feared that she would die without immediate care.

By the time the Lees arrived at the hospital, the seizures had stopped. With no clear symptoms to treat, the doctors were at a loss. The hospital had no translator, and the Lees spoke no English. The resident on call misdiagnosed the remaining symptoms as an infection, prescribed medication, and sent the family home. Unfortunately, the prescription and medication instructions were written in English, which the Lees could not understand. Lia Lee was misdiagnosed at the hospital again on November 11. Finally, on March 3, 1983, the family arrived with Lia still convulsing. A young family member who spoke some English translated. The resident on call diagnosed the cause as epilepsy. Then the child was subjected to a battery of invasive tests, including a spinal tap, a CT scan, a chest X-ray, and blood work—none of which the hospital staff could adequately explain to Lia's parents. The child had experienced five months of seizures small and large without proper diagnosis and medication, and now she endured a terrifying night at the hospital.

Between the ages of eight months and four and a half years, Lia Lee was admitted to MCMC seventeen times and made more than one hundred outpatient visits for treatment of her seizures. Over the same period, her doctors prescribed fourteen different medications in different combinations and dosages, changing her prescription twenty-three times—all with a family unfamiliar with English, Western medical practices, or the U.S. system of weights and measures needed to determine the proper dosage.

The collision of cultures escalated when doctors decided that Lia Lee's ongoing seizures were caused by her parents' failure to comply with the medication prescriptions. This, the lead doctor determined, qualified as child neglect and child abuse. Acting on the doctor's concerns, the county courts ordered Lia Lee removed from her parents' custody and placed in foster care so that her medicines could be properly administered. The doctors thought they were acting to protect the child. Her parents, however, unable to understand the medical, legal, or moral logic of removing a child from her family and convinced that they were doing everything in their power to care for their daughter, could only imagine that they were being punished for some unknown reason.

The courts eventually returned Lia Lee to her parents after nearly a year in foster care. Her condition had not improved. Her parents, in fact, felt that her cognitive abilities and social skills had deteriorated during the year away. Despite the parents' efforts to comply with Lia's drug regimen, another series of catastrophic epileptic seizures landed her in MCMC again and finally in a children's hospital in nearby Fresno. Treatment of the seizures was ultimately ineffective. Despite what hospital staff considered heroic measures, Lia was left with the dramatically reduced brain activity that doctors call a "persistent vegetative state." Doctors removed all life support and feeding tubes. She was returned to MCMC and finally to the Lees' home.

Considering her lingering fevers, the medical professionals expected her to die. But Lia's parents placed her in soothing herbal baths, fed her, carried her with them, slept with her in their bed, and continued the elaborate Hmong rituals of soul-calling to return her to health. Though her brain activity never returned, Lia did not die. Her parents were convinced that all the medicines the doctors had forced on her had left her in this condition. (Indeed, Fadiman found some evidence suggesting that Lia's massive final seizure may have been caused by a hospital-acquired infection.) They hoped that their traditional healing methods might still return her lost soul to her body.

Bridging Cultural Divides via Illness Narratives. Fadiman's interviews found that the parties in this cross-cultural health encounter held vastly different views of what had occurred. Most of the doctors criticized the parents as uncooperative. They debated whether this stemmed from cultural barriers, lack of intelligence, or character flaws that kept them from caring properly for their daughter. Many saw the parents as ungrateful for all the effort and resources that had been expended on their daughter's case. Few made any attempt to ask the Lees how they understood Lia's illness and how they would treat it. In contrast, the Lees considered most of the medical staff to be uncommunicative, arrogant, cold, and punitive; they also described the medical procedures Lia had undergone as invasive, culturally inappropriate, and ineffective. They never understood how the government could take their beloved daughter from them to be put in the care of strangers.

At the conclusion of her research, Fadiman contacted a preeminent medical anthropologist, Arthur Kleinman of Harvard University. Kleinman, a specialist in cross-cultural issues in health and illness, has been instrumental in formulating a concept of collecting illness narratives as a way to bridge cultural divides in treating illness and promoting health (Kleinman 1988). **Illness narratives** are the personal stories that people tell to explain their illness. The narratives reveal the psychological, social, and cultural aspects that give illness its context and meaning. These stories can provide healers with an essential framework for developing treatment strategies that will make sense to the patient and have the greatest chance of success.

Would Lia Lee's treatment would have been effective had the MCMC medical staff asked the family to provide this illness narrative—the cultural framework through which they viewed the cause and potential treatment of her illness? Doing so might have provided an avenue to engage the family in a cooperative treatment process. Through that process, multiple systems of healing and concepts of health and illness might have intersected to create a multifaceted approach to healing for Lia Lee.

Encounters of distinct medical systems like that experienced by Lia Lee and her family in the California health-care system will only increase as globalization continues to break down barriers to the flow of ideas, people, diseases, medical treatments, and health practitioners from one world region to another. These encounters will continue to challenge and expand our notions of disease, illness, and health care. As we have seen in this chapter, medical anthropologists are deeply engaged in the analysis and understanding of these transitions and in the articulation of strategies to develop and promote sophisticated, people-centered, and holistic approaches to the challenges of health and illness.

Foua Yang weeps as she talks about her daughter, Lia Lee, who died on August 31, 2012, at the age of 30 after a lifelong struggle for health. A collision of two cultural approaches to healing left her severely wounded in childhood.

illness narratives

The personal stories that people tell to explain their illnesses.

Toolkit

Thinking Like an Anthropologist:
Health in the Individual and in the Global Population

The human body is a spectacularly sophisticated organism. Its 10 trillion cells constitute complex cardiovascular, pulmonary, and digestive systems made up of muscles, ligaments, organs, veins, and arteries, all shaped and guided by approximately 20,000 protein-coding genes that form our DNA sequence. The body, which has evolved over millions of years, enables us to interact with one another, reproduce our species, and adapt to the remarkable variety of environments found on Earth.

Healthy bodies are produced through a complex interaction between genetics and culture. The human genetic code provides a basic framework for the body's growth, but culture and the natural environment influence how our bodies actually develop. Nutrition, disease, and exercise, along with our collective human health-care practices, affect what we look like, how we feel, how well we live, and how long we live. Even the human mind is not fully formed at birth. Nutrition, stimulation, affection, and trauma after birth continue to shape the contours of the brain.

When medical anthropologists consider issues of health, they think about both the individual body and the social body. As discussed in this chapter, we humans and our individual bodies do not live in isolation. Nor is our health created in isolation. We live in relation to one another as part of a social body—a collection of individuals whose health is tied to the success of the group as well (Scheper-Hughes and Lock 1987). The health of the football players discussed in the chapter opener, like the health of Lia Lee, is directly related to the health of those around them, to understandings of bodies, and to the system of health care created and shared by the larger culture in which they live.

As you think more about health and illness—perhaps your own personal experiences or those of people around you—remember the big questions we have been exploring:

- How does culture shape our ideas of health and illness?

- How do different cultural conceptions of the body affect health practices?

- How can anthropologists help solve health-care problems?

- Why does the distribution of health and illness mirror that of wealth and power?

- How is globalization changing the experience of health and illness and the practice of medicine?

After reading this chapter, are you able to apply these questions to specific situations?

As we have seen, medical anthropologists examine the diverse strategies that cultures have developed to protect and promote the health of the body. And they work to apply the methodological and analytical tools of anthropology to enhance and expand health care in the face of increasing global health inequalities. Debates about health and illness are all around us: Will all fifty U.S. states expand Medicaid eligibility for the poor as envisioned by the 2010 Affordable Care Act? Will the law address women's reproductive health needs? Will the Medicare eligibility age be raised, making it harder for seniors to find health coverage? Will your college or university adequately fund its student health center to provide for all of a student's health needs? Who sets the health center's policies and budget? Would you consider joining or supporting an organization like Paul Farmer's Partners in Health (see p. 412) to help address the health-care needs of people in another part of the world? How will you engage these debates? Thinking like an anthropologist can help you better understand and address these issues, whether they present themselves as your own personal issues of health and illness, those of your friends and family, or the health of the global human population.

Key Terms

Chapter 15
Art and Media

In a favela, or shantytown, set on a steep hillside above Rio de Janeiro, Brazil, a remarkable 4,000-square-foot miniature model of the city overlooks the sprawling metropolis below. Known as Morrinho ("Little Hill"), this virtual urban world began as a children's game in 1997 and today draws the attention of government officials, filmmakers, development agencies, and artists from around the world.

Working and playing together with other neighborhood kids, two brothers began to construct the miniature city out of discarded bricks, tiles, mortar, and borrowed masonry tools. As the game gradually grew in size and complexity, streets began to emerge, followed by homes, restaurants, stores, hospitals, and police stations. Each of the children began to inhabit the game, making avatars for themselves from bottle caps and batteries. The streets came alive with human interactions: friendships and fights, games and business. The constructed city took on a life of its own, yet it was a life that reflected and illuminated human relations and social conditions in the favela and the city of Rio.

Youth in a Brazilian shantytown have constructed a miniature city where they reenact their complex urban world in an elaborate game started in 1997.

Today thousands of avatars placed within the miniature city engage in an elaborate dramatization of community life. They live and die, work and play, break the law and make love. Battles rage between gangs and with police. Brazilian pennies have become currency, exchanged in the game for goods and services, motorcycle rides, and bags of drugs. Each youth controls his or her avatar and portion of the model.

Anthropologist Alessandro Angelini has conducted ethnographic fieldwork in this miniature world and the surrounding community since 2008. He notes the ways in which Morrinho has developed significance beyond the interactive model city, particularly as the youths' manipulation of miniature urban life has cast a spotlight on the intersection of poverty, class, power, kinship, identity, the state, and politics. For instance, Morrinho has drawn the attention of Brazilian political authorities. The community—now well known in Rio and beyond—became one of the first favelas to receive state infrastructure improvements, including sewage systems, housing, road paving, lighting, pathways, and railings. The community was also one of the first to be targeted with increased police presence and paramilitary security forces as the government sought to pacify and eliminate any undesirable elements.

Morrinho has also drawn the attention of artists and activists, crossing a boundary between play, creative expression, politics, and art. Tourists visit from Rio and beyond. Filmmakers document the story of the miniature city and its surrounding community through artistic films shown at international festivals. A small group of Morrinho's originators have been invited on multiple occasions since 2004 to reproduce a model of Morrinho at art festivals in cities such as Barcelona, Paris, Vienna, Munich, Venice, and Innsbruck, as well as in places in Holland, Colombia, and East Timor. Collaborating with local underprivileged youth from South London in the summer of 2010, the group created an installation of Morrinho at a prominent Brazilian arts festival in England, while adding to their miniature city certain elements of London—Big Ben, prisons, and other features important to London youth. In these settings what began as a game is admired as art, not as play (Angelini 2016).

In this chapter we will explore the array of human creative expression and interaction that anthropologists consider when exploring the world of art. Humans express themselves creatively and interact meaningfully through the visual and written arts, movement, sound, and more. An anthropological approach to art may include attention to paintings, drawings, design, weavings, photographs, film, sculpture, architecture, dance, music, songs, games, sports, clothing, cuisine, and even virtual online design and creativity. In addition, we will consider the intersection of art and globalization, art and politics, and art and media as technologies such as television, radio, film, and Internet-based social media establish new venues for creative expression and new avenues for communicating and engaging those expressions. In particular, we will consider the following questions:

- **What is art?**
- **What is unique about how anthropologists study art?**
- **What is the relationship between art and power?**
- **How do art and media intersect?**

By the end of the chapter you will have gained an understanding of the unique approach that anthropologists take to the study of art, the many ways in which art reflects and transforms culture, and the ways in which globalization and new forms of media are transforming art and its dissemination.

What Is Art?

Anthropologists define **art** broadly as all the ideas, forms, techniques, and strategies that humans employ to express themselves creatively and to communicate their creativity and inspiration to others. Art may include a vast array of music, songs, stories, paintings, plays, design, sculpture, architecture, clothing, food, and games. But art is not limited to the artist.

art
All ideas, forms, techniques, and strategies that humans employ to express themselves creatively and to communicate their creativity and inspiration to others.

THE ANTHROPOLOGY OF ART

Art is both created and received. Cooking and building, fashion and oratory, decorating and dressing, sewing and play all represent media through which artists and audience communicate. Through these often dynamic encounters, art takes its shape not only in creation but also in perception. In the chapter-opening story, for example, the full impact of the game created by the young people of Morrinho emerges in the interaction of those who are creating it with those who are perceiving it, interpreting it, and making it come alive for the community—a community that stretches far beyond local boundaries.

When thinking anthropologically about art in its global context, it is helpful to first consider some of the common but flawed assumptions that Western traditions have developed about how to evaluate what is and is not art. In particular, we will examine how the anthropology of art challenges commonplace notions of (1) a distinction between fine art and popular art, (2) the existence of a universal art aesthetic, and (3) the assumption of qualitative differences between Western art and so-called primitive art.

Fine Art versus Popular Art.
Art in Western traditions has often been associated with notions of "high culture" or "fine art," especially elite representations of visual and performance arts experienced in formal venues. Paintings and sculptures displayed in museums and art galleries; operas, symphonies, and ballets performed in recital halls; musicals and plays performed in theaters; fashion shows on runways; and fine cuisine prepared in expensive restaurants fit a view of **fine art** as the province of the elite. Such art is often evaluated and portrayed in contrast to **popular art**—less refined and less sophisticated creative expressions associated with the general population—in the same way that high culture might be simplistically compared to popular culture.

fine art
Creative expression and communication often associated with cultural elites.

popular art
Creative expression and communication often associated with the general population.

What is art? Art can be expressed in various venues and through an array of media. (*left to right*): *Maman* by Louise Bourgeois at the Guggenheim Museum, Bilbao, Spain; Chinese artists performing Beijing Opera at the National Theater in Algeria; and Stingray Mola, a fabric design of the Kuna Indians of Panama, Central America.

From an anthropological perspective, however, art is not the sole province of the elites or professional artists. Art is integral to all of human life. As such, it can be expressed through elaborate performances in specialized venues as well as through routine activities in mundane settings. Seen from a broad anthropological perspective, any members of a group can create and experience art.

The significance of art cannot be underestimated as anthropologists consider the full expression of human life. All creativity expressed through cultural products such as songs, paintings, dance, architecture, clothing, games, and food carries rich deposits of information about culture as a system of meaning and as a system of power. In fact, the very distinction between fine art and popular art may have more to do with political choices and hierarchies of power than with an intrinsic character of the art itself. Who decides, for instance, what will be performed in an opera house or displayed in a national museum? Who directs and who funds the selection, acquisition, and presentation (Thornton 2009; Werner 2006)? Can you identify other cultural dynamics of power and stratification—perhaps race, gender, class, religion, or sexuality—that might be reflected in these decisions and representations of what is fine art and what is popular art? (Marcus and Myers 1995; see Perkins and Morphy 2006; Schneider and Wright 2006.)

Considering Aesthetics across Cultures. The human encounter with art entails an aesthetic experience—broadly speaking, the perception through one's senses in contrast with the perception through intellect and logic.

Western art traditions, specifically those in Europe and North America, have tended to focus primarily on the aesthetic value of art and on a particular concept of aesthetics associated with certain standards of beauty, creativity, and innovation that are presumed to represent the most refined expressions of a group's culture. But is there a universal art aesthetic found across cultures that informs what people consider to be art and not art? Is there a **universal gaze**—an intrinsic way of perceiving art—that guides the ways people respond to art? Anthropologists of art have been deeply involved in this debate.

The Western concept of a universal art aesthetic traces back to the German philosophers Immanuel Kant (1724–1804) and Georg W. F. Hegel (1770–1831). They suggested that nature creates a universal aesthetic in humans—particularly a sense of what is beautiful—and that it establishes the foundation of a universal gaze through which all art can be seen. Through this universal gaze, art can provide viewers with a "transcendental" aesthetic experience, lift them out of the day-to-day, and transform their vision of the world (Stoller 2003).

A presumption of a universal art aesthetic was prevalent in much of the Western art world throughout most of the twentieth century. Reflecting this, Western art institutions, particularly those focusing on fine art, strove to reinforce this aesthetic experience through their style of presentation. Beginning in the last half of the twentieth century, curators displayed art in a minimalist manner, perhaps only accompanied by a piece's title, date, and name of artist, in an attempt to allow the art to speak for itself. Neutral, objective presentation encouraged the contemplation of objects removed from their worldly context, including their social and economic conditions of production, marketing, and consumption. Similarly, architects designed the physical spaces of Western art galleries and museums to symbolize this universal aesthetic, constructing high ceilings, bare white walls, and open areas that offered unique spaces for experiencing objects' transcendental qualities. The intent was for people to experience art as art—the intrinsic aesthetic of art objects re-created through a universal gaze.

Anthropologists of art have actively challenged the widespread belief in and representation of a universal art aesthetic. Not all cultures have the same aesthetic. Perceptions of beauty, imagination, skill, and style vary widely across cultures, as do approaches to artistic ideas, objects, and practices. In fact, what many people have considered to be a universal aesthetic has frequently proven to be a unique product of Western history and culture (Alexander 1996; Alpers 1991; Karp and Lavine 1991; Price 1989).

The expectations of art and the cultural frameworks for perceiving art may also vary from place to place and even within different cultures. Art may be viewed as beautiful and inspirational: A painting, sculpture, dance, or song may bring pleasure and joy to those who experience it. But the perception and response to art is not limited to only those emotions. Art may also shock, terrify,

How does the presentation of art—for instance, in this minimalist gallery—affect your experience and understanding of it?

horrify, or anger its audience. Like other key elements of culture, art is deeply embedded in the processes of enculturation that shape the observer's perceptions, expectations, and experience when evaluating art.

To further illustrate the vast range of possible aesthetic perspectives, consider the following simple contrasts. Whereas Western art traditions may emphasize innovation and originality—creating something entirely new—other traditions may celebrate improvisation on already-existing themes (Boas 1927; Price 1989). In such traditions, artistic value is created as the artist explores variations on established themes (Vogel 1991). Likewise, whereas many Western cultures may idealize the artist as an individual genius—as a cultural outsider separated from mundane daily life—other cultures may prioritize engagement with the audience and interaction with the community as the highest aspects of artistic expression. In such instances, the artist may be celebrated for playing a central role in the community's life rather than for his or her individual behavior (Perkins and Morphy 2006).

Beyond "Primitive" Art. Western art traditions have often created a problematic distinction between Western art and so-called primitive art. Early anthropologists played key roles in the nineteenth and early twentieth centuries in building great ethnographic museum collections to store and display the art and life ways of "other" cultures for a Western audience, though these treasure troves were often acquired through the colonial encounter (that is, taken rather than purchased or borrowed).

The Western art world became interested in what came to be known as "primitive art" in the early twentieth century. At that time, modernist European artists such as Pablo Picasso began to incorporate African and Oceanic art features and themes into their own work, though largely without reference to the art's original cultural context. In the twentieth century, museums and galleries mounted prominent displays, dioramas, and collections of "primitive" art itself (typically, the art of Africa, Oceania, and Latin America).

In contrast to the anthropological approach to world art, which seeks to understand the development and meaning of local art forms within their unique and complex cultural contexts, the tendency in Western art traditions to draw clear distinctions between Western and "primitive" art reinforced the perception of a hierarchy of world art and an evolutionary trajectory in its development from simple to complex, primitive to civilized. The tendency to display art from other cultures without reference to its original context or meaning reinforced the stereotypes about non-Western people and their relationship to Western civilization.

Anthropologists of art (as well as economic anthropologists and political anthropologists) reject an evolutionary framing and evaluation. As noted, through their research and writing, as well as through direct engagement with Western art institutions, anthropologists of art have been instrumental in challenging and transforming the ways museums and other institutions of art depict non-Western cultures and their creative expressions. These anthropologists have also been encouraging an ethnographic turn toward a thorough contextualization of the processes and meaning of art as it emerges in each local context, investigating art's "social life" as it moves beyond local borders, and even reconsidering Western art within its own indigenous, local cultural context (Alexander 1996; Alpers 1991; Karp and Lavine 1991; Price 1989).

ART IN HUMAN HISTORY

An examination of art in human history provides a crucial context for our deliberations as we consider the question "What is art?" Although common images of our human ancestors may not depict them as artists, the expanding archaeological record reveals a deep historical connection between humans and art that reaches back tens of thousands of years. Art appears to be a fundamental aspect of what it means to be human. Though the archaeological record of human artistic work expands dramatically around 40,000 years ago, clear evidence has emerged of human creative expression dating back at least 100,000 years.

Blombos Cave, South Africa. Archaeological discoveries over the past two decades in South Africa's Blombos Cave—set high in a cliff overlooking the Indian Ocean—reveal that as early as 75,000 years ago, anatomically modern

MAP 15.1
South Africa

humans were making finely crafted stone weapon points, carving tools out of animal bones, and engraving symbols on blocks of a red stone called ochre.

In 2008 Norwegian archaeologist Christopher Henshilwood and his colleagues uncovered what amounts to a 100,000-year-old painters' workshop: bone tools for mixing paint, stones for pounding and grinding, yellow and red ochre for color (Henshilwood et al. 2011; Larsen 2014). Archaeologists are uncertain what the paint was used for. Though perhaps applied to the skin or clothing as camouflage for hunting, paint might also have been used symbolically to convey a social message, perhaps in a group's social or ritual practices beyond the immediate group. Finds from this early date suggest that humans had already developed a rudimentary knowledge of chemistry and engaged in complex social practices, including the long-range planning required to find, store, and combine the materials found in Blombos Cave. And, perhaps most significant, the finds push back the date of the earliest indications of human capacity for symbolic thought.

A comprehensive study of artifacts gleaned from various African sites reveals the gradual emergence of human artistic expression that later spread to other world regions. Recent archaeological evidence suggests that our human ancestors in Africa may have become cognitively and behaviorally "modern" as early as 300,000 to 400,000 years ago. Later, the development of bone and stone tools— along with the processing and use of pigment, art, and decoration at sites across Africa and from various eras—suggests that our human ancestors in Africa gradually assembled the package of modern human behaviors associated with art, eventually carrying them to other regions of the world (McBrearty and Brooks 2000).

Paleolithic Cave Paintings in Europe. Perhaps the best-known examples of early art outside Africa are the spectacular Paleolithic cave paintings that have been discovered in areas of southern France (Lascaux Cave and Chauvet-Pont-d'Arc Cave) and northern Spain (Altamira Cave). The artwork dates from 32,000 to 10,000 years ago. The early artists elaborately depicted reindeer, bison, mammoth, horses, lions, and other animals prevalent in that period. Carved human figurines, jewelry, ritual objects, and bone and ivory carvings accompany elaborate burial sites found in the caves.

The cave art reveals highly developed artistic skills, including the incorporation of the contours of partially sculpted cave walls to provide a sense of dynamism and movement in the paintings. Analysis of the paintings reveals that the cave art was not the work of a few individuals or small groups but rather developed over a 20,000-year period through the efforts of many different artists who reused, modified, and painted over the artwork of their predecessors (Herzog 2010; Larsen 2014).

The connection between humans and art reaches back tens of thousands of years. Here, archaeologists excavate a 100,000-year-old "artists' studio" in Blombos Cave, South Africa, with artifacts in the foreground.

MAP 15.2
Spain and France

This elaborate wall painting in Lascaux Cave, France, depicting horses, bison, mammoth, and lions and dating between 32,000 to 12,000 BCE, reveals the highly developed artistic skills of our immediate ancestors.

The purpose of the cave paintings is not clear. Our ancestors may have used them in storytelling, recordkeeping, rituals, ceremonies, or perhaps all of these. Despite the uncertainty over their purpose, it is clear that the complexity of materials, subjects, and symbolism reveals an elaborate social life and an advanced level of cognitive development that does not fit contemporary stereotypes of "cavemen" living during the most recent ice age in Europe.

Whether through a 100,000-year-old painters' studio in southern Africa, Paleolithic cave art in southern France, or a fine art museum in a contemporary global city, we see that art is integral to all of human life. It can be expressed in elaborate displays or through simple craftwork. But through these events, objects, and expressions, anthropologists can gather crucial insights into people and their cultures. Anthropologists bring a unique perspective to the study of art. As we will explore in the following section, one of these unique contributions lies in careful ethnographic analysis and attention to the cultural production and transaction of art. This focus illuminates the complex social life of art as it is produced and exchanged between people and across geographic spaces and cultural boundaries.

What Is Unique about How Anthropologists Study Art?

Anthropologists' unique approach to art includes particular attention to how art is embedded in a community—how art connects to social norms and values and economic and political systems and events. Who makes it and why? What does it mean to the people who create it and to those who perceive it? What are its functional and inspirational roles? As ethnographers, anthropologists of art attend not only to the form of the art itself—its designs, movements, and sounds—but also to its context. We consider not only the creative production of a piece of art but also each work's unique and often complex history as it journeys through human culture. After all, as we will see, art is embedded in everyday exchanges, social networks, business negotiations, and other struggles over profit, power, and prestige.

THE ETHNOGRAPHY OF ART

Placing art in context has become more complicated and interesting in recent years. Today, in an era of intensifying globalization, local art is created in a global landscape. Local art practices, objects, and events intersect with global movements of people and ideas. Art is often a key juncture through which local communities engage the global economy (Kopytoff 1986). Within this global "artscape" (Appadurai 1986), the creation of local art may provide not only a means of economic activity but also a venue to demonstrate cultural skills and values and to assert local cultural identity in the face of rapid change (Perkins and Morphy 2006). As a result, contemporary anthropologists of art explore the journeys of objects across boundaries and the implications of the "traffic in culture" for both those who produce art and those who consume it (Marcus and Myers 1995; Schneider and Wright 2006; Venbrux, Rosi, and Welsch 2006).

Let's consider a few case studies that illuminate contemporary anthropological approaches to the study of art through ethnography.

The Trade in West African Art. In *African Art in Transit* (1994), anthropologist Christopher Steiner explores the dynamic role of art in human culture through an ethnographic study of art traders in Abidjan, the main port city of Côte d'Ivoire in West Africa. Abidjan's art traders, mostly Muslims, serve as middlemen in the flow of African art between its creators (mostly rural villagers) and its consumers (Western tourists and international art collectors).

Within this flow, itinerant African traders circulate among upcountry villages, purchasing wooden carvings and clay figurines. The traders sometimes buy unique ritual items and family heirlooms directly from individuals, but generally they acquire mass-produced objects from artisan workshops that cater to the tourist and export art trade. The traders then sell to urban dealers, small and large, who resell the pieces to street hawkers, market stands, and upscale galleries. Within this milieu, Steiner investigates the intricate business practices and networks that link traders, suppliers, and consumers. And he details the elaborate production, presentation, description, alteration, authentication, and pricing of local art pieces within an increasingly globalized art market driven by tourists, Western and non-Western art dealers, and art connoisseurs.

MAP 15.3
Abidjan

As is true in all art markets, whether for carvings, paintings, fabrics, jewelry, or cuisine, an object's aesthetic value translates into a monetary value. Steiner examines the process by which West African art objects acquire value as they move through the art market. For example, how does a piece of carved wood become a desired object for purchase and collection? In Côte d'Ivoire, it is primarily a few Western tourists and art dealers who determine these values. For the most highly valued objects, an influential and wealthy elite of dealers, scholars, collectors, and exhibitors establishes their worth.

Key to the creation of value in the African art market is the perception of art objects as "authentic" or "genuine." Indeed, buyers and collectors are drawn to objects perceived to be of a certain origin and initial use. In turn, Côte d'Ivoire's local traders actively engage in the construction of **authenticity**—the perception of an object's antiquity, uniqueness, and originality within a local culture. Art objects are dirtied, artificially aged, stained, made to appear "primitive" to Western eyes, and altered to fit the buyers' ideals. Local traders tell stories about the objects'

authenticity

The perception of an object's antiquity, uniqueness, and originality within a local culture.

What makes art "authentic"? A woodworker in West Africa makes carved figurines for market.

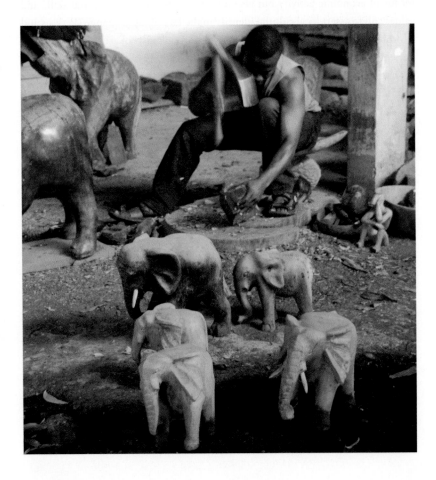

origin, meaning, and use to enhance the impression of authenticity. For tourists, traders create stories that appeal to the buyers' aesthetic tastes and desires to acquire a genuine, authentic object. For high-end collectors, traders provide an elaborate market history—a description of when, where, and how the object was collected, as well as its origins. Most of these stories, Steiner finds, are fabricated to meet the tastes of Western consumers and thereby raise the objects' value.

The aesthetic values of Western tourists and collectors, expressed in their consumption patterns, significantly influence the production, marketing, and display of West African art. In fact, West African art traders continually move between local and global art markets, communicating between image creators and image consumers, between artists and audiences. In this context, the production of art does not occur solely for art's sake but is part of an economic strategy that engages multiple levels of the art market. Steiner notes, "West African traders leave each negotiation with a new sense of the aesthetic sense of the Western buyers, a sense that the traders and manufacturers must be closely in tune with as they go about their business of making a living in a rapidly globalizing world and in their niche in a rapidly globalizing art market" (1995, 164). In this way, West African art traders play a sophisticated role in a global art market. They serve as cultural brokers and mediators who communicate Western desires to the native artists and who promote a particular image of African art and culture to the West (Beidelman 1994; Gell 1995; Zilberg 1996).

Think about your own perception of art. What makes a piece of art "authentic" in your eyes?

Transforming West African "Wood" and "Mud" into Global Art.
In recent years, facilitated by increased migration and enhanced global transportation and communication systems, West African art traders have extended their business networks across the Atlantic Ocean to New York and throughout the United States. As a result, the long-distance trade of West African artwork, particularly "wood" (carved statues and masks) and "mud" (terra-cotta clay figurines), is leading to encounters between cultures and commerce at the intersection of two worlds (Stoller 2003).

The hub of the West African art trade in the United States is New York City—in particular, a multistory building on the west side of Midtown Manhattan called the Warehouse. The Warehouse is packed with stalls and shelves and display tables, each overflowing with "wood" and "mud." Every day, moving vans unload newly arrived shipments from West Africa while others on-load pieces to be distributed by itinerant traders across the United States. West African traders cater to a wide array of clients: high-end art collectors, middle-class shoppers, and low-end street markets. High-end collectors search the New York galleries and art shows for what they consider fine art. At the same time, male and

How do wood and mud become art? West African traders have transformed a Manhattan warehouse into an African art market, full of stalls, shelves, and tables from which art is circulated to markets, vendors, galleries, and private collections across the United States, including this African art stall (*right*) at the San Diego, California, County Fair.

female West African art traders crisscross the country delivering mass-produced art objects for sale at boutiques, street markets, flea markets, and cultural festivals. They even deliver directly to some individual clients. The traders rely on networks of "cousins" and other fictive kin who provide housing, marketing advice, cultural interpretation, and shared transport in an extension of practices developed in West African long-distance trade networks.

Stoller reflects on the power of global flows of people, art, and ideas to shape worlds of work and worlds of meaning. The introduction of West African art pieces into Western art worlds expands Western cultural notions of art and beauty. Simultaneously, Western notions of art affect West African patterns of production and marketing, including what traders will buy from artisans in the mud and wood workshops in towns and villages throughout West Africa.

Moreover, on a practical level, these encounters at the crossroads of immigration and trade enable West African traders to meet their own social and economic obligations. They can pay off debts acquired in the immigration process and in starting up their small businesses. They can send remittances home to West Africa to support close family and extended kin groups. They can provide small amounts of start-up capital for rural and urban family enterprises. In the process of meeting these obligations, the traders themselves receive honor and respect from their home communities.

The studies by Steiner and Stoller provide an insightful ethnographic analysis of the power of movement, encounter, and exchange to shape key aspects of human life, including categories such as art. By considering the production, marketing, and consumption of art within this framework, Steiner and Stoller challenge notions of ideal art types and universal standards of aesthetic beauty. They discuss how aesthetic perceptions, commonly viewed as timeless and universal, can be constructed and negotiated in the encounters among humans—person to person, group to group, locally and globally.

What Is the Relationship between Art and Power?

Anthropologists do not approach art for art's sake. Instead, they inquire about the intersection of art with key systems of power such as race, ethnicity, class, gender, sexuality, politics, religion and economics (Marcus and Myers 1995; Perkins and Morphy 2006). Creative expressions, performances, and interactions through music, dance, song, museum displays, art events, and other art forms can produce venues for staging dynamic engagements with these systems of power, unmasking patterns of stratification, making the unconscious conscious, and opening space for alternative visions of reality (see Downey 2005; Dunham 1969; Shannon 2006). Artistic expressions enable people to explore and perform alternative identities to those that seem "normal" within the dominant culture. In some instances, they may also however, unintentionally create and reinforce stereotypes and misunderstandings.

ART EXHIBITIONS AND DISPLAYS OF POWER: PLAYING THE HUMANITY GAME

How might art exhibits, special events, and museum displays that are designed to educate, illuminate, and build bridges of understanding across cultures instead reinforce stereotypes and create and maintain narratives of difference and exclusion? After September 11, 2001, many local and national institutions, universities, and grassroots organizations in the United States for the first time organized Middle Eastern art exhibits and special events. Established art institutions increased displays of Middle Eastern and Islamic art, and art funders including the Rockefeller, Soros, Mellon, and Flora Family foundations contributed generously to underwrite the events and exhibits. All hoped to mobilize galleries and exhibit spaces to counter growing anti-Muslim rhetoric and rising talk of an inevitable "clash of civilizations" between Islam and the West. Art, they believed, would provide a unique venue for building bridges of cross-cultural understanding and an awareness of a common humanity.

How do museums choose what to exhibit? Anthropologist Jessica Winegar critiques the narrow slice of Middle Eastern art considered appropriate for display: (*left*) more frequently displayed "good Middle Eastern art" like this photograph "Speechless" from the series Women of Allah by Shirin Neshat, an Iranian woman artist living in New York; and (*right*) less frequently displayed controversial pieces like "Suffurya," a display of ceramic sacks by Palestinian artist Mervat Essa, memorializing the depopulation and destruction of Al Biram, her family's village, and many other Palestinian villages in 1948 at the creation of the state of Israel.

But did the art events have the intended effect?

Anthropologist Jessica Winegar, a scholar of Middle Eastern art and politics, suggests that in fact these art events may have had the opposite effect of what was intended. That is, they may have reinforced stereotypes and dichotomies rather than built bridges of understanding (see Marcus and Myers 1995; Price 1989). Winegar had a front-row seat to observe this phenomenon as virtual gallery operator for ArteEast, a nonprofit organization promoting cultural exchange between the United States, the Middle East, and North Africa. Drawing on her fieldwork in Egypt and her ethnography *Creative Reckonings: The Politics of Art and Culture in Contemporary Egypt* (2006), Winegar was surprised to discover that displays of Middle Eastern art in Egypt and the United States differed dramatically, with U.S. art events presenting an extremely narrow slice of the Middle Eastern art world. Three selection biases were most frequent: historical art focusing on Islam's past achievements; music and rituals of Sufi-ism, a mystical tradition within Islam, rather than mainstream orthodox Islam; and events featuring female Middle Eastern visual artists and filmmakers.

Why, wondered Winegar, were these the only categories considered "good Middle Eastern art" and selected for exhibition? Exhibitions largely ignored works celebrating contemporary orthodox Islam, despite the success of shows of art from Buddhist, Hindu, African, and Native American religious traditions. Male artists were seldom featured. Middle Eastern art such as abstract painting or sculptures with no explicit reference to Islam or the Middle East could have been shown but was not. Missing was art representing resistance to occupation, music critical of the United States or Israel, political cartoons and graffiti, graphic art from Islamic publications, or even the genre of martyr posters and videos—all representing cultural practices involving significant creativity. Winegar suggests that what the U.S. art market would bear—what would attract funders and audiences—was shaped not by some objective notion of art but rather by the post-9/11 political landscape of war in Afghanistan and Iraq and a War on Terror that had established Islam and the Middle East as the enemy.

Winegar warns that by focusing on certain limited categories of art as "good Middle Eastern art" worthy of exhibition, these events actually served to reinforce perceived differences. So while work by Middle Eastern women artists was popular, its representation played upon stereotypes of Middle Eastern women and assumptions about gender inequality in Islam. For instance, exhibits featuring Middle Eastern women artists were often presented and viewed as if critiquing Middle Eastern culture, particularly gender inequalities presumed to be derived from Islam. The artists themselves were often born in the Middle East but now residing in the West. While they were frequently viewed as human bridges of understanding, they were also seen as uniquely positioned and actively engaged in critiquing the culture from which they had come. In interviews with Winegar, audience members described the art as reflecting the submission of Middle Eastern and Muslim women and the desire of those women for freedom and liberty, even if these were not the intended meanings of the artist or presenter, or were clearly contradicted by the exhibition booklets or wall descriptions.

Is it possible that rather than bringing clarity to a complicated situation and building bridges of understanding, by framing so-called Islamic art to make it attractive, interesting, and palatable to funders and audiences, exhibitors actually reinforced the clash of civilizations and War on Terror frameworks? In the process of trying to accentuate common humanity through art—what Winegar calls "The Humanity Game"—could curators and funders' narrow selections have reinforced assumed oppositions between freedom and oppression, understanding and ignorance, civilization and barbarism? Winegar's research reveals the narrow limits imposed on the role of art as bridge builder and suggests that the potential of art to serve as an avenue for expressing and perceiving common humanity is severely limited by the political context in which art is selected, funded, marketed, and viewed (Winegar 2008).

BLACK GIRLS' PLAYGROUND GAMES AND THE CONSTRUCTION OF GENDER IDENTITY

When we think of kids jumping rope on the sidewalk or standing in a circle in the playground calling out rhymes and clapping to keep the beat, we may not

How have the rhyming, syncopations, dancelike gestures, melodies, and lyrics from black girls' game songs (*right*) shaped commercial music, like that performed by rap artist Nelly (*left*)?

ethnomusicology

The study of music in cultural context.

kinetic orality

A musical genre combining body movement and voice.

automatically think of art. But in *The Games Black Girls Play* (2006), ethnomusicologist Kyra Gaunt explores the sophisticated musical forms that are taught and learned, particularly by young black girls, on the playground.

Gaunt, herself a gifted musician and an anthropologist trained in **ethnomusicology**—the study of music and culture (see Nettl 2005)—applies a unique combination of musical analysis and gender analysis in her study of games that black girls play. According to Gaunt, the girls' hand-clapping and rope-jumping games embody a unique musical genre that combines body movement and voice to produce what she calls a **kinetic orality**. Hand clapping, foot stomping, and highly percussive singing create a musical expression deeply tied to the body—a performance that does not rely on musical instruments but only on body and voice.

These performances may appear to be improvised on the playground, street corner, or schoolyard. But Gaunt argues that they are learned in an elaborate process of enculturation. Through this process, complex rhythmic syncopations, chants, call-and-response vocal patterns, dances, and melodies are transferred from generation to generation as central lessons of socialization for young African American girls. Gaunt challenges the stereotypes that attribute musical patterns and bodily movement in black children's games to biology. Instead, she traces the enculturation processes of what she calls "learned musical blackness" that begins at an early age as part of African American identity construction.

Gaunt also explores how black girls' games and songs influence the development of commercially popular music associated with the African American community—namely, hip-hop, soul, and rhythm and blues. In particular, she details the ways in which the rhyming, syncopations, dancelike gestures, melodies, and lyrics from black girls' game songs have been adopted from and borrowed by the commercial music of black male artists from the 1950s to the present.

Although others have suggested that black girls' games and songs imitate music from radio and television, borrowing from genres such as rhythm and blues and hip-hop, Gaunt documents a dynamic circular relationship. Commercial songs may indeed be adopted, modified, and played within the girls' games and songs, but their games, musical styles, and group play are also sampled, borrowed, and appropriated by the popular music industry. Moreover, this occurs with a particular gender twist, as they are incorporated into music predominately associated with men and masculinity.

As an example of this borrowing, Gaunt documents how a common song in black girls' games, "Down, Down Baby," was appropriated into the chorus of the 2000 song "Country Grammar" by Grammy award–winning rap artist Nelly. In "Country Grammar," Nelly incorporates significant lyrical, rhythmic, melodic, and linguistic features of the game-song while revising the lyrics to fit commercial, masculine-centered mainstream hip-hop expectations.

By examining musical performance through the lens of gender, Gaunt raises important questions about the performance of gender and the patterns of interaction between women and men that are reflected through music. This is occurring as women transfer embodied music across generations as a form of socialization while men appropriate women's music for commercial purposes, often without attribution. Nelly's rewritten lyrics, complete with macho references to being "cocked ready to let it go" and marijuana culture, stand in sharp contrast to the language and tone of girls' performances on the playground. Unlike many artists who have borrowed from girls' games, Nelly has publicly acknowledged the borrowing from a chant in a popular "children's game," although he fails to acknowledge girls as the primary performers of schoolyard songs.

Gaunt's examination of kinetic orality in the games black girls play opens a window on the dynamic process of identity construction, including the construction of racial and gender identities, that emerges at the intersection of play, performance, creative expression, and art (Jamison 2006).

How Do Art and Media Intersect?

Historically, anthropologists have carefully analyzed visual systems and visible culture as part of their ethnographic fieldwork. Art, media, material culture, and even museums become objects of anthropological inquiry. But visual media, including photography, film, television, videos, and web-based techniques, can also become tools of anthropological inquiry, drawing attention to the imaginative and sensory in a way ethnographic writing may not and opening up new possibilities for understanding the world.

Since the late nineteenth century anthropologists like Franz Boaz have incorporated photography and recorded film footage into their research, both to document their ethnographic projects and to provide visual support for their public educational work at home. Margaret Mead and her husband Gregory Bateson set new standards for integrating the visual into their work, taking 25,000 photos and 22,000 feet of film in Bali, Indonesia, between 1931 and 1938. With the technological advance of portable, synchronous sound cameras in the 1960s, ethnographic filmmaking entered a new and expansive era (Ruby and Banks 2011).

Just as globalization has intensified the worldwide movement of people, money, data, goods, and services, so globalization has transformed the flow of images and sounds through new media technologies (Askew and Wilk 2007). The anthropologist Arjun Appadurai (1990) calls this new formation a **global mediascape**: Global cultural flows of media and visual images enable linkages and communication across boundaries of culture, language, geography, economics, and politics in ways unimaginable one hundred years ago. Faye Ginsberg and colleagues (2002) have introduced the concept of **media worlds**, to reflect more textured local realities and the tensions that exist when political, economic and visual worlds collide in the context of contemporary globalization.

Just as newspapers dominated the mediascape in the late nineteenth century, radio, audio recordings, film, television, and the Internet have shaped communication in the twentieth and twenty-first centuries. In contemporary culture the image, whether in photograph, film, or video, has replaced written texts as the primary educator. New forms of **social media**, including Facebook, YouTube, Twitter, Instagram, and Tumblr, have transformed communication for many people, and computer- and Internet-based technologies serve as sources of pleasure and social engagement, not merely as tools for work (Boellstorff 2008).

Today, media reach every corner of the globe and permeate all aspects of daily life. The decentralized production and circulation of new media, facilitated by satellites, computers, and handheld communication devices, has undermined the old media empires and has challenged the state's ability to control media content and media flows. In turn, new media have facilitated opportunities for activism, as indigenous and marginalized groups use photographs, film, text, and video to mobilize movements for social change and to challenge existing power structures (Askew and Wilk 2007; Ginsburg, Abu-Lughod, and Larkin 2002; Juris and Khasnabish 2013).

VISUAL IMAGES AND CULTURAL IDENTITY

Visual anthropology explores the production, circulation, and consumption of visual images, including photographs, film, television, and new media, focusing on the power of visual representations in art, performance, museums, and the mass media to influence culture and cultural identity (Hockings 2003). As you read the following discussion, you may be surprised to discover the power that photographs have to wield such influence.

National Geographic's Photographic Gaze.
In a classic work of visual anthropology, *Reading National Geographic* (1993), anthropologists Catherine Lutz and Jane Collins examine the photographs of the popular U.S. magazine *National Geographic* to reveal the power of visual images to shape cultural perspectives and behavior. Launched in 1888, *National Geographic* has successfully blended science, art, photojournalism, and entertainment to become one of the most popular and influential U.S. sources of information about other cultures. Indeed, it collects "the world between its covers." At its peak, the reasonably priced magazine attracted more than ten million monthly subscribers (97 percent white and middle-class) and, with multiple reads in classrooms, lobbies, and doctors' offices, perhaps 40 million total viewers. *National*

How might the visual images of *National Geographic*—its photographic gaze—shape readers' perspectives on the world? What messages emerge from these photos? (*left to right*): An Egyptian girl and man sit in front of the Sphinx, Giza, Egypt (Nov. 1955); a Mayan man reads to a crowd from his Bible during Holy Week, Guatemala (March 1960); an Imperial Bodyguard member rides in a war game, Ethiopia (March 1964); a Swazi princess accepts a new suitcase at her wedding ceremony, Swaziland (Jan. 1978); and a highland girl gathers wild cosmos flowers near Lake Itasy, Madagascar (Oct. 1967).

visual anthropology
A field of anthropology that explores the production, circulation, and consumption of visual images, focusing on the power of visual representation to influence culture and cultural identity.

Geographic's beautiful photos of smiling people from around the globe have inspired world travel, scientific exploration, and even sexual fantasies for generations of U.S. readers.

National Geographic may at first glance appear to offer a straightforward presentation of evidence about human nature and the natural world. But Lutz and Collins, using the analytical frameworks of visual anthropology, ask how the particular "gaze" of *National Geographic* photographs may reflect the worldview of those behind the lens—that is, the magazine's owners, editors, photographers, and graphic designers. This gaze, the authors suggest, can shape the understandings of the magazine's readers as they think about humanity, the natural world, and their own culture's position in the global arena.

To investigate this claim, Lutz and Collins interviewed editors and readers and analyzed photographs from the magazine's nearly 600 articles published about non-Western topics between 1950 and 1986. The researchers asked: What messages did these images convey? What was their intent?

According to the magazine's mission statement, issued in 1915, "only what is of a kindly nature is printed about any country or people; everything unpleasant or unduly critical is to be avoided" (1993, 27). Indeed, underlying the exquisite photos of seemingly happy people, elaborate rituals, and exotic costumes, Lutz and Collins perceive a particular editorial perspective and philosophical worldview. They draw the following conclusion: "Clearly, photographic practice at *National Geographic* is geared to a classic form of humanism, drawing readers' attention through its portrayal of difference, and then showing that under the colorful dress and skin, as it were, we are all more or less the same" (1993, 61). Even though this editorial viewpoint—expressed in the **photographic gaze**—appeared neutral, it projected a particular perspective on human nature, the natural world, history, and difference.

In projecting an almost magical sense of unity, the magazine's photographic gaze tended to overlook key aspects of human history. Photographers and editors selected and framed images to limit political and economic contexts. Conflict, inequality, poverty, and hunger were downplayed or completely avoided. In keeping with this editorial approach, photos of the period under study rarely portrayed dramatic world events of the time. Struggles for decolonization, the Cold War, the Vietnam War, or movements for civil rights, women's rights, and gay rights in the United States were left out of the magazine's photographic gaze. Lutz and Collins note that the magazine's editorial choices consistently minimized diversity and difference, especially along the lines of race and gender.

The authors suggest that during the period they studied, the gaze of *National Geographic*'s images created a cultural lens that mediated U.S. readers' experience of the world and its diverse people. The photographs avoided

photographic gaze

The presumed neutral viewpoint of the camera that in fact projects the perspective of the person behind the camera onto human nature, the natural world, and history.

images that might disrupt readers' views of the world and the United States' place in it. Instead, as a primary source for U.S. middle-class information about the world, the magazine's gaze provided reassurance that (1) in essential ways the world that seems so diverse is actually quite familiar; (2) fundamentally, all is well with the world; and (3) the readers and their country play a benevolent role in world events. Here, Lutz and Collins suggest, the power of *National Geographic*'s photographs to shape the U.S. cultural worldview held deep implications for the way the magazine's primarily middle-class readers engaged in debates about the nation's domestic and foreign policy (Fernea 1996; Goldstein 1998).

National Geographic's photographic gaze has continued to change over the years. But the concept of the gaze, central to visual anthropology, provides an important tool for thinking about how the form and content of media are shaped by those "behind the camera." As you engage with media throughout your day— through television shows, news broadcasts, websites, tweets, YouTube channels, movies, Facebook pages—can you use the concept of the photographic gaze as a tool to analyze the intentionally and unintentionally expressed worldviews of the owners, editors, designers, videographers, and others behind the scenes?

ETHNOGRAPHIC FILM AND INDIGENOUS MEDIA

Ethnographic filmmaking, with a long history in anthropology, has emerged in recent decades as the dominant force in visual anthropology. Classic ethnographic films like Robert Flaherty's silent film *Nanook of the North* (1922), shot among the indigenous Inuit of Canada, John Marshall's many films about the Ju/'hoansi of Namibia, Napoleon Chagnon and Tim Asch's *The Ax Fight* (1975) about the Yanomami in southern Venezuela, and Robert Gardner's *Dead Birds* (1963), set in New Guinea, broke significant ground in promoting the use of images for the description, analysis, and interpretation of human behavior, often focusing on individuals and communities in rural, tribal, and seemingly isolated settings. More contemporary ethnographic films strive to show local communities in their rapidly shifting, friction-filled global contexts, including the complex and changing web of relationships between humans, diverse species, and their environments (Grimshaw and Ravetz 2009; MacDougall 2005; Young 1995).

In today's interconnected global age, digital video filmmaking has taken on a key role in giving voice to the concerns of local communities through what visual anthropologists refer to as **indigenous media**. The power of media to overcome boundaries of time and space is increasingly used by people who have experienced massive economic, political, and geographic disruption to mediate rapid change and build alternative strategies for communication, survival, and empowerment.

indigenous media
The use of media by people who have experienced massive economic, political and geographic disruption to build alternative strategies for communication, survival, and empowerment.

Chinese Villagers Stay Connected through Festival Videos.

For new immigrants far from home, for instance, the creation and circulation of new media forms like digital video has tremendous potential to unify immigrants, resist dominant narratives of otherness, and reinforce their solidarity with their native communities. My own experience bears out this observation.

In early 2007 I attended a temple festival in a small village on China's southeast coast. I had visited the village previously, but the opportunity to participate in a full two weeks of festivities at the invitation of the temple master was a unique privilege. Vivid rituals, raucous processions, solemn prayers, and bountiful banquets filled the days. But the constant presence of a small film crew documenting every element of temple life surprised me. One afternoon the temple master asked if I would be willing to be interviewed on camera to say a few words about the festival. As a grateful guest—and an oddity as the only non-Chinese at the festival—I readily agreed, gave an interview at the foot of a beautiful new pagoda overlooking the harbor, and thought little more about the matter.

Back in New York a few weeks later, I placed a call to a young woman from the village now living in Flushing, Queens. Her mother, still living in China, had entrusted me to deliver some baby clothes for her new granddaughter. We agreed to meet the next day on a corner of Main Street in Flushing—a meeting that, despite her assurances, I doubted would go smoothly on one of the busiest intersections in New York City.

I patiently waited the next day on the appointed corner. Much to my surprise, at the agreed-upon time a car pulled up, a window rolled down, and a young woman said in Chinese, "Professor Guest, get in!" Over dumplings and tea she explained, "Everyone from the village knows you! You're in the video!" It turns out that in order to keep immigrant villagers connected to the home temple and engaged in its spiritual and financial life, the master regularly produces and circulates festival videos to his devotees now living in the New York metropolitan area. Video of the festival I attended had traversed the globe from a rural Chinese village to the streets of New York City, serving to build solidarity among immigrant villagers now in the United States and to strengthen connections with their kinfolk, fellow townspeople, and religious co-adherents in China. The forces of globalization move people, money, things—and images. A Chinese village festival had now entered the global mediascape.

Can you also imagine some of the power dynamics that may be revealed by such a video production? Consider all of the players involved: funders, filmmakers, editors, an anthropologist, distributors, and recipients. How might the global exchange of media intersect and affect existing relationships of power?

Today media is reshaping human life in every part of the world as it increasingly permeates the routines of daily life. As you think about the expanding global mediascape, can you see how your everyday actions—friendships, education, love life, job, entertainment, religion, political engagements, communications, and more—are mediated by new technologies in ways unimaginable even two decades ago? The anthropology of media will continue to develop as this global mediascape expands and deepens. What will the next two decades bring? How will anthropologists use the tools of our discipline to understand the impact of these changes on people and their communities across the globe?

Toolkit

Thinking Like an Anthropologist:
The Landscape of World Art

Art is everywhere in our lives. From the games we play and the songs we sing to the way we dress and the food we eat, we humans express ourselves creatively and interact with one another through creative expression. As we have seen throughout this chapter, communication between artist and audience through art objects, performances, events, and experiences is not limited to elite actors or venues but is present throughout human cultures and deeply rooted in the activities of everyday life. This chapter's opening story described the creative ways in which young people in a Brazilian favela have built community, challenged the political and economic assumptions of the state, and projected their concerns into a national and international dialogue. When do games take on a life of their own? How do they become political action or efforts at community building? How do they become art? What is the relationship among creative expression, play, performance, and art?

Through Morrinho, imaginative young people engage in an evolving drama that performs, imitates, and examines life, constructing artificial scenarios and relationships through which the players explore their own emotional and social worlds. By telling an untold story or history, speaking the truth of a community back to its members and the surrounding culture and political structures, the virtual world of Morrinho explores those boundaries among real life, play, and the creative expressions and engagements that anthropologists call art.

In this chapter we have begun to consider the vast landscape of world art. Where can you find these dynamics in your own life? In what ways are you an artist? How do you use new forms of media technology to express your creativity and communicate with others through the global mediascape?

As you think more about the world of art, remember the opening questions that framed this chapter's inquiries:

- **What is art?**

- **What is unique about how anthropologists study art?**

- **What is the relationship between art and power?**

- **How do art and media intersect?**

After reading this chapter, you should be able to apply these questions to situations in which you encounter art and media and the intersections of real life, play, politics, and creative expression. Thinking like an anthropologist about the world of art can give you a more complete set of tools for comprehending this complex part of human culture, understanding your own creativity, and engaging the world around you.

Key Terms

art (p. 427)

fine art (p. 428)

popular art (p. 428)

universal gaze (p. 430)

authenticity (p. 436)

ethnomusicology (p. 442)

kinetic orality (p. 442)

global mediascape (p. 444)

media worlds (p. 444)

social media (p. 444)

visual anthropology (p. 445)

photographic gaze (p. 446)

indigenous media (p. 447)

References

Abu-Lughod, Janet L. 1989. *Before European Hegemony: The World System A.D. 1250–1350.* New York: Oxford University Press.

———. 2000. *Veiled Sentiments: Honor and Poetry in a Bedouin Society.* Berkeley: University of California Press.

Abu-Lughod, Lila. 2005. *Dramas of Nationhood: The Politics of Television in Egypt.* Chicago: University of Chicago Press.

Agrama, Hussein Ali. 2010. "Ethics, Tradition, Authority: Toward an Anthropology of the Fatwa." *American Ethnologist* 37(1): 2–18.

———. 2012. *Questioning Secularism: Islam, Sovereignty and the Rule of Law in Modern Egypt.* Chicago: Chicago University Press.

Ahearn, Laura M. 2012. *Living Language: An Introduction to Linguistic Anthropology.* Malden, MA: Wiley-Blackwell.

Aiyer, Ananthakrishnan. 2007. "The Allure of the Transnational: Notes on Some Aspects of the Political Economy of Water in India." *Cultural Anthropology* 22(4): 640–58.

Alexander, Edward P. 1996. "What Is a Museum?" In *Museums in Motion: An Introduction to the History and Functions of Museums,* edited by Edward P. Alexander and Mary Alexander. Walnut Creek, CA: AltaMira. Published in cooperation with the American Association for State and Local History.

Alexander, Michelle. 2012. *The New Jim Crow: Mass Incarceration in the Age of Colorblindness* (rev. ed.). New York: The New Press.

Allison, Anne. 1994. *Nightwork: Sexuality, Pleasure, and Corporate Masculinity in a Tokyo Hostess Club.* Chicago: University of Chicago Press.

Alpers, Svetlana. 1991. "Museums as a Way of Seeing." In *Exhibiting Cultures: The Poetics and Politics of Museum Display,* edited by Ivan Karp and Steven Lavine, 25–32. Washington, DC: Smithsonian Institution.

American Academy of Pediatrics. 2000. "Evaluation of the Newborn with Developmental Anomalies of the External Genitalia." *Pediatrics* 106(1): 138–42.

American Anthropological Association. 2004. "Statement on Marriage and the Family." www.aaanet.org/issues/policy-advocacy/Statement-on-Marriage-and-the-family.cfm

———. 2015. "What Is Anthropology?" www.americananthro.org/AdvanceYourCareer/Content.aspx?ItemNumber=2150&navItemNumber=740

Anand, Nikhil. 2011a. "Infrapolitics: The Social Life of Water in Mumbai." Unpublished dissertation, Department of Anthropology, Stanford University.

———. 2011b. "PRESSURE: The PoliTechnics of Water Supply in Mumbai." *Cultural Anthropology* 26(4): 542–64.

———. 2012. "Municipal Disconnect: On Abject Water and Its Urban Infrastructures." *Ethnography* 12(4): 487–509.

Anderson, Benedict. 1983. *Imagined Communities: Reflections on the Origin and Spread of Nationalism.* London: Verso.

Anderson, E. N. 2005. *Everyone Eats: Understanding Food and Culture.* New York: NYU Press.

Angelini, Alessandro. 2016. "Favela in Replica: Iterations and Itineraries of a Miniature City." *Journal of Latin American and Caribbean Anthropology* 20(3): 39-60.

Anglin, Mary K. 2002. *Women, Power, and Dissent in the Hills of Carolina.* Urbana: University of Illinois Press.

Appadurai, Arjun, ed. 1986. *The Social Life of Things: Commodities in Cultural Perspective.* Cambridge, UK: Cambridge University Press.

———. 1990. "Disjuncture and Difference in the Global Cultural Economy." *Public Culture* 2(2): 1–24.

Appiah, Kwame Anthony. 2006. *Cosmopolitanism: Ethics in a World of Strangers.* New York: Norton.

Armstrong, Thomas D. 2013. "China's 'Floating' Population." *Southern California International*

Review. http://scir.org/2013/10/chinas-floating -population/

Arobba, Biagio, Robert E. McGrath, Joe Futrelle, and Alan B. Craig. 2010. *A Community-Based Social Media Approach for Preserving Endangered Languages and Culture.* www.ideals.illinois.edu /bitstream/handle/2142/17078/lat-comm-info -2-sep-2010.pdf?sequence=2

Asad, Talal, ed. 1973. *Anthropology and the Cultural Encounter.* London: Ithaca Press.

———. 1992. *Anthropology & the Colonial Encounter.* Atlantic Highlands, NJ: Humanity Books.

———. 1993. *Genealogies of Religion: Discipline and Reasons of Power in Christianity and Islam.* Baltimore: Johns Hopkins University Press.

Askew, Kelly Michelle, and Richard R. Wilk, eds. 2007. *The Anthropology of Media: A Reader.* Malden, MA: Blackwell.

Baer, Hans A., Merrill Singer, and Ida Susser. 2003. *Medical Anthropology and the World System.* Westport, CT: Praeger.

Baker, Lee D. 1995. "Racism in Professional Settings: Forms of Address as Clues to Power Relations." *Journal of Applied Behavioral Science* 31(2): 186–201.

———. 2004. "Franz Boas out of the Ivory Tower." *Anthropological Theory* 4(1): 29–51.

Bank for International Settlements. 2016. "About Derivatives Statistics." www.bis.org/statistics /about_derivatives_stats.htm

Barth, Fredrik. 1959. *Political Leadership among Swat Pathans.* London: Athlone Press.

———. 1969. "Introduction." In *Ethnic Groups and Boundaries,* edited by Fredrik Barth. Boston: Little, Brown.

Beidelman, T. O. 1994. "*African Art in Transit* [Review]." *Anthropos* 89(4/6): 653–54.

Bellah, Robert. 1980. *Varieties of Civil Religion.* San Francisco: Harper & Row.

Bellamy, Carla. 2011. *The Powerful Ephemeral: Everyday Healing in an Ambiguously Islamic Place.* Berkeley: University of California Press.

Benedict, Ruth. 1934. *Patterns of Culture.* Boston: Houghton Mifflin.

———. 1946. *The Chrysanthemum and the Sword: Patterns of Japanese Culture.* Boston: Houghton Mifflin.

Bennett, R.R., et al. 2002. "Genetic Counseling and Screening of Consanguineous Couples and Their Offspring: Recommendations of the National Society of Genetic Counselors." *Journal of Genetic Counseling* 11(2): 97–119.

Berger, Peter, ed. 1999. *The Desecularization of the World: Resurgent Religion and World Politics.* Grand Rapids, MI: Eerdmans.

Bern, Sandra Lipsitz. 1981. "Gender Schema Theory: A Cognitive Account of Sex Typing." *Psychological Review* 88: 354–64.

———. 1983. "Gender Schema Theory and Its Implications for Child Development: Raising Gender-Aschematic Children in a Gender-Schematic Society." *Signs: Journal of Women in Culture and Society* 8: 598–616.

Bernal, Victoria. 2014. *Nation as Network: Diaspora, Cyberspace and Citizenship.* Chicago and London: The University of Chicago Press.

Besteman, Catherine L., ed. 2002. *Violence: A Reader.* New York: New York University Press.

Besteman, Catherine L., and Lee V. Cassanelli. 1996. *The Struggle for Land in Southern Somalia: The War Behind the War.* Boulder, CO: Westview Press.

Bestor, Theodore C. 2001. "Supply-Side Sushi: Commodity, Market, and the Global City." *American Anthropologist* 102(1): 76–95.

———. 2004. *Tsukiji: The Fish Market at the Center of the World.* Berkeley: University of California Press.

Bickford, Andrew. 2011. *Fallen Elites: The Military Other in Post-unification Germany.* Stanford, CA: Stanford University Press.

Blackless, Melanie, Anthony Charuvastra, Amanda Derryck, Anne Fausto-Sterling, Karl Lauzanne, and Ellen Lee. 2000. "How Sexually Dimorphic Are We? Review and Synthesis." *American Journal of Human Biology* 12: 151–66.

Board of Governors of the Federal Reserve System. 2012. "Changes in U.S. Family Finances from 2007 to 2010: Evidence from the Survey of Consumer Finances." www.federalreserve.gov /pubs/bulletin/2012/pdf/scf12.pdf

———. 2016a. "Consumer Credit-G.19." www .federalreserve.gov/releases/g19/current/

———. 2016b. "Mortgage Debt Outstanding." www.federalreserve.gov/econresdata/releases /mortoutstand/current.htm

Boas, Franz. 1912. "Changes in the Bodily Form of Descendants of Immigrants." *American Anthropologist* 14(3).

———. 1927. *Primitive Art.* New York: Dover.

———. 1966. *Kwakiutl Ethnography* (Classics of Anthropology), edited by Helen F. Codere. Chicago: University of Chicago Press.

Boehm, Christopher. 1999. *Hierarchy in the Forest: The Evolution of Egalitarian Behavior*. Cambridge, MA: Harvard University Press.

Boellstorff, Tom. 2007. "Queer Studies in the House of Anthropology." *Annual Review of Anthropology* 36: 17–35.

———. 2008. *Coming of Age in Second Life: An Anthropologist Explores the Virtually Human*. Princeton, NJ: Princeton University Press.

Boellstorff, Tom, and Cymene Howe. 2015. "Queer Futures." http://culanth.org/fieldsights /709-queer-futures

Bohannan, Laura. 1966. "Shakespeare in the Bush: An American Anthropologist Set Out to Study the Tiv of West Africa and Was Taught the True Meaning of *Hamlet*." *Natural History* 75: 28–33.

Bolin, Anne. 1992. "Families We Choose: Lesbians, Gays, Kinship [Review]." *American Anthropologist* 94(4): 947–48.

Bonilla, Yarimar, and Jonathan Rosa. 2015. "#Ferguson: Digital Protest, Hashtag Ethnography, and the Racial Politics of Social Media in the United States." *American Ethnologist* 42(1): 4–17.

Bonilla-Silva, Eduardo. 2010. *Racism without Racists: Color-Blind Racism and Racial Inequality in Contemporary America* (3rd ed.). New York: Rowman & Littlefield.

Bonvillain, Nancy. 2007. *Women and Men: Cultural Constructions of Gender* (4th ed.). Upper Saddle River, NJ: Prentice Hall.

Bourdieu, Pierre. 1982. *Ce que parler veut dire*. Paris: Fayard.

———. 1984. *Distinction: A Social Critique of the Judgment of Taste*, translated by R. Nice. Cambridge, MA: Harvard University Press.

Bourdieu, Pierre, with Jean-Claude Passeron. (1970) 1990. *Reproduction in Education, Society and Culture* (2nd ed.) (Theory, Culture, and Society Series vol. 4), translated by Lois Wacquant. New York: Sage.

Bourgois, Philippe I. 2003. *In Search of Respect: Selling Crack in El Barrio* (2nd ed.). Cambridge, UK: Cambridge University Press.

Bowen, John R. 2006. *Why the French Don't Like Headscarves: Islam, the State, and Public Space*. Princeton, NJ: Princeton University Press.

Bowie, Fiona. 2006. *The Anthropology of Religion: An Introduction* (2nd ed.). Malden, MA: Blackwell.

Brash, Julian. 2011. *Bloomberg's New York: Class and Governance in the Luxury City*. Athens: University of Georgia.

Braudel, Fernand. (1979) 1992. *Civilization and Capitalism, 15th to 18th Centuries*, vol. 3, *The Perspective of the World*, translated by Siân Reynolds. Berkeley: University of California Press.

Brettell, Caroline B., and C. F. Sargent, eds. 2009. *Gender in Cross-Cultural Perspective* (5th ed.). Upper Saddle River, NJ: Pearson/ Prentice Hall.

Bridges, Khiara M. 2011. *Reproducing Race: An Ethnography of Pregnancy as a Site of Racialization*. Berkeley: University of California Press.

Bridges, Tristan S. 2007. "Dude You're a Fag: Masculinity and Sexuality in High School [Review]." *Gender and Society* 21(5): 776–78.

Bringa, Tone. 1993. *Bosnia: We Are All Neighbors*. Granada Television.

———. 1995. *Being Muslim the Bosnian Way: Identity and Community in a Central Bosnian Village*. Princeton, NJ: Princeton University Press.

Bringa, Tone, and Peter Loizos. 2002. *Returning Home: Revival of a Bosnian Village*. Sage Film and Video (Sarajevo).

Brodkin, Karen. 1998. *How the Jews Became White Folks: And What That Says about Race in America*. New Brunswick, NJ: Rutgers University Press.

———. 2007. "Foreword." In *The Gender of Globalization: Women Navigating Cultural and Economic Marginalities*, edited by Nandini Gunewardena and Ann Kingsolver. Santa Fe, NM: School for Advanced Research Press.

Brown, Jacqueline Nassy. 2007. "Suriname, Sweet Suriname [Review]." *GLQ: A Journal of Lesbian and Gay Studies* 13(2–3): 406–8.

Brubaker, Rogers. 2004. *Ethnicity without Groups*. Cambridge, MA: Harvard University Press.

Brundage, W. Fitzhugh. 1993. *Lynching in the New South: Georgia and Virginia, 1880–1930*. Chicago: University of Illinois Press.

Buck, Pem Davidson. 2001. *Worked to the Bone: Race, Class, Power, and Privilege in Kentucky*. New York: Monthly Review Press.

———. 2009. *In/equality: An Alternative Anthropology*. Redding, CA: CAT Publishing.

Budrys, Grace. 2010. *Unequal Health: How Inequality Contributes to Health or Illness*. Lanham, MD: Rowman & Littlefield.

Butler, Judith. 1990. *Gender Trouble: Feminism and the Subversion of Identity*. New York: Routledge.

Calderwood, Brent. 2008. "Be Butch or Be Bashed." *Gay and Lesbian Review* 155(1): 38–39.

Cameron, Deborah. 2007. *The Myth of Mars and Venus*. Oxford, UK: Oxford University Press.

Cardoso, Fernando Henrique, and Enzo Faletto. 1969. *Dependencia y desarrollo en American Latina: ensayo de interpretación sociologica*. Mexico City: Siglo Veintiuno Editores.

Carneiro, Robert. 1978. "Political Expansion as an Expression of the Principle of Competitive Exclusion." In *Origins of the State*, edited by Ronald Cohn and Elman Service. Philadelphia: Institute for the Study of Human Issues.

———. 1981. "The Chiefdom: Precursor of the State." In *The Transition to Statehood in the New World*, edited by Grant Jones and Robert Kautz, 37–79. Cambridge, UK: Cambridge University Press.

Carroll, John B., ed. 1956. *Language, Thought, and Reality: Selected Writings of Benjamin Lee Whorf*. Cambridge, MA: MIT Press.

Carsten, Janet. 1997. *The Heat of the Hearth: The Process of Kinship in a Malay Fishing Community*. Oxford, UK: Clarendon Press.

———. 2004. *After Kinship*. Cambridge, UK: Cambridge University Press.

Casanova, Jose. 1994. *Public Religions in the Modern World*. Chicago: University of Chicago Press.

Cawthon Lang, Kristina. 2005. "Primate Factsheets: Gorilla Taxonomy, Morphology, & Ecology." Primate Info Net. http://pin.primate.wisc.edu /factsheets/entry/gorilla/taxon

Cazenave, Noel A. 2011. *The Urban Racial State: Managing Race Relations in American Cities*. Lanham, MD: Rowman & Littlefield.

Césaire, Aimé Fernand David. 1955. *Discourse on Colonialism*. Paris: Preĺsence africaine.

Chagnon, Napoleon A. 1968. *Y[[aogonek]]nomamö: The Fierce People*. New York: Holt, Rinehart and Winston.

Chagnon, Napoleon A., Timothy Asch, and Paul E. Bugos. 1975. *The ax fight*. Watertown, MA: Documentary Educational Resources.

Chan, Selina Ching. 2006. "Love and Jewelry: Patriarchal Control, Conjugal Ties, and Changing Identities." In *Modern Loves: The Anthropology of Romantic Courtship and Companionate Marriage*, edited by Jennifer S. Hirsch and Holly Wardlow, 35–50. Ann Arbor: University of Michigan Press.

Chapman, Gary. 2010. *The 5 Love Languages: The Secret to Love That Lasts*. Chicago: Northfield Publishing.

Chapman, Rachel R., and Jean R. Berggren. 2005. "Radical Contextualization: Contributions to an Anthropology of Racial/Ethnic Health Disparities." *Health* 9(2): 145–67.

Checker, Melissa. 2005. *Polluted Promises: Environmental Racism and the Search for Justice in a Southern Town*. New York: New York University Press.

Chio, Jenny. 2014. *A Landscape of Travel: The Work of Tourism in Rural Ethnic China*. Seattle: University of Washington Press.

Chodorow, Nancy. 1974. "Strategies, Cooperation and Conflict among Women in Domestic Groups." In *Woman, Culture and Society*, edited by Michelle Z. Rosaldo and Louise Lamphere, 97–113. Stanford, CA: Stanford University Press.

Chomsky, Noam. 1957. *Syntactic Structures*. The Hague/Paris: Mouton.

CNN/ORC International. 2015. "Poll: Do you approve or disapprove of the way Barack Obama is handling his job as president?" http:// i2.cdn.turner.com/cnn/2015/images/09/12 /iranpoll.pdf

Cohen, Yehudi A. 1974. *Man in Adaptation: The Cultural Present*. Chicago: Aldine.

Coles, Kimberly. 2007. *Democratic Designs: International Intervention and Electoral Practices in Postwar Bosnia-Herzegovina*. Ann Arbor: University of Michigan Press.

Comaroff, John L., and Jean Comaroff. 2009. *Ethnicity, Inc*. Chicago: University of Chicago Press.

Coontz, Stephanie. 1988. *The Social Origins of Private Life: A History of American Families 1600–1900*. New York: Verso.

———. 1992. *The Way We Never Were: American Families and the Nostalgia Trap*. New York: Basic Books.

Counihan, Carole, and Penny Van Esterik, eds. 2013. *Food and Culture: A Reader* (3rd ed.). New York: Taylor and Francis.

Cowen, M. P., and R. W. Shenton. 1996. *Doctrines of Development*. London: Routledge.

Curtis, Debra A. 1996. "Review of *Nightwork: Sexuality, Pleasure, and Corporate Masculinity in a Tokyo Hostess Club*." *Gender and Society* 10(2): 215–16.

———. 2009. *Pleasures and Perils: Girls' Sexuality in a Caribbean Consumer Culture.* New Brunswick, NJ: Rutgers University Press.

Dahlberg, Frances, ed. 1981. *Woman the Gatherer.* New Haven, CT: Yale University Press.

Davidson, Julia O'Connell. 1997. "Review of *Nightwork: Sexuality, Pleasure, and Corporate Masculinity in a Tokyo Hostess Club*." *Signs* 22(3): 759–61.

Davies, James B., Susanna Sandstrom, Anthony Shorrocks, and Edward N. Wolff. 2007. *Estimating the Level and Distribution of Global Household Wealth.* Helsinki: UNU-WIDER.

Davis, Georgiann. 2015. *Contesting Intersex: The Dubious Diagnosis.* New York: NYU Press.

Davis-Floyd, Robbie. 1992. *Birth as an American Rite of Passage.* Berkeley: University of California Press.

Davis-Floyd, Robbie, and Joseph Dumit, eds. 1997. *Cyborg Babies: From Techno-Sex to Techno-Tots.* London: Routledge.

Deloria, Vine, Jr. 1969. *Custer Died for Your Sins: An Indian Manifesto.* New York: Macmillan.

D'Emilio, John, and Estelle B. Freedman. 1998. *Intimate Matters: A History of Sexuality in America* (2nd ed.). Chicago: University of Chicago Press.

de Waal, Frans. 2002. "Primate Behavior and Human Aggression." In *Must We Fight?: From the Battlefield to the Schoolyard, a New Perspective on Violent Conflict and Its Prevention*, edited by William L. Ury, 13–25. San Francisco: Jossey-Bass.

Diamond, Jared. 1997. "The Animal with the Weirdest Sex Life." In *Constructing Sexualities: Readings in Sexuality, Gender and Culture*, edited by Suzanne LaFont. Upper Saddle River, NJ: Prentice Hall, 2002.

DiGangi, Christine. 2016. "How Many Credit Cards Does the Average American Have?" Credit.com. http://blog.credit.com/2016/01/how-many-credit-cards-does-the-average-american-have-132997/

Dill, Bonnie Thornton. 1983. "Race, Class and Gender: Prospects for an All-Inclusive Sisterhood." *Feminist Studies* 9: 131–50.

Dolan, Kerry A., and Luisa Kroll. 2016. "Forbes 2016 World's Billionaires: Meet the Richest People on the Planet." *Forbes*, March 1.

Domhoff, G. William. 2012. "Power in America: Wealth, Income, and Power." *Who Rules America?* http://sociology.ucsc.edu/whorulesamerica/power/wealth.html

Downey, Greg. 2005. *Learning Capoeira: Lessons in Cunning from an Afro-Brazilian Art.* New York: Oxford University Press.

Dudley, Kathryn Marie. 2000. *Debt and Dispossession: Farm Loss in America's Heartland.* Chicago: University of Chicago Press.

Dunham, Katherine. 1969. *Island Possessed.* Garden City, NY: Doubleday.

Durkheim, Émile. (1912) 1965. *The Elementary Forms of Religious Life.* New York: Free Press.

Durrenberger, E. Paul, and Suzan Erem. 2010. *Anthropology Unbound: A Field Guide to the 21st Century* (2nd ed.). Boulder, CO: Paradigm.

Edelman, Marc. 1999. *Peasants against Globalization: Rural Social Movements in Costa Rica.* Stanford, CA: Stanford University Press.

———. 2001. "Social Movements: Changing Paradigms and Forms of Politics." *Annual Review of Anthropology* 30: 285–317.

Edelman, Marc, and Angelique Haugerud. 2005. *The Anthropology of Development and Globalization: From Classical Political Economy to Contemporary Neoliberalism.* Malden, MA: Blackwell.

Ehrenreich, Barbara, and Arlie Russell Hochschild, eds. 2004. *Global Woman: Nannies, Maids, and Sex Workers in the New Economy.* New York: Holt Paperbacks.

Eller, Jack David. 1999. *From Culture to Ethnicity to Conflict: An Anthropological Perspective on Ethnic Conflict.* Ann Arbor: University of Michigan Press.

El Issa, Erin. 2015. "2015 American Household Credit Card Debt Study." NerdWallet.com. www.nerdwallet.com/blog/credit-card-data/average-credit-card-debt-household/

England, Sarah. 2002. "The Production and Consumption of Pink-Collar Identities in the Caribbean." *Current Anthropology* 43(3): 522–23.

Englund, Harri. 1999. "A Different Kind of War Story [Review]." *Journal of the Royal Anthropological Institute* 5(1): 141–42.

Ericksen, Thomas Hylland. 2010. *Ethnicity and Nationalism* (3rd ed.). Boulder, CO: Pluto Press.

Evans-Pritchard, E. E. 1937. *Witchcraft, Oracles and Magic among the Azande.* Oxford, UK: Clarendon Press.

———. 1940. *The Nuer: A Description of the Modes of Livelihood and Political Institutions of a Nilotic People.* Oxford, UK: Clarendon Press.

———. 1951. *Kinship and Marriage among the Nuer.* Oxford, UK: Clarendon Press.

Fadiman, Anne. 1997. *The Spirit Catches You and You Fall Down: A Hmong Child, Her American Doctors, and the Collision of Two Cultures.* New York: Farrar, Straus, and Giroux.

Falk, R. 1993. "The Making of Global Citizenship." In *Global Visions: Beyond the New World Order,* edited by Jeremy Brecher, John B. Childs, and Jill Cutler, 39–50. Boston: South End.

Fanon, Frantz. 1961. *The Wretched of the Earth.* Paris: F. Maspero.

Farmer, Paul. 1985. "The Anthropologist Within." *Harvard Medical Alumni Bulletin* 59(1): 23–28.

———. 2003. *Pathologies of Power: Health, Human Rights and the New War on the Poor.* Berkeley: University of California Press.

———. 2006. *AIDS and Accusation: Haiti and the Geography of Blame.* Berkeley: University of California Press.

Farquhar, Judith Brooke. 1986. "Knowledge and Practice in Chinese Medicine." Ph.D. dissertation, University of Chicago, Department of Anthropology.

———. 1994. *Knowing Practice: The Clinical Encounter of Chinese Medicine.* Boulder, CO: Westview Press.

Fausto-Sterling, Anne. 1993. "The Five Sexes: Why Male and Female Are Not Enough." *The Sciences* May/April: 20–24.

Feagin, Joe R., and Clairece Booher Feagin. 2011. *Racial and Ethnic Relations* (9th ed.). New York: Pearson.

Feagin, Joe R., and Melvin P. Sikes. 1994. *Living with Racism: The Black Middle-Class Experience.* Boston: Beacon Press.

Fedigan, Linda. 1982. *Primate Paradigms: Sex Roles and Social Bonds.* Montreal: Eden Press.

———. 1986. "The Changing Role of Women in Models of Human Evolution." *Annual Reviews of Anthropology* 15: 25–66.

Feldman, Jeffrey D. 2001. "Reproducing Jews: A Cultural Account of Assisted Conception in Israel [Review]." *American Ethnologist* 28(4): 924–25.

Ferguson, Brian R. 2002. "The History of War: Fact vs. Fiction." In *Must We Fight?: From the Battlefield to the Schoolyard, a New Perspective on Violent Conflict and Its Prevention,* edited by William L. Ury, 26–37. San Francisco: Jossey-Bass.

———. 2011. "Tribal Warfare." In *Encyclopedia of War,* 1–13. Malden, MA: Blackwell.

Ferguson, James, and Akhil Gupta. 2002. "Spatializing States: Toward an Ethnography of Neoliberal Governmentality." *American Ethnologist* 29(4): 981–1002.

Fernandez-Kelly, Maria Patricia. 1983. *For We Are Sold, I and My People: Women and Industry in Mexico's Frontier.* Albany: State University of New York Press.

Fernea, Robert. 1996. "Photographic Politics." *Current Anthropology* 37(1): 183–84.

FinAid. 2016. "Student Loan Debt Clock." www.finaid.org/loans/studentloandebtclock.phtml

Finkler, Kaja. 2002. "Reproducing Jews: A Cultural Account of Assisted Conception in Israel [Review]." *Journal of Anthropological Research* 58(2): 299–301.

Finnstrom, Sverker. 2005. "Shadows of War: Violence, Power and International Profiteering in the Twenty-First Century [Review]." *Anthropological Quarterly* 78(2): 491–96.

Fisher, Bonnie, Leah E. Daigle, and Francis T. Cullen. 2010. *Unsafe in the Ivory Tower: The Sexual Victimization of College Women.* Los Angeles: Sage Publications.

Fisher, Helen. 2004. *Why We Love: The Nature and Chemistry of Romantic Love.* New York: Henry Holt.

Flaherty, Robert Joseph. 1922. *Nanook of the North.* [France?]: Révillon Frères.

Floyd, Charlene J. 1996. "A Theology of Insurrection? Religion and Politics in Mexico." *Journal of International Affairs* 50(1): 142–65.

Flueckiger, Joyce. 2006. *In Amma's Healing Room: Gender and Vernacular Islam in South India.* Bloomington: Indiana University Press.

Fluehr-Lobban, Carolyn. 2006. *Race and Racism: An Introduction.* Lanham, MD: Altamira Press.

Fortes, Meyer. 1949. "Time and Social Structure: An Ashanti Case Study." In *Social Structure: Studies Presented to A. R. Radcliffe-Brown,* edited by Meyer Fortes. Oxford, UK: Clarendon Press.

Fortes, Meyer, and E. E. Evans-Pritchard. 1940. *African Political Systems.* London: Published for the International Institute of African Languages & Cultures by the Oxford University Press.

Foucault, Michel. (1976) 1990. *The History of Sexuality*, vol. 1: *An Introduction*. New York: Vintage Books.

———. 1977. *Discipline and Punish: The Birth of the Prison*. New York: Pantheon.

———. 1978. *The History of Sexuality*. New York: Pantheon.

Fouts, Roger. 1997. *Next of Kin: What Chimpanzees Have Taught Me about Who We Are*. New York: William Morrow.

Frank, Andre Gunder. 1969. *Latin America: Underdevelopment or Revolution: Essays on the Development of Underdevelopment and the Immediate Enemy*. New York: Monthly Review Press.

———. 1998. *ReORIENT: Global Economy in the Asian Age*. Berkeley: University of California Press.

Franklin, Sarah. 1997. *Embodied Progress: A Cultural Account of Assisted Conception*. London: Routledge.

Frazer, James George. 1890. *The Golden Bough: A Study in Comparative Religion*. New York: Macmillan.

Freeman, Carla. 2000. *High Tech and High Heels in the Global Economy*. Durham, NC: Duke University Press.

Freud, Sigmund. 1952. *Totem and Taboo: Some Points of Agreement between the Mental Lives of Savages and Neurotics*. New York: Norton.

Freyre, Gilberto. (1933) 1944. *The Masters and the Slaves: A Study in the Development of Brazilian Civilization*. New York: Knopf.

Friedman, Jaclyn, and Jessica Valenti. 2008. *Yes Means Yes! Visions of Female Sexual Power and a World without Rape*. Berkeley, CA: Seal Press.

Friedner, Michele. 2015. *Valuing Deaf Worlds in Urban India*. Rutgers, NJ: Rutgers University Press.

Fuentes, Augustin. 2013. "Blurring the Biological and Social in Human Becomings." In *Biosocial Becomings: Integrating Social and Biological Anthropology*, edited by Tim Ingold and Gisli Palsson, 42–58. New York: Cambridge University Press.

Gardner, Robert. 1963. *Dead birds*. Cambridge, MA: Harvard University Film Study Center.

Gaudio, Rudolf. 2009. *Allah Made Us: Sexual Outlaws in an Islamic African City*. Malden, MA: Wiley-Blackwell.

Gaunt, Kyra Danielle. 2006. *The Games Black Girls Play: Learning the Ropes from Double-Dutch to Hip-Hop*. New York: New York University Press.

Geertz, Clifford. 1973a. "Deep Play: Notes on a Balinese Cockfight." In *The Interpretation of Cultures*. New York: Basic Books.

———. 1973b. "Religion as a Cultural System." In *The Interpretation of Cultures*. New York: Basic Books.

———. 1973c. "Thick Description: Toward an Interpretive Theory of Culture." In *The Interpretation of Cultures*. New York: Basic Books.

Gell, A. F. 1995. "*African Art in Transit* [Review]." *Journal of the Royal Anthropological Institute* 1(4): 841–42.

Gellner, Ernest. 1983. *Nations and Nationalism*. Ithaca, NY: Cornell University Press.

Geyer, Michael. 1989. "The Militarization of Europe, 1914–1945." In *The Militarization of the Western World*, edited by John Gillis, 65–102. New Brunswick, NJ: Rutgers University Press.

Gibson, Jane. 1996. "The Social Construction of Whiteness in Shellcracker Haven, Florida." *Human Organization* 55(4): 379–89.

Giddens, Anthony. 1985. *The Nation-State and Violence*. Cambridge, UK: Polity.

Ginsburg, Faye D., Lila Abu-Lughod, and Brian Larkin, eds. 2002. *Media Worlds: Anthropology on New Terrain*. Berkeley: University of California Press.

Ginsburg, Faye and Rayna Rapp. 2013. "Disability Worlds." *Annual Review of Anthropology* 42:53–68.

Glazer, Nathan, and Daniel Patrick Moynihan. 1970. *Beyond the Melting Pot* (2nd ed.). Cambridge, MA: MIT Press.

Gledhill, John. 2000. *Power and Its Disguises: Anthropological Perspectives on Politics*. London: Pluto.

Global Footprint Network. 2016. http://footprintnetwork.org

Global Witness. 2007. *Hot Chocolate: How Cocoa Fuelled the Conflict in Côte D'Ivoire*. www.globalwitness.org/sites/default/files/pdfs/cotedivoire.pdf

Gluckman, Max. 1954. *Rituals of Rebellion in South-East Africa*. Manchester, UK: Manchester University Press.

Gmelch, George. 1992. "Superstition and Ritual in American Baseball." *Elysian Fields Quarterly* 11(3): 25–36.

Goldstein, Daniel M. 2016. *Owners of the Sidewalk: Security and Survival in the Informal City*. Durham, NC: Duke University Press.

Goldstein, Donna M. 2003. *Laughter out of Place: Race, Class, Violence, and Sexuality in a Rio Shantytown.* Berkeley: University of California Press.

Goldstein, Judith L. 1998. "Reading *National Geographic* [Review]." *American Ethnologist* 25(1): 9–10.

Goode, Judith, and Jeff Maskovsky, eds. 2001. *The New Poverty Studies: The Ethnography of Power, Politics, and Impoverished People in the United States.* New York: New York University Press.

Gough, Kathleen. 1971. "Nuer Kinship: A Reexamination." In *The Translation of Culture: Essays to E. E. Evans-Pritchard,* edited by Thomas O. Beidelman, 79–121. London: Tavistock Publications.

Graeber, David. 2011. *Debt: The First Five Thousand Years.* Brooklyn, NY: Melville House.

Gramsci, Antonio. 1971. *Selections from the Prison Notebooks,* translated and edited by Quintin Hoare and Geoffrey Nowell Smith. New York: International Publishers.

Gray, John. 1992. *Men Are from Mars, Women Are from Venus: The Classic Guide to Understanding the Opposite Sex.* New York: Harper.

Green, Edward C. 1999. *Indigenous Theories of Contagious Disease.* Walnut Creek, CA: AltaMira.

Green, L. J. 2002. *African American English: A Linguistic Introduction.* Cambridge, MA: Cambridge University Press.

Gregg, Jessica L. 2003. *Virtually Virgins: Sexual Strategies and Cervical Cancer in Recife, Brazil.* Stanford, CA: Stanford University Press.

Gregory, Steven. 1998. *Black Corona: Race and the Politics of Place in an Urban Community.* Princeton, NJ: Princeton University Press.

Gregory, Steven, and Roger Sanjek, eds. 1994. *Race.* New Brunswick, NJ: Rutgers University Press.

Grimshaw, Ana, and Amanda Ravetz. 2009. *Observational Cinema: Anthropology, Film, and the Exploration of Social Life.* Bloomington: Indiana University Press.

Gudmundson, Lowell. 2001. "Peasants Against Globalization: Rural Social Movement in Costa Rica [Review]." *Agricultural History* 75(4): 504–6.

Guest, Kenneth J. 2003. *God in Chinatown: Religion and Survival in New York's Evolving Immigrant Community.* New York: New York University Press.

———. 2011. "From Mott Street to East Broadway: Fuzhounese Immigrants and the Revitalization of New York's Chinatown." *Journal of Chinese Overseas* 7(1): 24–44.

Gusterson, Hugh. 1996. *Nuclear Rites: A Weapons Laboratory at the End of the Cold War.* Berkeley: University of California Press.

———. 1997. "Studying Up Revisited." *Political and Legal Anthropology Review* 20(1): 114–19.

———. 2004. *People of the Bomb: Portraits of America's Nuclear Complex.* Minneapolis: University of Minnesota Press.

———. 2008. "When Professors Go to War: Why the Ivory Tower and the Pentagon Don't Mix." *Foreign Policy,* July 21.

Gutmann, Matthew C. 2007. *The Meanings of Macho: Being a Man in Mexico City.* Berkeley: University of California Press. (Originally published in 1996.)

Hannerz, Ulf. 1996. *Transnational Connections: Culture, People, Places.* London: Routledge.

Harding, Jennifer. 1998. "Investigating Sex: Essentialism and Constructionism." In *Sex Acts,* 8–22. London: Sage Publications.

Hargrove, Melissa D. 2009. "Mapping the 'Social Field of Whiteness': White Racism as Habitus in the City Where History Lives." *Transforming Anthropology* 17(2): 93–104.

Harris, Marvin. 1964. *Patterns of Race in the Americas.* New York: Walker.

———. 1970. "Referential Ambiguity in the Calculus of Brazilian Racial Identity." *Southwestern Journal of Anthropology* 21(1): 1–14.

———. 1974. *Cows, Pigs, Wars, & Witches: The Riddles of Culture.* New York: Random House.

Harris, Reginald. 2009. "Allah Made Us [Review]." *Gay and Lesbian Review Worldwide* 16(6): 42.

Harrison, Faye V. 1998. "Introduction: Expanding the Discourse on 'Race.'" *American Anthropologist* 100(3): 609–31.

———. 2002a. "Subverting the Cultural Logics of Marked and Unmarked Racisms in the Global Era." In *Discrimination and Tolerations,* edited by K. Hastrup and G. Ulrich, 97–125. London: Kluwer Law International.

———. 2002b. "Unraveling 'Race' for the 21st Century." In *Exotic No More: Anthropology on the Front Lines,* edited by Jeremy MacClancy. Chicago: University of Chicago Press.

Harrison, K. David. 2007. *When Languages Die: The Extinction of the World's Languages and the Erosion of Human Knowledge.* New York: Oxford University Press.

Hartigan, John Jr. 1999. *Racial Situations: Class Predicaments of Whiteness in Detroit*. Princeton, NJ: Princeton University Press.

———. 2005. *Odd Tribes: Toward a Cultural Analysis of White People*. Durham, NC: Duke University Press.

Harvey, David. 1990. *The Condition of Postmodernity: An Enquiry into the Origins of Cultural Change*. Malden, MA: Blackwell.

———. 1996. *Justice, Nature and the Geography of Difference*. Oxford: Blackwell.

———. 2003. *The New Imperialism*. Oxford: Oxford University Press.

Haugerud, Angelique. 1998. "Purity and Exile: A Book Review." *International Journal of African Historical Studies* 31(1): 214–16.

Haugerud, Angelique, Margaret Priscilla Stone, and Peter D. Little. 2000. *Commodities and Globalization: Anthropological Perspectives*. Lanham, MD: Rowman & Littlefield.

Hearn, Jonathan. 2006. *Rethinking Nationalism: A Critical Introduction*. New York: Palgrave Macmillan.

Helmreich, Stefan. 2009. *Alien Ocean: Anthropological Voyages in Microbial Seas*. Berkeley: University of California Press.

Henshilwood, Christopher S., et al. 2011. "A 100,000-Year-Old Ochre-Processing Workshop at Blombos Cave, South Africa." *Science* 334(6053): 219–22.

Herzog, Werner (director). 2010. *Cave of Forgotten Dreams*. IFC Films.

Higgenbotham, Evelyn Brooks. 1992. "African-American Women's History and the Metalanguage of Race." *Signs: Journal of Women in Culture and Society* 17: 251–74.

Hirsch, Jennifer. 2007. "'Love Makes a Family': Globalization, Companionate Marriage, and the Modernization of Gender Equality." In *Love and Globalization: Transformations of Intimacy in the Contemporary World*, edited by Mark Padilla, Jennifer Hirsch, Miguel Munoz-Laboy, Richard Sember, and Richard Parker, 93–106. Nashville, TN: Vanderbilt University Press.

Ho, Karen. 2009. *Liquidated: An Ethnography of Wall Street*. Durham, NC: Duke University Press.

Hobhouse, L. T. 1915. *Morals in Evolution; A Study in Comparative Ethics*. New York: Holt.

Hobsbawm, Eric, and Terence Ranger. 1983. *Invented Traditions*. Cambridge, UK: Cambridge University Press.

Hockings, Paul Edward, ed. 2003. *Principles of Visual Anthropology* (3rd ed.). Berlin: Mouton De Gruyter.

Holmes, Janet. 1998. "Women's Talk: The Question of Sociolinguistic Universals." In *Language and Gender: A Reader*, edited by Jennifer Coates, 461–83. Oxford, UK: Blackwell.

Hondagneu-Sotelo, Pierrette. 2001. *Domestica: Immigrant Workers Cleaning and Caring in the Shadows of Affluence*. Berkeley: University of California Press.

Honwana, Alcinda. 1999. "A Different Kind of War Story [Review]." *American Ethnologist* 26(2): 504–5.

Hopkins, Nancy. 1999. "A Study on the Status of Women Faculty in Science at MIT." *MIT Faculty Newsletter*, 11(4): 1–15.

Hostetler, John A. 1993. *Amish Society* (4th ed.). Baltimore: Johns Hopkins University Press.

———. 1997. *Hutterite Society* (2nd ed.). Baltimore: Johns Hopkins University Press.

Hubbard, Ruth. 1990. "The Social Construction of Sexuality." In *The Politics of Women's Biology*. New Brunswick, NJ: Rutgers University Press.

Hurston, Zora Neale. 1935. *Mules and Men*. Philadelphia: Lippincott.

———. 1938. *Tell My Horse*. Philadelphia: Lippincott.

Hutchinson, Sharon. 1996. *Nuer Dilemmas: Coping with Money, War and the State*. Berkeley: University of California Press.

Ignatiev, Noel. 1995. *How the Irish Became White*. New York: Routledge Press.

Illouz, Eva. 1997. *Consuming the Romantic Utopia: Love and Cultural Contradictions of Capitalism*. Berkeley: University of California Press.

Inda, Jonathan Xavier, and Renato Rosaldo. 2002. *The Anthropology of Globalization: A Reader*. Malden, MA: Blackwell.

India Resource Center. 2015. www.indiaresource.org/index.html

Ingold, Tim, and Gisli Palsson, eds. 2013. *Biosocial Becomings: Integrating Social and Biological Anthropology*. New York: Cambridge University Press.

Ingraham, Chrys. 2008. *White Weddings: Romancing Heterosexuality in Popular Culture*, (rev. ed.). New York: Routledge. (Originally published in 1999.)

Ingstad, Benedicte, and Susan R Whyte, eds. 2007. *Disability in Local and Global Worlds*. Berkeley: University of California Press

Inhorn, Marcia. 1996. *Infertility and Patriarchy: The Cultural Politics of Gender and Family Life in Egypt.* Philadelphia: University of Pennsylvania Press.

Instituto Cervantes. 2015. "El español: un lengua viva." http://eldiae.es/wp-content/uploads/2015/06/espanol_lengua-viva_20151.pdf

International Monetary Fund. 2014. "World Economic Outlook Database." www.imf.org/external/pubs/ft/weo/2014/02/weodata/index.aspx

International Telecommunication Union. 2015. "Statistics." www.itu.int/en/ITU-D/Statistics/Pages/stat/default.aspx

Ivana, Greti-Julia. 2015. "Nation as Network: A Book Review." *Information, Communication and Society* 18(12): 1481–83.

Jacobs, A. J. 2005. "Tsukiji: The Fish Market at the Center of the World [Review]." *Contemporary Sociology* 34(4): 373–75.

Jacobs, Sue-Ellen, ed. 1997. *Two-Spirit People: Native American Gender Identity, Sexuality, and Spirituality.* Champaign: University of Illinois Press.

Jamison, Sandra L. 2006. "The Games Black Girls Play [Review]." *Black Issues Book Review,* 8(3): 43–44.

Jaynes, Gregory. 1982. "A Louisiana Lawsuit Asks What It Means to Be Black, White, or 'Colored' in America." *Providence Sunday Journal,* October 14, A-19.

Jenkins, Richard. 1996. *Social Identity.* New York: Routledge.

———. 2008. *Rethinking Ethnicity* (2nd ed.). Thousand Oaks, CA: Sage.

Jones, Camara Phyllis. 2000. "Levels of Racism: A Theoretic Framework and a Gardener's Tale." *American Journal of Public Health* 90(8): 1212–15.

Jordan, Brigitte. 1993. *Birth in Four Cultures: A Cross-cultural Investigation of Childbirth in Yucatan, Holland, Sweden, and the United States.* Rev. and expanded by Robbie Davis-Floyd. Prospect Heights, IL: Waveland Press.

Jordan, Miriam. 2010. "Arizona Grades Teachers on Fluency: State Pushes School Districts to Reassign Instructors with Heavy Accents or Other Shortcomings in Their English." *Wall Street Journal,* April 30.

Juris, Jeffrey S. 2012. "Reflections on #Occupy Everywhere: Social Media, Public Space, and Emerging Logics of Aggregation." *American Ethnologist* 39(2): 259–79.

Juris, Jeffrey S., and Alex Khasnabish. 2013. *Insurgent Encounters: Transnational Activism, Ethnography, and the Political.* Durham, NC: Duke University Press.

Kahn, Susan Martha. 2000. *Reproducing Jews: A Cultural Account of Assisted Conception in Israel.* Durham, NC: Duke University Press.

Kant, Immanuel. 1790. *Critique of Judgement.* Translated by J. H. Bernard. London: Collier Macmillan.

Karp, Ivan, and Steven Lavine. 1991. *Exhibiting Cultures: The Poetics and Politics of Museum Display.* Washington, DC: Smithsonian Institution.

Katz, Jonathan Ned. 2007. *The Invention of Heterosexuality,* with a new preface. Chicago: University of Chicago Press. (Originally published in 1995.)

Kearney, M. 1995. "The Local and the Global: The Anthropology of Globalization and Transnationalism." *Annual Review of Anthropology* 24: 547–65.

Keynes, John Maynard. (1936) 2007. *The General Theory of Employment Interest and Money.* Houndmills, UK: Palgrave Macmillan.

Kidder, Tracy. 2003. *Mountains beyond Mountains: The Quest of Dr. Paul Farmer, A Man Who Would Cure the World.* New York: Random House.

Kinsey, Alfred C. 1953. *Sexual Behavior in the Human Female.* Philadelphia: W. B. Saunders.

Kinsey, Alfred C., Wardell Baxter Pomeroy, and Clyde E. Martin. 1948. *Sexual Behavior in the Human Male.* Philadelphia: W. B. Saunders.

Kleinman, Arthur. 1988. *The Illness Narratives: Suffering, Healing, and the Human Condition.* New York: Basic Books.

Knauft, Bruce M. 1991. "Violence and Sociality in Human Evolution." *Current Anthropology* 32(4): 391–408.

Kohrman, Matthew. 2005. *Bodies of Difference: Experiences of Disability and Institutional Advocacy in the Making of Modern China.* Berkeley: University of California Press

Kolbert, Elizabeth. 2014. *The Sixth Extinction: An Unnatural History.* New York: Henry Holt.

Kopytoff, Igor. 1986. "The Cultural Biography of Things: Commoditization as Process." In *The Social Life of Things: Commodities in Cultural Perspective,* edited by Arjun Appadurai, 64–91. Cambridge, UK: Cambridge University Press.

Kottak, Conrad P. 2006. *Assault on Paradise: The Globalization of a Little Community in Brazil* (4th ed.). New York: McGraw-Hill.

Kromidas, Maria. 2004. "Learning War/Learning Race: Fourth-Grade Students in the Aftermath of September 11th in New York City." *Critique of Anthropology* 24(1).

Krugman, Paul R. 2015. "Ending Greece's Bleeding." *New York Times*, July 5.

Kulick, Don, and Jens Rydstrom. 2015. *Loneliness and Its Opposite: Sex, Disability, and the Ethics of Engagement*. Durham, NC: Duke University Press.

Kuper, Adam. 1983. *Anthropology and Anthropologists: The Modern British School*. London: Routledge & Kegan Paul.

Kurtz, Donald V. 2001. *Political Anthropology: Power and Paradigms*. Boulder, CO: Westview Press.

Kuzawa, Christopher, et al. 2009. "Fatherhood, Pair-Bonding, and Testosterone in the Philippines." *Hormones and Behavior* 56(4): 429–35.

Labov, William. 1972. *Language in the Inner City: Studies in the Black English Vernacular*. Philadelphia: University of Pennsylvania Press.

Lakoff, Robin T. 2004. *Language and Woman's Place: Text and Commentaries*, edited by Mary Bucholtz. New York: Oxford University Press.

Lan, Pei-Chia. 2006. *Global Cinderellas: Migrant Domestics and Newly Rich Employers in Taiwan*. Durham, NC: Duke University Press.

Lancaster, Roger N. 1994. *Life Is Hard: Machismo, Danger, and the Intimacy of Power in Nicaragua*. Berkeley: University of California Press.

Landers, Melissa A., and Gary Alan Fine. 1996. "Learning Life's Lessons in Tee Ball: The Reinforcement of Gender and Status in Kindergarten Sport." *Sociology of Sport Journal* 13(1).

Larrain, Jorge, 1989. *Theories of Development: Capitalism, Colonialism and Dependency*. London: Polity Press.

Larsen, Clark Spencer. 2014. *Our Origins: Discovering Physical Anthropology* (3rd ed.). New York: Norton.

Leach, Edmund. 1954. *Political Systems of Highland Burma: A Study of Kachin Social Structure*. Cambridge, MA: Harvard University Press.

Leacock, Eleanor Burke. 1971. *The Culture of Poverty: A Critique*. New York: Simon & Schuster.

———. 1981. *Myths of Male Dominance: Collected Articles on Women Cross-Culturally*. New York: Monthly Review Press.

Leap, William L. 2010. "Allah Made Us [Review]." *Journal of the Royal Anthropological Institute* 16: 938–39.

Lee, Richard B. 1984. *The Dobe !Kung*. New York: Holt, Rinehart and Winston.

———. 2003. *The Dobe JuHoansi* (3rd ed.) (Case Studies in Cultural Anthropology). Belmont, CA: Wadsworth Publishing.

Lee, Richard B., and Irven Devore, eds. 1968. *Man the Hunter: The First Intensive Survey of a Single Crucial Stage of Human Development—Man's Once Universal Hunting Way of Life*. New York: The Wenner-Gren Foundation for Anthropological Research.

Lessinger, Johanna. 1995. *From the Ganges to the Hudson: Indian Immigrants in New York City*. Boston: Allyn & Bacon.

Lewellen, Ted C. 2002. *The Anthropology of Globalization: Cultural Anthropology Enters the 21st Century*. Westport, CT: Praeger.

———. 2003. *Political Anthropology: An Introduction*. Westport, CT: Praeger.

Lewin, Ellen. 1992. "Families We Choose: Lesbians, Gays, Kinship [Review]." *American Ethnologist* 19(4): 825–26.

———. 1995. "Life Is Hard [Review]." *American Ethnologist* 22(2): 441–42.

Lewis, Oscar. 1959. *Five Families: Mexican Case Studies in the Culture of Poverty*. New York: Basic Books.

———. 1966. *La Vida: A Puerto Rican Family in the Culture of Poverty—San Juan and New York*. New York: Random House.

Leys, Colin. 1996. *The Rise and Fall of Development Theory*. Oxford, UK: James Currey.

Liang, Zai. 2012. "Recent Migration Trends in China: Geographic and Demographic Aspects of Development Implications." Presentation for UN Expert Group Meeting on New Trends in Migration: Demographic Aspects, New York, December 3. www.un.org/esa/population/meetings/EGM_MigrationTrends/UN_presentation_Dec_2012_FINAL_SH.pdf

Liang, Zai, Zhen Li, and Zhongdang Ma. 2014. Changing Patterns of the Floating Population in China, 2000–2010. *Population and Development Review* 40(4): 695–716.

Limon, Jose E. 1997. "The Meanings of Macho: Being a Man in Mexico City [Review]." *American Anthropologist* 99(1): 185.

LiPuma, Edward, and Benjamin Lee, 2004. *Financial Derivatives and the Globalization of Risk*. Duke University Press.

Lock, Margaret M. 1993. *Encounters with Aging: Mythologies of Menopause in Japan and North America*. Berkeley: University of California Press.

———. 2002. *Twice Dead: Organ Transplants and the Reinvention of Death.* Berkeley: University of California Press.

Lopez, Ian Haney. 2006. *White by Law: The Legal Construction of Race* (2nd ed.). New York: New York University Press.

Lorber, Judith. 1994. *Paradoxes of Gender.* New Haven, CT: Yale University Press.

Low, Setha, and Sally Engle Merry. 2010. "Engaged Anthropology: Diversity and Dilemmas: An Introduction to Supplement 2." *Current Anthropology* 51(S2): 203–26.

Lowie, Robert Harry. 1920. *Primitive Society.* New York: Harper & Brothers.

Lutz, Catherine. 2001. *Homefront: A Military City and the American Twentieth Century.* Boston: Beacon.

———. 2004. "Militarization." In *A Companion to the Anthropology of Politics*, edited by David Nugent and Joan Vincent, 318–31. Malden, MA: Blackwell.

Lutz, Catherine, and Jane L. Collins. 1993. *Reading National Geographic.* Chicago: University of Chicago Press.

MacClancy, Jeremy, ed. 1996. *Sport, Identity and Ethnicity.* Oxford, UK: Berg.

MacDougall, David. 2005. *Film, Ethnography, and the Senses: The Corporeal Image.* Princeton, NJ: Princeton University Press.

Malinowski, Bronislaw. (1922) 2002. *Argonauts of the Western Pacific.* London: Routledge.

———. 1927. *Sex and Repression in Savage Society.* London: Kegan Paul, Trench, Trübner & Co.

———. 1929. *The Sexual Life of Savages in North Western Melanesia: An Ethnographic Account of Courtship, Marriage and Family Life among the Natives of the Trobriand Islands, British New Guinea.* London: Kegan Paul, Trench, Trübner & Co.

———. 1930. "Parenthood—The Basis of Social Structure." In *The New Generation: The Intimate Problems of Modern Parents and Children*, edited by Victor F. Calverton and Samuel D. Schmalhausen. London: George Allen & Unwin.

Malkki, Liisa. 1995. *Purity and Exile: Violence, Memory, and National Cosmology Among Hutu Refugees in Tanzania.* Chicago: University of Chicago Press.

Mallory, J. P., and D. Q. Adams. 2006. *The Oxford Introduction to Proto-Indo-European and the Proto-Indo-European World.* Oxford, UK: Oxford University Press.

Mamdani, Mahmood. 2002. *When Victims Become Killers: Colonialism, Nativism, and the Genocide in Rwanda.* Princeton, NJ: Princeton University Press.

Marable, Manning. 2002. "Whither Whiteness." *Souls: A Critical Journal of Black Politics, Culture and Society* 4(4): 45–73.

Marcus, George E., and Fred R. Myers. 1995. *The Traffic in Culture: Refiguring Art and Anthropology.* Berkeley: University of California Press.

Mardi Gras: Made in China. 2005. Directed by David Redmon. Carnivalesque Films.

Marks, Jonathan. 1995. *Human Biodiversity: Genes, Race, and History.* New York: Aldine de Gruyter.

Marlowe, Frank. 2010. *The Hadza: Hunter-Gatherers of Tanzania.* Berkeley: University of California Press.

Martin, Emily. 1991. "The Egg and the Sperm: How Science Has Constructed a Romance Based on Stereotypical Male-Female Roles." *Signs: Journal of Women in Culture and Society* 16(3): 485–501.

Martin, Joann. 1999. "Women and Social Movements in Latin America: Power from Below [Review]." *American Ethnologist* 26(2): 482–83.

Marx, Karl. 1867. *Capital.* Reprint, London: Penguin, 1986.

Marx, Karl, and Friedrich Engels. 1848. *The Communist Manifesto.* Reprint, London: Penguin, 1967.

———. 1957. *On Religion.* Moscow: Foreign Languages Publishing House.

Mascia-Lees, Frances E. 2009. *Gender and Difference in a Globalizing World: Twenty-First Century Anthropology.* Prospect Heights, IL: Waveland Press.

Mauss, Marcel. 1979. "Body Techniques." In *Sociology and Psychology: Essays by Marcel Mauss*, translated by Ben Brewster. London: Routledge and Kegan Paul.

Maybury-Lewis, David. 2002. *Indigenous Peoples, Ethnic Groups and the State.* Boston: Allyn and Bacon.

McAdam, Doug, John D. McCarthy, and Mayer N. Zald. 1996. *Comparative Perspectives on Social Movements: Political Opportunities, Mobilizing Structures, and Cultural Framings.* Cambridge, UK: Cambridge University Press.

McAdoo, Harriette Pipes. 2000. "All Our Kin: Strategies for Survival in a Black Community

[Review]." *Journal of Marriage and Family* 62(3): 864–65.

McBrearty, Sally, and Alison S. Brooks. 2000. "The Revolution That Wasn't: A New Interpretation of the Origin of Modern Human Behaviour." *Journal of Human Evolution* 39(5): 453–563.

McClaurin, Irma. 2007. "Finding Zora." www .research.ufl.edu/publications/explore/v07n1 /zora.htm

McCracken, Grant. 1991. *Culture and Consumption: New Approaches to the Symbolic Character of Consumer Goods and Activities*. Bloomington: Indiana University Press.

———. 2005. *Culture and Consumption II: Markets, Meaning, and Brand Management*. Bloomington: Indiana University Press.

McFate, Montgomery. 2005. "Anthropology and Counterinsurgency: The Strange Story of Their Curious Relationship." *Military Review* (March-April): 24–38.

McGrath, Charles. 2005. "In Fiction, a Long History of Fixation on the Social Gap." *New York Times*, June 8.

McIntosh, Peggy. 1989. "White Privilege: Unpacking the Invisible Knapsack." *Peace and Freedom* (July–August): 10–12.

McKibben, William. 2010. *Earth: Making a Life on a Tough New Planet*. New York: Henry Holt.

———. 2012. "Global Warming's Terrifying New Math." *Rolling Stone*, July 19.

McKinnon, Susan, and Sydel Silverman, eds. 2005. *Complexities: Beyond Nature and Nurture*. Chicago: University of Chicago Press.

McWhorter, John H. 2001. *The Power of Babel: A Natural History of Language*. New York: HarperCollins.

Mead, Margaret. 1928. *Coming of Age in Samoa: A Psychological Study of Primitive Youth for Western Civilization*. New York: William Morrow.

———. 1935. *Sex and Temperament in Three Primitive Societies*. New York: William Morrow.

———. 1940. "Warfare Is Only an Invention—Not a Biological Necessity." *Asia: A Journal of the American Asiatic Association*. August. 402–405.

Medeiros, Melanie A. 2014. "The Other End of the Bargain: The Socioeconomics of Marital Dissolution in Rural Northeast Brazil." *Transforming Anthropology* 22(2): 105–20.

Miles, H. Lyn White. 1993. "Language and the Orangutan: The Old 'Person of the Forest.'" In *The Great Ape Project*, edited by Paola Cavalieri

and Peter Singer, 45–50. New York: St. Martin's Press.

Miller, Raegen, and Diana Epstein. 2011. "There Still Be Dragons: Racial Disparity in School Funding Is No Myth." Center for American Progress. www.americanprogress.org/issues/education /report/2011/07/05/9943/there-still-be-dragons/

Mills, Mary Beth. 2003. "Gender and Inequality in the Global Labor Force." *Annual Review of Anthropology* 32: 41–62.

Miner, Horace. 1956. "Body Ritual among the Nacirema." *American Anthropologist* 58(3): 503–7.

Mintz, Sidney W. 1985. *Sweetness and Power: The Place of Sugar in Modern History*. New York: Viking Penguin.

Molyneux, Maxine. 1999. "Women and Social Movements in Latin America: Power from Below [Review]." *Journal of Latin American Studies* 31(2): 535–37.

Monnier, Oliver. 2013. "Agribusiness: Smoothing Out the Bumps in Côte d'Ivoire." *The Africa Report*. July 25. www.theafricareport.com /West-Africa/agribusiness-smoothing -out-the-bumps-in-Cote-divoire.html

Moore, Mignon R. 2011. *Invisible Families: Gay Identities, Relationships, and Motherhood among Black Women*. Berkeley: University of California Press.

———. 2012. "Intersectionality and the Study of Black, Sexual Minority Women." *Gender and Society* 26: 33–39.

Moran, Emilio F. 2006. *People and Nature: An Introduction to Human Ecological Relations*. Malden, MA: Blackwell.

Morgan, Lewis Henry. (1877) 1964. *Ancient Society*. Cambridge, MA: Belknap Press.

Morrell, Virginia. 2008. "Inside Animal Minds: Birds, Apes, Dolphins and a Dog with a World-Class Vocabulary." *National Geographic*, March.

Mukhopadhyay, Carol C., Rosemary Henze, and Yolanda T. Moses. 2007. *How Real Is Race? A Sourcebook on Race, Culture, and Biology*. Lanham, MD: Rowman & Littlefield.

Muller, Martin N. et al., 2009. "Testosterone and Paternal Care in East African Foragers and Pastoralists." *Proceeding of the Royal Society: Biological Sciences* 276: 347–354.

Mullings, Leith. 2005a. "Interrogating Racism: Toward an Anti-Racist Anthropology." *Annual Review of Anthropology* 34: 667–93.

―――. 2005b. "Resistance and Resilience: The Sojourner Syndrome and the Social Context of Reproduction in Central Harlem." *Transforming Anthropology* 13(2): 79–91.

Mullings, Leith, and Alaka Wali. 2001. *Stress and Resilience: The Social Context of Reproduction in Central Harlem.* New York: Kluwer Academic/ Plenum Publishers.

Myerhoff, Barbara G. 1974. *Peyote Hunt: The Sacred Journey of the Huichol Indians.* Ithaca, NY: Cornell University Press.

―――. 1978. *Number Our Days.* New York: Dutton.

Nader, Laura. 1972. "Up the Anthropologist: Perspectives Gained from Studying Up." In *Reinventing Anthropology*, edited by Dell H. Hymes, 284–311. New York: Pantheon.

Nahman, Michal Rachel. 2002. "Reproducing Jews: A Cultural Account of Assisted Conception in Israel [Review]." *Canadian Review of Sociology and Anthropology* 39(3): 359–61.

Nakamura, Karen. 2006. *Deaf in Japan: Signing and Politics of Identity.* Ithaca, NY: Cornell University Press.

Nanda, Serena. 1998. *Neither Man nor Woman: The Hijras of India* (2nd ed.). Florence, KY: Wadsworth.

National Aeronautics and Space Administration. 2015. "The Consequences of Climate Change." http://climate.nasa.gov/effects/

Nelson, Diane M. 1999. *A Finger in the Wound: Body Politics in Quincentennial Guatemala.* Berkeley: University of California Press.

Nettl, Bruno. 2005. *The Study of Ethnomusicology: Thirty-One Issues and Concepts.* Urbana: University of Illinois Press.

Neubeck, Kenneth J., and Noel A. Cazenave. 2001. *Welfare Racism: Playing the Race Card Against America's Poor.* New York: Routledge.

Newman, Andrew. 2015. *Landscape of Discontent: Urban Sustainability in Immigrant Paris.* Minneapolis: University of Minnesota Press.

Nordstrom, Carolyn. 1997. *A Different Kind of War Story.* Philadelphia: University of Pennsylvania Press.

―――. 2004. *Shadows of War: Violence, Power, and International Profiteering in the Twenty-First Century.* Berkeley: University of California Press.

North, James. 2011. "The Roots of the Côte d'Ivoire Crisis: How the Demand for Chocolate—Yes, Chocolate!—Helped Fuel the Country's Civil War." *The Nation*, April 25.

Norton, M. I., and D. Ariely. 2011. "Building a Better America—One Wealth Quintile at a Time." *Perspectives on Psychological Science* 6(1): 9–12.

Nugent, David, and Joan Vincent, eds. 2004. *A Companion to the Anthropology of Politics.* Malden, MA: Blackwell.

Ogasawara, Yuko. 1995. "Review of *Nightwork: Sexuality, Pleasure, and Corporate Masculinity in a Tokyo Hostess Club.*" *American Journal of Sociology* 100(4): 1071–73.

Ogden, Cynthia L., Cheryl D. Fryar, Margaret D. Carroll, and Katherine M. Flegal. 2004. "Mean Body Weight, Height, and Body Mass Index, United States 1960–2002." *Advance Data from Vital and Health Statistics* 347(October 27).

Omi, Michael, and Howard Winant. 1994. *Racial Formation in the United States from the 1960s to the 1990s* (2nd ed.). New York: Routledge.

Ong, Aihwa. 1987. *Spirits of Resistance and Capitalist Discipline.* Albany: State University of New York Press.

Ore, Tracy. 2010. *The Social Construction of Difference and Inequality: Race, Class, Gender, and Sexuality.* New York: McGraw-Hill.

Ortner, Sherri. 1974. "Is Female to Male as Nature Is to Culture?" In *Woman, Culture and Society*, edited by Michelle Z. Rosaldo and Louise Lamphere. Stanford, CA: Stanford University Press.

Palsson, Gisli. 2013. "Ensembles of Biosocial Relations." In *Biosocial Becomings: Integrating Social and Biological Anthropology*, edited by Tim Ingold and Gisli Palsson, 23–41. New York: Cambridge University Press.

Parker, Richard. 1999. "The Meanings of Macho [Review]." *American Ethnologist* 26(2): 497–98.

Parsons, Talcott. 1964. *Theory of Social and Economic Organization.* New York: Simon & Schuster.

Pascoe, C. J. 2007. *Dude, You're a Fag: Masculinity and Sexuality in High School.* Berkeley: University of California Press.

Payer, Lynn. 1996. *Medicine and Culture: Varieties of Treatment in the United States, England, West Germany, and France.* New York: Henry Holt.

PayScale. 2015. www.payscale.com

Peletz, Michael G. 1999. "The Heat of the Hearth [Review]." *American Ethnologist* 26(1): 251–52.

Pérez-Alemán, Paola. 1994. "Life Is Hard [Review]." *American Journal of Sociology* 99(5): 1393–95.

Perkins, Morgan, and Howard Morphy, eds. 2006. *The Anthropology of Art: A Reader.* Malden, MA: Blackwell.

Petersen, Glenn. 2009. *Traditional Micronesian Societies: Adaptation, Integration, and Political Organization*. Honolulu: University of Hawaii Press.

———. 2015. "American Anthropology's 'Thailand Controversy': An Object Lesson in Professional Responsibility." *SOJOURN: Journal of Social Issues in Southeast Asia* 30(2): 528–49.

Pew Forum on Religion & Public Life. 2015. "America's Changing Religious Landscape." www.pewforum.org/2015/05/12/americas-changing-religious-landscape

Pew Research Center. 2013. "Second Generation Americans: A Portrait of the Adult Children of Immigrants." www.pewsocialtrends.org/2013/02/07/second-generation-americans/

Phillips, Sarah. 2011. *Disability and Mobile Citizenship in Postsocialist Ukraine*. Bloomington: Indiana University Press.

Polanyi, Karl. (1944) 2001. *The Great Transformation*. Boston: Beacon.

Pollitt, Katha. 2005. "Summers of Our Discontent." *The Nation*, February 21.

Pordié, Laurent. 2008. *Tibetan Medicine in the Contemporary World: Global Politics of Medical Knowledge and Practice*. London: Routledge.

Portes, Alejandro, Patricia Fernández-Kelly, and William Haller. 2009. "The Adaptation of the Immigrant Second Generation in America: Theoretical Overview and Recent Evidence." *Journal of Ethnic and Migration Studies* 35(7): 1077–1104.

Portes, Alejandro, and Rubén G. Rumbaut. 2006. *Immigrant America: A Portrait*. Berkeley: University of California Press.

Price, David. 2004. *Threatening Anthropology*. Durham, NC: Duke University Press.

———. 2011. *Weaponizing Anthropology: Social Science in Service of the Militarized State*. Oakland, CA: AK Distribution.

Price, Sally. 1989. *Primitive Art in Civilized Places*. Chicago: University of Chicago Press.

Quinn, Naomi. 1977. "Anthropological Studies on Women's Status." *Annual Review of Anthropology* 6: 181–222.

Radcliffe-Brown, A. R. 1950. "Introduction," In *African Systems of Kinship and Marriage*, edited by A. R. Radcliffe-Brown and Daryll Forde. London: Oxford University Press.

Rebhun, L. A. 1999. *The Heart Is Unknown Country: Love in the Changing Economy of Northeast Brazil*. Stanford, CA: Stanford University Press.

Redfield, Robert. 1941. *The Folk Culture of the Yucatan*. Chicago: University of Chicago Press.

Richards, Audrey. 1956. *Chisungu: A Girl's Initiation Ceremony among the Bemba of Northern Rhodesia*. London: Faber.

Richards, Paul. 1999. "A Different Kind of War Story [Review]." *American Anthropologist* 101(1): 214–15.

Richman, Karen. 2001. "High Tech and High Heels in the Global Economy [Review]." *American Ethnologist* 28(4): 954–55.

Rickford, John R., and Russell J. Rickford. 2000. *Spoken Soul: The Story of Black English*. New York: Wiley.

Robbins, Richard H. 2013. *Global Problems and the Culture of Capitalism* (6th ed.). Boston: Pearson.

Roberts, Elizabeth F. S., and Nancy Scheper-Hughes. 2011. "Introduction: Medical Migrations." *Body and Society* 17(2–3): 1–30.

Rodriguez, Clara. 2000. *Changing Race: Latinos, the Census, and the History of Ethnicity*. New York: New York University Press.

Rodseth, L., R. W. Wrangham, A. M. Harrigan, and B. Smuts. 1991. "The Human Community as a Primate Society." *Current Anthropology* 32: 221–54.

Roediger, David. 1992. *The Wages of Whiteness: Race and the Making of the American Working Class*. New York: Verso.

Rosaldo, Michelle Z. 1974. "Women, Culture and Society: A Theoretical Overview." In *Woman, Culture and Society*, edited by Michelle Z. Rosaldo and Louise Lamphere. Stanford, CA: Stanford University Press.

———. 1980. "The Use and Abuse of Anthropology: Reflections on Feminism and Cross-Cultural Understanding." *Signs: Journal of Women in Culture and Society* 5(3): 389–417.

Roscoe, Will. 1991. *The Zuni Man-Woman*. Albuquerque: University of New Mexico Press.

Roseberry, William. 1997. "Review Essay: On Historical Consciousness." *Current Anthropology*, 38(5): 926–32.

Roth-Gordon, Jennifer. 2016. *Race and the Brazilian Body: Blackness, Whiteness and Everyday Life in Rio de Janeiro*. New York: Macmillan.

Rouse, Roger. 1994. "Life Is Hard [Review]." *Contemporary Sociology* 23(1): 57–9.

Rubin, Gayle. 1975. "The Traffic in Women: Notes on the 'Political Economy' of Sex." In *Toward an Anthropology of Women*, edited by Rayna Reiter. New York: Monthly Review Press.

Ruby, Jay, and Marcus Banks. 2011. *Made to Be Seen: Historical Perspectives on Visual Anthropology.* Chicago: University of Chicago Press.

Rumbaut, Ruben G., and Alejandro Portes, eds. 2001. *Ethnicities: Children of Immigrants in America.* Berkeley: University of California Press.

Sachs, Jeffrey. 2005. *The End of Poverty: Economic Possibilities for Our Time.* New York: Penguin.

Safa, Helen. 1995. *The Myth of the Male Breadwinner: Women and Industrialization in the Caribbean.* Boulder, CO: Westview Press.

Sahlins, Marshall D. 1971. *Social Stratification in Polynesia.* Seattle: University of Washington Press.

———. (1974) 2004. *Stone Age Economics.* New York: Routledge.

Saillant, Francine, and Serge Genest, eds. 2007. *Medical Anthropology: Regional Perspectives and Shared Concerns.* Malden, MA: Blackwell.

Sanday, Peggy. 1990. *Fraternity Gang Rape: Sex, Brotherhood, and Privilege on Campus.* New York: New York University Press.

Sanders, Stephanie A., and June Machover Reinisch. 2006. "Would You Say You 'Had Sex' If . . . ?" In *The Language and Sexuality Reader*, edited by Deborah Cameron and Don Kulick. New York: Routledge.

Sanjek, Roger. 1994. "The Enduring Inequalities of Race." In *Race*, edited by Steven Gregory and Roger Sanjek, 1–17. New Brunswick, NJ: Rutgers University Press.

Sapir, Edward, and Morris Swadesh. 1946. "Word 2." In *American Indian Grammatical Categories*, 103–12. Reedited for Dell Hymes in *Language in Culture and Society*, 100–7. New York: Harper & Row, 1964.

Savage, Michael, and Karel Williams, eds. 2008. *Remembering Elites.* Malden, MA: Blackwell.

Scheid, Volker. 2002. *Chinese Medicine in Contemporary China: Plurality and Synthesis.* Durham, NC: Duke University Press.

Scheid, Volker, and Hugh MacPherson. 2012. *Integrating East Asian Medicine into Contemporary Healthcare.* Edinburgh, UK: Churchill Livingstone Elsevier.

Scheper-Hughes, Nancy. 1989. "Death without Weeping: Has Poverty Ravaged Mother Love in the Shantytowns of Brazil?" *Natural History* 98(10): 8–16.

———. 1992. *Death without Weeping: The Violence of Everyday Life in Brazil.* Berkeley: University of California Press.

———. 1995. "The Primacy of the Ethical: Propositions for a Militant Anthropology." *Current Anthropology* 36(3): 409–20.

———. 2002. "Min(d)ing the Body: On the Trail of Organ-Stealing Rumors." In *Exotic No More: Anthropology on the Front Lines*, edited by Jeremy MacClancy, 33–63. Chicago: University of Chicago Press.

———. 2013. "No More Angel Babies on the Alto do Cruzeiro: A Dispatch from Brazil's Revolution in Child Survival." *Natural History*. www.naturalhistorymag.com/features/282558/no-more-angel-babies-on-the-alto-do-cruzeiro

Scheper-Hughes, Nancy, and Margaret M. Lock. 1987. "The Mindful Body: A Prolegomenon to Future Work in Medical Anthropology." *Medical Anthropology Quarterly* 1(1): 6–41.

Scheper-Hughes, Nancy, and Philippe Bourgois. 2004. *Violence in War and Peace: An Anthology.* New York: Wiley.

Schneider, Arnd, and Christopher Wright. 2006. *Contemporary Art and Anthropology.* Oxford, UK: Berg.

Schneider, David M. 1980. *American Kinship: A Cultural Account* (2nd ed.). Chicago: University of Chicago Press.

Schneider, Jane. 1977. "Was There a Pre-Capitalist World System?" *Peasant Studies* 6(1): 20–29.

Schoendorf, Kenneth C., Carol J. R. Hogue, and Joel C. Kleinman. 1992. "Mortality among Infants of Blacks as Compared to White College-Educated Parents." *New England Journal of Medicine* 326(23): 1522–26.

Schulz, Amy J., and Leith Mullings. 2006. *Gender, Race, Class, and Health: Intersectional Approaches.* San Francisco: Jossey-Bass.

Scott, A. O. 2013. "Or Would You Rather Be a Fish?" *New York Times*, February 28.

Scott, James C. 1985. *Weapons of the Weak: Everyday Forms of Peasant Resistance.* New Haven, CT: Yale University Press.

Sebeok, Thomas A., and Donna J. Umiker-Sebeok, eds. 1980. *Speaking of Apes: A Critical Anthology of Two-Way Communication with Man.* New York: Plenum Press.

Service, Elman R. 1962. *Primitive Social Organization; An Evolutionary Perspective.* New York: Random House.

———. 1966. *The Hunters.* Englewood Cliffs, NJ: Prentice Hall.

Severson, Kim. 2011. "Race-Based Names Dot the Landscape." *New York Times*, October 6.

Shanklin, Eugenia. 1998. "The Profession of the Color Blind: Sociocultural Anthropology and Racism in the 21st Century." *American Anthropologist* 100(3): 669–79.

Shannon, Jonathan Holt. 2006. *Among the Jasmine Trees: Music and Modernity in Contemporary Syria.* Middletown, CT: Wesleyan University Press.

Sharma, Aradhana, and Akhil Gupta, eds. 2006. *The Anthropology of the State: A Reader.* Malden, MA: Blackwell.

Shaw, Stephanie. 1996. *What a Woman Ought to Be and to Do: Black Professional Women Workers during the Jim Crow Era.* Chicago: University of Chicago Press.

Shiva, Vandana. 2006. "Building Water Democracy: People's Victory against Coca-Cola in Plachimada." In *Beyond Borders: Thinking Critically about Global Issues,* edited by Paula S. Rothenberg, 580–83. New York: Worth Publishers.

Simons, Gary F. and Charles D. Fennig, eds. 2017. *Ethnologue: Languages of the World, Twentieth edition.* Dallas, TX: SIL International. Online version: http://www.ethnologue.com.

Singer, Merrill, and Hans A. Baer. 2007. *Introducing Medical Anthropology: A Discipline in Action.* Lanham, MD: AltaMira.

Smedley, Audrey. 1993. *Race in North America: Origins and Evolution of a Worldview.* Boulder, CO: Westview Press.

Smith, Adam. 1776. *Wealth of Nations.* New York: Simon & Brown. (Reprint 2010.)

Smith, Christen. 2016. *Afro-Paradise: Blackness, Violence and Performance in Brazil.* Champaign: University of Illinois Press.

Smith, Neil. 2006. "There's No Such Thing as a Natural Disaster." *Understanding Katrina: Perspectives from the Social Sciences.* Social Science Research Council. http://understandingkatrina.ssrc.org/Smith.

Smith, Robert C. 2006. *Mexican New York: Transnational Lives of New Immigrants.* Berkeley: University of California Press.

Smith, Roberta. 2014. "In a Mattress, a Lever for Art and Political Protest." *New York Times,* September 21.

Speed, Shannon. 2006. "At the Crossroads of Human Rights and Anthropology: Toward a Critically Engaged Activist Research." *American Anthropologist* 108(1): 66–76.

———. 2007. *Rights in Rebellion: Indigenous Struggle and Human Rights in Chiapas.* Stanford, CA: Stanford University Press.

Spence, Jonathan D. 2013. *The Search for Modern China* (3rd ed.). New York: Norton.

Stack, Carol B. 1974. *All Our Kin: Strategies for Survival in a Black Community.* New York: Harper & Row.

Stange, Mary Zeiss. 1997. *Woman the Hunter.* Boston: Beacon Press.

Stark, Rodney, and William Sims Bainbridge. 1985. *The Future of Religion: Secularization, Revival, and Cult Formation.* Berkeley: University of California Press.

Steiner, Christopher Burghard. 1994. *African Art in Transit.* Cambridge, UK: Cambridge University Press.

———. 1995. "The Art of the Trade: On the Creation of Authenticity in the African Art Market." In *The Traffic in Culture,* edited by George E. Marcus and Fred R. Myers, 151–66. Berkeley: University of California Press.

Stephen, Lynn. 1995. "Women's Rights Are Human Rights: The Merging of Feminine and Feminist Interests among El Salvador's Mothers of the Disappeared (CO-MADRES)." *American Ethnologist* 22(4): 807–27.

Sterk, Claire E. 2000. *Tricking and Tripping: Prostitution in the Era of AIDS.* Putnam Valley, NY: Social Change.

Stevens, Carolyn S. 2005. "Tsukiji: The Fish Market at the Center of the World [Review]." *Journal of Asian Studies,* 64(4): 1022–23.

Steward, Julian H. 1956. *The People of Puerto Rico: A Study in Social Anthropology.* Urbana: University of Illinois Press.

Stiglitz, Joseph E. 2010. *Freefall: America, Free Markets, and the Sinking of the World Economy.* New York: Norton.

———. 2012. *The Price of Inequality: How Today's Divided Society Endangers Our Future.* New York: Norton.

Stocking, George W. Jr. 1968. *Race, Culture and Evolution: Essays in the History of Anthropology.* Chicago: University of Chicago Press.

———. 1983. *Observers Observed: Essays on Ethnographic Fieldwork.* Madison: University of Wisconsin Press.

———, ed. 1989. *A Franz Boas Reader: The Shaping of American Anthropology, 1883–1911.* Chicago: University of Chicago Press.

Stoller, Paul. 2003. "Circuits of African Art/Paths of Wood: Exploring an Anthropological Trail." *Anthropological Quarterly* 76(2): 207–34.

Stoller, Paul, and Cheryl Olkes. 1987. *In Sorcery's Shadow: A Memoir of Apprenticeship among the Songhay of Niger*. Chicago: University of Chicago Press.

Stone, Amy L. 2007. "Sexuality and Social Change: Sexual Relations in a Capitalist System." *American Anthropologist* 109(4): 753–55.

Stone, Linda. 2009. *Kinship and Gender: An Introduction* (4th ed.). Boulder, CO: Westview Press.

Sue, Derald Wing. 2010. *Microaggressions in Everyday Life: Race, Gender, and Sexual Orientation*. Hoboken, NJ: Wiley.

———. 2015. *Race Talk and the Conspiracy of Silence: Understanding and Facilitating Difficult Dialogues on Race*. (Hoboken, NJ: John Wiley and Sons).

Tannen, Deborah. 2001. *You Just Don't Understand: Women and Men in Conversation* (2nd ed.). New York: Ballantine.

Tax Policy Center. 2015. "Tax Facts." www.taxpolicycenter.org/taxfacts/displayafact.cfm?Docid=47

Taylor, Robert Joseph. 2000. "All Our Kin: Strategies for Survival in a Black Community [Review]." *Journal of Marriage and Family* 62(3): 865–67.

Terrace, Herbert S., L. A. Petitto, R. J. Sanders, and T. G. Bever. 1979. "Can an Ape Create a Sentence?" *Science* 206(4421): 891–902.

Tett, Gillian. 2010. *Fool's Gold: The Inside Story of J. P. Morgan and How Wall Street Greed Corrupted Its Bold Dream and Created a Financial Catastrophe*. New York: Free Press.

Thayer, Zeneta M., and Amy L. Non. 2015. "Anthropology Meets Epigenetics: Current and Future Directions." *American Anthropologist* 117(4): 722–35.

Thornton, Sarah. 2009. *Seven Days in the Art World*. New York: Norton.

Tierney, Patrick. 2000. *Darkness in El Dorado: How Scientists and Journalists Devastated the Amazon*. New York: Norton.

Tilly, Charles. 1975. "Reflections on the History of European State-Making." In *The Formation of National States in Western Europe*, edited by Charles Tilly. Princeton, NJ: Princeton University Press.

Trivedi, Bijal P. 2001. "Scientists Identify a Language Gene." *National Geographic News,* October 4.

Trouillot, Michel-Rolph. 1994. "Culture, Color, and Politics in Haiti." In *Race*, edited by Steven Gregory and Roger Sanjek, 146–74. New Brunswick, NJ: Rutgers University Press.

———. 2003. *Global Transformations: Anthropology and the Modern World*. New York: Palgrave Macmillan.

Turnbull, Colin M. (1961) 2010. *The Forest People*. New York: Simon & Schuster.

Turner, Victor. 1957. *Schism and Continuity in an African Society: A Study of Ndembu Village Life*. Manchester, UK: Manchester University Press.

———. 1969. *The Ritual Process: Structure and Anti-Structure*. Chicago: Aldine.

Tylor, Edward. 1920 [1871]. *Primitive Culture*. New York: J. P. Putnam's Sons.

United Nations. 2015. "The Millennium Development Goals Report 2015." www.un.org/millenniumgoals/2015_MDG_Report/pdf/MDG%202015%20rev%20(July%201).pdf

———. 2015b. "Sustainable Development Goals: 17 Goals to Transform our World." www.un.org/sustainabledevelopment/development-agenda/

United Nations Department of Economic and Social Affairs, Population Division. 2013. "Population Facts." http://esa.un.org/unmigration/documents/The_number_of_international_migrants.pdf

———. 2015a. *International Migrant Stock 2015*. www.un.org/en/development/desa/population/migration/data/estimates2/estimates15.shtml

———. 2015b. "World Population Prospects: The 2015 Revision, Key Findings and Advance Tables." Working Paper No. ESA/P/WP.241.

United Nations Development Programme. 2015. "The Millennium Development Goals: Eight Goals for 2015." www.undp.org/mdg/

United Nations High Commissioner for Refugees. 2015. "UNHCR Global Trends: Forced Displacement in 2014." http://unhcr.org/556725e69.html

Ury, William, ed. 2002. *Must We Fight? From the Battlefield to the Schoolyard—A New Perspective on Violent Conflict and Its Prevention*. San Francisco: Jossey-Bass.

Useem, Elizabeth. 1992. "Middle Schools and Math Groups: Parents' Involvement in Children's Math Placement." *Sociology of Education* 65: 263–79.

U.S. Census Bureau. 2010. "America's Families and Living Arrangements: 2010," Table FG3. www.census.gov/hhes/families/files/cps2010/tabFG4-all.xls

———. 2011. "Native North American Languages Spoken at Home in the United States and

Puerto Rico: 2006–2010." www.census.gov /prod/2011pubs/acsbr10-10.pdf

———. 2013. "People in Poverty by Selected Characteristics: 2012 and 2013." www.census.gov/hhes /www/poverty/data/incpovhlth/2013/table3.pdf

———. 2014. "Families and Living Arrangements." www.census.gov/hhes/families/data/families.html

———. 2016. "Income and Poverty in the United States, 2015." www.census.gov/content/dam /Census/library/publications/2016/demo/p60 -256.pdf

U.S. Centers for Disease Control. 2012. "Births: Final Data for 2010." *National Vital Statistics Reports.* www.cdc.gov/nchs/data/nvsr/nvsr61 /nvsr61_01.pdf#table02

U.S. Department of Justice. 2015. Civil Rights Division. "Investigation of the Ferguson Police Department." www.justice.gov/sites/default/files /opa/press-releases/attachments/2015/03/04 /ferguson_police_department_report.pdf

Van Gennep, Arnold. (1908) 1960. *The Rites of Passage.* Chicago: University of Chicago Press.

Venbrux, Eric, Pamela Sheffield Rosi, and Robert L. Welsch. 2006. *Exploring World Art.* Long Grove, IL: Waveland Press.

Vitelli, Romeo. 2013. "Television, Commercials, and Your Child." *Psychology Today,* July 22.

Vogel, Susan Mullin. 1991. *Africa Explores: 20th Century African Art.* New York: Center for African Art.

Wade, Lisa, and Myra Marx Ferree. 2015. *Gender: Ideas, Interactions, Institutions.* New York: Norton.

Wakin, Eric. 1992. *Anthropology Goes to War: Professional Ethics & Counterinsurgency in Thailand.* Madison: University of Wisconsin, Center for Southeast Asian Studies.

Walker, Sheila S. 2002. "Africanity vs. Blackness: Race, Class and Culture in Brazil." *NACLA Report on the Americas* 35(6)16–20.

Wallace, Anthony F. C. 1957. "Political Organization and Land Tenure among the Northwestern Indians, 1600–1830." *Southwest Journal of Anthropology* 13: 301–21.

Wallerstein, Immanuel Maurice. 1974. *World-Systems Analysis: An Introduction.* Durham, NC: Duke University Press.

Wardhaugh, Ronald. 2009. *An Introduction to Sociolinguistics* (6th ed.). London: Blackwell.

Wardlow, Holly. 2006. *Wayward Women: Sexuality and Agency in a New Guinea Society.* Berkeley: University of California Press.

Warriner, Christina, and Cecil M. Lewis Jr. 2015. "Microbiome and Health in Past and Present Human Populations." *American Anthropologist* 117(4): 740–41.

Waterston, Alisse. 2009. *An Anthropology of War: Views from War Zones.* New York: Berghahn.

Watson, James L., ed. 1998. *Golden Arches East: McDonald's in East Asia.* Stanford, CA: Stanford University Press.

Watson, James L., and Melissa L. Caldwell, eds. 2004. *The Cultural Politics of Food and Eating: A Reader.* New York: Wiley.

Weber, Eugen. 1976. *Peasants into Frenchmen: The Modernization of Rural France, 1870–1914.* Stanford, CA: Stanford University Press.

Weber, Max. 1905. *The Protestant Ethic and the Spirit of Capitalism.* London: Routledge, 2002.

———. 1919. *Politics as a Vocation.* Philadelphia: Fortress, 1965.

———. 1920 (1993). *Sociology of Religion.* Boston: Beacon Press.

———. (1920) 1946. "Class, Status and Party." In *From Max Weber: Essays in Sociology,* edited and translated by Hans Gerth and C. Wright Mills. New York: Free Press.

Weiner, Annette. 1976. *Women of Value, Men of Renown: New Perspectives in Trobriand Exchange.* Austin: University of Texas Press.

———. 1988. *The Trobrianders of Papua New Guinea.* New York: Holt, Rinehart and Winston.

Weiss, Margot. 2011. "The Epistemology of Ethnography: Method in Queen Anthropology." *GLQ: A Journal of Lesbian and Gay Studies* 17(4): 649–664.

Wekker, Gloria. 1999. "What's Identity Got to Do with It? Rethinking Identity in Light of the Mati Work in Suriname." In *Female Desires: Same-Sex and Transgender Practices across Cultures,* edited by Evelyn Blackwood and Saskia E. Wieringa, 119–38. New York: Columbia University Press.

———. 2006. *The Politics of Passion: Women's Sexual Culture in Afro-Surinamese Diaspora.* New York: Columbia University Press.

Welch, Cliff. 2001. "Peasants against Globalization: Rural Social Movement in Costa Rica [Review]." *Latin American Politics and Society* 43(4): 166–68.

Werner, Paul. 2006. *Museum Inc.: Inside the Global Art World.* Chicago: Prickly Paradigm Press.

West, Candace. 1998. "When the Doctor Is a 'Lady': Power, Status and Gender in Physician-Patient Encounters." In *Language and Gender: A Reader,* edited by Jennifer Coates, 396–412. London: Blackwell.

Weston, Kath. 1991. *Families We Choose: Lesbians, Gays, Kinship*. New York: Columbia University Press.

———. 1993. "Lesbian/Gay Studies in the House of Anthropology." *Annual Review of Anthropology* 22: 339–67.

Whitehouse, Bruce. 2012. *Migrants and Strangers in an African City: Exile, Dignity, Belonging*. Bloomington: Indiana University Press.

Wilkins, Amy C. 2008. "Dude You're a Fag: Masculinity and Sexuality in High School [Review]." *Contemporary Sociology* 37(3): 242–43.

Williams, Brackette F. 1995. "The Public I/Eye: Conducting Fieldwork to Do Homework on Homelessness and Begging in Two U.S. Cities." *Current Anthropology* 36(1): 25–51.

Williams, Brett. 2004. *Debt for Sale: A Social History of the Credit Trap*. Philadelphia: University of Pennsylvania Press.

Williams, Walter. 1992. *The Spirit and the Flesh: Sexual Diversity in American Indian Cultures* (2nd ed.). Boston: Beacon Press.

Wilson, William Julius. 1987. *The Truly Disadvantaged: The Inner City, the Underclass, and Public Policy*. Chicago: University of Chicago Press.

Winegar, Jessica. 2006. *Creative Reckonings: The Politics of Art and Culture in Contemporary Egypt*. Stanford, CA: Stanford University Press.

———. 2008. "The Humanity Game: Art, Islam and the War on Terror." *Anthropological Quarterly* 81(3), 651–81.

Wittfogel, Karl. 1957. *Oriental Despotism: A Comparative Study of Total Power*. New Haven, CT: Yale University Press.

Wolcott, Victoria W. 2001. *Remaking Respectability: African American Women in Interwar Detroit*. Chapel Hill: University of North Carolina Press.

Wolf, Eric R. 1982. *Europe and the People without History*. Berkeley: University of California Press.

———. 1990. "Distinguished Lecture: Facing Power—Old Insights, New Questions." *American Anthropologist* 92: 586–96.

———. 1999. *Envisioning Power: Ideologies of Dominance and Crisis*. Berkeley: University of California Press.

———. 2001. "Ethnicity and Nationhood." In *Pathways of Power: Building an Anthropology of the Modern World*. Berkeley: University of California Press.

Wolf, Eric, and Joseph Jorgensen. 1970. "Anthropology on the Warpath in Thailand." *New York Review of Books*, November 19.

Wolf-Meyer, Matthew J. 2012. *The Slumbering Masses: Sleep, Medicine, and Modern American Life*. Minneapolis: University of Minnesota Press.

World Food Programme. 2013. www.wfp.org.

World Health Organization. 2015a. "Drinking-water: Fact sheet no. 391." www.who.int /mediacentre/factsheets/fs391/en/

———. 2015b. "Life expectancy." http://who.int /gho/mortality_burden_disease/life_tables/en/

———. 2015c. "Trends in Maternal Mortality: 1990 to 2015: Estimates by WHO, UNICEF, UNFPA, World Bank Group and the United Nations Population Division." http://apps.who.int/iris/bitstream /10665/194254/1/9789241565141_eng.pdf?us=1.

Worm, Boris, et al. 2006. "Impacts of Biodiversity Loss on Ocean Ecosystem Systems." *Science* 314(5800): 787–90.

Yan, Yunxiang. 2003. *Private Life under Socialism: Love, Intimacy, and Family Change in a Chinese Village, 1949–1999*. Stanford, CA: Stanford University Press.

———. 2004. "Of Hamburgers and Social Space: Consuming McDonalds in Beijing." In *The Cultural Politics of Food and Eating: A Reader*, edited by James L. Watson and Melissa L. Caldwell. New York: Wiley.

Young, Colin. 1995. "Observational Cinema." In *Principles of Visual Anthropology*. edited by Paul Hockings, 99–113. Berlin: Mouton de Gruyter.

Younge, Gary. 2010. "What Soccer Says about Us." *The Nation*, July 19.

Zaloom, Caitlin. 2006. *Out of the Pits: Traders and Technology from Chicago to London*. University of Chicago Press.

Zhan, Mei. 2009. *Other-Worldly: Making Chinese Medicine through Transnational Frames*. Durham, NC: Duke University Press.

Zilberg, Jonathan. 1996. "African Art in Transit [Review]." *International Journal of African Historical Studies* 29(1): 147–49.

Zimmer, Carl. 2010. "How Microbes Defend and Define Us." *New York Times*, July 13.

———. 2011. "Bacterial Ecosystems Divide People into 3 Groups, Scientists Say." *New York Times*, April 20.

Zinn, Howard. 2005. *A People's History of the United States: 1492–Present* (rev. ed.). New York: Harper Perennial.

Credits

PART 1
PHOTOGRAPH: 2–3 Pavel Rahman / AP Photo

CHAPTER 1
PHOTOGRAPHS: 4 Raveendran / AFP / Getty Images; **7** © Yann Arthus-Bertrand / Getty Images; **10** David Grossman / Alamy Stock Photo; **11** HIP / Art Resource, NY; **13** Tarmizy Harva / Reuters; **14** Michael Nichols / National Geographic Creative; **16** Jeff Smith / Alamy; **18** Italian Coast Guard, Francesco Malavolta, HO; **23** © Chris Jordan, courtesy of Kopeikin Gallery, Los Angeles; **25** Courtesy of Kenneth Guest

CHAPTER 2
PHOTOGRAPHS: 30 Lea Suzuki / San Francisco Chronicle; **33 top left** Kay Maeritz / LOOK-foto / Getty Images; **33 right** Reza / Getty Images; **33 bottom left** Sean Locke / Stocksy; **35** Ozier Muhammad / The New York Times / Redux; **38** Koen van Weel / AFP / Getty Images; **40 left** NurPhoto / NurPhoto via Getty Images; **40 right** Parwiz Parwiz / Reuters; **41** © Pitt Rivers Museum, University of Oxford; **42** The Granger Collection, New York; **44** Hamilton / REA / Redux; **46** Charles Platiau / Reuters; **49 left** Khaled Elfiqi / epa; **49 right** Chris Stowers / Panos; **53** Dina Litocsky / The New York Times / Redux; **55** Chris Stowers / Panos; **57** Mark Henley / Panos

CHAPTER 3
PHOTOGRAPHS: 59 Eneraldo Carniero/ BrazilPhoto; **62** Nancy Scheper-Hughes; **66** Sergei Starus / Shutterstock; **67** Biblioteca Estense, Modena, Italy / Scala / Art Resource, NY; **69** American Philosophical Society; **70** From LSE Library's collections, MALINOWSKI/3/18/3 © London School of Economics and Political Science; **71** © Pitt Rivers Museum, University of Oxford; **72** Bettmann / Getty Images; **74** University Archives, University of Southern California East Library Building; **80 left** Courtesy of Kenneth Guest; **80 right** Capucine Bailey / Redux; **83 left** Philip Jones Griffiths / Magnum Photos; **83 right** Marco di Lauro / Getty Images; **86** Pat Rogue / AP

CHAPTER 4
PHOTOGRAPHS: 90 Matt York / AP Photo; **93** Vincent J. Musi / National Geographic; **94** Gorilla Foundation; **97 top left** The Print Collector / Alamy; **97 top right** Jason Lindsey / Alamy; **97 bottom** Shutterstock; **101** Guillaume Baptiste / AFP / Getty Images; **103 left** Brian Summers / First Light / Getty Images; **103 right** Kevin Dodge / Getty Images; **107** AP Photo / Ben Margo; **113** Lynn Johnson / National Geographic Stock

PART 2
PHOTOGRAPH: 116–117 Stuart Freedman / Panos Pictures

CHAPTER 5
TEXT: 137-138: Reproduced by permission of SAGE Publications Ltd., London, Los Angeles, New Delhi, Singapore and Washington DC, from Maria Kromidas, "Learning War/Learning Race: Fourth-grade Students in the Aftermath of September 11th in New York City," *Critique of Anthropology*, Vol. 2, No. 1, March 2004, pp. 15-33. Copyright © 2004, SAGE Publications.

PHOTOGRAPHS: 118 AP Photo / Jeff Roberson; **122 left** Image Source / SuperStock; **122 center** Corbis / SuperStock; **122 right** Jon Feingersh Photography / SuperStock; **123 left** Jon Feingersh Photography / SuperStock; **123 center** Image Source / Alamy; **123 right** Jorge Rohan / Alamy; **127** Wikimedia Commons; **130 left** United States Census Bureau; **130 right** United States Census Bureau; **132 left** The Granger Collection, New York; **132 right** Bettmann / Getty Images; **133** Everett Collection Inc / Alamy; **135** Library of Congress; **141** Carl Iwasaki / Time & Life Pictures / Getty Images; **143** Jim West / Alamy; **146 left** Brenda Ann Kenneally; **146 top right** Brenda Ann Kenneally; **146 bottom right** Brenda Ann Kenneally

CHAPTER 6

PHOTOGRAPHS: 150 Reuters / Kai Pfaffenbach; **153** AP Photo / Desmond Scholtz; **156 left** The Granger Collection, New York; **156 right** AP Photo / Jeff Christensen; **158** Richard Levine / Alamy Stock Photo; **161** A. Demotes / Photononstop / Alamy; **163** AP Photo / Amel Emric; **164 top left** Shiho Fukada / The New York Times / Redux; **164 top right** Shiho Fukada / The New York Times / Redux; **164 bottom left** Shiho Fukada / The New York Times / Redux; **164 bottom right** Shiho Fukada / The New York Times / Redux; **169** Keystone-France / Gamma-Keystone via Getty Images

CHAPTER 7

PHOTOGRAPHS: 176 U.S. Army photo by Staff Sgt. Scott Brooks; **181** Adek Berry / AFP / Getty Images; **183** Toni L. Sandys / The Washington Post / Getty Images; **185** Melanie Stetson Freeman / The Christian Science Monitor via Getty Images; **188** Louise Batella Duran / Alamy; **189 left** Anne Medley Missoula Independent; **189 right** Kevin Winter / Getty Images for Nederlander; **192 left** Images & Stories / Alamy; **192 right** Caroline Penn / Alamy; **194** Clouds Hill Imaging Ltd. / Science Source; **195** Hassan Ammar / AFP / Getty Images; **197** COMADRES@comadres.org; **200** AP Photo / Stacey Benedict

CHAPTER 8

PHOTOGRAPHS: 204 Andrew Burton / Getty Images; **208** Richard Levine / Alamy; **209 left** Tony Camacho/Science Source; **209 right** F. Stuart Westmoreland / Science Source; **212 top left** Roberto Herrett / Alamy; **212 right** Andrew Harrer / Bloomberg via Getty Images; **212 bottom left** Bob Daemmrich / The Image Works; **213** Frans Lemmens / Alamy; **218** Bettmann / Getty Images; **220** AP Photo / Vadim Ghirda; **221** Marco Gualazzini / LUZ / Redux; **223** Reuters / Jim Young; **225** Belinda Mason-Lovering; **227** Ruolf Gaudio and Rob Scarpa

CHAPTER 9

LINE ART 240 From Dennis O'Neil, "Kin Naming Systems: Part 1, The Nature of Kinship," http://anthro.palomar.edu/kinship/kinship_5.htm. Copyright © 1997-2013 by Dennis O'Neil. All rights reserved. Reprinted with permission.

PHOTOGRAPHS: 232 Amazon Studios / Photofest; **237 left** © London School of Economics and Political Science; **237 top right** Bachrach / Getty Images; **237 bottom right** Wikimedia Commons; **239 top left** © Pitt Rivers Museum, University of Oxford; **239 top right** ASUYOSHI CHIBA/AFP/Getty Images; **239 bottom right** George Steinmetz / Getty Images; **239 bottom left** © Pitt Rivers Museum, University of Oxford; **243** Courtesy of Kenneth Guest; **248 left** AP Photo / Michael Stravato; **248 right** Francis Miller / Time & Life Pictures / Getty Images; **250 left** Janet Carsten / Oxford University Press; **250 right** Janet Carsten / Oxford University Press; **253** Eddie Gerald / Laif / Redux; **255** Qilai Shen / Panos; **257** Erik S. Lesser / EPA

CHAPTER 10

PHOTOGRAPHS: 260 Jim West / Alamy Stock Photo; **263** Ryan Garza / Detroit Free Press / ZUMA; **264** J. Irwin / ClassicStock / Alamy; **266** B. Anthony Stewart / National Geographic Creative / Getty Images; **268** Frances Roberts / Alamy; **271** Tomas Abad / Alamy; **273** Ozier Muhammad / The New York Times / Redux; **275** Joshua Anderson / The New York Times / Redux; **277** David Preutz / Alamy; **281** AP Photo / Bismarck Tribune, Tom Stromme; **285** Popperfoto / Getty Images

PART 3

PHOTOGRAPH: 292–293 AP Photo / Pavel Rahman

CHAPTER 11

PHOTOGRAPHS: 294 Reuters / Thierry Gouegnon; **297** Luc Gnago; **299** Kim Walker / Robert Harding World Imagery / Alamy; **300** Joerg Boethling / Alamy; **303** World History Archive / Alamy; **307** The Everett Collection; **311 top left** Alessandro Bianchi / Reuters; **311 right** Reuters / David Gray; **311 bottom left** Imaginechina; **312** Reuters / Erik de Castro; **315** George Panagakis / Pacific Press / LightRocket via Getty Images; **317** Travel Pictures / Alamy; **321** Andrew C. Mace / Getty Images; **323** ZUMA Press, Inc. / Alamy Stock Photo; **324** AP Photo / Denver Post; **326** Godong / Universal Images Group via Getty Images; **328** AP Photo / John Minchillo

CHAPTER 12

PHOTOGRAPHS: 332 Ayesha D'souza / 350.org; **335** EPA / Etienne Laurent / Alamy; **337** Louise Murray / Alamy; **342 left** Xinhua / Alamy Stock Photo; **342 center** ZUMA Press, Inc. / Alamy;

342–343 Reuters / Jorge Luis Gonzales; **343 center** Reuters / Bogdan Cristel; **343 right** Robert Mora / Alamy; **345** Joshua Trujillo, seattlepi.com; **347** Frans Lanting / National Geographic Creative; **349** Jewel Samad / AFP / Getty Images; **351 left** Reuters / Muhammad Hamed; **351 center** Reuters / Paul Hackett; **351 right** Roger Hutchings / Alamy; **353** Reuters / Navesh Chitrakar; **354** Reuters / Juan Carlos Ulate; **355** Q. Sakamaki / Redux; **358** Faith Pinar / Anzenberger / Redux

CHAPTER 13

PHOTOGRAPHS: 362 Stephen Crowley / The New York Times / Redux; **367** © Ed Kashi; **370** Carla Bellamy; **371** Pictorial Press Ltd / Alamy; **372** Audrey Richards; **374** Ahmad Faizal Yahya / Alamy; **375** Glasshouse Images / Alamy; **376** Paul Springett C / Alamy; **377** Hulton Archive / Getty Images; **381** Images & Stories / Alamy; **382 left** CBW / Alamy; **382 right** FRANCES M. ROBERTS / Newscom; **383 left** AP Photo / Mary Schwalm; **383 right** Keith Torrie / NY Daily News Archive via Getty Images; **385** Reuters / Baz Ratner; **387** ORIANA ELICABE Agence France Presse / Newscom; **389** Nick Sinclair / Alamy

CHAPTER 14

PHOTOGRAPHS: 394 Jim Rogash / Getty Images; **399 left** Eye Ubiquitous / Newscom; **399 right** © Erich Schlegel; **401** Earl & Nazime Kowall / Corbis Documentary / Getty Images; **403** Siewert Falco / picture-alliance / dpa / AP Images; **404** Ian MacNicol / Getty Images; **405 left** Courtesy Everett Collection / age photostock; **405 right** Fuse / Getty Images; **408 left** Ginger Horsburgh / Earthside Birth Photography; **408 right** Family Childbirth Center at Swedish / Ballard; **409 left** © Alice Proujansky; **409 right** Mira / Alamy; **412 left** Daniel Wallace / ZUMAPRESS / Newscom; **412 center** Wallace, Daniel / St. Petersburg Times / PSG / Newscom; **412 right** AP Photo / Dieu Nalio Chery; **416** AP Photo / Eric Gay; **418 top** Michael Thornton / Media Bakery; **418 bottom left** AP Photo/ Aijaz Rahi; **418 bottom right** Andrew Holbrooke / Corbis via Getty Images; **421** Manny Crisostomo / MCT / ZUMAPRESS.com

CHAPTER 15

PHOTOGRAPHS: 424 © Alessandro Angelini; **426 left** © Alessandro Angelini; **426 right** © Alessandro Angelini; **428 left** Keith Corcoran / Alamy; **428 right** Xinhua / Mohamed Kadri / eyevine / Redux; **429** Kevin Schafer / Alamy; **431** Mario Fourmy / Redux; **433** John Reader / Science Source; **434** JM Labat / Science Source; **436** Danita Delimont / Gailo Images / Getty Images; **438** David Kilpatrick / Alamy; **440 left** © 2015 Museum Associates / LACMA Art Resource, NY; **440 right** Mervat Essa, Suffurya, © 2000. Courtesy of the Station Museum, Houston, Texas; **442 left** Ethan Miller / Reuters; **442 right** Tom Williams / Roll Call / Getty Images; **444 left** David Boyer / National Geographic / Getty Images; **444 center** David Boyer / National Geographic / Getty Images; **444–445** James P. Blair / National Geographic / Getty Images; **445 center** Volkmar K. Wentzel / National Geographic / Getty Images; **445 right** Albert Moldvay / National Geographic / Getty Images

Glossary/Index

anal penetration, 208

Anand, Nikhil, 286, 287

Anderson, Benedict, 168, 251

Angelini, Alessandro, 426

Angola, Africa, agriculture in, *300*

animals, language and, 93, *93*

"The Animal with the Weirdest Sex Life"
    (Diamond), 209

anomie, 372

anonymity, 84–85 Protecting the identities of the people involved in a study by changing or omitting their names or other identifying characteristics.

Anthropocene, 22 The current historical era in which human activity is reshaping the planet in permanent ways.

anthropologist's toolkit, 75–76 The tools needed to conduct fieldwork, including information, perspectives, strategies and even equipment.

anthropology, 5–27 The study of the full scope of human diversity, past and present, and the application of that knowledge to help people of different backgrounds better understand one another.
    applied, 9
    approach of, 9–12
        focus on local level, 10–11
        global scope, 9–10, *10*
        people and power structures, 11
        shared connections, 11–12
    of art, 427–432
    challenge of, 6–7
    defined, 8
    four-field approach of, 11–18
        archaeology, 15–16, *16*
        cultural anthropology, 17–18
        linguistic anthropology, 16–17
        physical anthropology, 13–15, *13, 14*
    globalization and, 18–27
    health and illness and, 411–13
    historical background of, 8–9
    overview of, 7–8
    term origin, 8

anti-apartheid movement, 127

anti-colonialism, 170–71, 307–8, *307*

anti-gay rhetoric, 229

Antioch College, 206

anti-racist liberation movements, 127

apartheid, 36, 127

apes, 34

Appadurai, A., 318, 444

applied anthropology, 9

archaeology, 15–16, *16* The investigation of the human past by means of excavating and analyzing artifacts.

arctic drilling, *345*

Argentina
    same-sex marriage in, 248
    sleep in, 50

Argonauts of the Western Pacific (Malinowski), 43, 69

Arizona, immigration and language in, *90*, 91

arranged marriage, 244–45 Marriage orchestrated by the families of the involved parties.

art All ideas, forms, techniques, and strategies that humans employ to express themselves creatively and to communicate their creativity and inspiration to others.
    aesthetics in, 429–431
    anthropology of, 427–432
    authenticity of, 436–37
    community vs. individualism in, 430
    defined, 427
    ethnography of, 435–39
    fine, 428–29, *429*
    in human history, 432–34
    media's intersection with, 443–49
        ethnographic film and indigenous media, 447–49
        visual images and cultural identity, 445–47
    Middle Eastern, 439–441, *440*
    miniature city model, 424–27, *424, 426*
    popular, 428–29, *429*
    post-9/11, 439–440

power and, 429, 439–443
    art exhibitions and, 439–441, *440*
    gender identity and, 441–43, *442*
    "primitive," 431–32
    style of presentation, 430
    West African, 435–39, *435, 436, 438*
    Western cultures and, 430–32
    women and, 439–440, 442–43, *442*

artificial insemination, 252–53, *253*
Asad, Talal, 385, 586
Asch, Tim, 447

asexuality, 216 A lack of erotic attraction to others.

Asia
    anti-colonial struggles in, 308
    trade routes through, *303*
Asians
    in interracial marriages, *48*
    poverty and, *280*
    racism and, 140

assimilation The process through which minorities accept the patterns and norms of the dominant culture and cease to exist as separate groups.
    defined, 166
    versus multiculturalism, 166–67

assisted reproductive technologies, 252–53, *253*, 255–56
Australia, life expectancy in, *415*

authenticity, 436–37 The perception of an object's antiquity, uniqueness, and originality within a local culture.

authorizing process, 385 The complex historical and social developments through which symbols are given power and meaning.

The Ax Fight (Asch), 447
Aymar Indians, 99
ayurvedic medicines, 399

Azande, South Sudan, magic in, 380–81, *380*
Azerbaijan, food and culture, *33*

B
Bafokeng, Inc., 165–66
balanced reciprocity, 301, 302
Bali, cockfights in, 44, *44*

band, 337–38 A small kinship-based group of foragers who hunt and gather for a living over a particular territory.

Bangkok, Thailand, street markets in, *33*
Bangladesh, coast of, 24, *332*, 333–34
Barbados, women in labor force, 199–200, *199*
Barrios, Steven, *189*

barter, 302–3 The exchange of goods and services, one for the other.

Barth, Fredrik, 155
Bateson, Gregory, 444
The Battle of Algiers (film), 307
Being Muslim the Bosnian Way (Bringa), 163–64
Belgium
    role in ethnic conflict in Rwanda, 160
    same-sex marriage in, 248
Bemba people, 9, *372*
Benedict, Ruth, 42, *42*
Bengal tiger, protests to protect, *332*, 333–34
Bernal, Victoria, 169, 170
Bestor, Theodore, 318
Beyond the Melting Pot (Glazer and Moynihan), 167
bifurcate collateral kinship systems, 238
bifurcate merging kinship systems, 238
biological anthropology (physical anthropology), 13–15, *13, 14. See also* biology and genetics; evolution
biology and genetics
    consanguineous unions, 247
    culture versus, 49
        culture and behavior, 51–52
        human evolution and individual development, 51
        nature versus nurture, 49–51

epigenetics, 51

generational kinship systems, 238

genetic similarities, 124

interconnected gene pool, 123–24

intersection of sexuality and, 208–11

language and, 94–95

races, biological similarities of, 122–26

    interconnected gene pool, 123–24

    linking phenotype to genotype, 124–26

    overview, 122–23

sexual dimorphism, 179–180

biomedicine, 402–3 A practice, often associated with Western medicine, that seeks to apply the principles of biology and the natural sciences to the practice of diagnosing disease and promoting healing.

    biomedical conceptions of body, 406

    defined, 402

biopower, 187

Birth in Four Cultures (Jordan and Davis-Floyd), 407

bisexuality, 216 Attraction to and sexual relations with members of both sexes.

Black Corona (Gregory), 142

Black Lives Matter movement, 120

Blacks. *See also* African Americans

    distribution of wealth to, 279

    girls, gender identity and games played by, 441–43, *442*

    in interracial marriages, *48*

    poverty and, *280*

    racism against, in medical profession, 416–17

    religions of, in United States, *385*

Blombos Cave, South Africa, art in, 432–33, *432, 433*

blue-collar workers, 268

Boas, Franz, 8, 41, 42, 68, 69, *69*, 75, 78

Boateng, Jerome, *150*, 151, *151*, 152

Boateng, Kevin-Prince, *150*, 151, *151*, 152, 157

"Body Ritual among the Nacirema" (Miner), 65

Boehm, Christopher, 338

Bohannan, Laura, 98, 99

Bolivia

    Cancha outdoor market in, 285–86, *285*

    language usage in, 99

Bonilla-Silva, Eduardo, 142

bonobos

    aggressiveness in, 347, *347*

    sexuality in, 209, *209*

Borgoglio, Jorge M., 363

Bosnia, ethnic conflict in, 162–63, *162, 163*

Bosnia: We Are All Neighbors (film), 163

Bourdieu, Pierre, 104, 267, 269, 270

Bourgeois, Louise, *429*

bourgeoisie, 267–68 Marxist term for the capitalist class that owns the means of production.

Bourgois, Philippe, 85

BP Deepwater Horizon oil spill, 23

Brahmans, 246

Brazil, *60, 127, 245*

    changes in ethnographic fieldwork, 85–86

    class in, 127–29

    economic independence and martial dissolution, 245

    ethics in anthropology, 83–84

    gender in, 127–29

    infant mortality in, 61–62, *62*

    offshoring to, 20

    organ trafficking in, *86*

    race in, 40, 127–29

    same-sex marriage in, 248

Brazzaville, Republic of Congo, migration to, 325–27, *326*

bread and wine, as symbols in Christianity, 384

breath (*qi*), 403–4

bridewealth, 248–49 The gift of goods or money from the groom's family to the bride's family as part of the marriage process.

bridges and barriers, 319 The factors that enable or inhibit migration.

Bridges, Khiara, 414, 416, 417

Bringa, Tone, 163, 164

British health system, 402–3
Brodkin, Karen, 136
Brogodo, Brazil, 245
Brown, Linda, *141*
Brown, Michael, 119, 120, 284
Brown, O., 140
Brown, Terry Lynn, *141*
Brown v. Board of Education, 140
Brubaker, Rogers, 159
Buck, Pem D., 132, 274, 275, 276, 280
Buddha, G., 38, 378
Buddhism
    healing practices of, 400–402, *401*
    in United States, *385*

built environment, 77 The intentionally designed features of human settlement, including buildings, transportation and public service infrastructure, and public spaces.

Bush, George H. W., *237*
Bush, George W., *237*
Bush, Jeb, *237*

C
Caesarean section, 408–9
Cairo, Egypt, Islamic Fatwa Councils in, 356–58
California
    Ebonics in, 107, *107*
    "fag discourse" in, 184
call centers, offshore, *312*
"Call of Duty" (video game), *349*
call systems, 93
Canada, same-sex marriage in, 248
Cange, Haiti, public health care system in, 411–13, *412*
capitalism
    consumerism and, 53–54
    history of, 313–14
capitalist (bourgeoisie) class, 267–68
Caribbean, plantation economy in, 305

carrying capacity, 300 The number of people who can be supported by the resources of the surrounding region.

Carry That Weight group, 206
Carsten, Janet, 249, 251
Carter, Ash, 178
carved statues and masks, West African, 437–38, *438*
Catalan Atlas, *67*
catequistas (lay teachers), 386–87, *387*
Catholic Church
    revolution in Mexico and, 386–88, *387*
    theology and practice of, changes in, 386–87
    in United States, *385*
cave paintings, in Europe, 433–34, *433*, *434*
CDO (collateralized debt obligations), 315
CDS (credit default swaps), 315
census, U.S., 130–31, *130*
Chagnon, Napolean, 83, 447
Chiapas, Mexico, religion and revolution in, 386–88, *387*
Chicago, Illinois, black networks near, 251, *251*

chiefdom, 339–340 An autonomous political unit composed of a number of villages or communities under the permanent control of a paramount chief.

childbirth, 407–10
chimpanzees
    common ancestry with other primates, 13, 14
    language and, 94
    learned behaviors, 34
China
    agriculture in other countries by, *300*
    archaeology in, 15
    chosen families, *255*
    cousin marriage, 246
    Dai Minority Park, Yunnan Province, *164*
    festival videos, 448–49
    food and culture, 50
    Gregorian calendar, 39
    identifying sex of unborn children, 256
    increasing migration within, 21
    kinship and descent, 242–44, *243*
    language continuum, 108–9
    life expectancy in, *415*
    migration to U.S. from, 134–35, 319–321
    migration within, 319

multi-sited ethnography, *25*

offshoring to, 20, 312–13

sleep in, 50

sweatshop factories in, 79, *80*

time zones, 39

women in military, 177

Chinese medicine, 403–5, *405*

Chinese religious communities, in New York City, 389–390

chisungu (Bemban coming-of-age initiation ceremony), *372*

Chisungu (Richards), 9

chocolate, as example in global economy, 295–97

Chomsky, Noam, 98

Christianity. *See also* Catholic Church

bread and wine as symbols in, 384

world distribution of, *369*

chronic traumatic encephalopathy (CTE), 396

The Chrysanthemum and the Sword (Benedict), 42

citizenship Legal membership in a nation-state.

defined, 168

kinship and, 252

city model, 424–27, *424*, *426*

civil rights movement, 127

civil society organization, 344–45 A local nongovernmental organization that challenges state policies and uneven development, and advocates for resources and opportunities for members of its local communities.

clan, 236 A type of descent group based on a claim to a founding ancestor but lacking genealogical documentation.

class A system of power based on wealth, income, and status that creates an unequal distribution of a society's resources.

in Brazil, 127–29

distribution of health and illness and, 414–17

economic statistics on, 277–79

egalitarian societies, 264–65

ethnographic studies of class in, 274–77

Flint water contamination crisis example, 261–63

globalization and, 284–89

division of world income, *288*

street vendors, 285–86, *285*

water circulation in Mumbai, 286–87

masking of, 282–84

poverty

as pathology, 280–81

roots of, 279–280

as structural economic problem, 281–82

ranked societies, 265–66

theories of class, 267–273

bourgeoisie (capitalist) class, 267–68

education and social reproduction, 269–270

intersectionality among race, gender, and class, 271–73

prestige and life chances, 269

clay figurines, West African, 437–38, *438*

climate change, 327–29, 328, 334, 335 Changes to Earth's climate, including global warming produced primarily by increasing concentrations of greenhouse gases created by the burning of fossil fuels.

defined, 24

income level and, 289

Pope on, 364

clines, 124

Clinton, Bill, 208

Coca-Cola, *4*, 5–6

Cochabamba, Bolivia, Cancha outdoor market in, 285–86, *285*

cockfighting, 44, *44*

cocoa, as example in global economy, 295–97

code switching, 105 Switching back and forth between one linguistic variant and another depending on the cultural context.

Cohen, Yehudi, 298, 299

collateralized debt obligations (CDO), 315

college students
    credit cards and debt, 54
    culture, 6, 35
    sexual assault on, 205–6
    sleep and, 50
Collins, Jane, 445, 446, 447
Colombia, same-sex marriage in, 248

colonialism, 304 The practice by which a
nation-state extends political, economic, and
military power beyond its own borders over an
extended period of time to secure access to raw
materials, cheap labor, and markets in other
countries or regions.
    anthropology and, 8, 68, 72–73, 83, *83*
    defined, 126, 304
    language and, 106, 109
    race and, 126–29
        in Brazil, 127–29
        overview, 126–27
    role in ethnic conflict in Rwanda, 160

color, people of, racism and, 140, 416–17
CO-MADRES, 196–99, *197*
Comaroff, Jean, 165
Comaroff, John, 165
Coming of Age in Samoa (Mead), 42, 71

commodity chains, 316–17 The hands an item
passes through between producer and consumer.

Communist Manifesto (Engels and Marx), 268

communitas, 373 A sense of camaraderie, a
common vision of what constitutes a good life,
and a commitment to take social action to move
toward achieving this vision that is shaped by the
common experience of rites of passage.

communities, globalization and changes in,
    24–25

companionate marriage, 245 Marriage built
on love, intimacy, and personal choice rather than
social obligation.

Concerned Community Adults (CCA), 143
Congo, Africa, migration to, 325–27, *326*
consumerism, 52–54, *53*
    advertising, 53–54
    and class masking in U.S., 283–84
    credit cards, 54
    financial services, 54
consumers, linking workers with, 316–18
Consuming the Romantic Utopia (Illouz), 283

contagious magic, 379 Ritual words or
performances that achieve efficacy as certain
materials that come into contact with one person
carry a magical connection that allows power to
be transferred from person to person.

coprolites, 15

core countries, 309, 310, *310* Industrialized
former colonial states that dominate the world
economic system.

Corona, Queens, NY, racism resistance in,
    142–44
corporations, global economy and, 311–13
Cortéz, Hernando, 92
cosmopolitanism, 56–57
Costa Rica, rural social movements in, 353–55, *353,*
    354
Côte d'Ivoire
    art in, 435–39, *435, 436*
    as example in global economy, 295–97
cotton plantations, 306
"Country Grammar" (Nelly), 443
cow, as symbol in Hinduism, 384
Creative Reckonings (Winegar), 440
credit cards, 54, 283–84
credit default swaps (CDS), 315
credit derivatives, 315

critical medical anthropology, 397, 414 An
approach to the study of health and illness that
analyzes the impact of inequality and stratification
within systems of power on individual and group
health outcomes.

cross-cousins, 246

Crow people, kinship classification, 238, *241*

CTE (chronic traumatic encephalopathy), 396

cultural anthropology, 17–18 The study of people's communities, behaviors, beliefs, and institutions, including how people make meaning as they live, work, and play together.

cultural capital, 270 The knowledge, habits, and tastes learned from parents and family that individuals can use to gain access to scarce and valuable resources in society.

cultural construction of gender, 181–84 The ways humans learn to behave as a man or woman and to recognize behaviors as masculine or feminine within their cultural context.

cultural materialism, 375 A theory that argues that material conditions, including technology, determine patterns of social organization, including religious principles.

cultural relativism, 69 Understanding a group's beliefs and practices within their own cultural context, without making judgments.

culture, 31–58 A system of knowledge, beliefs, patterns of behavior, artifacts, and institutions that are created, learned, shared, and contested by a group of people.

  biology versus, 49

    culture and behavior, 51–52

    human evolution and individual development, 51

    nature versus nurture, 49–51

  common core of, 35–40

    mental maps of reality, 38–40

    norms, 36–37

    symbols, 37–38

    values, 37

  contested, 35

  creation of, 52–54

  defined, 32, 34

  development of concept, 41–45

  gender and, 180–84

  globalization and, 54–57

    cosmopolitanism, 56–57

    homogenization versus diversification, 55–56

    migration, 56

  influences on ideas of health and illness, 398–405

    body concepts, 405–11

    ethnomedicine, 400–402

  overview of, 33–34

  power and, 45

    cultural institutions, 46–47

    hegemony, 47–48

    human agency, 48–49

  process of learning, 34, *35*

  sexuality and, 211–12

  shared, 35

D

Dai Minority Park, Yunnan Province, China, *164*

dargah (Muslim saint shrine), 368–370, *370*

Darkness in El Dorado (Tierney), 83

Darwin, Charles, 41

Davis-Floyd, Robbie, 407, 408, 409, 410

Dawei, Chen, 320

Death without Weeping: The Violence of Everyday Life in Brazil (Scheper-Hughes), 61

debt, 283–84

"Deep Play: Notes on the Balinese Cockfight" (Geertz), 44

dementia, 396

Denmark, *224*

  people with disabilities, sex and, 224–26

  same-sex marriage, 248

dependency theory, 309 A critique of modernization theory arguing that despite the end of colonialism, the underlying economic relations of the modern world economic system had not changed.

derivatives, financial, 315

descent group, 236–244, *237, 239, 243* A kinship group in which primary relationships are traced through certain consanguineous ("blood") relatives.

> ambilineal, 237, 241
> clans, 237
> defined, 236
> lineages, 237
> matrilineal, 237
> patrilineal, 237–38, 241–42
> systems of kinship classification, 238–242, *240–41*
> unilineal, 237

descriptive linguistics, 17, 95 The study of the sounds, symbols, and gestures of a language, and their combination into forms that communicate meaning.

descriptive linguists, 17 Those who analyze languages and their component parts.

development, 308 Post– World War II strategy of wealthy nations to spur global economic growth, alleviate poverty, and raise living standards through strategic investment in national economies of former colonies.

dialect, 104 A nonstandard variation of a language.

Diamond, Jared, 209, 210

diaspora, 170 A group of people living outside their ancestral homeland yet maintaining emotional and material ties to home.

Dick, Ramona, *113*
difference model, 102
A Different Kind of War Story (Nordstrom), 350
diffusion, 42
Dinka people, 242
disability, 410–11
Discipline and Punish (Foucault), 47
discrimination, 139

disease, 398 A discrete natural entity that can be clinically identified and treatedby a health professional.

distribution and exchange, 301–3
diversity, human, 14–15
divestment actions, 334
division of labor, 180, 191, 194–96, *195*, 311–12
DNA, physical anthropology and, 13–14
dogs, communication and, 93, *93*
dolphins
> communication and, 93
> sexuality in, 209
dominance model, 102–3
"do no harm" mandate, 82–84
dopamine, 210
"Down, Down Baby" (song), 443
Down Syndrome, sexuality of individuals with, 224–25, *225*

dowry, 249 The gift of goods or money from the bride's family to the groom's family as part of the marriage process.

Dramas of Nationhood: The Politics of Television in Egypt (Abu-Lughod), 56–57
Dude, You're a Fag (Pascoe), 184
Durkheim, Émile, 371, 372

E
Ebonics, 107, *107*
economics. *See also* global economy
> consumerism, 53–54
> economic independence and martial dissolution, 245
> economic liberalism, 313–14
> Kula ring, 69–70
> money as symbol, 39, *39*
> role of women, 73

economy A cultural adaptation to the environment that enables a group of humans to use the available land, resources, and labor to satisfy their needs and to thrive.

defined, 298
distribution and exchange in, 301–3

Edelman, Marc, 353, 355
education and schools
  code switching in academia, 105
  debate over Muslim head coverings, 46–47
  Ebonics, 107
  enculturation, 34, *35*
  in France, 169
  gender enculturation, 183–84
  income level and, 289
  race and racism and, 140–41
  sex education class, *212*
  social reproduction and, 269–270

egalitarian society, 264–65 A group based on the sharing of resources to ensure success with a relative absence of hierarchy and violence.

egg, gender stereotypes and, 193–94, *194*
Egypt, *57*
  archaeology in, 15
  brother-sister marriage, 246
  hieroglyphs, *97*
  Islamic Fatwa Councils in, 356–58
  McDonald's menu adaptations, 55
  protests, *49*
  television, 56–57, *57*
Elementary Forms of Religious Life (Durkheim),
    371–72
El Salvador, CO-MADRES, 196–99, *196, 197*
Emancipation Proclamation, 132

emic, 80 An approach to gathering data that investigates how local people think and how they understand the world.

emoticons and emoji, 97, *97*
employment and labor
  sweatshop factories, 79, *80*
  women in, 199–200, *199*

enculturation, 34 The process of learning culture.

endogamy, 38, 247 Marriage to someone within the kinship group.

engaged anthropology, 74 Applying the research strategies and analytical perspectives of anthropology to address concrete challenges facing local communities and the world at large.

Engels, Friedrich, 268
England
  food and culture in, *33*
  Greenwich meridian, 39
  "90-minute nation," 152

entrepreneurial immigrants, 323 Persons who move to a new location to conduct trade and establish a business.

environment, 22–24
  climate change, 24, 327–29, *328*, 334, *335*
    defined, 24
    income level and, 289
    Pope on, 364
  human shaping of natural world, 22–23

epigenetics, 51 An area of study in the field of genetics exploring how environmental factors directly affect the expression of genes in ways that may be inherited between generations.

epilepsy (*qaug dab peg*), 419–420
Eritrea, *169*
  transnational citizenship in, 169–170
  women in military, 177
Eskimo people, kinship classification, 238, *240*
Essa, Mervat, *440*
ethics, 82–85, *83*
  anonymity, 84–85
  "do no harm" mandate, 82–84
  informed consent, 84

ethnic boundary marker, 156 A practice or belief, such as food, clothing, language, shared name, or religion, used to signify who is in a group and who is not.

ethnic cleansing, 163 Efforts by representatives of one ethnic or religious group to remove or destroy another group in a particular geographic area.

ethnic groups. *See* tribes

ethnicity A sense of historical, cultural, and sometimes ancestral connection to a group of people who are imagined to be distinct from those outside the group.
    defined, 154
    identity and, 154–58
    relationship to nation, 167–173
    as source of conflict, 159–164
        in former Yugoslavia, 162–64
        Hutu refugees in Tanzania, 162
        in Rwanda, 159–161
    as source of opportunity, 164–66
    in U.S., 166–67
    World Cup soccer and, 151–54

Ethnicity, Inc. (Comaroff), 165
Ethnicity without Groups (Brubaker), 159

ethnocentrism, 9, 64, 66, 68–69 The belief that one's own culture or way of life is normal and natural; using one's own culture to evaluate and judge the practices and ideals of others.

ethnographic authority, 82

ethnographic fieldwork, 17–18, 61–87 A primary research strategy in cultural anthropology typically involving living and interacting with a community of people over an extended period to better understand their lives.
    as art, 66
    defined, 10, 63
    development of, 67–75
    effects of on anthropologists, 64–66
    engaged anthropology, 74–75
    focus on people, 64
    globalization and, 85–87
    as informing daily life, 66–67
    moral and ethical concerns, 82–85

    professionalization of, 68–74
    as social science, 66
    techniques in, 75–80
        analysis, 79–80
        mapping, 77–78
        preparation, 75–76
        skills and perspectives, 78–79
        strategies, 76–77

ethnographic film, 447–49
ethnographies, writing, 80–82
    ethnographic authority, 82
    moral and ethical concerns, 82–85
    polyvocality, 81
    reflexivity, 81–82
Ethnologue (SIL), 113

ethnology, 18, 80 The analysis and comparison of ethnographic data across cultures.

ethnomedicine, 400–402 Local systems of health and healing rooted in culturally specific norms and values.

ethnomusicology, 442 The study of music in cultural context.

ethnopharmacology, 400 The documentation and description of the local use of natural substances in healing remedies and practices.

etic, 80 Description of local behavior and beliefs from the anthropologist's perspective in ways that can be compared across cultures.

Eurocentrism, 68
Europe
    Industrial Revolution in, 306–7
    neoliberalism and, 314
    Paleolithic cave paintings in, 433–34, *433, 434*
    trade routes through, *303*
    trade with Africa and Americas, 304–6
Europe and the People Without History (Wolf), 72
Evans-Pritchard, E. E., 43, 70, 71, *71*, 73, 79, 81, 99, 238, 242, 379, 380, 381

evolution, 13–14, 22
    development of concept of culture, 41
    human becomings, 51
    influence of culture, 51–52
    language and, 93–95
    unilineal cultural, 41–42

exogamy, 38, 238, 247 Marriage to someone outside the kinship group.

F
facial expressions. *See* gestures and facial expressions
factory assembly line, 311–12
Fadiman, Anne, 419, 421
Families We Choose (Weston), 255
family. *See* kinship and family

family of orientation, 253 The family group in which one is born, grows up, and develops life skills.

family of procreation, 254 The family group created when one reproduces and within which one rears children.

Farmer, Paul, 411, 412, *412*, 413
Fatwa Councils, 356–58, *358*
Fausto-Sterling, Anne, 186
favela, model of, 424–27, *426*
Feagin, Joe, 145

femininity, 182, 184–85 The ideas and practices associated with womanhood.

feminism, 73
Ferguson, J., 140, 342
Ferguson, Missouri, *118*, 119–120
Ferron, Zoe, 222
festival videos, 448–49
fictive kin, 251

field notes, 77 The anthropologist's written observations and reflections on places, practices, events, and interviews.

figurines, clay, West African, 437–38, *438*
fijos (stall vendors), 285–86, *285*
film, ethnographic, 447–49
financial derivatives, 315
financial services, 54
Fine, G. A., 182

fine art, 428–29, *429* Creative expression and communication often associated with cultural elites.

Finland, same-sex marriage, 248
first cousins, 246
Fisher, Helen, 210, 211
The 5 Love Languages (Chapman), 102
"The Five Sexes" (Fausto-Sterling), 186
flags, 39
Flaherty, Robert, 447

flexible accumulation, 20, 262, 281, 312–13 The increasingly flexible strategies that corporations use to accumulate profits in an era of globalization, enabled by innovative communication and transportation technologies.

Flint water contamination crisis, 261–63, *263*
Florida, U.S., intersections of race and class in, 145–46
Floyd, Charlene, 586

focal vocabulary, 98, 99–100 The words and terminology that develop with particular sophistication to describe the unique cultural realities experienced by a group of people.

folk religions, world distribution of, *369*
food and nutrition
    access to, 32
    agriculture, 299–301
    culture and, 32, *33*, 50
    fast food, *30*, 31–32
    foraging, 298, *299*, 337–38, *337*
    horticulture, 299
    hunter-gatherer stereotype, 194–96
    McDonald's menu adaptations, 55, *55*
    pastoralism, 299

food foragers, 298 Humans who subsist by hunting, fishing, and gathering plants to eat.

Food for Peace program, 353–54
football, American, health and, 395–96
foraging, 298, *299*, 337–38, *337*
Ford, Henry, 311

Fordism, 311–12 The dominant model of industrial production for much of the twentieth century, based on a social compact between labor, corporations, and government.

Ford Motor Company, 311–12
Fossil Free UC, 334
Foucault, Michel, 47, 187, 222

four-field approach, 11–18, 68 The use of four interrelated disciplines to study humanity: physical anthropology, archaeology, linguistic anthropology, and cultural anthropology.
    archaeology, 15–16, *16*
    cultural anthropology, 17–18
    defined, 12
    linguistic anthropology, 16–17
    physical anthropology, 13–15, *13*, *14*

Fourteenth Amendment, U.S. Constitution, 131
FOXP2 gene, 95

framing process, 355 The creation of shared meanings and definitions that motivate and justify collective action by social movements.

France, *168*
    in Côte d'Ivoire conflict, 296
    ethnicity and nationalism in, 152–53
    French classroom in 1829, *169*
    infrastructure projects, 169
    language continuum, 108
    national soccer team, *153*
    Paleolithic cave paintings in, 433–34, *433*
    religious symbols in, 46–47, *46*
    Sykes-Picot Agreement, 172
    women in military, 177

Francis, Pope, 363, *363*, 364
Frazer, James, 41, 42, 379
Freeman, Carla, 199
free market, 313–14
Freud, Sigmund, 247
From the Ganges to the Hudson (Lessinger), 157
fur trade, in North America, 306
Fuzhou City, China, *25*, 26, 242–44, *243*, 319–321

G

The Games Black Girls Play (Gaunt), 442–43
garbology, *16*
Garcia, Alicia P. de, 198
Gardener, Robert, 447
Gardener's Dead Birds (Gardener), 447
Garner, Tyron, *248*
Gaudio, Rudolf, 227, 228
Gaunt, Kyra, 442, 443
gays and lesbians
    anti-gay rhetoric, 229
    black gay women in U.S., 222–24
    chosen families, 255, *255*
    engaged anthropology, 74
    families of same-sex partners, 256–57, *257*
    machismo and, 214–15
    mati work, 213–14
    in Nigeria, 226–28
    same-sex marriage, 246, 248, *248*, 256–57, *257*
    South Asian Lesbian and Gay Alliance (SALGA), 158
Gbagbo, Laurent, 296
Geertz, Clifford, 43, 44, 45, 81, 384, 385, 586

gender, 177–201 The expectations of thought and behavior that each culture assigns to people of different sexes.
    alternate genders, 188–190
    art and, 441–43, *442*
    biology and, 179–180
    Black gay women in U.S., 222–24
    in Brazil, 127–29
    culture and, 180–84
    defined, 179
    distribution of health and illness and, 414–17

globalization and
    labor force, 199–200, *200*
    migration, 201
ideologies
    defined, 193
    fairy tale of the egg and the sperm, 193–94, *194*
    hunter-gatherer stereotype, 194–96, *195*
intersectionality among race, class and, 271–73
lack of biological basis for inequality and
    stereotyping, 50–51
language and, 100, 102–3, *103*
performance of, 184–86
power and, 190–99
    challenging, 196–99
    early research on, 191–92
    gender ideologies, 193–96
sex versus, 179
stereotypes about, 193
stratification of, 193
theory of five sexes, 186–88

gender ideology, 193 A set of cultural ideas, usually stereotypical, about the essential character of different genders that functions to promote and justify gender stratification.

gender performance, 184 The way gender identity is expressed through action.

gender stereotypes, 193 Widely held preconceived notions about the attributes of, differences between, and proper roles for men and women in a culture.

gender stratification, 193 An unequal distribution of power in which gender shapes who has access to a group's resources, opportunities, rights, and privileges.

gender studies, 178 Research into masculinity and femininity as flexible, complex, and historically and culturally constructed categories.

Genealogies of Religion (Asad), 385
generalized reciprocity, 301

General Motors, 20
genetics. *See* biology and genetics
Gennep, Arnold van, 372

genocide, 159 The deliberate and systematic destruction of an ethnic or religious group.

genotype, 124–26 The inherited genetic factors that provide the framework for an organism's physical form.

geographic information system (GIS) devices and
    data, 78
Germany
    health system in, 403
    life expectancy in, *415*
    McDonald's menu adaptations in, 55
    Nuremburg Laws, 36
gestures and facial expressions
    kinesics, 96–97
    winking, 43–44
Ghandi, Mohandas, 307
GI Bill of Rights, 136
Gibson, Jane, 146
Ginsberg, Faye, 444
GIS (geographic information system) devices and
    data, 78
Glazer, Nathan, 167
global economy, 327–29. *See also* globalization
    corporations and, 311–13
    human ecological footprint and, 327–29
    instability of, 315–16
    linking workers with consumers, 316–18
    migration and, 318–327
        bridges and barriers, 319–321
        patterns of, 321–22, *322*
        pushes and pulls, 319
        types of immigrants, 322–27
    organizing principles of, 313–16
    overview, 295–98
    roots of, 303–13
        anti-colonial struggles, 307–8
        colonialism, 304
        flexible accumulation, 312–13
        Fordism, 311–12

Industrial Revolution, 306–7
    long-distance trade routes, 303–4
    modern world economic system, 308–11
    triangle trade, 304–6
successes and failures of, 327

globalization, 18–27 The worldwide intensification of interactions and increased movement of money, people, goods, and ideas within and across national borders.
    anthropology and, 18–27
        changing communities, 24–25
        changing research strategies, 25–26
    class and inequality and, 284–89
        division of world income, *288*
        street vendors, 285–86
        water circulation in Mumbai, 286–87
    culture and, 54–57
        cosmopolitanism, 56–57
        homogenization versus diversification,
            55–56
        migration, 56
    defined, 18
    environment and, 22–24
    ethnicity and, 155, 173
    health and illness and, 417–421
        biomedicine, 402–3
        Chinese medicine, 403–5
    key dynamics of, 19
        flexible accumulation, 20
        increasing migration, 20–21
        time-space compression, 20
        uneven development, 21
    kinship and, 253
        assisted reproductive technologies,
            255–56
        chosen families, 255, *255*
        families of same-sex partners, 256–57, *257*
        nuclear family, 253–55
    language and, 109–13
        diminishing diversity, 109, 111
        language loss, 112–13, *113*
        preserving endangered languages, 113, *113*
        revitalizing languages, 112–13
    religion and, 388–391

sexuality and, 226–29
    homogenization, 228–29
    Nigeria, 226–28
transnational citizenship in Eritrea, 169–170
war and, 349–351

global mediascape, 444 Global cultural flows of media and visual images that enable linkages and communication across boundaries in ways unimaginable a century ago.

Gluckman, Max, 43, 336
Gmelch, George, 379, 382, 383
God in Chinatown (Guest), 81, 319
Golden Arches East: McDonald's in East Asia
    (Watson), 55
The Golden Bough (Frazer), 379
Goldstein, Daniel, 285, 286
Goldstein, Donna, 128, 129
Goodall, Jane, *14*
Goode, Judith, 281, 282
gorillas, 13, 14, *14*
    language and, 94, *94*
    sexual dimorphism, 180
Gough, Kathleen, 73, 241, 242

grammar, 96 The combined set of observations about the rules governing the formation of morphemes and syntax that guide language use.

Gramsci, Antonio, 47
grants, 75
Great Britain, Sykes-Picot Agreement, 172
Greece
    neoliberalism and, 314, *315*
    Syrian refugees, *18*
Greenland, same-sex marriage in, 248
Gregorian calendar, 39
Gregory, Steven, 142, 144
Griest, Kristen, 177, *177*, 178
Guba, Azerbaijan, *33*
Guidelines about Sexuality— Regardless of
    Handicap, 225
Gupta, A., 342
Gutmann, Matthew, 185, 186

H

habitus, 270 Bourdieu's term to describe the self-perceptions, sensibilities, and tastes developed in response to external influences over a lifetime that shape one's conceptions of the world and where one fits in it.

Haiti
    independence of, 307
    life expectancy in, *415*
    public health care system in, 411–13, *412*
half-siblings, 246
Hanna-Attisha, Mona, 261
The Harlem Birth Right Project, 271–73
Harris, Marvin, 375, 376, 377
Harris, Neil P., 256
Harry Potter series (Rowling), *382*
Harsha, Edna, *418*
Harvey, David, 312
Haver, Shaye, 177, 178
Hawaii
    brother-sister marriage in, 246
    kinship classification in, 238, *240*
He, Zheng, 67
healing remedies, 400–402, *401*

health The absence of disease and infirmity, as well as the presence of physical, mental, and social well-being.
    anthropologists and, 411–13
    cultural influences on body concepts, 405–11
        biomedical conceptions of body, 406
        childbirth, 407–10
        disability, 410–11
        human microbiome, 406–7
    cultural influences on ideas of, 398–405
        biomedicine, 402–3
        Chinese medicine, 403–5
        ethnomedicine, 400–402
    definition of health, 398
    distribution of, 413–17
        critical medical anthropology and, 414
        health transition, 413–14
        income level and, 288–89
        race, class, and gender, 414–17
    globalization and, 417–421
        medical migration, 417–18
        multiple systems of healing, 418–421

health-care professionals, migration to U.S., 323

health transition, 413–14 The significant improvements in human health made over the course of the twentieth century that were not, however, distributed evenly across the world's population.

Hegel, Georg W. F., 430

hegemony, 47, 343–44 The ability of a dominant group to create consent and agreement within a population without the use or threat of force.

Henshilwood, Christopher, 433

heterosexuality, 216–18 Attraction to and sexual relations between individuals of the opposite sex.

Hidalgo y Costilla, Miguel, 387
Hierarchy in the Forest (Boehm), 338
High Tech and High Heels in the Global Economy (Freeman), 199
hijras, 188–89
Hindus and Hinduism
    alternative gender constructions, 188, *188*
    cow as symbol, 384
    world distribution of, *369*
hip-hop music, 442–43
Hispanics, 131
    children of, 174
    distribution of wealth to, 279
    in interracial marriages, *48*
    poverty and, *280*
    racism and, 140

historical linguistics, 17, 108–9 The study of the development of language over time, including its changes and variations.

historical particularism, 42 The idea, attributed to Franz Boas, that cultures develop in specific ways because of their unique histories.

historic archaeology, 16 The exploration of the more recent past through an examination of physical remains and artifacts as well as written or oral records.

historic linguists, 17 Those who study how language changes over time within a culture and how languages travel across cultures.

Hite, Shere, 218
Hmong refugees, U.S. health-care and, 419–421, *419*
Ho, Karen, 276
Hobsbawm, Eric, 168
Hogan, Nick, *225*
holidays, 53, *53*, 79, *80*

holism, 12 The anthropological commitment to look at the whole picture of human life—culture, biology, history, and language— across space and time.

Holland, viewpoint on birth, 407, 409–10
Homefront (Lutz), 349
homelessness, 67
homogenization, 55–56
Homo sapiens, 13, 14

homosexuality, 216 Attraction to and sexual relations between individuals of the same sex. *See* gays and lesbians

Hong Kong, life expectancy in, 414, *415*
Hopi people, 98
hormones, sex, 210

horticulture, 299 The cultivation of plants for subsistence through nonintensive use of land and labor.

How the Jews Became White Folks (Brodkin), 136
Huichol Indians, 73

human becomings, 51
human ecological footprint, 327–29

human microbiome, 51, 406–7 The complete collection of microorganisms in the human body's ecosystem.

Human Terrain Systems program, *83*, 84
humor, as coping strategy, 129
hunger, 288
hunter-gather bands, 337–38
Hurricane Katrina, 289
Hurston, Zora N., 74
Husain Tekri shrine, 368–370, *370*
Hussein, Saddam, 172
Hutus, 159–162
hydro-social processes, 262–63

hypodescent, 128, 133–34 Sometimes called the "one drop of blood rule"; the assignment of children of racially "mixed" unions to the subordinate group.

I
Iceland
    historic archaeology in, 16
    life expectancy in, *415*
    same-sex marriage, 248
identity, ethnic, 154–55
    creating, 155–58
    Indian identity in U.S., 157
    Rwandan identity cards, *161*

identity entrepreneurs, 159 Political, military, or religious leaders who promote a worldview through the lens of ethnicity and use war, propaganda, and state power to mobilize people against those whom they perceive as a danger.

Idrisi, Muhammad al-, *303*

illness, 399 The individual patient's experience of being unwell. *See* health

illness narratives, 421 The personal stories that people tell to explain their illnesses.

Illouz, Eva, 283
images, cultural identity and, 445–47
Imagined Communities (Anderson), 251

imagined community, 168 The invented sense of connection and shared traditions that underlies identification with a particular ethnic group or nation whose members likely will never all meet.

IMF (International Monetary Fund), 314

imitative magic, 379 A ritual performance that achieves efficacy by imitating the desired magical result.

immigration and immigrants. *See* migration
Inca people, 246
incense, chunks of (*loban*), 369–370, *370*

incest taboo, 246–47 Cultural rules that forbid sexual relations with certain close relatives.

income What people earn from work, plus dividends and interest on investments, along with rents and royalties.
    defined, 277
    distribution of, 277–78, *288*
    taxes on, 312

increasing migration, 20 The accelerated movement of people within and between countries.

indentured workers, 131
India, *157*, 286–87
    Buddhist healing practices in, 400–402, *401*
    Coca-Cola and water usage, *4*, 5–6, *6*, 23
    cousin marriage in, 246
    dowries in, 248
    healing practices in, 368–370
    hijras, 188–89
    Indian identity in U.S., 157
    life expectancy in, *415*

    outsourcing to, 20
    polyandry in, 246
    sex of unborn children in, identifying, 256
    surgery in, *418*
    water circulation in, 286–87
    women and labor in, 180–81
India Day Parade, 157–58, *158*

indigenous media, 447 The use of media by people who have experienced massive economic, political and geographic disruption to build alternative strategies for communication, survival, and empowerment.

indigenous people
    climate change demonstrations by, *335*
    media use by, 446, 447–49
individualism, art and, 430

individual racism, 139 Personal prejudiced beliefs and discriminatory actions based on race.

Indonesia, migration of women from, 201, *201*, *323*
industrial agriculture, 300–301
industrial mass production, 311–12
Industrial Revolution, 267, 306–7
inequality. *See* class and inequality
infant mortality, mothers' perception of, 61–62, *62*
informal economy, 285–86
informatics, 199–200

informed consent, 84 A key strategy for protecting those being studied by ensuring that they are fully informed of the goals of the project and have clearly indicated their consent to participate.

infrastructure projects, France, 169
Ingraham, Chrys, 219, 220, 221
In Sorcery's Shadow (Stoller), 381–82

institutional racism, 139–141 Patterns by which racial inequality is structured through key cultural institutions, policies, and systems.

defined, 139
overview, 139–140
U.S. educational system, 140–41
InterACT: Advocates for Intersex Youth,
187
interbreeding, 123
internally displaced persons, 323

internal migration, 322 The movement of
people within their own national borders.

International Monetary Fund (IMF), 314
International Phonic Alphabet, 96
Internet
advertising on, 53–54
language and, 17
in least-developed countries, 21
time-space compression and, 20

interpretivist approach, 43–44 A conceptual
framework that sees culture primarily as a symbolic system of deep meaning.

interracial marriage
in Brazil, 128
in U.S., 132

intersectionality An analytic framework for
assessing how factors such as race, gender, and
class interact to shape individual life chances and
societal patterns of stratification.
defined, 145, 271
of race, gender, and class, 271–73
of race and sexuality for black gay women,
222–23
of sexuality and biology, 208–11
of whiteness and racism, 145–47

intersex, 187 The state of being born with a
combination of male and female genitalia, gonads,
and/or chromosomes.

Intersex Society of North America, 187
interviews, 76
Inuit people, *69*

Invisible Families (Moore), 222
iPhone, resources for/production of, *311*
Iraq, 46, 171–73, *171*
Ireland
migration to U.S. from, 135
neoliberalism and, 314
same-sex marriage in, 248
Iroquois people, kinship classification, 238, *241*
ISIS (Islamic State in Iraq and the Levant), 172
Islam. *See* Muslims and Islam
Israel, *252*
artificial insemination and kinship in, 252–53,
253
life expectancy in, *415*
McDonald's menu adaptations in, 55
women in military, 177
Italy
language and, 108
life expectancy in, *415*

J
Japan
life expectancy in, *415*
McDonald's menu adaptations in, 55
race in, 40
sexuality in, 215–16
Jay-Z, *101*
Jenner, Bruce (later Caitlyn), *189*
Jesus Christ, 378, 384
Jews and Judaism
artificial insemination and kinship, 252–53
fieldwork at senior center, 73, *74*
interfaith Passover Seder, *33*
migration of, 136
Torah scroll as symbol, 384, *385*
in United States, *385*
world distribution of, *369*
Jill Soloway, 234

Jim Crow, 132 Laws implemented after the U.S.
Civil War to legally enforce segregation, particularly in the South, after the end of slavery.

John, Elton, 256
Johnson, Virginia, 218

John XXIII, Pope, 387
Jordan, Brigitte, 407, 408, 409, 410
Judaism. *See* Jews and Judaism
Julian calendar, 39
Juris, Jeffrey, 356

K

Kahn, Susan, 252
Kant, Immanuel, 430
Kathmandu, Nepal, activists in, *353*
Katrina, Hurricane, 289
Katz, Jonathan, 217
kayakctivists, *345*
Kennedy, John F., *237*
Kennedy, Joseph Sr., *237*
Kennedy, Robert, *237*
Kentucky, rural, poor Whites in,
    272–73
Kenya, same-sex marriage in, 248

key informant, 76 A community member who
advises the anthropologist on community issues,
provides feedback, and warns against cultural
miscues. Also called *cultural consultant.*

Keynes, John M., 313, 316
Keynesian economics, 313–14
kindred exogamy, 247

kinesics, 96–97 The study of the relationship
between body movements and communication.

kinetic orality, 442 A musical genre combining
body movement and voice.

Kinsey, Alfred C., *218*

kinship analysis, 76 A fieldwork strategy of
examining interlocking relationships of power
built on marriage and family ties.

kinship, 233–257 The system of meaning and
power that cultures create to determine who
is related to whom and to define their mutual
expectations, rights, and responsibilities.

acquisition through co-residence and
    co-feeding, 249–250, *250*
analysis of kinship, 76–77
defined, 234
ethnicity as version of, 155
globalization and, 253
    assisted reproductive technologies, 255–56
    chosen families, 255, *255*
    families of same-sex partners, 256–57, *257*
    nuclear family, 253–55
marriage and affinal ties, 244–49
    arranged marriages, 244–45
    bridewealth, 248–49
    companionate marriages, 245
    endogamy, 247
    exogamy, 247
    incest taboos, 246–47
    interracial marriage, 36–37, 47–48, *48*, 247,
        248
    monogamy, 246
    polyandry, 246
    polygyny, 246
    same-sex marriage, 246, 248, *248*, 256–57,
        257
nation-states and, 251–53
nuclear family, 234
as poverty survival strategy, 251
relationship organization, 236–244, *237, 239, 240,*
    241, 243
kissing, 208
Kleinman, Arthur, 421
Krafft Ebing, Richard von, 217
Kromidas, Maria, 136, 137, 138
Ku Klux Klan, 132
Kula ring, 69–70
Kulick, Don, 224, 225, 226
!Kung san people, *299*
Kurds, 171–72
Kwakiutl people, 42, 68, 265

L

labor immigrants, 322–23 Persons who
move in search of a low-skill and low-wage job,
often filling an economic niche that native-born
workers will not fill.

Labov, W., 106
Ladakh, India, Buddhist healing practices in, 400–402, *401*
Lafontant, Fritz, 411, 412
laissez-faire (leave it alone) capitalism, 313
Lakoff, Robin, 99
Lakota people, 113
Lan, Pei-chia, 201
Lancaster, Roger, 214, 215
Landers, M. A., 182
Langkawi people, 249–250, *250*

language, 91–113 A system of communication organized by rules that uses symbols such as words, sounds, and gestures to convey information.
    continuum of, 108–9
    defined, 93
    descriptive linguistics, 95–96
    effects of on thinking, 98–100
    gender enculturation, 184
    globalization and, 109–13
        diminishing diversity, 109, 111
        language loss, 112–13, *113*
        preserving endangered languages, 113, *113*
        revitalizing languages, 112–13
    linguistic anthropology, 16–17
    loss of, 112
    nonverbal communication, 96–97
    number of by country, *110*
    origins of, 93–95
    power systems and, 100–109
        dialects, 104
        gender, 102–3, *103*
        historical linguistics, 108–9
        use of the "N-word," 100–102, *101*
        variation in the US, 104–8
    sexuality and, 226–27
    top twenty, *111*

language continuum, 108–9 The idea that variation in languages appears gradually over distance so that groups of people who live near one another speak in a way that is mutually intelligible.

language loss, 112 The extinction of languages that have very few speakers.

Laos, life expectancy in, *415*
Lascaux Cave, France, paintings in, *434*
Laughter Out of Place (Goldstein), 128–29
Lawrence, John, *248*
Lawrence v. Texas, *248*
lay teachers (*catequistas*), 386–87, *387*
Leacock, Eleanor B., 281
lead poisoning, 261–63
League of Nations, 172
leave it alone (*laissez-faire*) capitalism, 313
Lee, Lia, 419, 420, 421, *421*
LeFrak City, 143
lesbians. *See* gays and lesbians
Lessinger, Johanna, 157
Levi-Strauss, Claude, 98
Lewinsky, Monica, 208
Lewis, Oscar, 280, 281

lexicon, 99 All the words for names, ideas, and events that make up a language's dictionary.

life chances, 269 An individual's opportunities to improve quality of life and realize life goals.

life expectancy, 414, *415*

life history, 76 A form of interview that traces the biography of a person over time, examining changes in the person's life and illuminating the interlocking network of relationships in the community.

Life Is Hard (Lancaster), 214–15
life span, 40

liminality, 373 One stage in a rite of passage during which a ritual participant experiences a period of outsiderhood, set apart from normal society, that is key to achieving a new perspective on the past, future, and current community.

Lincoln, Abraham, 132

lineage, 236 A type of descent group that traces genealogical connection through generations by linking persons to a founding ancestor.

lineal kinship systems, 238
linguistics, 16–17, 108–9. *See also* language

linguistic anthropology, 16–17 The study of human language in the past and the present.

Linnaeus, Carolus, 39
Liquidated (Ho), 276
listening skills, 78
literature review, 75
"Little Hill" (Morrinho), Rio de Janeiro, Brazil, 424–27, *424, 426*
Living with Racism (Feagin and Sikes), 145
loans, 283–84
loban (chunks of incense), 369–370, *370*
Lock, Margaret, 406
London, England, *33*
Loneliness and Its Opposite (Kulick and Rydstrom), 224
long-distance trade routes, 303–4
Lord of the Rings trilogy (Tolkien), *382*
Loving, Mildred, *248*
Loving, Richard, *248*
Loving v. Virginia, 248
Lutz, Catherine, 349, 445, 446, 447
Luxemborg, same-sex marriage, 248
Lynn, Terry, *141*

M
machismo, 185–86, *185*, 214–15

magic, 379–383, 390–91 The use of spells, incantations, words, and actions in an attempt to compel supernatural forces to act in certain ways, whether for good or for evil.

Makah Nation, *266*
Malaysia, 249–250, *249, 250*
    McDonald's menu adaptations in, 55
    protests in, *49*

Malendoski, Savanna E., *181*
Mali
    migration from, 324–27, *326*
    Mopti port, *7*
    trade routes, *11*
Malinowski, Bronislaw, 41, 43, 69, 70, *70*, 73, 75, 192, 206, 247
Malkki, Liisa, 162
Maman (Bourgeois), *429*
managers, 268
Manila, Philippines, *55*

mapping, 77–78 The analysis of the physical and/or geographic space where fieldwork is being conducted.

Mardi Gras, 79, *80*
Mardi Gras: Made in China (film), 79
market exchange, 302–3
Marks, Jonathan, 125

marriage, 244–49 A socially recognized relationship that may involve physical and emotional intimacy as well as legal rights to property and inheritance.
    arranged marriages, 244–45
    bridewealth, 248–49
    companionate marriages, 245
    endogamy, 247
    exogamy, 247
    incest taboos, 246–47
    interracial marriage, 36–37, 47–48, *48*, 247, *248*
    marriage defined, 244
    monogamy, 246
    norms regarding, 36–37
    polyandry, 246
    polygyny, 246
    same-sex marriage, 246, 248, *248*, 256–57, *257*

Marshall, John, 447
Martin, Emily, 193, 194, 196

martyr, 369 A person who sacrifices his or her life for the sake of his or her religion.

Marx, Karl, 266, 267, 268, 269, 371, 374, *375*, 377

Marxism, religion and, 374–77

masculinity, 182, 184–85 The ideas and practices associated with manhood. *See also machismo*

Maskovsky, Jeff, 281, 282

masks, West African, 437–38, *438*

mass production, industrial, 311–12

Masters, William, 218

masturbation, 217

Mata, Bahuchara, 188

material power, 47

mati work, Suriname, 213–14

matrilineal descent groups, 237

Mayans, viewpoint on birth, 407–8, 410

McDonald's, *30*, 31–32, 55–56, *55*

McIntosh, Peggy, 144, 145

MCMC (Merced Community Medical Center), 419–420

Mead, Margaret, 42, 71, 72, *72*, 75, 178, 206, 207, 348, 444

meaning, in religion, 384, 386–88

means of production, 267 The factories, machines, tools, raw materials, land, and financial capital needed to make things.

Medeiros, Melanie, 245

media, 443–49

    ethnographic film and indigenous media, 447–49

    media worlds, 444

    visual images and cultural identity, 445–47

media worlds, 444 An ethnographic and theoretical approach to media studies that focuses on the tensions that may exist when visual worlds collide in the context of contemporary globalization.

Medicaid patients, 416

medical anthropology, 395–98

medical migration, 415, 417–18 The movement of diseases, medical treatments, and entire health-care systems, as well as those seeking medical care, across national borders.

Medicine, Beatrice, 74

melting pot, 166 A metaphor used to describe the process of immigrant assimilation into U.S. dominant culture.

Men Are from Mars, Women Are from Venus (Gray), 102

mental maps of reality, 38–40 Cultural classifications of what kinds of people and things exist, and the assignment of meaning to those classifications.

Merced Community Medical Center (MCMC), 419–420

Merensky Reef geologic formation, 165

meritocracy, 142

Mesopotamia, 172

Mexican New York (Smith), 56

Mexico, 56, *185*

    archaeology in, 15

    life expectancy in, *415*

    machismo, 185–86, *185*

    McDonald's menu adaptations in, 55

    offshoring to, 20

    prescription drugs from, 417–18, *418*

    religion and revolution in, 386–88, *387*

    viewpoint on birth, 407, 410

Mexico City, *185*

Michaels, Jillian, 256

Michigan, water crisis in, 261–63, *263*

microaggressions, 139 Common, everyday verbal or behavioral indignities and slights that communicate hostile, derogatory, and negative messages about someone's race, gender, sexual orientation, or religion.

microbes, 406–7

middle class, 268

Middle East
    art exhibits and events originating from,
        439–441, *440*
    immigrants from, 136–38
    trade routes through, *303*
Migrants and Strangers in an African City
        (Whitehouse), 324
migration, 8, 318–327
    anti-immigrant cartoon, *135*
    bridges and barriers, 319–321
    effect on religion, 388–391, *389*
    effects of culture on, 42
    global flow of culture, 56
    increasing, 20–21
    kinship connections, 243–44
    language and, *90*, 91–92, 104–5
    multi-sited ethnography, *25*, 26
    patterns of, 321–22, *322*
    pushes and pulls, 319
    race and, 134–38
        Chinese, 134–35
        Irish, 135
        Middle Easterners, 136–38
        overview, 134
    religion and, *389*
    types of immigrants, 322–27
    women and, 201
Miles, Lyn, 94

militarization, 349 The contested social process
through which a civil society organizes for the
production of military violence.

military
    anthropology and, 83–84, *83*
    women in, *176*, 177–78, 181, *181*
Miner, Horace, 65
Minerva Initiative, 84
miniature city model, 424–27, *424, 426*
Mintz, Sydney, 72

miscegenation, 127 A demeaning historical
term for interracial marriage.

modernization theories, 308 Post–World
War II economic theories that predicted that with

the end of colonialism, less-developed countries
would follow the same trajectory toward modernization as the industrialized countries.

modern world economic system, 308–11
money. *See* economics; global economy

monogamy, 246 A relationship between only
two partners.

Moore, Mignon, 222, 223, 224
Mopti, Mali, *7*
Morgan, Lewis H., 41, 42, 68
Mormon religion, in United States, *385*
Morocco, McDonald's menu adaptations in, 55

morphemes, 96 The smallest units of sound
that carry meaning on their own.

morphology, 96 The study of patterns and rules
of how sounds combine to make morphemes.

Morrinho ("Little Hill"), Rio de Janeiro, Brazil,
        424–27, *424, 426*
Mountains beyond Mountains (Kidder), 411
Moynihan, Daniel P., 167, 251
Mozambique, war in, 350–51
muftis, 357–58
Muhammad, 368, 369
Mulatto race category, 130
Mullings, Leith, 267, 271, 272, 281

multiculturalism A pattern of ethnic relations in which new immigrants and their children
enculturate into the dominant national culture
and yet retain an ethnic culture.
    versus assimilation, 166–67
    defined, 167

multiple systems of healing, 418–421
multi-sited ethnography, 25–26, *25*
Mumbai, India, water circulation in, 286–87
music, gender identity and, 442–43, *442*
Muslims and Islam, 367–370
    art exhibits and events of, 439–441
    in Bosnia, 162–64

Fatwa Councils, 356–58, *358*
in France, 153
homosexuality and, 228–29
interfaith Passover Seder, *33*
religious symbols, 46–47, *46*
religious law (Sharia), 356–57, 386
saint shrines (*dargahs*), 368–370, *370*
in United States, *385*
world distribution of, *369*

mutual transformation, 64–66, 78–79 The potential for both the anthropologist and the members of the community being studied to be transformed by the interactions of fieldwork.

Myerhoff, Barbara, 73, *74*
mythico-histories, 162

N

"Nacirema" people, 65–66, *66*
Nanda, Serena, 188
Nandi people, 248
Nanook of the North (Flaherty), 447

nation, 168 A term once used to describe a group of people who shared a place of origin; now used interchangeably with *nation-state.*

National Geographic magazine, photographs in, 445–47

nationalism The desire of an ethnic community to create and/or maintain a nation-state.
anti-colonialism and, 170–71
challenges to sense of nationhood, 171–73
defined, 168
kinship and, 251
World Cup soccer and, 151–54

nation state, 168 A political entity, located within a geographic territory with enforced borders, where the population shares a sense of culture, ancestry, and destiny as a people.

Native Americans, *113*
engaged anthropology, 74

languages of, 104, 112–13
transgender, 189–190, *189*

nativism, 134 The favoring of certain long-term inhabitants, namely whites, over new immigrants.

natural healing remedies, 400–402
naturheilkunde (natural cure), 403
Nazism, Nuremburg Laws, 36
Neandertals, language and, 95
Neel, James, 83
negative reciprocity, 301, 302
"The Negro Family" (Moynihan), 251
Neither Man nor Woman (Nanda), 188
Nelly, *442*, 443
neocolonialism, 309

neoliberalism, 314–15, 344 An economic and political worldview that sees the free market as the main mechanism for ensuring economic growth, with a severely restricted role for government.

Nepal
activists in, *353*
polygyny and polyandry in, 246
Neshat, Shirin, *440*
Netherlands
life expectancy in, *415*
mati work, 213–14
same-sex marriage in, 248
stock exchange, *39*
New Orleans, Louisiana, Mardi Gras beads used in, 79–80, *80*
New York City, *67*, *157*
homelessness and begging in, 67
immigrant connections with homeland, 25–26, 56
kindergartners learning Mandarin in, *35*
migration from Fuzhou, China to, 319–321
multi-sited ethnography, 25–26
West African art sold via, 437–38
New Zealand, same-sex marriage, 248
NGOs (nongovernmental organizations), 344–45
Nicaragua, sexuality in, 214–15, *214*
Niger, magic in, 381–82

patience, 78–79

patrilineal descent groups, 237–38, 241–42

Patterns of Culture (Benedict), 42

Patterson, Francine, *94*

Pediatrics (journal), 187

The People of Puerto Rico (Steward), 72

A People's History of the United States (Zinn), 156

periphery countries, 309–10, *310* The least-developed and least-powerful nations; often exploited by the core countries as sources of raw materials, cheap labor, and markets.

Personal Status courts, in Egypt, 356–58

Peru, brother-sister marriage in, 246

petroglyphs, *195*

petting, 208

Peyote Hunt (Myerhoff), 73

Phelps, Michael, *404*

phenotype, 124–26 The way genes are expressed in an organism's physical form as a result of genotype interaction with environmental factors.

Philippines, *201*

    McDonald's menu adaptations in, 55, *55*

    offshoring to, *312*

    organ trafficking in, *86*

    outsourcing to, 20

    pointing in, 97

    women and migration, 201

Phipps, Susie, 133, 134

phonemes, 96 The smallest units of sound that can make a difference in meaning.

phonology, 96 The study of what sounds exist and which ones are important in a particular language.

photographic gaze, 446 The presumed neutral viewpoint of the camera that in fact projects the perspective of the person behind the camera onto human nature, the natural world, and history.

physical anthropology (biological anthropology), 13–15, *13, 14* The study of humans from a biological perspective, particularly how they have evolved over time and adapted to their environments.
See also biology and genetics; evolution

Picasso, Pablo, 432

pilgrimage, 373 A religious journey to a sacred place as a sign of devotion and in search of transformation and enlightenment.

Plachimada, India, *4*, 5–6, *6*, 23, 180–81

plantation economy, in Caribbean and South America, 305

Plessy, H., 140

Plessy v. Ferguson (1896), 140

political anthropology, 336–37

political systems

    bands, 337–38

    chiefdoms, 339–340

    state, 340–45

        defined, 340

        origin of, 341

        power of, 343–44

        Western model, 341–42

    tribes, 338–39

politics, style of presentation, 429

Politics of Passion (Wekker), 213

pollution, 23, *23*

Polo, Marco, 67

polyandry, 246 Marriage between one woman and two or more men.

polygyny, 246 Marriage between one man and two or more women.

Polynesia, chiefdoms in, 339–340

polyvocality, 81 The practice of using many different voices in ethnographic writing and research question development, allowing the reader to hear more directly from the people in the study.

popular art, 428–29, *429* Creative expression and communication often associated with the general population.

Pordié, Laurent, 400, 401, 402
Portugal
  neoliberalism and, 314
  same-sex marriage in, 248

potlatch, 265, *266*, 339–340 Elaborate redistribution ceremony practiced among the Kwakiutl of the Pacific Northwest.

poverty
  "culture of," 280–81
  increase in, 21, 287–88
  as pathology, 280–81
  poor Whites in rural Kentucky, 274–76
  roots of, 279–280
  as structural economic problem, 281–82
Powell, John W., 74

power The ability or potential to bring about change through action or influence.
  art and, 429, 439–443
    exhibitions, 439–441, *440*
    gender identity and, 441–43, *442*
  culture and, 45
    cultural institutions, 46–47
    hegemony, 47–48
    human agency, 48–49
  defined, 45
  distribution of health and illness and, 413–17
  gender and, 190–99
    challenging, 196–99
    early research on, 191–92
    gender ideologies, 193–96
  language and
    dialects, 104
    gender, 102–3, *103*
    historical linguistics, 108–9
    use of the "N-word," 100–102, *101*
    variation in the US, 104–8

  outside state control, 352–59
    alternative legal structures, 356–59
    social movements, 352–56
  religion and, 385–88
  sexuality and, 222–26
    black gay women in U.S., 222–24
    rights of disabled in Denmark and Sweden, 224–26
  of state, 343–44

prehistoric archaeology, 15–16 The reconstruction of human behavior in the distant past (before written records) through the examination of artifacts.

prescription drugs, 417–18, *418*

prestige, 269 The reputation, influence, and deference bestowed on certain people because of their membership in certain groups.

prestige language, 104 A particular language variation or way of speaking that is associated with wealth, success, education, and power.

primates, 14
  aggressiveness in, 346–47, *347*
  language and, 94
  sexuality in, 209, *209*

primatology, 14–15 The study of living non-human primates as well as primate fossils to better understand human evolution and early human behavior.

"primitive" art, 431–32
Primitive Culture (Tylor), 41
procreation, family of, 254

profane, 371 Anything that is considered unholy.

professional immigrants, 323 Highly trained individuals who move to fill economic niches in a middle-class profession often marked by shortages in the receiving country.

professionals, 268

proletariat, 267 Marxist term for the class of laborers who own only their labor.

The Protestant Ethic and the Spirit of Capitalism (Weber), *377*

Protestantism
    secularization and, 377–78
    in United States, *385*

protests and resistance
    against Coca-Cola and water usage, *4*, 5–6, *6*
    CO-MADRES of El Salvador, 196–99, *197*
    against dominant power relationships and structures, 49, *49*
    Emma Sulkowicz, *204*, 205
    Ferguson, Missouri, *118*, 120
    institutional racism, *143*
    against suspicion based on language, *90*
Psychopathia Sexualis (Krafft-Ebing), 217
public health care system, in Haiti, 411–13
Puerto Rico, ethnographic fieldwork in, 71–72
Purity and Exile (Malkki), 162

pushes and pulls, 319 The forces that spur migration from the country of origin and draw immigrants to a particular new destination country.

Q

qaug dab peg (epilepsy), 419–420
qi (breath or air), 403–4

qualitative data, 76 Descriptive data drawn from nonstatistical sources, including personal stories, interviews, life histories, and participant observation.

quantitative data, 78 Statistical information about a community that can be measured and compared.

Queens, New York, resisting racism in, 142–44, *142*

R

race A flawed system of classification, with no biological basis, that uses certain physical characteristics to divide the human population into supposedly discrete groups.
    biological similarities, 122–26
        interconnected gene pool, 123–24
        linking phenotype to genotype, 124–26
        overview, 122–23
    classifications of, lack of biological basis for, 15, 39–40
    colonialism and, 126–29
        in Brazil, 127–29
        overview, 126–27
    concepts of, 40
    defined, 121
    distribution of health and illness and, 414–17
    distribution of wealth and, 279
    general discussion, 119–122
    ideologies, 141–42
    intersectionality among gender, class and, 271–73
    intersection of sexuality with, 222–23
    in U.S. culture, 129–138
        census, 130–31
        constructing whiteness, 131–33
        hypodescent, 133–34
        immigration, 134–38
        overview, 129–130
    whiteness and, 144–47
        intersectionality, 145–47
        white privilege, 144–45
racial democracy thesis, Brazil, 128

racial ideology, 141–42 A set of popular ideas about race that allows the discriminatory behaviors of individuals and institutions to seem reasonable, rational, and normal.

racialization, 138 The process of categorizing, differentiating, and attributing a particular racial character to a person or group of people.

racism Individuals' thoughts and actions and institutional patterns and policies that create or reproduce unequal access to power, privilege, resources, and opportunities based on imagined differences among groups.

ranked society, 265–66 A group in which wealth is not stratified but prestige and status are.

reciprocity, 264, *264*, 301–2 The exchange of resources, goods, and services among people of relatively equal status; meant to create and reinforce social ties.

redistribution, 265, *266*, 302 A form of exchange in which accumulated wealth is collected from the members of the group and reallocated in a different pattern.

reflexivity, 73, 81–82 A critical self- examination of the role the anthropologist plays and an awareness that one's identity affects one's fieldwork and theoretical analyses.

refugees, 319 Persons who have been forced to move beyond their national borders because of political or religious persecution, armed conflict, or disasters.

religion, 363–391 A set of beliefs and rituals based on a unique vision of how the world ought to be, often focused on a supernatural power and lived out in community.

rite of passage, 372 A category of ritual that enacts a change of status from one life stage to another, either for an individual or for a group.

ritual, 371, 372–74 An act or series of acts regularly repeated over years or generations that embody the beliefs of a group of people and create a sense of continuity and belonging.

S

sacred, 371 Anything that is considered holy.

saint, 369 An individual considered exceptionally close to god and who is then exalted after death.

salvage ethnography, 69 Fieldwork strategy developed by Franz Boas to collect cultural, material, linguistic, and biological information about Native American populations being devastated by the westward expansion of European settlers.

Sapir-Whorf hypothesis, 98 The idea that different languages create different ways of thinking.

sex, 179 The observable physical differences between male and female, especially biological differences related to human reproduction.

sexual dimorphism, 179–80 The phenotypic differences between males and females of the same species.

sexuality The complex range of desires, beliefs, and behaviors that are related to erotic physical contact and the cultural arena within which people debate about what kinds of physical desires and behaviors are right, appropriate, and natural.

Mardi Gras beads and nudity, 79, *80*
overview, 206–7
power and, 222–26
  black gay women in U.S., 222–24
  rights of disabled in Denmark and Sweden,
    224–26
sexual assault on college campuses, 205–6
Sulkowicz, Emma, *204*, 205
theory of five sexes, 186–88
in United States, 216–221
  heterosexuality, 216–18
  wedding culture/wedding industry,
    219–221
Victorian ideal of, 217

Shadows of War (Nordstrom), 350
"Shakespeare in the Bush" (Bohannan), 99

shaman, 378–79 Part-time religious practitioners with special abilities to connect individuals
with supernatural powers or beings.

Sharia (Islamic religious law), 356–57, 386
Shia, 171–72

sickness, 399 An individual's public expression
of illness and disease, including social expectations about how one should behave and how others will respond.
See also health

Sierre Leone, outsourcing to, 20
sign languages, 94, *94*, 97
Sikes, Melvin, 145
SIL (Summer Institute of Linguistics), 112–13
Singapore, life expectancy in, *415*

situational negotiation of identity, 157 An
individual's self-identification with a particular
group that can shift according to social location.

skin color, 123, *123*, 124, 128
slavery, 16
  in Brazil, 127
  efforts to eliminate in U.S., 132

  slave auction advertisement, *132*
  slave family working cotton fields, *132*
  slave trade, *127*, 305–6
sleep, 50
Smith, Adam, 313, 314
Smith, Neil, 289
Smith, Robert, 56
Smith, Roberta, 205
social learning, 34

social media, 444 New forms of communication based on computer- and Internet-based technologies that facilitate social engagement, work,
and pleasure.

social mobility, 269 The movement of one's
class position, upward or downward, in stratified
societies.

social movement, 352 Collective group actions
that seek to build institutional networks to transform cultural patterns and government policies.

social network analysis, 77 A method for
examining relationships in a community, often
conducted by identifying whom people turn to in
times of need.

social reproduction, 269–270 The phenomenon whereby social and class relations of prestige
or lack of prestige are passed from one generation
to the next.

society, 43 The focus of early British anthropological research whose structure and function
could be isolated and studied scientifically.

sociolinguistics, 17, 100 The study of the ways
culture shapes language and language shapes culture, particularly the intersection of language with
cultural categories and systems of power such as
age, race, ethnicity, sexuality, gender, and class.

sociolinguists, 17 Those who study language in
its social and cultural contexts.

Sociology of Religion (Weber), *377*
Sojourner syndrome, 272–73
Songhay region, Niger, magic in, *381*
sorcery, 381–82
South Africa, *165*
    apartheid in, 36, 127
    art in, 432–33, *432, 433*
    Bafokeng, Inc., 165–66
    same-sex marriage in, 248
    women in military, 177
South America, plantation economy in,
    305
South Asian Lesbian and Gay Alliance
    (SALGA), 158
South Sudan, magic in, 380–81, *380*
Spain
    life expectancy in, *415*
    neoliberalism and, 314
    Paleolithic cave paintings in, 433
    same-sex marriage, 248
"Speechless" (Neshat), *440*
sperm, 193–94, *194*
The Spirit Catches You and You Fall Down
    (Fadiman), 419
spiritism, 378–383, 390–91
spirituality. *See* religion and spirituality
sports and athleticism, gender enculturation in,
    182, *183*
SSAE (Standard Spoken American English), 105,
    106
Stack, Carol, 251
stall vendors (*fijos*), 285–86, *285*
Standard Spoken American English (SSAE), 105,
    106

state, 340–45 An autonomous regional structure of political, economic, and military rule with
a central government authorized to make laws
and use force to maintain order and defend its
territory.
    defined, 167, 340
    origin of, 341
    power of, 343–44
    violence and, 347–350
    Western model, 341–42

statues, West African, 437–38, *438*
Steiner, Christopher, 435, 437, 439
Stephen, Lynn, 198
stereotypes, poor whites, 146–47
Sterk, Claire, 85
Steward, Julian, 72
stocks, ownership of, 279
Stoller, Paul, 379, 381, 382, 438, 439

stratification, 45 The uneven distribution of
resources and privileges among participants in a
group or culture.

street vendors (*ambulantes*), 285–86, *285*

structural functionalism, 43 A conceptual
framework positing that each element of society
serves a particular function to keep the entire system in equilibrium.

structural racism. *See* institutional racism
Sudan. *See also* Nuer people
    kinship classification, 238, 240, *240*
    magic in, 380–81, *380*
"Suffurya" (Essa), *440*
sugarcane plantations, 305
Sulkowicz, Emma, 205, *205*, 206
Summer Institute of Linguistics (SIL), 112–13
Sundarbans, Bangladesh, protests to protect envi-
    ronment of, *332*, 333–34
Sunnis, 171–72
surgery, in foreign countries, *418*
Suriname, sexuality in, 213–14, *213*

survey, 76 An information-gathering tool for
quantitative data analysis.

Swaziland, life expectancy in, 414, *415*
Sweden, *224*
    life expectancy in, *415*
    rune stones, *97*
    same-sex marriage in, 248
    sexuality and disabilities in, 224–26
    viewpoint on birth, 407, 409
Sweetness and Power (Mintz), 72

symbol, 37–38 Anything that represents something else.
  defined, 384
  in religion, 384–85

synchronic approach, 70

syntax, 96 The specific patterns and rules for combining morphemes to construct phrases and sentences.

Syria, refugees from, *18*

T

Tabula Rogeriana, *303*
Taiwan, women and migration, 201
Tannen, Deborah, 102
Tanzania, Hutu refugees in, 162
Tel Aviv, Israel, *253*
television, cosmopolitanism and, 56–57, *57*
terra-cotta clay figurines, West African, 437–38, *438*
terrorism, debate over Muslim head coverings and, 46–47
testosterone, 210
Thailand
  food and culture in, *33*
  offshoring to, 20
Thanksgiving, American identity and, *156*

thick description, 44 A research strategy that combines detailed description of cultural activity with an analysis of the layers of deep cultural meaning in which those activities are embedded.

Thind, Bhagat S., 135
Tibet, polyandry in, 246
Tibetan Buddhism, healing practices of, 400–402, *401*
Tierney, Patrick, 83
Tihuateca, Mexico, migration and, 56
time, concepts of, 39–40

time-space compression, 20, 226 The rapid innovation of communication and transportation technologies associated with globalization

that transforms the way people think about space (distances) and time.

time zones, 39
Tiv people, 99
Togotala, Mali, migration from, 325–27, *326*
Tokyo, Japan, *215*
  seafood trade in, 317–18, *317*
  sexuality in, 215
Torah scroll, as symbol in Judaism, 384, *385*
Totti, Francesco, *311*
trade routes, *303*

transgender, 188, 189, *189*, **233–34** A gender identity or performance that does not fit with cultural norms related to one's assigned sex at birth.

transnational citizenship in Eritrea, 169–170
Transparent (TV series), *232*, 233–34
triangle trade, 304–6, *305*

tribe, 338–39 Originally viewed as a culturally distinct, multiband population that imagined itself as one people descended from a common ancestor; currently used to describe an indigenous group with its own set of loyalties and leaders living to some extent outside the control of a centralized authoritative state.

Trobriand Islands, *43, 70*
  exchange system in, 68–69
  women economy of, *73*
Troxler, Julia, *257*
Trump, Donald J., 91
Tsukiji Fish Market, 317–18, *317*
Tucson, Arizona, 67, *67*
tuna trade, 317–18, *317*
Turner, Victor, 43, 73, 373, 374
Tutsis, 159–161
Two-Spirits, 189–190, *189*
Tylor, Edward B., 41, *41*, 42, 68

U

underdevelopment, 309 The term used to suggest that poor countries are poor as a result of their relationship to an unbalanced global economic system.

uneven development, 21 The unequal distribution of the benefits of globalization.

unilineal cultural evolution, 41, 42 The theory proposed by nineteenth-century anthropologists that all cultures naturally evolve through the same sequence of stages from simple to complex.

universal gaze, 430 An intrinsic way of perceiving art— thought by many in the Western art world to be found across cultures— that informs what people consider to be art or not art.

V

values, 37 Fundamental beliefs about what is important, what makes a good life, and what is true, right, and beautiful.

vasopressin, 210

Vázquez de Coronado, Francisco, 92

Vietnam War, 83, *83*

violence

    state and, 347–48

    whether natural to humans, 346–48

Virchow, Rudolf, 413

visual anthropology, 445 A field of anthropology that explores the production, circulation, and consumption of visual images, focusing on the power of visual representation to influence culture and cultural identity.

visual images, cultural identity and, 445–47

W

Waal, Frans de, 346, 347

wages, 312

Wallerstein, Immanuel, 309, 310, 318

Wall Street, 276–77, *277*

Walmart, in China, 20

Walter, LeeAnne, *263*

war

    globalization and, 349–351

    glorification of by popular culture, *349*

    militarization and, 349

    state and, 348–49

Warehouse, in New York, NY, 437–38

"Warfare Is Only an Invention—Not a Biological Necessity" (Mead), 348

Washoe people, *113*

water crisis

    in Flint, Michigan, 261–63, *263*

    in Mumbai, India, 286–87

water resources

    access to, 32

    beef production and, 32

    India, *4*, 5–6, *6*, 23

    stress caused by human activity, 23

wealth, 278–79 The total value of what someone owns, minus any debt.

The Wealth of Nations (Smith), 313

Weapons of the Weak (Scott), 49

Weber, Max, 266, 269, 284, 343, 371, 377, *377*, 378, 380, 384, 385

Webster, Mike, 396

wedding culture/wedding industry, 219–221

    constructing heterosexuality, 219–220

    inequality and unequal access, 220–21

    same-sex weddings, *221*

Weiner, Annette, 73, 192

Weinreich, Max, 104

Wekker, Gloria, 213, 214

Wendell, Turk, *383*

West, Kanye, *101*

West Africa

    art from, 435–39, *435*, *436*, *438*

    magic in, 381–82

    migration from, 324–27, *326*

Western cultures

    art and, 430–32

    development model of, 308–9

    health care and, 399, 402–3, 408–9

    religion in, 377–78, 385

    state model, 341–42

Weston, Kath, 255

whales, communication and, 93

white-collar workers, 268

Whitehouse, Bruce, 324

whiteness A culturally constructed concept originating in 1691 Virginia designed to establish clear boundaries of who is white and who is not, a process central to the formation of U.S. racial stratification.

    constructing in U.S. culture, 131–33

    defined, 131

    race and racism and, 144–47

        intersectionality, 145–47

        white privilege, 144–45

    "unmarked" category, *146*

"White Privilege" (McIntosh), 144

Whites

    distribution of wealth to, 279

    in interracial marriages, *48*

    poverty and, 146–47, 274–76, *280*

white-supremacist groups, 132–33

white supremacy, 131 The belief that whites are biologically different from and superior to people of other races.

zeros, 78 Elements of a story or a picture that are not told or seen and yet offer key insights into issues that might be too sensitive to discuss or display publicly.